SEX AND GENDER ISSUES

SEX AND GENDER ISSUES

A Handbook of Tests and Measures

CAROLE A. BEERE

GREENWOOD PRESS
New York • Westport, Connecticut • London

Library of Congress Cataloging-in-Publication Data

Beere, Carole A.
Sex and gender issues : a handbook of tests and measures / Carole A. Beere.
p. cm.
Includes bibliographical references.
ISBN 0-313-27462-2 (lib. bdg. : alk. paper)
1. Sex (Psychology)—Testing—Handbooks, manuals, etc. I. Title.
BF692.B38 1990
155.3'028'7—dc20 90-32466

British Library Cataloguing in Publication Data is available.

Library of Congress Catalog Card Number: 90-32466
ISBN: 0-313-27462-2

First published in 1990

Greenwood Press, 88 Post Road West, Westport, CT 06881
An imprint of Greenwood Publishing Group, Inc.

Printed in the United States of America

The paper used in this book complies with the Permanent Paper Standard issued by the National Information Standards Organization (Z39.48-1984).

10 9 8 7 6 5 4 3 2 1

Contents

Acknowledgments

Completing two handbooks in a two-year period requires the help and cooperation of many people. I am grateful to my many friends who encouraged me during this time. Without them I would not have begun the work that led to these handbooks.

Financial support from the Rockefeller Foundation and Central Michigan University (CMU) was crucial to the completion of this work. CMU supported me with a sabbatical leave, a Faculty Research and Creative Endeavors Grant, and a Research Professorship award.

Colleagues at CMU answered many questions for me. I am grateful to Professors Dan King and Lynda King, who answered my statistical questions without ever reminding me that I had already asked the questions before. Thanks go to Richard Hartley and Sherwood Bridges, who provided me with computer assistance when my computers and printers refused to cooperate and gave me moral support at other times. Rose Marie Fisher of the CMU Psychology Department helped me with my periodic struggles to wend my way through CMU's bureaucracy, and Michael Kent, chairperson of psychology, supported me in numerous ways.

The help I received from librarians and library staff was immeasurable. I extend my sincerest thanks to Sue Miles, Bill Miles, David Ginsburg, Ruth Helwig, Beth Macleod, Judy Porter, and Tom Moore. I cannot enumerate the variety of services they provided me; I called on Sue, Bill, and David for help at least weekly and often daily. They were consistently supportive and managed to answer all of my questions, no matter how outlandish some were. I miss the daily contact with all my library friends now that I have moved out of the library and back into my office in the Psychology Department.

Special thanks go to Mary Cannon. Without her help, I expect that this book would have been at least six months behind schedule and filled with many errors. She served as my local editor-proofreader, verifying the consistency of my style and the accuracy of my citations. She did a great job.

Thank you, most of all, to my family. Two members of my family live hundreds of miles from me and still managed to help. My sister, Rochelle Elstein, is a librarian at Northwestern University. I called on her for help locating citations on several occasions. She was most efficient in assisting me. My mother is retired and lives 300 miles from me; however, on every visit to our town, she went to work and helped me with locating materials, filing, or proofreading. It was a wonderful experience to have her help and support. My immediate family deserves special accolades. My children, Jennifer and Jonathan, helped me with my work, as well as tolerating my lengthy preoccupation with my research and writing. Despite her young age, Jennifer is adept at locating materials within our library and is an excellent proofreader. Jonathan helped with miscellaneous tasks, and best of all, he helped me to improve my writing. I have learned a lot from him.

My deepest appreciation is for my husband, Don, himself a psychologist, who is a wonderful colleague and a marvelous husband and father. He supported me through every step of my work, even staying up with me most of the night when my computer and printer finally joined forces to print out the entire manuscript. He is my best friend.

SEX AND GENDER ISSUES

1

Introduction

To conduct research, a scientist must locate or develop measures for assessing the relevant variables. Unlike physical scientists who can often rely on well-established measurement procedures, social scientists frequently have difficulty locating high-quality measures. If the selected measures are unreliable or invalid, the research is of limited, if any, value. Comparing research studies that have used different measures may lead to erroneous conclusions. In an ideal world, researchers would identify the variables they need to measure and then consult the "Standard Guide for Measures" to locate one extremely reliable, extremely valid measure for assessing each variable. Unfortunately this is not an ideal world, and no such book exists, but we can work toward solving some of the problems. We can try to facilitate the researcher's task of locating reliable, valid measures appropriate for his or her research.

As a step toward this goal, I wrote *Women and Women's Issues: A Handbook of Tests and Measures* (Beere, 1979). Based on searching the psychological, sociological, and educational literature from the 1920s through 1977, I described 235 measures, organized into 11 chapters: Sex Roles (59 scales), Sex Stereotypes (25 scales), Sex Role Prescriptions (7 scales), Children's Sex Roles (11 scales), Gender Knowledge (5 scales), Marital and Parental Roles (23 scales), Employee Roles (16 scales), Multiple Roles (20 scales), Attitudes Toward Women's Issues (41 scales), Somatic and Sexual Issues (17 scales), and Unclassified (11 scales). Users' and reviewers' comments have made it clear that the book serves a useful purpose.

The field of women's research has grown phenomenally during the past decade: areas not previously researched have become the foci of study, some measures formerly used were discarded, and researchers have developed new measures. Considering the changes that have taken place, it is clear that my 1979 book is of limited use for future research. For this reason, I have written a new book, providing researchers with more recent information about appropriate measures.

I conducted a thorough literature search using two databases: SilverPlatter's PsycLIT and its ERIC. PsycLIT is the computerized version of *Psychological Abstracts*, which abstracts articles from about 1,300 journals in psychology and related disciplines. ERIC is the computerized version of *Current Index to Journals in Education (CIJE)*, which abstracts articles from over 740 education journals, and *Resources in Education (RIE)*, which abstracts the documents comprising the microfiche collection of the Education Resources Information Center (ERIC).

After reviewing search terms listed in the *Thesaurus of Psychological Index Terms* (American Psychological Association, 1985), I selected the following 58 terms for searching PsycLIT:

amenorrhea	androgyny	anorexia nervosa
appetite disorders	birth	bulimia
childbirth training	daughters	divorce
dual career	dysmenorrhea	family planning attitudes
family structure	family violence	fathers
femininity	feminism	gender identity
housewives	human females	husbands
hysterectomy	incest	induced abortion
labor-childbirth	lesbianism	marital relations
marriage	masculinity	mastectomy
matriarchy	menarche	menopause
menstrual disorders	menstrual cycle	menstruation
mother-child relations	mothers	natural childbirth
obscenity	ovariectomy	parental role
pornography	pregnancy	premenstrual tension
prostitution	rape	sex discrimination
sex role	sexual harassment	sexual attitude
sisters	spontaneous abortion	unwed mothers
widows	wives	women's liberation movement
working women		

From the *Thesaurus of ERIC Descriptors* (Houston, 1987), I selected 49 terms for my ERIC search:

abortion	anorexia nervosa	androgyny
battered women	birth	bulimia
contraception	daughters	displaced homemakers
divorce	employed parents	employed women
family attitudes	family planning	family role
family violence	fathers	femininity
feminism	gynecology	homemakers
homosexuality	incest	lesbianism
marital satisfaction	marital status	marriage
masculinity	mother attitudes	mothers
obscenity	parent role	pornography
pregnancy	pregnant students	rape
sex bias	sex education	sex fairness
sex role	sex stereotypes	sexual abuse
sexual harassment	sexual identity	sexuality
sons	spouses	unwed mothers
women's studies		

I searched the two databases for articles entered between January 1978 and December 1988. Additionally I identified selected journal titles and hand searched issues not entered into the database as of December 1988. The hand-searched journals were: *Adolescence, Behaviour Research and Therapy, Child Development, Developmental Psychology, Family Relations, Journal of Clinical Psychology, Journal of Counseling Psychology, Journal of Marriage and the Family, Journal of Sex Research, Journal of Sex and Marital Therapy, Journal of Social Psychology, Journal of Vocational Behavior, Perceptual and Motor Skills, Personality and Social Psychology Bulletin, Psychological Reports, Psychology of Women Quarterly,* and *Sex Roles.*

Not surprisingly, my procedures produced a tremendous number of articles and hence a very large number of scales. The computer search yielded 36,000 references, reduced to 6,900 references as a result of reviewing the abstracts. Articles from the hand-searched journals made the final total slightly higher. I identified 1,450 measures of widely varying quality. I developed criteria for determining which scales to include in the new handbook: (1) any scale described in my original handbook would be included if used in research published since the completion of my original literature search (about 1978); (2) any relevant scale for which there was evidence of reliability or validity and which had been used in more than one published article or ERIC document would be included; (3) if a published article or ERIC document focused on a measure's development, that measure would be included; or (4) if the measure assessed a relevant variable not measured by other scales I located, that measure was included. Despite these criteria, it soon became apparent that I had too much material for a single handbook. The rather obvious solution was to prepare two handbooks.

In the first, *Gender Roles: A Handbook of Tests and Measures* (Beere, 1990), I described 211 scales in seven chapters: Gender Roles (39 scales), Children and Gender (18 scales), Stereotypes (18 scales), Marital and Parental Roles (26 scales), Employee Roles (24 scales), Multiple Roles (30 scales), and Attitudes Toward Gender Role Issues (56 scales). Of the 211 scales in the gender roles handbook, 67 (32%) were described in my original handbook (Beere, 1979).

This handbook, *Sex and Gender Issues: A Handbook of Tests and Measures*, describes 197 scales organized into 11 chapters: Heterosocial Relations (17 scales), Sexuality (41 scales), Contraception and Abortion (17 scales), Pregnancy and Childbirth (20 scales), Somatic Issues (16 scales), Homosexuality (10 scales), Rape and Sexual Coercion (25 scales), Family Violence (9 scales), Body Image and Appearance (17 scales), Eating Disorders (20 scales), and Other Scales (5 scales). Only 6 (3%) of these scales were described in my 1979 handbook.

SOURCE OF INFORMATION FOR SCALE DESCRIPTIONS

I wrote all the scale descriptions for this book, relying primarily on information from articles, books, and ERIC documents. In some cases, I used information from dissertations or master's theses. Generally I did not consider a scale for inclusion unless I could review a copy of it. Most scales were readily available in the published literature or in ERIC documents; some I purchased from commercial test publishers. When I could not obtain the scale by these means, I contacted the scale authors to request a copy of the measure. Many scale authors sent me additional information that I incorporated into the scale description.

FORMAT FOR SCALE DESCRIPTIONS

For the 191 scales not described in my 1979 handbook, I used a consistent format for writing the scale descriptions, including the following information:

TITLE: The title of the scale is written as it was by the scale's author. If the authors did not assign a title to the scale, I assigned one, generally starting with the authors' names. If the scale name is commonly abbreviated, the abbreviation is given in parentheses following the scale's title. Sometimes several scales have the same abbreviation.

AUTHORS: For most scales, the author or authors are listed as they appear on the earliest publication mentioning the scale. Occasionally information contained in a publication or in personal correspondence from the author indicated different authors or a different order for the authors' names. I used the best information I had for identifying the authors' names and their order.

DATE: Generally the date given is the earliest date that the scale was mentioned in a publication. Occasionally information contained in a publication or in personal correspondence from the author indicated an earlier date. Information showing that the test was used earlier or revised later is listed in parentheses following the date.

VARIABLE: I provide a brief statement of the variables that the scale is intended to measure, usually based on the author(s)' claims. Of course, researchers sometimes use a measure for a different purpose than its authors intended, and a scale does not always measure the variable it is intended to measure.

TYPE OF INSTRUMENT: Of the 197 measures described, 134 (68%) are summated rating scales. There are also multiple choice measures, alternate choice measures, semantic differentials, observational measures, physiological measures, checklists, forced choice measures, Guttman scales, visual analogue scales, role plays, and open-ended questionnaires.

DESCRIPTION: I provide a general description of the scale, including information regarding length, item content, and response options. Subscales are described.

SAMPLE ITEMS: One sample item is usually given for each subscale; if there are no subscales, one or two items are given from the test as a whole.

PREVIOUS SUBJECTS: The most salient characteristic of each group who completed the scale is given. College students are listed separately from adults in general, but no differentiation is made for college major or class standing (e.g., freshman vs. sophomore, undergraduate vs. graduate). If the scale was used in foreign countries, they are listed here.

APPROPRIATE FOR: Since authors rarely provide information regarding who can complete their measure, I made a judgment on this issue for most scales. I reviewed the items on the scale and considered the difficulty of the task. My judgments should be considered tentative, and researchers should pilot test a measure with groups comparable to the ones they intend to study. One cannot presume that measures are reliable and valid for different populations.

ADMINISTRATION: Most of the measures are self-administered. When a measure requires special administration, I briefly describe the procedures. Time requirements are given here; usually they are my own estimates. They should be considered tentative and be verified with pilot testing.

SCORING: Information is provided on the number of scores, names of the scores, range of scores, and scoring procedures. Availability of normative data is indicated in this section.

DEVELOPMENT: Information I obtained regarding theoretical or empirical bases for scale development is described here.

RELIABILITY: Reliability data are presented here, including alpha, Kuder-Richardson (KR) 20, split-half, test-retest, and alternate form reliabilities, as well as item-total or item-subscale correlations. The most commonly reported reliability reflects internal consistency of the scale, generally an alpha coefficient; test-retest is next most frequently reported. Researchers rarely report both internal consistency and test-retest reliabilities. Do not presume that evidence regarding reliability is proof the scale is sufficiently reliable. Reliability coefficients are often too low to allow generalizing from the results; this is particularly true for short subscales.

VALIDITY: There are numerous ways to provide evidence relevant to a scale's validity. Information on content validity, concurrent validity, and construct validity (including convergent and discriminant validity) is reported in this section. Often the validity data were inferred from studies involving hypothesis testing or factor analysis; that is, if the hypothesis was supported or the obtained factor structure paralleled the intended factor structure, that provided indirect evidence of the measure's construct validity. It was difficult to decide whether factor analytic and hypothesis testing studies were best reported in this section or under NOTES & COMMENTS. I entered each study where I felt it best fit, without regard to consistency. For scales used extensively, it was not possible to summarize all the studies in the validity section; I described the significant validity studies in this section and listed other studies under NOTES & COMMENTS. As with reliability, validity data were not always positive. Although some evidence supports the validity, some refutes it, and some is ambiguous. When factor analysis is used to provide evidence of validity, one should interpret findings in light of the sample size. Too often researchers use a small number of subjects relative to the size of the item pool.

NOTES & COMMENTS: I provide information here that does not readily fit into any of the other headings. For example, I describe scale modifications, enumerate criticisms of the scale, and describe research using the scale.

AVAILABLE FROM: This section provides the information necessary to acquire the measure. For commercially published scales, the publisher or distributor is listed. Other measures are available from journal articles, books, ERIC documents, dissertations, or the National Auxiliary Publication Service (NAPS). Some unpublished measures are available from the author(s) of the scale. Regardless of the measure's source, researchers are cautioned to obtain all necessary permissions before using copyrighted materials. Obtaining the necessary permissions sometimes reaps unexpected benefits; the person or organization contacted may tell the researcher about a newer edition of the scale or direct the researcher to new information regarding the psychometric properties or uses of the scale.

USED IN: This section lists the articles and ERIC documents that report research using the scale. I wish these lists were comprehensive, but many are not. Since my literature search did not consider the years prior to 1979, reference lists for the older scales are incomplete. Articles from journals not in *Psychological Abstracts* are likely omitted. My search terms defined the topics that would be located; if a scale was used in a research study that was not indexed on any of my search terms, I would not have identified that article for inclusion. I did not systematically search *Dissertation Abstracts International*, but if I serendipitously located a relevant dissertation, it is listed. Most dissertations, however, are omitted. Researchers interested in amending my lists are advised to use SilverPlatter's PsycLIT for newer references, and to use *Social Sciences Citation Index* for comprehensiveness.

BIBLIOGRAPHY: Listed here are citations to materials that are referred to in the scale's description, but do not report research using the measure.

Abbreviated descriptions are provided for the six scales described in my 1979 handbook. The abbreviated descriptions include the following information: TITLE, AUTHOR, DATE, VARIABLE, DESCRIPTION, ARTICLES LISTED IN BEERE, 1979, NOTES & COMMENTS, AVAILABLE FROM, USED IN, and BIBLIOGRAPHY. All but one of these headings were described above: "ARTICLES LISTED IN BEERE, 1979" reports the number of references that accompanied my earlier description of the scale.

OTHER REFERENCES

There are numerous books that are useful for researchers seeking information about scales not described in this handbook. Some of these books are mentioned in the introductions to the relevant chapters. Others are listed below.

Gender Roles: A Handbook of Tests and Measures (Beere, 1990) contains descriptions of 211 measures used in gender role research. It also includes a thorough description of the procedures I used to develop the two handbooks (more complete than what is included in this book) and a chapter describing the measurement problems common in gender-related research.

Women and Women's Issues: A Handbook of Tests and Measures (Beere, 1979) includes descriptions of 235 measures, but clearly it is a dated source of information.

Measures for Clinical Practice: A Sourcebook (Corcoran & Fischer, 1987) contains descriptions and copies of 127 scales selected "because they measure most of the common problems seen in clinical practice, they are relatively short, easy to score and administer" (p. xxv).

Sexuality-Related Measures: A Compendium (Davis, Yarber, & Davis, 1988) describes 109 measures dealing with a variety of sexuality-related topics. Many of these scales are reproduced in the book. The scales are organized into 38 topics. Unfortunately, there are no indexes to facilitate using the book.

Marriage and Family Assessment: A Sourcebook for Family Therapy (Filsinger, 1983) contains five chapters on observational techniques, five chapters on marital questionnaires, and four chapters regarding family questionnaires.

Family Assessment: A Guide to Methods and Measures (Grotevant & Carlson, 1989) contains descriptions of 70 family assessment measures. The descriptions were written by the book's authors, but each description is followed by a comment—about half a page—written by the scale's author.

Dictionary of Behavioral Assessment Techniques (Hersen & Bellack, 1988) contains descriptions of 287 behavioral assessment measures. Author and subject indexes facilitate locating scales.

Handbook of Family Measurement Techniques (Touliatos, Perlmutter, & Straus, 1989) provides descriptions of 976 measures with relatively detailed information on 504 of them. The scales pertain to dimensions of family interaction, intimacy and family values, parenthood, family roles and power, and family adjustment. Author, title, and classification indexes facilitate locating scales.

Sourcebook of Measures of Women's Educational Equity (Parks, Bogart, Reynolds, Hamilton, & Finley, 1982) contains descriptions of 198 measures used to evaluate programs to eliminate sex stereotyping. Three indexes—title, subject, and author—facilitate locating scales.

There are very good references available that deal with published tests. The *Mental Measurements Yearbooks* (MMY) have been published at irregular intervals since 1938 (the predecessor of the MMYs was published in 1933); the most recent volume is the tenth edition published in 1989 (Conoley & Kramer, 1989). Related to the MMYs is *Tests in Print* (TIP), also published at irregular intervals. The most recent TIP is *Tests in Print III* (Mitchell, 1983). The Test Corporation of America has published two series of books that deal primarily with commercially published tests:

Tests: A Comprehensive Reference for Assessments in Psychology, Education and Business (Sweetland & Keyser, 1983, 1986) and *Test Critiques*, a multivolume series edited by Keyser and Sweetland. The series began in 1984; the newest volume was published in 1988.

Among older books that provide information on measures are *Sociological Measurement: An Inventory of Scales and Indices* (Bonjean, Hill, & McLemore, 1967), *Measures for Psychological Assessment: A Guide to 3,000 Original Sources and Their Applications* (Chun, Cobb, & French, 1975), *A Sourcebook of Mental Health Measures* (Comrey, Backer, & Glaser, 1973), *Directory of Unpublished Experimental Mental Measures* (Vols. 1 & 2) (Goldman & Busch, 1978; Goldman & Saunders, 1974), *Tests and Measurements in Child Development: Handbook I* (Johnson & Bommarito, 1971), *Tests and Measurements in Child Development: Handbook II* (Johnson, 1976), *Handbook of Research Design and Social Measurement* (Miller, 1970), *Measures of Occupational Attitudes and Occupational Characteristics* (Robinson, Athanasiou, & Head, 1969), *Measures of Political Attitudes* (Robinson, Rusk, & Head, 1968), *Scales for the Measurement of Attitudes* (Shaw & Wright, 1967), and *Socioemotional Measures for Preschool and Kindergarten Children* (Walker, 1973).

Another source for obtaining information on measures is the Health Instruments File database, an online database service containing information on more than 4,500 health-related measures, including measures for the behavioral sciences. The Health Instruments File database is accessible through BRS Information Technologies, 1200 RT 7, Latham, NY 12110 (telephone: 1–800–345–4277).

BIBLIOGRAPHY:

American Psychological Association. (1985). *Thesaurus of psychological index terms* (4th ed.). Washington, DC: Author.

Beere, C. A. (1979). *Women and women's issues: A handbook of tests and measures*. San Francisco: Jossey-Bass.

Beere, C. A. (1990). *Gender roles: A handbook of tests and measures*. Westport, CT: Greenwood.

Bonjean, C. M., Hill, R. J., & McLemore, S. D. (1967). *Sociological measurement: An inventory of scales and indices*. San Francisco: Chandler.

Chun, K. T., Cobb, S., & French, J. R. P., Jr. (1975). *Measures for psychological assessment: A guide to 3,000 original sources and their applications*. Ann Arbor: Survey Research Center of the Institute for Social Research.

Comrey, A. L., Backer, T. E., & Glaser, E. M. (1973). *A sourcebook of mental health measures*. Los Angeles: Human Interaction Research Institute.

Conoley, J. C., & Kramer, J. J. (1989). *The tenth mental measurements yearbook*. Lincoln, NE: Buros Institute of Mental Measurements, University of Nebraska.

Corcoran, K., & Fischer, J. (1987). *Measures for clinical practice: A sourcebook*. New York: Free Press.

Davis, C. M., Yarber, W. L., & Davis, S. L. (Eds.). (1988). *Sexuality-related measures: A compendium*. Syracuse: Editors.

Filsinger, E. E. (Ed.). (1983). *Marriage and family assessment: A sourcebook for family therapy*. Beverly Hills: Sage.

Goldman, B. A., & Busch, J. C. (1978). *Directory of unpublished experimental mental measures* (Vol. 2). New York: Human Sciences Press.

Goldman, B. A., & Saunders, J. L. (1974). *Directory of unpublished experimental mental measures* (Vol. 1). New York: Behavioral Publications.

Grotevant, H. D., & Carlson, C. I. (1989). *Family assessment: A guide to methods and measures*. New York: Guilford Press.

Hersen, M., & Bellack, A. S. (Eds.). (1988). *Dictionary of behavioral assessment techniques*. New York: Pergamon Press.

Houston, J. E. (Ed.). (1987). *Thesaurus of ERIC descriptors* (11th ed.). Phoenix: Oryx Press.

Johnson, O. G. (1976). *Tests and measurements in child development: Handbook II*. San Francisco: Jossey-Bass.

Johnson, O. G., & Bommarito, J. W. (1971). *Tests and measurements in child development: Handbook I*. San Francisco: Jossey-Bass.

Keyser, D. J., & Sweetland, R. C. (Eds.). (1988). *Test critiques* (Vol. 7). Kansas City: Test Corporation of America.

Miller, D. C. (1970). *Handbook of research design and social measurement* (2nd ed.). New York: McKay.

Mitchell, J. V., Jr. (1983). *Tests in print III*. Lincoln, NE: Buros Institute of Mental Measurements, University of Nebraska.

Parks, B. J., Bogart, K., Reynolds, D. F., Hamilton, M., & Finley, C. J. (1982). *Sourcebook of measures of women's educational equity*. Palo Alto: American Institutes for Research.

Robinson, J. P., Athanasiou, R., & Head, K. B. (1969). *Measures of occupational attitudes and occupational characteristics*. Ann Arbor: Institute for Social Research, University of Michigan.

Robinson, J. P., Rusk, J. G., & Head, K. B. (1968). *Measures of political attitudes*. Ann Arbor: Institute for Social Research, University of Michigan.

Shaw, M. E., & Wright, J. M. (1967). *Scales for the measurement of attitudes*. New York: McGraw-Hill.

Sweetland, R. C., & Keyser, D. J. (Eds.). (1983). *Tests: A comprehensive reference for assessments in psychology, education and business*. Kansas City: Test Corporation of America.

Sweetland, R. C., & Keyser, D. J. (Eds.). (1986). *Tests: A comprehensive reference for assessments in psychology, education and business* (2nd ed.). Kansas City: Test Corporation of America.

Touliatos, J., Perlmutter, B. F., & Straus, M. A. (1989). *Handbook of family measurement techniques*. Newbury Park, CA: Sage.

Walker, D. K. (1973). *Socioemotional measures for preschool and kindergarten children*. San Francisco: Jossey-Bass.

2

Heterosocial Relations

The 17 scales described in this chapter deal with heterosocial relations. The first 5 scales relate to heterosocial competence, the next 6 pertain specifically to love, and the balance cover a variety of topics. Since I did not cover these topics in my original handbook (Beere, 1979), none of these scales was described in that book, but 5 of them are old enough to have been included. Three of the older scales deal with love: Attitudes Toward Love (Knox & Sporakowski, 1968), Rubin Liking Scale/Rubin Love Scale (Rubin, 1970), and Scale of Feelings and Behavior of Love (Fiore & Swensen, 1977). The other 2 older scales are the Attitudes Toward Marital Exclusivity Scale (Neubeck & Schletzer, 1962), the oldest scale in this chapter, and the Survey of Heterosexual Interactions (Twentyman & McFall, 1975). Had the search procedures for this book covered the years before 1978, it is likely that additional older scales would have been located for this chapter, but these would have been scales that are no longer used.

Fifteen of the 17 scales in this chapter are summated rating scales, 1 is an observational rating scale, and 1 is a multiple choice measure. The scales tend to be fairly short, ranging from 7 to 42 items with two exceptions: the Heterosocial Assessment Inventory for Women (Kolko, 1985) contains 60 items, and the Scale of Feelings and Behavior of Love (Fiore & Swensen, 1977) contains 120 items. The scales in this chapter are appropriate for high school and/or college students and for adults, with some measures restricted to one sex. Only 1 scale—the Male-Female Relations Questionnaire (Spence, Helmreich, & Sawin, 1980)—is available in separate forms for female and male respondents.

There were some data relevant to the reliability of 16 of the 17 scales in this chapter. Alpha coefficients were reported for 13 of the measures, and test-retest reliability was reported for 8 measures. Only the Munro-Adams Love Attitude Scale (Munro & Adams, 1978) lacked any information regarding reliability. Of course, data relevant to reliability are not always data supportive of reliability. In fact, the reliability for some scales was marginal, and for others it was unacceptably low. When scales and subscales are short, reliability is more likely to be low.

There were data relevant to the validity of all scales in this chapter. Sometimes the data strongly supported the scale's validity; other times, the data were equivocal, but at least validity was considered.

There is considerable variability in the extent to which the scales in this chapter have been used. The Rubin Liking Scale and Rubin Love Scale (Rubin, 1970) have been used more often than the other measures; the next most commonly used measure is the Adversarial Sexual Beliefs scale (Burt, 1980).

It was a challenge to decide which scales to include in this chapter and which to omit; there are many scales closely related to the 17 described here. For example, "relationship" scales focus on dating relationships or on marital relationships. Those in the former group are included here; those in the latter group are not. Some relationship scales might be readily adapted for both dating and marital relationships. Researchers interested in studying relationships might be interested in some of the scales excluded from this book. Their exclusion was not a function of their quality; rather their exclusion reflects the fact that they are less relevant than the scales that were included. Following are brief descriptions of some excluded scales.

The Relationship Inventory (Barrett-Lennard, 1962, 1978) was originally developed in 1957 to measure "five theoretically critical variables of therapist counselor-to-client response" (Barrett-Lennard, 1978, p. [i]). Since then it has been used extensively to measure relationships within marriage. The scale was reproduced in Barrett-Lennard's (1978) article.

The Relationship Belief Inventory (Eidelson & Epstein, 1982) was developed to measure "dysfunctional relationship beliefs" (p. 715). Used to study married couples' relationships, the inventory has five subscales: Disagreement is destructive; Mindreading is expected; Partners cannot change; Sexual perfectionism; and the Sexes are different. The measure can be obtained from Norman Epstein at the University of Maryland.

The Caring Relationship Inventory (Shostrom, 1975) measures "the essential elements of love or caring in human relationships" (p. 3). The scale contains 83 true/false items representing five subscales: Affection, Friendship, Eros, Empathy, and Self-Love. The scale has been used to study marital relationships as well as nonmarital relationships. It can be purchased from EdITS, P.O. Box 7234, San Diego, CA 92107.

An interesting and related scale that has been used to study married couples is Ryder's Lovesickness Scale. It consists of 32 true/false items pertaining to whether "the husband or wife paid enough attention or was adequately loving" (Ryder, 1973, p. 604). The Lovesickness Scale can be obtained from Robert Ryder at the University of Connecticut.

Another scale for assessing relationships was described by Peplau, Cochran, Rook, and Padesky (1978) and later used by Peplau and Cochran (1981) and Cochran and Peplau (1985). The scale, designed to measure relationship values, contains between 20 and 23 items representing two or three factors, depending on the group completing the scale. The different versions of the scale appear in the different articles cited here.

Two other relationship measures that may be of interest to researchers were developed by Snell; they are not described in this handbook because they have not yet appeared in any published materials, although both have been the focus of convention presentations. The first scale, the Relationship Awareness Scale, is a 30-item summated rating scale with items representing three factors: relationship-consciousness, relationship-monitoring, and relationship-anxiety. Snell (1988) defined the factors as follows: "relationship-consciousness refers to people's tendency to be aware of the nature and dynamics of their intimate relationships; relationship-monitoring refers to the tendency to be concerned with the public image of one's intimate relationship; and relationship-anxiety deals with the tendency to feel anxious, tense, and inhibited in intimate relationships" (p. 2). The second scale is the Relationship Assessment Scale, another 30-item summated rating scale with items representing three factors: relationship-esteem, relationship-depression, and relationship-preoccupation. Snell and Finney (1988) defined the factors as follows: "relationship-esteem [is] a generalized tendency to positively evaluate one's capacity to relate intimately to another person; relationship-depression [is] a tendency to feel depressed about one's capability to relate in an intimate way to a close partner; and relationship-preoccupation [is] the tendency to become highly absorbed in thoughts about intimate relationships" (p. 2). The Relationship Awareness Scale and the Relationship Assessment Scale can be obtained from William Snell at Southeast Missouri State University, Cape Girardeau, Missouri.

In addition to the heterosocial competence scales described in this chapter, a variety of scales measuring social competence have appeared in the literature. There are a number of reasons that such scales have been omitted from this chapter: they focus on general social competence rather than specifically heterosocial competence, they have not been used in the past decade, they have not been used by more than one researcher, or I was unable to obtain a copy of the measure. Because researchers might want to know more about these scales, they are briefly described here.

Watson and Friend (1969) developed two measures dealing with social competence. The Fear of Negative Evaluation Scale is a 30-item true/false measure designed to measure "apprehension about others' evaluations, distress over their negative evaluations, avoidance of evaluative situations, and the expectation that others would evaluate oneself negatively" (Watson & Friend, 1969, p. 449). The Social Avoidance and Distress Scale (SADS) is a 28-item true/false measure containing two subscales: "Social avoidance . . . defined as avoiding being with, talking to, or escaping from others for any reason [and] social distress . . . defined as the reported experience of a negative emotion, such as being upset, distressed, tense, or anxious, in social interactions, or the reported lack of negative emotions" (p. 449). Both scales have been used by other researchers, and both scales appear in Watson and Friend's article.

Rehm and Marson (1968) briefly described a 30-item summated rating scale to measure heterosocial anxiety. It is titled the Situation Questionnaire, and different versions of the scale are needed for male and female respondents. The Situation Questionnaire can be obtained from Lynn Rehm at the University of Houston.

Arkowitz, Lichtenstein, McGovern, and Hines (1975) briefly described the Social Activity Questionnaire, a "multiple choice survey inquiring about frequency of dating, and self-reports of comfort, skill, and satisfaction with present dating behavior" (p. 4). Because I was unable to obtain a copy of this measure, I did not describe it in this chapter; it has, however, been used by other researchers during the past decade.

Perri and Richards (1979) described the development of a behavioral approach to assessing heterosocial skills in college men. A complete description of the procedure is available in Perri's (1977) doctoral dissertation. For more information on role-playing approaches to assessing social skills, see Bellack, Hersen, and Lamparski (1979) and Fawcett (1988).

There are several topics that seem to relate, at least indirectly, to social competence, in particular, assertiveness, self-disclosure, and intimacy. These topics are not included in this book because I had to place some limits on the scope of coverage. Nevertheless, researchers may find it useful to know a little about the scales most often used to measure these variables.

Five assertiveness measures have been used extensively. The Rathus Assertiveness Schedule (Rathus, 1973) is a 30-item summated rating scale and probably the most commonly used measure of assertiveness. For a copy of the scale, consult Rathus's (1973) article. Gambrill and Richey (1975) developed the Assertion Inventory, a 40-item self-report scale for assessing assertiveness. Gambrill and Richey (1988) provided an overview of the measure, and the items are printed in their 1975 article. Galassi, DeLo, Galassi, and Bastien (1974) described the development of a 50-item assertiveness measure appropriate for college students. Titled the College Self-Expression Scale, the scale measures three aspects of assertiveness: positive assertiveness, which is the expression of positive feelings; negative assertion, which is the expression of negative feelings; and self-denial, which involves "overapologizing, excessive interpersonal anxiety, and exaggerated concern for the feelings of others" (Galassi et al., 1974, p. 168). The College Self-Expression Scale is described in Galassi and Galassi (1988b), and the items are provided in Galassi et al. (1974). The Adult Self-Expression Scale (Gay, Hollandsworth, & Galassi, 1975) is a 48-item summated rating scale appropriate for measuring assertiveness in an adult population. The scale is described in Galassi and Galassi (1988a) and can be obtained from Melvin Gay at Central Piedmont Community College, Charlotte, North Carolina. MacDonald (1978) described a 52-item role-play measure of assertion, the College Women's Assertion Sample. The scale is described in MacDonald (1988); the items are available from MacDonald (1974/1975).

Although these five are the most commonly used measures of assertiveness, others might prove useful to researchers. Callner and Ross (1976) developed a 40-item measure of assertiveness. The items are presented in their article; the scale is described by Ammerman and VanHasselt (1988). O'Leary and Curley (1986) developed the Spouse Specific Assertion/Aggression Scale, a 29-item measure containing 17 assertion items and 12 aggression items. The scale is intended for use with married couples. The scale is available from K. Daniel O'Leary at the State University of New York at Stony Brook. Bakker, Bakker-Rabdau, and Breit (1978) developed the Bakker Assertiveness-Aggressiveness Inventory, a 32-item measure of "(a) defensive, responsive behaviors which protect territory and privileges, and (b) initiating behaviors which augment the person's territory or status" (p. 277). Their article includes the full scale. Osborn and Harris (1975) described the Assertive Behavior Assessment for Women, a 60-item summated rating scale that is reproduced in the appendix of their book. Eisler, Miller, and Hersen (1973) described the development of a role-play measure of assertiveness. Eisler (1988) described the Behavioral Assertiveness Test-Revised, a 32-item role-play measure. The original role-play situations are given in Eisler et al. (1973); the revised measured can be obtained from Richard Eisler at Virginia Polytechnic Institute, Blacksburg, Virginia. McFall and Lillesand (1971) developed a role-playing measure of assertiveness, titled the Behavioral Role-Playing Assertion Test. The measure was described by St. Lawrence (1988) and can be obtained from Richard McFall at the University of Indiana.

The topic of self-disclosure also relates to social competence. The most commonly used measure of self-disclosure, the Jourard Self-Disclosure Questionnaire (Jourard, 1971), contains 10 items for each of six areas: attitudes and opinions, tastes and interests, work, money, personality, and body. Respondents indicate the extent to which they have talked about each item with a particular disclosure recipient. Jourard (1971) listed all of the items on the scale. Snell, Miller, and Belk (1988) developed the Emotional Self-Disclosure Scale to measure persons' willingness to disclose information about specific emotions with different disclosure recipients. Snell, Belk, and Hawkins (1986) developed the Masculine and Feminine Self-Disclosure Scale described in Chapter 12 of this handbook.

The third area that seems related to social competence is intimacy. The most frequently used measures of intimacy that I located were the Personal Assessment of Intimacy in Relationships (PAIR) (Schaefer & Olson, 1981) and the Intimacy Status Interview (Orlofsky, Marcia, & Lesser, 1973). The former measure "provides systematic information on five types of intimacy: emotional, social, sexual, intellectual and recreational" (Schaefer & Olson, 1981, p. 47). For information on purchasing the PAIR, contact David Olson at the University of Minnesota in St. Paul. The Intimacy Status Interview relies on a semistructured interview "to assess the level of intimacy in the individual's relationship with close friends and lover(s)" (Orlofsky, undated, p. 1). Intimacy is based on involvement, commitment, depth of communication, and dependency or autonomy in relationships. For complete information regarding this measure, contact Jacob Orlofsky at the University of Missouri, St. Louis. Researchers might also be interested in other measures of intimacy developed by Walker and Thompson (1983), Waring and Reddon (1983), and Christensen and Carpenter (1962).

Some references described in Chapter 1 might prove useful for researchers who seek measures to meet their research needs. *Gender Roles: A Handbook of Tests and Measures* (Beere, 1990) includes a chapter dealing with marital roles; some of those measures are useful for assessing nonmarital relationships. Touliatos, Perlmutter, and Straus (1989) provided descriptions of 976 measures that were selected because of their relevance to the needs of family researchers. Many of those scales are relevant for researchers interested in heterosocial relations. Hersen and Bellack's *Dictionary of Behavioral Assessment Techniques* (1988) describes a variety of measures that are likely to relate to heterosocial assessment. Similarly, Corcoran and Fischer's *Measures for Clinical Practice* (1987) describes numerous measures relevant to heterosocial assessment. Although it is somewhat outdated, researchers might also find it useful to review Hersen and Bellack's (1977) "Assessment of Social Skills."

BIBLIOGRAPHY:

Ammerman, R. T., & VanHasselt, V. B. (1988). Callner-Ross Assertion Questionnaire. In M. Hersen & A. S. Bellack (Eds.), *Dictionary of behavioral assessment techniques* (pp. 90–91). New York: Pergamon.

Arkowitz, H., Lichtenstein, E., McGovern, K., & Hines, P. (1975). The behavioral assessment of social competence in males. *Behavior Therapy*, *6*, 3–13.

Bakker, C. B., Bakker-Rabdau, M. K., & Breit, S. (1978). The measurement of assertiveness and aggressiveness. *Journal of Personality Assessment*, *42*, 277–284.

Barrett-Lennard, G. T. (1962). Dimensions of therapist response as causal factors in therapeutic change. *Psychological Monographs*, *76*(43). (Whole No. 562)

Barrett-Lennard, G. T. (1978). The Relationship Inventory: Development and adaptations. *Catalog of Selected Documents in Psychology*, *8*, 68. (Ms. No. 1732)

Beere, C. A. (1979). *Women and women's issues: A handbook of tests and measures*. San Francisco: Jossey-Bass.

Beere, C. A. (1990). *Gender roles: A handbook of tests and measures*. Westport, CT: Greenwood.

Bellack, A. S., Hersen, M., & Lamparski, D. (1979). Role-play tests for assessing social skills: Are they valid? Are they useful? *Journal of Consulting and Clinical Psychology*, *47*, 335–342.

Burt, M. R. (1980). Cultural myths and supports for rape. *Journal of Personality and Social Psychology*, *38*, 217–230.

Callner, D. A., & Ross, S. M. (1976). The reliability and validity of three measures of assertion in a drug addict population. *Behavior Therapy*, *7*, 659–667.

Christensen, H. T., & Carpenter, G. R. (1962). Value-behavior discrepancies regarding premarital coitus in three Western cultures. *American Sociology Review*, *27*, 66–74.

Cochran, S. D., & Peplau, L. A. (1985). Value orientations in heterosexual relationships. *Psychology of Women Quarterly*, *9*, 477–488.

Corcoran, K., & Fischer, J. (1987). *Measures for clinical practice: A sourcebook*. New York: Free Press.

Eidelson, R. J., & Epstein, N. (1982). Cognition and relationship maladjustment: Development of a measure of dysfunctional relationship beliefs. *Journal of Consulting and Clinical Psychology*, *50*, 715–720.

Eisler, R. M. (1988). Behavioral Assertiveness Test—Revised. In M. Hersen & A. S. Bellack (Eds.), *Dictionary of behavioral assessment techniques* (pp. 48–50). New York: Pergamon.

Eisler, R. M., Miller, P. M., & Hersen, M. (1973). Components of assertive behavior. *Journal of Clinical Psychology*, *29*, 295–299.

Fawcett, S. B. (1988). Role-playing assessment instruments. In M. Hersen & A. S. Bellack (Eds.), *Dictionary of behavioral assessment techniques* (pp. 385–389). New York: Pergamon.

Fiore, A., & Swensen, C. H. (1977). Analysis of love relationships in functional and dysfunctional marriages. *Psychological Reports*, *40*, 707–714.

Galassi, J. P., DeLo, J. S., Galassi, M. D., & Bastien, S. (1974). The College Self-Expression Scale: A measure of assertiveness. *Behavior Therapy*, *5*, 165–171.

Galassi, J. P., & Galassi, M. D. (1988a). Adult Self-Expression Scale. In M. Hersen & A. S. Bellack (Eds.), *Dictionary of behavioral assessment techniques* (pp. 18–20). New York: Pergamon.

Galassi, J. P., & Galassi, M. D. (1988b). College Self-Expression Scale. In M. Hersen & A. S. Bellack (Eds.), *Dictionary of behavioral assessment techniques* (pp. 127–129). New York: Pergamon.

Gambrill, E. D., & Richey, C. A. (1975). An assertion inventory for use in assessment and research. *Behavior Therapy, 6*, 550–561.

Gambrill, E., & Richey, C. (1988). Assertion Inventory. In M. Hersen & A. S. Bellack (Eds.), *Dictionary of behavioral assessment techniques* (pp. 32–34). New York: Pergamon.

Gay, M. L., Hollandsworth, J. G., Jr., & Galassi, J. P. (1975). An assertiveness inventory for adults. *Journal of Counseling Psychology, 22*, 340–344.

Hersen, M., & Bellack, A. S. (1977). Assessment of social skills. In A. R. Ciminero, K. S. Calhoun, & H. E. Adams (Eds.), *Handbook of behavioral assessment*. New York: Wiley.

Hersen, M., & Bellack, A. S. (Eds.). (1988). *Dictionary of behavioral assessment techniques*. New York: Pergamon.

Jourard, S. M. (1971). *The transparent self* (pp. 213–217). New York: Van Nostrand Reinhold.

Knox, D. H., Jr., & Sporakowski, M. J. (1968). Attitudes of college students toward love. *Journal of Marriage and the Family, 30*, 638–642.

Kolko, D. J. (1985). The Heterosocial Assessment Inventory for Women: A psychometric and behavioral evaluation. *Journal of Psychopathology and Behavioral Assessment, 7*, 49–64.

MacDonald, M. L. (1975). A behavioral assessment methodology applied to the measurement of assertion (Doctoral dissertation, University of Illinois, 1974). *Dissertation Abstracts International, 35*, 6101B.

MacDonald, M. L. (1978). Measuring assertion: A model and method. *Behavior Therapy, 9*, 889–899.

MacDonald, M. L. (1988). College Women's Assertion Sample. In M. Hersen & A. S. Bellack (Eds.), *Dictionary of behavioral assessment techniques* (pp. 129–131). New York: Pergamon.

McFall, R. M., & Lillesand, D. B. (1971). Behavior rehearsal with modeling and coaching in assertion training. *Journal of Abnormal Psychology, 77*, 313–323.

Munro, B., & Adams, G. R. (1978). Love American style: A test of role structure theory on changes in attitudes toward love. *Human Relations, 31*, 215–228.

Neubeck, G., & Schletzer, V. M. (1962). A study of extra-marital relationships. *Marriage and Family Living, 24*, 279–281.

O'Leary, K. D., & Curley, A. D. (1986). Assertion and family violence: Correlates of spouse abuse. *Journal of Marital and Family Therapy, 12*, 281–289.

Orlofsky, J. L. (undated). *Abstract: Intimacy Status Interview and rating manual*. Unpublished manuscript, University of Missouri, St. Louis.

Orlofsky, J. L., Marcia, J. E., & Lesser, I. M. (1973). Ego identity status and the intimacy versus isolation crisis of young adulthood. *Journal of Personality and Social Psychology, 27*, 211–219.

Osborn, S. M., & Harris, G. G. (1975). *Assertive training for women*. Springfield, IL: Charles C. Thomas.

Peplau, L. A., & Cochran, S. D. (1981). Value orientations in the intimate relationships of gay men. *Journal of Homosexuality, 6*, 1–19.

Peplau, L. A., Cochran, S., Rook, K., & Padesky, C. (1978). Loving women: Attachment and autonomy in lesbian relationships. *Journal of Social Issues, 34*, 7–27.

Perri, M. G. (1977). *The empirical development of a behavioral role-playing test for the assessment of heterosocial skills in male college students*. Unpublished doctoral dissertation, University of Missouri, Columbia.

Perri, M. G., & Richards, C. S. (1979). Assessment of heterosocial skills in male college students: Empirical development of a behavioral role-playing test. *Behavior Modification, 3*, 337–354.

Rathus, S. A. (1973). A 30-item schedule for assessing assertive behavior. *Behavior Therapy, 4*, 396–406.

Rehm, L. P., & Marson, A. R. (1968). Reduction of social anxiety through modification of self-reinforcement: An instigation therapy technique. *Journal of Consulting and Clinical Psychology, 32*, 565–574.

Rubin, Z. (1970). Measurement of romantic love. *Journal of Personality and Social Psychology, 16*, 265–273.

Ryder, R. G. (1973). Longitudinal data relating marriage satisfaction and having a child. *Journal of Marriage and the Family, 35*, 604–606.

Schaefer, M. T., & Olson, D. H. (1981). Assessing intimacy: The Pair Inventory. *Journal of Marital and Family Therapy, 7*, 47–60.

Shostrom, E. L. (1975). *Caring Relationship Inventory Manual*. San Diego: Educational and Industrial Testing Service.

Snell, W. E., Jr. (1988, April). *The Relationship Awareness Scale: Measuring relationship-consciousness, relationship-monitoring, and relationship-anxiety*. Paper presented at the meeting of the Southwestern Psychological Association, Tulsa.

Snell, W. E., Jr., Belk, S. S., & Hawkins, R. C., II. (1986). The Masculine and Feminine Self-Disclosure Scale: The politics of masculine and feminine self-presentation. *Sex Roles, 15*, 249–267.

Snell, W. E., Jr., & Finney, P. (1988, April). *The Relationship Assessment Scale: Measuring relationship-esteem, relationship-depression, and relationship-preoccupation*. Paper presented at the meeting of the Southwestern Psychological Association, Tulsa.

Snell, W. E., Jr., Miller, R. S., & Belk, S. S. (1988). Development of the Emotional Self-Disclosure Scale. *Sex Roles, 18*, 59–73.

Spence, J. T., Helmreich, R. L., & Sawin, L. L. (1980). The Male-Female Relations Questionnaire: A self-report inventory of sex-role behaviors and preferences and its relationships to masculine and feminine personality traits, sex role attitudes, and other measures. *Catalog of Selected Documents in Psychology, 10*, 87. (Ms. No. 2123)

St. Lawrence, J. (1988). Behavioral Role-Playing Assertion Test. In M. Hersen & A. S. Bellack (Eds.), *Dictionary of behavioral assessment techniques* (pp. 67–69). New York: Pergamon.

Touliatos, J., Perlmutter, B. F., & Straus, M. A. (1989). *Handbook of family measurement techniques*. Newbury Park, CA: Sage.

Twentyman, C. T., & McFall, R. M. (1975). Behavioral training of social skills in shy men. *Journal of Consulting and Clinical Psychology, 43*, 384–395.

Walker, A. J., & Thompson, L. (1983). Intimacy and intergenerational aid and contact among mothers and daughters. *Journal of Marriage and the Family, 45*, 841–849.

Waring, E. M., & Reddon, J. R. (1983). The measurement of intimacy in marriage:

The Waring Intimacy Questionnaire. *Journal of Clinical Psychology, 39*, 53–57.

Watson, D., & Friend, R. (1969). Measurement of social-evaluative anxiety. *Journal of Consulting and Clinical Psychology, 33*, 448–457.

DATING AND ASSERTION QUESTIONNAIRE

AUTHORS: Robert W. Levenson and John M. Gottman

DATE: 1978

VARIABLE: Social competence in regard to dating and assertiveness

TYPE OF INSTRUMENT: Summated rating scale

DESCRIPTION: The Dating and Assertion Questionnaire is a two-part measure with nine items on each of the two parts. The first part contains a list of nine behaviors: four reflecting assertiveness and five related to dating. Each behavior is to be rated on a 4-point scale: "1 = I never do this; 2 = I sometimes do this; 3 = I often do this; 4 = I do this almost always." The second part of the questionnaire contains descriptions of nine situations, each ending with a statement of something the respondent would like to say or do in response to the situation. Five situations relate to assertiveness, and four relate to dating. For each situation, respondents use a 5-point scale to rate their response to the situation: "1 = I would be so uncomfortable and so unable to handle this situation that I would avoid it if possible; 2 = I would feel very uncomfortable and would have a lot of difficulty handling this situation; 3 = I would feel somewhat uncomfortable and would have some difficulty in handling this situation; 4 = I would feel quite comfortable and would be able to handle this situation fairly well; 5 = I would feel very comfortable and be able to handle this situation very well."

SAMPLE ITEMS: (Behaviors—Assertiveness) Stand up for your rights

(Situations—Dating) You have enjoyed this date and would like to see your date again. The evening is coming to a close and you decide to say something.

PREVIOUS SUBJECTS: College students, bulimics with and without a prior history of anorexia nervosa, nonbulimic binge eaters

APPROPRIATE FOR: College students

ADMINISTRATION: Self-administered; less than 10 minutes

SCORING: The ratings assigned to each item are used to obtain separate scores on two subscales: Dating Competence and Social Assertiveness. Higher scores reflect greater comfort and competence.

DEVELOPMENT: Two measures, a Situations Questionnaire and a Behavior Inventory, served as the basis for the Dating and Assertion Questionnaire. To develop the Situations Questionnaire, 8 college students each interviewed 10 college students, asking them to describe four social situations that "the interviewee had recently found to be 'difficult to handle' " (Levenson & Gottman, 1978, p. 455). This procedure produced 320 situations, later reduced to "97 nonredundant items that could be potentially relevant to both sexes and that struck a balance between being overly general or overly specific" (p. 455). The situations represented eight areas: refusal, getting what you want, expressing feelings, requesting behavior change, formal situations, conversation skills, close interpersonal situations, and dating. Durham (cited in Levenson & Gottman, 1978) tested the items using three different sets of rating scales: a scale based on competence/incompetence, a scale based on comfort/discomfort, and a scale including both competence/incompetence and comfort/discomfort. Test-retest reliability, alpha coefficients, and split-half reliability were all highest using the scale involving both competence and comfort. As a result, this was the rating scale adopted for the final form of the Dating and Assertion Questionnaire. Durham, using item analysis data, reduced the 97-item questionnaire to 40 items that still covered the eight areas. The Behavior Inventory, containing 26 items, was also developed. The Behavior Inventory contained five subscales: friendship, self-confidence, assertiveness, intimacy, and dating.

The Situations Questionnaire and the Behavior Inventory were administered to 46 college students who experienced problems in dealing with dating situations (called dating clients), to 46 college students who experienced problems in dealing with assertion situations (called assertion clients), and to 69 college students enrolled in an introductory psychology class. The Dating and Assertion Questionnaire was developed from the 26-item Behavior Inventory and the 40-item Situations Questionnaire "by selecting only those items that both successfully discriminated clients from normals and successfully discriminated dating clients from assertion clients" (Levenson & Gottman, 1978, p. 458). Nine items on the Dating and Assertion Questionnaire posed greater problems for the dating clients, and the other 9 items posed greater problems for the assertion clients. Half of the items were from the Behavior Inventory and half from the Situations Questionnaire.

RELIABILITY: Using data from the 92 clients and the 69 persons in the comparison group, the authors computed coefficient alpha to be .92 for the Dating Competence subscale and .85 for the Social Assertiveness subscale (Levenson & Gottman, 1978). The test-retest reliability coefficient, based on data from 28 college students tested on two occasions separated by 2 weeks, was .71 for the Dating Competence subscale and .71 for the Social Assertiveness subscale. Using data from a different group of 39 college students tested on two occasions separated by 6 weeks, the authors found that test-retest reliability coefficient was .62 for the Dating Competence subscale and .70 for the Social Assertiveness subscale (Levenson & Gottman, 1978).

Newcomb (1984) reported an internal consistency reliability of .81 for the Dating Competence subscale and .71 for the Social Assertiveness subscale.

VALIDITY: Levenson and Gottman (1978) compared the scores from 92 clients and 69 "normals." Clients scored significantly lower on both the Dating Competence and Social Assertiveness subscales; that is, they felt less competent and less comfortable. Additionally when the dating clients and the assertion clients were compared, the former group had significantly lower scores on the Dating Competence subscale, and the latter group had significantly lower scores on the Social Assertiveness subscale.

Levenson and Gottman (1978) provided further evidence for the scale's validity when they showed that significant pretest/posttest changes occurred when dating and assertion clients participated in programs to help them overcome their dating and assertion problems. In particular, there was a significant pretest/posttest score increase for the dating clients on the Dating Competence subscale. For the assertion clients, there were significant pretest/posttest increases for both the Dating Competence and Social Assertiveness subscales, but the gains on the Social Assertiveness subscale were greater.

Kolko and Milan (1985) developed a new measure to assess heterosocial competence. The measure, called the Heterosocial Skill Observational Rating System (HESORS) (see separate entry), required trained raters to observe subjects doing role plays and to rate the subjects on 11 verbal behaviors and 5 nonverbal behaviors. In validating the HESORS, Kolko and Milan found that 14 of the 16 HESORS behaviors were significantly correlated with scores on the Dating Competence subscale of the Dating and Assertion Questionnaire, and 13 of the 16 behaviors were significantly correlated with scores on the Social Assertiveness subscale.

Kolko (1985) correlated scores on the Dating and Assertion Questionnaire with scores on the five factors of his Heterosocial Assessment Inventory for Women (see separate entry). The five correlations were statistically significant, ranging in magnitude from .43 to .59.

NOTES & COMMENTS: Reis, Wheeler, Kernis, Spiegel, and Nezlek (1985) used the Dating and Assertion Questionnaire as one of several social competence measures in a study looking at the relationships between social competence and physical and psychological health. In a similar study, Wittenberg and Reis (1986) looked at the relationship between social competence and loneliness. Newcomb (1984, 1986) looked at the relationships between sexual behavior and a variety of other variables, including general assertiveness and dating competence. Katzman and Wolchik (1983) compared bulimics with and without anorexia nervosa on a variety of measures, including the Dating and Assertion Questionnaire. Similarly, Katzman and Wolchik (1984) compared bulimics, binge eaters, and a control group on a variety of measures, including the Dating and Assertion Questionnaire. Kobak and Sceery (1988) used the Dating and Assertion Questionnaire along with numerous other measures in a study of attachment in first-year college students.

AVAILABLE FROM: Levenson and Gottman, 1978; Corcoran and Fischer, 1987

USED IN:

Katzman, M. A., & Wolchik, S. A. (1983, April). *Bulimics with and without prior anorexia nervosa: A comparison of personality characteristics*. Paper presented at the meeting of the Rocky Mountain Psychological Association. (ERIC Document Reproduction Service No. ED 236 463)

Katzman, M. A., & Wolchik, S. A. (1984). Bulimia and binge eating in college women: A comparison of personality and behavioral characteristics. *Journal of Consulting and Clinical Psychology, 52*, 423–428.

Kobak, R. R., & Sceery, A. (1988). Attachment in late adolescence: Working models, affect regulation, and representations of self and others. *Child Development, 59*, 135–146.

Kolko, D. J. (1985). The Heterosocial Assessment Inventory for Women: A psychometric and behavioral evaluation. *Journal of Psychopathology and Behavioral Assessment, 7*, 49–64.

Kolko, D. J., & Milan, M. A. (1985). A women's heterosocial skill observational rating system. *Behavior Modification, 9*, 165–193.

Levenson, R. W., & Gottman, J. M. (1978). Toward the assessment of social competence. *Journal of Consulting and Clinical Psychology, 46*, 453–462.

Newcomb, M. D. (1984). Sexual behavior, responsiveness, and attitudes among women: A test of two theories. *Journal of Sex and Marital Therapy, 10*, 272–286.

Newcomb, M. D. (1986). Notches on the bedpost: Generational effects of sexual experience. *Psychology, 23*(2/3), 37–46.

Reis, H. T., Wheeler, L., Kernis, M. H., Spiegel, N., & Nezlek, J. (1985). On specificity in the impact of social participation on physical and psychological health. *Journal of Personality and Social Psychology, 48*, 456–471.

Wittenberg, M. T., & Reis, H. T. (1986). Loneliness, social skills, and social perception. *Personality and Social Psychology Bulletin, 12*, 121–130.

BIBLIOGRAPHY:

Corcoran, K., & Fischer, J. (1987). *Measures for clinical practice: A sourcebook* (pp. 137–140). New York: Free Press.

HETEROSOCIAL ASSESSMENT INVENTORY FOR WOMEN (HAI-W)

AUTHOR: David J. Kolko

DATE: 1985

VARIABLE: Heterosocial skills

TYPE OF INSTRUMENT: Summated rating scale

DESCRIPTION: The Heterosocial Assessment Inventory for Women (HAI-W) consists of brief descriptions of 12 situations representing three areas of heterosocial behavior: "finding dates, making conversation, and initiating physical or sexual activity" (Kolko, 1985, p. 52). The situations all focus on men. Each situation is followed by five questions covering the following areas: likelihood of carrying out a particular behavior in regard to the man, degree of anxiety associated with the behavior, degree of skill in carrying out the behavior, impact of one's own physical attractiveness, and the likely response from the man. Each question is followed by a 9-point rating scale with the endpoints labeled with extreme ratings (e.g., "very rejecting: displeased/disinterested" and "very encouraging: delighted/interested"). The respondent answers each question in terms of her own "thoughts, feelings, behaviors, expectations, etc."

SAMPLE ITEMS: (situation) You have just finished working and begin to think about tomorrow's busy schedule. As you begin to think about the day's events, you start thinking about a male friend whom you haven't spoken to in a few weeks. You consider contacting him.

(questions) What is the likelihood of your calling him? How anxious/uncomfortable would you feel if you were to make the call? How skillful would you be in carrying this out? How would your physical attractiveness influence your effectiveness in this situation? What would your male friend's response be to your phone call?

PREVIOUS SUBJECTS: Unmarried college women

APPROPRIATE FOR: Unmarried women

ADMINISTRATION: Self-administered; about 15–20 minutes

SCORING: Items are individually scored on a 9-point scale. Each of the five questions accompanying a description of a situation contributes to a different subscale score. Thus, there are five scores, each based on 12 items. The five scores, expressed as item means, are: likelihood, anxiety, skill, attractiveness, and expectation. On four of the subscales, higher scores reflect greater heterosocial skill; on the anxiety subscale, higher scores reflect greater anxiety. Kolko (1985) tested 250 college women. For each subscale, he reported the mean, standard deviation, median, mode, skewness, kurtosis, and range. Kolko also used factor scores for the HAI-W (see NOTES & COMMENTS).

DEVELOPMENT: The 12 situations used on the HAI-W were selected "on the basis of their high factor loadings from a recent factor-analytic study of the Situation Questionnaire (SQ) using undergraduates (Heimberg et al., 1980)" (Kolko, 1985, p. 52). The situations were modified by two female research assistants who ensured that each situation included a potentially interactive situation. The five questions associated with each situation were chosen because they related to variables that heterosocial competence literature has shown to be significant.

RELIABILITY: The responses from the 250 college women were used to compute both split-half correlations and alpha coefficients. The split-half correlations were .74 for likelihood, .77 for anxiety, .83 for skillfulness, .94 for attractiveness, and .79 for expectation. The alpha coefficients were .88 for likelihood, .90 for anxiety, .91 for skillfulness, .96 for attractiveness, and .93 for expectation. Since the split-half reliabilities were all lower than the alpha coefficients, it is likely that the split-half reliabilities were not corrected with the Spearman-Brown formula.

A sample of 31 college women completed the HAI-W on a second occasion, 3 weeks after the first testing. Test-retest reliability was .83 for likelihood, .81 for anxiety, .80 for skillfulness, .87 for attractiveness, and .84 for expectation.

VALIDITY: To demonstrate the validity of the HAI-W, Kolko (1985) correlated factor scores (see NOTES & COMMENTS) with several other indicators of heterosocial competence, including the Social Activity Questionnaire (Christensen & Arkowitz, 1974), the Survey of Heterosexual Interactions (SHI) (Twentyman & McFall, 1975) (see separate entry), the Dating and Assertion Questionnaire (Levenson & Gottman, 1978) (see separate entry), and five global self-ratings (heterosocial skill, heterosocial anxiety, physical attractiveness, the quality of one's intimate relationships, and satisfaction with one's social life). The five factor scores of the HAI-W were significantly correlated with scores on the SHI and the Dating and Assertion Questionnaire. Relating the eight scores from the Social Activity Questionnaire to the five factor scores from the HAI-W produced 40 correlations. Eighteen of the correlations were statistically significant. All of the correlations between the five global self-ratings and the five factor scores on the HAI-W were statistically significant.

For a sample of 20 college women, Kolko (1985) reported correlations between HAI-W scores and scores on three other measures presumed to relate to heterosocial competence: the Self-Monitoring Scale (Snyder, 1974), Miller Opener Scale (Miller, Berg, & Archer, 1979), and the Generalized Expectations of Others Questionnaire (Eisler, Frederiksen, & Peterson (1978). Twelve of the 15 correlations were statistically significant.

Kolko (1985) had expert judges, peer judges, and a male confederate rate each of 20 women's performance in two role-play situations that involved a male confederate. Each woman was assigned nine ratings; ratings were made by the confederate, the expert judges, and the peer judges on three variables: skill, anxiety, and attractiveness. The ratings were correlated with the HAI-W factor scores. Of the 45 correlations, 34 were statistically significant. All but 1 of the correlations between ratings of skill and HAI-W scores were significant, and 8 of the correlations between ratings of attractiveness and HAI-W factor scores were nonsignificant.

NOTES & COMMENTS: Kolko (1985) factor analyzed the item responses from the 250 college women. He extracted five factors. Factor I was labeled Attractiveness Impact and contained the 12 attractiveness items from the HAI-W. The factor loadings ranged from .67 to .86. Factor II consisted of 17 items and was labeled Casual Conversation with Friends; it involved face-to-face and telephone conversations with male friends. Factor loadings ranged from .36 to .83. Factor III, Potentially Intimate Initiations with Strangers, contained 15 items pertaining to becoming friends with a man one meets. Factor loadings ranged from .51 to .79. Factor IV consisted of 8 items with loadings between .46 and .78; labeled Physical Contact, it dealt with actions such as holding hands or putting an arm around a man. Factor V, Physical Intimacy, consisted of 8 items with factor loadings ranging from .38 to .82. A factor analysis involving 60 items and data from only 250 persons cannot be presumed to produce stable results.

AVAILABLE FROM: David J. Kolko, University of Pittsburgh, School of Medicine, CPTS Inpatient Unit, WPIC, 3811 O'Hara Street, Pittsburgh, PA 15213–2593

USED IN:

Kolko, D. J. (1985). The Heterosocial Assessment Inventory for Women: A psychometric and behavioral evaluation. *Journal of Psychopathology and Behavioral Assessment, 7,* 49–64.

BIBLIOGRAPHY:

Christensen, A., & Arkowitz, H. (1974). Preliminary report on practice dating and feedback as treatment for college dating problems. *Journal of Counseling Psychology, 21,* 92–95.

Eisler, R. M., Frederiksen, L. W., & Peterson, G. L. (1978). The relationship of cognitive variables to the expression of assertiveness. *Behavior Therapy, 9,* 419–427.

Heimberg, R. G., Harrison, D. F., Montgomery, D., Madsen, C. H., & Sherfey, J. A. (1980). Psychometric and behavioral analysis of a social anxiety inventory: The Situation Questionnaire. *Behavioral Assessment, 2,* 403–416.

Levenson, R. W., & Gottman, J. M. (1978). Toward the assessment of social competence. *Journal of Consulting and Clinical Psychology, 46,* 453–462.

Miller, L., Berg, J., & Archer, R. (1979, August). *Who becomes intimate with whom? Two personality variables that affect self-disclosure.* Paper presented at the meeting of the American Psychological Association, Los Angeles.

Snyder, M. (1974). Self-monitoring of expressive behavior. *Journal of Personality and Social Psychology, 30,* 526–537.

Twentyman, C. T., & McFall, R. M. (1975). Behavioral training of social skills in shy males. *Journal of Consulting and Clinical Psychology, 43,* 384–395.

HETEROSOCIAL SKILL OBSERVATIONAL RATING SYSTEM (HESORS)

AUTHORS: David J. Kolko and Michael A. Milan

DATE: 1985

VARIABLE: Women's heterosocial skill

TYPE OF INSTRUMENT: Observational rating system
DESCRIPTION: The Heterosocial Skill Observational Rating System (HESORS) consists of 11 verbal behaviors and 5 nonverbal behaviors. Each behavior is accompanied by a 3-point behaviorally referenced rating scale. Trained observers record their ratings while watching a female subject during two 4-minute role plays involving a male confederate. One role play, for example, involves a situation at a New Year's Eve party in which the female is attracted to and approaches a lone male. The subject is told, "Your task is to initiate a conversation with him and to make a favorable impression" (Kolko & Milan, 1985, p. 169).
SAMPLE ITEMS:

Topic development

2 = Enhanced conversation, added important or interesting material, or embellished content

1 = Some or brief development, somewhat inadequate coverage, stuck occasionally

0 = Rambled from one topic/issue to another, or excessively questioned about numerous areas

PREVIOUS SUBJECTS: College women
APPROPRIATE FOR: College women; the scale might also be used with older high school girls and young adult women not in college
ADMINISTRATION: The use of HESORS requires a trained observer; about 10–12 minutes should be allowed to complete the two 4-minute role plays.
SCORING: Kolko and Milan (1985) did not report any score totals. They reported only information regarding results on individual items. They also reported means and standard deviations on each item for two sets of five respondents who were high in heterosocial competence and two sets of five respondents who were low in heterosocial competence.
DEVELOPMENT: Kolko and Milan (1985) provided extensive information on the development of the measure. The first stage in scale development was to identify appropriate role-play situations. A sample of 50 unmarried college women kept logs of difficult heterosocial situations they encountered in the course of a week. Their logs produced 63 situations that were reduced to 35 situations by the elimination of redundancies. Another sample of 50 college women rated these situations, and their ratings were used to reduce the pool to 7 situations. From this pool of 7, 4 nonredundant situations that could be used in role-play situations were selected for use in scale development.

Several paper-and-pencil measures were used to identify a sample of 10 college women who were "high" on heterosocial competence (HHC) and 10 college women who were "low" on heterosocial competence (LHC). Half of each group participated in the development phase of the research, and the other half participated in the validation phase. Those in the development sample performed in all four role plays, playing the role of the initiator in two role plays and the role of the responder in the other two. The two role plays in which the subject was the initiator were rated by trained experts and also by 90 undergraduate students, called peer judges. Both sets of judges made global ratings of skill, anxiety, and physical attractiveness. In addition, the peer judges listed the behaviors and/or characteristics that had affected their choice of ratings to assign. That is, they listed the cues or aspects of the subject's behavior that influenced their ratings. A total of 5,998 cues were listed. These were classified, relying largely on a system drawn from the work of Conger, Wallander, Mariotto, and Ward (1980). Ten most frequently listed cue categories were identified. Another set of peer judges rated videotapes of the role plays done by the development sample of HHC and LHC subjects. The new set of judges rated the tapes in terms of the 10 identified cue categories and then listed the cues they used for making their ratings. A total of 6,631 referents were listed across the 10 cue categories. The 5 most frequently listed behavioral referents were identified for each of the 10 categories. Four judges refined and clarified the list; the result was a set of 34 behaviors, each accompanied by 3-point behaviorally referenced rating scales.

The validation sample of five HHC women and five LHC women was used for the balance of the scale development. They participated in role plays that four trained observers rated on the 34 behaviors. The consistency of the ratings assigned by two judges rating the same set of behaviors was estimated using Cohen's kappa. A total of 28 behaviors satisfied the criterion of interrater reliability greater than .70. When the ratings assigned to the HHC group and the LHC group were compared, statistically significant differences were found on 16 of the 28 reliable scales. These 16 behaviors comprise the final version of the scale.

RELIABILITY: Interrater reliability was at least .70 for each item in the scale.

VALIDITY: All 16 behaviors were shown to discriminate between the HHC and LHC groups used in scale development.

The 10 women in the validation sample completed two other measures that were expected to relate to ratings on HESORS: the Dating and Assertion Questionnaire (Levenson & Gottman, 1978) (see separate entry) and the Miller Opener Scale (Miller, Berg, & Archer, 1979). With 16 items on the HESORS, one score on the Miller Opener Scale, and two scores on the Dating and Assertion Questionnaire, there were 48 correlation coefficients. Of these, 41 were statistically significant. Only one behavior—follow-up answers to questions—was not significantly correlated with any of the three criterion scores.

Global ratings of skill, anxiety, and attractiveness were made by the confederate, the expert judges, the peer judges, and the subjects themselves. These global ratings were correlated with the ratings on the HESORS. The correlation coefficients ranged from .01 to .92; the average correlation was .46. Across all rater sources, 26% of the correlations with verbal behaviors were significant, and 27% of the correlations with nonverbal behaviors were significant. The global ratings given by the subjects to themselves were the least likely of all ratings to correlate with scores on the HESORS.

NOTES & COMMENTS: (1) Kolko and Milan (1985) reported the intercorrelations between the ratings of the 16 behaviors. The average intercorrelation for the verbal behaviors was .66; the average intercorrelation for the nonverbal behaviors was .56. Although Kolko and Milan acknowledged that these correlations may have resulted from the halo effect influencing judgments, they also stated that it is more likely that "a particular skillful performance may beget and even predict the execution of other skillful performances" (p. 189).

(2) Because the number of subjects used for scale development was quite small, Kolko and Milan (1985) suggested caution in generalizing the usefulness of the scale to other populations and situations unless additional validation data are obtained. In a general sense, the authors suggested the scale is useful for "assessing an individual client's strengths and weaknesses, prescribing specific skills to be mastered, evaluating the clinical impact of training programs, and documenting maintenance and generalization" (p. 190).

(3) Determining whether scores can successfully differentiate between a group of HHC and a group of LHC other than the persons used in scale development would be useful for providing further evidence regarding the scale's validity.

AVAILABLE FROM: David J. Kolko, University of Pittsburgh, School of Medicine, CPTS Inpatient Unit, WPIC, 3811 O'Hara Street, Pittsburgh, PA 15213–2593

USED IN:

Kolko, D. J., & Milan, M. A. (1985). A women's Heterosocial Skill Observational Rating System. *Behavior Modification, 9,* 165–192.

BIBLIOGRAPHY:

Conger, A. J., Wallander, J. L., Mariotto, M. J., & Ward, D. (1980). Peer judgments of heterosexual-social anxiety and skill: What do they pay attention to anyhow? *Behavioral Assessment, 2,* 261–266.

Levenson, R. W., & Gottman, J. M. (1978). Toward the assessment of social competence. *Journal of Consulting and Clinical Psychology, 46,* 453–462.

Miller, L., Berg, J., & Archer, R. (1979, August). *Who becomes intimate with whom? Two personality variables that affect self-disclosure.* Paper presented at the meeting of the American Psychological Association, Los Angeles.

SURVEY OF HETEROSEXUAL INTERACTIONS (SHI)

AUTHORS: Craig T. Twentyman and Richard M. McFall

DATE: 1975

VARIABLE: Ability to initiate and continue interactions with women; past dating behavior
TYPE OF INSTRUMENT: Summated rating scale
DESCRIPTION: The Survey of Heterosexual Interactions (SHI) asks four general questions about past dating behavior and then presents brief descriptions of 20 heterosocial situations. Each situation is followed by a 7-point response scale, with 1 indicating an inability to respond and 7 reflecting the ability to carry out the interaction successfully; verbal descriptors are provided to anchor the scale at three points.
SAMPLE ITEMS: You want to call a woman up for a date. This is the first time you are calling her up as you only know her slightly. When you get ready to make the call, your roommate comes into the room, sits down on his bed, and begins reading a magazine. In this situation you would . . . (be unable to call in every case, be able to call in some cases, be able to call in every case).

You are at a dance. You see a very attractive woman whom you do not know. She is standing alone and you would like to dance with her. You would . . . (be unable to ask her in every case, be able to ask her in some cases, be able to ask her in every case).
PREVIOUS SUBJECTS: College men; prison inmates, including rapists, child molesters, and non–sex offenders; adult men; women (scale was modified)
APPROPRIATE FOR: College men
ADMINISTRATION: Self-administered; about 10 minutes
SCORING: Items are individually scored on a 7-point scale, with higher scores reflecting greater heterosocial skill. Item scores are summed to yield an overall score that can range from 20 (extremely low self-rating of heterosocial skill) to 140 (extremely high self-rating of heterosocial skill). Twentyman, Boland, and McFall (1981) reported means and standard deviations for several large groups of college males; they also reported item means and standard deviations based on testing one large sample of college men.
DEVELOPMENT: No information was provided.
RELIABILITY: Twentyman et al. (1981) reported a split-half reliability of .85 and a test-retest reliability of .85, given a 4-month interval between test and retest. They also reported that interitem correlations ranged from .15 to .78, with a median of .35.
VALIDITY: Twentyman and McFall (1975) found that the SHI was significantly correlated with a variety of other measures, such as self-reported anxiety in a forced interaction test ($r = -.69$), self-reported anxiety in a simulated telephone call situation ($r = -.42$), self-reported behavior in social situations ($r = .79$-$.84$), observers' skill ratings ($r = .34$-$.48$), and observers' anxiety ratings ($r = -.45$).

Segal and Marshall (1986) tested a variety of men, including incarcerated child molesters, rapists, non–sex offenders, and nonincarcerated men from both high and low socioeconomic status groups. Among other things, the subjects completed the SHI and rated their own ability to enact four behaviors in an upcoming role-play situation: introducing themselves, starting a conversation, asking questions, and answering questions. SHI scores were significantly correlated with responses to all but the first question.

NOTES & COMMENTS: (1) Williams and Ciminero (1978) have developed a version of the SHI for women (Survey of Heterosexual Interactions for Females [SHI-F]—see separate entry) that is very similar to the SHI.

(2) Twentyman et al. (1981) used the SHI in a series of studies designed to identify the skill deficits of nondating college men. Glass and Biever (1981) used the SHI, as well as the version for women (SHI-F), as one measure of social competence in a study designed to look at the relationship between psychological androgyny and social competence.

(3) Leary and Dobbins (1983) modified the SHI by asking respondents how "nervous or uneasy" they would feel in each of the 20 situations. Responses were recorded on a 5-point scale ranging from "not at all" to "extremely." Based on responses from 260 college students, the modified SHI had a coefficient alpha of .91. Scores on the modified SHI were compared with scores on measures of sexual behavior and contraceptive use.

(4) Kolko (1985) apparently modified the SHI for use with women. He then used the SHI as one of several scales against which to validate a new measure he was developing, the Heterosocial Assessment Inventory for Women (see separate entry). Correlations between the SHI and factor scores on the new measure were all statistically significant and positive; they ranged from .51 to .78.

(5) Kagel and Schilling (1985) used the SHI with both college men and college women (presumably modifying it for women) "to provide a measure of sexual orientation differences between father-absent and father-present male subjects" (p. 361). Females were used as a comparison group.

(6) Gilmartin (1985) used the SHI to identify shy and nonshy men. Scores above 105 were considered indicative of nonshyness. Gilmartin then compared nonshy men, shy college-age men, and shy older men on several family background variables. Robins (1986) used the SHI, as well as the version developed for women (SHI-F), as one of several measures in a study examining the relationship between sex role characteristics, anxiety, and skill in same-sex and opposite-sex social situations. Kuhlenschmidt and Conger (1988) conducted a study to look at the behavioral concomitants of social competence. They used the SHI to select participants for the research.

(7) Martinez-Diaz and Edelstein (1980) looked at the predictive and

construct validity of several measures of heterosocial competence, including the SHI. Wallander, Conger, Mariotto, Curran, and Farrell (1980) compared several different measures of social competence.

AVAILABLE FROM: Twentyman, Boland, and McFall, 1981; Corcoran and Fischer, 1987

USED IN:

Bruch, M. A., & Hynes, M. J. (1987). Heterosocial anxiety and contraceptive behavior. *Journal of Research in Personality, 21,* 343–360.

Cole, D. A., Howard, G. S., & Maxwell, S. E. (1981). Effects of mono- versus multiple-operationalization in construct validation efforts. *Journal of Consulting and Clinical Psychology, 49,* 395–405.

Gilmartin, B. G. (1985). Some family antecedents of severe shyness. *Family Relations, 34,* 429–438.

Glass, C. R., & Biever, J. L. (1981). Sex-roles and social skill: A cognitive-behavioral analysis. *Behavioral Counseling Quarterly, 1,* 244–260.

Gormally, J., Sipps, G., Raphael, R., Edwin, D., & Varvil-Weld, D. (1981). The relationship between maladaptive cognitions and social anxiety. *Journal of Consulting and Clinical Psychology, 49,* 300–301.

Gormally, J., Varvil-Weld, D., Raphael, R., & Sipps, G. (1981). Treatment of socially anxious college men using cognitive counseling and skills training. *Journal of Counseling Psychology, 28,* 177–187.

Kagel, S. A., & Schilling, K. M. (1985). Sexual identification and gender identity among father-absent males. *Sex Roles, 13,* 357–370.

Kolko, D. J. (1985). The Heterosocial Assessment Inventory for Women: A psychometric and behavioral evaluation. *Journal of Psychopathology and Behavioral Assessment, 7,* 49–64.

Kuhlenschmidt, S., & Conger, J. C. (1988). Behavioral components of social competence in females. *Sex Roles, 18,* 107–112.

Leary, M. R., & Dobbins, S. E. (1983). Social anxiety, sexual behavior, and contraceptive use. *Journal of Personality and Social Psychology, 45,* 1347–1354.

Martinez-Diaz, J. A., & Edelstein, B. A. (1980). Heterosocial competence: Predictive and construct validity. *Behavior Modification, 4,* 115–129.

Robins, C. J. (1986). Sex role perceptions and social anxiety in opposite-sex and same-sex situations. *Sex Roles, 14,* 383–395.

Segal, Z. V., & Marshall, W. L. (1986). Discrepancies between self-efficacy predictions and actual performance in a population of rapists and child molesters. *Cognitive Therapy and Research, 10,* 363–376.

Twentyman, C., Boland, T., & McFall, R. M. (1981). Heterosexual avoidance in college males. *Behavior Modification, 5,* 523–552.

Twentyman, C. T., & McFall, R. M. (1975). Behavioral training of social skills in shy men. *Journal of Consulting and Clinical Psychology, 43,* 384–395.

Wallander, J. L., Conger, A. J., Mariotto, M. J., Curran, J. P., & Farrell, A. D. (1980). Comparability of selection instruments in studies of heterosexual social problem behaviors. *Behavior Therapy, 11,* 548–560.

BIBLIOGRAPHY:

Corcoran, K., & Fischer, J. (1987). *Measures for clinical practice: A sourcebook* (pp. 345–350). New York: Free Press.

Williams, C. L., & Ciminero, A. R. (1978). Development and validation of a heterosocial skills inventory: The Survey of Heterosexual Interactions for Females. *Journal of Consulting and Clinical Psychology, 46*, 1547–1548.

SURVEY OF HETEROSEXUAL INTERACTIONS FOR FEMALES (SHI-F)

AUTHORS: Carolyn L. Williams and Anthony R. Ciminero

DATE: 1978

VARIABLE: Heterosocial skill in women

TYPE OF INSTRUMENT: Summated rating scale

DESCRIPTION: The Survey of Heterosexual Interactions for Females (SHI-F) contains 25 items: 4 items pertain to frequency of heterosexual dating, 1 item asks about the respondent's physical appearance, and 20 items are brief descriptions of social situations. For each social situation, the respondent indicates how she would respond in that situation. A 5-point response scale accompanies each item. One end of the continuum indicates that the respondent would be unable to perform a particular behavior (e.g., be unable to initiate a conversation), and the other end indicates that she would be able to perform the particular behavior.

SAMPLE ITEMS: You want to call a guy you like about a homework assignment. This is the first time you have talked to him on the phone as you only know him slightly. When you get ready to make the call, your roommate comes into the room, sits down on her bed, and begins reading a magazine. In this situation you would . . . (response 1 is labeled "be unable to call in every case," and response 5 is labeled "be able to call in every case").

You are walking to your mailbox in the large apartment building where you live. When you get there you notice that two guys are putting their names on the mailbox of the vacant apartment beneath yours. In this situation you would . . . (response 1 is labeled "be unable to go over and initiate a conversation," and response 5 is labeled "be able to go over and initiate a conversation in every case").

PREVIOUS SUBJECTS: College women

APPROPRIATE FOR: College women

ADMINISTRATION: Self-administered; about 10 minutes

SCORING: Responses to the 20 social situations are individually scored on a 5-point scale, with 1 point assigned to the end of the continuum reflecting less heterosocial skill and 5 points assigned to the opposite end of the continuum. Total scores can range from 20 (low self-rating of heterosocial skill) to 100 (high self-rating of heterosocial skill). For a sample of 256 college women, Williams and Ciminero (1978) reported a range of 32 to 98, a mean of 68.28, and a standard deviation of 11.78.

DEVELOPMENT: The SHI-F is based on Twentyman and McFall's (1975) Survey of Heterosexual Interactions (SHI) (see separate entry). Williams

and Ciminero (1978) reworded the questions on the SHI to make them appropriate for females. The question regarding physical attractiveness that appeared on the SHI-F did not have a counterpart on the SHI.
RELIABILITY: Forty college women completed the SHI-F on two occasions, with a 1-month interval between testings. Test-retest reliability was .62. Based on testing 117 college women, Williams and Ciminero (1978) obtained a coefficient alpha of .89.
VALIDITY: Williams and Ciminero (1978) identified two subgroups from their sample of 256 respondents: high scorers were at least one standard deviation above the mean; low scorers were at least one standard deviation below the mean. In comparing the two groups, the researchers found that "high scorers reported dating a significantly greater number of different males per year . . . , rated themselves as participating in a greater amount of heterosocial behavior . . . , and rated themselves as significantly more attractive" (p. 1547). The two groups did not differ in terms of the number of dates they had during the prior 4 weeks.

Williams and Ciminero (1978) also administered the Rathus Assertiveness Scale (Rathus, 1973) and the State-Trait Anxiety Inventory (Speilberger, Gorsuch, & Lushene, 1968) to the 256 college women they tested with the SHI-F. The researchers reported significant correlations between the SHI-F and the Rathus Assertiveness Scale ($r = .56$) and between the SHI-F and the Trait portion of the State-Trait Inventory ($r = -.40$).

Williams and Ciminero (1978) also reported obtaining measures during brief heterosocial interactions that took place over an intercom between each female subject and a male confederate. The high and low scorers on the SHI-F did not differ in terms of heart rate during their interactions nor did they differ on an observer rating of anxiety, but they did differ in terms of observer-rated social skills, interest, and initiation. Furthermore, the two groups differed in terms of self-ratings of social skill and anxiety during the situations. The low scorers also rated themselves as less physically attractive.

As predicted, Burgio, Glass, and Merluzzi (1981) found a significant relationship between social anxiety and scores on the SHI-F: high socially anxious women, compared to low socially anxious women, obtained lower scores on the SHI-F.
NOTES & COMMENTS: Glass and Biever (1981) used the SHI-F as one measure of social competence in a study designed to look at the relationship between psychological androgyny and social competence. Robins (1986) used the SHI-F as one of several measures in a study examining the relationship among sex role characteristics, anxiety, and skill in same-sex and opposite-sex social situations. Kuhlenschmidt and Conger (1988) conducted a study to look at the behavioral concomitants

of social competence in young women. They used the SHI-F to select women who were low, middle, and high on social competence.
AVAILABLE FROM: Carolyn L. Williams, Division of Epidemiology, University of Minnesota, Stadium Gate 27, Minneapolis, MN 55455
USED IN:

Burgio, K. L., Glass, C. R., & Merluzzi, T. V. (1981). The effects of social anxiety and videotape performance feedback on cognitions and self-evaluations. *Behavioral Counseling Quarterly, 1,* 288–301.

Glass, C. R., & Biever, J. L. (1981). Sex-roles and social skill: A cognitive-behavioral analysis. *Behavioral Counseling Quarterly, 1,* 244–260.

Kuhlenschmidt, S., & Conger, J. C. (1988). Behavioral components of social competence in females. *Sex Roles, 18,* 107–112.

Robins, C. J. (1986). Sex role perceptions and social anxiety in opposite-sex and same-sex situations. *Sex Roles, 14,* 383–395.

Williams, C. L., & Ciminero, A. R. (1978). Development and validation of a heterosocial skills inventory: The Survey of Heterosexual Interactions for Females. *Journal of Consulting and Clinical Psychology, 46,* 1547–1548.

Williams, C. L., & Ciminero, A. R. (undated). *Extended report: Development and validation of a heterosocial skills inventory: The Survey of Heterosexual Interactions for Females.* Unpublished paper, University of Minnesota, Minneapolis.

BIBLIOGRAPHY:

Rathus, S. (1973). A 30 item schedule for assessing assertive behavior. *Behavior Therapy, 4,* 398–406.

Speilberger, C. D., Gorsuch, R., & Lushene, R. (1968). *Manual for the self-evaluation questionnaire.* Palo Alto: Consulting Psychologist Press.

Twentyman, C. T., & McFall, R. M. (1975). Behavioral training of social skills in shy males. *Journal of Consulting and Clinical Psychology, 43,* 384–395.

ATTITUDES TOWARD LOVE

AUTHORS: David H. Knox, Jr. and Michael J. Sporakowski
DATE: 1968
VARIABLE: Support for romantic versus conjugal views of love
TYPE OF INSTRUMENT: Summated rating scale
DESCRIPTION: The Attitudes Toward Love scale contains 29 items relating to love and to love and marriage. The items are phrased to reflect a romantic view of love. Each item is rated on a 5-point scale: "1—Strongly agree (definitely yes); 2—Mildly agree (I believe so); 3—Undecided (not sure); 4—Mildly disagree (probably not); 5—Strongly disagree (definitely not)."
SAMPLE ITEMS: When you are really in love, you just aren't interested in anyone else.

Love doesn't make sense. It just is.

PREVIOUS SUBJECTS: College students
APPROPRIATE FOR: Ages 16 and older

ADMINISTRATION: Self-administered; about 15 minutes
SCORING: Items are scored on a 5-point scale, with 5 points assigned to the response reflecting a conjugal view of love and 1 point assigned to the response reflecting a romantic view of love. Item scores are summed to yield a total score that can range from 29 to 145. Lower scores represent a romantic view of love; higher scores represent a conjugal view of love. Hinkle and Sporakowski (1975) suggested using factor scores for the Attitudes Toward Love scale. The factor scores are described under NOTES & COMMENTS.

Knox (1970a), Knox and Sporakowski (1968), and Munro and Adams (1978a) provided means and standard deviations for various groups who completed the Attitudes Toward Love scale.
DEVELOPMENT: Scale development began with the establishment of definitions of "romantic" and "conjugal" love. Characteristics of romantic love were specified; they reflected the fact that romantic love is highly emotional and exciting and transcends the problems of the real world. Conjugal love was viewed as the opposite of romantic love; it was seen as a "more calm, solid, and comforting type of love" (Knox & Sporakowski, 1968, p. 639). Based on a review of the relevant professional literature, a pool of 200 items was generated and reviewed by 10 professionals in the field of marriage and family living. Based on the professionals' review of the items, 85 items were retained and administered to 200 college students. Twenty-nine items that differentiated between the top 25% of the scorers and the bottom 25% of the scorers were retained for the final version of the scale.
RELIABILITY: Knox and Sporakowski (1968) administered the scale to a group of over 20 students on two occasions about 1 week apart. There was 78.4% agreement between the two testings.
VALIDITY: Knox and Sporakowski (1968) found that both college men and college women tended to be more conjugal than romantic, but college women were significantly more conjugal than men in their orientation toward love. Knox and Sporakowski also showed that attitudes toward love became more conjugal as one advanced in college from freshman to senior, and they showed that engaged college men were significantly more conjugal in their attitudes than were nonengaged males.

Lester (1985) replicated some of these findings. Based on testing 807 college students with the Attitudes Toward Love scale, he found that men compared to women had significantly more romantic attitudes toward love, and younger students compared to older students also had significantly more romantic attitudes toward love.

Munro and Adams (1978b) correlated scores from the Attitudes Toward Love scale with scores from the Munro-Adams Love Attitude Scale (see separate entry) and from the Rubin Love Scale (Rubin, 1970) (see separate entry). They found that scores on the Attitudes Toward Love scale were significantly correlated with both of the other love measures. Furthermore they correlated the factor scores from the Attitudes Toward Love scale (see NOTES & COMMENTS for a description of the factors) with scores from the Munro-Adams Love Attitude Scale. The pattern of intercorrelations provided further evidence for the validity of the Attitudes Toward Love scale.

NOTES & COMMENTS: (1) Knox (1970a, 1970b) used an 84-item version of the Attitudes Toward Love scale. (It appears that Knox omitted 1 item from the item set retained after the review by professionals in the field.) Knox compared responses from high school seniors, persons married fewer than 5 years, and persons married more than 20 years.

(2) Hinkle and Sporakowski (1975) factor analyzed responses from 234 college students. Eight factors had eigenvalues greater than 1.0. All items loaded positively on the first factor; factor loadings ranged from .27 to .61, with 28 of the 29 items having factor loadings above .30. This evidence, combined with data from additional analyses, provided strong support for the idea that the scale was unidimensional. Through further analysis and review, the authors identified three interrelated factors: Factor I, Traditional Love—One Person, contained 11 items; Factor II, Love Overcomes All, contained 6 items; and Factor III, Irrationality, contained 8 items. The remaining four items showed moderate loadings on more than one factor. The intercorrelations among the factors ranged from .21 to .28. Hinkle and Sporakowski suggested that item weights, derived from factor analysis, should be used in scoring the Attitudes Toward Love scale. They provided item weights and suggested that three factor scores could be computed or the factor scores could be combined to produce a single overall score.

(3) Scores on the Attitudes Toward Love scale have been related to other variables, including internal-external locus of control (Munro & Adams, 1978a), level of education (Munro & Adams, 1978a), androgyny (Lester, Brazill, Ellis, & Guerin, 1984), self-disclosure (Lester et al., 1984), experience of love (Lester, 1985), jealousy (Lester, Deluca, Hellinghausen, & Scribner, 1985), self-esteem (Lester et al., 1985), affiliative tendencies (Lester et al., 1985), hysteroid personality (Lester, 1987), and romantic behaviors (McGrath & Lester, 1988).

AVAILABLE FROM: Knox and Sporakowski, 1968

USED IN:

Hinkle, D. E., & Sporakowski, M. J. (1975). Attitudes toward love: A reexamination. *Journal of Marriage and the Family, 37*, 764–767.

Knox, D. H., Jr. (1970a). Conceptions of love at three developmental levels. *Family Coordinator, 19*, 151–157.

Knox, D. H., Jr. (1970b). Conceptions of love by married college students. *College Student Survey, 4*, 28–30.

Knox, D. H., Jr., & Sporakowski, M. J. (1968). Attitudes of college students toward love. *Journal of Marriage and the Family, 30*, 638–642.

Lester, D. (1985). Romantic attitudes toward love in men and women. *Psychological Reports, 56*, 662.

Lester, D. (1987). Hysteroid-obsessoid personality and romantic love. *Psychological Reports, 60*, 258.

Lester, D., Brazill, N., Ellis, C., & Guerin, T. (1984). Correlates of romantic attitudes toward love: Androgyny and self-disclosure. *Psychological Reports, 54*, 554.

Lester, D., Deluca, G., Hellinghausen, W., & Scribner, D. (1985). Jealousy and irrationality in love. *Psychological Reports, 56*, 210.

McGrath, J. N., III, & Lester, D. (1988). Romantic attitudes toward love and romantic behavior. *Perceptual and Motor Skills, 66*, 486.

Munro, B., & Adams, G. R. (1978a). Correlates of romantic love revisited. *Journal of Psychology*, 211–214.

Munro, B., & Adams, G. R. (1978b). Love American style: A test of role structure theory on changes in attitudes toward love. *Human Relations, 31*, 215–228.

Rubin, Z. (1970). Measurement of romantic love. *Journal of Personality and Social Psychology, 9*, 256–273.

LOVE ATTITUDES SCALE

AUTHORS: Clyde Hendrick, Susan Hendrick, Franklin H. Foote, and Michelle J. Slapion-Foote

DATE: 1984 (revised 1986)

VARIABLE: Six aspects of love: Eros, Ludus, Storge, Pragma, Mania, and Agape

TYPE OF INSTRUMENT: Summated rating scale

DESCRIPTION: The Love Attitudes Scale is a 42-item scale with 7 items representing each of six factors: Eros, Ludus, Storge, Pragma, Mania, and Agape. Eros refers to "strong physical preferences, early attraction, and intensity of emotion . . . along with strong commitment to the lover" (C. Hendrick & Hendrick, 1986, p. 400). Ludus reflects the idea that love is "an interaction game to be played out with diverse partners . . . deception of the lover is acceptable within proper role limits . . . there is not great depth of feeling . . . [and] love has a manipulative quality to it" (p. 400). Storge "reflects an inclination to merge love and friendship" (p. 400). Pragma reflects the idea that "rational calculation with a focus on desired attributes of the lover is central to . . . love" (p. 400). Mania is " 'symptom love,' based on uncertainty of self and the lover . . . [and] may be most characteristic of adolescents" (p. 401). Agape "is an all-giving, nondemanding love" (p. 401). Items are accompanied by five response options: "strongly agree, moderately agree, neutral, moderately disagree, strongly disagree."

SAMPLE ITEMS: (Eros) My lover and I were attracted to each other immediately after we first met.

(Ludus) I try to keep my lover a little uncertain about my commitment to him/her.

(Storge) The best kind of love grows out of a long friendship.

(Pragma) I consider what a person is going to become in life before I commit myself to him/her.

(Mania) When things aren't right with my lover and me, my stomach gets upset.

(Agape) I would rather suffer myself than let my lover suffer.

PREVIOUS SUBJECTS: College students, heterosexual dating couples

APPROPRIATE FOR: College students and older

ADMINISTRATION: Self-administered; about 15–20 minutes

SCORING: Items are individually scored on a 5-point scale and summed to yield six factor scores. The "strongly agree" end of the continuum is assigned 1 point; therefore lower scores reflect greater commitment to the love style being measured. Scores on each subscale range from 7 to 35. C. Hendrick and Hendrick (1986) reported means and standard deviations for each individual item. S. S. Hendrick and Hendrick (1987a) reported item means and standard deviations for each of the six subscales.

DEVELOPMENT: The Love Attitudes Scale was based on Lee's (1973) typology of love. "Lee identified three primary types of love styles: Eros (romantic, passionate love), Ludus (game-playing love), Storge (friendship love), and three main secondary styles: Mania (possessive, dependent love), Pragma (logical, 'shopping list' love), and Agape (all-giving, selfless love)" (C. Hendrick & Hendrick, 1986, p. 393). The first version of the Love Attitudes Scale was based on a true/false scale developed earlier by Lasswell and Lasswell (1976). C. Hendrick, Hendrick, Foote, and Slapion-Foote (1984) adapted the 50 items from the Lasswell and Lasswell measure by changing the item format from true/false to Likert format and adding 4 more items to create a 54-item scale. The scale was completed by 374 college men and 439 college women. A factor analysis of their responses produced six factors and led the authors to conclude that "the secondary styles of Mania, Pragma, and Agape emerged clearly as separate factors. However, each of the primary styles (Eros, Ludus, and Storge) tended to combine with another style instead of emerging as independent factors, and it was unclear whether Eros existed at all" (C. Hendrick & Hendrick, 1986, p. 393).

The Love Attitudes Scale was substantially revised and administered to a sample of 807 college students. Their responses were factor analyzed, and six factors were extracted. On Factor 1, Eros, the seven items had factor loadings between .36 and .68; on Factor 2, Ludus, the seven items had factor loadings between .50 and .70; on Factor 3, Storge, the seven items had factor loadings between .36 and .69; on Factor 4, Pragma, the seven items had factor loadings between .54 and .72; on

Factor 5, Mania, the seven items had factor loadings between .45 and .76; and on Factor 6, Agape, the seven items had factor loadings between .30 and .79.

C. Hendrick and Hendrick (1986) conducted a second study involving 368 college women and 199 college men. For this study, they changed six items on the Love Attitudes Scale.

RELIABILITY: C. Hendrick and Hendrick (1986) used the data from 807 college students to compute coefficient alpha for the first 42-item version of the scale. They obtained the following coefficients: Eros = .70, Ludus = .76, Storge = .62, Pragma = .81, Mania = .73, and Agape = .84. A subset of 112 of these students completed the Love Attitudes Scale a second time, 4 to 6 weeks later. Their data were used to compute the test-retest reliability of the scale. C. Hendrick and Hendrick obtained the following reliability test-retest coefficients: Eros = .60, Ludus = .72, Storge = .72, Pragma = .78, Mania = .75, and Agape = .73. Using data from another sample of 567 students who completed the revised version of the Love Attitudes Scale (six items changed), C. Hendrick and Hendrick obtained the following values for coefficient alpha: Eros = .70, Ludus = .74, Storge = .69, Pragma = .74, Mania = .72, and Agape = .83. They obtained the following test-retest reliabilities based on data from a subset of 55 students: Eros = .74, Ludus = .82, Storge = .74, Pragma = .71, Mania = .70, and Agape = .81.

S. S. Hendrick and Hendrick (1987a) tested 218 college students and obtained the following alpha coefficients: Eros = .71, Ludus = .76, Storge = .67, Pragma = .79, Mania = .75, and Agape = .83.

Based on data from 30 males and 30 females, S. S. Hendrick, Hendrick, and Adler (1988) reported alpha coefficients above .70 for all factor scores except Mania, which had an alpha coefficient of .62.

VALIDITY: The factor analysis, described in the DEVELOPMENT section, provided support for the factorial validity of the scale. The factors resulting from the factor analysis confirmed the theoretical factors.

NOTES & COMMENTS: (1) C. Hendrick and Hendrick (1986) intercorrelated the factor scores. Based on data obtained in their first study of 807 college students, 7 of the 15 intercorrelations were statistically significant. However, the magnitude of the correlations was rather low, with the largest correlation being .30 (Agape with Mania). In their second study, based on 567 students, C. Hendrick and Hendrick obtained 8 significant intercorrelations. The two largest correlations were −.42 (Agape with Ludus) and .32 (Agape with Eros). Overall, Agape seemed to be the factor most closely related to the other factor scores.

(2) C. Hendrick and Hendrick (1986) related factor scores on the Love Attitudes Scale to other variables, including age, gender, ethnic background, domestic versus international student, number of times in love, current love status, and self-esteem.

(3) Bailey, Hendrick, and Hendrick (1987) intercorrelated scores on the Love Attitudes Scale, the Sexual Attitudes Scale (S. Hendrick & Hendrick, 1987b) (see separate entry), the Bem Sex Role Inventory (BSRI) (Bem, 1974) (see Beere, 1990), which is a measure of gender identity, and the Rosenberg Self-Esteem Scale (Rosenberg, 1965, 1979). The researchers also looked at scores on the Love Attitudes Scale in relation to sex and to gender role, as measured by the BSRI. S. Hendrick and Hendrick (1987a, 1987b) intercorrelated scores on the Love Attitudes Scale and the Sexual Attitudes Scale using data from different groups of subjects. In the former article, they also related scores to measures of self-disclosure and sensation seeking. In the latter article, they performed a factor analysis of the six scores from the Love Attitudes Scale and the four scores from the Sexual Attitudes Scale. S. S. Hendrick et al. (1988) intercorrelated scores on the Love Attitudes Scale, self-esteem, and relationship satisfaction, as measured by the Dyadic Adjustment Scale (Spanier, 1976) and the Relationship Assessment Scale (S. S. Hendrick, 1981). S. S. Hendrick et al. used regression analysis to identify the predictors of relationship satisfaction. For each factor score, S. S. Hendrick et al. also reported the correlations between partners. The researchers looked at a person's love attitudes in relationship to his or her partner's prediction of the person's love attitudes, and they looked at the love attitudes of "couples together" as compared to "couples apart." S. S. Hendrick (1988) correlated scores on the Love Attitudes Scale with scores on the Relationship Assessment Scale.

(4) C. Hendrick et al. (1984) and S. Hendrick, Hendrick, Slapion-Foote, and Foote (1985) used the original 54-item version of the Love Attitudes Scale.

AVAILABLE FROM: C. Hendrick, Hendrick, Foote, and Slapion-Foote, 1984, provided the original version of the Love Attitudes Scale; C. Hendrick and Hendrick, 1986, provided the current version of the Love Attitudes Scale

USED IN:

Bailey, W. C., Hendrick, C., & Hendrick, S. S. (1987). Relation of sex and gender role to love, sexual attitudes, and self-esteem. *Sex Roles, 16*, 637–648.

Hendrick, C., & Hendrick, S. (1986). A theory and method of love. *Journal of Personality and Social Psychology, 50*, 392–402.

Hendrick, C., Hendrick, S., Foote, F. H., & Slapion-Foote, M. J. (1984). Do men and women love differently? *Journal of Social and Personal Relationships, 1*, 177–195.

Hendrick, S. S. (1988). A generic measure of relationship satisfaction. *Journal of Marriage and the Family, 50*, 93–98.

Hendrick, S. S., & Hendrick, C. (1987a). Love and sexual attitudes, self-disclosure and sensation seeking. *Journal of Social and Personal Relationships, 4*, 281–297.

Hendrick, S., & Hendrick, C. (1987b). Multidimensionality of sexual attitudes. *Journal of Sex Research, 23*, 502–526.

Hendrick, S. S., Hendrick, C., & Adler, N. L. (1988). Romantic relationships: Love, satisfaction, and staying together. *Journal of Personality and Social Psychology, 54,* 980–988.

Hendrick, S., Hendrick, C., Slapion-Foote, M. J., & Foote, F. H. (1985). Gender differences in sexual attitudes. *Journal of Personality and Social Psychology, 48,* 1630–1642.

BIBLIOGRAPHY:

Beere, C. A. (1990). *Gender roles: A handbook of tests and measures.* Westport, CT: Greenwood.

Bem, S. L. (1974). The measurement of psychological androgyny. *Journal of Consulting and Clinical Psychology, 42,* 155–162.

Hendrick, S. S. (1981). Self-disclosure and marital satisfaction. *Journal of Personality and Social Psychology, 40,* 1150–1159.

Lasswell, T. E., & Lasswell, M. E. (1976). "I love you but I'm not in love with you." *Journal of Marriage and Family Counseling, 38,* 211–224.

Lee, J. A. (1973). *The colors of love: An exploration of the ways of loving.* Don Mills, Ontario: New Press.

Rosenberg, M. (1965). *Society and the adolescent self-image.* Princeton: Princeton University Press.

Rosenberg, M. (1979). *Conceiving the self.* New York: Basic Books.

Spanier, G. B. (1976). Measuring dyadic adjustment: New scales for assessing the quality of marriage and similar dyads. *Journal of Marriage and the Family, 38,* 15–28.

MUNRO-ADAMS LOVE ATTITUDE SCALE

AUTHORS: Brenda Munro and Gerald R. Adams

DATE: 1978

VARIABLE: Attitudes toward romantic and conjugal love

TYPE OF INSTRUMENT: Summated rating scale

DESCRIPTION: The Munro-Adams Love Attitude Scale consists of 26 items representing three factors. Factor I, Romantic Ideal, contains 9 items that reflect a very idealized view of love and the belief that love is an ultimate goal in life. Factor II, Conjugal-Rational Love, contains 8 items that reflect a warm and more settled view of love. Factor III, Romantic Power, contains 9 items that reflect the beliefs that love gives one the power to handle life and is a powerful interpersonal force. Each item is accompanied by five response options ranging from "strongly agree" to "strongly disagree."

SAMPLE ITEMS: (Romantic Ideal) Love is the highest goal between a man and a woman.

(Conjugal-Rational Love) Erotic and romantic feelings toward another are poor signs toward indicating a long and stable love relationship.

(Romantic Power) There can be no real happiness or success in life for those in a poor love relationship.

PREVIOUS SUBJECTS: College students; engaged, married, and divorced persons; single adults; married adults; married persons with and

without children. The scale has been used in Canada, the United States, Uganda, Senegal, South Africa, Barbados, and St. Lucia.
APPROPRIATE FOR: Ages 16 and older
ADMINISTRATION: Self-administered; about 10–15 minutes
SCORING: Items are individually scored, with 5 points assigned to the "strongly agree" end of the continuum. Item scores are summed to yield a score on each of the three factors: Romantic Ideal, Conjugal-Rational Love, and Romantic Power. Higher scores represent greater support for the factor. For example, a high score on Romantic Ideal reflects strong support for a romantic and idealized view of love. The articles listed under USED IN provide means and standard deviations on the three factor scores for a variety of different groups who completed the measure.
DEVELOPMENT: A sample of 302 college students responded to a pool of 57 items—31 literary quotations selected from popular romantic literature and 26 items describing love as "a strong sense of mutual, personal trust" (Munro & Adams, 1978b, p. 217). Their responses were factor analyzed using both orthogonal and oblique rotations. Three factors were identified, and items representing each factor were selected for the final version of the scale.
RELIABILITY: No information was provided.
VALIDITY: Thirty college students were asked to respond to the items of the Munro-Adams Love Attitude Scale as they believed an engaged person would respond; another 30 college students were asked to respond to the items as they believed a married person with children would respond. Consistent with predictions, those responding "as engaged" scored significantly higher than those responding "as married" on the Romantic Ideal and the Romantic Power factors and significantly lower on the Conjugal-Rational Love factor (Munro & Adams, 1978b).

The Munro-Adams Love Attitude Scale was completed by three groups of respondents: 25 engaged persons, 25 married persons, and 15 divorced persons. Engaged persons scored significantly higher than the other two groups on the Romantic Ideal factor and the Romantic Power factor; divorced and married persons scored significantly higher than engaged persons on the Conjugal-Rational Love factor (Munro & Adams, 1978b).

Munro and Adams (1978b) tested 236 high school-educated persons and 92 college-educated persons with three measures regarding love: the Rubin Love Scale (Rubin, 1970) (see separate entry), Knox's (1970a, 1970b) Attitudes Toward Love scale (see separate entry), and the Munro-Adams Love Attitude Scale. For the group with a high school education, scores on Romantic Idealism were significantly correlated with the Rubin Love Scale (r = .42) and the Attitudes Toward Love scale (r = .16); scores on Romantic Power were also significantly correlated with scores on the Rubin Love Scale (r = .36) and the Attitudes Toward Love Scale (r = .41). Romantic Power scores and Romantic Idealism scores of the high school group were significantly correlated with each other (r = .53). The results were somewhat different for the college-educated sample. The Romantic Power scores were significantly correlated with the Rubin Love Scale scores (r = .41), but not with the Attitudes Toward Love scores (r = .05), and the Romantic Idealism scores were significantly correlated with the Attitudes Toward Love scores (r = .38) but not with the Rubin Love Scale scores (r = .05). The Romantic Idealism scores and Romantic Power scores were significantly correlated with each other (r = .54).

NOTES & COMMENTS: (1) Munro and Adams (1978b) referred to the scale as the New Love Attitudes Scale, but the name used here—Munro-Adams Love Attitude Scale—has been used more commonly in the literature.

(2) For each item on each factor, Munro and Adams (1978b) reported factor loadings for the orthogonal rotation and for the oblique rotation.

(3) Munro and Adams (1978b) looked at responses on the Munro-Adams Love Attitude Scale in relation to respondent's sex, educational attainment (high school or college), and stage of life (single, married without children, married with children, or married with children no longer at home). Munro and Adams (1978a) looked at the relationship between locus of control and attitudes regarding love, and they considered attitudes regarding love in relation to educational level, sex, and stage of life.

AVAILABLE FROM: Munro and Adams, 1978b

USED IN:

Munro, B. E., & Adams, G. R. (1978a). Correlates of romantic love revisited. *Journal of Psychology, 98,* 211–214.

Munro, B., & Adams, G. R. (1978b). Love American style: A test of role structure theory on changes in attitudes toward love. *Human Relations, 31,* 215–228.

Payne, M., & Vandewiele, M. (1987). Attitudes toward love in the Caribbean. *Psychological Reports, 60,* 715–721.

Philbrick, J. L. (1987). Sex differences in romantic attitudes toward love among engineering students. *Psychological Reports, 61,* 482.

Philbrick, J. L., & Opolot, J. A. (1980). Love style: Comparison of African and American attitudes. *Psychological Reports, 46,* 286.

Philbrick, J. L., & Stones, C. R. (1988a). Love attitudes in black South Africa: A comparison of school and university students. *Psychological Record, 38,* 249–251.

Philbrick, J. L., & Stones, C. R. (1988b). Love attitudes of white South African adolescents. *Psychological Reports, 62,* 17–18.

Philbrick, J. L., Thomas, F. F., Cretser, G. A., & Leon, J. J. (1988). Sex differences in love-attitudes of black university students. *Psychological Reports, 62,* 414.

Vandewiele, M., & Philbrick, J. L. (1983). Attitudes of Senegalese students toward love. *Psychological Reports, 52,* 915–918.
BIBLIOGRAPHY:
Knox, D. (1970a). Conceptions of love at three developmental levels. *Family Coordinator, 19,* 151–157.
Knox, D. (1970b). Conceptions of love by married college students. *College Students Survey, 4,* 28–30.
Rubin, Z. (1970). Measurement of romantic love. *Journal of Personality and Social Psychology, 9,* 265–273.

RUBIN LIKING SCALE/RUBIN LOVE SCALE
AUTHOR: Zick Rubin
DATE: 1970
VARIABLE: The Rubin Love Scale was designed to measure "romantic love," defined as "love between unmarried opposite-sex peers, of the sort which could possibly lead to marriage" (Rubin, 1970, p. 266). The Rubin Liking Scale was designed to measure an attraction for another person, as in a platonic friendship.
TYPE OF INSTRUMENT: Summated rating scale
DESCRIPTION: Each of the two Rubin scales contains 13 items. The items on the Rubin Love Scale represent three components of romantic love: "affiliative and dependent need, a predisposition to help, and an orientation of exclusiveness and absorption" (Rubin, 1970, p. 265). The items on the Rubin Liking Scale include "components of favorable evaluation and respect for the target person, as well as the perception that the target is similar to oneself" (p. 268). Responses are recorded on a line, with the endpoints labeled "not at all true; disagree completely" and "definitely true; agree completely" and the midpoint labeled "moderately true; agree to some extent." Respondents mark their responses anywhere on the line. There are also 9- item versions of the two scales.
SAMPLE ITEMS: (Love Scale) If ______were feeling bad, my first duty would be to cheer him (her) up.

(Liking Scale) When I am with ______, we almost always are in the same mood.

PREVIOUS SUBJECTS: Dating college couples, college students, married and divorced adults, gay and lesbian couples. The scales have been used in the United States, Canada, and India.
APPROPRIATE FOR: High school students and older
ADMINISTRATION: Self-administered; the two scales together require less than 10 minutes
SCORING: A 9-point scale is laid over the response line, and each item is assigned a score between 1 and 9 points. Higher scores are assigned to the "agree" end of the continuum and reflect more liking and more loving. Item scores are summed to yield a total score on each scale. Total scores can range from 13 (no liking or loving) to 117 (strong liking or

loving). Rubin (1970, 1973) provided normative data for college men and women.

DEVELOPMENT: A pool of about 80 items was compiled, with approximately half the items based on the literature regarding the nature of love: "these items referred to physical attraction, idealization, a predisposition to help, the desire to share emotions and experiences, feelings of exclusiveness and absorption, felt affiliative and dependent needs, the holding of ambivalent feelings, and the relative unimportance of universalistic norms in the relationship" (Rubin, 1970, p. 266). The remaining items were based on the literature regarding interpersonal attraction: "they included references to the desire to affiliate with the target in various settings, evaluation of the target on several dimensions, the salience of norms of responsibility and equity, feelings of respect and trust, and the perception that the target is similar to oneself" (p. 266). The item pool was independently reviewed by two panels of students and faculty, who sorted the items into "loving" and "liking" categories. This led to a revised pool of 70 items that were administered to 198 introductory psychology students. The students completed the items with regard to a girlfriend or boyfriend and with regard to a nonromantic friend of the opposite sex. Separate factor analyses were performed for the girlfriend/boyfriend responses and for the nonromantic friend responses. Each factor analysis produced a general factor that accounted for a large portion of the variance. The results of the factor analyses were used to construct the two 13-item scales.

RELIABILITY: The Rubin Love Scale and Rubin Liking Scale were administered to 158 college-level dating couples. Coefficient alpha for the Rubin Love Scale was .84 for female respondents and .86 for male respondents. Coefficient alpha for the Rubin Liking Scale was .81 for women and .83 for men (Rubin, 1970).

VALIDITY: Rubin (1970) computed the correlation between the Liking and Love Scales using the data from 158 dating couples. Rubin expected low correlations because he intended for the two scales to measure different constructs. The correlation for women was .39, and the correlation for men was .60. The correlation for the men was significantly higher than the correlation for women.

Using the responses from the 158 dating couples, Rubin (1970) found that men's scores on the Rubin Love Scale were almost identical to women's scores when the men and women were rating their opposite-sex partner. When using the Rubin Liking Scale to rate their opposite-sex partner, women had significantly higher scores, meaning that they expressed more liking for their boyfriends than their boyfriends expressed for them. When rating same-sex friends, there was no sex difference on the Rubin Liking Scale, but women expressed significantly more love on the Rubin Love Scale. These results are consistent with expectations; our society is more tolerant of women expressing love for a same-sex friend, less tolerant of men admitting to loving a same-sex friend. Another finding provided additional evidence for the validity of the two measures: both men and women expressed significantly more love for their dating partner than they did for their same-sex friend, but they expressed only slightly more liking for their dating partner than they did for their same-sex friend.

Rubin (1970) correlated scores on the Liking and Love Scales with responses to three questions: "Would you say that you and ______ are in love? What is your best estimate of the likelihood that you and ______ will marry one another? How long have you been dating each other?" For both men and women, responses to the "in love" question and the marriage probability question were more strongly correlated with Rubin Love scores than with Rubin Liking scores, but all of the correlations were statistically significant at the .01 level. For women, the correlation between Love scores and the "in love" question was .59, and the correlation between Love scores and marriage probability was also .59. The comparable correlations for the Liking Scale were .28 and .32. For men, the correlations between the Love scores and "in love" and the love scores and marriage probability were .52 and .59, respectively. For men's Liking scores, the comparable correlations were both .35. For women, the correlation between dating length and Love score was low but statistically significant; for men, it was nonsignificant. For both men and women, the correlation between Liking score and dating length was nonsignificant.

Consistent with expectations, Rubin (1970) found that love for one's dating partner was only slightly correlated with love for one's same-sex friend. For women, the correlation was .18; for men, the correlation was .15.

As further evidence of the validity of the Rubin Love Scale, Rubin (1970) showed that scores on the Love Scale were essentially independent of scores on the Marlowe-Crowne Social Desirability Scale (Crowne & Marlowe, 1964); the correlation was .01 for both males and females.

Rubin (1970) obtained a correlation of .42 for the male and female partners' responses to the Rubin Love Scale. The comparable correlation for the Rubin Liking Scale was .28.

Rubin (1970, 1973) identified two groups of dating couples. One group, called strong love couples, included couples who both scored high on the Rubin Love Scale when rating their partner; the couples in the other group, called weak love couples, scored low on the scale when rating their partner. Rubin found that there was a tendency, although nonsignificant, for strong love couples to engage in more mutual gazing (eye contact) than weak love couples. Rubin also found that strong love couples compared to weak love couples were significantly more likely to engage in mutual focus behaviors. (Mutual focus refers to the percentage of gazing time that was mutual gazing.) Rubin (1973) failed to confirm two hypotheses regarding Love Scale scores and behavior. The first hypothesis was that partners in strong love couples would tend to underestimate the time they are together and overestimate the time they are apart. The second hypothesis was that love score would relate to helping behavior directed toward the loved partner. Failure to support these hypotheses may have been the result of methodological flaws in the research.

In a follow-up study of dating couples, Rubin (1973) found a positive but low correlation between Love scores obtained in October and reported relationship progress measured the following April (r = .20 for women and .19 for men). However, the results were different when the participants were divided into two groups—romantic and nonromantic—as a function of their support for a romantic ideal of love. For the romantic students, Rubin Love scores obtained in October were significantly correlated with a couple's progress in their relationship, measured in April (r = .41 for women and .37 for men). Interestingly, for the romantic students, the correlation between Rubin Liking scores and the couple's progress in their relationship was also significant (r =.30 for women and .33 for men). For the nonromantic students, the correlations were all nonsignificant.

Munro and Adams (1978b) correlated scores from the Rubin Love Scale with three other scores. They obtained the following correlations: with Knox's Attitude Toward Love scale (Knox, 1970a, 1970b) (see separate entry), the correlation was .18 for a high school–educated sample and .17 for a college-educated sample; with the Romantic Power subscale of the Munro-Adams Love Attitude Scale (Munro & Adams, 1978b) (see separate entry), the correlation was .36 for a high school–educated sample and .41 for a college-educated sample; and with the Romantic Idealism subscale of the Munro-Adams Love Attitude Scale, the correlation was .42 for a high school–educated sample and .05 for a college-educated sample. (The correlation of .05 is so different from the others that it appears to be an error.)

NOTES & COMMENTS: (1) The Rubin Love Scale and the Rubin Liking Scale have been related to a variety of other variables, including jealousy (Mathes & Severa, 1974); childhood father absence (Hainline & Feig, 1978); educational level (Munro & Adams, 1978a); Bem Sex Role Inventory scores (Kurdek & Schmitt, 1986a; Small, Gross, Erdwins, & Gessner, 1979); self-disclosure (Rubin, Hill, Peplau, & Dunkel-Schetter, 1980); dyadic trust (Larzelere & Huston, 1980); identity (Kacerguis & Adams, 1980); cohabitation (Risman, Hill, Rubin, & Peplau, 1981); arranged versus love marriages (Gupta & Singh, 1982); tendency to have mystical experiences (Mathes, 1982); hypnotic susceptibility (Mathes, 1982); strategies used to avoid unwelcome persuasion attempts from one's partner (Belk, Martin, & Snell, 1982); egalitarian autonomy and dyadic attachment (Cochran & Peplau, 1985); homophobia (Devlin & Cowan, 1985); lifestyle, including heterosexual married, heterosexual cohabiting, gay, and lesbian lifestyles (Kurdek & Schmitt, 1986b); age and sexual experience (Newcomb, 1986); Type A/Type B personality (Rosenberger & Strube, 1986); loneliness (Sadava & Matejcic, 1987); feminism (Rose & Roades, 1987); and courtship violence (Samios, Arias, & O'Leary, 1985). The data obtained from some of these studies provide evidence for the validity of the scales.

(2) The Rubin Love Scale and Rubin Liking Scale have been used to study lesbian relationships (Caldwell & Peplau, 1984; Peplau, Padesky, & Hamilton, 1982).

(3) In a study of college students' stereotypes of physically disabled persons, Robillard and Fichten (1983) asked college students to complete a variety of measures, including the two Rubin scales, as they believed a physically disabled person would complete them. Berman (1988) used the Rubin scales to determine divorced women's views of their former spouse. The women responded to the scales in terms of their feelings prior to the divorce. Thomas (1985) studied the effect that spouses have on each other. Among the measures used in the study were the Rubin Love Scale and the Rubin Liking Scale.

AVAILABLE FROM: Rubin, 1970, 1973

USED IN:

Belk, S. S., Martin, H. P., & Snell, W. E., Jr. (1982, April). *Avoidance strategies in intimate relationships*. Paper presented at the meeting of the Southwestern Psychological Association, Dallas.

Berman, W. H. (1988). The role of attachment in the post-divorce experience. *Journal of Personality and Social Psychology, 54*, 496–503.

Caldwell, M. A., & Peplau, L. A. (1984). The balance of power in lesbian relationships. *Sex Roles, 10*, 587–599.

Cochran, S. D., & Peplau, L. A. (1985). Value orientations in heterosexual relationships. *Psychology of Women Quarterly, 9*, 477–488.

Devlin, P. K., & Cowan, G. A. (1985). Homophobia, perceived fathering, and male intimate relationships. *Journal of Personality Assessment, 49*, 467–473.

Gupta, U., & Singh, P. (1982). An exploratory study of love and liking and type of marriages. *Indian Journal of Applied Psychology, 19*, 92–97.

Hainline, L., & Feig, E. (1978). The correlates of childhood father absence in college-aged women. *Child Development, 49*, 37–42.

Kacerguis, M. A., & Adams, G. R. (1980). Erikson stage resolution: The relationship between identity and intimacy. *Journal of Youth and Adolescence, 9*, 117–126.

Kurdek, L. A., & Schmitt, J. P. (1986a). Interaction of sex role self-concept with relationship quality and relationship beliefs in married, heterosexual cohabiting, gay, and lesbian couples. *Journal of Personality and Social Psychology, 51*, 365–370.

Kurdek, L. A., & Schmitt, J. P. (1986b). Relationship quality of partners in heterosexual married, heterosexual cohabiting, and gay and lesbian relationships. *Journal of Personality and Social Psychology, 51,* 711–720.

Larzelere, R. E., & Huston, T. L. (1980). The Dyadic Trust Scale: Toward understanding interpersonal trust in close relationships. *Journal of Marriage and the Family, 42,* 595–604.

Mathes, E. W. (1982). Mystical experiences, romantic love, and hypnotic susceptibility. *Psychological Reports, 50,* 701–702.

Mathes, E. W., & Severa, N. (1974). *Jealousy, romantic love, and liking.* Unpublished paper, Western Illinois University, Macomb. (ERIC Document Reproduction Service No. ED 147 671)

Munro, B. E., & Adams, G. R. (1978a). Correlates of romantic love revisited. *Journal of Psychology, 98,* 211–214.

Munro, B., & Adams, G. R. (1978b). Love American style: A test of role structure theory on changes in attitudes toward love. *Human Relations, 31,* 215–228.

Newcomb, M. D. (1986). Notches on the bedpost: Generational effects of sexual experience. *Psychology, 23,* 37–46.

Peplau, L. A., Padesky, C., & Hamilton, M. (1982). Satisfaction in lesbian relationships. *Journal of Homosexuality, 8,* 23–35.

Risman, B. J., Hill, C. T., Rubin, Z., & Peplau, L. A. (1981). Living together in college: Implications for courtship. *Journal of Marriage and the Family, 43,* 77–83.

Robillard, K., & Fichten, C. S. (1983). Attributions about sexuality and romantic involvement of physically disabled college students: An empirical study. *Sexuality and Disability, 6,* 197–212.

Rose, S., & Roades, L. (1987). Feminism and women's friendships. *Psychology of Women Quarterly, 11,* 243–254.

Rosenberger, L. M., & Strube, M. J. (1986). The influence of Type A and B behavior patterns on the perceived quality of dating relationships. *Journal of Applied Social Psychology, 16,* 277-286.

Rubin, Z. (1970). Measurement of romantic love. *Journal of Personality and Social Psychology, 16,* 265–273.

Rubin, Z. (1973). *Liking and loving: An invitation to social psychology.* New York: Holt, Rinehart, & Winston.

Rubin, Z., Hill, C. T., Peplau, L. A., & Dunkel-Schetter, C. (1980). Self-disclosure in dating couples: Sex roles and the ethic of openness. *Journal of Marriage and the Family, 42,* 305–317.

Sadava, S. W., & Matejcic, C. (1987). Generalized and specific loneliness in early marriage. *Canadian Journal of Behavioural Science, 19,* 56–66.

Samios, M., Arias, I., & O'Leary, K. D. (1985, March). *Prevalence and correlates of courtship violence.* Paper presented at the meeting of the Eastern Psychological Association, Boston. (ERIC Document Reproduction Service No. ED 259 264)

Small, A., Gross, R., Erdwins, C., & Gessner, T. (1979). Social attitude correlates of sex role. *Journal of Psychology, 101,* 115-121.

Thomas, C. C. (1985, August). *Social power: Effect on spouses' quality of personal life.* Paper presented at the meeting of the American Psychological As-

sociation, Los Angeles. (ERIC Document Reproduction Service No. ED 269 682)
BIBLIOGRAPHY:
Crowne, D. P., & Marlowe, D. (1964). *The approval motive*. New York: John Wiley.
Knox, D. (1970a). Conceptions of love at three developmental levels. *Family Coordinator, 19,* 151–157.
Knox, D. (1970b). Conceptions of love by married college students. *College Students Survey, 4,* 28–30.

SCALE OF FEELINGS AND BEHAVIOR OF LOVE (SFBL)
AUTHOR: Clifford H. Swensen
DATE: 1977 (modified 1989)
VARIABLE: Various aspects of love
TYPE OF INSTRUMENT: Summated rating scale
DESCRIPTION: The Scale of Feelings and Behavior of Love (SFBL) consists of 120 statements representing six subscales: "(1) verbal expression of affection; (2) self-disclosure of intimate facts about oneself; (3) tolerance for the less desirable characteristics of the loved person; (4) non-material evidence—interest, concern, encouragement, moral support of the loved person; (5) unexpressed feelings—feelings you have for the loved person, but which you have not expressed to them; and (6) material evidence—providing financial support, giving gifts, doing chores" (Fiore & Swensen, 1977, p. 710). Some of the items focus on the expression or giving of love and others on the receipt of love. When completing the scale, respondents are directed to think of a particular love; the object of the love might be a parent, a dating partner, or a spouse. On the earlier version of the SFBL, a statement is followed by three response options phrased in such a way as to be compatible with the phrasing of the item. An example of a set of options is "(a) He (She) *never* tells you this; (b) He (She) *occasionally* tells you this; (c) He (She) *frequently* tells you this." In the 1989 revision of the SFBL, a response key is given at the top of the page, and respondents record the number of their response to the left of each item. The response key gives five options: "1 = Never, 2 = Seldom, 3 = Sometimes, 4 = Often, 5 = Always." The 1989 version is tailored to the respondent; that is, if the love object is a spouse, there is a separate form for husbands and for wives.
SAMPLE ITEMS: (Husband's form of 1989 revision)

Your wife tells you that she feels good about how well you get along together.

Your wife provides direct support when you are in a difficult situation.

PREVIOUS SUBJECTS: College students, married couples, adults
APPROPRIATE FOR: College students and older
ADMINISTRATION: Self-administered; about 40 minutes

SCORING: Items are individually scored on a 5-point scale and summed to yield scores on each of the six subscales. In addition, a Love Scale Index is computed by finding the weighted sum of the subscale scores. Swensen, Eskew, and Kohlhepp (1981) provided means for groups of persons who were at different points in the life cycle (e.g., with preschool and school-aged children).

DEVELOPMENT: Scale development began about thirty years ago. About 300 college students were asked to "describe the feelings or incidents connected with people they loved which distinguished this relationship from that with people they only liked" (Swensen, 1961, p. 167). Fiore and Swensen (1977) reported that about 200 individuals were interviewed and asked to describe their love relationships. From these steps, a pool of 383 items was compiled. The item pool represented eight areas: "material evidence of love (material support, performing chores, etc.); non-material evidence of love (encouragement, advice, etc.); shared activities (games, church, shows, etc.); similarity of outlook on life, values, etc.; self-disclosure (disclosing intimate facts about yourself); verbal expression of feelings; feelings that were not verbally expressed; and physical expression of love" (Swensen & Gilner, 1964, p. 186). The item pool was administered to about 1,200 persons of various ages who completed the scale for love relationships with "parents, children, brothers, sisters, husbands, wives and friends" (Fiore & Swensen, 1977, p. 709). The item pool was factor analyzed 42 times, and the results of the factor analyses were used to develop the first version of the SFBL. For the 1989 revision of the SFBL, items from the earlier version were rephrased and are now consistent with more contemporary patterns of speech.

RELIABILITY: Alpha coefficients were computed for the earlier version of the SFBL and for the 1989 version. The alpha coefficient for the earlier version is given first, with the coefficient for the 1989 version in parentheses: verbal expression = .93 (.95), self-disclosure = .88 (.91), tolerance = .82 (.78), nonmaterial evidence = .91 (.92), unexpressed feelings = .93 (.97), material evidence = .84 (.93), and total score = .95 (.95) (C. H. Swensen, personal communication, June 1989).

Swensen et al. (1981) reported test-retest reliabilities for the subscales and total scores ranging from .77 to .96.

VALIDITY: Fiore and Swensen (1977) compared functional and dysfunctional married couples with the SFBL. They found that dysfunctional married couples compared to functional married couples received less love and received less love than they had expected to receive.

Scores on the SFBL have been related to gender role identity as measured by the Bem Sex Role Inventory (BSRI) (Bem, 1974) (see Beere, 1990). As predicted, Coleman and Ganong (1985) found that persons classified differently on the BSRI responded differently to most scales of the SFBL when they completed the SFBL in terms of their current love relationship. Ganong and Coleman (1987) found similar results when respondents completed the SFBL in terms of their love feelings for a family member.

NOTES & COMMENTS: (1) Swensen (1961) and Swensen and Gilner (1964) reported early work on the development of a love scale.

(2) The SFBL has been used to study marital relationships (Eskew, 1981; Swensen et al., 1981; Swensen & Trahaug, 1985).

AVAILABLE FROM: Clifford H. Swensen, Department of Psychological Sciences, Purdue University, West Lafayette, IN 47907

USED IN:

Coleman, M., & Ganong, L. H. (1985). Love and sex role stereotypes: Do macho men and feminine women make better lovers? *Journal of Personality and Social Psychology, 49,* 170–176.

Eskew, R. W. (1981, November). *Cohort influences in older marriages.* Paper presented at the joint meeting of the Scientific Gerontological Society and the Scientific and Educational Canadian Association on Gerontology, Toronto. (ERIC Document Reproduction Service No. ED 214 086)

Fiore, A., & Swensen, C. H. (1977). Analysis of love relationships in functional and dysfunctional marriages. *Psychological Reports, 40,* 707–714.

Ganong, L. H., & Coleman, M. (1987). Sex, sex roles, and familial love. *Journal of Genetic Psychology, 148,* 45–52.

Swensen, C. H. (1961). Love: A self-report analysis with college students. *Journal of Individual Psychology, 17,* 167–171.

Swensen, C. H., Eskew, R. W., & Kohlhepp, K. A. (1981). Stage of family life cycle, ego development, and the marriage relationship. *Journal of Marriage and the Family, 43,* 841–853.

Swensen, C. H., & Gilner, F. (1964). Factor analysis of self-report statements of love relationships. *Journal of Individual Psychology, 20,* 186–188.

Swensen, C. H., & Trahaug, G. (1985). Commitment and the long-term marriage relationship. *Journal of Marriage and the Family, 47,* 939–945.

BIBLIOGRAPHY:

Beere, C. A. (1990). *Gender roles: A handbook of tests and measures.* Westport, CT: Greenwood.

Bem, S. L. (1974). The measurement of psychological androgyny. *Journal of Consulting and Clinical Psychology, 42,* 155–162.

SEX-LOVE-MARRIAGE ASSOCIATION SCALE (SLM)

AUTHOR: David L. Weis

DATE: 1981

VARIABLE: Cognitive association of sex, love, and marriage

TYPE OF INSTRUMENT: Summated rating scale

DESCRIPTION: The Sex-Love-Marriage Association Scale (SLM) contains eight items. Three items pertain to the pairing of sex and love, four items deal with sexual exclusivity (only one partner), and one item deals with sex and marriage. Five items are phrased to support the pairing of sex, love, and marriage; three items are phrased in the reverse

direction. Each item is accompanied by five response options: "strongly disagree, disagree, neither agree nor disagree, agree, strongly agree."
SAMPLE ITEMS: A man can't have a satisfactory and satisfying sex life without being in love with his partner.

Sex thoughts about someone other than the sex partner during intercourse with the partner are a form of unfaithfulness.
PREVIOUS SUBJECTS: College students
APPROPRIATE FOR: College students and older
ADMINISTRATION: Self-administered; about 5 minutes
SCORING: Items are individually scored on a 5-point scale, with 5 points assigned to the end of the continuum representing support for the pairing of sex, love, and marriage. Item scores are summed to yield a total score that can range from 8 (sex is not associated with love and marriage) to 40 (strong support for associating sex with love and marriage). Weis, Slosnerick, Cate, and Sollie (1986) provided means and standard deviations for various groups of college students who completed the SLM Scale.
DEVELOPMENT: The items on the SLM were taken from McHugh and McHugh's (1976) Sex Attitudes Survey. The items were selected because they appeared to reflect some aspect of the sex-love-marriage relationship. Later analyses showed that the eight items on the SLM yielded a higher reliability coefficient than various subsets of the eight items (Weis et al., 1986). Thus, all eight items were retained on the SLM Scale.
RELIABILITY: Coefficient alpha for a sample of 321 college students was .80. Furthermore, all item-total correlations were significant at the .001 level (Weis & Slosnerick, 1981). For three other samples of college students (sample sizes ranging from 240 to 318), coefficient alpha was .75, .75, and .77 (Weis et al., 1986).
VALIDITY: Weis and Slosnerick (1981) found that SLM scores of 321 college students were significantly related to scores on their Attitudes Toward Marital Exclusivity Scale (see separate entry). Persons who supported marital exclusivity were more likely to believe that sex, love, and marriage were strongly associated. In fact, SLM scores were the strongest of seven predictor variables in a multiple regression equation predicting scores on the Attitudes Toward Marital Exclusivity Scale. Similar results were found by Weis and Felton (1987), who tested 379 college women. Using stepwise multiple regression, they found that SLM scores were the second strongest predictor of Attitudes Toward Marital Exclusivity scores; the strongest predictor was jealousy.

Based on data from the 321 students, Weis et al. (1986) reported that persons with high SLM scores were less likely to approve of premarital and extramarital sex and had fewer premarital sex partners. SLM scores were not significantly related to age and sex. Data collected with another sample of college students showed that SLM scores were again significantly related to attitudes toward extramarital activities. Stepwise regression yielded seven significant variables predictive of SLM scores. In decreasing order of importance, they were: frequency of church attendance, number of premarital coital partners, guilt associated with premarital sex, gender role egalitarianism, current involvement or noninvolvement in a steady relationship, experience with a variety of heterosexual behaviors, and age at first coitus.

NOTES & COMMENTS: (1) Weis et al. (1986) reported that the scale was dominated by a single factor that accounted for 75% of the variance.

(2) Although the items are readily available in the publications listed here, the Sex Attitudes Survey, from which the items were excerpted, is a copyrighted instrument. For more information on the Sex Attitudes Survey, contact Family Life Publications, Inc., P.O. Box 427, Saluda, NC 28773.

AVAILABLE FROM: Weis and Slosnerick, 1981; Weis, Slosnerick, Cate, and Sollie, 1986; Weis, 1988

USED IN:

Weis, D. L. (1988). The Sex-Love-Marriage Association Scale. In C. M. Davis, W. L. Yarber, & S. L. Davis (Eds.), *Sexuality-related measures: A compendium* (pp. 221–222). Syracuse: Editors.

Weis, D. L., & Felton, J. R. (1987). Marital exclusivity and the potential for future marital conflict. *Social Work, 32*, 45–49.

Weis, D. L., & Slosnerick, M. (1981). Attitudes toward sexual and nonsexual extramarital involvements among a sample of college students. *Journal of Marriage and the Family, 43*, 349–358.

Weis, D. L., Slosnerick, M., Cate, R., & Sollie, D. L. (1986). A survey instrument for assessing the cognitive association of sex, love, and marriage. *Journal of Sex Research, 22*, 206–220.

BIBLIOGRAPHY:

McHugh, G., & McHugh, T. G. (1976). *The Sex Attitudes Survey and profile*. Saluda, NC: Family Life Publications.

ADVERSARIAL SEXUAL BELIEFS (ASB)

AUTHOR: Martha R. Burt

DATE: 1980 (used 1977)

VARIABLE: Belief that male-female relationships are basically adversarial, manipulative, or coercive

TYPE OF INSTRUMENT: Summated rating scale

DESCRIPTION: The Adversarial Sexual Beliefs (ASB) scale contains nine items reflecting a negative relationship between men and women. Two items suggest that men must be the boss in the relationship; two items indicate that women are manipulative when trying to "catch" a man; two items suggest that sexual demands are excessive (one of those items says men make the excessive demands; the other says women make them); one item says women like to "put men down"; one item says women "take advantage" of men; and one item says men are inadequate sexually. The tone of all of the items is clearly negative. Seven items reflect a negative view of women, and two items reflect a negative view of men. Each item is accompanied by a 7-point response scale ranging from "strongly agree" to "strongly disagree."

SAMPLE ITEMS: A woman will only respect a man who will lay down the law to her.

Many women are so demanding sexually that a man just can't satisfy them.

PREVIOUS SUBJECTS: College students; adults, ages 18 and older; convicted rapists; child molesters

APPROPRIATE FOR: Ages 18 and older

ADMINISTRATION: Self-administered (although the scale has been administered in an interview format); a few minutes

SCORING: Items are individually scored on a 7-point scale, with the higher number of points assigned to "strongly agree," the response reflecting adversarial sexual beliefs. Item scores are summed to yield a total score that can range from 9 to 63. Burt (1980) tested 598 adults in Minnesota and obtained a mean score of 29.0 and a standard deviation of 8.5.

DEVELOPMENT: This scale was developed concurrently with four other scales: the Sex Role Stereotyping Scale (see Beere, 1990), the Sexual Conservatism scale (see separate entry), the Acceptance of Interpersonal Violence (AIV) scale (see separate entry), and the Rape Myth Acceptance Scale (RMA) (see separate entry). Pretesting involving a large item pool was conducted, and based on the results, about twice the number of items to be included on each of the final scales was included on an interview form. The interview was administered to 598 adults in Minnesota, and item analyses were performed on their responses. Based on these analyses, the "best items" were selected for the scale.

RELIABILITY: Based on testing 598 adults, Burt (1980, 1983) obtained a coefficient alpha of .80. Item-total correlations ranged from .38 to .58.

VALIDITY: Burt (1980) tested 598 adults and found that high scores on the ASB were associated with greater acceptance of rape myths, as measured by the RMA. Check and Malamuth (1983) tested college students with the Sex Role Stereotyping Scale and correlated their results with scores on the ASB. As predicted, the correlation was significant (r = .46).

NOTES & COMMENTS: (1) Although I have presented Burt's measures as five separate scales and they can be used independently of each other, Burt actually developed her five measures together. The five scales are: AIV, ASB, RMA, Sex Role Stereotyping Scale, and Sexual Conservatism. A subset of 37 items from the Burt scales has been used in research looking at the characteristics of rape victims who never reported their assault (Koss, 1985) and sexual offenders who were never detected (Koss, Leonard, Beezley, & Oros, 1985). When these researchers factor analyzed responses to the 37 items, they identified five factors that were quite comparable to the scales Burt developed. The factors were labeled "Acceptance of Sexual Aggression; Conservative Attitudes Toward Female Sexuality; Rejection of Rape Myths; Heterosexual Relationships as Game-playing; and Unacceptability of Aggression" (Koss, 1985, p. 198).

(2) Briere, Malamuth, and Check (1985) factor analyzed the responses from 452 male college students. They identified two factors: "Male Dominance is Justified" and "Adversarial Sexual Beliefs (Purified)."

(3) In Burt and Albin's (1981) study, subjects heard one of six rape depictions that varied in terms of the victim's reputation (good or bad), the relationship between assailant and victim (no relationship or dating), and the amount of force used (low or high force). The subjects completed a variety of measures including the ASB, and they answered two questions: "How much do you feel the situation was a rape or was not a rape?" and "How strongly do you feel that you would convict or would not convict the man?" (p. 219).

(4) In order to compare the perceptions of rapists with the perceptions of the general public, Burt (1983) conducted a study in which subjects heard a description of a scene involving a man and a woman. The scene varied according to the degree of violence described (three levels) and the closeness of the relationship between the man and woman (strangers, acquaintances, and married persons). The respondents were asked to rate the violence and the man in the story and to indicate what the woman did to "deserve" the violence. In addition, respondents completed several attitude scales including the ASB.

(5) Briere and Malamuth (1983) sought to identify the variables that could predict likelihood to rape or likelihood to use sexual force. They tested college men with a variety of measures, including the RMA, the AIV, and the ASB. To examine the impact of these three scales, they reformed the responses into nine attitude scales using results of earlier research.

(6) Check and Malamuth (1985) conducted a study to determine whether scores on the ASB scale and other attitude scores can predict "(a) reactions to fictional rape, (b) reactions to a report of a real rape, and (c) males' actual predictions about their own likelihood of raping" (p. 417). They also looked at how scores on the ASB scale were affected by observing a sexually violent film as compared to watching a control film (Malamuth & Check, 1981).

(7) Rapaport and Burkhart (1984) investigated the relationship between college men's coercive sexual behaviors and their responses on a variety of measures, including the ASB scale. Overholser and Beck (1986) compared incarcerated rapists, incarcerated child molesters, and three con-

trol groups on a variety of measures, including the ASB. Pryor (1987) studied college men and compared their scores on a measure of their likelihood to commit sexual harassment with their scores on a variety of other measures including the ASB. Muehlenhard and Linton (1987) used the ASB as one of several measures in their study of the risk factors for date rape and other forms of male-to-female sexual aggression. Demare, Briere, and Lips (1988) used the ASB as one of several measures in order to study the relationships between violent pornography and sexual aggression. Malamuth (1989a, 1989b) used the ASB to study sexual aggression in men.

(8) Mayerson and Taylor (1987) conducted a study with 98 college women. They used eight items from the Sex Role Stereotyping Scale and selected those females scoring in the highest third and in the lowest third on stereotyping. They then compared these two groups in terms of how pornography affects them. More specifically, they looked at how pornographic depictions that varied in degree of consent and degree of sexual arousal affected the two groups of women's scores on a variety of measures, including seven items from the ASB.

AVAILABLE FROM: Burt, 1980, 1983; Burt and Albin, 1981

USED IN:

Briere, J., & Malamuth, N. M. (1983). Self-reported likelihood of sexually aggressive behavior: Attitudinal versus sexual explanations. *Journal of Research in Personality, 17*, 315–323.

Briere, J., Malamuth, N., & Check, J. V. P. (1985). Sexuality and rape-supportive beliefs. *International Journal of Women's Studies, 8*, 398–403.

Burt, M. R. (1980). Cultural myths and supports for rape. *Journal of Personality and Social Psychology, 38*, 217–230.

Burt, M. R. (1983). Justifying personal violence: A comparison of rapists and the general public. *Victimology: An International Journal, 8*, 131–150.

Burt, M. R., & Albin, R. S. (1981). Rape myths, rape definitions, and probability of conviction. *Journal of Applied Social Psychology, 11*, 212–230.

Check, J. V. P., & Malamuth, N. M (1983). Sex role stereotyping and reactions to depictions of stranger versus acquaintance rape. *Journal of Personality and Social Psychology, 45*, 344–356.

Check, J. V. P., & Malamuth, N. M. (1985). An empirical assessment of some feminist hypotheses about rape. *International Journal of Women's Studies, 8*, 414–423.

Demare, D., Briere, J., & Lips, H. M. (1988). Violent pornography and self-reported likelihood of sexual aggression. *Journal of Research in Personality, 22*, 140–153.

Koss, M. P. (1985). The hidden rape victim: Personality, attitudinal, and situational characteristics. *Psychology of Women Quarterly, 9*, 193–212.

Koss, M. P., Leonard, K. E., Beezley, D. A., & Oros, C. J. (1985). Nonstranger sexual aggression: A discriminant analysis of the psychological characteristics of undetected offenders. *Sex Roles, 12*, 981–992.

Malamuth, N. M. (1989a). The Attraction to Sexual Aggression Scale: Part one. *Journal of Sex Research, 26*, 26–49.

Malamuth, N. M. (1989b). The Attraction to Sexual Aggression Scale: Part two. *Journal of Sex Research, 26*, 324–354.

Malamuth, N. M., & Check, J. V. P. (1981). The effects of mass media exposure on acceptance of violence against women: A field experiment. *Journal of Research in Personality, 15*, 436–446.

Mayerson, S. E., & Taylor, D. A. (1987). The effects of rape myth pornography on women's attitudes and the mediating role of sex role stereotyping. *Sex Roles, 17*, 321–338.

Muehlenhard, C. L., & Linton, M. A. (1987). Date rape and sexual aggression in dating situations: Incidence and risk factors. *Journal of Counseling Psychology, 34*, 186–196.

Overholser, J. C., & Beck, S. (1986). Multimethod assessment of rapists, child molesters, and three control groups on behavioral and psychological measures. *Journal of Consulting and Clinical Psychology, 54*, 682–687.

Pryor, J. B. (1987). Sexual harassment proclivities in men. *Sex Roles, 17*, 269–290.

Rapaport, K., & Burkhart, B. R. (1984). Personality and attitudinal characteristics of sexually coercive college males. *Journal of Abnormal Psychology, 93*, 216–221.

BIBLIOGRAPHY:

Beere, C. A. (1990). *Gender roles: A handbook of tests and measures*. Westport, CT: Greenwood.

ATTITUDES TOWARD MARITAL EXCLUSIVITY SCALE

AUTHORS: Gerhard Neubeck and Vera M. Schletzer, modified by Ralph E. Johnson, later modified by David L. Weis

DATE: 1962 (modified 1970, 1981)

VARIABLE: Attitudes toward sexual and nonsexual extramarital involvements when the spouse is not present

TYPE OF INSTRUMENT: Summated rating scale

DESCRIPTION: The Attitudes Toward Marital Exclusivity Scale consists of a brief description of a hypothetical situation in which a husband (or wife) is in a situation where his (or her) spouse is out of town and the spouse of very close friends is also out of town. Thus, the two in-town, opposite-sex spouses have an opportunity to be together. The description is followed by a list of seven activities, and the respondent is to indicate the extent to which he or she would accept or reject participating in each activity. Five response options are provided: "Total rejection, Moderate rejection, No feelings either way, Moderate acceptance, Total acceptance."

SAMPLE ITEMS: Spending an evening or evenings with him (her) in his (her) living room?

Becoming sexually involved.

PREVIOUS SUBJECTS: College students

APPROPRIATE FOR: Ages 16 and older

ADMINISTRATION: Self-administered; less than 5 minutes

SCORING: Items are individually scored on a 5-point scale, with 1 point assigned to the end of the continuum stating "total rejection" and 5 points assigned to the end of the continuum stating "total acceptance." Item scores are summed to yield a total score that can range from 7 (total rejection of extramarital activities) to 35 (total acceptance of extramarital activities). For each item and for the total score, Weis and Felton (1987) reported the mean, standard deviation, and percentage accepting the behavior. Their data were based on responses from 379 college women.

DEVELOPMENT: In 1962, Neubeck and Schletzer (1962) reported the results of a study dealing with attitudes regarding extramarital involvement. Participants responded to a measure that presented a brief description of a situation that was similar to the situation in the Attitudes Toward Marital Exclusivity Scale. The situation was followed by three activities, also similar to those in the Attitudes Toward Marital Exclusivity Scale, and participants were asked to indicate how they would feel about each of the activities. Several years later, Johnson (1970) conducted a study using a variation of the Neubeck and Schletzer measure. Johnson described a situation that was quite similar to Neubeck and Schletzer's and followed it with a list of seven activities. These seven activities are the same as those now on the Attitudes Toward Marital Exclusivity Scale. The scale's name was introduced by Weis (Weis & Slosnerick, 1981), who also modified slightly the wording of the situation and introduced the five response options currently used.

RELIABILITY: Weis and Slosnerick (1981) administered the Attitudes Toward Marital Exclusivity Scale to 112 college men and 209 college women. Coefficient alpha was .87. Although Weis and Slosnerick did not report the values of the item-total correlations, they did indicate that all were statistically significant ($p < .001$). Weis and Felton (1987) administered the scale to 379 college women and obtained a coefficient alpha of .81. Weis (1988) reported that coefficient alpha for three different samples of college students ranged from .85 to .88.

VALIDITY: Weis and Slosnerick (1981) related scores on the Attitudes Toward Marital Exclusivity Scale to the following variables: age, marital status, size of home town, religion, gender, number of premarital coital partners, scores on a series of items measuring the extent to which persons associate sex, love, and marriage (The Sex-Love-Marriage Association Scale [Weis, Slosnerick, Cate, & Sollie, 1986] [see separate entry]), premarital petting permissiveness, premarital coital permissiveness, marital motivations for extramarital sex, and individual motivations for extramarital sex. There were significant correlations between scores on the Attitudes Toward Marital Exclusivity Scale and five of the other measures: Sex-Love-Marriage Association, premarital petting permissiveness, premarital coital permissiveness, marital motivations for extramarital sex, and individual motivations for extramarital sex. A multiple regression analysis showed that the Sex-Love-Marriage Association, followed by premarital coital permissiveness and gender, explained the most variance in the Attitudes Toward Marital Exclusivity scores.

Weis and Felton (1987) conducted a similar study to look at the predictors of college women's attitudes toward marital exclusivity. They found that the women who supported marital exclusivity were "most likely to score high on a measure of jealousy, to associate sex and love, to score low on intimacy diffusion (that is, they believed that persons in love wish to spend time only with each other), to view themselves as conservative, and to attend church frequently" (p. 47).

Weis et al. (1986) showed that college students who supported marital exclusivity were more likely to associate sex, love, and marriage.

Weis (1988) reported that a study of three samples of college students showed that students who were supportive of marital exclusivity were likely to have had less sexual and dating experience, to have experienced less variety of sexual behaviors, and to believe that they could not form intimate relationships with several partners. These students were more likely to associate sex, love, and marriage, and they were more likely to be involved in an exclusive relationship at the time of the study.

NOTES & COMMENTS: Weis and Slosnerick (1981) reported the correlations among each item on the Attitudes Toward Marital Exclusivity Scale and the following variables: age, marital status, population of home town, Judaism, Protestantism, Catholicism, gender, number of premarital coital partners, Sex-Love-Marriage Association, premarital petting permissiveness, premarital coital permissiveness, marital motivations for extramarital sex, and individual motivations for extramarital sex.

AVAILABLE FROM: Weis and Slosnerick, 1981; Weis and Felton, 1987; Weis, 1988

USED IN:

Johnson, R. E. (1970). Extramarital sexual intercourse: A methodological note. *Journal of Marriage and the Family, 32*, 279–282.

Neubeck, G., & Schletzer, V. M. (1962). A study of extra-marital relationships. *Marriage and Family Living, 24*, 279–281.

Weis, D. L. (1988). Attitudes Toward Marital Exclusivity Scale. In C. M. Davis, W. L. Yarber, & S. L. Davis (Eds.), *Sexuality-related measures: A compendium* (pp. 105–106). Syracuse: Editors.

Weis, D. L., & Felton, J. R. (1987). Marital exclusivity and the potential for future marital conflict. *Social Work, 32*, 45–49.

Weis, D. L., & Slosnerick, M. (1981). Attitudes toward sexual and nonsexual extramarital involvements among a sample of college students. *Journal of Marriage and the Family, 43*, 349–358.

Weis, D. L., Slosnerick, M., Cate, R., & Sollie, D. L. (1986). A survey instrument for assessing the cognitive association of sex, love, and marriage. *Journal of Sex Research, 22*, 206–220.

DELUCIA DATING BEHAVIOR INDICES

AUTHOR: Janice L. DeLucia

DATE: 1987 (used 1983)

VARIABLE: Self-reported performance of masculine and feminine dating behaviors

TYPE OF INSTRUMENT: Multiple choice
DESCRIPTION: There are two parts to the DeLucia's Dating Behavior Indices: a masculine index and a feminine index, each containing 26 items. The items describe behaviors that might be exhibited in a dating relationship and cover such topics as the "sexual relationship, expression of feeling, problem solving and decision making, degree of relationship commitment and focus, manners, and finances" (DeLucia, 1987, p. 156). Each item is accompanied by four response options: "you, both of you, your partner, neither of you." The respondents use these options to indicate who performs the behavior in their dating relationship.
SAMPLE ITEMS: (masculine index) Carries packages for the other; Pays for activities you suggest

(feminine index) Confides in the other; Does favors for the other, even when not asked to
PREVIOUS SUBJECTS: College students involved in heterosexual dating relationships
APPROPRIATE FOR: Anyone involved in a sexually intimate, heterosexual dating relationship
ADMINISTRATION: Self-administered; about 15–20 minutes
SCORING: The responses "you" and "both of you" are each given 1 point per item. Thus, the higher the score, the more the person performs the behaviors listed in the index. Separate scores are obtained for the masculine index and the feminine index, with each index yielding a score between 0 and 26. DeLucia (1987) provided means and standard deviations on both forms of the scale for small numbers of males and females divided by sex role identity categories—androgynous, undifferentiated, feminine, and masculine—as measured by the Bem Sex Role Inventory (BSRI) (Bem, 1974) (see Beere, 1990).
DEVELOPMENT: A class of undergraduate students developed a list of dating behaviors that a second class of students then judged as either traditionally masculine or traditionally feminine. Items were included if there was 70% agreement regarding their classification.
RELIABILITY: Test-retest reliabilities were computed with a 2-week interval between testings. The reliability estimate was .98 for males and .96 for females. Internal consistency reliability, as measured by coefficient alpha, was .74 for the masculine index and .70 for the feminine index.
VALIDITY: DeLucia (1987) used the BSRI to classify respondents into four categories: androgynous, undifferentiated, masculine, and feminine. As expected, DeLucia found that males classified as androgynous or masculine scored significantly higher on the masculine index, and females classified as androgynous or feminine scored significantly higher on the feminine index. No significant differences were found when

looking at the masculine index scores for the females or the feminine index scores for the males.

NOTES & COMMENTS: (1) The correlation between the masculine and feminine indexes was fairly low: for males, r =.21; for females, r = .39.

(2) Additional research is needed to demonstrate whether the self-reports provided in response to this measure are accurate reflections of real behavior. Furthermore, it would be interesting to know whether there is a relationship between the performance of sex-typed dating behaviors and the length of the dating relationship.

AVAILABLE FROM: DeLucia, 1987

USED IN:

DeLucia, J. L. (1987). Gender role identity and dating behavior: What is the relationship? *Sex Roles, 17*, 153–161.

BIBLIOGRAPHY:

Beere, C. A. (1990). *Gender roles: A handbook of tests and measures*. Westport, CT: Greenwood.

Bem, S. L. (1974). The measurement of psychological androgyny. *Journal of Consulting and Clinical Psychology, 42*, 155–162.

HETEROSEXUAL RELATIONSHIPS SCALE

AUTHORS: Eleanor R. Hall, Judith A. Howard, and Sherrie L. Boezio

DATE: 1986

VARIABLE: Attitudes toward male-female relationships

TYPE OF INSTRUMENT: Summated rating scale

DESCRIPTION: There are two versions of the Heterosexual Relationships Scale, each intended to measure "beliefs that men should dominate women, perceptions of the opposite sex as sex objects, and views that sex involves conquest" (Hall, Howard, & Boezio, 1986, p. 108). A 12-item version of the scale is intended for use with adolescents; responses are recorded on a 5-point scale ranging from "strongly agree" to "strongly disagree." A 9-item version with slightly different wording is intended for use with college students; items are accompanied by a 9-point scale, but the endpoints are still "strongly agree" and "strongly disagree."

SAMPLE ITEMS: (wording used here is for adolescents) It's OK for a guy to punch a stranger who makes a pass at his girlfriend.

Most girls like kind, considerate guys better than tough ones.

PREVIOUS SUBJECTS: High school and college students

APPROPRIATE FOR: High school and college students

ADMINISTRATION: Self-administered; about 5 minutes

SCORING: Scores for the two versions of the scale are not comparable because both the number of items and the number of points per item are different on the two versions. Item scores are summed to yield one score on each version. Hall et al. (1986) reported means and standard deviations by sex for a sample of 973 adolescents and a sample of 293 college students.

DEVELOPMENT: A pool of items was administered to a sample of 973 adolescents between the ages of 14 and 17; a slightly different item pool was administered to 293 college students. When responses were analyzed, items with low item-total correlations were eliminated from the scale, leaving 12 items on the adolescent scale and 9 on the college student scale.

RELIABILITY: Coefficient alpha for both the college version and the adolescent version was .64. Item-total correlations for the 971 adolescent respondents ranged from .10 to .58. For the sample of 293 college students, the item-total correlations ranged from .17 to .54.

VALIDITY: Face validity of the items was demonstrated by having the items classified by students enrolled in a college-level sex roles course.

When the responses of males and females were compared, it was found that males were significantly more likely to favor male domination over women and to view women as sex objects. These findings were true at both the adolescent and college levels. Furthermore, there was a significant, positive relationship between rape attitudes and scores on the Heterosexual Relationships Scale. For both males and females, those who were tolerant of rape were more likely to favor male dominance over women and to perceive women as sex objects.

AVAILABLE FROM: Hall, Howard, and Boezio, 1986

USED IN:

Hall, E. R., Howard, J. A., & Boezio, S. L. (1986). Tolerance of rape: A sexist or antisocial attitude? *Psychology of Women Quarterly, 10,* 101–118.

HETEROSEXUAL TRUST SCALE (HTS)

AUTHOR: Michael B. Gurtman

DATE: 1979

VARIABLE: Extent to which females trust males in heterosexual interactions

TYPE OF INSTRUMENT: Summated rating scale

DESCRIPTION: The Heterosexual Trust Scale (HTS) consists of 18 items, each focusing on "a guy" or "most guys." Ten of the items are negative statements about "guys," and 8 are positive statements. Each item is accompanied by five response options ranging from "strongly agree" to "strongly disagree."

SAMPLE ITEMS: It's better not to trust a guy until you have proof of his sincerity.

You can rely on guys to be truthful about their feelings.

PREVIOUS SUBJECTS: College women

APPROPRIATE FOR: High school students and older
ADMINISTRATION: Self-administered; about 5–10 minutes
SCORING: Items are scored on a 5-point scale, with 5 points assigned to the response reflecting greater trust. Item scores are summed to yield a total score that can range from 18 (very low trust) to 90 (very high trust).

Gurtman (1979/1980) reported item means and standard deviations based on a sample of 85 college women. Gurtman also presented item means, item-remainder correlations, and alpha values with the item deleted for a sample of 145 sorority sisters who completed the scale. DEVELOPMENT: Scale development began with the following definition of heterosexual trust: "the generalized expectancy that the honesty, sincerity and benevolence of opposite sex peers can be relied upon in heterosexual interactions" (Gurtman, 1979/1980, p. 24). Patterning the scale after Rotter's (1967) Interpersonal Trust Scale, the authors developed a pool of about 40 items. From this item pool, the authors selected a subset of 22 items, but their procedure for selecting the subset was not specified. The 22-item version of the scale was administered to a sample of 23 college women. Item means, item variances, and item-remainder correlations were computed. A set of 18 items with item-remainder correlations of .30 or higher was selected for the final scale.

RELIABILITY: Gurtman (1979/1980) administered the HTS to a sample of 85 college women. Coefficient alpha was .83. Item-remainder correlations were statistically significant for 17 of the 18 items; they ranged from .20 to .66, with a mean of .48. Another sample of 145 college women completed the HTS. Coefficient alpha, based on responses from 139 of these women, was .88. Item-remainder correlations for this group were all significant at the .001 level; the correlations ranged from .32 to .65, with a mean of .51.

Southworth and Schwarz (1987) administered the HTS to 52 college women from divorced families and 52 college women from intact families. Internal consistency reliability for the women from divorced families was .90; for the women from intact families, the internal consistency reliability was .86.

VALIDITY: In order to obtain evidence of the validity of the HTS, a sample of 85 college women completed several other measures in addition to the HTS. In general, the correlations were as predicted. Women who scored high on the HTS—that is, they showed greater trust—were more likely to have a steady boyfriend and were likely to have been dating their partner for a longer period of time. Women scoring low on the HTS reported having a poorer dating adjustment in college and were more likely to maintain an "exchange orientation" in their current relationship, meaning that they were more likely to believe in strict reciprocity: If I do something for you, you must do something for me in return. Furthermore, there was a significant, positive correlation between scores on the HTS and scores on Rotter's (1967) Interpersonal Trust Scale (r = .52), a measure of more general trust. No significant relationships were found between HTS scores and age, religion, sexual experience, or sexual standards.

A peer nomination technique, referred to as the Interpersonal Behavior Survey (IBS), was administered to 145 college women to provide independent criteria by which to judge the validity of the HTS. The IBS covered 15 variables, "each presented as a descriptive paragraph of a particular interpersonal typology. . . . Subjects were required to nominate, in order, the three members of their group who best fit each of the descriptions" (Gurtman, 1979/1980, p. 29). It was predicted that HTS scores would be strongly related to peer ratings on four trust variables: trust, distrust, trustworthiness, and gullibility. The prediction was essentially unsupported.

For the sample of 145 college women, the correlation between the HTS and the Interpersonal Trust Scale was .60.

Some of the results reported as supporting the validity of the scale with the sample of 85 college women were not replicated when the scale was administered to a sample of 145 college women. For example, scores on the HTS were not related to having a steady boyfriend, nor were they related to the length of the relationship when there was one, nor were they related to a recent breakup in a heterosexual relationship.

NOTES & COMMENTS: (1) Gurtman (1979/1980) factor analyzed responses from 145 college women. Using an eigenvalue of 1.0 as the cutoff, he identified four orthogonal factors. These four factors accounted for 56.5% of the total variance, but one general factor accounted for 71.4% of the common variance. As a result Gurtman concluded that "the results thus indicate that a one factor solution may approximate the true dimensionality of the scale" (p. 43).

(2) Gurtman (1979/1980) related HTS to a variety of variables, a portion of them reported in the VALIDITY section. He concluded that there was not enough evidence to make a judgment regarding the scale's validity.

(3) Southworth and Schwarz (1987) compared college women from divorced and intact families on a variety of measures. One of the measures was the HTS.

AVAILABLE FROM: Gurtman, 1979/1980

USED IN:

Gurtman, M. B. (1980). Heterosexual trust: Theory and measurement (Doctoral dissertation, University of Connecticut, 1979). *Dissertation Abstracts International*, *41*, 689B.

Southworth, S., & Schwarz, J. C. (1987). Post-divorce contact, relationship with father, and heterosexual trust in female college students. *American Journal of Orthopsychiatry*, *57*(3), 371–382.

BIBLIOGRAPHY:
Rotter, J. B. (1967). A new scale for the measurement of interpersonal trust. *Journal of Personality, 35*, 651–665.

MALE-FEMALE RELATIONS QUESTIONNAIRE (MFRQ)
AUTHORS: Janet T. Spence, Robert L. Helmreich, and Linda Levitt Sawin
DATE: 1980
VARIABLE: Sex role behaviors and preferences
TYPE OF INSTRUMENT: Summated rating scale
DESCRIPTION: There are two 30-item forms of the Male-Female Relations Questionnaire (MFRQ), one for male respondents and the other for female respondents. Each form consists of three subscales. The Social Interaction subscale consists of 16 items describing "the individual's tendency to modify his or her behavior in social situations containing implicit sex-role demands" (Spence, Helmreich, & Sawin, 1980, p. [i]); the Marital Roles subscale consists of 10 items that deal with "preferred relationships between the individual and his or her spouse" (p. [i]). Unmarried respondents are urged to answer the marital items in terms of how they hope their spouse will be if they later marry. The third subscale is different on the two forms. On the male form, the third subscale is labeled "Expressivity" and contains 4 items concerning men's unwillingness to deal with their own emotional feelings. On the female form, the third subscale is labeled "Male Preference" and contains 4 items dealing with the characteristics desired in a male. In general, many of the items on the female form are parallel to items on the male form; some are even identical on the two forms. Each item is accompanied by a 5-point response scale, with the endpoints labeled "strongly agree" and "strongly disagree."
SAMPLE ITEMS: (Social Interaction; both forms) I'd rather have a man as a boss at work than a woman.

(Marital Roles; female form) One of my jobs should be to help my husband in his work by taking the pressure off him at home.

(Marital Roles; male form) One of my wife's jobs should be to help me in my work by taking the pressure off me at home.

(Expressivity; male form) If I tried to be very kind and aware of other people's feelings, it would make me too soft to be a good leader.

(Male Preference; female form) I don't have much respect for a man who allows himself to be led around by his wife or girlfriend, even if it's not done obviously.
PREVIOUS SUBJECTS: College students
APPROPRIATE FOR: College students and older
ADMINISTRATION: Self-administered; about 10–15 minutes
SCORING: Items are individually scored on a 5-point scale with item

scores ranging from 0 to 4. All items are keyed in the same direction. "Strongly agree," the traditional response, is assigned 4 points. Item scores are summed to yield scores on the three subscales and a total score. Spence et al. (1980) provided means, standard deviations, and ranges, by sex, for the three subscale scores on the MFRQ.

DEVELOPMENT: Scale development was based on the following definition of sex roles: "normative expectations about the duties, responsibilities, and rules for behavior in specific situations that men and women in a given society should assume" (Spence et al., 1980, p. 4). Items were developed to examine the tendency to conform to sex role expectations in social interactions and to identify preferences and expectations held for members of the opposite sex. Separate items were developed for male and female respondents, although in many cases, it was possible to include parallel items in the two item pools. Two preliminary versions of the scale were developed, one for males and one for females, each containing 56 items. A sample of 258 college women and 250 college men completed the preliminary subscales. Some items were deleted due to excessive skewness, and responses to the remaining items were factor analyzed. The factor analysis of the marital items produced similar results for both males and females. Four factors emerged, but only one had an eigenvalue over 1.0. The results for the nonmarital items were more complex and less consistent across sex. The male responses led to five factors with eigenvalues over 1.0; the female responses led to four factors with eigenvalues over 1.0. The current versions of the MFRQ were constructed using the results of the factor analyses and a cutoff value of .30 on factor loadings.

RELIABILITY: Responses from 250 college men and 258 college women were used to compute coefficient alpha. For males, alpha was equal to .87, .67, and .89 for Social Interaction, Expressivity, and Marital Roles, respectively. For females, alpha was equal to .84, .56, and .85 for Social Interaction, Male Preference, and Marital Roles, respectively (Spence et al., 1980).

VALIDITY: Spence et al. (1980) looked at the relationship between MFRQ scores and scores on the Attitudes Toward Women Scale (Spence & Helmreich, 1978) (see Beere, 1990). As expected, significant correlations were found between the two measures.

Contrary to expectations, Spence et al. (1980) did not find substantial correlations between MFRQ scores and ratings of preferences for sex stereotyped tasks. This may have resulted from the researchers' using tasks that were not sex stereotyped from the perspective of college students.

NOTES & COMMENTS: (1) Spence et al. (1980) reported the intercorrelations between the subscales. For both males and females, the correlations between Social Interaction and Marital Roles were quite high and statistically significant: .73 for males and .72 for females.

(2) Spence et al. (1980) factor analyzed responses from a different sample of 159 college men and 267 college women. The results confirmed the factor analytic results found earlier.

(3) Spence et al. (1980) related MFRQ scores to scores on several other measures, including the Texas Social Behavior Inventory (Helmreich & Stapp, 1974), which is a measure of social competence and self-esteem; the Work and Family Orientation Scale (Helmreich & Spence, 1978), which is a measure of achievement motivation and attitudes toward family and career (see Beere, 1990); and the Extended Personal Attributes Questionnaire (Spence, Helmreich, & Holahan, 1979), which is a measure of gender role identity (see Beere, 1990).

(4) Belk, Martin, and Snell (1982) and Belk and Snell (1988) looked at the relationship between MFRQ scores and the strategies people use to avoid being influenced by others.

(5) Belk and Snell (1986) used two subscales from the MFRQ as criterion measures for establishing the convergent validity of their Beliefs About Women Scale (see Beere, 1990). Snell (1986) used the MFRQ as a criterion measure in establishing the validity of the Masculine Role Inventory (see Beere, 1990).

(6) Swann, Pelham, and Chidester (1988) used a subset of items from the MFRQ to select a sample of college students who "possessed relatively liberal beliefs concerning women's roles" (p. 271).

AVAILABLE FROM: Spence, Helmreich, and Sawin, 1980

USED IN:

Belk, S. S., Martin, H. P., & Snell, W. E., Jr. (1982, April). *Avoidance strategies in intimate relationships.* Paper presented at the meeting of the Southwestern Psychological Association, Dallas.

Belk, S. S., & Snell, W. E., Jr. (1986). Beliefs about women: Components and correlates. *Personality and Social Psychology Bulletin, 12,* 403–413.

Belk, S. S., & Snell, W. E., Jr. (1988). Avoidance strategy use in intimate relationships. *Journal of Social and Clinical Psychology, 7,* 80–96.

Edwards, V. J., & Spence, J. T. (1987). Gender-related traits, stereotypes, and schemata. *Journal of Personality and Social Psychology, 53,* 146–154.

Snell, W. E., Jr. (1986, April). *Convergent and discriminant validity of the Masculine Role Inventory.* Paper presented at the meeting of the Southwestern Psychological Association, Fort Worth.

Snell, W. E., Jr., Belk, S. S., & Hawkins, R. C., II. (1986). The Stereotypes About Male Sexuality Scale (SAMSS): Components, correlates, antecedents, consequences and counselor bias. *Social and Behavioral Science Documents, 16,* 9. (Ms. No. 2746)

Spence, J. T., Helmreich, R. L., & Sawin, L. L. (1980). The Male-Female Relations Questionnaire: A self-report inventory of sex-role behaviors and preferences and its relationships to masculine and feminine personality traits, sex role attitudes, and other measures. *Catalog of Selected Documents in Psychology, 10,* 87. (Ms. No. 2123)

Swann, W. B., Jr., Pelham, B. W., & Chidester, T. R. (1988). Change through paradox: Using self-verification to alter beliefs. *Journal of Personality Social Psychology, 54,* 268–273.

BIBLIOGRAPHY:

Beere, C. A. (1990). *Gender roles: A handbook of tests and measures.* Westport, CT: Greenwood.

Helmreich, R. L., & Spence, J. T. (1978). The Work and Family Orientation Scale (WOFO): An objective instrument to assess components of achievement motivation and attitudes toward family and career. *Catalog of Selected Documents in Psychology, 8,* 35. (Ms. No. 1677)

Helmreich, R. L., & Stapp, J. (1974). Short forms of the Texas Social Behavior Inventory, an objective measure of self-esteem. *Bulletin of the Psychonomic Society, 4,* 473–475.

Spence, J. T., & Helmreich, R. L. (1978). *Masculinity and femininity: Their psychological dimensions, correlates and antecedents.* Austin: University of Texas Press.

Spence, J. T., Helmreich, R. L., & Holahan, C. K. (1979). Negative and positive components of psychological masculinity and femininity and their relationships to neurotic and acting out behaviors. *Journal of Personality and Social Psychology, 37,* 1673–1682.

3

Sexuality

Chapter 3 is the largest chapter in this handbook, both in terms of number of scales described and total length. Furthermore, unlike many of the other chapters in this handbook, many scales described here have been used by a variety of researchers.

All 41 scales in this chapter pertain to sexuality. I have organized the scales into five sections and within each section present the scales alphabetically. The first section contains 4 scales dealing with sexual experiences. Two of them—the Heterosexual Behavior Assessment Inventory (Bentler, 1968a, 1968b) and the Heterosexual Experience Scales (Zuckerman, 1973)—are similar. Both include only heterosexual activities, and there are male and female forms of both scales. They have been used by a variety of researchers. In the scale descriptions, I list 34 references to studies using Bentler's scale and 11 references to studies using Zuckerman's scale. Brady and Levitt's (1965) Sexual Experience Inventory includes homosexual experiences as well as heterosexual ones. It is appropriate only for males, although Mosher and Cross (1971) modified the scale, and their modified version is appropriate for both males and females. The Depth of Sexual Involvement Scale (McCabe & Collins, 1979) is also appropriate for both males and females. It has not been as widely used as the other scales. Generally there was evidence to suggest that the sexual experience scales are adequately reliable and also evidence supportive of the validity of these scales. Since sexual experience scales ask respondents to report on their sexual experiences, motivation can have a significant effect on validity. If respondents are motivated to provide an honest report of their prior sexual experiences, they should have little difficulty in doing so. On the other hand, it is easy to provide responses that give a completely distorted picture of one's experiences.

The second section of this chapter describes 17 scales pertaining to sexual functioning, sexual dysfunction, and sexual satisfaction. The oldest scale in this section is the Mosher Guilt Inventory (Mosher, 1968, 1988), listed in this book as the Revised Mosher Guilt Inventory and described in my original handbook (Beere, 1979). The newest measure described in this section is the Pinney Sexual Satisfaction Inventory (Pinney, Gerrard, & Denney, 1987). There were no data regarding the reliability of 4 of these 17 measures. Where there were reliability data, they were slightly more likely to pertain to the internal consistency of the scale than to the stability of the measure over time. There was some evidence relating to the validity of all but 2 scales in this section. Sometimes the data that were available raised questions about the scale's validity. Factor analysis was used in the development or further examination of 10 of the 17 measures. Several of the measures in this section were used extensively. The most popular measures were the Revised Mosher Guilt Inventory (81 citations including those listed in Beere, 1979) (Mosher, 1988), the Sexual Interaction Inventory (34 citations) (LoPiccolo & Steger, 1974), the Derogatis Sexual Functioning Inventory (33 citations) (Derogatis & Melisaratos, 1979), and the Sexual Opinion Survey (31 citations) (Fisher, 1978/1979).

The third section of this chapter contains descriptions of five measures of sexual arousal. Three of the five are physiological measures. The strain gauge—either mercury (Fisher, Gross, & Zuch, 1965) or mechanical (Barlow, Becker, Leitenberg, & Agras, 1970)—is for use with male subjects, and the vaginal plethysmograph (Sintchak & Geer, 1975) and labial thermistor-clip (Henson, Rubin, Henson, & Williams, 1977) are for use with females. These three physiological measures have been widely used. The remaining two measures in this section—the Sexual Arousability Inventory (Hoon, Hoon, & Wincze, 1976) (described in my original handbook) and the Subjective Sexual Arousal scales (Mosher & Abramson, 1977)—are self-report measures.

The fourth section contains attitude measures. Most of these are summated rating scales designed to measure some aspect of sexual attitudes, sexual behavior, and premarital or extramarital sexual behavior. I considered the Attitudes Toward Marital Exclusivity (Neubeck & Schletzer, 1962) for inclusion here, but since it focuses on nonsexual behaviors more than sexual behaviors, it appears in Chapter 2. There was evidence regarding the reliability of 9 of the 11 scales in this section; most often the reliability data pertained to internal consistency. There was evidence pertaining to the validity of 8 scales, and factor analysis was used in the development or further examination of 7 of the measures. None of the measures was described in my original handbook, but 5 of them are old enough to have been included. The most commonly used measure in this section was the Reiss Premarital Sexual Permissiveness Scale (Reiss, 1964) with 44 citations; many of these 44 citations are old since the scale was first used in 1959.

The final section in this chapter contains four scales dealing with sexual knowledge. The Sexual Knowledge and Attitude Test (SKAT) (Lief, 1974) has 39 citations, making it the most commonly used scale. The number of citations would have been longer had the years between 1971 and 1978 been searched for references. There was evidence regarding the reliability of three of the four measures in this section, and there were some data relevant to the validity of all four. One measure in this section stands out as different from the others. The Aging Sexual Knowledge and Attitudes Scale (White, 1982) is unique in its focus on sexuality in aged persons. As senior citizens represent an increasing percentage of our population, there is likely to be an increase in interest in sexuality among the elderly; we can therefore expect this scale to be used more in coming years.

For the most part, the topics covered in this chapter were not included in my original handbook. As a result, the references listed under USED IN must be considered incomplete, particularly for the years preceding 1979. Even for the more recent years, however, the reference list may be incomplete because these measures have been used in conjunction with studies that would not have been identified by the search terms that I used. (See Chapter 1 for a list of the search terms.)

Researchers interested in the topics included in this chapter might also be interested in articles reviewing measurement techniques used to study specific aspects of sexuality. Measuring sexual arousal is discussed in Hoon's (1979) chapter titled "The Assessment of Sexual Arousal in Women" and in Barlow's (1977) chapter titled "Assessment of Sexual Behavior." Conte authored two relevant articles. The first deals with self-report measures for assessing sexual functioning (Conte, 1983), and the second reviews and critiques measures of sexual dysfunction (Conte, 1986). Eyman and Eyman (1984) also reviewed methods of assessing sexual dysfunction.

BIBLIOGRAPHY:

Barlow, D. H. (1977). Assessment of sexual behavior. In A. R. Ciminero, K. S. Calhoun, & H. E. Adams (Eds.), *Handbook of behavioral assessment* (pp. 461–508). New York: Wiley.

Barlow, D. H., Becker, R., Leitenberg, H., & Agras, W. S. (1970). A mechanical strain gauge for recording penile circumference change. *Journal of Applied Behavior Analysis, 3,* 73–76.

Beere, C. A. (1979). *Women and women's issues: A handbook of tests and measures.* San Francisco: Jossey-Bass.

Bentler, P. M. (1968a). Heterosexual Behavior Assessment—I. Males. *Behaviour Research and Therapy, 6,* 21–25.

Bentler, P. M. (1968b). Heterosexual Behavior Assessment—II. Females. *Behaviour Research and Therapy, 6*, 27–30.

Brady, J. P., & Levitt, E. E. (1965). The scalability of sexual experiences. *Psychological Record, 15*, 275–279.

Conte, H. R. (1983). Development and use of self-report techniques for assessing sexual functioning: A review and critique. *Archives of Sexual Behavior, 12*, 555–576.

Conte, H. R. (1986). Multivariate assessment of sexual dysfunction. *Journal of Consulting and Clinical Psychology, 54*, 149–157.

Derogatis, L. R., & Melisaratos, N. (1979). The DSFI: A multidimensional measure of sexual functioning. *Journal of Sex and Marital Therapy, 5*, 244–281.

Eyman, J., & Eyman, S. K. (1984). Sexual dysfunction: A review of assessment strategies. In P. McReynolds & G. Chelune (Eds.), *Advances in psychological assessment* (Vol. 6, pp. 151–193). San Francisco: Jossey-Bass.

Fisher, C., Gross, J., & Zuch, J. (1965). Cycle of penile erection synchronous with dreaming (REM) sleep. *Archives of General Psychiatry, 12*, 29–45.

Fisher, W. A. (1979). Affective, attitudinal, and normative determinants of contraceptive behavior among university men (Doctoral dissertation, Purdue University, 1978). *Dissertation Abstracts International, 39*, 4613B.

Henson, D. E., Rubin, H. B., Henson, C., & Williams, J. R. (1977). Temperature change of the labia minora as an objective measure of female eroticism. *Journal of Behavior Therapy and Experimental Psychiatry, 8*, 401–410.

Hoon, P. W. (1979). The assessment of sexual arousal in women. In M. Hersen, R. M. Eisler, & P. M. Miller (Eds.), *Progress in behavior modification* (Vol. 7, pp. 1–61). New York: Academic Press.

Hoon, E. F., Hoon, P. W., & Wincze, J. P. (1976). An inventory for the measurement of female sexual arousability: The SAI. *Archives of Sexual Behavior, 5*, 291–300.

Lief, H. I. (1974). Sexual knowledge, attitudes and behavior of medical students: Implications for medical practice. In W. Abse, E. M. Nash, & L. M. R. Louden (Eds.), *Marital and sexual counseling in medical practice* (2nd ed.) (pp. 474–494). Hagerstown, MD: Harper & Row.

LoPiccolo, J., & Steger, J. C. (1974). The Sexual Interaction Inventory: A new instrument for assessment of sexual dysfunction. *Archives of Sexual Behavior, 3*, 585–595.

McCabe, M. P., & Collins, J. K. (1979). Sex role and dating orientation. *Journal of Youth and Adolescence, 8*, 407–425.

Mosher, D. L. (1968). Measurement of guilt in females by self-report inventories. *Journal of Consulting and Clinical Psychology, 32*, 690–695.

Mosher, D. L. (1988). Revised Mosher Guilt Inventory. In C. M. Davis, W. L. Yarber, & S. L. Davis (Eds.), *Sexuality-related measures: A compendium* (pp. 152–155). Syracuse: Editors.

Mosher, D. L., & Abramson, P. R. (1977). Subjective sexual arousal to films of masturbation. *Journal of Consulting and Clinical Psychology, 45*, 796–807.

Mosher, D. L., & Cross, H. J. (1971). Sex guilt and premarital sexual experiences of college students. *Journal of Consulting and Clinical Psychology, 36*, 27–32.

Neubeck, G., & Schletzer, V. M. (1962). A study of extra-marital relationships. *Marriage and Family Living, 24*, 279–281.

Pinney, E. M., Gerrard, M., & Denney, N. W. (1987). The Pinney Sexual Satisfaction Inventory. *Journal of Sex Research, 23,* 233–251.

Reiss, I. L. (1964). The scaling of premarital sexual permissiveness. *Journal of Marriage and the Family, 26,* 188–198.

Sintchak, G., & Geer, J. H. (1975). A vaginal plethysmograph system. *Psychophysiology, 12,* 113–115.

White, C. B. (1982). A scale for the assessment of attitudes and knowledge regarding sexuality in the aged. *Archives of Sexual Behavior, 11,* 491–502.

Zuckerman, M. (1973). Scales for sex experience for males and females. *Journal of Consulting and Clinical Psychology, 41,* 27–29.

DEPTH OF SEXUAL INVOLVEMENT

AUTHORS: Marita P. McCabe and John K. Collins

DATE: 1979

VARIABLE: Depth of desired and experienced sexual involvement at various stages in the dating relationship

TYPE OF INSTRUMENT: Alternate choice

DESCRIPTION: The Depth of Sexual Involvement scale contains 12 items, each naming a sexual activity. Respondents are generally asked to complete the scale six times, indicating which behaviors they had experienced and which behaviors they would desire to experience for each of three stages in a dating relationship: at the time of the first date, after several dates, and when going steady.

SAMPLE ITEMS: (first item) Hand holding: holding hands or locking arms, generally while walking.

(last item) Intercourse

PREVIOUS SUBJECTS: High school and college students in Australia

APPROPRIATE FOR: High school students and older, unmarried

ADMINISTRATION: Self-administered; about 20 minutes for completing the scale six times

SCORING: Six scores can be obtained, one for each time the scale is completed. Each score is the sum of the number of affirmative responses; thus, scores range from 0 to 12.

DEVELOPMENT: A list of 16 sexual activities was developed by extending the work of Collins (1974) and Luckey and Nass (1969). A sample of high school and university students completed the scale. Using their responses, the authors reduced the scale from 16 to 12 items "by combining adjacent scale items which showed similar responses by males and females in each of the age categories over each of the stages of dating" (McCabe & Collins, 1984, p. 380). "Hand holding" and "light embrace" were combined into one item; "necking," "deep kissing," and "general body contact" were combined into one item; and "simulated intercourse" and "mutual masturbation" were combined into one item.

RELIABILITY: The 12-item scale was administered to 61 college students on two occasions, about 8 weeks apart (McCabe & Collins, 1984). Each respondent completed the scale six times. Test-retest reliability for experiences on a first date was .86; for experiences after several dates, it was .73; and for experiences when going steady, it was .96. For desires on a first date, test-retest reliability was .86; for desires after several dates, it was .80; and for desires when going steady, it was .78.

To study the reliability of the scale further, it was administered to 1,027 males and 974 females between the ages of 16 and 25 (McCabe & Collins, 1984). Guttman scale analysis was performed to determine the coefficients of reproducibility and the coefficients of scalability. The coefficient of reproducibility for experiences was .95 for first date, .94 for several dates, and .94 for going steady. Identical results were obtained for desires. The coefficient of scalability for experiences was .74 for first date, .77 for several dates, and .79 for going steady. The coefficient of scalability for desires was .70 for first date, .76 for several dates, and .79 for going steady. Coefficient alpha for experiences was .98 for first date, .98 for several dates, and .99 for going steady. Coefficient alpha for desires was .87 for first date, .88 for several dates, and .91 for going steady.

McCabe and Collins (1984) administered the Depth of Sexual Involvement scale to 156 persons between the ages of 18 and 48 years. They then computed item-total correlations for each of the six sets of directions, that is, experience and desire for each of three degrees of dating involvement. All item-total correlations were statistically significant, and most were of substantial magnitude. For prior experiences at all three levels of dating involvement, the item-total correlations ranged from .52 to .96. For desires at all three levels of dating involvement, the item-total correlations ranged from .16 to .88.

VALIDITY: In order to provide data regarding the validity of the Depth of Sexual Involvement scale, McCabe and Collins (1984) administered the scale to 199 males and 140 females at three age levels: 16–17 years, 19–20 years, and 24–25 years. Following standard procedures, each respondent completed the scale six times. As predicted, males scored higher than females for first date and for several dates in each age group. These sex differences diminished with increasing involvement in the relationship. Also as predicted, for both sexes and all ages, desired levels of sexual involvement increased with increasing involvement in the relationship. Another predicted finding was that females showed a greater interest in sexual involvement as their ages increased, but this trend was not apparent on the first date responses. Males did not show a significantly greater interest in sexual activity with increasing age.

Twenty-nine couples, ages 19 to 27, who were going steady independently completed the Depth of Sexual Involvement scale, providing information on their sexual desires when steady dating. Responses from the two members of each dyad were compared. It was found that for

62% of the couples, the partners indicated the identical number of "yes" responses, and for 77% of the couples, the partners scored within one "yes" response of each other.

NOTES & COMMENTS: (1) McCabe and Collins (1979) used an earlier version of the scale with 120 males and 139 females in three age groups: 16–17 years, 19–20 years, and 24–25 years. The researchers compared responses to the Depth of Sexual Involvement scale with responses to a series of 16 psychoaffectional items and to gender role classifications based on the Bem Sex Role Inventory (BSRI) (Bem, 1974) (see Beere, 1990).

(2) McCabe and Collins (1981) used the Depth of Sexual Involvement scale, calling it the Psychosexual Scale. They related scores on the Psychosexual Scale to stage of dating, migrant status of respondent and respondent's parents, and rural versus urban residence. McCabe (1982) conducted a similar study relating responses on the Psychosexual Scale to sex and to gender role as measured by the BSRI. McCabe and Collins (1983) compared responses on the Psychosexual Scale to the following other variables: "stages of dating, age, socioeconomic status, church attendance, and type of school attended" (p. 525).

AVAILABLE FROM: McCabe and Collins, 1984, 1988

USED IN:

McCabe, M. P. (1982). The influence of sex and sex role on the dating attitudes and behavior of Australian youth. *Journal of Adolescent Health Care, 3,* 29–36.

McCabe, M. P., & Collins, J. K. (1979). Sex role and dating orientation. *Journal of Youth and Adolescence, 8,* 407–425.

McCabe, M., & Collins, J. K. (1981). Dating desires and experiences: A new approach to an old question. *Australian Journal of Sex, Marriage and Family, 2,* 165–173.

McCabe, M. P., & Collins, J. K. (1983). The sexual and affectional attitudes and experiences of Australian adolescents during dating: The effects of age, church attendance, type of school, and socioeconomic class. *Archives of Sexual Behavior, 12,* 525–539.

McCabe, M. P., & Collins, J. K. (1984). Measurement of depth of desired and experienced sexual involvement at different stages of dating. *Journal of Sex Research, 20,* 377–390.

McCabe, M. P., & Collins, J. K. (1988). Depth of Sexual Involvement scale. In C. M. Davis, W. L. Yarber, & S. L. Davis (Eds.), *Sexuality-related measures: A compendium* (pp. 186–188). Syracuse: Editors.

BIBLIOGRAPHY:

Beere, C. A. (1990). *Gender roles: A handbook of tests and measures.* Westport, CT: Greenwood.

Bem, S. L. (1974). The measurement of psychological androgyny. *Journal of Consulting and Clinical Psychology, 42,* 155–162.

Collins, J. K. (1974). Adolescent dating intimacy: Norms and peer expectations. *Journal of Youth and Adolescence, 3,* 317–28.

Luckey, E., & Nass, G. A. (1969). A comparison of sexual attitudes and behavior in an international sample. *Journal of Marriage and the Family, 31*, 364–379.

HETEROSEXUAL BEHAVIOR ASSESSMENT INVENTORY
AUTHOR: Peter M. Bentler
DATE: 1968
VARIABLE: Experience with heterosexual behavior
TYPE OF INSTRUMENT: Cumulative hierarchy (Guttman scale); alternate choice
DESCRIPTION: There are two forms of the Heterosexual Behavior Assessment Inventory, one for males and one for females. Each form is a list of 21 heterosexual behaviors ordered from "most likely to have experienced" to "least likely to have experienced." The male and female forms contain the same items, but the hierarchical placement of two items differs on the two forms. Respondents indicate which behaviors they have experienced.

Short forms of the Heterosexual Behavior Assessment Inventories each contain 10 items taken from the full-length versions of the inventories. The 10 items are parallel on the male and female versions of the short forms.
SAMPLE ITEMS: (The items below are on both the male and female forms. They are the first and last items on both the full-length versions and the short forms of the scales.)

1. One minute continuous lip kissing.

21. Mutual oral manipulation of genitals to mutual orgasm.

PREVIOUS SUBJECTS: College students, married and unmarried women, newly married couples, couples in which the female is suffering from secondary orgasmic dysfunction, nurses. The inventory has been used in South Africa and Canada, as well as in the United States.
APPROPRIATE FOR: Persons with at least some sexual experience
ADMINISTRATION: Self-administered; about 5–10 minutes
SCORING: Because the items form a hierarchy, a person can be located on the hierarchy by indicating the number of the last item endorsed. Bentler (1968a, 1968b) provided normative information for college students. Stillerman and Shapiro (1979) provided normative information for persons in South Africa.
DEVELOPMENT: In developing the male form, Bentler compiled a list of 56 heterosexual behaviors, which he administered to 175 college males. The homogeneity scaling of the 56 items revealed that the items could be scaled on a single dimension. A set of 21 items was selected to comprise the final form of the inventory. The selected items covered the range of sexual behaviors and had high loadings on the underlying dimension. The selection of the subset of 10 items for the short form

followed the same guidelines: the items covered the range of sexual behaviors and had high loadings on the underlying dimension.

The development of the female version of the Heterosexual Behavior Assessment Inventory paralleled the development of the male version. The item pool for the female version began with 63 heterosexual behaviors, and the original sample for scale development included 175 college women. As was the case with the pool of items for the male version, the item pool for the female version had one underlying dimension. Items for the full-length and the short-form female versions were selected to parallel the items selected for the two male versions.

RELIABILITY: Kuder-Richardson reliability (KR 20) was computed for the male versions using data from the 175 college men on whom the inventory was developed and data from a cross-validation sample of 108 college men. For the former group, KR 20 was .95 for the full-length version and .90 for the short form. For the latter group, KR 20 was .95 for the full-length version and .88 for the short version. Two different indicators of the scalability of the items were computed; the Bentler coefficient of homogeneity is similar to Guttman's coefficient of reproducibility, and Loevinger's coefficient of homogeneity is a measure of scalability. Using data from the sample on whom the inventory was developed, the authors determined that the Bentler coefficient was .98 for the full-length version and .98 for the short version. The Loevinger coefficient was .76 and .81 for the full-length and short versions, respectively. The analyses were repeated using data from the cross-validation sample. The Bentler coefficients were .99 and .98 for the full-length and short versions, respectively; and the Loevinger coefficients were .79 and .81 for the full-length and short versions respectively (Bentler, 1968a).

Comparable data analyses were performed on the female forms of the inventories. Data were analyzed from three samples: the 175 college women on whom the inventory was developed, a cross-validation sample of 79 college women, and a second cross-validation sample of 135 college women. When KR 20 was computed, the following results were obtained: for the full-length version, the coefficients were .95 for each of the three sets of data; for the short version, the coefficients were .90, .89, and .90 for the three groups. The Bentler coefficient for the full-length version was .99 for each of the three groups; for the short version, the Bentler coefficient was .98 for each of the three groups. The Loevinger coefficients for the full-length version were .79, .80, and .83 for the three samples, respectively. For the short version, the Loevinger coefficients were .83, .81, and .87 (Bentler, 1968b).

Stillerman and Shapiro (1979) used the short form of the Heterosexual Behavior Assessment Inventory with persons in South Africa. For each of four samples, they obtained a coefficient of reproducibility greater than .91. They obtained the following values for the coefficient of scalability: .71, .47, .68, and .81.

VALIDITY: For both the male forms and the female forms, the correlation between the full-length and short versions was .98 (Bentler, 1968a, 1968b).

NOTES & COMMENTS: (1) Because the Heterosexual Behavior Assessment Inventory asks for a report of previous behavior that is likely to be remembered by the respondent, validity is primarily a function of the respondent's motivation to provide honest answers.

(2) The Heterosexual Behavior Assessment Inventory has been used to ensure that a subject pool includes persons with varying degrees of sexual experience (Hoon, Wincze, & Hoon, 1977; Julien & Over, 1988; Prerost, 1983, 1984; Smith & Over, 1987).

(3) The Heterosexual Behavior Assessment Inventory has been used in studies dealing with sexual experience and response to erotic materials (Fisher & Byrne, 1978; Kenrick, Stringfield, Wagenhals, Dahl, & Ransdell, 1980; Mosher & White, 1980; Saunders, Fisher, Hewitt, & Clayton, 1985; Steinman, Wincze, Sakheim, Barlow, & Mavissakalian, 1981; Wincze, Venditti, Barlow, & Mavissakalian, 1980).

(4) Abramson, Michalak, and Alling (1977) looked at the relationship between sexual experience, as measured by the Heterosexual Behavior Assessment Inventory, and sex guilt, perceptions of parental sex guilt, and sexual arousal. Keller, Eakes, Hinkle, and Hughston (1978) looked at the relationship between variety of sexual experience and age among married women. Although they also looked at the relationship between sex guilt and age, they did not compare sexual experience and sex guilt. Bentler and Newcomb (1978) used the Heterosexual Behavior Assessment Inventory in a longitudinal study designed to identify the predictors of marital success and failure. Kelley (1979) studied the relationship between attitudes about contraceptives and a variety of other variables, including sexual experience, as measured by the Heterosexual Behavior Assessment Inventory. Bentler and Peeler (1979) used the Heterosexual Behavior Assessment Inventory in a study designed to develop a model of women's subjective responsiveness to orgasm. Fisher, Miller, Byrne, and White (1980) were interested in how situational and personality factors affected college students' responses to communicating a sexual message. One of the personality factors they considered was sexual experience as measured by the Heterosexual Behavior Assessment Inventory. Istvan and Griffitt (1980) studied whether a target person's prior sexual experience affects college students' perceptions of the target person's desirability as a dating and marriage partner. The researchers also considered the sexual experience of the students who were rating the target person. A somewhat similar study was conducted by Garcia (1982), who looked at whether the sexual experiences of the respondent

and the sexual experiences attributed to a target person would affect the respondent's ratings of erotic slides and the respondent's perceptions of the target person's ratings of the slides. The researchers also looked at the respondents' ratings of the target person's personality. Perlman and Abramson (1982) used the Heterosexual Behavior Assessment Inventory as one of several measures in a study designed to identify the correlates of sexual satisfaction among married and cohabiting adults. Malamuth and Check (1983, 1985) and Malamuth (1986) conducted research relating men's sexual experiences, as measured by the Heterosexual Behavior Assessment Inventory, to sexual aggression and rape. Weidner and Griffitt (1984) looked at how college students perceive women who have had abortions and men who have impregnated women and advised abortion. The researchers also looked at the relationships between these perceptions and a variety of other variables, including scores on the Heterosexual Behavior Assessment Inventory. Barnes, Malamuth, and Check (1984) examined the relationships between personality and a variety of measures related to sexuality. The Heterosexual Behavior Assessment Inventory was one of their measures regarding sexuality. Smith and Over (1987) also looked at sexuality, in particular male sexual arousal, and sexual experience as measured by the Heterosexual Behavior Assessment Inventory. Byers and Wilson (1985) conducted a study to determine how men responded to a woman's refusal of further sexual advances and how women expected men to respond. The researchers looked at whether scores on the Heterosexual Behavior Assessment Inventory interacted with the results. Byers (1988) conducted another study, which looked at how sexual experience mediates responses to sexual refusals.

(5) Everaerd and Dekker (1982) modified the Heterosexual Behavior Assessment Inventory to measure sexual anxiety and inhibitions. The items on the inventory were rated on a 5-point scale ranging from "very pleasant" to "not pleasant." Similarly, Andersen and Jochimsen (1985) modified the Heterosexual Behavior Assessment Inventory to measure anxiety associated with sexual behaviors. They presented the items with a 7-point response scale ranging from "no anxiety" to "very much anxiety." Saunders et al. (1985) reported using an expanded version of the Heterosexual Behavior Assessment Inventory but did not provide details regarding the relationship between the expanded version and the original scale.

(6) Jensen, Witcher, and Upton (1987) reported that the reading level of the instructions accompanying the Heterosexual Behavior Assessment Inventory is at the 7th-grade level. They reported that the reading level for the items on the female form is at the 12th-grade level, and the reading level for the items on the male form is at the college level.

AVAILABLE FROM: The general wording for each item on the long and short forms of the male version is in Bentler, 1968a, and the general wording for each item on the long and short forms of the female version is in Bentler, 1968b. The general wording of the short forms is also in Stillerman and Shapiro, 1979. For the precise wording of each item, contact Peter M. Bentler, University of California—Los Angeles, Department of Psychology, 1282A Franz Hall, 405 Hilgard Avenue, Los Angeles, CA 90024–1563

USED IN:

Abramson, P. R., Michalak, P., & Alling, C. (1977). Perception of parental sex guilt and sexual behavior and arousal of college students. *Perceptual and Motor Skills, 45,* 337–338.

Andersen, B. L., & Jochimsen, P. R. (1985). Sexual functioning among breast cancer, gynecologic cancer, and healthy women. *Journal of Consulting and Clinical Psychology, 53,* 25–32.

Barnes, G. E., Malamuth, N. M., & Check, J. V. P. (1984). Personality and sexuality. *Personality and Individual Differences, 5,* 159–172.

Bentler, P. M. (1968a). Heterosexual Behavior Assessment—I. Males. *Behaviour Research and Therapy, 6,* 21–25.

Bentler, P. M. (1968b). Heterosexual Behavior Assessment—II. Females. *Behaviour Research and Therapy, 6,* 27–30.

Bentler, P. M., & Newcomb, M. D. (1978). Longitudinal study of marital success and failure. *Journal of Consulting and Clinical Psychology, 46,* 1053–1070.

Bentler, P. M., & Peeler, W. H. (1979). Models of female orgasm. *Archives of Sexual Behavior, 8,* 405–423.

Byers, E. S. (1988). Effects of sexual arousal on men's and women's behavior in sexual disagreement situations. *Journal of Sex Research, 25,* 235–254.

Byers, E. S., & Wilson, P. (1985). Accuracy of women's expectations regarding men's responses to refusals of sexual advances in dating situations. *International Journal of Women's Studies, 8,* 376–387.

Everaerd, W., & Dekker, J. (1982). Treatment of secondary orgasmic dysfunction: A comparison of systematic desensitization and sex therapy. *Behaviour Research and Therapy, 20,* 269–274.

Fisher, W. A., & Byrne, D. (1978). Individual differences in affective, evaluative, and behavioral responses to an erotic film. *Journal of Applied Social Psychology, 8,* 355–365.

Fisher, W. A., Miller, C. T., Byrne, D., & White, L. A. (1980). Talking dirty: Responses to communicating a sexual message as a function of situational and personality factors. *Basic and Applied Social Psychology, 1,* 115–126.

Garcia, L. T. (1982). Sex-role orientation and stereotypes about male-female sexuality. *Sex Roles, 8,* 863–876.

Hoon, P. W., Wincze, J. P., & Hoon, E. F. (1977). A test of reciprocal inhibition: Are anxiety and sexual arousal in women mutually inhibitory? *Journal of Abnormal Psychology, 86,* 65–74.

Istvan, J., & Griffitt, W. (1980). Effects of sexual experience on dating desirability and marriage desirability: An experimental study. *Journal of Marriage and the Family, 42,* 377–385.

Jensen, B. J., Witcher, D. B., & Upton, L. R. (1987). Readability assessment of questionnaires frequently used in sex and marital therapy. *Journal of Sex and Marital Therapy, 13,* 137–141.

Julien, E., & Over, R. (1988). Male sexual arousal across five modes of erotic stimulation. *Archives of Sexual Behavior, 17,* 131–143.

Keller, J. F., Eakes, E., Hinkle, D., & Hughston, G. A. (1978). Sexual behavior and guilt among women: A cross-generational comparison. *Journal of Sex and Marital Therapy, 4,* 259–265.

Kelley, K. (1979). Socialization factors in contraceptive attitudes: Roles of affective responses, parental attitudes, and sexual experience. *Journal of Sex Research, 15,* 6–20.

Kenrick, D. T., Stringfield, D. O., Wagenhals, W. L., Dahl, R. H., & Ransdell, H. J. (1980). Sex differences, androgyny, and approach responses to erotica: A new variation on the old volunteer problem. *Journal of Personality and Social Psychology, 38,* 517–524.

Malamuth, N. M. (1986). Predictors of naturalistic sexual aggression. *Journal of Personality and Social Psychology, 50,* 953–962.

Malamuth, N. M. (1989). The Attraction to Sexual Aggression Scale: Part two. *Journal of Sex Research, 26,* 324–354.

Malamuth, N. M., & Check, J. V. P. (1983). Sexual arousal to rape depictions: Individual differences. *Journal of Abnormal Psychology, 92,* 55–67.

Malamuth, N. M., & Check, J. V. P. (1985). The effects of aggressive pornography on beliefs in rape myths: Individual differences. *Journal of Research in Personality, 19,* 299–320.

Mosher, D. L., & White, B. B. (1980). Effects of committed or casual erotic guided imagery on females' subjective sexual arousal and emotional response. *Journal of Sex Research, 16,* 273–299.

Perlman, S. D., & Abramson, P. R. (1982). Sexual satisfaction among married and cohabiting individuals. *Journal of Consulting and Clinical Psychology, 50,* 458–460.

Prerost, F. J. (1983). Changing patterns in the response to humorous sexual stimuli: Sex roles and expression of sexuality. *Social Behavior and Personality, 11,* 23–28.

Prerost, F. J. (1984). Reactions to humorous sexual stimuli as a function of sexual activeness and satisfaction. *Psychology, 21,* 23–27.

Saunders, D. M., Fisher, W. A., Hewitt, E. C., & Clayton, J. P. (1985). A method for empirically assessing volunteer selection effects: Recruitment procedures and responses to erotica. *Journal of Personality and Social Psychology, 49,* 1703–1712.

Smith, D., & Over, R. (1987). Correlates of fantasy-induced and film-induced male sexual arousal. *Archives of Sexual Behavior, 16,* 395–409.

Steinman, D. L., Wincze, J. P., Sakheim, B. A., Barlow, D. H., & Mavissakalian, M. (1981). A comparison of male and female patterns of sexual arousal. *Archives of Sexual Behavior, 10,* 529-547.

Stillerman, E. D., & Shapiro, C. M. (1979). Scaling sex attitudes and behavior in South Africa. *Archives of Sexual Behavior, 8,* 1–13.

Weidner, G., & Griffitt, W. (1984). Abortion as a stigma: In the eyes of the beholder. *Journal of Research in Personality, 18,* 359–371.

Wincze, J. P., Venditti, E., Barlow, D., & Mavissakalian, M. (1980). The effects of a subjective monitoring task in the physiological measure of genital response to erotic stimulation. *Archives of Sexual Behavior, 9,* 533–545.

HETEROSEXUAL EXPERIENCE SCALES

AUTHOR: Marvin Zuckerman

DATE: 1973 (revised 1976)

VARIABLE: Experience with heterosexual behavior

TYPE OF INSTRUMENT: Guttman scale, scored as summated rating scale

DESCRIPTION: There are two forms of the Heterosexual Experience Scales, one for male respondents and the other for female respondents. Originally each form was a list of 12 behaviors, but the newer versions each list 14 behaviors. The items on the two forms are parallel to each other, but the order is slightly different, and the wording is altered to make each form sex appropriate. For each item, respondents rate their experience from "never" to "10 times or more."

SAMPLE ITEMS: (The items given here are the first and last items from the 14-item male form.)

Kissing without tongue contact

Sexual intercourse, entering vagina from rear

PREVIOUS SUBJECTS: College students

APPROPRIATE FOR: Persons with at least some sexual experience

ADMINISTRATION: Self-administered; less than 5 minutes

SCORING: Each item is scored on a 5-point scale, with higher points assigned to the responses representing greater frequency. Thus, scores can range from 14 (no experience with the behaviors listed) to 70 (frequent experience with the behaviors listed). Zuckerman (1973) reported the percentage of males and of females who said "yes" to each item.

DEVELOPMENT: The ordering of the items in the hierarchy was based on responses from 83 unmarried college men and 101 unmarried college women. The size of the item pool was not provided, but items were selected for the final scale if they had endorsement rates in the range of 10 to 90%. In order to make the male and female forms parallel to each other, this rule was violated for one item on the male form.

In expanding from the 12-item versions of the Heterosexual Experience Scales to the 14-item versions, 2 items that had previously had high endorsement rates were added to the scale.

RELIABILITY: Based on data obtained from 83 unmarried college men, the coefficient of reproducibility for the 12-item version was .97. Based on data obtained from 101 unmarried college women, the coefficient of reproducibility for the 12-item version was again .97. The correlation between the ordering of the items on the 12-item male and female forms was .95 (Zuckerman, 1973).

Reliability data were obtained for the 14-item versions of the scale by testing 224 unmarried college men and 331 unmarried college women. The coefficient of reproducibility was .94 for the women and .93 for the men. The coefficient of scalability was .81 for the women and .77 for the men.

Test-retest reliability for the 14-item version was estimated using responses from 47 college men and 50 college women in a control group, and it was estimated again using responses from 41 college men and 96 college women in the experimental group (meaning they were taking a class in human sexuality). Test-retest reliability for the men was .94 and .80 for the control and experimental groups, respectively. Test-retest reliability for the women was .92 and .95 for the control and experimental groups, respectively.

VALIDITY: As evidence of the validity of the Heterosexual Experience Scales, Zuckerman (1973) stated that his results were similar to results obtained by other researchers using other measures of sexual experience.

NOTES & COMMENTS: (1) Rader, Bekker, Brown, and Richardt (1978) modified the Heterosexual Experience Scales by asking respondents to indicate how comfortable they felt (or would feel) if involved in each of the listed behaviors. They also asked respondents to indicate which behaviors they had engaged in. This revised measure was used in a study looking at the correlates of unwanted pregnancy. Wishnoff (1978) modified the Heterosexual Experience Scales by asking college women to indicate which behaviors they intended to engage in. The scale was administered after the women had seen one of three videotapes varying in degree of sexual explicitness. Zuckerman and Myers (1983) used a 7-item version of the Heterosexual Experience Scales and related scores to "sensation seeking."

(2) Joe, Jones, Noel, and Roberts (1979) used the Heterosexual Experience Scales to divide a group of college women into two groups: sexually experienced and sexually inexperienced. The researchers then looked at the contraceptive behavior of the two groups.

(3) Zuckerman, Tushup, and Finner (1976) used the Heterosexual Experience Scales in a study looking at the impact of a course on human sexuality. Daitzman and Zuckerman (1980) looked at a variety of correlates of male hormone levels. One variable they considered was sexual experience as measured by the Heterosexual Experience Scales. As one step in validating the Sex Anxiety Inventory (SAI) (see separate entry), Janda and O'Grady (1980) tested whether SAI scores could predict scores on the Heterosexual Experience Scales. Using a variety of measures, Kozma and Zuckerman (1983) compared convicted rapists, convicted murderers, and men convicted for property offenses. One measure they used was the Heterosexual Experience Scales. In a study comparing

college students and their parents, Yarber and Greer (1986) used the Heterosexual Experience Scales as the measure of college students' sexual experience.

AVAILABLE FROM: Zuckerman, 1973; Wishnoff, 1978; Zuckerman, 1988, p. 97

USED IN:

Daitzman, R., & Zuckerman, M. (1980). Disinhibitory sensation seeking, personality and gonadal hormones. *Personality and Individual Differences, 1,* 103–110.

Janda, L. H., & O'Grady, K. E. (1980). Development of a Sex Anxiety Inventory. *Journal of Consulting and Clinical Psychology, 48,* 169–175.

Joe, V. C., Jones, R. N., Noel, A. S., & Roberts, B. (1979). Birth control practices and conservatism. *Journal of Personality Assessment, 43,* 536–540.

Kozma, C., & Zuckerman, M. (1983). An investigation of some hypotheses concerning rape and murder. *Personality and Individual Differences, 4,* 23–29.

Rader, G. E., Bekker, L. D., Brown, L., & Richardt, C. (1978). Psychological correlates of unwanted pregnancy. *Journal of Abnormal Psychology, 87,* 373–376.

Wishnoff, R. (1978). Modeling effects of explicit and nonexplicit sexual stimuli on the sexual anxiety and behavior of women. *Archives of Sexual Behavior, 7,* 455–461.

Yarber, W. L., & Greer, J. M. (1986). The relationship between the sexual attitudes of parents and their college daughters' or sons' sexual attitudes and sexual behavior. *Journal of School Health, 56,* 68–72.

Zuckerman, M. (1973). Scales for sex experience for males and females. *Journal of Consulting and Clinical Psychology, 41,* 27–29.

Zuckerman, M. (1988). Human sexuality questionnaire. In C. M. Davis, W. L. Yarber, & S. L. Davis (Eds.), *Sexuality-related measures: A compendium* (pp. 92–98). Syracuse: Editors.

Zuckerman, M., & Myers, P. L. (1983). Sensation seeking in homosexual and heterosexual males. *Archives of Sexual Behavior, 12,* 347–356.

Zuckerman, M., Tushup, R., & Finner, S. (1976). Sexual attitudes and experience: Attitude and personality correlates and changes produced by a course in sexuality. *Journal of Consulting and Clinical Psychology, 44,* 7–19.

SEXUAL EXPERIENCE INVENTORY

AUTHORS: John Paul Brady and Eugene E. Levitt

DATE: 1965

VARIABLE: Experience with homosexual and heterosexual activities

TYPE OF INSTRUMENT: Multiple choice; Guttman scale

DESCRIPTION: The Sexual Experience Inventory consists of 16 sexual activities, with 10 items referring to heterosexual activities and 6 items referring to homosexual activities. In contrast to other sexual experience inventories that present items in order of increasing intimacy or decreasing rates of endorsement, the items on the Sexual Experience Inventory are presented in random order. Each item is accompanied by three response alternatives for respondents to indicate their experience with the named activity: "sometime in life, during last five years, never." Mosher's modification of the Sexual Experience Inventory (Mosher & Cross, 1971) has been used more often than Brady and Levitt's original scale. (See NOTES & COMMENTS.)

SAMPLE ITEMS: Oral contact with female breast

Oral contact with your genitalia by a male

PREVIOUS SUBJECTS: Male college students

APPROPRIATE FOR: Males, ages 16 and older; females can complete Mosher and Cross's (1971) modified version of the Sexual Experience Inventory.

ADMINISTRATION: Self-administered; about 10 minutes

SCORING: Brady and Levitt (1965a, 1965b) did not score the Sexual Experience Inventory. Rather they reported results across persons for individual items. The Sexual Experience Inventory could be scored by counting the number of experiences a respondent reports having.

DEVELOPMENT: Brady and Levitt (1965b) administered the 16-item Sexual Experience Inventory to 68 male graduate students. Before performing a Guttman analysis, they eliminated items with an endorsement frequency greater than 90% or less than 10%. This led to the elimination of 4 frequently endorsed items and 3 rarely endorsed items.

RELIABILITY: Using data from unmarried college students, Brady and Levitt (1965b) obtained a coefficient of reproducibility of .94 for the 9-item version of the Sexual Experience Inventory. For 38 married students, they obtained a coefficient of reproducibility of .98. When data for the two groups were combined, the coefficient of reproducibility was .97.

VALIDITY: Brady and Levitt (1965a) administered the Sexual Experience Inventory to 68 college men who also rated each of 19 photographs in terms of how sexually stimulating they judged them to be. Since all respondents indicated they had engaged in kissing with tongue contact at least "sometime in life," the item was not included in the correlational analyses. Correlating the sexual arousability of each of the 19 photographs with the respondents' experiences with each of 15 items from the Sexual Experience Inventory produced 285 correlations. Only 16 of the 285 correlations were statistically significant. Brady and Levitt pointed out that all 6 homosexual experience items were significantly correlated with responses to a picture of a partially clad male.

Mosher and Cross (1971) and Mosher (1973) used a modification of the Sexual Experience Inventory (see NOTES & COMMENTS) and showed that sex experience scores "relate to sex guilt, sexual attitudes, and reactions to explicitly sexual films in ways that support the validity of the measure" (Abramson & Mosher, 1975, p. 486).

NOTES & COMMENTS: (1) Brady and Levitt (1965a) reported that ordering the items according to their overall endorsement rate led to the same order regardless of whether the response "sometime in life" or the response "during last five years" served as the basis for computing endorsement rates. It is not clear, therefore, whether including both of these response options adds to the usefulness of the scale. Responses that allow for reporting relative frequencies, such as "once in last five years, a few times in the last few years, several times a year, several times a month, at least once a week" might produce more useful results.

(2) Mosher and Cross (1971) modified the Sexual Experience Inventory. They reduced the number of items from 16 to 12 by adding a new item about kissing and combining the 6 items pertaining to various homosexual activities into 1 item, "homosexual relations." In addition, they phrased the items so that both males and females could respond to them. Mosher and Cross posed four questions about the items. The questions pertained to "experiences, feelings, reasons for nonparticipation, and sexual standards" (p. 28). They scored the scale by counting 1 point for each experience the respondent had. They also obtained scores "for sexual experiences with loved and unloved partners in the last year or in the past, and for premarital and postmarital standards for males and females" (p. 30). Mosher and Cross summarized their findings and reported correlations between the various sexual experience scores and scores from the Mosher Forced-Choice Guilt Inventory (Mosher, 1966) (see separate entry for Revised Mosher Guilt Inventory). Mosher (1973) and Mosher and Abramson (1977) used the 12-item version of the Sexual Experience Inventory and asked college students to circle each activity they had experienced. Abramson and Mosher (1975) also used the 12-item version of the Sexual Experience Inventory with college students and related their scores to scores on Abramson and Mosher's Negative Attitudes Toward Masturbation scale (see separate entry), the Mosher Forced-Choice Guilt Inventory, a measure of the average frequency of masturbation per month, and a measure of the maximum frequency of masturbation per day. Mosher (1979) related college students' scores on the 12-item version of the Sexual Experience Inventory to scores on Mosher's Sex Myth Inventory (see separate entry) and scores on the Mosher Forced-Choice Guilt Inventory.

(3) Morokoff (1985) used Mosher's modification of the Sexual Experience Inventory in a study designed to assess "the relation[ship] of inventory measures of sex guilt, repression-sensitization, sexual 'arousability,' and sex experience to sexual arousal during erotic stimuli" (p. 177). Morokoff (1986) used Mosher's modification of the Sexual Experience Inventory as one of several measures in a study comparing college women who did and did not volunteer to participate in a psychophysiological study of female sexuality.

AVAILABLE FROM: Brady and Levitt, 1965a, 1965b

USED IN:
Abramson, P. R., & Mosher, D. L. (1975). Development of a measure of negative attitudes toward masturbation. *Journal of Consulting and Clinical Psychology, 43*, 485–490.
Brady, J. P., & Levitt, E. E. (1965a). The relation of sexual preferences to sexual experiences. *Psychological Record, 15*, 377–384.
Brady, J. P., & Levitt, E. E. (1965b). The scalability of sexual experiences. *Psychological Record, 15*, 275–279.
Morokoff, P. J. (1985). Effects of sex guilt, repression, sexual "arousability," and sexual experience on female sexual arousal during erotica and fantasy. *Journal of Personality and Social Psychology, 49*, 177–187.
Morokoff, P. J. (1986). Volunteer bias in the psychophysiological study of female sexuality. *Journal of Sex Research, 22*, 35–51.
Mosher, D. L. (1973). Sex differences, sex experience, sex guilt, and explicitly sexual films. *Journal of Social Issues, 29*, 95–112.
Mosher, D. L. (1979). Sex guilt and sex myths in college men and women. *Journal of Sex Research, 15*, 224–234.
Mosher, D. L., & Abramson, P. R. (1977). Subjective sexual arousal to films of masturbation. *Journal of Consulting and Clinical Psychology, 45*, 796–807.
Mosher, D. L., & Cross, H. J. (1971). Sex guilt and premarital sexual experiences of college students. *Journal of Consulting and Clinical Psychology, 36*, 27–32.
BIBLIOGRAPHY:
Mosher, D. L. (1966). The development and multitrait-multimethod matrix analysis of three measures of three aspects of guilt. *Journal of Consulting Psychology, 30*, 25–29.

AWARENESS OF PHYSIOLOGICAL CHANGES DURING SEXUAL ACTIVITY (APC)

AUTHORS: John P. Wincze, Emily Franck Hoon, and Peter W. Hoon
DATE: 1976
VARIABLE: A woman's awareness of her own physiological changes during sexual activity
TYPE OF INSTRUMENT: Summated rating scale
DESCRIPTION: The Awareness of Physiological Changes During Sexual Activity (APC) measure is a brief scale that requires a woman to rate the extent to which she is aware of her own physiological changes in nine areas: "vaginal lubrication, nipple erection, sex flush, heart rate increase, breast swelling, muscular tension, pelvic warmth, hyperventilation, and decreasing awareness of the environment" (Wincze, Hoon, & Hoon, 1976, p. 446).
PREVIOUS SUBJECTS: Sexually well-adjusted women, sexually dysfunctional women, women who have had mastectomies
APPROPRIATE FOR: Females who have experienced sexual arousal
ADMINISTRATION: Self-administered; a few minutes
SCORING: Little information was provided except to note that lower scores reflect less awareness of one's own physiological changes.
DEVELOPMENT: No information was provided.

RELIABILITY: No information was provided.
VALIDITY: In a comparison of "normal" women and sexually dysfunctional women, both exposed to a sexually arousing stimulus, Wincze et al. (1976) found that the latter group had significantly lower scores; that is, the sexually dysfunctional women were less aware of their own physiological changes during sexual activity. The researchers also found a positive and significant correlation between APC scores and vaginal blood volume and between APC scores and skin conductance response. Nonsignificant correlations were found between APC scores and four other physiological measures: systolic blood pressure, diastolic blood pressure, skin conductance, and heart rate.
NOTES & COMMENTS: (1) Although little is known about the psychometric properties of the APC scale, it is described here because it measures a variable that is not measured by the other scales.

(2) Gerard (1982) used the APC as one of several measures in a study comparing postmastectomy patients' and "normal" women's reactions to erotic video and audio material.
AVAILABLE FROM: Wincze, Hoon, and Hoon, 1976
USED IN:

Gerard, D. (1982). Sexual functioning after mastectomy: Life vs. lab. *Journal of Sex and Marital Therapy, 8*, 305–315.

Wincze, J. P., Hoon, E. F., & Hoon, P. W. (1976). Physiological responsivity of normal and sexually dysfunctional women during erotic stimulus exposure. *Journal of Psychosomatic Research, 20*, 445–451.

DEROGATIS SEXUAL FUNCTIONING INVENTORY (DSFI)

AUTHOR: Leonard R. Derogatis
DATE: 1975 (modified 1978)
VARIABLE: Current sexual functioning
TYPE OF INSTRUMENT: There are a variety of item types included on the measure.
DESCRIPTION: The Derogatis Sexual Functioning Inventory (DSFI) is a lengthy measure with 11 sections and 256 items. Section I, Information, contains 26 true/false items to measure the respondent's knowledge regarding sexual behavior. There are right and wrong answers for these 26 items. Section II, Experience, contains a list of 24 sexual behaviors. For each behavior, the respondent is to check "yes" if he or she has ever experienced the behavior and "no" if he or she has not experienced the behavior. A third column is provided for respondents to indicate, for those behaviors that they have experienced, whether they have experienced the behavior within the past 60 days. The behaviors in the list range from casual to very intimate; they are not listed in order of increasing intimacy. Section III, Drive, contains 7 items. The first 4 items are sexual activities; each is to be rated on a 9-point scale to show "the

frequency with which you typically engage in certain sexual activities." The 9-point scale ranges from "not at all" to "4 or more [times] per day." The remaining 3 items are open-ended questions pertaining to ideal frequency of intercourse, age at initial sexual interest, and age at first intercourse. Section IV, Attitudes, contains 30 statements; half reflect a liberal attitude and half a conservative attitude. For each statement, the respondent selects one of five responses ranging from "−2, strongly disagree" to " + 2, strongly agree." Section V, Psychological Symptoms, contains 53 psychological symptoms, each rated on a 5-point scale: "not at all, slightly, moderately, quite a bit, extremely." Ratings are to reflect the extent to which the respondent has been bothered by the particular symptom in the prior 2 weeks. Section VI, Affects, contains a list of 40 feelings, half positive and half negative. Respondents are to rate the frequency with which they experienced the feelings during the prior 2 weeks. A 5-point response scale is provided: "never, rarely, sometimes, frequently, always." Section VII, Gender Role Definition, is a list of 30 adjectives, most of which refer to positive traits. Respondents are to rate the extent to which each adjective is typical of them. A 5-point response scale is provided: "not at all, a little bit, moderately, quite a bit, extremely." Section VIII, Fantasy, is a list of 20 sexually related fantasies. The fantasies range from common sexual practices to highly unusual sexual practices. Respondents are asked to check each fantasy they have experienced "either in daydreams or dreams while asleep." Section IX, Body Image, contains 20 items: the first 10 items are answered by both men and women, the next 5 items are for men only, and the last 5 items are for women only. Each item is a first-person statement regarding one's physical appearance. For each statement, respondents are to indicate how true the statement is for them. Five response options are provided: "not at all, slightly, moderately, quite a bit, extremely." Section X, Sexual Satisfaction, contains 10 true/false items regarding satisfaction with one's current sexual activities. Following Section X is a single question asking respondents to "record your personal evaluation of how satisfying your sexual relationship is." Nine response options are provided. The response to this item is used as the General Sexual Satisfaction Index (GSSI).

SAMPLE ITEMS: (Information) Usually men achieve orgasm more quickly than women.

(Experience) Male lying prone on female (clothed)

(Drive) Intercourse

(Attitudes) Premarital intercourse is beneficial to later marital adjustment.

(Psychological Symptoms) Nervousness or shakiness inside

(Affects) Sad

(Gender Role Definition) Sympathetic

(Fantasy) Having more than one sexual partner at the same time
(Body Image) I am less attractive than I would like to be
(Sexual Satisfaction) Usually, I am satisfied with my sexual partner

PREVIOUS SUBJECTS: College students; married and cohabiting couples; sexually dysfunctional men; vulvectomy patients; women with breast cancer; diabetic women; women with gynecologic cancer; anorgasmic women; male transsexuals, homosexuals, and heterosexuals; men and women seeking treatment for infertility; female transsexuals

APPROPRIATE FOR: College students and older

ADMINISTRATION: Self-administered; about 30–40 minutes

SCORING: Scoring algorithms and profile sheets are available from the publisher of the DSFI. A *T* score is computed for each of the 10 sections, and *T* scores are combined to produce an overall score. Different norms are used for converting male and female scores to *T* scores.

DEVELOPMENT: The first step in developing the DSFI was to identify the substantive domains. According to Derogatis and Melisaratos (1979), "A combination of clinical experience, broadly based theory, and empirical research all went into the selection of our substantive domains" (p. 247). The original version of the DSFI, completed in 1975, included eight domains. In preparing the 1978 version, two domains were added—Body Image and Sexual Satisfaction—and the number of items on the Fantasy section was reduced from 35 to 20 items.

Some of the sections on the DSFI were adopted from other measures. Section V, Psychological Symptoms, is a 53-item version of the SCL-90-R (Derogatis, 1977). This version is called the Brief Symptom Inventory (Derogatis, 1975b) and yields scores on nine symptoms (somatization, obsessive-compulsive, interpersonal sensitivity, depression, anxiety, hostility, phobic anxiety, paranoid ideation, and psychoticism) and three global indices of distress. One of these global indexes—General Severity Index—contributes to the DSFI score.

Section VI of the DSFI, Affects, is actually the Affects Balance Scale (Derogatis, 1975a). In explaining their selection of this measure, Derogatis and Melisaratos (1979) stated: "Because dysphoric affect is such a pervasive concomitant of sexual disorders and because of its etiologic significance, we decided that affects on the DSFI should also be measured by a proven psychometric instrument" (p. 252).

RELIABILITY: Derogatis and Melisaratos (1979) computed internal consistency reliabilities based on testing 325 persons. For three sections—Attitudes, Affects, and Gender Role Definition—they reported the reliability separately for each of the two components of the section. Derogatis and Melisaratos obtained the following reliabilities: Information = .56, Experience = .97, Drive = .60, Attitudes-Liberalism = .81, Attitudes-Conservatism = .86, Affect-Positive Total = .93, Affect-Negative Total = .94, Gender Role—Masculinity = .84, Gender Role—Femininity

= .76, Fantasy = .82, Body Image = .58, and Sexual Satisfaction = .71. Instead of reporting the internal consistency for the Psychological Symptoms section, they reported the internal consistency for each of the nine primary symptoms comprising the scale: Somatization = .80, Obsessive-compulsive = .83, Interpersonal sensitivity = .74, Depression = .85, Anxiety = .81, Hostility = .78, Phobic anxiety = .77, Paranoid ideation = .77, and Psychoticism = .69. Derogatis and Melisaratos also reported test-retest reliability for 8 of the 10 sections. The test-retest reliabilities were based on testing 60 persons on two occasions, separated by a 14-day interval. The results were: Information = .61, Experience = .92, Drive = .77, Attitudes = .96, Psychological Symptoms = .90, Affects = .81, Gender Role Definition = .84, and Fantasy = .93. They also reported the test-retest reliabilities for the scores on Attitudes, Affects, and Gender Role Definition. They obtained the following results: Attitudes-Liberalism = .92, Attitudes-Conservatism = .72, Affects—Positive Total = .75, Affects—Negative Total = .42, Gender Role Definition—Masculinity = .60, and Gender Role Definition—Femininity = .58.

Howell et al. (1987) tested 26 male outpatients suffering from major depressive disorders and a control group of 20 normal men. The patients completed the measure on two occasions, with a 1-month interval between testings. For 7 of the 10 sections on the DSFI, test-retest reliability exceeded .70 for both the depressives and the control group. For the control group, 2 sections had lower reliabilities: Psychological Symptoms = .54 and Affects = .40. Two sections also had lower test-retest reliabilities for the depressed men: Experience = .68 and Affects = .68.

VALIDITY: Derogatis and Melisaratos (1979) compared DSFI scores, separately by sex, for 150 sexually dysfunctional persons and 230 nonpatient normals. For males, they found significant differences on 9 of the 10 sections. The Attitudes section failed to show a significant difference. In addition, there was a large and statistically significant difference on the overall DSFI score and on the GSSI (the General Sexual Satisfaction Index). Females showed statistically significant differences on 5 of the 10 sections: Information, Symptoms, Affects, Body Image, and Sexual Satisfaction. Females also showed statistically significant differences on the overall DSFI score and the GSSI.

Derogatis and Melisaratos (1979) reported results of a discriminative analysis using data obtained from sexually normal and sexually dysfunctional adults who completed the original version of the DSFI (i.e., the version with eight subtests). The researchers found that the analysis produced 77% correct assignment among males and 75% correct assignment among females. For females, Information, Symptoms, Affects, and Fantasy contributed significantly to the discrimination. For males, these four sections plus Drive contributed significantly to the discrimination.

Other researchers have shown that the DSFI can discriminate between groups of respondents. Derogatis, Meyer, and Dupkin (1976) compared men with organic causes for impotence with men having psychogenic causes for impotence. The two groups differed significantly on two of the eight subtests on the earlier version of the DSFI. Derogatis, Meyer, and Vazquez (1978) compared results from male transsexuals with results from normal males; they found significant differences on all subtests except Fantasy. Derogatis, Meyer, and Boland (1981) compared results from female transsexuals with results from normal heterosexual females. There were significant differences on Information, Experience, Drive, Positive Affects, Gender Role Definition (including the Masculinity and Femininity scores), and the GSSI. Derogatis and Meyer (1979a) found differences in the DSFI scores of persons married to someone with a sexual dysfunction and a normal control group. Derogatis and Meyer (1979b) found that normal and sexually dysfunctional persons differed significantly on seven of the eight scores of the original DSFI. Andersen and Hacker (1983) showed that the DSFI profiles from vulvar cancer patients were different from those of sexually active healthy women. Newman and Bertelson (1986) compared diabetic women with and without sexual dysfunction. They found that the two groups were significantly different on three scores: Psychological Symptoms, Gender Role Definition, and Sexual Satisfaction. Schreiner-Engel, Schiavi, Vietorisz, De Simone Eichel, and Smith (1985) found DSFI differences between diabetic women and a matched control group. Schreiner-Engel, Schiavi, Vietorisz, and Smith (1987) found less clear-cut results. They concluded that Type I diabetic women (early onset, greater morbidity, and more severe complications) did not differ from a control group in terms of DSFI scores, but Type II diabetic women (onset usually occurs much later in life, probably after many years of marriage) differed in terms of Experience scores and Body Image scores. Derogatis, Fagan, Schmidt, Wise, and Gilden (1986) compared DSFI scores obtained by anorgasmic women and scores obtained by a matched control group. There were significant differences on only one score: Sexual Satisfaction. In addition, they divided the group into two subgroups: those with conscious homosexual fantasies and those without conscious homosexual fantasies. The researchers found significant differences between the two groups on five of the sections: Information, Attitudes, Psychological Symptoms, Fantasy, and Body Image. Wincze et al. (1988) found that a nondysfunctional group of men compared to men with several types of sexual dysfunction obtained significantly different scores on the Experience and Fantasy sections of the DSFI but not on the Information section. They did not compare scores from the other sections.

Skrapec and MacKenzie (1981) compared DSFI scores of male transsexuals, homosexuals, and heterosexuals. Although they reported the differences between means for each of the sections, they did not perform any statistical tests to determine if the differences were statistically significant.

Segraves, Schoenberg, Zarins, Knopf, and Camic (1981) studied two groups of men with erectile dysfunction: those with an organic cause for their dysfunction and those with a psychogenic cause for their dysfunction. The researchers found that the DSFI could not differentiate between the two groups. These findings conflict with those from Derogatis et al. (1976).

NOTES & COMMENTS: (1) Jensen, Witcher, and Upton (1987) evaluated the readability of several psychological tests including the DSFI. They concluded that the instructions for the DSFI require a ninth-grade reading level, and the items on the DSFI require college-level reading ability.

(2) Derogatis and Melisaratos (1979) factor analyzed data from 380 persons, including sexually dysfunctional men and women as well as nonpatient men and women. The factor analysis included 21 variables: Information, Experience, seven Drive scores (Intercourse, Masturbation, Kissing and Petting, Fantasy, Ideal Frequency, First Interest, and First Intercourse), two Attitudes scores (Liberalism and Conservatism), two Symptoms scores (General Severity Index and Positive Symptom Distress Index), two Affects scores (positive and negative), two Gender Role Definition scores (Femininity and Masculinity), Body Image, Fantasy, Sexual Satisfaction, and General Sexual Satisfaction. Seven factors were identified and accounted for 52% of the variance. The factors were named: Psychological Distress, Body Image, Heterosexual Drive, Autoeroticism, Gender Role, General Satisfaction, and Sexual Precociousness. Between one and five scores loaded on each factor; Information, Liberalism, and Conservatism did not load on any of the factors.

(3) The DSFI has been used to study various patient populations, including vulvectomy patients (Stellman, Goodwin, Robinson, Dansak, & Hilgers, 1984), women with gynecologic cancer (Andersen & Hacker, 1983; Andersen & Jochimsen, 1985), women with breast cancer (Andersen & Jochimsen, 1985; Wolberg, Tanner, Romsaas, Trump, & Malec, 1987), diabetic women (Newman & Bertelson, 1986; Schreiner-Engel et al., 1985; Schreiner-Engel et al., 1987), and depressed men (Howell et al., 1987).

(4) Some researchers have used only selected sections of the DSFI (e.g., Andersen & Jochimsen, 1985; McEwan, Costello, & Taylor, 1987; Perlman & Abramson, 1982; Robillard, 1983).

(5) Kuriansky, Sharpe, and O'Connor (1982) used the DSFI as a pretest/posttest measure to evaluate the effectiveness of a behavioral group therapy approach to treating anorgasmia. Meisler, Carey, Krauss, and Lantinga (1988) used the DSFI as one of several measures in a study looking at the effects of penile prosthesis surgery.

(6) Perlman and Abramson (1982) used portions of the DSFI to study sexual satisfaction among married and cohabiting persons. Robillard (1983) used the DSFI as one of several measures to study college students' stereotypes of physically disabled persons. Seidner, Calhoun, and Kilpatrick (1985) compared persons who had a childhood sexual experience with a matched group of control subjects. They used several measures, including the DSFI. McEwan et al. (1987) used portions of the DSFI as part of a battery of tests to study male and female adjustment to infertility. Beck, Barlow, Sakheim, and Abrahamson (1987) used the DSFI to verify that the subjects in their research were normal in terms of sexual interest and experience. Fagan, Schmidt, Wise, and Derogatis (1988) used the DSFI as one of several measures in a study looking at the question of whether "sexual dysfunction is a discrete problem or... symptomatic of more elaborate psychiatric disorder" (p. 278).

(7) Conte (1983) reviewed a variety of self-report instruments for assessing various aspects of sexual functioning. Conte criticized the DSFI for low reliability on several sections, excessive length, and possible irrelevancies on the Psychological Symptoms and Affects sections. She also felt that the items may be difficult for some persons to understand. However, Conte concluded that "for general clinical use, Derogatis' DSFI appears to be the most comprehensive and potentially useful inventory; it also provides the most complete psychometric data" (p. 574).

(8) The DSFI is entry 317 in the *Ninth Mental Measurements Yearbook* (Mitchell, 1985).

AVAILABLE FROM: Clinical Psychometric Research, Inc., P.O. Box 619, Riderwood, MD 21139; telephone 1–800–245–0277

USED IN:

Andersen, B. L., & Hacker, N. F. (1983). Treatment for gynecologic cancer: A review of the effects on female sexuality. *Health Psychology*, *2*, 203–221.

Andersen, B. L., & Jochimsen, P. R. (1985). Sexual functioning among breast cancer, gynecologic cancer, and healthy women. *Journal of Consulting and Clinical Psychology*, *53*, 25–32.

Beck, J. G., Barlow, D. H., Sakheim, D. K., & Abrahamson, D. J. (1987). Shock threat and sexual arousal: The role of selective attention, thought content, and affective states. *Psychophysiology*, *24*, 165–172.

Conte, H. R. (1983). Development and use of self-report techniques for assessing sexual functioning: A review and critique. *Archives of Sexual Behavior*, *12*, 555–576.

Derogatis, L. R. (1980). Psychological assessment of psychosexual functioning. In J. K. Meyer (Ed.), *The psychiatric clinics of North America: Symposium on sexuality*. Philadelphia: W. B. Sauders.

Derogatis, L. R., Fagan, P. J., Schmidt, C. W., Wise, T. N., & Gilden, K. S. (1986). Psychological subtypes of anorgasmia: A marker variable approach. *Journal of Sex and Marital Therapy*, *12*, 197–210.

Derogatis, L. R., Lopez, M. C., & Zinzeletta, E. M. (1988). Clinical applications of the DSFI in the assessment of sexual dysfunctions. In R. A. Brown & J. R. Field (Eds.), *Treatment of sexual problems in individual and couples therapy* (pp. 167–186). Great Neck, NY: PMA Publishing.

Derogatis, L. R., & Melisaratos, N. (1979). The DSFI: A multidimensional measure of sexual functioning. *Journal of Sex and Marital Therapy, 5,* 244–281.

Derogatis, L. R., & Meyer, J. K. (1979a). The invested partner in sexual disorders: A profile. *American Journal of Psychiatry, 136,* 1545–1549.

Derogatis, L. R., & Meyer, J. K. (1979b). A psychological profile of the sexual dysfunctions. *Archives of Sexual Behavior, 8,* 201–223.

Derogatis, L. R., Meyer, J. K., & Boland, P. (1981). A psychological profile of the transsexual: II. The female. *Journal of Nervous and Mental Disease, 169,* 157–168.

Derogatis, L. R., Meyer, J. K., & Dupkin, C. N. (1976). Discrimination of organic versus psychogenic impotence with the DSFI. *Journal of Sex and Marital Therapy, 2,* 229–240.

Derogatis, L. R., Meyer, J. K., & Vazquez, N. (1978). A psychological profile of the transsexual: I. The male. *Journal of Nervous and Mental Disease, 166,* 234–254.

Fagan, P. J., Schmidt, C. W., Wise, T. N., & Derogatis, L. R. (1988). Sexual dysfunction and dual psychiatric diagnoses. *Comprehensive Psychiatry, 29,* 278–284.

Howell, J. R., Reynolds, C. F., III, Thase, M. E., Frank, E., Jennings, J. R., Houck, P. R., Berman, S., Jacobs, E., & Kupfer, D. J. (1987). Assessment of sexual function, interest and activity in depressed men. *Journal of Affective Disorders, 13,* 61–66.

Jani, N. N., Wise, T. N., Kass, E., & Sessler, A. (1988). Trazodone and anorgasmia. *American Journal of Psychiatry, 145,* 896.

Jensen, B. J., Witcher, D. B., & Upton, L. R. (1987). Readability assessment of questionnaires frequently used in sex and marital therapy. *Journal of Sex and Marital Therapy, 13,* 137–141.

Kuriansky, J. B., Sharpe, L., & O'Connor, D. (1982). The treatment of anorgasmia: Long-term effectiveness of a short-term behavioral group therapy. *Journal of Sex and Marital Therapy, 8,* 29–43.

McEwan, K. L., Costello, C. G., & Taylor, P. J. (1987). Adjustment to infertility. *Journal of Abnormal Psychology, 96,* 108–116.

Meisler, A. W., Carey, M. P., Krauss, D. J., & Lantinga, L. J. (1988). Success and failure in penile prosthesis surgery: Two cases highlighting the importance of psychosocial factors. *Journal of Sex and Marital Therapy, 14,* 108–119.

Newman, A. S., & Bertelson, A. D. (1986). Sexual dysfunction in diabetic women. *Journal of Behavioral Medicine, 9,* 261–270.

Perlman, S. D., & Abramson, P. R. (1982). Sexual satisfaction among married and cohabiting individuals. *Journal of Consulting and Clinical Psychology, 50,* 458–460.

Robillard, K. (1983). Attributions about sexuality and romantic involvement of physically disabled college students: An empirical study. *Sexuality and Disability, 6,* 197–212.

Schreiner-Engel, P., Schiavi, R. C., Vietorisz, D., De Simone Eichel, J., & Smith,

H. (1985). Diabetes and female sexuality: A comparative study of women in relationships. *Journal of Sex and Marital Therapy, 11*, 165–175.

Schreiner-Engel, P., Schiavi, R. C., Vietorisz, D., & Smith, H. (1987). The differential impact of diabetes type on female sexuality. *Journal of Psychosomatic Research, 31*, 23–33.

Segraves, R. T., Schoenberg, H. W., Zarins, C. K., Knopf, J., & Camic, P. (1981). Discrimination of organic versus psychological impotence with the DSFI: A failure to replicate. *Journal of Sex and Marital Therapy, 7*, 230–238.

Seidner, A. L., Calhoun, K. S., & Kilpatrick, D. G. (1985, August). *Childhood and/or adolescent sexual experiences: Predicting variability in subsequent adjustment*. Paper presented at the meeting of the American Psychological Association, Los Angeles. (ERIC Document Reproduction Service No. ED 262 317)

Skrapec, C., & MacKenzie, K. R. (1981). Psychological self-perception in male transsexuals, homosexuals, and heterosexuals. *Archives of Sexual Behavior, 10*, 357–370.

Stellman, R. E., Goodwin, J. M., Robinson, J., Dansak, D., & Hilgers, R. D. (1984). Psychological effects of vulvectomy. *Psychosomatics, 25*, 779–783.

Wincze, J. P., Bansal, S., Malhotra, C., Balko, A., Susset, J. G., & Malamud, M. (1988). A comparison of nocturnal penile tumescence and penile response to erotic stimulation during waking states in comprehensively diagnosed groups of males experiencing erectile difficulties. *Archives of Sexual Behavior, 17*, 333–348.

Wolberg, W. H., Tanner, M. A., Romsaas, E. P., Trump, D. L., & Malec, J. F. (1987). Factors influencing options in primary breast cancer treatment. *Journal of Clinical Oncology, 5*, 68–74.

BIBLIOGRAPHY:

Derogatis, L. R. (1975a). *The Affect Balance Scale*. Baltimore: Clinical Psychometrics.

Derogatis, L. R. (1975b). *The Brief Symptom Inventory*. Baltimore: Clinical Psychometrics.

Derogatis, L. R. (1977). *The SCL-90 manual I: Scoring, administration and procedures for the SCL-90-R*. Baltimore: Clinical Psychometrics.

Mitchell, J. V., Jr. (1985). *The ninth mental measurements yearbook* (entry 317). Lincoln, NE: Buros Institute of Mental Measurements, University of Nebraska.

DESIRED CHANGES IN SEX LIFE CHECKLIST

AUTHORS: J. Kenneth Davidson, Sr. and Carol A. Darling

DATE: 1986

VARIABLE: Changes desired in one's sex life

TYPE OF INSTRUMENT: Checklist

DESCRIPTION: The Desired Changes in Sex Life Checklist is a list of 43 changes one might desire in one's sex life. Respondents are to check all items that represent changes they would like in their current sex life.

SAMPLE ITEMS: More foreplay

Use of vibrator during foreplay by partner

End current sexual relationship
PREVIOUS SUBJECTS: College students, nurses
APPROPRIATE FOR: College students and older
ADMINISTRATION: Self-administered; less than 10 minutes
SCORING: The researcher can count the number of items checked; the score reflects the extent to which the respondent desires change in his or her sex life. Alternatively the researcher might simply report the percentage of respondents who marked each change given in the list.
DEVELOPMENT: No information was provided.
RELIABILITY: No information was provided.
VALIDITY: No information was provided.
NOTES & COMMENTS: (1) Although data are lacking to demonstrate the reliability and validity of this measure, and in fact, it is arguable as to whether the items actually constitute a scale, the Desired Changes in Sex Life Checklist is included in this book because it measures a variable different from the other measures in this book.

(2) Darling and Davidson (1986a) compared college students on a variety of sexual measures, including the Desired Changes in Sex Life Checklist. The researchers listed, in priority order, the changes that respondents desired in their sex lives, and the researchers reported significant sex differences for numerous items. Darling and Davidson (1986b) asked nurses to complete a variety of sexual measures, including the Desired Changes in Sex Life Checklist. Again, the researchers listed, in priority order, the changes that respondents desired in their sex lives. The researchers compared the responses from nurses who faked orgasm with the responses from nurses who did not fake orgasm.
AVAILABLE FROM: J. Kenneth Davidson, Department of Sociology, University of Wisconsin—Eau Claire, Eau Claire, WI 54702–4004
USED IN:

Darling, C. A., & Davidson, J. K., Sr. (1986a). Coitally active university students: Sexual behaviors, concerns, and challenges. *Adolescence, 21,* 403–419.

Darling, C. A., & Davidson, J. K., Sr. (1986b). Enhancing relationships: Understanding the feminine mystique of pretending orgasm. *Journal of Sex and Marital Therapy, 12,* 182–196.

DYADIC SEXUAL REGULATION SCALE (DSR)

AUTHORS: Joseph A. Catania, Lois J. McDermott, and Jo Anna Wood
DATE: 1984
VARIABLE: Locus of control in regard to dyadic sexual relations
TYPE OF INSTRUMENT: Summated rating scale
DESCRIPTION: The Dyadic Sexual Regulation Scale (DSR) contains 11 statements regarding whether persons feel they have control in dyadic sexual relations. Six statements express an internal locus of control, and

5 express an external locus of control. Each item is accompanied by a 7-point scale ranging from "strongly disagree" to "strongly agree."
SAMPLE ITEMS: I often take the initiative in beginning sexual activity.

If my sexual relations are not satisfying there is little I can do to improve the situation.
PREVIOUS SUBJECTS: Heterosexual college students who had a regular sexual partner
APPROPRIATE FOR: College students and adults with a regular sexual partner
ADMINISTRATION: Self-administered; a couple of minutes
SCORING: Items are individually scored on a 7-point scale, with the higher number of points assigned to the response reflecting an internal locus of control. Total scores range from 11 (external locus of control) to 77 (internal locus of control).
DEVELOPMENT: Little information was provided regarding scale development. Catania, McDermott, and Wood (1984) simply stated that "items were initially developed from open-ended interviews with heterosexual and homosexual (gay and lesbian) couples" (p. 315).
RELIABILITY: Coefficient alpha for a sample of 59 college men and 92 college women was .74. Coefficient alpha for another sample of 27 college men and 43 college women was .83. The latter sample completed the DSR on a second occasion, about 2 weeks after the first administration. Test-retest reliability was .77.
VALIDITY: In order to provide evidence of the validity of the DSR, 151 college students completed the DSR, the Nowicki-Strickland Adult Internal-External Control Scale (NSLC) (Nowicki & Duke, 1974), and single-item measures assessing frequency of intercourse, frequency of genital masturbation, receipt of oral-genital stimulation from partner, frequency of orgasms, and sexual anxiety. The DSR and NSLC were expected to have a low but significant correlation with each other since both measured locus of control but in different areas. The correlation was .19 ($p < .05$). As predicted, DSR scores were significantly correlated with frequency of intercourse ($r = .40$), receipt of oral-genital stimulation from partner ($r = .30$), frequency of orgasms ($r = .36$), and sexual anxiety ($r = .47$). Also as predicted, the DSR did not correlate significantly ($r = .06$) with the frequency of masturbation. Contrary to predictions, DSR scores were not related to sex. The DSR, compared to the NSLC, had significantly larger correlations with frequency of intercourse, frequency of orgasms, and sexual anxiety but not with receipt of oral-genital stimulation.

Another sample of 70 college students completed the DSR, the Index of Sexual Satisfaction (ISS) (Hudson, Harrison, & Crosscup, 1981) (see separate entry), an item regarding frequency of genital masturbation, an item regarding frequency of sexual relations, and an item regarding frequency of affectionate behaviors. As predicted, DSR scores were not significantly related to the measure of genital masturbation (r = .13), but DSR scores were significantly correlated with the other three measures: ISS (r = .68), frequency of sexual relations (r = .46), and frequency of affectionate behaviors (r = .30). Again, sex was not significantly related to DSR scores.

NOTES & COMMENTS: Separate factor analyses were conducted using the responses from two groups of college students. Both analyses suggested that items loaded on a single factor.

AVAILABLE FROM: Catania, McDermott, and Wood, 1984

USED IN:

Catania, J. A., McDermott, L. J., & Wood, J. A. (1984). Assessment of locus of control: Situational specificity in the sexual context. *Journal of Sex Research, 20*, 310–324.

BIBLIOGRAPHY:

Hudson, W. W., Harrison, D. R., & Crosscup, P. C. (1981). A short-form scale to measure sexual discord in dyadic relationships. *Journal of Sex Research, 17*, 157–174.

Nowicki, S., & Duke, M. (1974). A locus of control scale for noncollege as well as college adults. *Journal of Personality Assessment, 38*, 136–137.

GOLOMBOK-RUST INVENTORY OF SEXUAL SATISFACTION (GRISS)

AUTHORS: John Rust and Susan Golombok

DATE: 1984

VARIABLE: Sexual dysfunction

TYPE OF INSTRUMENT: Summated rating scale

DESCRIPTION: There are two forms of the Golombok-Rust Inventory of Sexual Satisfaction (GRISS). The blue form is for males; the green form is for females. Each form contains 28 items accompanied by five response options: "never, hardly ever, occasionally, usually, always." The respondent circles the correct number to show the frequency with which the statement applies to him or her. Each partner in the couple completes one form of the GRISS.

SAMPLE ITEMS: (items taken from female form)

Do you feel uninterested in sex?

Do you ask your partner what he likes or dislikes about your sexual relationship?

PREVIOUS SUBJECTS: Sexually dysfunctional couples and normal couples

APPROPRIATE FOR: Persons involved in a sexually active, heterosexual relationship

ADMINISTRATION: Self-administered; about 10 minutes

SCORING: The GRISS yields 14 scores: Impotence, Premature Ejaculation, Male Nonsensuality, Male Avoidance, Male Dissatisfaction, Infrequency, Noncommunication, Female Dissatisfaction, Female Avoidance, Female Nonsensuality, Vaginismus, Anorgasmia, an overall sexual functioning score for the female, and an overall sexual functioning score for the male. Scoring the items and subscales and converting scores to a standardized scale requires about 3 minutes per couple when done by hand. Scoring can also be computerized. Scores are reported on a 9-point "pseudo-stanine" scale where 5 is considered a borderline score and scores above 5 are indicative of a sexual functioning problem. The standardization sample for the GRISS included 88 sex therapy clients from the United Kingdom.

DEVELOPMENT: "A 'think tank' of sex therapists at the Sexual Dysfunction Clinic of The Maudsley Hospital, London" (Rust & Golombok, 1986, p. 158) developed the specifications for the GRISS. They listed seven major areas relating to sexual satisfaction: "frequency, satisfaction, interest, dysfunctions, anxiety, communication, and touching" (Rust & Golombok, 1985, p. 63). A pilot version of the measure was constructed containing 48 items for the female form and 48 items for the male form. The pilot test was administered to 51 couples seeking help for sexual dysfunction and 36 couples who were not known to have sexual dysfunction. An item analysis of their responses led to the elimination of "items with extreme scores or with a large amount of response refusal" (Rust & Golombok, 1986, p. 159). The remaining items were subjected to a factor analysis. Four items were selected for each of the 12 subscales. The items were selected by applying the following criteria: "(1) stability of the factor structure, with a common factor accounting for more than 50% of the variance, (2) an equal number of items (four), two with positive and two with negative loadings, (3) content continuity along the full length of the indicated dimension, (4) factorial consistency between the clinical and student samples, and (5) face validity" (Rust & Golombok, 1986, p. 159). Further factor analysis led to the development of the two overall scales—one for males and one for females. Eight items contributed to these overall scales but not to the subscales. Thus, there are 56 items on the two forms combined: 4 items on each of 12 subscales plus 8 items contributing to the overall scores.

RELIABILITY: Rust and Golombok (1986) reported reliability estimates for the GRISS. Split-half reliability for the overall female score was .94; for the overall male score, it was .87. Internal consistency reliability was computed for the 12 subscales: Impotence = .78, Premature Ejaculation = .78, Male Nonsensuality = .69, Male Avoidance = .76, Male Dissatisfaction = .69, Infrequency = .79, Noncommunication = .61, Female Dissatisfaction = .64, Female Avoidance = .82, Female Nonsensuality = .78, Vaginismus = .73, and Anorgasmia = .83. Test-retest reliabilities were calculated using data from 41 couples; 21 couples had sex therapy, and 20 couples had marital therapy. The test-retest reliabilities were based on their pretest and posttest scores, so the reliability estimates can be considered quite conservative as one would expect score changes to result from therapy programs. For the overall scores, the test-retest reliability for the males was .76, and for the females, it was .65. The following test-retest reliabilities were computed for the subscales: Impotence = .79, Premature Ejaculation = .84, Male Nonsensuality = .57, Male Avoidance = .64, Male Dissatisfaction = .61, Infrequency = .66, Noncommunication = .52, Female Dissatisfaction = .47, Female Avoidance = .62, Female Nonsensuality = .61, Vaginismus = .82, and Anorgasmia = .61.

VALIDITY: Rust and Golombok (1986) reported that the GRISS discriminated between sexually dysfunctional (clinical) and nondysfunctional (control) groups. The point biserial correlation for the overall female scale and clinical/control status was .63; for the overall male scale, it was .37. Four of 42 women in the clinical group scored below the mean for the control group; 14 of 57 men in the clinical group scored below the mean for the control group. Therapists identified clinic patients with four different diagnoses: impotence, premature ejaculation, vaginismus, and anorgasmia. For all four groups, there was a significant difference on the target subscale between those in the diagnostic category and a control group. The clinical and control groups also differed on five of the eight subscales that did not reflect specific dysfunction. They did not differ significantly on Noncommunication, Male Nonsensuality, and Male Avoidance.

Using a 4-point scale, therapists rated the overall severity of the sexual dysfunction experienced by persons seeking therapy (Rust & Golombok, 1986). These scores were correlated with overall scale scores. For 63 females, the correlation was .56 ($p < .001$); for 68 males, the correlation was .53 ($p < .001$). Therapists also used 4-point scales to rate the improvement in the clients as a result of therapy. The improvement ratings were correlated with the change in the overall score. For males, the correlation was .54; for females, the correlation was .43. Both correlations were statistically significant.

NOTES & COMMENTS: (1) Golombok, Rust, and Pickard (1984) used the GRISS to determine the prevalence of sexual dysfunction in the general public.

(2) The GRISS has been used to predict and/or evaluate the effectiveness of programs for treating sexual dysfunction (Bennun, 1984, 1985a, 1985b; Bennun, Rust, & Golombok, 1985).

(3) Rust, Bennun, Crowe, and Golombok (1986) developed the Golombok Rust Inventory of Marital State (GRIMS) to assess the quality of a marital relationship. GRIMS is a companion measure for the GRISS and, like the GRISS, contains 28 items. Split-half reliability for the GRIMS was .90 for women and .92 for men.

(4) The GRISS is entry 127 in the *Tenth Mental Measurements Yearbook* (Conoley & Kramer, 1989).

AVAILABLE FROM: May be purchased from NFER-Nelson, Darville House, 2 Oxford Road East, Windsor, Berkshire SL4 1DF, England

USED IN:

Bennun, I. (1984). Evaluating marital therapy: A hospital and community study. *British Journal of Guidance and Counselling, 12*, 84–91.

Bennun, I. (1985a). Behavioral marital therapy: An outcome evaluation of conjoint, group and one spouse treatment. *Scandinavian Journal of Behaviour Therapy, 14*, 157–168.

Bennun, I. (1985b). Prediction and responsiveness in behavioural marital therapy. *Behavioural Psychology, 13*, 186–201.

Bennun, I., Rust, J., & Golombok, S. (1985). The effects of marital therapy on sexual satisfaction. *Scandinavian Journal of Behaviour Therapy, 14*, 65–72.

Golombok, S., Rust, J., & Pickard, C. (1984). Sexual problems encountered in general practice. *British Journal of Sexual Medicine, 11*, 210–212.

Rust, J., Bennun, I., Crowe, M., & Golombok, S. (1986). The Golombok Rust Inventory of Marital State (GRIMS). *Sexual and Marital Therapy, 1*, 55–60.

Rust, J., & Golombok, S. (1985). The Golombok-Rust Inventory of Sexual Satisfaction (GRISS). *British Journal of Clinical Psychology, 24*, 63–64.

Rust, J., & Golombok, S. (1986). The GRISS: A psychometric instrument for the assessment of sexual dysfunction. *Archives of Sexual Behavior, 15*, 157–165.

BIBLIOGRAPHY:

Conoley, J. C., & Kramer, J. J. (1989). *The tenth mental measurements yearbook* (entry 127). Lincoln, NE: Buros Institute of Mental Measurements, University of Nebraska.

INDEX OF SEXUAL SATISFACTION (ISS)

AUTHOR: W. W. Hudson

DATE: 1981 (used 1976)

VARIABLE: Sexual discord in dyadic relationships

TYPE OF INSTRUMENT: Summated rating scale

DESCRIPTION: The Index of Sexual Satisfaction (ISS) consists of 25 items, with most items referring to the quality of the sexual relationship between the respondent and his or her partner. Some of the items refer to specific aspects of the sexual relationship, and others are statements about the overall quality of the sexual relationship. Two items pertain to the respondent's feelings about sex in general. Twelve of the 25 items are positive statements; the other 13 items are negative statements. Respondents express their views on each statement using the following five options: "Rarely or none of the time, A little of the time, Some of the time, Good part of the time, Most or all of the time."

SAMPLE ITEMS: I feel that my partner enjoys our sex life.

When we have sex it is too rushed and hurriedly completed.

PREVIOUS SUBJECTS: College students and adults in stable sexual re-

lationships, abused wives, alcoholic women and wives of alcoholics, couples being treated for infertility
APPROPRIATE FOR: Persons in a stable sexual relationship
ADMINISTRATION: Self-administered; about 10 minutes
SCORING: The negatively phrased items are scored by assigning 5 points to the option "Most or all of the time" and 1 point to "Rarely or none of the time." The positively phrased items are reverse scored. Total scores are computed by using the following formula:

$$\text{score} = (\Sigma Y - N)(100)/[(N)(4)]$$

where Y represents an item score and N represents the total number of items completed by the respondent. This formula yields total scores ranging from 0 (sexually very satisfied) to 100 (sexually very dissatisfied). Although the formula adjusts for missing responses, Hudson, Harrison, and Crosscup (1981) recommended disregarding scores when respondents complete fewer than 20 items. If no items are omitted, the formula can be simplified:

$$\text{score} = \Sigma Y - 25.$$

Hudson et al. (1981) recommended using a cutoff score of 28 to identify persons who have a sexual problem in their relationship. The researchers showed, however, that a cutoff score of 30 did not appreciably affect the rate of misclassifications.
DEVELOPMENT: The items on the ISS "were developed on the basis of clinical and personal experience, and they reflect a number of the common complaints that clients provide when they are discussing dissatisfaction with the sexual component of their relationship" (Hudson et al., 1981, p. 159).
RELIABILITY: To determine the test-retest reliability of the ISS, Hudson et al. (1981) tested 79 graduate students enrolled in a social work program. The participating students were either married or in a stable sexual relationship. Using a 1-week interval between test and retest, the reliability coefficient was computed to be .93.

Hudson (1982) reported coefficient alpha for six different samples of respondents. The coefficients ranged from .91 to .94. Based on a combined sample of 1,738 persons, Hudson obtained a coefficient alpha of .92.
VALIDITY: To determine the discriminant validity of the ISS, Hudson et al. (1981) tested 100 persons seeking personal counseling. The respondents were divided into two groups. One group included the 49 persons whom therapists had determined were having a sexual relationship problem with their spouse or partner; the other group included

the 51 people whom therapists judged did not have a significant sexual relationship problem. The difference between the two groups was statistically significant ($p < .001$). The point-biserial correlation between ISS scores and the two groups was .76. The two groups also completed two other measures: the Index of Marital Satisfaction (IMS) (Cheung & Hudson, 1982), which assessed marital discord, and the Sexual Attitude Scale (SAS) (Hudson, Murphy, & Nurius, 1983) (see separate entry), which measured liberal versus conservative orientation toward sexual expression. Of the three measures, the ISS showed the strongest correlation with group membership, and the mean difference between the two groups was largest for the ISS. Based on these data, Hudson et al. (1981) concluded that "since the ISS correlates very highly with a criterion it is supposed to be related to (the existence of a sex problem), and the other two scales correlate lower with the same criterion, these data also provide some evidence in support of the claim that the ISS also has good construct validity" (p. 165).

Using a cutoff score of 28 to identify persons with a sexual problem in their relationship, the misclassification rate was 11.8% for those without a sex problem (false positives) and 14.3% for those with a sex problem (false negatives). Overall the misclassification rate was 13%.

In order to provide further evidence of the scale's validity, Hudson et al. (1981) correlated ISS scores with a variety of other variables: the IMS (Cheung & Hudson, 1982); the SAS (Hudson et al., 1983); the Generalized Contentment Scale (GCS) (Byerly, 1979), which measures depression; the Index of Self-Esteem (ISE) (McIntosh, 1979); and sex, age, educational level, and income. They obtained the following correlations: with the IMS, $r = .68$; with the GCS, $r = .47$; with the ISE, $r = .44$; with the SAS, $r = .14$; with sex, $r = .01$; with age, $r = -.06$; with educational level, $r = -.10$; and with income, $r = .01$. Based on these correlations, the authors "concluded that the ISS has good construct validity" (Hudson et al., 1981, p. 172).

Hudson and McIntosh (1981) administered the ISS to women who were victims of spouse abuse and to women who were not abused by their spouses. There was a significant difference in the means obtained by the two groups ($p < .0001$), and the point-biserial correlation between group membership and ISS scores was .43.

As predicted, Cheung and Hudson (1982) obtained a significant and relatively high correlation between ISS scores and scores on the IMS ($r = .67$). For three samples, Cheung and Hudson obtained correlations of .72, .64, and .69 between ISS and IMS scores. Correlations between the ISS and the SAS were predicted to be low and nonsignificant. For three samples, the correlations were .10, .18, and .18; only the last correlation was significant at the .05 level.

Perlman and Abramson (1982) administered the ISS along with two measures of social desirability: the Marlowe-Crowne Social Desirability Scale (Crowne & Marlowe, 1964) and the Jemail-LoPiccolo Sexual Defensiveness Scale (Jemail & LoPiccolo, 1982). From their analysis, they concluded that "the data are not unduly confounded by social-desirability effects" (Perlman & Abramson, 1982, 459).

Catania, McDermott, and Wood (1984) administered their Dyadic Sexual Regulation scale (DSR) (see separate entry), a measure of locus of control in regard to dyadic sexual situations, and the ISS to 27 college men and 43 college women who were involved in an ongoing sexual relationship. The correlation between the two measures was .68 ($p <$ .0001). Increasing perceptions of internal control were associated with higher levels of sexual satisfaction.

Link and Darling (1986) studied 43 married couples who were undergoing treatment for infertility. The couples independently completed the ISS, the GCS, and the IMS. For wives, scores on the ISS were significantly correlated with the GCS (r = .48) and the IMS (r = .73). Similarly, for husbands, scores on the ISS were significantly correlated with the GCS (r = .37) and the IMS (r = .81). Furthermore, scores on the ISS were significantly correlated for the husband-wife pairs (r = .57).

NOTES & COMMENTS: (1) Item analysis procedures involving the items from the ISS as well as items from several other scales led Hudson et al. (1981) to conclude that four items on the ISS should be replaced with four new items. They provided substitute items for the four unacceptable items. Hudson (1982) suggested that an additional item on the ISS be replaced with a new item, and so he provided replacements for five items.

(2) One purpose of the ISS is to monitor and assess progress in treatment, and thus the scale is often administered to the same client on several occasions. Hudson et al. (1981) recommended that score changes of less than 4 points be disregarded since the SEM is 3.83. Score changes of at least 8 points are likely to be indicative of genuine change in the client.

(3) Hudson's (1982) Clinical Measurement Package includes nine measures of "variables that define and influence the quality of personal and social functioning among individuals, couples, families, and small groups" (p. 1). Each measure is intended for use by researchers or therapists. The ISS is one of the nine measures. The balance of the Clinical Measurement Package includes the GCS to measure depression, the ISE to measure self-esteem problems, the IMS to measure marital discord, the Index of Parental Attitudes to measure discord with a child, the Child's Attitude Toward Mother to measure discord with the mother, the Child's Attitude Toward Father to measure discord with the father, the Index of Family Relations to measure intrafamilial stress, and the Index of Peer Relations to measure peer discord. Hudson's (1982) book

describing the Clinical Measurement Package provides considerable information regarding all of these measures, including the ISS.

(4) Dailey (1979) used the ISS as one of seven measures to compare the relationship success of 10 homosexual and 26 heterosexual couples. Perlman and Abramson (1982) looked at the relationship between sexual satisfaction and nine potentially relevant variables: "attitudes toward sex, attitudes toward one's body, previous sexual experience, factual knowledge about sex, sexual communication, pleasure, anxiety, affective connection, and life stress" (p. 458). Darling and Hicks (1983) studied the sexual attitudes and sexual satisfaction of 80 college students. One of their measures was the ISS. The authors did not explain how the students who were not involved in stable sexual relationships were able to respond to the items. Peterson, Hartsock, and Lawson (1984) compared ISS responses from four groups of women: alcoholic women, women married to alcoholic men, women seeking counseling for problems unrelated to alcohol abuse, and women not seeking counseling. Adkins and Jehu (1985) used the ISS as one of several dependent measures in a research study evaluating the effectiveness of a treatment program to help nonorgasmic women attain orgasm. In a study designed to explore the long-term consequences of various childhood sexual experiences, Kilpatrick (1986) administered five scales from the Clinical Measurement Package to 501 women. The ISS was one of the scales administered. Gold (1986) administered several scales, including some items from the ISS, to 103 women who had been sexually victimized as children. She was interested in the relationship between childhood sexual victimization and adult functioning.

AVAILABLE FROM: Both the original version and the version with four items changed appear in Hudson, Harrison, and Crosscup, 1981; the version with five items changed appears in Hudson, 1982. The ISS is available for purchase from the WALMYR Publishing Co., P.O. Box 3554, Leon Station, Tallahassee, FL 32315. The entire Clinical Measurement Package is available for purchase from Dorsey Press, 1818 Ridge Road, Homewood, Il 60430. Corcoran and Fischer, 1987

USED IN:

Adkins, E., & Jehu, D. (1985). Analysis of a treatment program for primary orgastic dysfunction. *Behaviour Research and Therapy, 23,* 119–126.

Catania, J. A., McDermott, L. J., & Wood, J. A. (1984). Assessment of locus of control: Situational specificity in the sexual context. *Journal of Sex Research, 20,* 310–324.

Cheung, P. P. L., & Hudson, W. W. (1982). Assessment of marital discord in social work practice: A revalidation of the Index of Marital Satisfaction. *Journal of Social Service Research, 5,* 101-118.

Dailey, D. M. (1979). Adjustment of heterosexual and homosexual couples in pairing relationships: An exploratory study. *Journal of Sex Research, 15,* 143–157.

Darling, C. A., & Hicks, M. W. (1983). Recycling parental sexual messages. *Journal of Sex and Marital Therapy, 9,* 233–243.

Gold, E. R. (1986). Long-term effects of sexual victimization in childhood: An attributional approach. *Journal of Consulting and Clinical Psychology, 54,* 471–475.

Hudson, W. W. (1982). *The Clinical Measurement Package: A field manual.* Homewood, IL: Dorsey.

Hudson, W. W., Harrison, D. F., & Crosscup, P. C. (1981). A short-form scale to measure sexual discord in dyadic relationships. *Journal of Sex Research, 17,* 157–174.

Hudson, W. W., & McIntosh, S. R. (1981). The assessment of spouse abuse: Two quantifiable dimensions. *Journal of Marriage and the Family, 43,* 873–885.

Kilpatrick, A. C. (1986). Some correlates of women's childhood sexual experiences: A retrospective study. *Journal of Sex Research, 22,* 221–242.

Link, P. A., & Darling, C. A. (1986). Couples undergoing treatment for infertility: Dimensions of life satisfaction. *Journal of Sex and Marital Therapy, 12,* 46–59.

Perlman, S. D., & Abramson, P. R. (1982). Sexual satisfaction among married and cohabiting individuals. *Journal of Consulting and Clinical Psychology, 50,* 458–460.

Peterson, J. S., Hartsock, N., & Lawson, G. (1984). Sexual dissatisfaction of female alcoholics. *Psychological Reports, 55,* 744–746.

BIBLIOGRAPHY:

Byerly, F. C. (1979). Comparison between inpatients, outpatients, and normals on three self-report depression inventories (Doctoral dissertation, Western Michigan University, 1979). *Dissertation Abstracts International, 40,* 904B.

Corcoran, K., & Fischer, J. (1987). *Measures for clinical practice: A sourcebook* (pp. 190–191). New York: Free Press.

Crowne, D., & Marlowe, D. (1964). *The approval motive: Studies in evaluative dependency.* New York: Wiley.

Hudson, W. W., Murphy, G. J., & Nurius, P. S. (1983). A short-form scale to measure liberal vs. conservative orientations toward human sexual expression. *Journal of Sex Research, 19,* 258–272.

Jemail, J., & LoPiccolo, J. (1982). A sexual and a marriage defensiveness scale for each sex. *American Journal of Family Therapy, 10,* 33–40.

McIntosh, S. R. (1979). *Validation of scales to be used in research on spouse abuse.* Unpublished master's thesis, University of Hawaii, Honolulu.

JUHASZ-SCHNEIDER SEXUAL DECISION-MAKING QUESTIONNAIRE (JSSDMQ)

AUTHORS: Anne McCreary Juhasz and Mary Sonnenshein-Schneider

DATE: 1979

VARIABLE: Importance of various factors that influence sexual decision-making

TYPE OF INSTRUMENT: Summated rating scale

DESCRIPTION: The Juhasz-Schneider Sexual Decision-Making Questionnaire (JSSDMQ) contains 135 items organized around six decisions relating to sexual intercourse and its possible ramifications. The first decision, "To have or not to have sexual intercourse," is followed by 43 items, each a factor that might influence a person's decision to have or not to have sexual intercourse. The second decision, "To have or not to have children," is followed by 8 items. These items pertain to the respondent's feelings, as well as his or her perceptions of other persons' feelings. The third decision pertains to the use of birth control and is followed by 7 items. Some of the items focus on the respondent's perceptions of other persons' feelings. The fourth decision concerns the choice between delivering a child or having an abortion and is followed by 38 items. Many of the pregnancy-related items focus on the impact of a child on the new mother and the new father. The abortion-related items focus on the impact of the abortion on the partners' and other people's perceptions of abortion. Decision 5 relates to the choice between keeping a child and giving him or her up for adoption and is followed by 15 items. Items pertain to the female, the male, and other people. The final decision, "To marry or stay single," is followed by 24 items. These items focus on characteristics of the partner and the relationship and on the long-term impact of marriage on each of the two individuals. Again, there are questions regarding the impact of other persons' perceptions. Respondents express their feelings on each item by selecting one of five response options: "of no importance, of little importance, of some importance, quite important, extremely important."

SAMPLE ITEMS: (To have or not to have sexual intercourse) My partner's personality.

(To have or not to have children) I have the characteristics of a good parent.

(To use or not to use birth control) The risks involved in using birth control.

(If pregnancy, to deliver the child or have an abortion) There might be negative physical effects of delivery on the mother.

(If you [or your partner] delivered a child . . . to keep the baby or give it up for adoption) Our decision to stay together.

(To marry or stay single) My partner's race.

PREVIOUS SUBJECTS: Ages 13–19

APPROPRIATE FOR: High school students and older

ADMINISTRATION: Self-administered; about 45 minutes

SCORING: Items are individually scored on a 5-point scale, with 1 point assigned to the response "of no importance" and 5 points to the response "extremely important." Item scores are summed to yield scores on six factors: Family Establishment Competence, External Morality, Consequences of Childbearing, Self-Enhancement through Sexual Intercourse,

Intimacy Considerations regarding Intercourse, and Consequences of Marriage.

DEVELOPMENT: The theory underlying the development of the JSSDMQ was first described by Juhasz (1975). The revised JSSDMQ, which is described here, is based on the original Juhasz Sexual Decision-Making Questionnaire, a 78-item measure concerning the same six decision areas covered by the revised measure (see McCreary-Juhasz & Kavanagh, 1978). A factor analysis of the original scale yielded six factors accounting for 48.55% of the variance: "Effect of pregnancy on the couple and on the child's development; Social, religious and family mores and sanctions; Responsibility and the idea of mutual sharing (other than intercourse); Egocentric reasons for intercourse; Other influences on intercourse; and Psychological aspects of abortion" (Juhasz & Sonnenshein-Schneider, 1979, p. 183). Because the original version of the scale was intended for college students, the vocabulary and sentence structure of the measure was altered to make it more appropriate for an adolescent population. Inputs from 260 high school students were used to identify changes needed in wording and structure. Additionally the response scale was changed from a 3-point scale to the current 5-point scale; "the clustered items were split into separate items to avoid contamination of response regarding each item" (Sonnenshein-Schneider, 1978, p. 82); and 18 items were added to the scale.

To identify the factors for scoring the JSSDMQ, a factor analysis was done using data from 502 adolescents. Six factors were extracted, accounting for 34.67% of the variance. The factor names were the result of discussions between "four experts in the field" (Sonnenshein-Schneider, 1978, p. 107).

Factor 1, Family Establishment Competence, contained 29 items with factor loadings ranging from .32 to .68. The items related to three of the decisions on the scale: the decision to deliver the child or seek an abortion, to keep the child or give him or her up for adoption, and to marry or remain single. Scores on this factor "correlate highly with personal autonomy and the influence of one's partner on the decisions to have a child . . . and to marry" (Sonnenshein-Schneider, 1978, p. 107).

Factor 2, External Morality, contained 25 items with factor loadings ranging from .30 to .64. The items were from all six decision-making areas of the scale and related to the idea that moral judgments should be determined by other persons rather than by an internal sense of morality. Scores on Factor 2 "correlate positively with religiosity . . . , negatively with age . . . , sexual permissiveness . . . , and the beliefs that it is all right to engage in heavy petting . . . , sexual intercourse . . . , or cohabitation" (Sonnenshein-Schneider, 1978, p. 109).

Factor 3, Consequences of Childbearing, contained 25 items with factor loadings ranging from .31 to .71. The items were from two decision-making areas: to deliver the child or have an abortion and to keep the baby or give him or her up for adoption. The items pertained to the consequences of childbirth on the lives of the new father and new mother. Scores on Factor 3 "correlate negatively with the desire for pregnancy . . . , intelligence . . . , and . . . tender-mindedness" (Sonnenshein-Schneider, 1978, p. 112).

Factor 4, Self-Enhancement through Sexual Intercourse, contained 19 items with factor loadings between .32 and .69. Most items on this factor related to the decision to have or not to have sexual intercourse; item content emphasized the gains or benefits associated with intercourse. Scores on Factor 4 "correlate positively with sexual permissiveness . . . and the beliefs that it is alright to engage in heavy petting . . . , sexual intercourse . . . and cohabitation . . . [and with] tough-mindedness . . . , weak superego strength . . . , and low self-sentiment integration" (Sonnenshein-Schneider, 1978, p. 112).

Factor 5, Intimacy Considerations regarding Intercourse, contained 13 items with factor loadings between .38 and .53. All 13 items were from one decision-making area: to have or not to have sexual intercourse. Scores on Factor 5 "correlate negatively with the belief that premarital sexual intercourse is permissible . . . , positively with personal autonomy regarding the decisions involving intercourse . . . , having children . . . , employing birth control . . . , delivering or aborting . . . , keeping a child or giving it up for adoption . . . [and] self-assuredness" (Sonnenshein-Schneider, 1978, p. 114).

Factor 6, Consequences of Marriage, contained 10 items with factor loadings between .38 and .76. All of these items referred to the decision to marry or remain single. Item content focused primarily on how marriage limits one's personal autonomy.

Fifteen items on the JSSDMQ did not load on any of the six factors, and 4 items loaded on more than one factor. Those 4 items loaded on Factor 3, Consequences of Childbearing, and Factor 6, Consequences of Marriage.

RELIABILITY: Coefficient alpha was computed for each factor score using responses from 502 high school students. The results were: Family Establishment Competence = .91, External Morality = .89, Consequences of Childbearing = .92, Self-Enhancement through Sexual Intercourse = .86, Intimacy Considerations regarding Intercourse = .81, and Consequences of Marriage = .90 (Juhasz & Sonnenshein-Schneider, 1979; Sonnenshein-Schneider, 1978).

VALIDITY: The authors claimed content validity for the scale on the grounds that "the items in the original item pool were the result of a thorough review of the literature, which was supplemented by the suggestions of black and white, male and female students. Four judges in the field evaluated the content validity and wording of the original questionnaire" (Juhasz & Sonnenshein-Schneider, 1979, p. 183).

Juhasz and Sonnenshein-Schneider (1979) claimed that the factor analysis of the JSSDMQ provided evidence of the construct validity of the measure. This is only partially true.

Sonnenshein-Schneider (1978) and Juhasz and Sonnenshein-Schneider (1979) reported that scores on the JSSDMQ were not related to locus of control for a sample of 484 adolescents. However, when the sexes were considered separately, they found that males, but not females, showed a relationship between JSSDMQ and locus of control. In particular, they found that a regression analysis on the data from males identified two significant predictors of locus of control: Consequences of Childbearing and Self-Enhancement through Sexual Intercourse.

NOTES & COMMENTS: (1) There are some differences in the assignment of items to factors when the data reported by Juhasz (1988) are compared to the data reported by Sonnenshein-Schneider (1978).

(2) Juhasz, Kaufman, and Meyer (1986) reported results of a study involving 451 adolescents. Although the study was based on Juhasz's model regarding sexual decision making, the researchers did not actually use the JSSDMQ in their research.

AVAILABLE FROM: Juhasz, 1988 (Note: There is a typesetting error in Juhasz [1988]. Item 112 should begin a new section headed "Decision 6: TO MARRY OR STAY SINGLE); Sonnenshein-Schneider, 1978

USED IN:

Juhasz, A. M. (1988). The Juhasz-Schneider Sexual Decision-Making Questionnaire (JSSDMQ). In C. M. Davis, W. L. Yarber, & S. L. Davis (Eds.), *Sexuality-related measures: A compendium* (pp. 69-72). Syracuse: Editors.

Juhasz, A. M., Kaufman, B., & Meyer, H. (1986). Adolescent attitudes and beliefs about sexual behavior. *Child and Adolescent Social Work, 3,* 177–193.

Juhasz, A. M., & Sonnenshein-Schneider, M. (1979). Responsibility and control: The basis of sexual decision making. *Personnel and Guidance Journal, 58,* 181–185.

McCreary-Juhasz, A., & Kavanagh, J. A. (1978). Factors which influence sexual decisions. *Journal of Sex Education and Therapy, 4,* 35–39.

Sonnenshein-Schneider, M. (1978). *The relationship between factors which influence adolescent sexual decisions, locus of control, and selected personality dimensions.* Unpublished doctoral dissertation, Loyola University, Chicago, IL.

BIBLIOGRAPHY:

Juhasz, A. M. (1975). A chain of sexual decision-making. *Family Coordinator, 24,* 43–49.

PINNEY SEXUAL SATISFACTION INVENTORY (PSSI)

AUTHORS: Elise M. Pinney, Meg Gerrard, and Nancy W. Denney

DATE: 1987

VARIABLE: Women's sexual satisfaction
TYPE OF INSTRUMENT: Summated rating scale
DESCRIPTION: The Pinney Sexual Satisfaction Inventory (PSSI) consists of 24 items representing two factors: General Sexual Satisfaction (14 items) and Satisfaction with Partner (10 items). All of the items on the General Sexual Satisfaction subscale reflect satisfaction, a positive attitude; all of the items on the Satisfaction with Partner subscale reflect dissatisfaction, a desire that things be different. Items on the General Sexual Satisfaction subscale are phrased in the present tense and begin with the phrase "I am" or "I feel." Items on the Satisfaction with Partner subscale are phrased in the future tense, and all begin with the phrase "I wish." Each item is accompanied by a 7-point response scale, with response options ranging from "strongly agree" to "strongly disagree."
SAMPLE ITEMS: (General Sexual Satisfaction) I feel that nothing is lacking in my sex life.

(Satisfaction with Partner) I wish my partner(s) were more loving and caring when we make love.
PREVIOUS SUBJECTS: Sexually active college women
APPROPRIATE FOR: Sexually active women
ADMINISTRATION: Self-administered; about 10 minutes
SCORING: Items are individually scored on a 7-point scale, with higher scores reflecting greater satisfaction. On the General Sexual Satisfaction subscale, "strongly agree" is assigned 7 points, and on the Satisfaction with Partner subscale, "strongly disagree" is assigned 7 points. Three total scores are obtained: one for each of the two factors and one overall score. Pinney, Gerrard, and Denney (1987) reported means and standard deviations for the items on the PSSI.
DEVELOPMENT: Sexual satisfaction was defined as "a subjective evaluation of the degree to which a woman is content with her sex life, independent of behavioral criteria" (Pinney et al., 1987, p. 236). That is, a woman is satisfied with her sex life if she says she is satisfied. A pool of 51 items was developed based on a review of the relevant literature. Using inputs from graduate students and faculty in psychology, the item pool was reduced to 36 items that were administered to over 200 college women. Factor analytic procedures using the responses from the college women led to the selection of the factors and items that comprise the scale. An initial factor analysis led to a reduction of the item pool; 24 items remained. The second factor analysis led to the identification of Factor 1, General Sexual Satisfaction, which contains 14 items with factor loadings ranging from .49 to .72, and Factor 2, Satisfaction with Partner, which contains 10 items with factor loadings ranging from .36 to .80. The two factors accounted for 42% of the variance. The correlation between the two factors was .57.

RELIABILITY: Coefficient alpha for the overall PSSI was .92. Split-half reliability was .90. Item-total correlations ranged from .24 to .69.

VALIDITY: To test the concurrent validity of the PSSI, scores from the PSSI were correlated with scores on four other indicators of sexual satisfaction. The other measures and their correlation with the PSSI were: Hudson's (1982) Index of Sexual Satisfaction (see separate entry), r = .68; one item from the PSSI ("Generally, I am satisfied with my sex life."), r = .66; a single-item measure reflecting the percentage of times the woman reaches orgasm, r = .37; and a measure of the frequency of sexual intercourse, r = .35.

The correlation between PSSI scores and scores on the Marlowe-Crowne Social Desirability Scale (Crowne & Marlowe, 1960) was low but statistically significant (r = .21).

NOTES & COMMENTS: Pinney et al. (1987) used the PSSI to study the correlates of women's sexual satisfaction. They used multiple regression procedures to determine how each of 11 variables contributed to the prediction of scores on each of the two subscales and the total score. The 11 predictor variables were: sex guilt as measured by the Mosher-Forced-Choice Sex Guilt Inventory—Langston Version (Langston, 1975) (see separate entry for Revised Mosher Guilt Inventory); religious intensity, as measured by a single item; religious commitment, as measured by a single item; number of sexual partners in one's lifetime; length of current relationship; contraceptive effectiveness, based on a 4-point scale; age when sexual intercourse first occurred; orgasm consistency, based on a single item; occurrence of masturbation, based on a single yes/no question; frequency of sexual intercourse, based on a single item; and diversity of sexual experience.

AVAILABLE FROM: Pinney, Gerrard, and Denney, 1987

USED IN:

Pinney, E. M., Gerrard, M., & Denney, N. W. (1987). The Pinney Sexual Satisfaction Inventory. *Journal of Sex Research, 23,* 233–251.

BIBLIOGRAPHY:

Crowne, D. P., & Marlowe, D. (1960). A new scale of social desirability independent of psychopathology. *Journal of Consulting Psychology, 24,* 349–354.

Hudson, W. (1982). *The Clinical Measurement Package: A field manual.* Homewood, IL: Dorsey Press.

Langston, R. (1975). Stereotyped sex role behavior and guilt. *Journal of Personality Assessment, 39,* 77–81.

REVISED MOSHER GUILT INVENTORY

AUTHOR: Donald L. Mosher

DATE: 1966 (revised mid-1980s)

VARIABLE: Sex-guilt, hostility-guilt, and guilty-conscience

TYPE OF INSTRUMENT: Summated rating scale

DESCRIPTION: There were two versions of the Mosher Inventories: the Mosher Forced-Choice Inventory in which statements were presented in pairs and the respondent was to select one item from each pair, and the Mosher "G" Inventory in which the respondent answered true or false for each item on the scale. The inventories have been revised since being described in Beere (1979). There is now one form, the Revised Mosher Guilt Inventory, which consists of 114 statements, presented in 72 pairs: 50 items reflect sex-guilt, 42 items reflect hostility guilt, and 22 items reflect guilty-conscience. Although items are presented in pairs, persons completing the scale respond to both items in the pair by rating each one on a 7-point scale with the endpoints labeled "not at all true of (for) me" and "extremely true of (for) me." The purpose of presenting the item in pairs, with a common stem, is "to permit subjects to compare the intensity of TRUENESS for them since people generally find one alternative is more or less TRUE for them" (Mosher, undated, p. 2).
ARTICLES LISTED IN BEERE, 1979: 5
NOTES & COMMENTS: (1) The research reports listed below used the Mosher Inventories primarily to measure sex guilt. There are other research studies not listed here that also used the Mosher Inventories, but they are not likely to be relevant to the focus of this book.

(2) O'Grady and Janda (1979) reported the results of a factor analytic study using the Mosher Forced-Choice Guilt Inventory.
AVAILABLE FROM: Donald Mosher, Department of Psychology, University of Connecticut, Storrs, CT 06268; Mosher, 1988
USED IN:

Abramson, P. R., & Handschumacher, I. W. (1978). The Mosher Sex Guilt Scale and the college population: A methodological note. *Journal of Personality Assessment, 42*, 635.

Abramson, P. R., & Imai Marquez, J. (1982). The Japanese-American: A cross-cultural, cross-sectional study of sex guilt. *Journal of Research in Personality, 16*, 227–237.

Abramson, P. R., Michalak, P., & Alling, C. (1977). Perception of parental sex guilt and sexual behavior and arousal of college students. *Perceptual and Motor Skills, 45*, 337–338.

Abramson, P. R., & Mosher, D. L. (1979). An empirical investigation of experimentally induced masturbatory fantasies. *Archives of Sexual Behavior, 8*, 27–39.

Abramson, P. R., Mosher, D. L., Abramson, L. M., & Woychowski, B. (1977). Personality correlates of the Mosher Guilt scales. *Journal of Personality Assessment, 41*, 375–382.

Allgeier, A. R., Allgeier, E. R., & Rywick, T. (1981). Orientations toward abortion: Guilt or knowledge? *Adolescence, 16*, 273–280.

Allgeier, A. R., Allgeier, E. R., & Rywick, T. (1982). Response to requests for abortion: The influence of guilt and knowledge. *Journal of Applied Social Psychology, 12*, 281–291.

Arndt, W. B., & Ladd, B. (1981). Sibling incest aversion as an index of oedipal conflict. *Journal of Personality Assessment, 45,* 52–58.

Berger, C., Jacques, J., Brender, W., Gold, D., & Andres, D. (1985). Contraceptive knowledge and use of birth control as a function of sex guilt. *International Journal of Women's Studies, 8,* 72–79.

Bernard, H. S., & Schwartz, A. J. (1977). Impact of a human sexuality program on sex related knowledge, attitudes, behavior and guilt of college undergraduates. *Journal of the American College Health Association, 25,* 182–185.

Bond, S. B., & Mosher, D. L. (1986). Guided imagery of rape: Fantasy, reality, and the willing victim myth. *Journal of Sex Research, 22,* 162–183.

Brown, I. S., & Pollack, R. H. (1982, August). *Sex knowledge, sex guilt and sexual behavior among university students.* Paper presented at the meeting of the American Psychological Association, Washington, DC. (ERIC Document Reproduction Service No. ED 226 295)

Davis, G. L., & Cross, H. J. (1979). Sexual stereotyping of black males in interracial sex. *Archives of Sexual Behavior, 8,* 269–279.

Embree, R. A. (1986, August). *Pro-recreational sex morality, religiosity, and causal attribution of homosexual attitudes.* Paper presented at the meeting of the American Psychological Association, Washington, DC. (ERIC Document Reproduction Service No. ED 283 080)

Evans, R. G. (1984). Hostility and sex guilt: Perceptions of self and others as a function of gender and sex-role orientation. *Sex Roles, 10,* 207–215.

Fehr, L. A. (1979). Media violence and catharsis in college females. *Journal of Social Psychology, 109,* 307–308.

Fehr, L. A. (1988). Guilt in alcoholics. *Psychological Reports, 62,* 92–94.

Fehr, L. A., & Stamps, L. E. (1979). Guilt and shyness: A profile of social discomfort. *Journal of Personality Assessment, 43,* 481–484.

Fisher, W. A., Byrne, D., White, L. A., & Kelley, K. (1988). Erotophobia-erotophilia as a dimension of personality. *Journal of Sex Research, 25,* 123–151.

Follingstad, D. R., & Kimbrell, C. D. (1986). Sex fantasies revisited: An expansion and further clarification of variables affecting sex fantasy production. *Archives of Sexual Behavior, 15,* 475.

Geis, B. D., & Gerrard, M. (1984). Predicting male and female contraceptive behavior: A discriminant analysis of groups high, moderate, and low in contraceptive effectiveness. *Journal of Personality and Social Psychology, 46,* 669–680.

Gerrard, M. (1977). Sex guilt in abortion patients. *Journal of Consulting and Clinical Psychology, 45,* 708.

Gerrard, M. (1980). Sex guilt and attitudes toward sex in sexually active and inactive female college students. *Journal of Personality Assessment, 44,* 258–261.

Gerrard, M. (1982). Sex, sex guilt, and contraceptive use. *Journal of Personality and Social Psychology, 42,* 153–158.

Gerrard, M. (1987). Sex, sex guilt, and contraceptive use revisited: The 1980s. *Journal of Personality and Social Psychology, 52,* 975–980.

Gerrard, M., & Gibbons, F. X. (1982). Sexual experience, sex guilt, and sexual moral reasoning. *Journal of Personality, 50*, 345–359.

Gibbons, F. X. (1978). Sexual standards and reactions to pornography: Enhancing behavioral consistency through self-focused attention. *Journal of Personality and Social Psychology, 36*, 976–987.

Gibbons, F. X., & Wright, R. A. (1981). Motivational biases in causal attributions of arousal. *Journal of Personality and Social Psychology, 40*, 588–600.

Gibbons, F. X., & Wright, R. A. (1983). Self-focused attention and reactions to conflicting standards. *Journal of Research in Personality, 17*, 263–273.

Green, S. E., & Mosher, D. L. (1985). A causal model of sexual arousal to erotic fantasies. *Journal of Sex Research, 21*, 1–23.

Greendlinger, V. (1985). Authoritarianism as a predictor of response to heterosexual and homosexual erotica. *High School Journal, 68*, 183–186.

Griffitt, W., & Kaiser, D. L. (1978). Affect, sex guilt, gender, and the rewarding-punishing effects of erotic stimuli. *Journal of Personality and Social Psychology, 36*, 850–858.

Gunderson, M. P., & McCary, J. L. (1979). Sexual guilt and religion. *Family Coordinator, 28*, 353–357.

Harrell, T. H., & Stolp, R. D. (1985). Effects of erotic guided imagery on female sexual arousal and emotional response. *Journal of Sex Research, 21*, 292–304.

Hawkins, R. C., Turell, S., & Jackson, L. J. (1983). Desirable and undesirable masculine and feminine traits in relation to students' dieting tendencies and body image dissatisfaction. *Sex Roles, 9*, 705–718.

Heiser, P., & Gannon, L. R. (1984). The relationship of sex-role stereotypy to anger expression and the report of psychosomatic symptoms. *Sex Roles, 10*, 601–611.

Hendrick, S., & Hendrick, C. (1987). Multidimensionality of sexual attitudes. *Journal of Sex Research, 23*, 502–526.

Hoddinott, E., & Follingstad, D. R. (1983). Effects of instructional set and personality variables on the use of touching. *Perceptual and Motor Skills, 56*, 299–309.

Janda, L. H., & O'Grady, K. E. (1980). Development of a sex anxiety inventory. *Journal of Consulting and Clinical Psychology, 48*, 169–175.

Janda, L. H., O'Grady, K. E., Nichelous, J., Harsher, D., Denny, C., & Denner, K. (1981). Effects of sex guilt on interpersonal pleasuring. *Journal of Personality and Social Psychology, 40*, 201–209.

Keller, J. F., Eakes, E., Hinkle, D., & Hughston, G. A. (1978). Sexual behavior and guilt among women: A cross-generational comparison. *Journal of Sex and Marital Therapy, 4*, 259–265.

Kelley, K. (1985). Sex, sex guilt, and authoritarianism: Differences in responses to explicit heterosexual and masturbatory slides. *Journal of Sex Research, 21*, 68–85.

Klenke-Hamel, K. E., & Janda, L. H. (1979). The Mosher Forced-Choice Guilt Scale as a measure of anxiety. *Journal of Personality Assessment, 43*, 150–154.

Lang, A. R., Searles, J., Lauerman, R., & Adesso, V. J. (1980). Expectancy, alcohol, and sex guilt as determinants of interest in and reaction to sexual stimuli. *Journal of Abnormal Psychology, 89*, 644–653.

Mendelsohn, M. J., & Mosher, D. L. (1979). Effects of sex guilt and premarital sexual permissiveness on role-played sex education and moral attitudes. *Journal of Sex Research, 15*, 174–183.

Moreault, D., & Follingstad, D. R. (1978). Sexual fantasies of females as a function of sex guilt and experimental response cues. *Journal of Consulting and Clinical Psychology, 46*, 1385–1393.

Morokoff, P. J. (1985). Effects of sex guilt, repression, sexual "arousability," and sexual experience on female sexual arousal during erotica and fantasy. *Journal of Personality and Social Psychology, 49*, 177–187.

Morokoff, P. J. (1986). Volunteer bias in the psychophysiological study of female sexuality. *Journal of Sex Research, 22*, 35–51.

Mosher, D. L. (undated). *Revised Mosher Guilt Inventory*. Unpublished manuscript.

Mosher, D. L. (1979). Sex guilt and sex myths in college men and women. *Journal of Sex Research, 15*, 224–234.

Mosher, D. L. (1988). Revised Mosher Guilt Inventory. In C. M. Davis, W. L. Yarber, & S. L. Davis (Eds.), *Sexuality-related measures: A compendium* (pp. 152–155). Syracuse: Editors.

Mosher, D. L., & Abramson, P. R. (1977). Subjective sexual arousal to films of masturbation. *Journal of Consulting and Clinical Psychology, 45*, 796–806.

Mosher, D. L., & O'Grady, K. E. (1979a). Homosexual threat, negative attitudes toward masturbation, sex guilt, and males' sexual and affective reactions to explicit sexual films. *Journal of Consulting and Clinical Psychology, 47*, 860–873.

Mosher, D. L., & O'Grady, K. E. (1979b). Sex guilt, trait anxiety, and females' subjective sexual arousal to erotica. *Motivation and Emotion, 3*, 235–249.

Mosher, D. L., & Vonderheide, S. G. (1985). Contributions of sex guilt and masturbation guilt to women's contraceptive attitudes and use. *Journal of Sex Research, 21*, 24–39.

Mosher, D. L., & White, B. B. (1980). Effects of committed or casual erotic guided imagery on females' subjective sexual arousal and emotional response. *Journal of Sex Research, 16*, 273–299.

Myers, L. S., & Morokoff, P. J. (1986). Physiological and subjective sexual arousal in pre- and postmenopausal women and post menopausal women taking replacement therapy. *Psychophysiology, 23*, 283–292.

O'Grady, K. E. (1982). Affect, sex guilt, gender, and the rewarding-punishing effects of erotic stimuli: A reanalysis and reinterpretation. *Journal of Personality and Social Psychology, 43*, 618–622.

O'Grady, K. E., & Janda, L. H. (1978). Psychometric correlates of the Mosher Forced-Choice Guilt Inventory. *Journal of Consulting and Clinical Psychology, 46*, 1581–1582.

O'Grady, K. E., & Janda, L. H. (1979). Factor analysis of the Mosher Forced-Choice Guilt Inventory. *Journal of Consulting and Clinical Psychology, 47*, 1131–1133.

O'Grady, K. E., Janda, L. H., & Gillen, H. B. (1979). A multidimensional scaling analysis of sex guilt. *Multivariate Behavioral Research, 14*, 415–434.

Perlman, S. D., & Abramson, P. R. (1982). Sexual satisfaction among married and cohabiting individuals. *Journal of Consulting and Clinical Psychology, 50*, 458–460.

Pinhas, V. (1980). Sex guilt and sexual control in women alcoholics in early sobriety. *Sexuality and Disability, 3*, 256–272.

Propper, S., & Brown, R. A. (1986). Moral reasoning, parental sex attitudes, and sex guilt in female college students. *Archives of Sexual Behavior, 25*, 123–151.

Rader, G. E., Bekker, L. D., Brown, L., & Richardt, C. (1978). Psychological correlates of unwanted pregnancy. *Journal of Abnormal Psychology, 87*, 373–376.

Rizzo, A. A., Fehr, L. A., McMahon, P. M., & Stamps, L. E. (1981). Mosher Guilt scores and sexual preference. *Journal of Clinical Psychology, 37*, 827–830.

Schill, T., Van Tuinen, M., & Doty, D. (1980). Repeated exposure to pornography and arousal levels of subjects varying in guilt. *Psychological Reports, 46*, 467–471.

Schover, L. R. (1980, September). *Gender differences in therapist responses to client sexual material.* Paper presented at the meeting of the American Psychological Association, Montreal. (ERIC Document Reproduction Service No. ED 201 915)

Schover, L. R. (1981). Male and female therapists' responses to male and female client sexual material: An analogue study. *Archives of Sexual Behavior, 10*, 477–492.

Slane, S., & Morrow, L. (1981). Race differences in feminism and guilt. *Psychological Reports, 49*, 45–46.

Snell, W. E., Jr., Belk, S. S., & Hawkins, R. C., II. (1986). The Stereotypes About Male Sexuality Scale (SAMSS): Components, correlates, antecedents, consequences and counselor bias. *Social and Behavioral Science Documents, 16*, 9. (Ms. No. 2746)

Wanlass, R. L., Kilmann, P. R., Bella, B. S., & Tarnowski, K. J. (1983). Effects of sex education on sexual guilt, anxiety, and attitudes: A comparison of instruction formats. *Archives of Sexual Behavior, 12*, 487–502.

Weis, C. B., & Dain, R. N. (1979). Ego development and sex attitudes in heterosexual and homosexual men and women. *Archives of Sexual Behavior, 8*, 341–356.

Yarber, W. L., & Anno, T. (1981). Changes in sex guilt, premarital sexual intimacy attitudes and sexual behavior during a human sexuality course. *Health Education, 12*(5), 17–21.

Yarber, W. L., & Yee, B. (1983). Heterosexuals' attitudes toward lesbianism and male homosexuality: Their affective orientation toward sexuality and sex guilt. *Journal of American College Health, 31*(5), 203–208.

Zuroff, D. C., Moskowitz, D. S., Wielgus, M. S., Powers, T. A., & Franko, D. L. (1983). Construct validation of the Dependency Self-Criticism Scales of the Depressive Experiences Questionnaire. *Journal of Research in Personality, 17*, 226–241.

BIBLIOGRAPHY:

Beere, C. A. (1979). *Women and women's issues: A handbook of tests and measures* (pp. 494–499). San Francisco: Jossey-Bass.

SEX ANXIETY INVENTORY (SAI)

AUTHORS: Louis H. Janda and Kevin E. O'Grady

DATE: 1980

VARIABLE: Anxiety concerning sex, defined as "a generalized expectancy for nonspecific external punishment for the violation of perceived normative sexual standards" (Janda & O'Grady, 1980, p. 169)

TYPE OF INSTRUMENT: Forced choice

DESCRIPTION: The Sex Anxiety Inventory (SAI) consists of 25 forced-choice items in which each sentence stem is followed by one response option that is indicative of sex anxiety and one option that is not. Respondents are to select the option that applies to them. Items pertain to a variety of sex-related topics such as specific sexual behaviors (e.g., petting, oral sex), sexual behavior in general, sexual thoughts, masturbation, extramarital sex, group sex, dirty jokes, pornography, and flirting. When the scale is administered, the 25 items are interspersed with 13 filler items.

SAMPLE ITEMS: Extramarital sex (a) is OK if everyone agrees. (b) can break up families.

If I were to flirt with someone (a) I would worry about his or her reaction. (b) I would enjoy it.

PREVIOUS SUBJECTS: College students

APPROPRIATE FOR: College students and older

ADMINISTRATION: Self-administered; about 15–20 minutes (including the filler items)

SCORING: For each item, there is a keyed response (Janda & O'Grady, 1980; Janda, 1988); that is, one response is indicative of sex anxiety. One point is assigned each time the respondent selects the keyed response. Thus, total scores can range from 0 (no sex anxiety) to 25 (high sex anxiety).

DEVELOPMENT: A pool of 40 forced-choice items was administered to 95 college men and 135 college women, who also completed the Mosher Forced Choice Guilt Inventory (MFCGI) (Mosher, 1966) (see separate entry for Revised Mosher Guilt Inventory) and the Marlowe-Crowne Social Desirability Scale (Crowne & Marlowe, 1964). Janda and O'Grady (1980) reported that "in writing the items, attention was paid to presenting pairs of endings for each item that could be considered equally good (or bad) and that we believed would have similar probability of endorsement in the population" (p. 170), but they did not present any data to demonstrate whether the pairs of endings were in fact of equal desirability. Items were selected for the final version of the SAI if they met four criteria: (1) a significant correlation between item and total SAI scores, (2) similar item-total correlation for males and for females, (3) an item-SAI correlation that is stronger than the item's correlation with the Sex Guilt subscale of the MFCGI, and (4) an item-SAI correlation that is stronger than the item's correlation with the Marlowe-Crowne Social Desirability Scale. The application of these criteria led to the selection of 25 items. Four were significantly correlated with the Marlowe-Crowne Social Desirability scores.

RELIABILITY: Kuder-Richardson reliability was estimated using the same data used to develop the scale. The reliability estimate was .86 (Janda & O'Grady, 1980). In order to estimate the test-retest reliability of the SAI, the scale was administered to a different sample of 66 college men and 72 college women on two occasions, separated by 10 to 14 days. Test-retest reliability was .84 for the college women and .85 for the college men (Janda & O'Grady, 1980).

VALIDITY: For the 95 college men and 135 college women used to develop the SAI (Janda & O'Grady, 1980), the correlation between SAI scores and scores on the Sex Guilt subscale of the MFCGI was .67, and the correlation between the SAI scores and scores on the Marlowe-Crowne Social Desirability Scale was .07. There was a significant difference between the mean scores of the college men and the college women, with the college women showing significantly more sex anxiety.

Janda and O'Grady (1980) used the results of their factor analysis (see NOTES & COMMENTS) to compute weighted composite scores on each of three factors. Correlating these factor scores with scores on the Sex Guilt subscale of the MFCGI, they obtained correlations of .37, .15, and .41 for the three factors, respectively. All three correlations were significant at the .001 level. When the three factor scores were correlated with scores on the Marlowe-Crowne Social Desirability Scale, only Factor III scores yielded a statistically significant correlation (r = .19).

In order to determine the effects of intentionally faking responses on the SAI, Janda and O'Grady (1980) administered the SAI to 20 college men and 20 college women. Each respondent completed the scale under three different sets of instructions: "answer honestly, attempt to create a favorable impression, and attempt to create an unfavorable impression" (p. 172). Both males and females had significantly higher scores when attempting to create a favorable impression (fake good). In addition, in the fake good condition, females had a significantly higher score than males. Surprisingly, some men had lower scores when they were asked to create a favorable impression and higher scores when they were asked to create an unfavorable impression. This was not true for any of the women. The authors concluded that "instructional and motivational variables are an important consideration when using the SAI" (p. 173).

In addition to factor analyzing responses to the SAI (see NOTES & COMMENTS), Janda and O'Grady (1980) combined items from the SAI with items from the Sex Guilt subscale of the MFCGI and factor analyzed responses to all 53 items using responses from 228 subjects. Seven factors were extracted. Twelve of the 25 SAI items loaded on the first factor; only 3 MFCGI items loaded on this factor. Seventeen of the 28 MFCGI items loaded on three factors; only 1 SAI item loaded on any of these three factors. The remaining three factors included items from both the SAI and MFCGI.

An independent sample of 72 college women and 113 college men completed the SAI, the MFCGI, and Zuckerman's (1973) Heterosexual Experience Scales (see separate entry). A regression analysis for women showed that both the SAI and the MFCGI contributed significantly to the prediction of scores on the Heterosexual Experience Scales. For men, only the SAI contributed significantly to the prediction.

Tolor and Barbieri (1981) tested 115 college students with the SAI and looked at the relationship between their SAI scores and results on two projective measures of sexual anxiety. A "highly experienced clinician" (p. 546) scored the students' responses on the Bender-Gestalt test and the Draw-A-Person test. Correlations between the SAI scores and these two measures were nonsignificant. Furthermore, global judgments on the part of the clinician did not differentiate between the high and low scorers on the SAI. Overall Tolor and Barbieri concluded that "there is very little clinically useful correspondence between scores on the new Sex Anxiety Inventory and projective measures of sex anxiety" (p. 546).

NOTES & COMMENTS: (1) In addition to defining sex anxiety (see VARIABLE), Janda and O'Grady (1980) differentiated sex anxiety from sex guilt by stating that "guilty individuals are concerned with what they will think of themselves, whereas sexually anxious individuals are concerned with what others will think of them" (p. 170).

(2) Janda and O'Grady (1980) factor analyzed responses from the 95 college men and 135 college women whose data were used to develop the scale. Three factors were extracted: Factor I "appeared to reflect feelings of discomfort in social situations in which sexuality is implied" (p. 172), Factor II "appeared to deal with socially unacceptable forms of sexual behavior" (p. 172), and Factor III "appeared to be related to sexuality experienced in private" (p. 172). The three factors, respectively, accounted for 50.8%, 13.0%, and 10.2% of the variance.

(3) Wanlass, Kilmann, Bella, and Tarnowski (1983) used the SAI as one of several measures to evaluate the effectiveness of different formats for teaching sex education. Geis and Gerrard (1984) conducted a study with college students to identify variables that could differentiate three contraceptive effectiveness groups (low, moderate, and high). Scores from the SAI were one of the variables they included in their multivariate analysis. In a related study, Burger and Inderbitzen (1985) used the SAI as one of several measures in a study designed to identify predictors of

college students' contraceptive use. Kilmann et al. (1987) used the SAI as one of several measures to compare the effectiveness of three approaches for treating secondary erectile dysfunction.

AVAILABLE FROM: Janda and O'Grady, 1980; Janda, 1988

USED IN:

Burger, J. M., & Inderbitzen, H. M. (1985). Predicting contraceptive behavior among college students: The role of communication, knowledge, sexual anxiety, and self-esteem. *Archives of Sexual Behavior, 14,* 343–350.

Geis, B. D., & Gerrard, M. (1984). Predicting male and female contraceptive behavior: A discriminant analysis of groups high, moderate, and low in contraceptive effectiveness. *Journal of Personality and Social Psychology, 46,* 669–680.

Janda, L. H. (1988). The Sex Anxiety Inventory. In C. M. Davis, W. L. Yarber, & S. L. Davis (Eds.), *Sexuality-related measures: A compendium* (pp. 19–20). Syracuse: Editors.

Janda, L. H., & O'Grady, K. E. (1980). Development of a sex anxiety inventory. *Journal of Consulting and Clinical Psychology, 48,* 169–175.

Kilmann, P. R., Milan, R. J., Jr., Boland, J. P., Nankin, H. R., Davidson, E., West, M. O., Sabalis, R. F., Caid, C., & Devine, J. M. (1987). Group treatment of secondary erectile dysfunction. *Journal of Sex and Marital Therapy, 13,* 168–182.

Tolor, A., & Barbieri, R. J. (1981). Different facets of sex anxiety. *Perceptual and Motor Skills, 52,* 546.

Wanlass, R. L., Kilmann, P. R., Bella, B. S., & Tarnowski, K. J. (1983). Effects of sex education on sexual guilt, anxiety, and attitudes: A comparison of instruction formats. *Archives of Sexual Behavior, 12,* 487–502.

BIBLIOGRAPHY:

Crowne, D., & Marlowe, D. (1964). *The approval motive.* New York: Wiley.

Mosher, D. L. (1966). The development and multitrait-multimethod matrix analysis of three measures of three aspects of guilt. *Journal of Consulting Psychology, 30,* 25–29.

Zuckerman, M. (1973). Scales for sex experience for males and females. *Journal of Consulting and Clinical Psychology, 41,* 27–29.

SEXUAL FANTASY QUESTIONNAIRES

AUTHORS: William B. Arndt, Jr., John C. Foehl, and F. Elaine Good

DATE: 1985

VARIABLE: Sexual fantasies: themes and frequency

TYPE OF INSTRUMENT: Summated rating scale

DESCRIPTION: There are two forms of the Sexual Fantasy Questionnaires: a female form and a male form. The female form lists 20 sexual fantasies that a female might experience. There are 5 fantasies representing each of four factors: Romance, Variety, Suffer, and Dominance. The male form lists 20 sexual fantasies that a male might experience. Again, there are 5 fantasies representing each of four factors: Force, Same Sex, Unpopular, and Macho. For each fantasy, respondents list

the frequency with which they had the fantasy during the prior year. Response options range from "(1) never" to "(7) once a day or more."
SAMPLE ITEMS: (The first four items are from the female form.)

(Romance) I'm a very glamorous woman and an extremely handsome man is having sex with me.

(Variety) A man is watching me masturbate.

(Suffer) Several boys are tied in a row. I bring each of them to erection.

(Dominance) An older man is seducing me.

(The last four items are from the male form.)

(Force) I'm spanking a woman because she's been naughty.

(Same Sex) Another man and I are having sex with a woman.

(Unpopular) A woman is watching me urinate.

(Macho) A woman tells me that she wants my body.

PREVIOUS SUBJECTS: College students
APPROPRIATE FOR: College students and adults
ADMINISTRATION: Self-administered; about 10 minutes
SCORING: Individual items are scored on a 7-point scale, with higher scores assigned to responses representing greater frequency. On each form, item scores are summed to yield four factor scores and a total score.
DEVELOPMENT: The fantasy themes for women were derived from Friday (1974, 1975) and Shanor (1977); the themes for men were based on Friday (1980) and Slattery (1975). Items were administered to 138 college women and 125 college men. Their responses were factor analyzed. Factor 1 for women, Romantic, included items presenting the woman as attractive and the male as admiring and gentle. Factor 2, Variety, contained fantasies involving both watching and being watched as one engages in sexual activities. Factor 3, Suffer, dealt with bondage, suffering, pain, and punishment. Factor 4, Dominance, concerned fantasies involving dominance or submission themes. Factor 1 for males, Force, included items dealing with the use of force in sexual encounters. Factor 2, Same Sex, contained fantasies that involved at least one other man. Factor 3, Unpopular, described three fantasies pertaining to urination, one pertaining to kissing large breasts, and one pertaining to women's legs. Factor 4, Macho, contained items dealing with a man's being very exciting and appealing to women. The scale, as described here, includes the five most salient fantasies on each factor.
RELIABILITY: No information was provided.
VALIDITY: Using total sexual fantasy scores and a median split procedure, the researchers divided women and men into two groups: high scorers and low scorers. A discriminant analysis on the women's data showed significant differences on all four factors. A discriminant analysis on the men's data showed a significant difference on only one factor: Same Sex (Arndt, Foehl, & Good, 1985).

Arndt et al. (1985) reported that, for women, the largest factor intercorrelations were between Romance and Dominance (r = .41) and between Variety and Dominance (r = .47). The remaining intercorrelations for females were less than .25. For males, the largest factor intercorrelations were between Force and Macho (r = .42) and between Force and Same Sex (r = .28). The remaining intercorrelations were all below .20.

Arndt et al. (1985) administered the Guilford-Zimmerman Temperament Survey (Guilford, Guilford, & Zimmerman, 1978) (see Beere, 1990) and a sexual behaviors questionnaire in addition to the Sexual Fantasy Questionnaires. They found that those scoring high on the various factors had identifiable personality traits or behaviors. Arndt et al. (1985) concluded that "the existence of four relatively independent male and female fantasy factors, each associated with differing personality and sexual patterns, support the contention that sexual fantasies are multidimensional" (p. 478).

NOTES & COMMENTS: Arndt et al. (1985) made no claims for their "scale." In fact, they never labeled it as a scale. However, the measure seems to hold promise for researchers, and there are not many competing measures in the area of sexual fantasy. Before the scale is used by other researchers, however, reliability estimates are needed. Furthermore, because scale development was based on factor analysis and the number of items was large relative to the number of subjects, there needs to be a replication of the factor structure.

AVAILABLE FROM: Arndt, Foehl, and Good, 1985

USED IN:

Arndt, W. B., Jr., Foehl, J. C., & Good, F. E. (1985). Specific sexual fantasy themes: A multidimensional study. *Journal of Personality and Social Psychology, 48,* 472–480.

BIBLIOGRAPHY:

Beere, C. A. (1990). *Gender roles: A handbook of tests and measures.* Westport, CT: Greenwood.

Friday, N. (1974). *My secret garden.* New York: Pocket Books.

Friday, N. (1975). *Forbidden flowers.* New York: Pocket Books.

Friday, N. (1980). *Men in love.* New York: Dell.

Guilford, J. P., Guilford, J. S., & Zimmerman, W. S. (1978). *The Guilford-Zimmerman Temperament Survey.* Beverly Hills, CA: Sheridan Psychological Services.

Shanor, K. (1977). *The fantasy files.* New York: Dial Press.

Slattery, W. J. (1975). *The erotic imagination.* New York: Bantam Books.

SEXUAL FUNCTION AFTER GYNECOLOGIC ILLNESS SCALE (SFAGIS)

AUTHORS: Diane D. Bransfield, Jean-Claude Horiot, and Abdenour Nabid

DATE: 1984

VARIABLE: Level of sexual functioning after treatment for gynecologic cancer
TYPE OF INSTRUMENT: Multiple choice
DESCRIPTION: The Sexual Function After Gynecologic Illness Scale (SFAGIS) consists of 30 sentence stems, each followed by five response options. Item content is varied and pertains to such topics as sexual desire, frequency, satisfaction, and fears. The last 2 items on the SFAGIS are appropriate only for patients who have had radiotherapy.
SAMPLE ITEMS: My sexual desire is (0) very low, (1) low, (2) normal for me, (3) strong, (4) very strong.

When I would like to have sexual relations, (0) this is not possible because I do not have a partner (husband/lover), (1) this does not concern me because I do not want sexual relations, (2) this is not possible because my partner cannot have sexual relations, (3) this is sometimes possible with my partner, (4) this is always possible with my partner.
PREVIOUS SUBJECTS: Surgical and radiotherapy patients with cervical, uterine, and ovarian cancer in the United States and France
APPROPRIATE FOR: Women treated for gynecological cancer
ADMINISTRATION: Self-administered; about 15–20 minutes
SCORING: Each response option is assigned a score, and the total score is the sum of the item scores. An item score of 0 reflects "no sexual desire, lack of a partner, anxiety or fear about sexual functioning, sexual inactivity, severe vaginal insufficiency, no previous discussion of sexual functioning with the physician, or no desire to discuss sexual functioning with a health provider" (Bransfield, Horiot, & Nabid, 1984, p. 14). An item score of 4 represents "high libido, availability of a partner, no anxiety or fear about sexual functioning, much sexual activity, no vaginal insufficiency, discussion of sexual functioning with the physician during the treatment, or desire to discuss sexual functioning with a health provider" (p. 14). Item scores of 2, 3, and 4 were regarded by Bransfield et al. as passing, and item scores of 0 or 1 were regarded as failing. Total scores can range from 0 to 112 for patients not receiving radiotherapy and from 0 to 120 for patients receiving radiotherapy.
DEVELOPMENT: Based on a review of the relevant literature, the authors identified 15 content areas to be represented on the scale: sexual desire, unavailability of a partner, patient's fears about sexual activity, partner's fear about sexual activity, sexual satisfaction, initiation of sexual activity, affectionate behavior, frequency of sexual intercourse, frequency of orgasm, vaginal dimensions and mucosal condition, potential for vaginal lubrication, intervention of health provider, desire for sexual information, changes in sexual activity after therapy, and compliance with a prescription for a dilator (for radiotherapy patients only). Two items were written representing each of these 15 factors. The 30 items were pilot tested with 10 patients, and their feedback was used to make

slight modifications in the items. The scale was then translated into French, and based on staff input, additional minor modifications were made.

RELIABILITY: Based on 30 gynecological cancer patients, corrected split-half reliability was .80, and Kuder-Richardson reliability was .76. Corrected item-total correlations ranged from −.10 to .84, with a mean of .54.

VALIDITY: No information was provided. Although Bransfield et al. (1984) made some general comments about the face validity, content validity, and concurrent validity of the SFAGIS, they did not provide data to support their contentions.

NOTES & COMMENTS: (1) Bransfield et al. (1984) developed a shorter form of the SFAGIS. Since each of the original 15 content areas was represented by 2 items, the authors selected the 1 item in each pair that had the larger range of responses and a response distribution closer to the normal curve. There were three exceptions to this. For 1 content area, the 2 items were not highly correlated with each other, and so both items were retained. For 2 other content areas, both items were considered to provide necessary information that was not available elsewhere in the SFAGIS. Thus, those 4 items were retained. As a result, the shortened version of the SFAGIS contains a total of 18 items.

(2) The SFAGIS is included here because no comparable scales were identified. However, one should be cautious in using the scale. Item content appears very heterogeneous. Item-total correlations were sometimes very low and even negative, but no scale revisions were made to correct this problem. Furthermore, the response options for some items do not appear to form a continuum. For example, in the second example listed under SAMPLE ITEMS, it is difficult to understand why options 0, 1, and 2 are scored differently from each other. Each one states that the respondent is not sexually active, but the cause of the sexual inactivity may be totally independent of the gynecological cancer. Furthermore, options 3 and 4 indicate that the respondent is sexually active. There appears to be no option indicating that the respondent is not sexually active and the sexual inactivity is caused by her or her partner's feelings about gynecological cancer. Researchers considering this scale must review the items very carefully.

AVAILABLE FROM: Bransfield, Horiot, and Nabid, 1984

USED IN:

Bransfield, D. D., Horiot, J. C., & Nabid, A. (1984). Development of a scale for assessing sexual function after treatment for gynecologic cancer. *Journal of Psychosocial Oncology*, *2*, 3–19.

SEXUAL FUNCTIONS SCALE

AUTHOR: Paul A. Nelson

DATE: 1978

VARIABLE: Motivations for engaging in sexual acts
TYPE OF INSTRUMENT: Summated rating scale
DESCRIPTION: The Sexual Functions Scale consists of 56 items, with 8 items representing each of seven subscales. The Hedonism subscale contains items relating to a need for pleasure; the Recognition subscale contains items relating to a need for positive recognition from others; the Dominance subscale contains items dealing with the need to control another person; the Submission subscale contains items dealing with the need to be controlled by others; the Conformity subscale contains items pertaining to the need to conform to others' expectations in order to gain acceptance; the Personal Love and Affection subscale contains items relating to the need for affection and intimacy; and the Novelty subscale contains items dealing with a need for excitement and novelty. Each item is a statement that may or may not describe a motivation for engaging in sexual behaviors. Using a 4-point scale ranging from "Very Important" to "Not Important at All," respondents indicate the importance of each potential source of motivation.
SAMPLE ITEMS: (Hedonism) Because I'm a pleasure seeker.
(Recognition) Because others admire a person who is sexually experienced.
(Dominance) Because it makes me feel masterful.
(Submission) Because sex allows me to feel.
(Conformity) Because I want to be like everyone else.
(Personal Love and Affection) Because it makes me feel as one with another person.
(Novelty) Because I'm stimulated by curiosity.
PREVIOUS SUBJECTS: College students
APPROPRIATE FOR: Sexually active persons; however, results may be very different for different age groups
ADMINISTRATION: Self-administered; about 20–30 minutes
SCORING: Items are individually scored on a 4-point scale, with higher scores assigned to the response indicating greater importance. Item scores can be summed to yield scores for each of the seven subscales: Hedonism, Recognition, Dominance, Submission, Conformity, Personal Love and Affection, and Novelty. Alternately scores can be obtained for each of five factor analytically derived subscales: Pleasurable Stimulation based on 15 items, Conformity-Acceptance based on 11 items, Personal Love and Affection based on 9 items, Power based on 8 items, and Recognition-Competition based on 4 items.
DEVELOPMENT: Nelson and Swanson (cited in Nelson, 1978) developed a scale to measure functions of sexual behavior. Since it was originally developed for use in a prison setting, the scale had to be revised for use with a college population. The only revision Nelson (1978) specifically described was the rewriting of some items "so as to elicit more

differentiated responding" (p. 29). This revision was done because some items were redundant.

RELIABILITY: Using responses from 395 college students, Nelson (1978) calculated coefficient alpha for each of the seven subscales and obtained the following results: Hedonism = .83, Recognition = .83, Dominance = .83, Submission = .77, Conformity = .85, Personal Love and Affection = .85, and Novelty = .84.

A subset of 30 subjects participating in Nelson's (1978) research was asked to take home a copy of the Sexual Functions Scale to be completed by a significant person, someone who would know him or her well. The significant person was to complete the scale as the subject would complete it. Calculation of alpha coefficients for this group were: Hedonism = .91, Recognition = .92, Dominance = .87, Submission = .86, Conformity = .86, Personal Love and Affection = .93, and Novelty = .87.

VALIDITY: To provide evidence of the convergent validity of the Sexual Functions Scale, Nelson (1978) correlated scores from 30 persons who completed the scale for themselves with the scores obtained when the scale was completed by these respondents' "significant others"; that is, each of 30 people asked a significant person to complete the scale as she or he thought the subject would. For five of the subscales, the correlations were statistically significant: Hedonism = .72, Recognition = .63, Dominance = .49, Submission = .47, and Novelty = .53. For two subscales, Conformity and Personal Love and Affection, the correlations were nonsignificant.

To provide evidence of the discriminant validity of the Sexual Functions Scale, Nelson (1978) compared subscale reliabilities with subscale intercorrelations. Although 19 of the 21 subscale intercorrelations were significant, and some were quite substantial, the subscale reliabilities were all higher than the highest subscale intercorrelation.

NOTES & COMMENTS: (1) Nelson (1978) factor analyzed the responses from 395 college students. He identified five factors that jointly accounted for all of the variance. Factor 1 was labeled "Pleasurable Stimulation" and contained items from the Hedonism and Novelty subscales. Factor 2 was labeled "Conformity-Acceptance" and contained items from the Recognition and Conformity subscales. Factor 3 was labeled "Personal Love and Affection" and contained items from the subscale of the same name. Factor 4 was labeled "Power" and contained items from the Dominance and Submission subscales. Factor 5 was labeled "Recognition-Competition" and contained items from the Recognition subscale. For an item to be included on a factor, it had to have a loading of at least .40. Given that the sample size was somewhat small relative to the number of items, the factor structure may be unstable.

(2) The Sexual Functions Scale has been used in studies looking at sexual aggression (Malamuth, 1986, 1989) and reactions to pornography

and rape depictions (Malamuth & Check, 1983, 1985). Nelson (1978) used the Sexual Functions Scale to examine the relationship between sexual behavior and personality variables. In particular, he wanted to test the hypothesis that scores on the Sexual Functions Scale used along with scores from measures of personality traits would more accurately predict sexual behavior than would personality measures used alone. His hypothesis was supported. Whitley (1988) looked at the relationships between gender, gender role, and sexual behavior of college students. He used three measures relating to sexual behavior, and one measure was the Sexual Functions Scale.

AVAILABLE FROM: Nelson, 1978

USED IN:

Malamuth, N. M. (1986). Predictors of naturalistic sexual aggression. *Journal of Personality and Social Psychology, 50*, 953–962.

Malamuth, N. M. (1989). The Attraction to Sexual Aggression Scale: Part two. *Journal of Sex Research 26*, 324–354.

Malamuth, N. M., & Check, J. V. P. (1983). Sexual arousal to rape depictions: Individual differences. *Journal of Abnormal Psychology, 92*, 55–67.

Malamuth, N. M., & Check, J. V. P. (1985). The effects of aggressive pornography on beliefs in rape myths: Individual differences. *Journal of Research in Personality, 19*, 299–320.

Nelson, P. A. (1978). Personality, sexual functions, and sexual behavior: An experiment in methodology (Doctoral dissertation, University of Florida, 1978). *Dissertation Abstracts International, 39*, 6134B. (University Microfilms No. 79–13307)

Whitley, B. E., Jr. (1988). The relation of gender-role orientation to sexual experience among college students. *Sex Roles, 19*, 619–638.

SEXUAL INTERACTION INVENTORY (SII)

AUTHORS: Joseph LoPiccolo and Jeffrey C. Steger

DATE: 1974

VARIABLE: Sexual adjustment and sexual satisfaction

TYPE OF INSTRUMENT: Summated rating scale

DESCRIPTION: The Sexual Interaction Inventory (SII) consists of 102 items. There are six questions for each of 17 heterosexual behaviors. The six questions pertain to frequency of the activity, desired frequency of the activity, reaction to the activity, perception of mate's reaction to the activity, ideal reaction to the activity for self, and ideal reaction to the activity for mate. Six response options are provided for each item. Response options range from "Never" to "Always" and from "Extremely Unpleasant" to "Extremely Pleasant." Both members of a couple independently must complete the SII in order for it to be scored.

SAMPLE ITEMS: The male seeing the female when she is nude.

The male and female having intercourse with both of them having an orgasm (climax).

PREVIOUS SUBJECTS: Sexually functional and sexually dysfunctional heterosexual couples, older couples, mastectomy patients
APPROPRIATE FOR: Heterosexual couples
ADMINISTRATION: Self-administered; about 40 minutes
SCORING: The SII yields scores on 11 scales. Scales 1 and 2 are titled "Frequency Dissatisfaction—Male" and "Frequency Dissatisfaction—Female." To compute each of these scores, the response to question 1 (current frequency of behavior) is subtracted from the response to question 2 (desired frequency of behavior), and the differences are summed across all 17 behaviors. High scores on this scale represent respondent dissatisfaction with his or her range and/or frequency of sexual behaviors. Scales 3 and 4 are titled "Self Acceptance—Male" and "Self Acceptance—Female." To compute each of these scores, responses to question 3 (self-satisfaction with activity) are subtracted from responses to question 5 (ideal satisfaction with activity), and the differences are again summed across all 17 behaviors. High scores on this scale represent respondent dissatisfaction with the level of pleasure derived from sexual behaviors. Scales 5 and 6 are titled "Pleasure Mean—Male" and "Pleasure Mean—Female." Scores on these scales are based on responses to question 3 (self-satisfaction with activity). The scores are found by averaging the answers across all 17 items. Higher scores represent greater pleasure. Scales 7 and 8 are titled "Perceptual Accuracy, Female of Male" and "Perceptual Accuracy, Male of Female." These scores are found by subtracting a respondent's answers to question 4 (perception of mate's satisfaction with activity) from the mate's answer to question 3 (self-satisfaction with activity). These scales provide an indication of the extent to which each partner is knowledgeable about the mate's satisfaction level. Higher scores represent greater disparity between the perception and the reality. Scales 9 and 10 are titled "Mate Acceptance, Male of Female" and "Mate Acceptance, Female of Male." Scores on these scales reflect the differences between responses to questions 4 (perception of mate's satisfaction with each activity) and 6 (desirable level of mate's satisfaction). Higher scores indicate that the respondent would like the partner to be more responsive. Scale 11, "Total Disagreement," is equal to the sum of the scores on scales 1 to 4 and 7 to 10. LoPiccolo and Steger (1974) provided a sample profile form showing how all scale scores can be standardized and displayed graphically.
DEVELOPMENT: The list of sexual behaviors on the SII was adapted from Bentler's (1968a, 1968b) Heterosexual Behavior Assessment Inventory (see separate entry). The development of the scales was based on LoPiccolo and Steger's clinical experiences.
RELIABILITY: LoPiccolo and Steger (1974) reported both test-retest reliability and internal consistency reliability for each of the 11 scales. Test-retest reliabilities were based on testing 15 couples on two occasions,

with a 2-week interval between testings. Coefficient alpha was computed using the responses from a different set of 78 couples. The test-retest reliabilities were .89, .65, .86, .71, .80, .89, .53, .67, .90, .69, and .82 for Scales 1 through 11, respectively. The alpha coefficients were .89, .85, .85, .89, .92, .93, .85, .80, .92, .90, and .88 for Scales 1 through 11, respectively.

VALIDITY: To provide evidence of the convergent validity of the SII, LoPiccolo and Steger (1974) correlated scores on the 11 scales with responses to a single question asking persons to rate their overall sexual satisfaction on a 6-point scale ranging from "extremely unsatisfactory" to "extremely satisfactory." Nine of the 11 correlations were significantly different from zero, but the magnitude of the correlations was fairly low. The highest correlation ($r = -.35$) was between the rating of sexual satisfaction and Scale 11, Total Disagreement. The balance of the correlations ranged from $-.34$ to $+.24$.

To provide evidence regarding the discriminant validity of the SII, LoPiccolo and Steger (1974) considered scores from 63 couples who were satisfied with their sex lives and compared them with the scores from 28 sexually dysfunctional couples. There were significant differences on 9 of the 11 scales. Scale 5, Pleasure Mean-Male, and Scale 10, Mate Acceptance, Female of Male, failed to produce significant differences. LoPiccolo and Steger also looked at responses given by 16 sexually dysfunctional couples who completed a 15-session treatment program. The researchers compared the pretest/posttest scores from the couples and found significant differences on all 11 scales. All changes were in the predicted direction.

Kilmann et al. (1984) compared SII results from couples in which only the wife experienced sexual dysfunction with results from couples who were sexually satisfied. There were significant differences on 9 of the 11 scales. The Mate Acceptance, Female of Male, and the Perceptual Accuracy, Female of Male, did not show significant differences. Overall the sexually satisfied couples showed greater sexual satisfaction on the SII compared to the couples in which the wife was experiencing sexual dysfunction.

NOTES & COMMENTS: (1) LoPiccolo and Steger (1974) recommended the SII as a diagnostic tool for sex therapists.

(2) Jensen, Witcher, and Upton (1987) investigated the readability of a variety of psychological measures including the SII. They concluded that the instructions on the SII require a sixth-grade reading level, and the items require college-level reading ability.

(3) In reviewing the SII, D'Augelli-Frankel (1986) noted that "its content validity is moderate" (p. 166) because it omits some general sexual activities and does not include specific sexual actions.

(4) The SII has been used to evaluate the effectiveness of various

methods of treating sexual dysfunction (Abramowitz & Sewell, 1980; Chesney, Blakeney, Chan, & Cole, 1981; De Amicis, Goldberg, LoPiccolo, Friedman, & Davies, 1985; Ersner-Hershfield & Kopel, 1979; Fichten, Libman, Takefman, & Brender, 1988; Hartman, 1983; Hartman & Daly, 1983; Kilmann et al., 1987a, 1987b; Libman et al., 1984; LoPiccolo, Heiman, Hogan, & Roberts, 1985; McMullen & Rosen, 1979; Morokoff & Heiman, 1980; Sotile & Kilmann, 1978; Sotile, Kilmann, & Follingstad, 1977; Takefman & Brender, 1984; Zimmer, 1987). The findings from these studies may provide further evidence regarding the validity of the SII.

(5) The SII has also been used to evaluate the effectiveness of various programs designed to improve the quality of the sexual relationship among nondysfunctional couples (Cooper & Stoltenberg, 1987; Nathan & Joanning, 1985; Rowland & Haynes, 1978)

(6) Frank, Dornbush, Webster, and Kolodny (1978) used a measure based on the SII to study the effect of mastectomy on sexual behavior. Kirkpatrick (1980) studied the relationship between sexual satisfaction for women, femininity, and feminism. They used Scale 1 on the SII as the measure of sexual satisfaction. Chesney, Blakeney, Chan, et al. (1981) used the SII as one of several measures in a study designed to identify the factors that differentiate couples who seek sex therapy from couples who do not seek sex therapy. Jemail and LoPiccolo (1982) developed a sexual and a marital defensiveness scale for each sex. The SII was used in the process of validating the new scales. Persky, Charney et al. (1982) used the SII to measure sexual adjustment in a study of the relationship between sexual adjustment and marital adjustment. Persky, Dreisbach et al. (1982) studied the relationships between women's hormones and their sexual behaviors and attitudes. The SII was one of several measures used in the study. Wheeler and Kilmann (1983) used the SII in a study comparing couples engaged in comarital sexual behavior and couples not engaged in such behavior. Coleman (1985) looked at the impact of male bisexuality on the quality of a marriage. One of the measures was the SII.

(7) Zimmer (1987) used the SII with a German sample and concluded that 4 of the 11 scales were reliable and valid.

(8) DeHaan and Wallander (1988) extended the SII to include more items and used the modified measure to compare college women with early and late onset of physical disability.

(9) Nowinski & LoPiccolo (1979) provided a thorough description of the scales on the SII.

AVAILABLE FROM: LoPiccolo and Steger, 1974

USED IN:

Abramowitz, S. I., & Sewell, H. H. (1980). Marital adjustment and sex therapy outcome. *Journal of Sex Research, 16*, 325–337.

Chesney, A. P., Blakeney, P. E., Chan, F. A., & Cole, C. M. (1981). The impact of sex therapy on sexual behaviors and marital communication. *Journal of Sex and Marital Therapy, 7*, 70–79.

Chesney, A. P., Blakeney, P. E., Cole, C. M., & Chan, F. A. (1981). A comparison of couples who have sought sex therapy with couples who have not. *Journal of Sex and Marital Therapy, 7*, 131–140.

Coleman, E. (1985). Integration of male bisexuality and marriage. *Journal of Homosexuality, 11*, 189–207.

Cooper, A., & Stoltenberg, C. D. (1987). Comparison of a sexual enhancement and a communication training program on sexual and marital satisfaction. *Journal of Counseling Psychology, 34*, 309–314.

D'Augelli-Frankel, J. (1986). Sexual Interaction Inventory. *American Journal of Family Therapy, 14*, 165–170.

De Amicis, L. A., Goldberg, D. C., LoPiccolo, J., Friedman, J., & Davies, L. (1985). Clinical follow-up of couples treated for sexual dysfunction. *Archives of Sexual Behavior, 14*, 467–489.

DeHaan, C. B., & Wallander, J. L. (1988). Self-concept, sexual knowledge and attitudes, and parental support in the sexual adjustment of women with early- and late-onset physical disability. *Archives of Sexual Behavior, 17*, 145–161.

Ersner-Hershfield, R., & Kopel, S. (1979). Group treatment of preorgasmic women: Evaluation of partner involvement and spacing of sessions. *Journal of Consulting and Clinical Psychology, 47*, 750–759.

Fichten, C. S., Libman, E., Takefman, J., & Brender, W. (1988). Self-monitoring and self-focus in erectile dysfunction. *Journal of Sex and Marital Therapy, 14*, 120–128.

Frank, D., Dornbush, R. L., Webster, S. K., & Kolodny, R. C. (1978). Mastectomy and sexual behavior: A pilot study. *Sexuality and Disability, 1*, 16–26.

Hartman, L. M. (1983). Effects of sex and marital therapy on sexual interaction and marital happiness. *Journal of Sex and Marital Therapy, 9*, 137–151.

Hartman, L. M., & Daly, E. M. (1983). Relationship factors in the treatment of sexual dysfunction. *Behavior Research Therapy, 21*, 153–160.

Jemail, J. A., & LoPiccolo, J. (1982). A sexual and a marital defensiveness scale for each sex. *American Journal of Family Therapy, 10*, 33–40.

Jensen, B. J., Witcher, D. B., & Upton, L. R. (1987). Readability assessment of questionnaires frequently used in sex and marital therapy. *Journal of Sex and Marriage, 13*, 137–141.

Kilmann, P. R., Milan, R. J., Jr., Boland, J. P., Mills, K. H., Caid, C., Davidson, E., Bella, B., Wanlass, R., Sullivan, J., & Montgomery, B. (1987a). The treatment of secondary orgasmic dysfunction II. *Journal of Sex and Marital Therapy, 13*, 93–105.

Kilmann, P. R., Milan, R. J., Boland, J. P., Nankin, H. R., Davidson, E., West, M. O., Sabalis, R. F., Caid, C., & Devine, J. M. (1987b). Group treatment of secondary erectile dysfunction. *Journal of Sex and Marital Therapy, 13*, 168–182.

Kilmann, P. R., Mills, K. H., Caid, C., Bella, B., Davidson, E., & Wanlass, R. (1984). The sexual interaction of women with secondary orgasmic dysfunction and their partners. *Archives of Sexual Behavior, 13*, 41–49.

Kirkpatrick, C. S. (1980). Sex roles and sexual satisfaction in women. *Psychology of Women Quarterly, 4,* 444–459.

Libman, E., Fichten, C. S., Brender, W., Burstein, R., Cohen, J., & Binik, Y. M. (1984). A comparison of three therapeutic formats in the treatment of secondary orgasmic dysfunction. *Journal of Sex and Marital Therapy, 10,* 147–159.

LoPiccolo, J., Heiman, J. R., Hogan, D. R., & Roberts, C. W. (1985). Effectiveness of single therapists versus cotherapy teams in sex therapy. *Journal of Consulting and Clinical Psychology, 53,* 287–294.

LoPiccolo, J., & Steger, J. C. (1974). The Sexual Interaction Inventory: A new instrument for assessment of sexual dysfunction. *Archives of Sexual Behavior, 3,* 585–595.

McMullen, S., & Rosen, R. C. (1979). Self-administered masturbation training in the treatment of primary orgasmic dysfunction. *Journal of Consulting and Clinical Psychology, 47,* 912–918.

Morokoff, P. J., & Heiman, J. R. (1980). Effects of erotic stimuli on sexually functional and dysfunctional women: Multiple measures before and after sex therapy. *Behavior Research and Therapy, 18,* 127–137.

Nathan, E. P., & Joanning, H. H. (1985). Enhancing marital sexuality: An evaluation of a program for the sexual enrichment of normal couples. *Journal of Sex and Marital Therapy, 11,* 157–164.

Nowinski, J. K., & LoPiccolo, J. (1979). Assessing sexual behavior in couples. *Journal of Sex and Marital Therapy, 5,* 225–243.

Persky, H., Charney, N., Strauss, D., Miller, W. R., O'Brien, C. P., & Lief, H. I. (1982). The relationship of sexual adjustment and related sexual behaviors and attitudes to marital adjustment. *American Journal of Family Therapy, 10,* 38–49.

Persky, H., Dreisbach, L., Miller, W. R., O'Brien, C. P., Khan, M. A., Lief, H. I., Charney, N., & Strauss, D. (1982). The relation of plasma androgen levels to sexual behaviors and attitudes of women. *Psychosomatic Medicine, 44,* 305–319.

Rowland, K. F., & Haynes, S. N. (1978). A sexual enhancement program for elderly couples. *Journal of Sex and Marital Therapy, 4,* 91–113.

Sotile, W. M., & Kilmann, P. R. (1978). Effects of group systematic desensitization on female orgasmic dysfunction. *Archives of Sexual Behavior, 7,* 477–491.

Sotile, W. M., Kilmann, P., & Follingstad, D. R. (1977). A sexual-enhancement workshop: Beyond group systematic desensitization for women's sexual anxiety. *Journal of Sex and Marital Therapy, 3,* 249–255.

Takefman, J., & Brender, W. (1984). An analysis of the effectiveness of two components in the treatment of erectile dysfunction. *Archives of Sexual Behavior, 13,* 321–340.

Wheeler, J., & Kilmann, P. R. (1983). Comarital sexual behavior: Individual and relationship variables. *Archives of Sexual Behavior, 12,* 295–306.

Zimmer, D. (1987). Does marital therapy enhance the effectiveness of treatment for sexual dysfunction? *Journal of Sex and Marital Therapy, 13,* 193–209.

BIBLIOGRAPHY:

Bentler, P. M. (1968a). Heterosexual Behavior Assessment—I. Males. *Behaviour Research and Therapy, 6,* 21–25.

Bentler, P. M. (1968b). Heterosexual Behavior Assessment—II. Females. *Behaviour Research and Therapy, 6,* 27–30.

SEXUAL OPINION SURVEY (SOS)

AUTHORS: Leonard A. White, William A. Fisher, Donn Byrne, and R. Kingma

DATE: 1977

VARIABLE: Erotophobia-erotophilia, defined as "the disposition to respond to sexual cues along a negative-positive dimension of affect and evaluation" (Fisher, Byrne, White, & Kelley, 1988, p. 124); erotophobia implies a negative emotional response to sexuality, and erotophilia implies a positive emotional response to sexuality

TYPE OF INSTRUMENT: Summated rating scale

DESCRIPTION: The Sexual Opinion Survey (SOS) consists of 21 items, each stating a positive or negative reaction to a sexual activity or sexual situation. The items pertain to "autosexual, heterosexual, homosexual behavior; sexual fantasies; and visual stimuli" (Fisher, Byrne et al., 1988, p. 124). Ten items express negative responses to sexual stimuli, and 11 items express positive responses. Each item is accompanied by a 7-point response scale, with the endpoints labeled "I strongly agree," and "I strongly disagree." In the original version of the SOS, 6 items related to "pornography" and 1 item concerned a "go-go dancer." Fisher, Byrne et al. (1988) recommended revising these items. For the revised version, the term *pornography* was replaced with the phrase "erotic (sexually explicit) . . . " in 6 items, and *go-go dancer* was replaced with *stripper*.

A short form of the SOS is described under NOTES & COMMENTS.

SAMPLE ITEMS: I think it would be very entertaining to look at erotica (sexually explicit books, movies, etc.).

Swimming in the nude with a member of the opposite sex would be an exciting experience.

PREVIOUS SUBJECTS: Parents, college students, couples about to have their first child, medical students, health science teachers

APPROPRIATE FOR: Ages 16 and older

ADMINISTRATION: Self-administered; about 10 minutes

SCORING: Items are individually scored on a 7-point scale, with higher scores assigned to the "I strongly disagree" end of the continuum. Scores on the positively phrased items are summed, and the total is subtracted from the sum of the scores on the negatively phrased items. A constant, 67, is added to the difference. Total scores can range from 0 (most erotophobic) to 126 (most erotophilic). Based on factor analytic research (described below), scores can be obtained on each of three factors.

Fisher (1988) cautioned that scores on the SOS may be affected by sexual orientation: "Homosexuals and bisexuals may respond more positively to homosexually oriented items than do heterosexuals, and there are more specifically homosexual than specifically heterosexual items on the scale" (p. 36).

Fisher, Byrne et al. (1988) presented normative data for males and females, college students and adults, and persons in Canada and the United States. They also presented normative data for persons from India, Hong Kong, and Israel and normative data by age, socioeconomic status, and religion. Gilbert and Gamache (1984) presented normative information by sex, marital status, age, socioeconomic status, and race. They also provided a chart for converting raw scores to percentile scores.

DEVELOPMENT: A pool of 53 items was developed and administered to a sample of 88 college men and 103 college women, who also viewed and responded to 19 erotic slides. Responses to 21 of the 53 items were significantly correlated with affective responses to the 19 slides; the correlations were significant for both males and females. These 21 items comprise the SOS. The overall correlation between scores on the 21-item SOS and responses to the slides was .61 for males and .72 for females. Both correlations were significant at the .001 level.

RELIABILITY: Coefficient alpha for the college men used for scale development was .88; for the college women, it was .90. A second sample of 149 college men and 118 college women completed the 21-item SOS. Coefficient alpha was .86 for the men and .82 for the women. Split-half reliability was .84.

Test-retest reliability, with a 2-month interval between testings, was assessed using responses from public school teachers training to become sex educators. For men, the test-retest reliability was .85; for women, it was .80 (Fisher, 1988). Tanner and Pollack (1988) tested monogamous college-age couples and reported a test-retest reliability of .84 based on a testing interval of about 2 weeks.

Based on testing 265 parents, Gilbert and Gamache (1984) obtained a coefficient alpha of .90. Fisher et al. (1979) administered the SOS to 230 unmarried college women. The split-half reliability was .86.

VALIDITY: To cross-validate the item selection procedures, Fisher, Byrne et al. (1988) administered the 21-item SOS to a sample of 149 college men and 118 college women, who also responded to a series of explicit erotic slides. These slides were different from those used in the original item selection procedures. For the college men, every item on the SOS was significantly correlated with responses to the erotic slides. For the women, 19 of the 21 items were significantly correlated with responses to the erotic slides. The correlation between the overall score on the SOS and responses to the erotic slides was .60 for the college men and .54 for the college women.

Fisher, Byrne et al. (1988) reported predictable differences between various groups: males scored higher (more positive) than females; younger respondents scored higher than older respondents; persons with higher socioeconomic status (SES) levels scored higher than persons with lower SES levels; and for males, agnostics scored higher than Protestants or Catholics. Gilbert and Gamache (1984) confirmed these findings in terms of sex, age, and SES. They did not obtain data to enable them to consider differences as a function of religious orientation. Walfish and Myerson (1980) also found a significant sex difference, with males scoring higher than females.

Evidence of the discriminant validity of the SOS was provided by Fisher, Byrne et al. (1988) who found a nonsignificant relationship between SOS scores and scores on the Marlowe-Crowne Social Desirability Scale (Crowne & Marlowe, 1964). Correlations between the two measures ranged from −.11 to +.05.

Fisher, Byrne et al. (1988) administered the SOS to 153 college men and 119 college women who also answered questions regarding their socialization to sex. As predicted, students with low scores (erotophobic) were more likely to report "parental strictness about sex, sex-related guilt, fears, inhibitions, and conservative attitudes . . . avoidance of masturbation, erotica, and (for women, at least) multiple premarital partners" (p. 135).

Researchers (Byrne, Becker, & Przybyla, 1987; Fisher & Gray, 1986; Lemery, 1983; all cited in Fisher, Byrne et al., 1988) have repeatedly found significant and substantial correlations between husbands' and wives' scores on the SOS.

Fisher, Grenier et al. (1988) found that medical students with low SOS scores were more likely to score low on a sex knowledge test.

Fisher, Byrne et al. (1988) recommended modifying the wording of seven items. When the original and revised versions of the SOS were administered to a sample of 323 college students, the correlation between scores on the two versions was .92. Because the revised scale is more consistent with the way people currently speak, the authors recommended using the revised wording.

NOTES & COMMENTS: (1) Semph (1979, as cited in Fisher, Byrne et al., 1988) used regression analyses to develop a short form of the SOS. Five items that were good predictors of SOS scores for each sex comprise the short form of the scale. For a sample of 72 college men, the correlation between the short form and the full-length SOS was .82; for a sample of 173 college women, the correlation was .71. Short form scores were correlated with scores on the Heterosexual Behavior Assessment Inventory (Bentler, 1968) (see separate entry), a measure of heterosexual experience. As expected, for both college men and college women, the correlations were statistically significant. For men, the correlation was .36; for women, the correlation was .38. Yarber and Whitehill (1981) used the short form SOS to study "if a relationship exists between parental affective orientation toward sexuality and how parents respond to questions involving sex-related experiences of their preschool-age children" (p. 36).

(2) Gilbert and Gamache (1984) factor analyzed SOS responses from 287 parents and extracted three factors accounting for 52% of the variance and including 20 of the 21 items; 1 item was included on two factors. Factor 1, accounting for 34% of the variance, contained 10 items and was named Open Sexual Display. This factor contained all of the items regarding pornography and other items expressing a willingness to be open about sexuality. Factor 2 contained 7 items, accounted for 11% of the variance, and was named Sexual Variety. The items deal with "various ways of achieving sexual pleasure or sexual arousal" (p. 301). Factor 3, accounting for 7% of the variance and containing 4 items, was named Homoeroticism. All of the items related to homosexuality. Factor 4, containing 2 items and accounting for 5% of the variance, was judged unreliable and difficult to define. Gilbert and Gamache advised against using Factor 4.

(3) Many researchers have studied the relationship between SOS scores and contraceptive behavior (Fisher, 1984; Fisher et al., 1979; Geis & Gerrard, 1984; Kelley, Smeaton, Byrne, Przybyla, & Fisher, 1987; Tanner & Pollack, 1988). Fisher, Byrne, and White (1983) described and summarized several research studies regarding the relationship between SOS scores and contraceptive behavior.

(4) Walfish and Myerson (1980) studied the relationship between Bem Sex Role Inventory scores (Bem, 1974) (see Beere, 1990) and SOS scores. Fisher, Miller, Byrne, and White (1980) were interested in how situational and personality factors affected college students' responses to communicating a sexual message. One of the personality factors they considered was erotophobia-erotophilia as measured by the SOS. Yarber and Yee (1982/1983) used a 5-item SOS in order to determine whether there is a relationship between erotophobia/erotophilia and attitudes toward male and female homosexuality. Weidner and Griffitt (1983) examined the relationship between SOS scores and perceptions of a rape victim and a rapist. Yarber and Fisher (1983) conducted a study to determine whether SOS scores were related to willingness to engage in behaviors aimed at preventing sexually transmitted diseases. Yarber and McCabe (1981, 1984) looked at whether health science teachers' responses to the SOS related to their ratings of the importance of various topics as part of a sex education program. Daugherty and Burger (1984) related SOS scores to responses to a variety of questions regarding sexual experience, sex guilt, contraceptive use, and sources of learning about sexuality. Weidner and Griffitt (1984) looked at how college students perceive women who have had abortions and men who have impregnated women and advised abortion. The researchers also looked at the relationships between these perceptions and a variety of other variables,

including SOS scores. Kelley (1984/1985) examined whether SOS scores related to the production of sexual fantasy and sexual arousal in response to erotic slides. Greendlinger (1985) looked at the relationship between SOS scores and authoritarianism. Saunders, Fisher, Hewitt, and Clayton (1985) looked at the SOS scores of college students who volunteered to participate in research regarding "Responses to Erotica" and those who volunteered to participate in research regarding "Personality Questionnaires." Becker and Byrne (1985) studied reactions to erotica in terms of SOS scores and Type A coronary-prone behavior. Kelley (1985a, 1985b) and Kelley and Musialowski (1986) conducted research to determine whether SOS scores mediate the impact of erotica. Pryor (1987) used the SOS to determine whether a relationship exists between a man's likelihood to harass a woman sexually and his attitudes toward sexual behaviors. Przybyla, Byrne, and Allgeier (1988) looked at the relationship between SOS scores and the amount of sexual and nonsexual detail that one includes on a nude drawing. Fisher and Gray (1988) used SOS scores to look at the relationship between erotophobia/erotophilia and the sexual behavior of pregnant and postpartum couples.

(5) Fisher et al. (1983) summarized research showing many of the correlates of erotophobia/erotophilia as measured by the SOS. Many of these findings can be interpreted as providing evidence for the construct validity of the SOS. Fisher, Byrne et al. (1988) reviewed a variety of research studies using the SOS. Many of the studies they discussed are unpublished.

(6) The SOS has been translated into French, Hebrew, German, and Finnish and has also been used in Canada, the United States, Hong Kong, and India.

AVAILABLE FROM: Fisher, 1988; Fisher, Byrne, and White, 1983; Fisher, Byrne, White, and Kelley, 1988; Gilbert and Gamache, 1984

USED IN:

Becker, M. A., & Byrne, D. (1985). Self-regulated exposure to erotica, recall errors, and subjective reactions as a function of erotophobia and Type A coronary-prone behavior. *Journal of Personality and Social Psychology, 48,* 760–767.

Daugherty, L. R., & Burger, J. M. (1984). The influence of parents, church, and peers on the sexual attitudes and behaviors of college students. *Archives of Sexual Behavior, 13,* 351–359.

Fisher, W. A. (1979). Affective, attitudinal, and normative determinants of contraceptive behavior among university men (Doctoral dissertation, Purdue University, 1978). *Dissertation Abstracts International, 39,* 4613B.

Fisher, W. A. (1984). Predicting contraceptive behavior among university men: The role of emotions and behavioral intentions. *Journal of Applied Social Psychology, 14,* 104–123.

Fisher, W. A. (1988). The Sexual Opinion Survey. In C. M. Davis, W. L. Yarber, & S. L. Davis (Eds.), *Sexuality-related measures: A compendium* (pp. 34–37). Syracuse: Editors.

Fisher, W. A., Byrne, D., Edmunds, M., Miller, C. T., Kelley, K., & White, L. A. (1979). Psychological and situational-specific correlates of contraceptive behavior among university women. *Journal of Sex Research, 15*, 38–55.

Fisher, W. A., Byrne, D., & White, L. A. (1983). Emotional barriers to contraception. In D. Byrne & W. A. Fisher (Eds.), *Adolescents, sex, and contraception*. Hillsdale, NJ: Lawrence Erlbaum.

Fisher, W. A., Byrne, D., White, L. A., & Kelley, K. (1988). Erotophobia-erotophilia as a dimension of personality. *Journal of Sex Research, 25*, 123–151.

Fisher, W. A., & Gray, J. (1988). Erotophobia-erotophilia and sexual behavior during pregnancy and postpartum. *Journal of Sex Research, 25*, 379–396.

Fisher, W. A., Grenier, G., Watters, W. W., Lamont, J., Cohen, M., & Askwith, J. (1988). Students' sexual knowledge, attitudes toward sex, and willingness to treat sexual concerns. *Journal of Medical Education, 63*, 379–385.

Fisher, W. A., Miller, C. T., Byrne, D., & White, L. A. (1980). Talking dirty: Responses to communicating a sexual message as a function of situational and personality factors. *Basic and Applied Social Psychology, 1*, 115–126.

Geis, B. D., & Gerrard, M. (1984). Predicting male and female contraceptive behavior: A discriminant analysis of groups high, moderate, and low in contraceptive effectiveness. *Journal of Personality and Social Psychology, 46*, 669–680.

Gilbert, F. S., & Gamache, M. P. (1984). The Sexual Opinion Survey: Structure and use. *Journal of Sex Research, 20*, 293–309.

Greendlinger, V. (1985). Authoritarianism as a predictor of response to heterosexual and homosexual erotica. *High School Journal, 68*, 183–186.

Kelley, K. (1984/1985). Sexual fantasy and attitudes as functions of sex of subject and content of erotica. *Imagination, Cognition, and Personality, 4*, 339–347.

Kelley, K. (1985a). The effects of sexual and/or aggressive film exposure on helping, hostility, and attitudes about the sexes. *Journal of Research in Personality, 19*, 472–483.

Kelley, K. (1985b). Sexual attitudes as determinants of the motivational properties of exposure to erotica. *Personality and Individual Differences, 6*, 391–393.

Kelley, K., & Musialowski, D. (1986). Repeated exposure to sexually explicit stimuli: Novelty, sex, and sexual attitudes. *Archives of Sexual Behavior, 15*, 487–498.

Kelley, K., Smeaton, G., Byrne, D., Przybyla, D. P. J., & Fisher, W. A. (1987). Sexual attitudes and contraception among females across five college samples. *Human Relations, 40*, 237–254.

Pryor, J. B. (1987). Sexual harassment proclivities in men. *Sex Roles, 17*, 269–290.

Przybyla, D. P. J., Byrne, D., & Allgeier, E. R. (1988). Sexual attitudes as correlates of sexual details in human figure drawing. *Archives of Sexual Behavior, 17*, 99–105.

Saunders, D. M., Fisher, W. A., Hewitt, E. C., & Clayton, J. P. (1985). A method for empirically assessing volunteer selection effects: Recruitment and responses to erotica. *Journal of Personality and Social Psychology, 49*, 1703–1712.

Tanner, W. M., & Pollack, R. H. (1988). The effect of condom use and erotic instructions on attitudes toward condoms. *Journal of Sex Research, 25,* 537–541.

Walfish, S., & Myerson, M. (1980). Sex role identity and attitudes toward sexuality. *Archives of Sexual Behavior, 9,* 199–203.

Weidner, G., & Griffitt, W. (1983). Rape: A sexual stigma? *Journal of Personality, 51,* 152–166.

Weidner, G., & Griffitt, W. (1984). Abortion as a stigma: In the eyes of the beholder. *Journal of Research in Personality, 18,* 359–371.

Yarber, W. L., & Fisher, W. A. (1983). Affective orientation to sexuality and venereal disease preventive behaviors. *Health Values, 7,* 19–23.

Yarber, W. L., & McCabe, G. P., Jr. (1981). Teacher characteristics and the inclusion of sex education topics in grades 6–8 and 9–11. *Journal of School Health, 51,* 288–291.

Yarber, W. L., & McCabe, G. P., Jr. (1984). Importance of sex education topics: Correlates with teacher characteristics and inclusion of topics in instruction. *Health Education, 15,* 36–41.

Yarber, W. L., & Whitehill, L. L. (1981). The relationship between parental affective orientation toward sexuality and response to sex-related situations of preschool-age children. *Journal of Sex Education and Therapy, 7,* 36–39.

Yarber, W. L., & Yee, B. (1982/1983). Heterosexuals' attitudes toward lesbianism and male homosexuality: Their affective orientation toward sexuality and sex guilt. *Journal of American College Health, 31,* 203–208.

BIBLIOGRAPHY:

Beere, C. A. (1990). *Gender roles: A handbook of tests and measures.* Westport, CT: Greenwood.

Bem, S. L. (1974). The measurement of psychological androgyny. *Journal of Consulting and Clinical Psychology, 42,* 155–162.

Bentler, P. M. (1968). Heterosexual Behavior Assessment. *Behaviour Research and Therapy, 6,* 21–30.

Crowne, D. P., & Marlowe, D. (1964). *The approval motive.* New York: Wiley.

SEXUAL RESPONSE SCALE

AUTHORS: Lorraine Dennerstein, Graham D. Burrows, Carl Wood, and Carol Poynton

DATE: 1977

VARIABLE: Sexual behavior

TYPE OF INSTRUMENT: Visual analogue

DESCRIPTION: The Sexual Response Scale consists of 15 questions pertaining to sexual activities including, for example, foreplay, intercourse, and autoeroticism. Each item is accompanied by a straight line, 100 mm long, with the endpoints labeled "No, not at all" and "Yes, a great deal." The written instructions state: "Please indicate how you have felt in your sexual relationship over the last month by placing a line in the appropriate space." Oral instructions indicate that the endpoints represent the extremes of feelings and the midpoint represents the middle of these feelings.

SAMPLE ITEMS: Do you enjoy kissing?

How often would you like to initiate sexual intercourse?

PREVIOUS SUBJECTS: Sexually dysfunctional women and sexually "normal" women in Australia

APPROPRIATE FOR: Sexually experienced women in Australia; it is likely that the scale would be appropriate in other countries, but there is no evidence regarding its use except in Australia

ADMINISTRATION: Self-administered; about 5 minutes

SCORING: Dennerstein, Burrows, Wood, and Poynton (1977) looked at responses to each individual item. They did not obtain subscale or total scores.

DEVELOPMENT: Following the work of Cullberg, Gelli, and Jonssen (1969), questions were written to measure two aspects of sexuality: sexual desire and ability to respond. Zuckerman's (1973) Heterosexual Experience Scales (see separate entry) provided a framework for writing questions.

RELIABILITY: Test-retest reliability was estimated using responses from 20 women who were tested twice, half an hour apart. When these women were tested, the questions were embedded in a longer questionnaire, including detractor questions that differed in the two administrations. Spearman correlations were calculated for each item. One item had a correlation of .62, one item had a correlation of .74, six items had correlations between .80 and .89, and seven items had correlations of .90 or higher.

VALIDITY: In order to determine whether the items could differentiate between sexually normal women and sexually dysfunctional women, the Sexual Response Scale was administered to 126 patients referred for treatment of sexual disorders and to 54 "normal" women, most of whom were seeing general practitioners about medical problems unrelated to sexuality. For 11 of the 15 items, there was a significant difference between the responses of the two groups. There were no significant differences on the 4 items dealing with autoeroticism.

A group of 20 of the sexually dysfunctional women completed the scale before and after treatment for their sexual problems. Only four items showed significant differences when pretreatment responses were compared with posttreatment responses.

NOTES & COMMENTS: Dennerstein et al. (1977) offered several explanations for the lack of significant differences on the autoeroticism questions when responses of normal women were compared with responses from sexually dysfunctional women. However, since they cannot offer a definitive explanation, they correctly suggested that further research is needed to explain the lack of significant differences. Similarly, more research is needed to explain why there were few significant differences between pretreatment and posttreatment responses.

AVAILABLE FROM: Dennerstein, Burrows, Wood, and Poynton, 1977

USED IN:

Dennerstein, L., Burrows, G. D., Wood, C., & Poynton, C. (1977). The development of a scale for the assessment of sexual behaviour in Australian women. *Australian and New Zealand Journal of Psychiatry, 11,* 233–240.

BIBLIOGRAPHY:

Cullberg, J., Gelli, M. G., & Jonssen, C. (1969). Mental and sexual adjustment before and after six months use of an oral contraceptive. *Acta Psychiatrica Scandinavia, 45,* 259.

Zuckerman, M. (1973). Scales for sex experiences for males and females. *Journal of Consulting and Clinical Psychology, 41,* 27–29.

SEXUAL SATISFACTION INVENTORY

AUTHOR: Marilyn Peddicord Whitley

DATE: 1974

VARIABLE: Sexual satisfaction among women

TYPE OF INSTRUMENT: Summated rating scale

DESCRIPTION: The Sexual Satisfaction Inventory consists of 23 items, each an activity "commonly engaged in before, during and directly after the time of sexual activity" (Whitley & Poulsen, 1975, p. 579). The items represent a range of activities from the nonsexual (e.g., Talking with your partner) to the intensely sexual (e.g., Orgasm with vaginal intercourse), but the items are randomly ordered, not ordered by degree of intensity. The degree of satisfaction associated with each activity is rated on a 5-point scale, with the endpoints labeled "None" and "Maximum."

SAMPLE ITEMS: Kissing with your partner.

Orgasm by fantasy and daydreams.

PREVIOUS SUBJECTS: Employed professional women, rape victims, adult women, college women who were victims of sexual coercion and college women who were not victims of coercion

APPROPRIATE FOR: Sexually active women

ADMINISTRATION: Self-administered; about 10 minutes

SCORING: Each item is scored on a 5-point scale, with 1 point assigned to the end of the continuum labeled "None" and 5 points assigned to the end of the continuum labeled "Maximum." Item scores are summed to yield a total score that can range from 23 (no satisfaction) to 115 (maximum satisfaction). Scores from a sample of 45 professional employed women ranged from 41 to 115 (Whitley & Poulsen, 1975).

DEVELOPMENT: A factor analytic study involving a small sample of women and a pool of 31 items led the author to reduce the pool to the 23 items on the scale.

RELIABILITY: Whitley (1988) reported a coefficient alpha of .78 based on using a somewhat longer (32-item) version of the Sexual Satisfaction Inventory.

VALIDITY: Feldman-Summers, Gordon, and Meagher (1979) administered a slightly modified version of the Sexual Satisfaction Inventory to rape victims. The rape victims completed the scale three times, first indicating for each item their level of satisfaction 1 week prior to the rape, next indicating for each item their satisfaction 1 week after the rape, and finally indicating for each item their level of satisfaction 2 months after the rape. A nonvictim control group completed the scale in terms of their current level of satisfaction with each item. As one would expect, sexual satisfaction declined considerably after the rape, but "autoerotic and primarily affectional experiences appeared to be unaffected" (Feldman-Summers et al., 1979, p. 101). Also as one would expect, rape victims reported considerably less sexual satisfaction than was reported by nonvictims.

Orlando and Koss (1983) asked college women who had experienced varying degrees of sexual coercion to complete the scale three times, reporting their levels of satisfaction for the month preceding the victimization experience, the month following the victimization experience, and 3 months after the victimization experience. A control group of nonvictimized college women also completed the scale three times, reporting their levels of sexual satisfaction over a 30-day period 19 months earlier, 18 months earlier, and 15 months earlier. The items on the scale were divided into two categories: behaviors likely to occur during a rape and behaviors unlikely to occur during a rape. For purposes of analysis, subjects were divided into five groups based on degree of victimization. An analysis of variance produced significant main effects for level of victimization, categories of behavior, and time period.

NOTES & COMMENTS: Whitley (1988) provided a 32-item version of the Sexual Satisfaction Inventory. The longer version omits 1 item from the shorter version and adds 10 items not on the shorter version. Some of the 10 items were in the original item pool from which the scale was developed. The rationale for returning these items to the scale was not provided.

AVAILABLE FROM: Whitley and Poulsen, 1975; Feldman-Summers, Gordon, and Meagher, 1979; Whitley, 1988 for a longer version

USED IN:

Feldman-Summers, S., Gordon, P. E., & Meagher, J. R. (1979). The impact of rape on sexual satisfaction. *Journal of Abnormal Psychology, 88,* 101–105.

Orlando, J. A., & Koss, M. P. (1983). The effect of sexual victimization on sexual satisfaction: A study of the negative-association hypothesis. *Journal of Abnormal Psychology, 92,* 104–106.

Whitley, M. P. (1974). *A correlational survey comparing the levels of assertiveness with levels of sexual satisfaction in employed sexually active professional women.* Unpublished master's thesis, University of Washington, Seattle.

Whitley, M. P. (1988). Sexual Satisfaction Inventory. In C. M. Davis, W. L. Yarber, & S. L. Davis (Eds.). *Sexuality-related measures: A compendium* (pp. 243–244). Syracuse: Editors.

Whitley, M. P., & Poulsen, S. B. (1975). Assertiveness and sexual satisfaction in employed professional women. *Journal of Marriage and the Family, 37,* 573–581.

LABIAL THERMISTOR-CLIP

AUTHORS: Donald E. Henson, H. B. Rubin, Claudia Henson, and Jessie R. Williams
DATE: 1977
VARIABLE: Sexual arousal in females
TYPE OF INSTRUMENT: Physiological measure
DESCRIPTION: The labial thermistor-clip is a thermistor attached to the end of one side of a brass "roach" clip using silicone glue. The end of the other side of the clip is coated with silicone glue to form a protective pad. A small bead at the top of the clip can be moved down the legs of the clip to increase the pressure from the clip and attach it to a surface. (To visualize the apparatus, think of the roach clip as a pair of tweezers, with the thermistor attached to the end of one branch of the tweezers while the opposing end is coated with silicone to form the pad. A bead is at the top of the tweezers and slides over both sides, reducing the space between the thermistor and the pad and simultaneously increasing the pressure between the two.) The labial thermistor-clip is attached to one of the labia minora. Another thermistor is taped to the chest to provide a reference point.
PREVIOUS SUBJECTS: Women
APPROPRIATE FOR: Post-pubescent females
ADMINISTRATION: The labial thermistor-clip should be used on an individual basis in a laboratory setting. It is important that the research subject feel relaxed and comfortable when the procedure is used. After the procedure for attaching the thermistor-clip is explained and the experimenter leaves the room, the subject attaches the clip to her labia minora.
DEVELOPMENT: Development of the labial thermistor-clip was based on the fact that an increase in blood volume in peripheral tissue is known to be accompanied by an increase in the surface temperature of the area of the tissue.
RELIABILITY & VALIDITY: D. E. Henson, Rubin, Henson, and Williams (1977) tested 10 women while they watched an erotic film and a nonerotic film. In addition to using the labial thermistor-clip, the women provided ratings of their subjective sexual arousal. For 9 of the 10 women, there were increases in the labial temperature during the erotic film. These increases were significantly higher than the temperature increases recorded during the nonerotic film. The reference temperature, measured on the chest, showed no consistent changes during either of the films. D. E. Henson et al. reported a significant correlation between the sub-

jective ratings of sexual arousal and labial temperature (r = .53) and a nonsignificant correlation between the subjective ratings and the reference temperature (r = .23). However, after the erotic film, subjective ratings of sexual arousal returned to prearousal levels more quickly than did the temperature readings.

In a study by D. E. Henson and Rubin (1978), eight women watched an erotic film and provided data using three measures of sexual arousal: the labial thermistor-clip, a subjective rating of sexual arousal, and the vaginal photoplethysmograph (Sintchak & Geer, 1975) (see separate entry). For six of the eight women, the two physiological measures—labial thermistor-clip and vaginal photoplethysmograph—were highly correlated with each other. Additionally, results from the labial thermistor-clip were significantly related to the subjective ratings of sexual arousal, but this was not true for the results from the vaginal photoplethysmograph. In attempting to explain these results, D. E. Henson and Rubin (1978) stated that "although highly speculative, it is possible that labial temperature was more highly correlated with subjective ratings of arousal because the labia minora, and the clitoris to which it is juxtaposed, are more richly supplied with sensory nerve endings than the vaginal wall. . . . Changes of the labia might be more easily perceived than changes of the vagina" (p. 149). Again subjective ratings returned to prearousal levels more quickly than did the physiological measures.

In another study to compare the vaginal photoplethysmograph and the thermistor-clip, C. Henson, Rubin, and Henson (1979) tested eight women who watched an erotic film. For six of the eight women, there were significant correlations between labial temperature and vaginal blood volume, a measure obtained with the vaginal photoplethysmograph; for seven of the eight women, there were significant correlations between labial temperature and vaginal blood pulse, another measure obtained with the vaginal photoplethysmograph. Overall, the correlation between vaginal blood volume and labial temperature was .37, and the correlation between vaginal blood pulse and labial temperature was .66. The correlations were considerably weaker in the time period following the presentation of the erotic film. Subjective reports of sexual arousal were significantly correlated with labial temperature (r = .82).

In a related study, D. E. Henson, Rubin, and Henson (1979) reported that labial temperatures across two film presentations were very highly correlated with each other, and labial temperature was significantly related to subjective ratings of sexual arousal.

D. E. Henson, Rubin, and Henson (1978) conducted a study with six women to determine the consistency of measurement using the labial thermistor-clip. The women participated in two experimental sessions, 4 weeks apart. During the first session, each woman viewed the same erotic film. During the second session, four women watched the same film, and two women watched another film. Using the Spearman rank-order correlation, D. E. Henson et al. showed a significant correlation between temperature changes during the two film presentations (r = .83, $p < .05$). Subjective ratings of sexual arousal were also significantly correlated with labial temperature changes. The correlation during the first testing session was .78; the correlation during the second testing session was .77.

In another study comparing the vaginal photoplethysmograph with the labial thermistor-clip, D. E. Henson, Rubin, and Henson (1982) found that the two measures produced similar results during both visual and physical stimulation, and the results for the two measures were similar after arousal if the woman did not experience orgasm. For women experiencing orgasm, the vaginal photoplethysmograph and the labial thermistor-clip showed different levels of arousal after orgasm.

NOTES & COMMENTS: (1) Hoon, Coleman, Amberson, and Ling (1981) described a different approach to measuring sexual arousal in women. They used a thermistor that is held against the vaginal wall by vacuum pressure. This device was used previously by Levin and Wagner (1978) and Levin (1980). Hoon, Bruce, and Kinchloe (1982) reported using an electronic thermometer to measure labial temperature.

(2) Because physiological measures are quite different from paper-and-pencil measures, researchers considering the labial thermistor-clip need to be completely familiar with the procedure and all of its ramifications. The references used here should be carefully reviewed, and the equipment should be carefully tested before the procedure is implemented.

AVAILABLE FROM: The apparatus is described in D. E. Henson, Rubin, Henson, and Williams, 1977

USED IN:

Henson, C., Rubin, H. B., & Henson, D. E. (1979). Women's sexual arousal concurrently assessed by three genital measures. *Archives of Sexual Behavior, 8*, 459–469.

Henson, D. E., & Rubin, H. B. (1978). A comparison of two objective measures of sexual arousal of women. *Behavior Research and Therapy, 16*, 143–151.

Henson, D. E., Rubin, H. B., & Henson, C. (1978). Consistency of the labial temperature change measure of human female eroticism. *Behavior Research and Therapy, 16*, 125–129.

Henson, D. E., Rubin, H. B., & Henson, C. (1979). Analysis of the consistency of objective measures of sexual arousal in women. *Journal of Applied Behavior Analysis, 12*, 701–711.

Henson, D. E., Rubin, H. B., & Henson, C. (1982). Labial and vaginal blood volume responses to visual and tactile stimuli. *Archives of Sexual Behavior, 11*, 23–31.

Henson, D. E., Rubin, H. B., Henson, C., & Williams, J. R. (1977). Temperature change of the labia minora as an objective measure of female eroticism. *Journal of Behavior Therapy and Experimental Psychiatry, 8*, 401–410.

Hoon, P. W., Bruce, K., & Kinchloe, B. (1982). Does the menstrual cycle play a role in sexual arousal? *Psychophysiology, 19,* 21–27.

Hoon, P. W., Coleman, E., Amberson, J., & Ling, F. (1981). A possible physiological marker of female sexual dysfunction. *Biological Psychiatry, 16,* 1101–1106.

BIBLIOGRAPHY:

Levin, R. (1980). The physiology of sexual function in women. *Clinical Obstetrics and Gynecology, 7,* 213–251.

Levin, R., & Wagner, G. (1978). Haemodynamic changes of the human vagina during sexual arousal assessed by a heated oxygen electrode. *Journal of Physiology, 275,* 23–24.

Sintchak, G., & Geer, J. H. (1975). A vaginal plethysmograph system. *Psychophysiology, 12,* 113–115.

SEXUAL AROUSABILITY INVENTORY (SAI)

AUTHORS: Emily Franck Hoon, Peter W. Hoon, and John P. Wincze

DATE: 1976

VARIABLE: Sexual arousability in women

TYPE OF INSTRUMENT: Summated rating scale

DESCRIPTION: The Sexual Arousability Inventory (SAI) consists of 28 items representing five factors: Foreplay, Erotic Visual and Verbal Stimuli, Breast Stimulation, Preparation for and Participation in Intercourse, and Genital Stimulation. Each item is a brief description of an experience that may be sexually arousing. The respondent rates the degree of arousal she would feel in response to experiencing what is described. In the SAI—Expanded, the respondent rates each item three times: once in terms of how arousing the experience would be, once in terms of how relaxing or anxiety producing the experience would be, and once in terms of how satisfying or dissatisfying the experience would be.

ARTICLES LISTED IN BEERE 1979: 1

NOTES & COMMENTS: (1) The SAI has been used extensively since its original publication in 1976. In addition to being used in the United States and Canada, it has been modified for use in Czechoslovakia. The SAI has been used with healthy adults and college women, rape and incest victims, psychiatric patients, neurotic women, anorectics, postmastectomy patients, women with breast and gynecological cancers, alcoholics, lesbians, and postmenopausal women. According to Jensen, Witcher, and Upton (1987), a college reading level is needed to understand both the scale instructions and the scale items.

(2) Researchers considering using the SAI should review Andersen, Broffitt, Karlsson, and Turnquist (1989). The article provided data regarding the reliability and validity of the scale and reported the results of a factor analytic study using the SAI.

AVAILABLE FROM: Hoon, Hoon, and Wincze, 1976; Hoon and Chambless, 1988; Corcoran and Fischer, 1987

USED IN:

Adkins, E., & Jehu, D. (1985). Analysis of a treatment program for primary orgastic dysfunction. *Behaviour Research and Therapy, 23,* 119–126.

Andersen, B. L., Broffitt, B., Karlsson, J. A., & Turnquist, D. C. (1989). A psychometric analysis of the Sexual Arousability Inventory. *Journal of Consulting and Clinical Psychology, 57,* 123–130.

Andersen, B. L., & Jochimsen, P. R. (1985). Sexual functioning among breast cancer, gynecologic cancer, and healthy women. *Journal of Consulting and Clinical Psychology, 53,* 25–32.

Beck, J. G., Barlow, D. H., Sakheim, D. K., & Abramson, D. J. (1987). Shock threat and sexual arousal: The role of selective attention, thought content, and affective states. *Psychophysiology, 24,* 165–172.

Becker, J. V., Skinner, L. J., Abel, G. G., & Cichon, J. (1984). Time limited therapy with sexually dysfunctional sexually assaulted women. *Journal of Social Work and Human Sexuality, 3,* 97–115.

Becker, J. V., Skinner, L. J., Abel, G. G., & Cichon, J. (1986). Level of postassault sexual functioning in rape and incest victims. *Archives of Sexual Behavior, 15,* 37–49.

Becker, J. V., Skinner, L. J., Abel, G. G., & Treacy, E. C. (1982). Incidence and types of sexual dysfunctions in rape and incest victims. *Journal of Sex and Marital Therapy, 8,* 65–74.

Chambless, D. L., & Lifshitz, J. L. (1984). Self-reported sexual anxiety and arousal: The Expanded Sexual Arousability Inventory. *Journal of Sex Research, 20,* 241–254.

Coleman, E. M., Hoon, P. W., & Hoon, E. F. (1983). Arousability and sexual satisfaction in lesbian and heterosexual women. *Journal of Sex Research, 19,* 58–73.

Cotten-Huston, A. L., & Wheeler, K. A. (1983). Preorgasmic group treatment: Assertiveness, marital adjustment and sexual function in women. *Journal of Sex and Marital Therapy, 9,* 296–302.

Gerard, D. (1982). Sexual functioning after mastectomy: Life vs. lab. *Journal of Sex and Marital Therapy, 8,* 305–315.

Hoon, E. F., & Chambless, D. (1988). Sexual Arousability Inventory (SAI) and Sexual Arousability Inventory-Expanded (SAI—E). In C. M. Davis, W. L. Yarber, & S. L. Davis (Eds.), *Sexuality-related measures: A compendium* (pp. 21–24). Syracuse: Editors.

Hoon, E. F., & Hoon, P. W. (1978). Styles of sexual expression in women: Clinical implications of multivariate analyses. *Archives of Sexual Behavior, 7,* 105–116.

Hoon, E. F., Hoon, P. W., & Wincze, J. P. (1976). An inventory for the measurement of female sexual arousability: The SAI. *Archives of Sexual Behavior, 5,* 291–300.

Hoon, P. W. (1983). A path analysis model of psychosexuality in young women. *Journal of Research in Personality, 17,* 143–152.

Jensen, B. J., Witcher, D. B., & Upton, L. R. (1987). Readability assessment of questionnaires frequently used in sex and marital therapy. *Journal of Sex and Marital Therapy, 13,* 137–141.

Mellan, J. (1978a). Sexual Arousability of Women I. *Ceskoslovenska Gynekologie, 5,* 359–361. (in Czech)

Mellan, J. (1978b). Sexual Arousability of Women II. *Ceskoslovenska Gynekologie, 6,* 432–434. (in Czech)

Morokoff, P. J. (1985). Effects of sex guilt, repression, sexual "arousability," and sexual experience on female sexual arousal during erotica and fantasy. *Journal of Personality and Social Psychology, 49,* 177–187.

Morokoff, P. J. (1986). Volunteer bias in the psychophysiological study of female sexuality. *Journal of Sex Research, 22,* 35–51.

Murphy, W. D., Coleman, E., Hoon, E., & Scott, C. (1980). Sexual dysfunction and treatment in alcoholic women. *Sexuality and Disability, 3,* 240–255.

Myers, L. S., & Morokoff, P. J. (1986). Physiological and subjective sexual arousal in pre- and postmenopausal women and postmenopausal women taking replacement therapy. *Psychophysiology, 23,* 283–292.

Raboch, J. (1984). The sexual development and life of female schizophrenic patients. *Archives of Sexual Behavior, 13,* 341–349.

Raboch, J. (1986). Sexual development and life of psychiatric female patients. *Archives of Sexual Behavior, 15,* 341–353.

Raboch, J., & Horejsi, J. (1982). Sexual life of women with the Kustner-Rokitansky Syndrome. *Archives of Sexual Behavior, 11,* 215–220.

Raboch, J., Kobilkova, J., Raboch, J., & Starka, L. (1985). Sexual life of women with the Stein-Leventhal Syndrome. *Archives of Sexual Behavior, 14,* 263–270.

Rogers, G. S., Van de Castle, R. L., Evans, E. S., & Critelli, J. W. (1985). Vaginal pulse amplitude response patterns during erotic conditions and sleep. *Archives of Sexual Behavior, 14,* 327–342.

Snow, L. J., & Parsons, J. L. (1983). Sex role orientation and female sexual functioning. *Psychology of Women Quarterly, 8,* 133–143.

Steinman, D. L., Wincze, J. P., Sakheim, B. A., Barlow, D. H., & Mavissakalian, M. (1981). A comparison of male and female patterns of sexual arousal. *Archives of Sexual Behavior, 10,* 529–547.

Thyer, B. A., & Papsdorf, J. D. (1981). Relationship between irrationality and sexual arousability. *Psychological Reports, 48,* 834.

Wincze, J. P., & Qualls, C. B. (1984). A comparison of structural patterns of sexual arousal in male and female homosexuals. *Archives of Sexual Behavior, 13,* 361–370.

Wincze, J. P., Venditti, E., Barlow, D., & Mavissakalian, M. (1980). The effects of a subjective monitoring task in the physiological measure of genital response to erotic stimulation. *Archives of Sexual Behavior, 9,* 533–545.

BIBLIOGRAPHY:

Beere, C. A. (1979). *Women and women's issues: A handbook of tests and measures* (pp. 501–503). San Francisco: Jossey-Bass.

Corcoran, K., & Fischer, J. (1987). *Measures for clinical practice: A sourcebook* (pp. 308–311). New York: Free Press.

STRAIN GAUGE

AUTHORS: The authors most often associated with the mercury strain gauge are Charles Fisher, Joseph Gross, and Joseph Zuch (1965) and J.

H. J. Bancroft, H. Gwynne Jones, and B. R. Pullan (1966); the names most often associated with the mechanical strain gauge are D. H. Barlow, R. Becker, H. Leitenberg, and W. S. Agras (1970) and D. R. Laws and R. A. Bow (1976)

VARIABLE: Sexual arousal in men as reflected in penile erection

TYPE OF INSTRUMENT: Physiological measure

DESCRIPTION: The mercury strain gauge, available in various diameters, is a rubber tube, filled with mercury, that circles the penis. When the penis becomes erect, the tube lengthens, the diameter of the column of mercury is reduced, and there is a change in the resistance. The changes in resistance are generally recorded on a polygraph. The gauge has the advantage of being lightweight, can be put on by the subject, and is unobtrusive so that it can be worn under the clothing. Although the gauge has a limited life, its life can be increased by using platinum rather than copper electrodes. Bancroft, Jones, and Pullan (1966) developed a modification of the mercury strain gauge. Their modification involves a plastic carriage that can be used with a range of penile circumferences. In this device, "the mercury-filled tubing forms one arm of a Wheatstone bridge circuit" (Barlow, 1977, p. 477).

Barlow (1977) provided a description of the mechanical strain gauge: "It is a thin, metal, ring-like device open at one end that is placed around the penis, forming a semicircle around it. At the base of the ring are located one or more strain gauges. During erection the 'wings' of the ring separate, which causes a slight bending of the strain gauge and produces increased electrical output" (p. 477). Laws and Bow (1976) improved upon the mechanical gauge. Their modifications have the following advantages: "(1) the use of heavier Elgiloy increases durability and obviates the need for construction of a gauge platform; (2) the use of strain gauges with a larger surface area permits easier handling, installation, and assembly of the circuit; (3) the greater strain range (20%) of the larger gauges allows rougher handling of the transducer and diminishes the possibility of stretching the gauge to the breaking point; (4) coating the gauge assembly with silicon rubber instead of Tygon eliminates the problem of brittleness; and (5) the longevity of this redesigned penile transducer exceeds that typically reported" (p. 598).

PREVIOUS SUBJECTS: College and adult men, homosexual men, men with erectile dysfunction, dialysis and kidney transplant patients, rapists, child sex offenders, incest offenders, exhibitionists, men incarcerated for nonrape offenses

APPROPRIATE FOR: Males

ADMINISTRATION: The strain gauge must be used in a laboratory setting with a researcher who is completely familiar with the equipment. The subject can be shown how to put on the strain gauge, and he can then put it on himself after the experimenter leaves the room.

RELIABILITY & VALIDITY: Laws and Bow (1976) reported adequate reliability for their modification of the mechanical strain gauge.

Farkas et al. (1979) showed that test-retest reliability over a short time period, using a mercury-in-rubber strain gauge, was very acceptable, but reliability during a full erection was somewhat lower. They also found that videotaped records of erectile angle yielded results that were quite comparable to those from a mercury-in-rubber strain gauge, particularly during initial arousal.

Earls and Jackson (1981) looked at the effects of temperature on the results obtained with a mercury strain gauge. They concluded that "the combined results of both experiments indicated that temperature should have little effect during the measurement of penile tumescence" (p. 145).

Laws (1977) compared results obtained with a mechanical strain gauge and results obtained with a mercury strain gauge. He found that differences between the two measures were not statistically significant. According to Laws, "with either device there is approximately a ±5% measurement error on the upper end of the scale" (p. 49).

Some researchers have shown that erections, as measured by a strain gauge, in response to different types of sexually related materials can be used to help identify sex offenders (Abel, Barlow, Blanchard, & Guild, 1977; Abel, Becker, Blanchard, & Djenderedjian, 1978; Barbaree, Marshall, & Lanthier, 1979; Fedora, Reddon, & Yeudall, 1986; Malamuth & Check, 1983; Marshall, Barbaree, & Christophe, 1986; Quinsey & Chaplin, 1982, 1984; Quinsey, Chaplin, & Upfold, 1984; Quinsey, Steinman, Bergersen, & Holmes, 1975). On the other hand, Murphy, Krisak, Stalgaitis, and Anderson (1984) found no significant differences in the responses elicited from incarcerated rapists and incarcerated nonrapists. Their results led them to question seriously the use of penile tumescence in identifying rapists.

To the extent that penile tumescence is subject to voluntary control, a strain gauge will not provide a valid indication of sexual arousal. Malcolm, Davidson, and Marshall (1985) found that the ability to suppress penile tumescence is a function of both the level of sexual arousal when suppression is attempted and the stimulus being attended to at the time of suppression. Other researchers have also studied sexual arousal in relation to voluntary control and instrumental conditioning (Abel, Blanchard, & Barlow, 1981; Callahan & Leitenberg, 1973; Laws & Rubin, 1969; Quinsey & Bergersen, 1976; Rosen, 1973).

Evidence for the validity of the strain gauge is provided when subjective ratings of sexual arousal yield results that are similar to those from the strain gauge (Barnes, Malamuth, & Check, 1984; Heiman, 1977; Julien & Over, 1988; Malamuth, 1981; Wincze & Qualls, 1984; Wincze, Venditti, Barlow, & Mavissakalian, 1980). Some researchers have found that strain gauge measures of sexual arousal produce results that differ from subjective ratings of sexual arousal (Blader & Marshall, 1984; Farkas, Sine, & Evans, 1979; Hinton, O'Neill, & Webster, 1980).

NOTES & COMMENTS: (1) Because the strain gauge is a technique rather than a specific scale, the usual format for describing a scale has been modified here.

(2) The research described in the references listed under USED IN involved either a mercury strain gauge or a mechanical strain gauge. The type of strain gauge used is listed in parentheses following each entry. If the type of strain gauge is not specified, the article deals with both types.

(3) The strain gauge has been used extensively for many years. A researcher interested in all of the prior research using the measure will need to supplement the reference list given below. Most of the references given here were published primarily since the mid-1970s, and most involved gender-related studies.

(4) For a discussion of some aspects of the validity of penile tumescence measures, see the following four articles: Davidson, Malcolm, Lanthier, Barbaree, and Ho (1981); Farkas (1978); Levin, Gambaro, and Wolfinsohn (1978); and Rosen and Kopel (1978).

(5) Laws (1977) compared the mercury and mechanical strain gauges. He concluded that "because the mercury transducer is accurate, is acceptable for use with all subjects, is easy to handle, is durable if properly used, and is inexpensive, we recommend it as the best circumferential device presently available" (p. 51).

(6) Rosen and Keefe (1978) provided a good summary of the various approaches to measuring penile tumescence.

(7) A rape index represents "the ratio of penile responses to rape stimuli over responses to stimuli depicting mutually consenting sex" (Davidson & Malcolm, 1985, p. 283). Krisak, Murphy, and Stalgaitis (1981) looked at the reliability of the rape index for 18 men incarcerated for nonsex offenses. They concluded that the reliability of the rape index tended to be low. Davidson and Malcolm (1985) conducted an empirical study of the reliability of the rape index and concluded that combining responses to various stimuli was more reliable over sessions than were the individual responses to various stimuli.

(8) Fuller, Barnard, Robbins, and Spears (1988) strongly suggested that the erotic stimulus materials used in research involving the sexual arousal of sex offenders should be based on Tanner's (1962, 1978) stages of sexual maturity rather than on age.

AVAILABLE FROM: The mercury strain gauge is described by Fisher, Gross, and Zuch (1965) and by Bancroft, Jones, and Pullan (1966). The mechanical strain gauge is described by Barlow, Becker, Leitenberg, and Agras (1970) and by Laws and Bow (1976).

USED IN:

Abel, G. G., Barlow, D. H., Blanchard, E. B., & Guild, D. (1977). The components of rapists' sexual arousal. *Archives of General Psychiatry, 34,* 895–903. (mechanical)

Abel, G. G., Becker, J. V., Blanchard, E. B., & Djenderedjian, A. (1978). Differentiating sexual aggressives with penile measures. *Criminal Justice and Behavior, 5,* 315–332. (mechanical)

Abel, G. G., Blanchard, E. B., & Barlow, D. H. (1981). Measurement of sexual arousal in several paraphilias: The effects of stimulus modality, instructional set and stimulus content on the objective. *Behavior Research and Therapy, 19,* 25–33. (mechanical)

Bancroft, J. H. J., Jones, H. G., & Pullan, B. R. (1966). A simple transducer for measuring penile erection, with comments on its use in the treatment of sexual disorders. *Behavior Research and Therapy, 4,* 239–241. (mercury)

Barbaree, H. E., Marshall, W. L., & Lanthier, R. D. (1979). Deviant sexual arousal in rapists. *Behavior Research and Therapy, 17,* 215–222. (mercury)

Barbaree, H. E., Marshall, W. L., Yates, E., & Lightfoot, L. O. (1983). Alcohol intoxication and deviant sexual arousal in male social drinkers. *Behaviour Research and Therapy, 21,* 365–373. (mercury)

Barlow, D. H. (1977). Assessment of sexual behavior. In A. R. Ciminero, K. S. Calhoun, & H. E. Adams (Eds.), *Handbook of behavioral assessment* (pp. 461–508). New York: John Wiley & Sons.

Barlow, D. H., Becker, R., Leitenberg, H., & Agras, W. S. (1970). A mechanical strain gauge for recording penile circumference change. *Journal of Applied Behavior Analysis, 3,* 73–76. (mechanical)

Barnes, G. E., Malamuth, N. M., & Check, J. V. (1984). Psychoticism and sexual arousal to rape depictions. *Personality and Individual Differences, 5,* 273–279. (mercury)

Beck, J. G., Barlow, D. H., Sakheim, D. K., & Abrahamson, D. J. (1987). Shock threat and sexual arousal: The role of selective attention, thought content, and affective states. *Psychophysiology, 24,* 165–172. (mechanical)

Blader, J. C., & Marshall, W. L. (1984). The relationship between cognitive and erectile measures of sexual arousal in non-rapist males as a function of depicted aggression. *Behavior Research and Therapy, 22,* 623–630. (mercury)

Callahan, E. J., & Leitenberg, H. (1973). Aversion therapy for sexual deviation: Contingent shock and covert sensitization. *Journal of Abnormal Psychology, 81,* 60–73. (mechanical)

Ceniti, J., & Malamuth, N. M. (1984). Effects of repeated exposure to sexually violent or nonviolent stimuli on sexual arousal to rape and nonrape depictions. *Behavior Research and Therapy, 22,* 535–548. (mercury)

Davidson, P. R., & Malcolm, P. B. (1985). The reliability of the rape index: A rapist sample. *Behavioral Assessment, 7,* 283–292. (mercury)

Davidson, P. R., Malcolm, P. B., Lanthier, R. D., Barbaree, H. E., & Ho, T. P. (1981). Penile response measurement: Operating characteristics of the Parks plethysmograph. *Behavioral Assessment, 3,* 137–143. (mercury)

Earls, C. M., & Jackson, D. R. (1981). The effects of temperature on the mercury-in-rubber strain gauge. *Behavioral Assessment, 3,* 145–149. (mercury)

Farkas, G. M. (1978). Comments on Levin et al. and Rosen and Kopel: Internal and external validity issues. *Journal of Consulting and Clinical Psychology, 46*, 1515–1516.

Farkas, G. M., Evans, I. M., Sine, L. F., Eifert, G., Wittlieb, E., & Vogelmann-Sine, S. (1979). Reliability and validity of the mercury-in-rubber strain gauge measure of penile circumference. *Behavior Therapy, 10*, 555–561. (mercury)

Farkas, G. M., Sine, L. F., & Evans, I. M. (1979). The effects of distraction, performance demand, stimulus explicitness and personality on objective and subjective measures of male sexual arousal. *Behaviour Research and Therapy, 17*, 25–32. (mercury)

Fedora, O., Reddon, J. R., & Yeudall, L. T. (1986). Stimuli eliciting sexual arousal in genital exhibitionists: A possible clinical application. *Archives of Sexual Behavior, 15*, 417–427. (mercury)

Fisher, C., Gross, J., & Zuch, J. (1965). Cycle of penile erection synchronous with dreaming (REM) sleep. *Archives of General Psychiatry, 12*, 29–45. (mercury)

Fuller, A. K., Barnard, G., Robbins, L., & Spears, H. (1988). Sexual maturity as a criterion for classification of phallometric stimulus slides. *Archives of Sexual Behavior, 17*, 271–276. (mercury)

Glass, C. A., Fielding, D. M., Evans, C., & Ashcroft, J. B. (1987). Factors related to sexual functioning in male patients undergoing hemodialysis and with kidney transplants. *Archives of Sexual Behavior, 16*, 189–207. (mechanical)

Heiman, J. R. (1977). A psychophysiological exploration of sexual arousal patterns in females and males. *Psychophysiology, 14*, 266–274. (mercury)

High, R. W., Rubin, H. B., & Henson, D. (1979). Color as a variable in making an erotic film more arousing. *Archives of Sexual Behavior, 8*, 263–267. (mercury)

Hinton, J. W., O'Neill, M. T., & Webster, S. (1980). Psychophysiological assessment of sex offenders in a security hospital. *Archives of Sexual Behavior, 9*, 205–216. (mercury)

Julien, E., & Over, R. (1984). Male sexual arousal with repeated exposure to erotic stimuli. *Archives of Sexual Behavior, 13*, 211–222. (mercury)

Julien, E., & Over, R. (1988). Male sexual arousal across five modes of erotic stimulation. *Archives of Sexual Behavior, 17*, 131–143. (mercury)

Krisak, J., Murphy, W. D., & Stalgaitis, S. (1981). Reliability issues in the penile assessment of incarcerants. *Journal of Behavioral Assessment, 3*, 199–207. (mechanical)

Langevin, R., Paitich, D., Hucker, S., Newman, S., Ramsay, G., Pope, S., Geller, G., & Anderson, C. (1979). The effect of assertiveness training, provera and sex of therapist in the treatment of genital exhibitionism. *Journal of Behavior Therapy and Experimental Psychiatry, 10*, 275–282. (mechanical)

Laws, D. R. (1977). A comparison of the measurement characteristics of two circumferential penile transducers. *Archives of Sexual Behavior, 6*, 45–51. (mechanical and mercury)

Laws, D. R., & Bow, R. A. (1976). An improved mechanical strain gauge for recording penile circumference change. *Psychophysiology, 13*, 596–599. (mechanical)

Laws, D. R., & Rubin, H. B. (1969). Instructional control of an autonomic sexual response. *Journal of Applied Behavior Analysis, 2,* 93–99. (mercury)

Levin, S. M., Gambaro, S., & Wolfinsohn, L. (1978). Penile tumescence as a measure of sexual arousal: A reply to Farkas. *Journal of Consulting and Clinical Psychology, 46,* 1517–1518.

Malamuth, N. M. (1981). Rape fantasies as a function of exposure to violent sexual stimuli. *Archives of Sexual Behavior, 10,* 33–45. (mercury)

Malamuth, N. M. (1983). Factors associated with rape as predictors of laboratory aggression against women. *Journal of Personality and Social Psychology, 45,* 432–442. (mercury)

Malamuth, N. M. (1989). The Attraction to Sexual Aggression Scale: Part two. *Journal of Sex Research, 26,* 324–354. (mercury)

Malamuth, N. M., & Check, J. V. P. (1980). Penile tumescence and perceptual responses to rape as a function of victim's perceived reactions. *Journal of Applied Social Psychology, 10,* 528–547. (mercury)

Malamuth, N. M., & Check, J. V. P. (1983). Sexual arousal to rape depictions: Individual differences. *Journal of Abnormal Psychology, 92,* 55–67. (mercury)

Malcolm, P. B., Davidson, P. R., & Marshall, W. L. (1985). Control of penile tumescence: The effects of arousal level and stimulus content. *Behavior Research and Therapy, 23,* 273–280. (mercury)

Marshall, W. L., Barbaree, H. E., & Christophe, D. (1986). Sexual offenders against female children: Sexual preferences for age of victims and type of behavior. *Canadian Journal of Behavioural Science, 18,* 424–439. (mercury)

Murphy, W. D., Krisak, J., Stalgaitis, S., & Anderson, K. (1984). The use of penile tumescence measures with incarcerated rapists: Further validity issues. *Archives of Sexual Behavior, 13,* 545–554. (mechanical)

Quinsey, V. L., & Bergersen, S. G. (1976). Instructional control of penile circumference in assessments of sexual preference. *Behavior Therapy, 7,* 489–493. (mercury)

Quinsey, V. L., & Chaplin, T. C. (1982). Penile responses to nonsexual violence among rapists. *Criminal Justice and Behavior, 9,* 372–381. (mercury)

Quinsey, V. L., & Chaplin, T. C. (1984). Stimulus control of rapists' and non-sex offenders' sexual arousal. *Behavioral Assessment, 6,* 169–176. (mercury)

Quinsey, V. L., Chaplin, T. C., & Carrigan, W. F. (1979). Sexual preferences among incestuous and nonincestuous child molesters. *Behavior Therapy, 10,* 562–565. (mercury)

Quinsey, V. L., Chaplin, T. C., & Upfold, D. (1984). Sexual arousal to non-sexual violence and sadomasochistic themes among rapists and non-sex-offenders. *Journal of Consulting and Clinical Psychology, 52,* 651–657. (mercury)

Quinsey, V. L., Chaplin, T. C., & Varney, G. (1981). A comparison of rapists' and non-sex offenders' sexual preferences for mutually consenting sex, rape, and physical abuse of women. *Behavioral Assessment, 3,* 127–135. (mercury)

Quinsey, V. L., Steinman, C. M., Bergersen, S. G., & Holmes, T. F. (1975). Penile circumference, skin conductance, and ranking responses of child molesters and "normals" to sexual and nonsexual visual stimuli. *Behavior Therapy, 6,* 213–219. (mercury)

Rosen, R. C. (1973). Suppression of penile tumescence by instrumental conditioning. *Psychosomatic Medicine, 35,* 509–514. (mercury)

Rosen, R. C., & Keefe, F. J. (1978). The measurement of human penile tumescence. *Psychophysiology, 15,* 366–376.

Rosen, R. C., & Kopel, S. A. (1978). Role of penile tumescence measurement in the behavioral treatment of sexual deviation: Issues of validity. *Journal of Consulting and Clinical Psychology, 46,* 1519–1521.

Rosen, R. C., Kostis, J. B., & Jekelis, A. W. (1988). Beta-blocker effects on sexual function in normal males. *Archives of Sexual Behavior, 17,* 241–255. (mercury)

Rubinsky, H. J., Eckerman, D. A., Rubinsky, E. W., & Hoover, C. R. (1987). Early-phase physiological response patterns to psychosexual stimuli: Comparison of male and female patterns. *Archives of Sexual Behavior, 16,* 45–56. (mercury)

Schaefer, H. H., & Colgan, A. H. (1977). The effect of pornography on penile tumescence as a function of reinforcement and novelty. *Behavior Therapy, 8,* 938–946. (mechanical)

Wincze, J. P., Bansal, S., Malhotra, C., Balko, A., Susset, J. G., & Malamud, M. (1988). A comparison of nocturnal penile tumescence and penile response to erotic stimulation during waking states of comprehensively diagnosed groups of males experiencing erectile difficulties. *Archives of Sexual Behavior, 17,* 333–348. (mercury)

Wincze, J. P., & Qualls, C. B. (1984). A comparison of structural patterns of sexual arousal in male and female homosexuals. *Archives of Sexual Behavior, 13,* 361–371. (mechanical)

Wincze, J. P., Venditti, E., Barlow, D., & Mavissakalian, M. (1980). The effects of a subjective monitoring task in the physiological measure of genital response to erotic stimulation. *Archives of Sexual Behavior, 9,* 533–545. (mechanical)

Yates, E., Barbaree, H. E., & Marshall, W. L. (1984). Anger and deviant sexual arousal. *Behavior Therapy, 15,* 287–294. (mercury)

BIBLIOGRAPHY:

Tanner, J. M. (1962). *Growth at adolescence* (2nd ed.). Oxford: Blackwell Scientific.

Tanner, J. M. (1978). *Foetus into man: Physical growth from conception to maturity.* Cambridge: Harvard University Press.

SUBJECTIVE SEXUAL AROUSAL

AUTHOR: Donald L. Mosher

DATE: 1977 (modified 1988)

VARIABLE: Subjective sexual arousal defined as a blend of cognition and affect, "awareness of physiological sexual arousal and sexual affects" (Mosher, Barton-Henry, & Green, 1988, p. 414)

TYPE OF INSTRUMENT: Rating scales

DESCRIPTION: There are three parts to the Subjective Sexual Arousal scales. Each part is completed in terms of a recent sexually arousing experience, often an experience in fantasy. The first part, Ratings of Sexual Arousal, contains five items. Each item is a phrase relating to sexual arousal (e.g., sexual warmth), followed by a definition of the phrase (e.g., "a subjective estimate of the amount of sexual warmth experienced in the genitals, breasts and body as a function of increasing vasocongestion, i.e., engorgement with blood."). Each item is followed by a 7-point rating scale with the endpoints labeled appropriately to the item (e.g., "no sexual warmth at all" and "extreme sexual warmth"). The left end of the scale is always labeled "1," and the verbal description always represents low arousal; similarly the right end is always labeled "7," and the verbal description always represents high arousal. The second part of the Subjective Sexual Arousal scales, Ratings of Affective Sexual Arousal, consists of five sexually related terms (e.g., *sensuous*) that are to be rated using the following scale: "1 = very slightly, 2 = slightly, 3 = moderately, 4 = considerably, 5 = very strongly." These items should be embedded in a longer list of adjectives. The third part of the Subjective Sexual Arousal scales, Ratings of Genital Sensations, is a single-item rating scale consisting of 11 points, each accompanied by a description ranging from "1. No genital sensations" to "11. Multiple orgasm—repeated orgasmic release in a single sexual episode." Respondents are to check the highest level of genital sensations they had experienced during the sexually arousing experience they are rating.

PREVIOUS SUBJECTS: College students

APPROPRIATE FOR: College students and older

ADMINISTRATION: The Subjective Sexual Arousal scales are administered after a person has had an opportunity to be sexually aroused, and the directions specify that the ratings made should reflect how the person felt during the sexually arousing experience. The scales are self-administered and can be completed in less than 10 minutes

SCORING: Ratings of Sexual Arousal is scored by summing the ratings assigned to the five items. The total score can range from 7 (no sexual arousal) to 35 (strong sexual arousal). Ratings of Affective Sexual Arousal is scored by summing the ratings assigned to the five key terms; other adjectives included in the list are not scored. Total scores range from 5 (no sexual arousal) to 25 (strong sexual arousal). Ratings of Genital Sensations is scored by using the numerical value of the rating selected by the respondent. That is, if the respondent selects item 4 as most descriptive, the score is 4 points.

DEVELOPMENT: To develop the Subjective Sexual Arousal scales, three scales were administered to 120 college men and 121 college women after they had listened to each of four sexually arousing audiotapes: one tape focused on recall of a heterosexual experience, one focused on recall of a masturbatory experience, one invited the participant to engage in any sexual fantasy, and one tape provided guided fantasy in which the voice on the tape described various activities that the participant was asked to imagine with an "ideal sex partner." The Ratings of Sexual Arousal contained 11 items, and the Ratings of Affective Sexual Arousal included 10 sexually related adjectives embedded in a 50-item adjective checklist. The length of the scales was reduced by using item analysis procedures including corrected item-total correlations, alpha coefficients, and a backward multiple regression approach and repeating the analysis for each of the four fantasy conditions. Based on these analyses, the authors selected the 5 best items for each of these two scales. The Ratings of Genital Sensations was modified from two other rating scales measuring genital sensations (Mosher & Abramson, 1977; Schmidt & Sigusch, 1970).

RELIABILITY: Mosher et al. (1988) administered the Subjective Sexual Arousal scales to 120 college men and 121 college women. For both the Ratings of Sexual Arousal and the Ratings of Affective Sexual Arousal, alpha coefficients across four sexually arousing fantasy conditions all exceeded .95.

VALIDITY: Mosher et al. (1988) provided a correlation matrix showing the intercorrelations of the three parts of the Subjective Sexual Arousal scales across the four fantasy conditions. They found that "the validity correlations, correlations of the same measure of subjective sexual arousal across erotic fantasy conditions, were all significant, ranging from .24 to .74 with a median of .51" (p. 420). They also found that, with two exceptions, correlations between the same measure used with different fantasy conditions were higher than the correlations between different measures used with different fantasy conditions. Mosher et al. also reported that the intercorrelations among the three parts of the Subjective Sexual Arousal scales within a single erotic condition were quite strong: the median intercorrelation of the Ratings of Sexual Arousal with the Ratings of Affective Sexual Arousal was .81; the median intercorrelation of the Ratings of Sexual Arousal with the Ratings of Genital Sensations was .74; and the median intercorrelation of the Ratings of Affective Sexual Arousal with Ratings of Genital Sensations was .69 (Mosher, 1988).

Mosher et al. (1988) reported that separate analyses by sex revealed "similar patterns of interrelationship among the correlations in the male and female matrices" (p. 422).

NOTES & COMMENTS: (1) Earlier versions of part or all of the Subjective Sexual Arousal scales were used by Mosher and Abramson (1977), Mosher and O'Grady (1979), Mosher and White (1980), Harrell and Stolp (1985), and Sirkin and Mosher (1985). The current version of the Ratings of Genital Sensations scale and 6-item versions of the Ratings of Sexual Arousal and Ratings of Affective Sexual Arousal were used by Mosher and Anderson (1986) who reported coefficient alpha reliabilities of .88

for a 6-item Ratings of Sexual Arousal and .94 for a 6-item Ratings of Affective Sexual Arousal. The reliabilities were based on testing 125 college men.

(2) The Subjective Sexual Arousal scales are recommended over single-item measures of subjective sexual arousal, which are likely to be less reliable and less valid than these multi-item measures. Mosher et al. (1988) showed that a different subset of items could be selected from the original item pool and used reliably to measure sexual arousal.

AVAILABLE FROM: Mosher, Barton-Henry, and Green, 1988; Mosher, 1988

USED IN:

Harrell, T. H., & Stolp, R. D. (1985). Effects of erotic guided imagery on female sexual arousal and emotional response. *Journal of Sex Research, 21,* 292–304.

Mosher, D. L. (1988). Multiple indicators of subjective sexual arousal. In C. M. Davis, W. L. Yarber, & S. L. Davis (Eds.), *Sexuality-related measures: A compendium* (pp. 25–27). Syracuse: Editors.

Mosher, D. L., & Abramson, P. R. (1977). Subjective sexual arousal to films of masturbation. *Journal of Consulting and Clinical Psychology, 45,* 796–807.

Mosher, D. L., & Anderson, R. D. (1986). Macho personality, sexual aggression, and reactions to guided imagery of realistic rape. *Journal of Research in Personality, 20,* 77–94.

Mosher, D. L., Barton-Henry, M., & Green, S. E. (1988). Subjective sexual arousal and involvement: Development of multiple indicators. *Journal of Sex Research, 25,* 412–425.

Mosher, D. L., & O'Grady, K. E. (1979). Homosexual threat, negative attitudes toward masturbation, sex guilt, and males' sexual and affective reactions to explicit sexual films. *Journal of Consulting and Clinical Psychology, 47,* 860–873.

Mosher, D. L., & White, B. B. (1980). Effects of committed or casual erotic guided imagery on females' subjective sexual arousal and emotional response. *Journal of Sex Research, 16,* 273–299.

Sirkin, M. I., & Mosher, D. L. (1985). Guided imagery of female sexual assertiveness: Turn on or turn off? *Journal of Sex and Marital Therapy, 11,* 41–50.

BIBLIOGRAPHY:

Schmidt, G., & Sigusch, V. (1970). Sex differences in responses to psychosexual stimulation by films and slides. *Journal of Sex Research, 6,* 268–283.

VAGINAL PHOTOPLETHYSMOGRAPHY

AUTHORS: George Sintchak and James H. Geer (1975) described the vaginal photoplethysmography that is most often referred to in the literature

DATE: 1975

VARIABLE: Sexual arousal in females

TYPE OF INSTRUMENT: Physiological measure

DESCRIPTION: The vaginal photoplethysmograph is a cylindrical clear acrylic probe that resembles a menstrual tampon in size and shape. It is ½ inch in diameter and 1¾ inches in length. Given simple instructions, the woman painlessly inserts the probe into her vagina. The probe includes a light source and a photoelectric transducer, a light detector. The light is directed toward the vaginal wall, and the light detector senses the amount of light reflected back. Because there is a difference in the transparency of blood and bloodless tissue, the vaginal photoplethysmograph can detect changes in blood volume, which are recorded from the photoelectric transducer. The probe is connected to a polygraph device to record the tracings. The device can be used to measure slowly developing changes in vaginal blood volume (VBV), and it can be used to measure vaginal pulse amplitude (VPA). Both VBV and VPA have been used as indicators of sexual arousal. Sintchak and Geer (1975) provided a detailed description and diagram of the vaginal photoplethysmograph.

PREVIOUS SUBJECTS: College and adult women, usually sexually aroused

APPROPRIATE FOR: Postpubescent females

ADMINISTRATION: The vaginal photoplethysmograph is used on an individual basis in a laboratory setting. It is important that the research subject feels relaxed and comfortable when the procedure is used.

DEVELOPMENT: Sintchak and Geer (1975) pilot tested different size probes and probes of different materials.

RELIABILITY & VALIDITY: Geer, Morokoff, and Greenwood (1974) used the vaginal photoplethysmograph with women who watched erotic and nonerotic films. They found that both the VBV and VPA reflected sexual arousal during the viewing of the erotic film, but VPA was a somewhat better indicator of arousal than was VBV. Heart rate was not a good indicator of sexual arousal. Self-report measures of sexual arousal were not related to the results of the physiological measures.

Heiman (1976, 1977) reported the following correlations between VBV and VPA: .43, .60, .41, and .47 for measures recorded during four different audiotapes. The same subjects heard the same tapes on a second occasion, and the correlations between the two measures were lower: .27, .45, .33, and .24. VPA seemed to relate better to a self-report measure of arousal, and Heiman concluded that: "vaginal pressure pulse seems to be the more reliable indicator of arousal" (Heiman, 1976, p. 198).

Geer and Quartararo (1976) found that VBV and VPA reflected sexual arousal during masturbation and postorgasm. Osborn and Pollack (1977) found that VBV did not discriminate between responses to hard-core pornography and erotically realistic stimulus materials, but VPA data showed that hard-core pornography produced significantly greater arousal. Zingheim and Sandman (1978) found that VPA and VBV were not significantly correlated in a study of women who were highly sexually aroused.

Hoon, Wincze, and Hoon (1976) compared seven physiological measures of sexual arousal, including the vaginal photoplethysmograph. They found that three measures—heart rate, heart rate variability, and skin conductance—failed to discriminate between sexually aroused and nonaroused states. Four measures—vaginal blood volume as measured by the vaginal photoplethysmograph, skin conductance, blood pressure, and forehead temperature—showed significant changes when women watched an erotic videotape. Of the four discriminating measures, the vaginal photoplethysmograph was the most sensitive measure.

D. E. Henson and Rubin (1978) compared the vaginal photoplethysmograph with a second physiological measure of sexual arousal, the labial thermistor-clip (see separate entry). They found that both measures increased as a function of sexual arousal, but whereas the labial thermistor-clip yielded results that significantly correlated with subjective ratings of sexual arousal, VBV was not significantly correlated with the subjective ratings. Furthermore, subjective ratings of arousal returned to prearousal levels more quickly than did the physiological measures.

D. E. Henson, Rubin, and Henson (1979) also compared results from the vaginal photoplethysmograph with results from the labial thermistor-clip. They found that VBV and the labial thermistor-clip were more reliable measures of sexual arousal than was VPA. They also found that VPA was significantly related to subjective ratings of arousal at two different testing times, but VBV was correlated significantly with subjective ratings only after the first testing session. In another study comparing the vaginal photoplethysmograph and the labial thermistor-clip, C. Henson, Rubin, and Henson (1979) found that, for most subjects who were watching an erotic film, the three measures were highly intercorrelated. However, measures taken after the film were not highly correlated. Subjective measures of sexual arousal were correlated with the physiological measures taken during the film but not after it.

D. E. Henson, Rubin, and Henson (1982) conducted another study to compare the vaginal photoplethysmograph and the labial thermistor-clip. They found considerable similarity in the response patterns recorded by the two measures except that orgasm affected the two measures differently.

Wincze, Venditti, Barlow, and Mavissakalian (1980) compared sexual arousal as measured by the vaginal photoplethysmograph to a subjective measure of sexual arousal. There was a statistically significant relationship between the two measures for only two of eight research subjects.

NOTES & COMMENTS: (1) The vaginal photoplethysmograph is quite different from most of the other measures described in this book, and thus some of the headings used to describe the other measures have been omitted here. Potential users of the technique are urged to review carefully the references listed here and, if necessary, seek consultative help before embarking on research using the vaginal photoplethysmograph.

(2) Beck, Sakheim, and Barlow (1983) compared the Sintchak and Geer (1975) vaginal photoplethysmograph with a modified light-emitting diode probe. Their results raised important questions regarding the usefulness of the vaginal photoplethysmograph, and potential users are urged to read this article before using the measure.

(3) For a description of the use of photoplethysmography in general, see Weinman (1967) and Novelly, Perona, and Ax (1973). Hatch (1979) provided a good discussion of the methodological considerations associated with using the vaginal photoplethysmograph. His article is strongly recommended for persons considering using the technique.

(4) Although there is some inconsistency in the findings, it appears that VPA is a better measure of sexual arousal than is VBV.

(5) Bohlen and Held (1979) described an anal probe for measuring blood volume and muscle.tension in both men and women.

(6) The vaginal photoplethysmograph has been used to study women's sexual arousal in regard to numerous other variables: amenorrhea (Van Dam, Honnebier, Van Zalinge, & Barendregt, 1976); biofeedback (Hoon, 1980; Hoon, Wincze, & Hoon, 1977a); anxiety (Beggs, Calhoun, & Wolchik, 1987; Hoon, Wincze, & Hoon, 1977b); physiology, affect, and context (Heiman, 1980); sexual dysfunction and the effects of sex therapy (Morokoff & Heiman, 1980); sex (Rubinsky, Eckerman, Rubinsky, & Hoover, 1987; Steinman, Wincze, Sakheim, Barlow, & Mavissakalian, 1981); phase of the menstrual cycle (Hoon, Bruce, & Kinchloe, 1982; Schreiner-Engel, Schiavi, & Smith, 1981; Schreiner-Engel, Schiavi, Smith, & White, 1981); mastectomy (Gerard, 1982); alcohol intake (Wilson & Lawson, 1976); acute alcohol intoxication (Malatesta, Pollack, Crotty, & Peacock, 1982); homosexuality (Wincze & Qualls, 1984); predictions of sexual arousability (Rogers, Van de Castle, Evans, & Critelli, 1985); "sex guilt, repression-sensitization, sexual experience, and sexual arousability" (Morokoff, 1985, p. 179); and menopausal stage (Myers & Morokoff, 1986). Cerny (1978) used the vaginal photoplethysmograph in a study to determine whether women could exercise voluntary control over physiological measures of sexual arousal. Messe and Geer (1985) studied the effectiveness of vaginal musculature contractions (Kegel exercises) as a method for increasing sexual arousability. Abel, Murphy, Becker, and Bitar (1979) looked at the VPA and VBV results for women who were sleeping.

(7) Armon, Weinman, and Weinstein (1978) described a slightly different vaginal photoplethysmograph that they used to monitor changes in blood volume during the menstrual cycle.

USED IN:

Abel, G. G., Murphy, W. D., Becker, J. V., & Bitar, A. (1979). Women's vaginal responses during REM sleep. *Journal of Sex and Marital Therapy, 5,* 5–14.

Armon, H., Weinman, J., & Weinstein, D. (1978). A vaginal photoplethysmographic transducer. *IEEE Transactions on Biomedical Engineering, 25,* 434–440.

Beck, J. G., Sakheim, D. K., & Barlow, D. H. (1983). Operating characteristics of the vaginal photoplethysmograph: Some implications for its use. *Archives of Sexual Behavior, 12,* 43–58.

Beggs, V. E., Calhoun, K. S., & Wolchik, S. A. (1987). Sexual anxiety and female sexual arousal: A comparison of arousal during sexual anxiety stimuli and pleasure stimuli. *Archives of Sexual Behavior, 16,* 311–319.

Bohlen, J. G., & Held, J. P. (1979). An anal probe for monitoring vascular and muscular events during sexual response. *Psychophysiology, 16,* 318–323.

Cerny, J. A. (1978). Biofeedback and the voluntary control of sexual arousal in women. *Behavior Therapy, 9,* 847–855.

Geer, J. H., Morokoff, P., & Greenwood, P. (1974). Sexual arousal in women: The development of a measurement device for vaginal blood volume. *Archives of Sexual Behavior, 3,* 559–564.

Geer, J. H., & Quartararo, J. D. (1976). Vaginal blood volume responses during masturbation. *Archives of Sexual Behavior, 5,* 403–413.

Gerard, D. (1982). Sexual functioning after mastectomy: Live vs. lab. *Journal of Sex and Marital Therapy, 8,* 305–315.

Hatch, J. P. (1979). Vaginal photoplethysmography: Methodological considerations. *Archives of Sexual Behavior, 8,* 357–374.

Heiman, J. R. (1976). Issues in the use of psychophysiology to assess female sexual dysfunction. *Journal of Sex and Marital Therapy, 2,* 197–204.

Heiman, J. R. (1977). A psychophysiological exploration of sexual arousal patterns in females and males. *Psychophysiology, 14,* 266–274.

Heiman, J. R. (1980). Female sexual response patterns: Interactions of physiological, affective, and contextual cues. *Archives of General Psychiatry, 37,* 1311–1316.

Henson, C., Rubin, H. B., & Henson, D. E. (1979). Women's sexual arousal concurrently assessed by three genital measures. *Archives of Sexual Behavior, 8,* 459–469.

Henson, D. E., & Rubin, H. B. (1978). A comparison of two objective measures of sexual arousal of women. *Behavior Research and Therapy, 16,* 143–151.

Henson, D. E., Rubin, H. B., & Henson, C. (1979). Analysis of the consistency of objective measures of sexual arousal in women. *Journal of Applied Behavior Analysis, 12,* 701–711.

Henson, D. E., Rubin, H. B., & Henson, C. (1982). Labial and vaginal blood volume responses to visual and tactile stimuli. *Archives of Sexual Behavior, 11,* 23–31.

Hoon, E. F. (1980). Biofeedback-assisted sexual arousal in females: A comparison of visual and auditory modalities. *Biofeedback and Self-Regulation, 5,* 175–191.

Hoon, P. W., Bruce, K., & Kinchloe, B. (1982). Does the menstrual cycle play a role in sexual arousal? *Psychophysiology, 19,* 21–27.

Hoon, P. W., Coleman, E., Amberson, J., & Ling, F. (1981). A possible physiological marker of female sexual dysfunction. *Biological Psychiatry, 16,* 1101–1106.

Hoon, P. W., Wincze, J. P., & Hoon, E. F. (1976). Physiological assessment of sexual arousal in women. *Psychophysiology, 13,* 196–204.

Hoon, P. W., Wincze, J. P., & Hoon, E. F. (1977a). The effects of biofeedback and cognitive mediation upon vaginal blood volume. *Behavior Therapy, 8,* 694–702.

Hoon, P. W., Wincze, J. P., & Hoon, E. F. (1977b). A test of reciprocal inhibition: Are anxiety and sexual arousal in women mutually inhibitory? *Journal of Abnormal Psychology, 86,* 65–74.

Malatesta, V. J., Pollack, R. H., Crotty, T. D., & Peacock, L. J. (1982). Acute alcohol intoxication and female orgasmic response. *Journal of Sex Research, 18,* 1–17.

Messe, M. R., & Geer, J. H. (1985). Voluntary vaginal musculature contractions as an enhancer of sexual arousal. *Archives of Sexual Behavior, 14,* 13–28.

Morokoff, P. J. (1985). Effects of sex guilt, repression, sexual "arousability," and sexual experience on female sexual arousal during erotica and fantasy. *Journal of Personality and Social Psychology, 49,* 177–187.

Morokoff, P. J., & Heiman, J. R. (1980). Effects of erotic stimuli on sexually functional and dysfunctional women: Multiple measures before and after sex therapy. *Behavior Research and Therapy, 18,* 127–137.

Myers, L. S., & Morokoff, P. J. (1986). Physiological and subjective sexual arousal in pre- and postmenopausal and postmenopausal women taking replacement therapy. *Psychophysiology, 23,* 283–292.

Osborn, C. A., & Pollack, R. H. (1977). The effects of two types of erotic literature on physiological and verbal measures of female sexual arousal. *Journal of Sex Research, 13,* 250–256.

Rogers, G. S., Van de Castle, R. L., Evans, W. S., & Critelli, J. W. (1985). Vaginal pulse amplitude response patterns during erotic conditions and sleep. *Archives of Sexual Behavior, 14,* 327–342.

Rubinsky, H. J., Eckerman, D. A., Rubinsky, E. W., & Hoover C. R. (1987). Early-phase physiological response patterns to psychosexual stimuli: Comparison of male and female patterns. *Archives of Sexual Behavior, 16,* 45–56.

Schreiner-Engel, P., Schiavi, R. C., & Smith, H., Jr. (1981). Female sexual arousal: Relation between cognitive and genital assessments. *Journal of Sex and Marital Therapy, 7,* 256–267.

Schreiner-Engel, P., Schiavi, R. C., Smith, H., & White, D. (1981). Sexual arousability and the menstrual cycle. *Psychosomatic Medicine, 43,* 199–214.

Sintchak, G., & Geer, J. H. (1975). A vaginal plethysmograph system. *Psychophysiology, 12,* 113–115.

Steinman, D. L., Wincze, J. P., Sakheim, B. A., Barlow, D. H., & Mavissakalian,

M. (1981). A comparison of male and female patterns of sexual arousal. *Archives of Sexual Behavior, 10,* 529–547.

Van Dam, F. S. A. M., Honnebier, W. J., Van Zalinge, E. A., & Barendregt, J. T. (1976). Sexual arousal measured by photoplethysmography. *Behavioral Engineering, 3,* 97–101.

Wilson, G. T., & Lawson, D. M. (1976). Effects of alcohol on sexual arousal in women. *Journal of Abnormal Psychology, 85,* 489–497.

Wincze, J. P., & Qualls, C. B. (1984). A comparison of structural patterns of sexual arousal in male and female homosexuals. *Archives of Sexual Behavior, 13,* 361–370.

Wincze, J. P., Venditti, E., Barlow, D., & Mavissakalian, M. (1980). The effects of a subjective monitoring task in the physiological measure of genital response to erotic stimulation. *Archives of Sexual Behavior, 9,* 533–545.

Zingheim, P. K., & Sandman, C. A. (1978). Discriminative control of the vaginal vasomotor response. *Biofeedback and Self-Regulation, 3,* 29–41.

BIBLIOGRAPHY:

Novelly, R. A., Perona, P. J., & Ax, A. F. (1973). Photoplethysmography: System calibration and light history effects. *Psychophysiology, 10,* 67–73.

Weinman, J. (1967). Photoplethysmography. In P. H. Venables & I. Martin (Eds.), *A manual of psychophysiological methods.* New York: Elsevier.

ATTITUDES TOWARD SEXUALITY SCALE (ATSS)

AUTHORS: Terri D. Fisher and Richard G. Hall

DATE: 1986 (used 1983)

VARIABLE: Sexual attitudes

TYPE OF INSTRUMENT: Summated rating scale

DESCRIPTION: The Attitudes Toward Sexuality Scale (ATSS) contains 14 statements relating to "such issues as nudity, abortion, contraception, premarital sex, pornography, prostitution, homosexuality, and venereal disease" (Fisher & Hall, 1988, p. 94). Half of the items reflect a sexually liberal attitude and the other half a sexually conservative attitude. Each item is accompanied by five response alternatives ranging from "strongly disagree" to "strongly agree."

SAMPLE ITEMS: Nudist camps should be made completely illegal.

Sexual intercourse should only occur between two people who are married to each other.

PREVIOUS SUBJECTS: Ages 12–23 and their parents

APPROPRIATE FOR: Ages 12 and up

ADMINISTRATION: Self-administered; less than 10 minutes

SCORING: Items are individually scored on a 5-point scale, with 5 points assigned to the response reflecting a liberal attitude and 1 point assigned to the response reflecting a conservative attitude. Item scores are summed to yield a total score that can range from 14 (extremely conservative) to 70 (extremely liberal). Fisher and Hall (1988) reported means and standard deviations, by sex, for various different age groups.

DEVELOPMENT: Based on the feedback obtained from earlier research (Fisher, 1986b), Fisher and Hall selected and adapted specific items from Calderwood's (1971) Checklist of Attitudes Toward Human Sexuality. In selecting items, those items "thought to be understandable and relatively unembarrassing for even a 12-year-old" (Fisher & Hall, 1988, p. 92) were adapted for the ATSS.

RELIABILITY: Fisher and Hall (1988) tested four groups of respondents: 35 early adolescents between the ages of 12 and 14; 47 middle adolescents between the ages of 15 and 17; 59 late adolescents between the ages of 18 and 20; and 141 adults. The alpha coefficients for the four groups were .76, .65, .80, and .84, respectively. When the three groups of adolescents were considered together, coefficient alpha was .75. When all persons were considered together, coefficient alpha was .80. An independent sample of 20 older adolescents, ages 18 to 20 years, was tested on two occasions with a 1-month interval between testings. Test-retest reliability was .90.

Fisher and Hall (1988) reported corrected item-total correlations ranging from .23 to .65, with a mean of .42. Item 3 had the lowest correlation ($r = .23$), followed by item 7, with a corrected item-total correlation of .26. Another item analysis was conducted using a different sample. In the new analysis, item 3 had a corrected item-total correlation of .54, but the item-total correlation for item 7 dropped to .18.

VALIDITY: The relationships among ATSS scores and several other variables provided some evidence of the scale's construct validity. Fisher and Hall (1988) found that the sexual attitudes of males were significantly more liberal than the sexual attitudes of females. They also found that middle adolescents (ages 15 to 17) were significantly more liberal than early adolescents or adults.

Fisher and Hall (1988) reported that several correlations between ATSS scores and demographic variables were significant. For all participants considered together, ATSS scores were negatively correlated with age ($r = -.18$), but for ages 12 through 17, ATSS scores were positively correlated with age ($r = .37$). For adults, education was significantly correlated with ATSS scores ($r = .20$). Religiosity was significantly correlated with ATSS scores for the middle adolescents ($r = -.32$), the older adolescents ($r = -.44$), and the adults ($r = -.41$).

Fisher and Hall (1988) gave a group of 42 college students the ATSS and the Sexual Knowledge and Attitude Test (SKAT) (Lief & Reed, 1972) (see separate entry). As predicted, ATSS scores were significantly correlated with the Heterosexual Relations subscale of the SKAT ($r = .83$) and the Abortion subscale of the SKAT ($r = .70$). Although no predictions were made, Fisher and Hall also found that ATSS scores were significantly correlated with the Autoeroticism subscale scores ($r = .54$) and the Sexual Myths subscale scores ($r = .59$).

NOTES & COMMENTS: (1) Because of its low item-total correlation in two independent analyses, Fisher and Hall (1988) recommended eliminating item 7 from the ATSS. They reported that coefficient alpha estimates using different subsamples and omitting item 7 were "not notably different" (p. 97).

(2) A factor analysis using the responses from 141 adults led to the identification of four factors. All items, except items 3 and 7, loaded heavily on the first factor. When the factor analysis was repeated without item 7, all 13 remaining items loaded heavily on the first factor, which accounted for 33.4% of the variance (Fisher & Hall, 1988).

(3) Fisher (1986a, 1987a, 1987b) conducted several studies looking at how parent-child communication about sex relates to the similarity in parent and adolescent attitudes about sex. The ATSS was used as the attitude measure for both the adolescents and their parents.

(4) The correlation between ATSS scores and age was negative for all ages combined but positive for the two early and middle adolescent groups combined. Without additional information, these findings are somewhat confusing. Is the relationship actually curvilinear? What would a scatterplot show? Is Pearson's r the best way to represent this relationship?

AVAILABLE FROM: Fisher and Hall, 1988

USED IN:

Fisher, T. D. (1986a). An exploratory study of parent-child communication about sex and the sexual attitudes of early, middle, and late adolescents. *Journal of Genetic Psychology, 147,* 543–557.

Fisher, T. D. (1987a). Family communication and the sexual behavior and attitudes of college students. *Journal of Youth and Adolescence, 16,* 481–495.

Fisher, T. D. (1987b, March). *Family relationships and parent-child discussion about sex.* Paper presented at the meeting of the Southeastern Psychological Association, Atlanta. (ERIC Document Reproduction Service No. ED 284 079)

Fisher, T. D., & Hall, R. G. (1988). A scale for the comparison of the sexual attitudes of adolescents and their parents. *Journal of Sex Research, 24,* 90–100.

BIBLIOGRAPHY:

Calderwood, D. (1971). *About your sexuality.* Boston: Beacon.

Fisher, T. D. (1986b). Parent-child communication and adolescents' sexual knowledge and attitudes. *Adolescence, 21,* 517–527.

Lief, H. I., & Reed, D. M. (1972). *Sex Knowledge and Attitude Test.* Philadelphia: Center for the Study of Sex Education in Medicine, University of Pennsylvania.

DEARTH CASSELL ATTITUDE INVENTORY

AUTHORS: Paul Dearth and Carol Cassell

DATE: 1976

VARIABLE: Attitudes regarding sexuality and related topics
TYPE OF INSTRUMENT: Summated rating scale
DESCRIPTION: The Dearth Cassell Attitude Inventory consists of 18 items covering a variety of topics related to sex and sexuality, such as homosexuality, contraception, childbirth, venereal disease, abortion, masturbation, sex education, sex laws, sex organs, and sexual practices. Each item is accompanied by five response options: "strongly agree, agree, undecided, disagree, strongly disagree."
SAMPLE ITEMS: Masturbation is an unhealthy behavior.
Sexual intercourse is the most meaningful expression of love.
PREVIOUS SUBJECTS: College students
APPROPRIATE FOR: High school students and older
ADMINISTRATION: Self-administered; about 10 minutes
SCORING: Rather than scoring across items, Dearth and Cassell (1976) analyzed responses to each item separately.
DEVELOPMENT: No information was provided.
RELIABILITY: No information was provided.
VALIDITY: Taylor (1982) reported a significant pretest-posttest difference when a slight variation of the Dearth Cassell Attitude Inventory was used to assess the impact of human sexuality courses at the undergraduate and graduate levels. In general, attitudes became more liberal as a result of the course, but the specific items that showed pretest-posttest changes were different for undergraduate students compared to graduate students.

Similarly Taylor (1983) found significant differences on some items when a variation of the Dearth Cassell Attitude Inventory was used to assess sexual attitudes before and after a course on human sexuality. No differences were found for the control group who did not take the sexuality class. She also found some differences in the responses from students at a southeastern university compared to students at a northeastern university.

Taylor and Adame (1986) compared responses from college men and women using data obtained from over 600 college students. They found that males and females differed significantly in their responses to 8 of the 18 items on a modified Dearth Cassell Attitude Inventory administered as a pretest. They also found that males and females differed significantly on 11 of the 18 items when the scale was used as a posttest. About half of the respondents who completed the posttest had also completed a class in human sexuality; the other half of the respondents were part of a control group that did not participate in the class.
NOTES & COMMENTS: (1) An examination of item content showed that there are both attitude items and knowledge items on the scale, but Dearth and Cassell refer to the measure as an attitude measure and ignore the factual nature of some items.

(2) The Dearth Cassell Attitude Inventory is not typical of the measures in this book in that this inventory does not produce an overall score for each respondent. However, it is included here because the inventory, or a slight modification of it, has been used in four published studies.
AVAILABLE FROM: Dearth and Cassell, 1976
USED IN:

Dearth, P., & Cassell, C. (1976). Comparing attitudes of male and female university students before and after a semester course on human sexuality. *Journal of School Health, 46*, 593–598.

Taylor, M. E. (1982). A discriminant analysis approach to exploring changes in human sexuality attitudes among university students. *Journal of American College Health, 31*, 124–129.

Taylor, M. E. (1983). Changing sexual attitudes among university students: A geographic comparison. *Health Education, 14*, 23–26.

Taylor, M. E., & Adame, D. D. (1986). Male and female sexuality attitudes: Differences and similarities. *Health Education, 17*, 8–12.

INVENTORY OF ATTITUDES TO SEX
AUTHOR: Hans J. Eysenck
DATE: 1970 (revised 1976)
VARIABLE: Sexual attitudes
TYPE OF INSTRUMENT: Most items are multiple choice items with three response alternatives
DESCRIPTION: The original Inventory of Attitudes to Sex contains 98 items. Most of the items assess attitudes, but some ask about the respondent's sexual experiences and preferences. The current version of the Inventory of Attitudes to Sex contains 158 items; most of the items assess attitudes, and the other items ask about the respondent's sexual experiences and preferences. The wording of 8 items on the Inventory must be modified depending on whether the respondents are males or females. The remaining 150 items are equally appropriate for both sexes.

A short form of the Inventory of Attitudes to Sex contains 96 items; 88 overlap the full-length version, and 8 are unique to the short form. Most items on the Inventory of Attitudes to Sex, regardless of the version, are accompanied by three response options: "yes, ?, no." Some items give the options "agree, ?, disagree" or "true, ?, false." The last 8 items on the full-length 1976 version of the scale use a variety of formats.
SAMPLE ITEMS: The opposite sex will respect you more if you are not too familiar with them.

Sex without love ("impersonal sex") is highly unsatisfactory.
PREVIOUS SUBJECTS: College students and adults, male members of a trade union, male alcoholics, sex offenders, infertile women, women at a family planning clinic, impotent men
APPROPRIATE FOR: Ages 16 and older

ADMINISTRATION: Self-administered; about 20–40 minutes for the 98-item version; about 40–60 minutes for the 158-item version

SCORING: Eysenck (1976) provided a scoring key indicating the direction of scoring for each item and the number of each item contributing to each subscale score. The following subscale scores can be computed: Permissiveness (14 items), Satisfaction (12 items), Neurotic Sex (13 items), Impersonal Sex (14 items), Pornography (8 items), Sexual Shyness (6 items), Prudishness (9 items), Sexual Disgust (6 items), Sexual Excitement (9 items), Physical Sex (10 items), Aggressive Sex (6 items), Sexual Satisfaction (a higher-order factor) (16 items), Sexual Libido (a higher-order factor) (36 items), and Masculinity-Femininity (50 items).

DEVELOPMENT: The original version of the Inventory of Attitudes to Sex was developed by adapting many items from Thorne's (1966) Sex Inventory and generating additional items based on a review of the relevant psychological and psychiatric literature. A factor analysis of 95 items from the Inventory of Attitudes to Sex produced the following oblique factors: Sexual Satisfaction, Sexual Excitement, Sexual Nervousness, Sexual Curiosity, Premarital Sex, Repression, Prudishness, Sexual Experimentation, Homosexuality, Censorship, Promiscuity, Sexual Hostility, and Guilt. Items loaded differently on these factors depending on whether data from males or from females were used as the basis for the analysis. The revised version of the Inventory of Attitudes to Sex, an extension of the original version, was administered to 427 males and 436 females ranging in age from 18 to 60 years. Due to the limitations of the available computing equipment, a factor analysis of all 158 items was not possible. Instead, the analysis involved 135 items that were selected by eliminating items with endorsements in excess of 90% or below 10% and eliminating redundant items. Separate factor analyses were performed by sex. Six factors were quite similar for males and females: Permissiveness, Satisfaction, Neurotic Sex, Impersonal Sex, Pornography, and Shyness. An additional six factors showed greater differences in item loadings for men and women: Prudishness, Dominance-Submission, Sexual Disgust, Sexual Excitement, Physical Sex, and Aggressive Sex. Eysenck (1976) also reported identifying two higher-order factors: Sexual Libido and Sexual Satisfaction. Using the results of these factor analyses, Eysenck devised subscales corresponding to 11 of the 12 primary factors. (For the Dominance-Submission factor, there were not enough items in common from the analysis of male data and the analysis of female data, so he did not create a Dominance-Submission subscale.) Eysenck also devised scales representing each of the two higher-order factors. To develop the Masculinity-Femininity subscale, Eysenck selected items that showed the largest differences between males and females.

RELIABILITY: Eysenck (1976) reported reliabilities, separately by sex, for each of the 11 primary factor scales. Following are the reliabilities for women, with the reliabilities for men given in parentheses: Permissiveness = .83 (.84), Satisfaction = .83 (.82), Neurotic Sex = .72 (.74), Impersonal Sex = .81 (.85), Pornography = .78 (.78), Sexual Shyness = .66 (.72), Prudishness = .61 (.58), Sexual Disgust = .65 (.54), Sexual Excitement = .77 (.66), Physical Sex = .61 (.65), and Aggressive Sex = .51 (.47). In reviewing these data, Eysenck (1976) noted: "Half the scales have reliabilities too low for serious consideration, except perhaps for group comparison" (p. 103).

For the Sexual Libido subscale, Eysenck (1976) reported a reliability of .90 for males and .89 for females. For the Sexual Satisfaction subscale, he reported a reliability of .82 for males and .81 for females. The reliability for the Masculinity-Femininity subscale was .80 for both sexes.

VALIDITY: In comparing the means on the primary factors, Eysenck (1976) found that males scored higher than females on Permissiveness, Impersonal Sex, Pornography, Excitement, and Physical Sex. The differences were consistent with expectations. Women had higher scores than men on Satisfaction, Disgust, and Prudishness. The differences on Disgust and Prudishness were consistent with expectations.

Eysenck (1976) reported a significant sex difference on the Sexual Libido subscale; as expected, males obtained higher scores. There was not a significant difference on the Sexual Satisfaction subscale.

Eysenck (1976) showed that "men and women of a given personality have similar attitude patterns" (p. 118) on the Inventory of Attitudes to Sex.

NOTES & COMMENTS: (1) The 98-item version of the Inventory of Attitudes to Sex was used in numerous research studies (e.g., Eysenck, 1970, 1971a, 1971b, 1972, 1973, 1976; Whalley, 1978; Whalley & McGuire, 1978). Eysenck (1970, 1971a, 1971b, 1973, 1976) related responses on the Inventory of Attitudes to Sex to personality variables. Whalley (1978) compared alcoholic men and nonalcoholic men on the Inventory.

(2) Whalley and McGuire (1978) used item analysis and factor analysis on the responses from 50 male alcoholics, 50 nonalcoholic males, and 35 sex offenders who completed the 98-item version of the Inventory of Attitudes to Sex. The researchers identified nine subscales: Sexual Satisfaction (8 items), Heterosexual Nervousness (6 items), Sexual Curiosity (9 items), Sexual Tension (12 items), Sexual Hostility (6 items), Pruriency (7 items), Sexual Repression (8 items), Heterosexual Distaste (7 items), and Sexual Promiscuity (7 items). They reported internal consistency reliability and test-retest reliability for each of the subscales. The internal consistency reliabilities were .80, .80, .63, .78, .60, .73, .36, .23, and .15 for the nine subscales, respectively. Obviously some of these coefficients were extraordinarily low. The test-retest reliabilities were .85, .76, .89, .79, .55, .83, .58, .79, and .75 for the nine subscales, respectively.

(3) Eysenck (1976) provided extensive information on the use of the 158-item version of the Inventory of Attitudes to Sex. He intercorrelated all of the primary and higher-order factor scores, separately by sex; he reported the intercorrelations between spouses for each of the primary and higher-order factor scores; he looked at the correlations, by sex, between each item and social class, occupation, age, marital status, and four personality scores (psychoticism, extraversion, neuroticism, and a lie scale); he related responses on the Inventory of Attitudes to Sex to responses on the Reiss Premarital Sexual Permissiveness Scale (Reiss, 1967) (see separate entry) and to a measure of sexual behavior.

(4) Paxton and Turner (1978) factor analyzed responses from 104 college women who completed the 158-item Inventory of Attitudes to Sex. The researchers identified four factors with internal consistency reliabilities ranging from .67 to .88: Sexual Satisfaction, Sexual Libido, Prudishness, and Permissiveness.

(5) Eysenck and Wakefield (1981) conducted a study of the correlates of marital satisfaction. Among the variables they related to marital satisfaction were scores on the Inventory of Attitudes to Sex.

(6) Slade (1981) used a subset of 32 items from the Inventory of Attitudes to Sex. The items represented six factors—Sexual Inhibition, Guilt, Hostility, Repression, Satisfaction, and Excitability—and were used to compare infertile women to a control group who were not known to have fertility problems.

(7) Segraves and Segraves (1986) compared men suffering from biogenic impotence with men suffering from psychogenic impotence and found no significant differences on any subscale scores.

AVAILABLE FROM: The 98-item version appears in Eysenck, 1970, 1971b, 1972, 1976; the 158-item version appears in Eysenck, 1976, 1988

USED IN:

Eysenck, H. J. (1970). Personality and attitudes to sex: A factorial study. *Personality, 1*, 355–376.

Eysenck, H. J. (1971a). Hysterical personality and sexual adjustment, attitudes and behaviour. *Journal of Sex Research, 7*, 274–281.

Eysenck, H. J. (1971b). Personality and sexual adjustment. *British Journal of Psychiatry, 118*, 593–608.

Eysenck, H. J. (1972). *Psychology is about people*. LaSalle, IL: Open Court.

Eysenck, H. J. (1973). Personality and attitudes to sex in criminals. *Journal of Sex Research, 9*, 295–306.

Eysenck, H. J. (1976). *Sex and personality*. London: Open Books.

Eysenck, H. J. (1988). The Eysenck Inventory of Attitudes to Sex. In C. M. Davis, W. L. Yarber, & S. L. Davis (Eds.), *Sexuality-related measures: A compendium* (pp. 28–34). Syracuse: Editors.

Eysenck, H. J., & Wakefield, J. A., Jr. (1981). Psychological factors as predictors of marital satisfaction. *Advances in Behaviour Research and Therapy, 3*, 151–192.

Paxton, A. L., & Turner, E. J. (1978). Self-actualization and sexual permissiveness, satisfaction, prudishness, and drive among female undergraduates. *Journal of Sex Research, 14,* 65–80.

Segraves, K. A., & Segraves, R. T. (1986). Differentiation of biogenic and psychogenic impotence with the Eysenck Personality Questionnaire and the Inventory of Sexual Attitudes. *Personality and Individual Differences, 7,* 423–425.

Slade, P. (1981). Sexual attitudes and social role orientations in infertile women. *Journal of Psychosomatic Research, 25,* 183–186.

Whalley, L. J. (1978). Sexual adjustment of male alcoholics. *Acta Psychiatrica Scandinavica, 58,* 281–298.

Whalley, L. J., & McGuire, R. J. (1978). Measuring sexual attitudes. *Acta Psychiatrica Scandinavica, 58,* 299–314.

BIBLIOGRAPHY:

Reiss, I. L. (1967). *The social context of premarital sexual permissiveness.* New York: Holt, Rinehart, & Winston.

Thorne, F. C. (1966). The Sex Inventory. *Journal of Clinical Psychology,* Monograph Supplement No. 21.

NEGATIVE ATTITUDES TOWARD MASTURBATION (NAM)

AUTHORS: Paul R. Abramson and Donald L. Mosher

DATE: 1975

VARIABLE: Masturbation guilt

TYPE OF INSTRUMENT: Summated rating scale

DESCRIPTION: The Negative Attitudes Toward Masturbation (NAM) scale contains 30 items: 20 statements reflect a negative attitude, and 10 statements reflect a positive attitude. Item content deals with the causes for masturbation, the feelings associated with masturbation, the consequences of masturbation, and judgments about masturbation. Each item is accompanied by five response alternatives ranging from "not at all true for me" to "extremely true for me."

SAMPLE ITEMS: People who masturbate will not enjoy sexual intercourse as much as those who refrain from masturbation.

Masturbation is a private matter which neither harms nor concerns anyone else.

PREVIOUS SUBJECTS: College students, high school students, rapists and molesters, women with sexually transmitted diseases

APPROPRIATE FOR: According to Mosher (1988), "the items are useful with educated populations of men and women" (p. 228).

ADMINISTRATION: Self-administered; about 10 minutes

SCORING: Items are individually scored and summed to yield a total score. Each item is scored on a 5-point scale, with the responses indicative of negative attitudes toward masturbation assigned the high scores. Total scores can range from 30 (very positive attitudes toward masturbation) to 150 (very negative attitudes toward masturbation). Abramson

and Mosher (1975) provided means and standard deviations for each of 30 items; they used data from 95 college men and 99 college women.
DEVELOPMENT: College students were asked to provide responses to open-ended questions concerning the consequences of masturbation (Abramson, 1973). Their responses were used to develop the 30 items comprising this scale.
RELIABILITY: Corrected split-half reliability, based on testing 96 college men and 102 college women, was .75 (Abramson & Mosher, 1975). Corrected item-total correlations ranged from .11 to .57. Only 1 of the 30 correlations was nonsignificant, and 24 of the 30 were significant at the .001 level.

Based on responses from 186 college women, Mosher and Vonderheide (1985) reported a coefficient alpha of .94.
VALIDITY: Abramson and Mosher (1975) related scores on the NAM to several other variables. For a sample of 96 college men and 102 college women, there were significant correlations between scores on the NAM and average frequency of masturbation per month ($r = -.26$ for men and $-.40$ for women). For females only, there was a significant correlation between scores on the NAM and maximum frequency of masturbation per day ($r = -.45$). There was a significant correlation between scores on the NAM and scores on the Sex Guilt subscale of the Mosher Forced-Choice Guilt Inventory (Mosher, 1968) (see separate entry for Revised Mosher Guilt Inventory) for both males ($r = .47$) and females ($r = .61$). For females only, there was a significant correlation between scores on the NAM and sex experience as measured by the Sexual Experience Inventory ($r = -.33$) (Brady & Levitt, 1965) (see separate entry).

Abramson and Mosher (1975) compared responses from males and females. There was no significant difference on total scores (in fact, the scores for males and females were nearly identical), but there were significant differences on 8 of the 30 items.

Mosher and Abramson (1977) administered the NAM to college students who saw a film of either a female or male masturbating until orgasm/ejaculation was achieved. The college students rated their arousal in response to the film, reported their genital sensations, and rated adjectives related to sexual arousal. Significant main effects showed that persons with negative attitudes toward masturbation were likely to experience less sexual arousal and less genital sensation than were persons with more positive attitudes toward masturbation. A significant three-way interaction (sex of subject, condition of film, and scores on the NAM) revealed that "males with negative attitudes toward masturbation reported the highest level of sexual arousal to the female film and the lowest level of affective sexual arousal to the film of the male masturbating" (Mosher & Abramson, 1977, p. 800); "women with greater negative attitudes toward masturbation were less aroused by the female film, whereas women with more positive attitudes toward masturbation reported the highest female level of sexual arousal after viewing the film of the male masturbating" (p. 800).

Mosher and O'Grady (1979) conducted a study with 215 college men who completed the following measures: NAM, Mosher Guilt Inventory (Mosher, 1968), Homosexual Threat Inventory, a questionnaire on masturbatory experience, and a heterosexual-homosexual orientation rating scale. The men then saw one of three films—a masturbation film, a homosexual pornographic film, or a heterosexual pornographic film—and afterward completed a sexual arousal rating scale, reported their genital sensations, responded to an affective adjective rating scale, and responded to four questions to determine their identification with persons in the film. Scores on the NAM were significantly correlated with scores on the Homosexual Threat Inventory ($r = .45$), Sex Guilt scores ($r = .23$), average weekly frequency of masturbation ($r = -.44$), and percentage of masturbatory orgasms ($r = -.44$). Scores on the NAM were not significantly related to heterosexual-homosexual orientation. Based on NAM scores, subjects were divided into two groups: high and low NAM. Ratings of sexual arousal and level of genital sensation were significantly different between the high and the low NAM groups. Men with more positive attitudes toward masturbation reported more sexual arousal and a higher level of genital sensation. There were significant interactions between NAM scores and film condition for the rating of sexual arousal and the level of genital sensation. Ratings of sexual arousal were significantly different for the high and low NAM groups who saw the masturbatory film or the homosexual film but not for those who saw the heterosexual film; the level of genital sensation was significantly different for the high and low NAM groups who saw the homosexual film but not the masturbatory or the heterosexual film. Regardless of the film seen, "men who held negative attitudes toward masturbation experienced more affective disgust . . . ; anger . . . ; shame . . . ; guilt . . . ; and depression . . . than did men with more positive attitudes toward masturbation" (Mosher & O'Grady, 1979, p. 869). The researchers also found that men "with more positive attitudes toward masturbation . . . found the masturbatory behavior in the film significantly more congruent with their sexual self-concept" (p. 869).

Bentler and Peeler (1979) studied 182 college women using a variety of measures to enable the researchers to identify "the dimensionality of women's subjective responsiveness to orgasm" (p. 405). Among their other findings, Bentler and Peeler concluded: "attitudes toward masturbation [as measured by the NAM] have a powerful influence on masturbatory behavior. Both coital and masturbatory orgasmic responsiveness were found to be the function of a subject's attitude toward masturbation, but these effects are indirect through sexual experience" (p. 420).

Abramson, Perry, Rothblatt, Seeley, and Seeley (1981) conducted a study to determine whether NAM scores related to an objective measure of sexual arousal. A group of 37 college women and 32 college men were assigned to one of three groups. They read a sexually arousing story or a comparably arousing but nonsexual story, or they stood still for 2 minutes, the amount of time required to read either of the two stories. Prior to reading the story, each person completed the NAM. In addition, both before and after the story reading, each person was scanned with a spectrotherm to measure pelvic vasocongestion, an indicator of sexual arousal. A significant statistical interaction showed that "women, with positive attitudes about masturbation, who read the erotic story, experienced the greatest increase in pelvic vasocongestion" (Abramson et al., 1981, p. 503).

Greendlinger and Byrne (cited in Fisher, Byrne, White, & Kelley, 1988) found a significant correlation between the Sexual Opinion Survey (see separate entry) and the NAM (r = .53 for males and .54 for females).

NOTES & COMMENTS: (1) A factor analysis using responses from 96 college men and 102 college women led to three factors. The first factor accounted for 31.9% of the variance and contained 12 items, with 9 of them reflecting positive attitudes toward masturbation; the second factor accounted for 6.7% of the variance and contained 11 items dealing with "false beliefs about the harmful nature of masturbation" (Abramson & Mosher, 1975, p. 487); and the third factor accounted for 5.7% of the variance and contained 7 items dealing with "personally experienced negative affects associated with masturbation" (p. 488). Because the sample size was small relative to the number of items, the results of the factor analysis cannot be presumed stable.

(2) Most of the studies using the NAM provided additional support for the validity of the measure. Abramson and Mosher (1979) studied the impact of sex guilt and masturbatory guilt (as measured by the NAM) on experimentally induced masturbatory fantasies. In another study (Cotten-Huston, 1983), male sex offenders and nonoffenders were assigned either to a control group or to participate in 14 sessions to learn about human sexuality. Following the treatment/control procedure, subjects completed two measures, including the NAM. Green and Mosher (1985) used the NAM in a study that looked at a variety of relationships, including the influence of masturbation guilt on sexual arousal. Lo Presto, Sherman, and Sherman (1985) sought to determine whether a single session seminar about masturbation could alter high school males' attitudes, beliefs, and behavior regarding the topic. The NAM was used to assess attitudes toward masturbation. Mosher and Vonderheide (1985) conducted a study to demonstrate that masturbation guilt (as measured

by the NAM) compared to sex guilt (as measured by the Mosher Guilt Inventory [Mosher, 1968]) specifically inhibits diaphragm use in college women. Greendlinger (1985) used the NAM to test the hypothesis that authoritarian persons would have more negative attitudes toward masturbation than would nonauthoritarian persons. Houck and Abramson (1986) conducted a study with 60 women suffering from sexually transmitted disease. The researchers tested two hypotheses: women with high masturbatory guilt (high NAM scores) who have sexually transmitted diseases "will have more clinical manifestations of their disorders, and . . . more stress as a result of contracting their disease" (p. 269).

AVAILABLE FROM: Abramson and Mosher, 1975; Mosher, 1988; Corcoran and Fischer, 1987

USED IN:

Abramson, P. R., & Mosher, D. L. (1975). Development of a measure of negative attitudes toward masturbation. *Journal of Consulting and Clinical Psychology, 43*, 485–490.

Abramson, P. R., & Mosher, D. L. (1979). An empirical investigation of experimentally induced masturbatory fantasies. *Archives of Sexual Behavior, 8*, 27–39.

Abramson, P. R., Perry, L. B., Rothblatt, A., Seeley, T. T., & Seeley, D. M. (1981). Negative attitudes toward masturbation and pelvic vasocongestion: A thermographic analysis. *Journal of Research in Personality, 15*, 497–509.

Bentler, P. M., & Peeler, W. H. (1979). Models of female orgasm. *Archives of Sexual Behavior, 8*, 405–423.

Cotten-Huston, A. L. (1983). Comparisons of sex offenders with nonoffenders on attitudes toward masturbation and female fantasy as related to participation in human sexuality sessions. *Journal of Offender Counseling, Services and Rehabilitation, 8*, 13–26.

Fisher, W. A., Byrne, D., White, L. A., & Kelley, K. (1988). Erotophobia-erotophilia as a dimension of personality. *Journal of Sex Research, 25*, 123–151.

Green, S. E., & Mosher, D. L. (1985). A causal model of sexual arousal to erotic fantasies. *Journal of Sex Research, 21*, 1–23.

Greendlinger, V. (1985). Authoritarianism as a predictor of response to heterosexual and homosexual erotica. *High School Journal, 68*, 183–186.

Houck, E. L., & Abramson, P. R. (1986). Masturbatory guilt and the psychological consequences of sexually transmitted diseases among women. *Journal of Research in Personality, 20*, 267–275.

Lo Presto, C. T., Sherman, M. F., & Sherman, N. C. (1985). The effects of a masturbation seminar on high school males' attitudes, false beliefs, guilt, and behavior. *Journal of Sex Research, 21*, 142–156.

Mosher, D. L. (1979). Negative attitudes toward masturbation in sex therapy. *Journal of Sex and Marital Therapy, 5*, 315–333.

Mosher, D. L. (1988). Negative Attitudes Toward Masturbation. In C. M. Davis, W. L. Yarber, & S. L. Davis (Eds.), *Sexuality-related measures: A compendium* (pp. 227–229). Syracuse: Editors.

Mosher, D. L., & Abramson, P. R. (1977). Subjective sexual arousal to films of masturbation. *Journal of Consulting and Clinical Psychology, 45,* 796–807.

Mosher, D. L., & O'Grady, K. E. (1979). Homosexual threat, negative attitudes toward masturbation, sex guilt, and males' sexual and affective reactions to explicit sexual films. *Journal of Consulting and Clinical Psychology, 47,* 860–873.

Mosher, D. L., & Vonderheide, S. G. (1985). Contributions of sex guilt and masturbation guilt to women's contraceptive attitudes and use. *Journal of Sex Research, 21,* 24–39.

BIBLIOGRAPHY:

Abramson, P. R. (1973). The relationship of the frequency of masturbation to several aspects of behavior. *Journal of Sex Research, 9,* 132–142.

Brady, J. P., & Levitt, E. E. (1965). The scalability of sexual experiences. *Psychological Record, 15,* 275–279.

Corcoran, K., & Fischer, J. (1987). *Measures for clinical practice: A sourcebook* (pp. 247–249). New York: Free Press.

Mosher, D. L. (1968). Measurement of guilt in females by self-report inventories. *Journal of Consulting and Clinical Psychology, 32,* 690–695.

PERMISSIVENESS OF WOMEN'S SEXUAL ATTITUDES

AUTHORS: Sanford A. Weinstein and Kathleen Borok

DATE: 1978

VARIABLE: Sexual permissiveness for women

TYPE OF INSTRUMENT: Summated rating scale

DESCRIPTION: The Permissiveness of Women's Sexual Attitudes scale consists of 18 items phrased in the third person (in terms of "a woman," not in terms of the respondent). The items "advocat[e] either conformity or non-conformity to social pressures and/or moralistic values limiting sexual behavior" (Weinstein & Borok, 1978, p. 55). Eight items are phrased in a permissive manner; 10 items are phrased in a conservative manner. Each item is accompanied by five response options.

SAMPLE ITEMS: When a woman is offered a sexual proposition by a man she finds sexually attractive, she should accept.

Sexual involvement for a woman should only occur in the context of well established loving relationships.

PREVIOUS SUBJECTS: College women and female nurses

APPROPRIATE FOR: Ages 16 and older

ADMINISTRATION: Self-administered; about 5–8 minutes

SCORING: Items are individually scored on a 5-point scale, with the least permissive response assigned 5 points. Items are summed to yield a total score that can range from 18 (very permissive) to 90 (not at all permissive).

DEVELOPMENT: Sexual permissiveness was defined as "the degree to which a woman feels free to act on her heterosexual impulses without acquiescence to social pressures and/or moralistic values that are in opposition to these impulses" (Weinstein & Borok, 1978, p. 55). A 20-item scale was constructed with items designed to measure sexual permissiveness as defined here. The scale was administered to 60 females, ages 17 to 42, and an item analysis was performed on their responses. Two items were eliminated from the scale due to low item-total correlations. The remaining 18 items comprise the scale.

RELIABILITY: For a sample of 30 female nurses, coefficient alpha was .72; for a sample of 30 college women, coefficient alpha was .88. Item-total correlations for all 60 women ranged from .17 to .79.

VALIDITY: No information was provided.

NOTES & COMMENTS: Weinstein and Borok (1978) used the Permissiveness of Women's Sexual Attitudes scale to determine whether the stereotype that nurses tend to be more sexually permissive than other groups was an accurate stereotype. They compared the mean scores from a group of 30 nurses with the mean scores from a group of 30 college women. There were no significant differences between the two groups.

AVAILABLE FROM: Weinstein and Borok, 1978

USED IN:

Weinstein, S. A., & Borok, K. (1978). The permissiveness of nurses' sexual attitudes: Testing a stereotype. *Journal of Sex Research, 14,* 54–58.

REISS PREMARITAL SEXUAL PERMISSIVENESS SCALE

AUTHOR: Ira L. Reiss

DATE: 1964 (used 1959)

VARIABLE: The acceptability of premarital sexual behavior; the extent to which premarital sexual behavior is equally acceptable for males and females

TYPE OF INSTRUMENT: Guttman scale

DESCRIPTION: There are two forms of the Reiss Premarital Sexual Permissiveness Scale. Each form consists of 12 parallel items, differing only in terms of the sex of the referent; one form asks about the acceptability of behavior on the part of males and the other about the acceptability of behavior on the part of females. The 12 items represent four levels of affection—engaged, love, strong affection, and no affection—crossed with three types of sexual behaviors—kissing, petting, and coitus. The four kissing items are given first, ordered from greatest emotional involvement to least emotional involvement; these are followed by the four petting questions and then the four coitus questions. The directions accompanying the scales provide the following definitions: "*Love* means the emotional state which is more intense than strong affection and which you would define as love. *Strong affection* means affection which is stronger than physical attraction, average fondness, or 'liking'—but less strong than love. *Petting* means sexually stimulating behavior more intimate than kissing and simple hugging but not including full sexual relations" (Reiss, 1964b, p. 190). For each statement, respondents are first to determine whether they agree or disagree with the statement and then to determine the degree of their agreement or disagreement: "Strong, Medium, Slight."

Depending on the needs of the researcher and the characteristics of the subjects being studied, Reiss (1964b, 1967, 1988) recommended using particular subsets of items rather than the entire Reiss Premarital Sexual Permissiveness Scale.

SAMPLE ITEMS: (These items are from the male standards form; the female standards form includes the same items with the word *female* substituted for the word *male*.)

1. I believe that kissing is acceptable for the male before marriage when he is in love.

12. I believe that full sexual relations are acceptable for the male before marriage even if he does not feel particularly affectionate toward his partner.

PREVIOUS SUBJECTS: Ages 12–90 years; high school students, college students, and adults, both black and white; parents of college students; persons in the United States, Canada, Malaysia, South Africa, Bangladesh, and Mexico

APPROPRIATE FOR: Ages 12 and up

ADMINISTRATION: Self-administered; about 5 minutes for both forms combined

SCORING: For scoring purposes, responses are dichotomized as "agree" or "disagree," but the differing levels of agreement and disagreement are retained on the scales so that respondents can feel more comfortable answering the items. An individual's own permissiveness score is equal to the number of items answered "agree" on the individual's same sex form. Similarly, a cross-sex permissiveness score can be found by counting the number of "agree" responses on the individual's cross-sex form. Support for equal sexual standards or a double sexual standard is determined by comparing an individual's responses on the two different forms.

Although many articles listed below provide normative information, the usefulness of the information may be limited by its age.

DEVELOPMENT: Reiss used a rational approach in developing items for the Reiss Premarital Sexual Permissiveness Scale. Because American sexual standards have been related to the degree of affection involved in the relationship, Reiss (1964b) developed items to represent four different levels of affection. Further he selected three levels of sexual behavior, ranging from somewhat casual to intense (i.e., from kissing to coitus).

RELIABILITY: Reiss (1964b) reported that results were not seriously affected by the order of the questions.

Reiss (1964a) reported a coefficient of reproducibility greater than .97

on each scale for each of two samples. The coefficient of scalability was greater than .88 on each scale for each of two samples. The minimal marginal reproducibility was greater than .68, and the percentage pure scale types was greater than .86 for each scale for each of two samples.

Libby, Gray, and White (1978) deleted the kissing items from the Reiss Premarital Sexual Permissiveness Scale and scored the scale as a summated rating scale. Using responses from 421 persons, they obtained an uncorrected, split-half reliability of .81.

VALIDITY: Reiss (1967) pointed out that the items cover the dimension of sexual permissiveness: "the first item in the scale . . . [received] about ninety-five to ninety-nine percent agreement and the last item only . . . [received] about seven to twenty-one percent agreement" (p. 28).

Reiss (1964a, 1964b) found that college students were more permissive than adults, and adult blacks were more permissive than adult whites. The black-white difference was not replicated in the research of DelCampo, Sporakowski, and DelCampo (1976), but it was in the research of Staples (1978).

Reiss (1967) and DelCampo et al. (1976) reported that males held more permissive attitudes than did females.

NOTES & COMMENTS: (1) In general, the scale order of the items paralleled the order in which the items were presented (Reiss, 1964b). However, item 4 (pertaining to kissing without affection) and item 8 (pertaining to petting without affection) tended to receive less support than more intense behaviors (petting and coitus) accompanied by greater involvement (in love or engaged). Furthermore, these two items (4 and 8) scaled differently for different samples of subjects.

(2) Stillerman and Shapiro (1979) obtained high mean marginal frequencies when they used the Reiss Premarital Sexual Permissiveness Scale with persons in South Africa, and their coefficients of scalability were unacceptably low. Stillerman and Shapiro concluded that "several items of the original set may be obsolete not only in addressing attitudes which are so frequently endorsed as to be redundant but also insofar as these items fail to satisfy the requirements for Guttman scaling" (p. 8). They recommended deleting the items that are very frequently endorsed (i.e., kissing behaviors) and substituting items that would elicit greater variability. Despite their conclusion that some items were obsolete, Stillerman and Shapiro's data provided strong support for the scale order originally obtained by Reiss.

(3) Mirande and Hammer (1974) presented data questioning the universality of the Reiss Premarital Sexual Permissiveness Scale. Reiss (1974) responded to their conclusions.

(4) Scores on the Reiss Premarital Sexual Permissiveness Scale (and on variations of the scales) have been related to numerous other variables (Caron, Carter, & Brightman, 1985; DelCampo et al., 1976; Eberhardt &

Schill, 1984; Glass, 1972; Heltsley & Broderick, 1969; Hendrick & Hendrick, 1987; Herold, 1981a, 1981b; Herold & Goodwin, 1981; Hornick, 1978; Hornick, Doran, & Crawford, 1979; Kaats & Davis, 1970; Libby et al., 1978; MacCorquodale & DeLamater, 1979; Maranell, Dodder, & Mitchell, 1970; Mendelsohn & Mosher, 1979; Perlman, Josephson, Hwang, Begum, & Thomas, 1978; Reiss, 1965; Roebuck & McGee, 1977; Weis & Slosnerick, 1981; Yarber & Greer, 1986).

(5) Researchers have modified the Reiss Premarital Sexual Permissiveness Scale (DeLamater & MacCorquodale, 1978; Eberhardt & Schill, 1984; Hepburn, 1981; Herold, 1981a, 1981b; Herold & Goodwin, 1981; Hornick, 1978; Hornick et al., 1979; Libby et al., 1978; MacCorquodale & DeLamater, 1979; Peplau, Rubin, & Hill, 1977; Roebuck & McGee, 1977; Wilcox & Udry, 1986). Researchers have also used subsets of items from the Reiss Premarital Sexual Permissiveness Scale (LaBeff & Dodder, 1981; Perlman et al., 1978).

(6) A significant revision of the Reiss Premarital Sexual Permissiveness Scale was developed by Sprecher, McKinney, Walsh, and Anderson (1988). They replaced the three sexual behaviors of kissing, petting, and full sexual relationships with heavy petting, which they defined as touching of genitals, sexual intercourse, and oral-genital sex. They also changed the levels of affection to be "first date, casually dating, seriously dating, pre-engaged (informal commitment to marriage) and engagement (formal commitment to marriage)" (p. 822). Crossing the three physical behaviors with the five degrees of relationship led to a 15-item scale. They named their scale the Revised Premarital Sexual Permissiveness Scale. Using their scale, they looked at premarital sexual standards as a function of the age and sex of the sexually active person.

(7) White and Houlihan (1978) factor analyzed responses from 108 college students. They identified three factors: "intercourse with affection, kissing with affection, and nonaffectional sexual activity" (p. 106). However, due to their small sample size, the results cannot be presumed stable. LaBeff and Dodder (1981, 1982) administered a subset of the Reiss Premarital Sexual Permissiveness Scale items to students in Mexico and the United States. Responses from the two groups were factor analyzed separately.

(8) Hobart (1983) compared Reiss Premarital Sexual Permissiveness Scale responses obtained in 1968 with those obtained in 1977. He also compared English-speaking and French-speaking Canadian college students.

(9) Eberhardt and Schill (1984) compared responses to the Reiss Premarital Sexual Permissiveness Scale with responses to a set of parallel items phrased in terms of behavioral intentions.

(10) Johnson (1986) used the INDSCAL technique (Carroll & Chang, 1970) to examine the dimensionality of attitudes toward sexual permis-

siveness. Johnson concluded that there are at least two underlying dimensions: "the physical act and the participants' relationship" (p. 105). Reiss (1986) wrote a letter to the editor replying to the Johnson article.

(11) Because the Reiss Premarital Sexual Permissiveness Scale was originally used more than 25 years ago, the list of research studies using the scale (see USED IN) is incomplete, particularly for the first 15 years of its use.

AVAILABLE FROM: Johnson, 1986; Reiss, 1964a, 1964b, 1965, 1967, 1988; Reiss and Miller, 1979

USED IN:

Caron, S. L., Carter, D. B., & Brightman, L. A. (1985). Sex-role orientation and attitudes towards women: Differences among college athletes and nonathletes. *Perceptual and Motor Skills, 61*, 803–806.

DeLamater, J., & MacCorquodale, P. (1978). Premarital contraceptive use: A test of two models. *Journal of Marriage and the Family, 40*, 235–247.

DelCampo, R. L., Sporakowski, M. J., & DelCampo, D. S. (1976). Premarital sexual permissiveness and contraceptive knowledge: A biracial comparison of college students. *Journal of Sex Research, 12*, 180–192.

Eberhardt, C. A., & Schill, T. (1984). Differences in sexual attitudes and likeliness of sexual behaviors of black lower-socioeconomic father-present vs. father-absent female adolescents. *Adolescence, 19*, 99–105.

Glass, J. C. (1972). Premarital sexual standards among church youth leaders: An exploratory study. *Journal for the Scientific Study of Religion, 11*, 361–367.

Heltsley, M. E., & Broderick, C. B. (1969). Religiosity and premarital sexual permissiveness: Reexamination of Reiss's traditionalism proposition. *Journal of Marriage and the Family, 31*, 441–443.

Hendrick, S., & Hendrick, C. (1987). Multidimensionality of sexual attitudes. *Journal of Sex Research, 23*, 502–526.

Hepburn, E. H. (1981). The father's role in sexual socialization of adolescent females in an upper and upper-middle class population. *Journal of Early Adolescence, 1*, 53–59.

Herold, E. S. (1981a). Contraceptive embarrassment and contraceptive behavior among young single women. *Journal of Youth and Adolescence, 10*, 233–242.

Herold, E. S. (1981b). Measurement issues involved in examining contraceptive use among young single women. *Population and Environment, 4*, 128–144.

Herold, E. S., & Goodwin, M. S. (1981). Premarital sexual guilt. *Canadian Journal of Behavioural Science, 13*, 65–75.

Hobart, C. W. (1983). Changing profession and practice of sexual standards: A study of young Anglophone and Francophone Canadians. *Journal of Comparative Family Studies, 15*, 231–255.

Hornick, J. P. (1978). Premarital sexual attitudes and behavior. *Sociological Quarterly, 19*, 534–544.

Hornick, J. P., Doran, L., & Crawford, S. H. (1979). Premarital contraceptives usage among male and female adolescents. *Family Coordinator, 28*, 181–190.

Johnson, M. P. (1986). The dimensionality of perspectives on premarital sex: A comparison of Guttman and INDSCAL dimensionality. *Journal of Sex Research, 22*, 94–107.

Kaats, G. R., & Davis, K. E. (1970). The dynamics of sexual behavior in college students. *Journal of Marriage and the Family, 32*, 390–399.

LaBeff, E. E., & Dodder, R. A. (1981). A comparison of attitudes toward sexual permissiveness in Mexico and the United States. *Interamerican Journal of Psychology, 15*, 29–40.

LaBeff, E. E., & Dodder, R. A. (1982). Attitudes toward sexual permissiveness in Mexico and the United States. *Journal of Social Psychology, 116*, 285–286.

Libby, R. W., Gray, L., & White, M. (1978). A test and reformulation of reference group and role correlates of premarital sexual permissiveness theory. *Journal of Marriage and the Family, 40*, 79–92.

MacCorquodale, P., & DeLamater, J. (1979). Self-image and premarital sexuality. *Journal of Marriage and the Family, 41*, 327–339.

Maranell, G. M., Dodder, R. A., & Mitchell, D. F. (1970). Social class and premarital sexual permissiveness: A subsequent test. *Journal of Marriage and the Family, 32*, 85–88.

Mendelsohn, M. J., & Mosher, D. L. (1979). Effects of sex guilt and premarital sexual permissiveness on role-played sex education and moral attitudes. *Journal of Sex Research, 15*, 174–183.

Mirande, A. M., & Hammer, E. L. (1974). Premarital sexual permissiveness: A research note. *Journal of Marriage and the Family, 36*, 356–358.

Parcel, G. S., Finkelstein, J., Luttman, D., & Nader, P. R. (1979). Sex concerns of young adolescents. *Birth and the Family Journal, 6*, 43–47.

Peplau, L. A., Rubin, Z., & Hill, C. T. (1977). Sexual intimacy in dating relationships. *Journal of Social Issues, 33*, 86–109.

Perlman, D., Josephson, W., Hwang, W. T., Begum, H., & Thomas, T. L. (1978). Cross-cultural analysis of students' sexual standards. *Archives of Sexual Behavior, 7*, 545–558.

Reiss, I. L. (1964a). Premarital sexual permissiveness among Negroes and whites. *American Sociological Review, 29*, 688–698.

Reiss, I. L. (1964b). The scaling of premarital sexual permissiveness. *Journal of Marriage and the Family, 26*, 188–198.

Reiss, I. L. (1965). Social class and premarital sexual permissiveness: A re-examination. *American Sociological Review, 30*, 747–756.

Reiss, I. L. (1967). *The social context of premarital sexual permissiveness* (pp. 15–37, 183–234). Chicago: Holt, Rinehart, & Winston.

Reiss, I. L. (1969). Response to the Heltsley and Broderick retest of Reiss's proposition one. *Journal of Marriage and the Family, 31*, 444–445.

Reiss, I. L. (1974). Comments on "Premarital Sexual Permissiveness." *Journal of Marriage and the Family, 36*, 445–446.

Reiss, I. L. (1986). Letter to the editor [replying to Johnson]. *Journal of Sex Research, 22*, 408–420.

Reiss, I. L. (1988). Reiss Male and Female Premarital Sexual Permissiveness Scales. In C. M. Davis, W. L. Yarber, & S. L. Davis (Eds.), *Sexuality-related measures: A compendium* (pp. 233–235). Syracuse: Editors.

Reiss, I. L., & Miller, B. C. (1979). Heterosexual permissiveness: A theoretical analysis. In W. R. Burr, R. Hill, F. I. Nye, & I. L. Reiss (Eds.), *Contemporary theories about the family* (Vol. 1, pp. 57–100). New York: Free Press.

Roebuck, J., & McGee, M. G. (1977). Attitudes toward premarital sex and sexual behavior among black high school girls. *Journal of Sex Research, 13,* 104–114.

Sprecher, S., McKinney, K., Walsh, R., & Anderson, C. (1988). A revision of the Reiss Premarital Sexual Permissiveness Scale. *Journal of Marriage and the Family, 50,* 821–828.

Staples, R. (1978). Race, liberalism-conservatism and premarital sexual permissiveness: A bi-racial comparison. *Journal of Marriage and the Family, 40,* 733–742.

Stillerman, E. D., & Shapiro, C. M. (1979). Scaling sex attitudes and behavior in South Africa. *Archives of Sexual Behavior, 8,* 1–13.

Weis, D. L., & Slosnerick, M. (1981). Attitudes toward sexual and nonsexual extramarital involvements among a sample of college students. *Journal of Marriage and the Family, 43,* 349–358.

Weis, D. L., Slosnerick, M., Cate, R., & Sollie, D. L. (1986). A survey instrument for assessing the cognitive association of sex, love, and marriage. *Journal of Sex Research, 22,* 206–220.

White, K. M., & Houlihan, J. (1978). The affectional component of sexual permissiveness: A factor-analytic study. *Journal of College Student Personnel, 19,* 106–108.

Wilcox, S., & Udry, J. R. (1986). Autism and accuracy in adolescent perceptions of friends' sexual attitudes and behavior. *Journal of Applied Social Psychology, 16,* 361–374.

Yarber, W. L., & Greer, J. M. (1986). The relationship between the sexual attitudes of parents and their college daughters' or sons' sexual attitudes and sexual behavior. *Journal of School Health, 56,* 68–72.

BIBLIOGRAPHY:

Carroll, J. D., & Chang, J. (1970). Analysis of individual differences in multidimensional scaling via an n-way generalization of "Eckart-Young" decomposition. *Psychometrika, 35,* 283–319.

SCALE OF ATTITUDES TOWARD PUBLIC EXPOSURE TO SEXUAL STIMULI

AUTHORS: JoEllen E. Crawford and Thomas J. Crawford

DATE: 1978 (used 1972)

VARIABLE: Attitudes regarding public exposure of sexually related stimuli

TYPE OF INSTRUMENT: Summated rating scale

DESCRIPTION: The Scale of Attitudes Toward Public Exposure to Sexual Stimuli consists of 10 items. Six items pertain to children, 2 pertain to pregnant or nursing women, and the remaining 2 pertain to public displays of affection and public nudity. Five items express a conservative attitude, and 5 express a permissive attitude. Respondents express their views regarding each item by selecting one of five response options: "strongly agree, agree, undecided, disagree, strongly disagree."

SAMPLE ITEMS: Pregnant women should not wear bikinis on a public beach.

Little girls should be taught that their bodies are private.

PREVIOUS SUBJECTS: College students, married women, mothers of two children, childless newlyweds

APPROPRIATE FOR: College students and older

ADMINISTRATION: Self-administered; about 5 minutes

SCORING: Items are individually scored on a 5-point scale, with higher scores assigned to responses indicative of a permissive attitude. Total scores range from 10 (very conservative) to 50 (very permissive).

DEVELOPMENT: A pool of 40 items was written by the senior author. After ambiguous, double-barreled, and irrelevant items were deleted, the pool contained 21 items, which were administered to several different samples. Corrected item-total correlations were computed for a sample of 61 married women and a sample of 61 college students. There were 11 items with corrected item-total correlations of at least .50 in both samples. These items were retained for the scale. One of these items was deleted because it lacked face validity. This left the current 10-item version of the Scale of Attitudes Toward Public Exposure to Sexual Stimuli.

RELIABILITY: The Kuder-Richardson reliability for the 21-item original version ranged from .87 to .91. The Kuder-Richardson reliability for the 11-item version was .92 for the sample of married women and .89 for the college students. For the final 10-item version of the Scale of Attitudes Toward Public Exposure to Sexual Stimuli, the Kuder-Richardson reliability was .87 for a sample of 59 mothers of two children and .84 for a sample of 38 childless newlyweds. Corrected item-total correlations for the sample of mothers ranged from .46 to .72; for the sample of childless newlyweds, they ranged from .40 to .67. Test-retest reliability was estimated for a sample of 33 college students who completed a 19-item version on two occasions about 4 weeks apart. The 19-item scale was formed by deleting 2 items concerning actual personal sexual behavior from the 21-item version. The test-retest reliability was .88.

VALIDITY: Evidence for the scale's validity was provided by correlating scores on the 11-item version of the Scale of Attitudes Toward Public Exposure to Sexual Stimuli with scores on the following other scales: Levinson and Huffman's (1955) Traditional Family Ideology Scale (TFI) (see Beere, 1990), Kaufman's (1957) Status-Concern scale, Faulkner and DeJong's (1965) Religious Orthodoxy scale, Kerlinger's (1967) Political Conservatism and Political Liberalism scales, and Gough's (1970) "Modernity" Trait Scale taken from Gough's Personal Values Abstract. For the sample of married women and the sample of college students, the correlations were in the predicted directions. That is, the correlations were positive between the Scale of Attitudes Toward Public Exposure to Sexual Stimuli and each of the first four measures, and the correlations were negative between the Scale of Attitudes Toward Public Exposure to Sexual Stimuli and each of the last two scales. The magnitude of the correlations ranged from .38 to .75.

Mothers of two children completed the Scale of Attitudes Toward Public Exposure to Sexual Stimuli plus the TFI, the Religious Orthodoxy scale, and the Modernity Trait Scale. Again, the correlations were in the predicted direction, and their magnitudes ranged from .48 to .71.

NOTES & COMMENTS: Despite the fact that the psychometric properties for this scale were encouraging, my literature search did not locate any subsequent uses of the scale. Perhaps researchers are more inclined to use the Suppression of Sex subscale from the Parental Attitude Research Instrument (Schaefer & Bell, 1958), which has been modified by Zuckerman (1959).

AVAILABLE FROM: Crawford and Crawford, 1978

USED IN:

Crawford, J. E., & Crawford, T. J. (1978). Development and construct validation of a measure of attitudes toward public exposure to sexual stimuli. *Journal of Personality Assessment*, *42*, 392–400.

BIBLIOGRAPHY:

Beere, C. A. (1990). *Gender roles: A handbook of tests and measures*. Westport, CT: Greenwood.

Faulkner, J. E., & DeJong, G. F. (1965, September). *Religiosity in 5-D: An empirical analysis*. Paper presented at the meeting of the American Sociological Association, Chicago.

Gough, H. G. (1970). *Personal Values Abstract from the California Psychological Inventory*. Palo Alto: Consulting Psychologists Press.

Kaufman, W. C. (1957). Status, authoritarianism, and anti-semitism. *American Journal of Sociology*, *62*, 379–382.

Kerlinger, F. N. (1967). The Social Attitudes Scale. In M. Shaw & J. Wright (Eds.), *Scales for the measurement of attitudes* (pp. 322–325). New York: McGraw-Hill.

Levinson, D., & Huffman, P. (1955). Traditional family ideology and its relation to personality. *Journal of Personality*, *23*, 251–273.

Schaefer, E. S., & Bell, R. Q. (1958). Development of a parental attitude research instrument. *Child Development*, *29*, 339–361.

Zuckerman, M. (1959). Reversed scales to control acquiescence response set in the Parental Attitude Research Instrument. *Child Development*, *30*, 523–532.

SEXUAL ATTITUDE SCALE (SAS)

AUTHORS: Walter W. Hudson, Gerald J. Murphy, and Paula S. Nurius

DATE: 1983

VARIABLE: Adherence to a liberal versus conservative orientation regarding sexual expression

TYPE OF INSTRUMENT: Summated rating scale

DESCRIPTION: The Sexual Attitude Scale (SAS) contains 25 statements; 23 reflect a conservative orientation toward sexual expression, and 2 reflect a liberal orientation. According to Hudson, Murphy, and Nurius (1983), a person with a conservative orientation toward sexual expression believes that sexual expression "should be considerably constrained and closely regulated" (p. 259), whereas a person with a liberal orientation toward sexual expression believes that it "should be open, free, and unrestrained" (p. 258). Item content deals with: sexual freedom; sex education; premarital and extramarital sex; acceptable forms of sexual expression; sex among the young, the elderly, and the handicapped; and sex in the media. Respondents express their views on each item by using the following key: "1 = strongly disagree, 2 = disagree, 3 = neither agree nor disagree, 4 = agree, 5 = strongly agree."
SAMPLE ITEMS: I think there is too much sexual freedom given to adults these days.

Sex education should be restricted to the home.
PREVIOUS SUBJECTS: Adults, college students
APPROPRIATE FOR: High school students and older
ADMINISTRATION: Self-administered; about 10 minutes
SCORING: The 23 conservatively phrased items are scored by assigning 5 points to the agree end of the continuum; scoring for the other 2 items is reversed. A total score is computed by using the following formula:

$$\text{score} = (\Sigma X - N)(100)/([N][4]),$$

where X represents an item score and N represents the total number of items that were properly completed. This formula produces scores in the range of 0 (very liberal orientation) to 100 (very conservative orientation). Although this formula corrects for omitted items, Hudson et al. (1983) recommended that users "disregard any SAS score that is based on fewer than 20 items" (p. 261).

If a respondent completes all items, the formula reduces to

$$\text{score} = \Sigma X - 25.$$

DEVELOPMENT: No information was provided.
RELIABILITY: Coefficient alpha was computed for two different groups—a group of 378 Hawaiian adults representing various ethnic groups and a similar group of 689 persons—and both alpha coefficients were equal to .92.
VALIDITY: In order to provide evidence of the discriminant validity of the SAS, Hudson et al. (1983) compared responses from members of churches that represented strongly religious denominations (conservative group) with responses from graduate students from a school of

social work (liberal group). They found a large and statistically significant difference between the means of the two groups ($p < .001$). Furthermore, the point-biserial correlation between group membership and SAS scores was .73. Hudson et al. also compared the Index of Marital Satisfaction (IMS) (Cheung & Hudson, 1982) scores of the liberal and conservative groups. As predicted, the difference in means between the two groups and the point-biserial correlation indicated that the SAS discriminated between the two groups better than did the IMS; "the SAS therefore appears to be about three times more powerful than the IMS in terms of its ability to discriminate between the two criterion groups" (Hudson et al., 1983, p. 265).

As further evidence of the validity of the SAS, Hudson et al. (1983) showed that the SAS items correlated very strongly with the SAS total scores and did not correlate highly with total scores on the IMS, the Index of Sexual Satisfaction (ISS) (Hudson, Harrison, & Crosscup, 1981) (see separate entry), the Generalized Contentment Scale (Byerly, 1979), which is a measure of depression, or the Index of Self-Esteem (Hudson, 1982). Furthermore, correlations among total scores on the SAS and total scores on these three measures were very low.

As predicted, Hudson et al. (1983) found that SAS scores were negatively correlated with education ($r = -.38$) and positively correlated with age ($r = .41$). SAS scores were independent of sex; the correlation between SAS scores and income was $-.23$.

The SAS, IMS, and ISS were administered to three groups (Cheung & Hudson, 1982). One group consisted of 110 persons seeking therapy; 50 of them were experiencing a marital relationship problem. The second group consisted of 100 persons; therapists judged 49 of them to be experiencing a significant sexual relationship problem and 49 to be free of any significant sexual relationship problem. The third group included 378 persons, ages 40 to 80. Cheung and Hudson predicted very small correlations between the SAS and each of the other two scales. Their predictions were substantiated for each of the three samples. The SAS-IMS correlations were .07, .19, and .08, respectively. The SAS-ISS correlations were .10, .18, and .18, respectively.

Troiden and Jendrek (1987) predicted that persons who were sexually liberal, as measured by the SAS, would engage in more varied sexual behaviors. Using data obtained from a sample of 191 college students, they found that their prediction was supported ($r = -.34$). Furthermore, the same pattern of results was obtained across both sexes ($r = -.38$ for men and $-.32$ for women) and across two levels of religious devoutness ($r = -.35$ for the devout and $-.24$ for the nondevout). Overall, more liberal attitudes on the SAS were associated with greater sexual experience.

NOTES & COMMENTS: Darling and Hicks (1983) studied the sexual attitudes and sexual satisfaction of 80 college students. One of their measures was the SAS. Nurius (1983) reported the results of a study examining the relationships among depression, self-esteem, marital discord, sexual discord, sexual activities and preferences, and SAS scores. Holland, Atkinson, and Johnson (1987) hypothesized that "subjects would rate a counselor expressing attitudes similar to their own more positively than one expressing dissimilar attitudes" (p. 323). To test this hypothesis, they conducted a study in which 209 college students completed the SAS and rated counselor effectiveness based on reading a description and a counseling transcript from one of four counselors: a male or female counselor who had sexual attitudes that were similar to or dissimilar from the respondent's. Fisher (1987) conducted a study to determine whether parent-child communication about sex is related to similarity in sexual attitudes for college students and their parents. The SAS was one of the measures used in the study.

AVAILABLE FROM: Hudson, Murphy, and Nurius, 1983

USED IN:

Cheung, P. P. L., & Hudson, W. W. (1982). Assessment of marital discord in social work practice: A revalidation of the Index of Marital Satisfaction. *Journal of Social Service Research, 5,* 101–118.

Darling, C. A., & Hicks, M. W. (1983). Recycling parental sexual messages. *Journal of Sex and Marital Therapy, 9,* 233–243.

Elwood, R. W., & Jacobson, N. S. (1988). The effects of observational training on spouse agreement about events in their relationship. *Behaviour Research and Therapy, 26,* 159–167.

Fisher, T. D. (1987, May). *Parent-child sexual attitude similarity as a function of communication about sex and proximity.* Paper presented at the meeting of the Midwestern Psychological Association, Chicago. (ERIC Document Reproduction Service No. ED 284 080)

Holland, A. L., Atkinson, D. R., & Johnson, M. E. (1987). Effects of sexual attitude and sex similarity on perceptions of the counselor. *Journal of Counseling Psychology, 34,* 322–325.

Hudson, W. W., Murphy, G. J., & Nurius, P. S. (1983). A short-form scale to measure liberal vs. conservative orientations toward human sexual expression. *Journal of Sex Research, 19,* 258–272.

Nurius, P. S. (1983). Mental health implications of sexual orientation. *Journal of Sex Research, 19,* 119–136.

Troiden, R. R., & Jendrek, M. P. (1987). Does sexual ideology correlate with level of sexual experience? Assessing the construct validity of the SAS. *Journal of Sex Research, 23,* 256–261.

BIBLIOGRAPHY:

Byerly, F. C. (1979). Comparison between inpatients, outpatients, and normals on three self-report depression inventories (Doctoral dissertation, Western Michigan University, 1979). *Dissertation Abstracts International, 40,* 904B.

Hudson, W. W. (1982). *The Clinical Measurement Package: A field manual.* Homewood, IL: Dorsey.

Hudson, W. W., Harrison, D. F., & Crosscup, P. C. (1981). A short-form scale to measure sexual discord in dyadic relationships. *Journal of Sex Research, 17*, 157–174.

SEXUAL ATTITUDES SCALE

AUTHORS: Clyde Hendrick, Susan Hendrick, Franklin H. Foote, and Michelle J. Slapion-Foote

DATE: 1984 (revised 1987)

VARIABLE: Sexual attitudes

TYPE OF INSTRUMENT: Summated rating scale

DESCRIPTION: The Sexual Attitudes Scale consists of 43 items representing four factors. Permissiveness contains 21 items dealing with such issues as premarital sex, extramarital sex, and other sexual relations; Sexual Practices contains 7 items dealing with birth control, sex education, masturbation, and "sex toys"; Communion contains 9 items reflecting "attitudes toward sex that focus on sharing, involvement, and more than a tinge of idealism" (S. Hendrick & Hendrick, 1987b, p. 523); and Instrumentality contains 6 items reflecting the idea that sex is pleasurable, a physical or bodily experience, and a game between men and women. Each item is accompanied by five response alternatives: "strongly agree, moderately agree, neutral, moderately disagree, strongly disagree."

SAMPLE ITEMS: (Permissiveness) I do not need to be committed to a person to have sex with him/her.

(Sexual Practices) Birth control is part of responsible sexuality.

(Communion) Sex is the closest form of communication between two people.

(Instrumentality) Sex is best when you let yourself go and focus on your own pleasure.

PREVIOUS SUBJECTS: College students; heterosexual dating couples

APPROPRIATE FOR: Ages 16 and older

ADMINISTRATION: Self-administered; about 15–20 minutes

SCORING: Items are scored on a 5-point scale, with the "strongly agree" end of the continuum assigned 1 point and the "strongly disagree" end of the continuum assigned 5 points. Before items are summed to form factor scores, the scoring of three items on the Permissiveness subscale must be reversed. Higher scores on the Permissiveness subscale reflect greater permissiveness; higher scores on the Sexual Practices subscale reflect stronger support for birth control responsibility and stronger support for other sexual practices; higher scores on the Communion subscale reflect a more idealistic view of sexual activity; and higher scores on the Instrumentality subscale reflect agreement with a pleasure-oriented view of sex that focuses on the physical, bodily, and game-playing aspects of

sexuality. S. S. Hendrick and C. Hendrick (1987a) reported item means and standard deviations separately by sex for each of the four subscales.
DEVELOPMENT: Susan Hendrick and Clyde Hendrick developed a pool of over 150 items, which they reduced to 102 items by eliminating ambiguous and redundant items. The items pertained to "some of the traditional sex attitude areas such as sexual permissiveness, premarital sex, and sexual practices, as well as areas such as the 'meaning' of sexuality, sexual responsibility, and power and dominance in sex" (S. Hendrick, Hendrick, Slapion-Foote, & Foote, 1985, p. 1633). The items were administered to over 800 college students, and their responses were factor analyzed. Nine factors were identified, although one was eliminated since it contained only 1 item with a substantial factor loading. The other factors were: Sexual Permissiveness, Sexual Responsibility, Sexual Communion, Sexual Instrumentality, Sexual Conventionality, Sex Avoidance, Sexual Control, and Sexual Power. Five of these factors were retained for the next step in scale development. A sample of 807 college students completed a 58-item version of the Sexual Attitudes Scale containing 29 Sexual Permissiveness items, 9 Sexual Responsibility items, 8 Sexual Communion items, 6 Sexual Instrumentality items, and 6 Sexual Conventionality items. Responses were factor analyzed, and items were retained if they loaded highly on only one factor. Some items were eliminated, and 7 items were revised. A 46-item version of the scale was administered to another sample of 567 college students, whose responses were also factor analyzed.
RELIABILITY: S. Hendrick and Hendrick (1987b) reported alpha coefficients for the 58-item version of the Sexual Attitudes Scale. Using data from 807 college students, they obtained the following coefficients: Permissiveness = .94, Sex Practices = .69, Communion = .79, and Instrumentality = .80. A subset of 112 students completed the scale on a second occasion about 4 weeks later. Test-retest reliability coefficients were: Permissiveness = .88, Sex Practices = .80, Communion = .67, and Instrumentality = .66. S. Hendrick and Hendrick also reported alpha coefficients based on 567 college students who completed the shorter (current) version of the scale: Permissiveness = .93, Sex Practices = .82, Communion = .74, and Instrumentality = .78.

S. S. Hendrick and Hendrick (1987a) tested 218 college students with the Sexual Attitudes Scale. They obtained the following values for coefficient alpha: Permissiveness = .94, Sexual practices = .78, Communion = .82, and Instrumentality = .79.
VALIDITY: In order to obtain information regarding the validity of the Sexual Attitudes Scale, S. Hendrick and Hendrick (1987b) correlated scores on the Sexual Attitudes Scale with five scores derived from the following measures: the Sexual Opinion Survey (SOS) (Fisher, Byrne, White, & Kelley, 1988) (see separate entry); the Reiss Premarital Sexual

Permissiveness Scale (Reiss, 1967) (see separate entry), from which separate scores for male permissiveness, female permissiveness, and total permissiveness were obtained; and the Revised Mosher Guilt Inventory (Green & Mosher, 1985) (see separate entry). The Permissiveness scores from the Sexual Attitudes Scale were significantly correlated with all five of the other scores; the magnitude of the correlations ranged from .53 to .63. The Sex Practices scores were also significantly correlated with the other five scores, but the magnitudes of the correlations were lower, ranging from .30 to .55. The Instrumentality scores, significantly correlated with the five other scores, had correlations of still lower magnitude, ranging from .23 to .28. Finally, the Communion scores were not significantly correlated with any of the other scores, except for the Revised Mosher Guilt Inventory scores where the correlation had a magnitude of .29.

NOTES & COMMENTS: (1) S. Hendrick and Hendrick (1987b) reported results from two different factor analyses that produced comparable results. The magnitude of the factor loadings for all items on the Permissiveness subscale exceeded .31, and most exceeded .50; for the Sexual Practices subscale, factor loadings exceeded .33, and most exceeded .50; on the Communion subscale, the lowest factor loading was .47; and on the Instrumentality subscale, the lowest factor loading was .52. S. Hendrick and Hendrick also reported the intercorrelations between the factor scores. The strongest relationships were between Instrumentality and Permissiveness and between Communion and Sex Practices.

(2) S. Hendrick and Hendrick (1987a, 1987b) correlated the 4 subscale scores from the Sexual Attitudes Scale with the 6 subscale scores obtained on the Love Attitudes Scale (C. Hendrick & Hendrick, 1986) (see separate entry). In the former study, they also related the subscales scores from the Sexual Attitude Scale with scores on measures of self-disclosure and sensation seeking. In the latter study, they also factor analyzed the 10 scores together, and they correlated scores from the Sexual Attitudes Scale with scores from the Sensation Seeking Scale (Zuckerman, Kolin, Price, & Zoob, 1964). S. Hendrick and Hendrick (1987b) also related factor scores from the Sexual Attitudes Scale to gender, ethnicity, international student status versus domestic student status, number of times in love, whether currently in love, and self-esteem.

(3) The 102-item version of the Sexual Attitudes Scale was used in two studies (C. Hendrick, Hendrick, Foote, & Slapion-Foote, 1984; S. Hendrick et al., 1985); C. Hendrick and Hendrick (1986) reported using the 58-item version of the Sexual Attitudes Scale.

(4) Bailey, Hendrick, and Hendrick (1987) intercorrelated scores on the Sexual Attitudes Scale, the Love Attitudes Scale, the Bem Sex Role Inventory (BSRI) (Bem, 1974) (see Beere, 1990), which is a measure of

gender role identity, and the Rosenberg Self-Esteem Scale (Rosenberg, 1965, 1979). The researchers also looked at scores on the Sex Attitudes Scale in relation to sex and in relation to gender role, as measured by the BSRI. S. S. Hendrick, Hendrick, and Adler (1988) related scores on Permissiveness, Communion, and Instrumentality to measures of relationship satisfaction, and for each of the three subscales, the researchers looked at the correlation between partners' scores. S. S. Hendrick (1988) correlated scores on the Sexual Attitudes Scale with scores on the Relationship Assessment Scale, developed by S. S. Hendrick.

AVAILABLE FROM: S. Hendrick and Hendrick, 1987b

USED IN:

Bailey, W. C., Hendrick, C., & Hendrick, S. S. (1987). Relation of sex and gender role to love, sexual attitudes, and self-esteem. *Sex Roles, 16*, 637–648.

Hendrick, C., & Hendrick, S. (1986). A theory and method of love. *Journal of Personality and Social Psychology, 50*, 392–402.

Hendrick, C., Hendrick, S., Foote, F. H., & Slapion-Foote, M. J. (1984). Do men and women love differently? *Journal of Social and Personal Relationships, 1*, 177–195.

Hendrick, S. S. (1988). A generic measure of relationship satisfaction. *Journal of Marriage and the Family, 50*, 93–98.

Hendrick, S. S., & Hendrick, C. (1987a). Love and sexual attitudes, self-disclosure and sensation seeking. *Journal of Social and Personal Relationships, 4*, 281–297.

Hendrick, S., & Hendrick, C. (1987b). Multidimensionality of sexual attitudes. *Journal of Sex Research, 23*, 502–526.

Hendrick, S. S., Hendrick, C., & Adler, N. L. (1988). Romantic relationships: Love, satisfaction, and staying together. *Journal of Personality and Social Psychology, 54*, 980–988.

Hendrick, S., Hendrick, C., Slapion-Foote, M. J., & Foote, F. H. (1985). Gender differences in sexual attitudes. *Journal of Personality and Social Psychology, 48*, 1630–1642.

BIBLIOGRAPHY:

Beere, C. A. (1990). *Gender roles: A handbook of tests and measures*. Westport, CT: Greenwood.

Bem, S. L. (1974). The measurement of psychological androgyny. *Journal of Consulting and Clinical Psychology, 42*, 155–162.

Fisher, W. A., Byrne, D., White, L. A., & Kelley, K. (1988). Erotophobia-erotophilia as a dimension of personality. *Journal of Sex Research, 25*, 123–151.

Green, S. E., & Mosher, D. L. (1985). A causal model of sexual arousal to erotic fantasies. *Journal of Sex Research, 21*, 1–23.

Reiss, I. L. (1967). *The social context of premarital sexual permissiveness*. Chicago: Holt, Rinehart, & Winston.

Rosenberg, M. (1965). *Society and the adolescent self-image*. Princeton: Princeton University Press.

Rosenberg, M. (1979). *Conceiving the self*. New York: Basic Books.

Zuckerman, M., Kolin, E. A., Price, L., & Zoob, I. (1964). Development of a sensation seeking scale. *Journal of Consulting Psychology, 28*, 477–482.

SEXUAL CONSERVATISM

AUTHOR: Martha R. Burt

DATE: 1980 (used 1977)

VARIABLE: Attitudes toward sexual behavior; in other words, "support for or opposition to restrictions on the appropriateness of sexual partners, sexual acts, conditions or circumstances under which sex should occur" (Burt, 1980, p. 218)

TYPE OF INSTRUMENT: Summated rating scale

DESCRIPTION: The Sexual Conservatism scale consists of 10 items, 1 of which pertains specifically to men and 5 of which pertain specifically to women and how freely they ought to engage in sexual activity. Of the remaining 4 items, 1 pertains to masturbation, 1 to oral sex, 1 to sex during menstruation, and 1 to the goals of sexual intercourse. Items are accompanied by 7-point response scales ranging from "strongly agree" to "strongly disagree."

SAMPLE ITEMS: A woman who initiates a sexual encounter will probably have sex with anybody.

Men have a biologically stronger sex drive than women.

PREVIOUS SUBJECTS: Adults, ages 18 and older; convicted rapists, convicted child molesters, and non-sex offender prisoners

APPROPRIATE FOR: Ages 16 and older

ADMINISTRATION: Self-administered (although it has been used in an interview format); a couple of minutes

SCORING: Items are scored on a 7-point scale, with 7 points assigned to the response that is most conservative. For eight items, the most conservative response is "strongly agree," and for two items, it is "strongly disagree." Item scores are summed to yield a total score that can range from 10 (very liberal) to 70 (very conservative). The mean score for 598 adults who completed the scale was 27.8, and the standard deviation was 10.5 (Burt, 1980).

DEVELOPMENT: This scale was developed concurrently with four other scales: Sex Role Stereotyping Scale (see Beere, 1990), Adversarial Sexual Beliefs scale (see separate entry), Acceptance of Interpersonal Violence scale (see separate entry), and Rape Myth Acceptance Scale (see separate entry). Pretesting involving a large item pool was conducted, and based on the results, about twice the number of items to be included on each of the final scales was included on an interview form. The interview was administered to 598 adults in Minnesota, and item analyses were performed on their responses. Based on these analyses, the "best items" were selected for the scale.

RELIABILITY: Based on testing 598 adults, Burt (1980) obtained a coefficient alpha of .81.

VALIDITY: Burt (1980) found that younger persons and persons with higher education levels had lower (more liberal) scores on the Sexual Conservatism scale. She also found that higher, more conservative scores were obtained by those who were more accepting of rape myths, those who supported adversarial sexual beliefs, and those who supported sex role stereotyping.

NOTES & COMMENTS: (1) Although I have presented Burt's scales as five separate scales and they can be used independently of each other, Burt actually developed her five measures together. The five scales are: Acceptance of Interpersonal Violence, Adversarial Sexual Beliefs, Rape Myth Acceptance Scale, Sex Role Stereotyping Scale, and Sexual Conservatism. A set of 37 items from the Burt scales has been used in research looking at the characteristics of rape victims who never reported their assault (Koss, 1985) and sexual offenders who were never detected (Koss, Leonard, Beezley, & Oros, 1985). When these researchers factor analyzed responses to the 37 items, they identified five factors that were quite comparable to the scales Burt developed. Koss (1985) and Koss et al. (1985) labeled their factors "Acceptance of Sexual Aggression; Conservative Attitudes Toward Female Sexuality; Rejection of Rape Myths; Heterosexual Relationships as Game-playing; and Unacceptability of Aggression" (Koss, 1985, p. 198).

(2) Using the results obtained from testing 598 adults, Burt (1980) reported the item-total correlations for each of the items. The values she obtained ranged from .405 to .595.

(3) Overholser and Beck (1986) compared incarcerated rapists, incarcerated child molesters, and three control groups on a variety of measures, including the Sexual Conservatism scale.

(4) Rapaport and Burkhart (1984) investigated the relationship between college men's coercive sexual behaviors and their responses on a variety of measures, including the Sexual Conservatism scale.

(5) Pryor (1987) studied college men and compared their scores on a measure of their likelihood to commit sexual harassment with their scores on a variety of other measures, including the Sexual Conservatism scale.

AVAILABLE FROM: Burt, 1980

USED IN:

Burt, M. R. (1980). Cultural myths and supports for rape. *Journal of Personality and Social Psychology, 38,* 217–230.

Koss, M. P. (1985). The hidden rape victim: Personality, attitudinal, and situational characteristics. *Psychology of Women Quarterly, 9,* 193–212.

Koss, M. P., Leonard, K. E., Beezley, D. A., & Oros, C. J. (1985). Nonstranger sexual aggression: A discriminant analysis of the psychological characteristics of undetected offenders. *Sex Roles, 12,* 981–992.

Overholser, J. C., & Beck, S. (1986). Multimethod assessment of rapists, child molesters, and three control groups on behavioral and psychological measures. *Journal of Consulting and Clinical Psychology*, *54*, 682–687.

Pryor, J. B. (1987). Sexual harassment proclivities in men. *Sex Roles*, *17*, 269–290.

Rapaport, K., & Burkhart, B. R. (1984). Personality and attitudinal characteristics of sexually coercive college males. *Journal of Abnormal Psychology*, *93*, 216–221.

BIBLIOGRAPHY:

Beere, C. A. (1990). *Gender roles: A handbook of tests and measures.* Westport, CT: Greenwood.

SEXUAL PERMISSIVENESS SCALE

AUTHORS: Mary Riege Laner, Roy H. Laner, and C. Eddie Palmer, excerpted from *Better Homes and Gardens*

DATE: 1972

VARIABLE: Attitudes toward premarital and extramarital permissiveness

TYPE OF INSTRUMENT: Summated rating scale or alternate choice: yes/no, approve/disapprove

DESCRIPTION: The Sexual Permissiveness Scale consists of either six or seven items, depending on the version that is being used. Item content pertains to premarital sex, premarital living together, communal living, and extramarital sex. When used as an alternate choice measure, the items are phrased as questions, and the response options are either "yes/no" or "approve/disapprove." When used as a summated rating scale, items are phrased as statements, and there is a 6-point response scale, ranging from "disagree completely" to "agree completely."

SAMPLE ITEMS: Do you think it's okay for a couple who are in love to have premarital sexual intercourse?

Among the couples you know, would the husband's unfaithfulness cause a divorce?

PREVIOUS SUBJECTS: College students in the United States and Australia, Australian adults

APPROPRIATE FOR: College students and older

ADMINISTRATION: Self-administered; a couple of minutes

SCORING: Laner, Laner, and Palmer (1978) and Laner and Housker (1980) did not obtain scores for individuals. Rather they collapsed responses across persons and reported the percentage of individuals agreeing and disagreeing with each item. Hong (1983, 1984) used the 6-item version of the scale with a 6-point response scale and obtained two scores; three items were summed to yield a premarital permissiveness score, and the other three items were summed to yield an extramarital score.

DEVELOPMENT: The items on the Sexual Permissiveness Scale were excerpted from a *Better Homes and Gardens* (1972, 1977) readership survey, "What's Happening to the American Family?"

RELIABILITY: No information was provided.
VALIDITY: No information was provided, but results from some applications of the Sexual Permissiveness Scale provided data regarding the scale's validity.
NOTES & COMMENTS: (1) Hong (1983) factor analyzed responses to a 6-item version of the Sexual Permissiveness Scale that was completed by 560 Australian college students. Two 3-item factors were extracted: Premarital Permissiveness and Extramarital Permissiveness.

(2) Laner et al. (1978) looked at college students' responses to the individual items on the Sexual Permissiveness Scale and related them to sex, year in school, attitudes toward divorce, marital intentions, and perceptions of parents' marriage. Laner and Housker (1980) looked at college students' responses to the individual items on the Sexual Permissiveness Scale and compared them to responses given by readers of *Better Homes and Gardens*. They also looked at responses in terms of sex, age, and year of data collection (1972 and 1978). Hong (1983) administered the Sexual Permissiveness Scale to Australian college students. He obtained a Premarital Permissiveness score and an Extramarital Permissiveness score for each respondent. Scores were then compared in terms of respondent's sex and church attendance. Hong (1984) compared the Premarital Permissiveness scores and Extramarital Permissiveness scores of college students and adults. He also looked at score differences as a function of sex, church attendance, education, and age.
AVAILABLE FROM: Laner and Housker, 1980; Laner, Laner, and Palmer, 1978; Hong, 1983
USED IN:

Hong, S. M. (1983). Gender, religion, and sexual permissiveness: Some recent Australian data. *Journal of Psychology, 115*, 17–22.

Hong, S. M. (1984). Permissiveness, more or less: Sexual attitudes in the general public. *Australian Journal of Sex, Marriage and Family, 5*, 89–96.

Laner, M. R., & Housker, S. L. (1980). Sexual permissiveness in younger and older adults. *Journal of Family Issues, 1*, 103–124.

Laner, M. R., Laner, R. H., & Palmer, C. E. (1978). Permissive attitudes toward sexual behaviors: A clarification of theoretical explanations. *Journal of Sex Research, 14*, 137–144.

BIBLIOGRAPHY:

What's happening to the American family. (1972, February). *Better Homes and Gardens*, pp. 33–36.

What's happening to the American family. (1977, September). *Better Homes and Gardens*, pp. 125–128.

AGING SEXUAL KNOWLEDGE AND ATTITUDES SCALE (ASKAS)

AUTHOR: Charles B. White
DATE: 1982 (used 1978)
VARIABLE: Knowledge and attitudes regarding sexuality in the aged

TYPE OF INSTRUMENT: Summated rating scale and alternate choice: true/false
DESCRIPTION: The Aging Sexual Knowledge and Attitudes Scale (ASKAS) consists of 61 items divided into two sections. The first section contains 35 items assessing knowledge of the sexuality changes associated with advancing age. Persons respond to these items by answering "true," "false," or "don't know." Since these are factual items, there is a correct answer for each item. The correct answer is "true" for 26 items and "false" for 9 items. The second part contains 26 statements assessing attitudes about sexual activity among elderly persons. Sixteen attitude items refer to sexuality within the context of a nursing home. Persons respond using a 7-point scale, with the endpoints labeled "disagree" and "agree." For 15 items, an "agree" response reflects a negative attitude toward sexuality among elderly persons; for 11 items, an "agree" response reflects a positive attitude.
SAMPLE ITEMS: (knowledge item) Sexual activity in aged persons is often dangerous to their health.
(attitude item) Aged people have little interest in sexuality (Aged = 65+ years of age).
PREVIOUS SUBJECTS: Nursing home residents, elderly persons living in the community, families of elderly persons, persons who work with the elderly, nursing home staff
APPROPRIATE FOR: College students and older
ADMINISTRATION: Self-administered; about 20–30 minutes
SCORING: ASKAS yields two separate scores: a knowledge score and an attitude score. For the knowledge items, 1 point is assigned for each correct answer, 2 points are assigned for each incorrect answer, and 3 points are assigned for each "don't know" response. Item scores are summed to yield a total score that can range from 35 (all items answered correctly) to 105 (all items answered "don't know"). Thus, lower scores reflect greater knowledge. The attitude items are scored on a 7-point scale, with higher scores assigned to the response reflecting a more permissive attitude. Item scores are summed to yield a total score that can range from 26 (most permissive attitude) to 182 (most conservative attitude). White (1982a) reported means and standard deviations for each part of the ASKAS for each of five samples of persons who completed the scale.
DEVELOPMENT: According to White (1982a), items for the ASKAS were adapted from the professional literature regarding physiological or social-psychological aspects of sexuality in the elderly. Item development was predicated on the assumption that attitudes toward the sexuality of persons in nursing homes predict attitudes toward the sexuality of elderly persons not in nursing homes.
RELIABILITY: White (1982a) reported reliabilities for various samples.

For the knowledge items, the corrected split-half reliability was .91 for 163 nursing home staff members and .90 for 279 nursing home residents. For these two groups, the alpha coefficients were .93 and .91. For three other groups—aged community residents, a nursing home staff, and immediate relatives of aged persons—alpha coefficients were all at least .90. Test-retest reliability was estimated for the knowledge items using two different samples: 15 aged members of the community and 30 persons including staff of a nursing home and immediate relatives of the aged. The reliability coefficients were .97 and .90. Somewhat lower reliabilities were obtained for the attitude items. For the 163 nursing home staff members and the 279 nursing home residents, the corrected split-half reliability was .86 and .83, respectively, and coefficient alpha was .85 and .76, respectively. For the other three groups—aged community residents, a nursing home staff, and immediate relatives of aged persons—the alpha coefficients were .87, .87, and .86, respectively. Test-retest reliability for the 15 aged members of the community was .96; for the 30 persons who were staff of a nursing home or relatives of the aged, test-retest reliability was .72.

VALIDITY: Hammond (cited in White, 1982a) used the ASKAS in a pretest-posttest design to evaluate the effectiveness of a sex education program for professionals working with aged persons and for members of community mental health center boards. She found that the sex education program was effective in lowering ASKAS scores; that is, the program resulted in an increase in knowledge regarding sexuality in the aged and an increase in permissiveness of attitudes toward sexuality in the aged.

White (1982b) tested 250 residents living in 15 nursing homes. Consistent with expectations, he found that "attitudes and knowledge regarding sexuality in the aged are significantly related to sexual activity" (p. 19).

Catania and White (1982) studied 30 elderly persons residing in the community and related their sexual knowledge scores from the ASKAS to frequency of masturbation, locus of control, and sexual status, defined as having or not having a sexual partner. They found that sexual knowledge scores were significantly correlated only with locus of control scores ($r = .37$).

Elderly members of the community, immediate relatives of elderly persons, and nursing home staff participated in a study to determine whether sexual knowledge and attitudes regarding the elderly would be changed by an educational program. The ASKAS was used as both a pretest and a posttest. As predicted, attitudes became more permissive and knowledge increased for all three groups relative to their own pretest and to scores obtained by control groups.

NOTES & COMMENTS: (1) White (1982a) reported the results of a factor analysis using pretest scores from about 525 persons who completed the ASKAS. Two factors were identified: a knowledge factor and an attitude factor. Using a factor loading cutoff of .35, two knowledge items and four attitude items failed to load sufficiently well on their own factor, but all six items loaded more heavily on their own factor than on the other factor.

(2) The scoring of the knowledge items is quite unusual in that an answer of "don't know" is considered to reflect less knowledge than an incorrect answer. (Remember that the wrong answer is assigned 2 points, and the "don't know" response is assigned 3 points.) It can be argued that people are more knowledgeable when they recognize that they do not know something than when they have misinformation, yet White seemed to believe that misinformation is closer to correct information than is a "don't know" response. White provided no justification for this unusual scoring system.

(3) A review of item content suggested that there is some redundancy in the items. For example, there is an item asking about masturbation for older males, another item asking about masturbation for older females, and a third item asking about masturbation (with no sex specified).

(4) White (1982b) reported a correlation of .13 between the two sections of the ASKAS. Glass, Mustiar, and Carte (1986) obtained completed ASKAS forms from 57 persons who worked in skilled care nursing homes. Surprisingly, there was a significant and *negative* correlation between knowledge and attitudes ($r = -.30$), showing that greater knowledge about sexuality in elderly persons was associated with more restrictive attitudes. The authors offered a possible explanation for this finding when they pointed out that the respondents with the higher knowledge scores were generally supervisory or administrative personnel who may have been more concerned with the smooth operation of their nursing home than they were with supporting the sexual needs of elderly residents.

(5) Glass et al. (1986) related ASKAS scores to a variety of other variables: sex, age, race, marital status, position, education, nursing education, time as geriatric caretaker, time in current position, continuing education courses, religion, and religiosity.

AVAILABLE FROM: White, 1982a, 1988

USED IN:

Catania, J. A., & White, C. B. (1982). Sexuality in an aged sample: Cognitive determinants of masturbation. *Archives of Sexual Behavior, 11*, 237–245.

Glass, J. C., Jr., Mustiar, R. D., & Carte, L. R. (1986). Knowledge and attitudes of health-care providers toward sexuality in the institutionalized elderly. *Educational Gerontology, 12*, 465–475.

White, C. B. (undated). *Aging Sexual Knowledge and Attitudes Scale*. Unpublished manuscript, Trinity University, San Antonio.

White, C. B. (1982a). A scale for the assessment of attitudes and knowledge regarding sexuality in the aged. *Archives of Sexual Behavior, 11,* 491–502.

White, C. B. (1982b). Sexual interest, attitudes, knowledge, and sexual history in relation to sexual behavior in the institutionalized aged. *Archives of Sexual Behavior, 11,* 11–21.

White, C. B. (1988). Aging Sexual Knowledge and Attitudes Scale. In C. M. Davis, W. L. Yarber, & S. L. Davis (Eds.), *Sexuality-related measures: A compendium* (pp. 12–15). Syracuse: Editors.

White, C. B., & Catania, J. A. (1982). Psychoeducational intervention for sexuality with the aged, family members of the aged, and people who work with the aged. *International Journal of Aging and Human Development, 15,* 121–138.

MILLER-FISK SEXUAL KNOWLEDGE QUESTIONNAIRE

AUTHORS: Warren Miller and Norman Fisk, shortened by Harrison G. Gough

DATE: Original version, 1969; 24-item shortened version, 1974

VARIABLE: Knowledge of contraceptive methods, reproductive physiology, and fertility/infertility

TYPE OF INSTRUMENT: Multiple choice and alternate choice: true/false

DESCRIPTION: The Miller-Fisk Sexual Knowledge Questionnaire described here consists of 24 items: half multiple choice items with four response options and half true/false items. Six items pertain to birth control, 11 items pertain to fertility, 4 items deal with menstruation and menopause, and the remaining 3 items cover related topics. There is one correct answer to each item.

SAMPLE ITEMS: The single most important factor in achieving pregnancy is (a) Time of exposure in the cycle; (b) Female's desire or wish to become pregnant; (c) Frequency of intercourse; (d) Female's overall state of health.

Pregnancy would be impossible in early adolescence when menstruation has not yet even begun or is not at all regularly established. (a) True (b) False

PREVIOUS SUBJECTS: 12 to 14-year-old adolescents, college students, adults, couples

APPROPRIATE FOR: High school students and older

ADMINISTRATION: Self-administered; about 15 minutes

SCORING: The score is derived by counting the number of correctly answered items.

DEVELOPMENT: The Miller-Fisk Sexual Knowledge Questionnaire, developed in 1969, was a 49-item test intended for use with the general public. Gough (1974) felt that some of the items were too difficult for the general public and believed that a shortened version of the test would prove to be more convenient for researchers. He administered the 49-item scale to 29 males and 75 females, some of them college students and some of them adults. Using their responses, he deleted items if the item-total correlation was low, if there was a large sex difference in the percentage getting the item correct or in the item-total correlation, or if the item was excessively easy or excessively difficult. Applying these criteria left a set of 24 questions that comprise the 24-item version of the Miller-Fisk Sexual Knowledge Questionnaire.

RELIABILITY: Corrected split-half reliability was .70 for 209 college men, .62 for 146 college women, and .67 for the combined group of 355 college students (Gough, 1974).

VALIDITY: Using the same data used to develop the 24-item version of the scale, Gough (1974) computed the correlation between the short version and the full-length version of the scale. For males, the correlation was .94; for females, the correlation was .92.

Females consistently scored significantly higher than males on the 24-item Miller-Fisk Sexual Knowledge Questionnaire. This is not surprising since the content of many items is directly related to female reproductive functioning.

NOTES & COMMENTS: (1) After correlating scores on the Miller-Fisk Sexual Knowledge Questionnaire with various indicators of cognitive performance and repeatedly obtaining rather low coefficients, Gough (1988) concluded: "sexual knowledge is specific, that is, only moderately related to academic performance and intellectual aptitude" (p. 199).

(2) Although there are other scales of sexual knowledge available, this questionnaire is included here because the majority of the questions focus on female physiology, pregnancy, and other topics of particular relevance for females.

(3) The 24-item version of the Miller-Fisk Sexual Knowledge Questionnaire has been translated into Italian.

(4) Fisher (1986) used the Miller-Fisk Sexual Knowledge Questionnaire in a study designed to determine whether adolescents whose parents frequently talk to them about sex were more knowledgeable about sex. Another purpose of Fisher's study was to determine whether parents who differed in the frequency with which they discussed sex with their adolescents also differed in their own knowledge about sex. Fisher (1987) conducted a similar study involving college students.

(5) Werner (1988) looked at the relationship between scores on the Miller-Fisk Sexual Knowledge Questionnaire and scores on a variety of personality measures.

AVAILABLE FROM: Gough, 1974, 1988

USED IN:

Fisher, T. D. (1986). Parent-child communication about sex and young adolescents' sexual knowledge and attitudes. *Adolescence, 21*, 517–527.

Fisher, T. D. (1987, May). *Parent-child sexual attitude similarity as a function of communication about sex and proximity.* Paper presented at the meeting of the Midwestern Psychological Association, Chicago. (ERIC Document Reproduction Service No. ED 284 080)

Gough, H. G. (1974). A 24-item version of the Miller-Fisk Sexual Knowledge Questionnaire. *Journal of Psychology, 87*, 183–192.

Gough, H. G. (1975). An attitude profile for studies of population psychology. *Journal of Research in Personality, 9*, 122–135.

Gough, H. G. (1988). A 24-item version of the Miller-Fisk Sexual Knowledge Questionnaire. In C. M. Davis, W. L. Yarber, & S. L. Davis (Eds.), *Sexuality-related measures: A compendium* (pp. 199–200). Syracuse: Editors.

Werner, P. D. (1988). Personality correlates of reproductive knowledge. *Journal of Sex Research, 25*(2), 219–234.

SEX KNOWLEDGE AND ATTITUDE TEST (SKAT)

AUTHORS: Harold I. Lief and David M. Reed

DATE: 1971 (revised 1972)

VARIABLE: Knowledge about sexuality and attitudes toward sexuality

TYPE OF INSTRUMENT: Summated rating scale and alternate choice: true/false

DESCRIPTION: The Sex Knowledge and Attitude Test (SKAT) is a five-part instrument, but only Parts I and II are scored for sex knowledge and attitudes. Part I contains 35 statements to measure attitudes regarding sexual behavior and covers the following topics: premarital sex, extramarital sex, marital sex, autoeroticism, abortion, and sexual variations. Five options are provided for responding to these items: "strongly agree, agree, uncertain, disagree, strongly disagree." Part I of the SKAT contains four subscales: Heterosexual Relations, Sexual Myths, Autoeroticism, and Abortion. The Heterosexual Relations score, based on 8 items, reflects attitudes regarding premarital and extramarital sexual experiences. The Sexual Myths score, based on 9 items, reflects one's acceptance of the common sexual myths. The Autoeroticism score, based on 7 items, reflects attitudes toward masturbation. The Abortion score, based on 8 items, reflects an individual's feelings about abortion from the social, medical, and legal perspectives. Three of the 35 items do not contribute to any of the subscales.

Part II of the SKAT contains 71 true/false items measuring knowledge of the physiological, psychological, and social aspects of sexual behavior. Fifty of these items are test items, and the other 21 items are intended to serve as the basis of lecture or discussion material in a human sexuality class.

The SKAT booklets include three other sections: the inside cover asks six questions about the status of the respondent (e.g., student status and major field of study), Part III contains 12 background questions (e.g., age, sex, and religion), and Part IV asks 27 questions, most of them pertaining to the sexual experiences of the respondent.

SAMPLE ITEMS: (attitudes) The spread of sex education is causing a rise in premarital intercourse.

(knowledge) Pregnancy can occur during natural menopause (gradual cessation of menstruation).

PREVIOUS SUBJECTS: Medical students; physicians; nursing students; registered nurses; high school students; college students and graduate students; law students; teachers; psychiatrists, clinical psychologists, and social workers; patients; married women; physicians; female schizophrenics, manic-depressives, neurotics, and hysterical psychopaths; pharmacists; and mothers of school children

APPROPRIATE FOR: College students and older

ADMINISTRATION: Individually administered; about 30 minutes

SCORING: SKAT tests can be hand scored or machine scored. Scoring keys are available from Harold Lief (see AVAILABLE FROM). Part I of the SKAT yields scores on the four subscales: Heterosexual Relations, Sexual Myths, Autoeroticism, and Abortion. Each item is assigned a score between 1 and 5. Subscale scores are equal to the sum of the scores for the items on the particular subscale. The Heterosexual Relations score ranges from 8 to 40, and higher scores reflect a more liberal attitude. The Sexual Myths score ranges from 9 to 45, and a high score indicates that the respondent does not accept these common myths. The Autoeroticism score ranges from 7 to 35; higher scores reflect an acceptance of masturbation. The Abortion score ranges from 8 to 40, and higher scores reflect a more accepting attitude regarding abortion. The authors recommended giving no score on a subscale if the respondent omits more than one item on that subscale. If only one item is omitted, it is assigned the mean score of the other items on the subscale.

Two scores are computed for the knowledge portion of the SKAT. One score is equal to the number of correctly answered items; the maximum score is 71. The second score is a *T* score, a standardized score reflecting the number correctly answered out of the 50 items on the sex knowledge test (i.e., ignoring the items intended for class discussion).

Normative data are available from Lief (see AVAILABLE FROM).

DEVELOPMENT: Lief and Reed began the development of the SKAT in 1965. They developed a pool of items based on the relevant human sexuality literature, their own clinical experiences, and their knowledge of controversial sex-related topics. Lief and Reed, as well as other researchers and practitioners, made suggestions that led to modifying and adding items. During the 1968–69 academic year, the pool of 180 items was completed by over 800 students in the United States, England, and Sweden. Data obtained from those testings led to the development of SKAT–Form 1.

Form 1 of SKAT contained 50 attitude items that were administered to 1,137 medical students. Their responses to the items were factor analyzed, and four factors were identified: Liberalism (later named Heterosexual Relations), Acceptance of Sexual Myths, Abortion, and Autoeroticism. Items were considered to contribute to a factor if they had loadings greater than .30. The factor analysis was cross-validated using another sample of 1,137 medical students. The data from the original sample were used to obtain the alpha coefficients for the four factors: .75, .71, .67, and .55 for Liberalism, Sexual Myths, Abortion, and Autoeroticism, respectively. The alpha coefficients declined somewhat when the data from the cross-validation sample were analyzed. The results were .73, .63, .65, and .50 for each of the four factors, respectively. The four scales from SKAT–Form 1 were expanded to their current form by adding items. The researchers sought to add items that were unique in content, but they were also interested in preserving the homogeneity of the scales. SKAT–Form 2 was administered to 850 medical students in 16 medical schools, and their responses were factor analyzed. The data supported the four-factor solution from the analysis of SKAT–Form 1.

Part II was intended to be both a research tool and a classroom teaching aid. To select the 21 teaching items, the authors used two criteria: they selected items that all medical and graduate students should know but that research had shown at least 10% of students did not know and items whose content could serve as the focal point for class lecture or group discussion. To select the 50 sex knowledge test items, Lief and Reed (according to Lief, undated) applied two criteria: an item difficulty between .25 and .75 and a point biserial correlation of at least .30. Lief and Reed also stated that the item had to add to the internal consistency of the scale.

RELIABILITY: Based on testing one sample of about 420 medical students in 15 medical schools, Lief (1988) reported the following values for coefficient alpha: Heterosexual Relations = .86, Sexual Myths = .71, Abortion = .80, and Autoeroticism = .81. Based on another sample of 425 medical students, the alpha coefficients were .86, .68, .77, and .84 for the four subscales, respectively. The Kuder-Richardson reliability (KR 21) for the 50-item sex knowledge test was estimated to be .87.

VALIDITY: As would be expected, scores on the sex knowledge items were significantly correlated with scores on the four attitude subscales. The largest correlation was with the Sexual Myths subscale (r = .57); the correlations with the other three subscales ranged from .32 to .49.

The correlations between the subscale scores on the sex attitudes measure and several of the items on Parts III and IV of the SKAT provided further evidence of the validity of the sex attitudes measure (Miller & Lief, 1979). The Heterosexual Relations score correlated most strongly (defined as correlations above .25) with responses regarding coital frequency (r = .28), variety of coital techniques (r = .32), variety of coital partners (r = .29), a rating of sexual experience (r = .30), conservative values (r = −.48), liberal values (r = .36), and religiously influenced values (r = −.43). The Sexual Myths score correlated most strongly with responses regarding conservative values (r = −.29). Abortion scores correlated most strongly with responses regarding conservative values (r = −.27), liberal values (r = .25), religiously influenced values (r = −.31), and Catholic (r = −.34). Autoeroticism scores correlated most strongly with responses regarding conservative values (r = −.46), liberal values (r =.27), and religiously influenced values (r = −.35).

The SKAT has frequently served as a pretest/posttest measure to evaluate the effectiveness of a human sexuality course or workshop (Adame, 1986; Alzate, 1982; Bernard & Schwartz, 1977; Elstein, Dennis, & Buckingham, 1977; Fyfe, 1979; Garrard, Vaitkus, Held, & Chilgren, 1976; Mims, Brown, & Lubow, 1976; Mims, Yeaworth, & Hornstein, 1974; Ray & Kirkpatrick, 1983; Schinke, Blythe, & Gilchrist, 1981; Schnarch & Jones, 1981; Smith, Flaherty, & Webb, 1981; Smith, Flaherty, Webb, & Mumford, 1984). The increase in scores between pretest and posttest demonstrated the effectiveness of the course and also provided evidence for the construct validity of the scale.

Other researchers obtained data that add support for the validity of the SKAT. Female medical students rejected sexual myths significantly more than did male medical students (Lief, 1974). For a sample of experienced family planning nurses, knowledge scores were significantly related to attitude scores; the correlations were .39, .64, .34, and .57 for Heterosexual Relations, Sexual Myths, Abortion, and Autoeroticism, respectively. For a sample of 67 senior nursing students, sex knowledge scores were significantly related to three of the four attitude scores: Heterosexual Relations = .33, Sexual Myths = .67, and Autoeroticism = .30 (Payne, 1976). Payne (1976) predicted that sex knowledge and sex attitudes would be significantly correlated with scores on the Professional Sexual Role Inventory (PSRI), a measure of comfort in professional situations that have sexual overtones. For experienced nurses, the correlation between sex knowledge and PSRI scores was significant (r = .55), but the correlation was nonsignificant for nursing students (r = .20). For the family planning nurses, the correlations between PSRI scores and the four subscales of the attitude measure were all significant: .39, .57, .32, and .54 for Heterosexual Relations, Sexual Myths, Abortion, and Autoeroticism, respectively. For the nursing students, PSRI scores were significantly correlated only with the Autoeroticism scores (r = .40).

NOTES & COMMENTS: (1) Lief (1988) indicated that the SKAT is not intended to assess or diagnose individuals; rather the measure is intended to describe groups of individuals.

(2) The intercorrelations among the four subscales of the sex attitudes

measure ranged from .31 (Abortion with Sexual Myths) to .59 (Autoeroticism with Heterosexual Relations). Payne (1976) obtained intercorrelations among the subscales ranging from .30 to .58 for a sample of experienced nurses and from .14 to .46 for a sample of nursing students.

(3) The SKAT has been used to understand the sex knowledge and attitudes of various groups, including Israeli medical students (Hoch, Kubat, Fisher, & Brandes, 1978); Arab medical students (Moracco & Zeidan, 1982); family physicians (Driscoll, Coble, & Caplan, 1982); female schizophrenics, manic-depressives, neurotics, and hysterical psychopaths (Raboch, 1984, 1986); pharmacists (Ray & Miederhoff, 1984); and Mexican-Americans (Padilla & O'Grady, 1987).

(4) The SKAT has been used to compare various groups of respondents: high school students, nursing students, medical students, law students, college students, graduate students, and registered nurses (Ebert & Lief, 1974; Lief, 1974; Lief & Payne, 1975; Marcotte, Kilpatrick, & Willis, 1977; Miller & Lief, 1976; Payne, 1976); males and females (Lief, 1974; Miller & Lief, 1976); students and their parents (McNab, 1976); homophobic and heterosexual men (Martin, 1983); married couples involved in mate swapping and married couples not involved in mate swapping (Wheeler & Kilmann, 1983); and women with and without physical disabilities (DeHaan & Wallander, 1988).

(5) McNab (1976) looked at the relationship between demographic variables and SKAT scores. Schover (1981) sought to determine whether sexual attitudes, as measured by the SKAT, mediated therapists' reactions to audiotapes of client-related sexual material. Schnarch (1981) asked medical students to predict patient responses to the SKAT and compared the students' projections with patients' actual responses. Schnarch (1982) asked medical students to predict patients' and physicians' responses to the SKAT and compared responses to actual responses from the two groups. Johnson and Boren (1982) used the SKAT to determine if there was a relationship between sexual knowledge and spouse abuse. Aja and Self (1986) used the SKAT in a study comparing different methods for changing the sexual attitudes of nursing home staff.

(6) The SKAT has been used in Israel (Hoch et al., 1978), Lebanon (Moracco & Zeidan, 1982), Colombia (Alzate, 1982), and Czechoslovakia (Raboch, 1984). Lief (1988) reported that it has also been used in England, Sweden, India, and Japan.

(7) Leary and Dobbins (1983) used a 15-item sex knowledge test based on the SKAT.

(8) The SKAT has been used extensively; in fact, it has been used with a larger number of respondents than almost all other measures described in this book. For example, Lief (1988) reported that, prior to 1979, over 35,000 medical students had taken the SKAT.

(9) The SKAT is entry 352 in the *Eighth Mental Measurements Yearbook*.

(10) Lief (1988) lists additional references that report on the use of the SKAT. These references should be consulted by anyone seeking information on the use of the scale prior to the period covered by this book (prior to the late 1970s).

AVAILABLE FROM: Harold I. Lief, 700 Spruce Street, Suite 503, Philadelphia, PA 19106. There is a charge for the materials.

USED IN:

Adame, D. D. (1986). Instruction and course content in sex knowledge and attitudes and internal locus of control. *Psychological Reports*, *58*, 91–94.

Aja, A., & Self, D. (1986). Alternate methods of changing nursing home staff attitudes toward sexual behavior of the aged. *Journal of Sex Education and Therapy*, *12*, 37–41.

Alzate, H. (1982). Effect of formal sex education on the sexual knowledge and attitudes of Colombian medical students. *Archives of Sexual Behavior*, *11*, 201–214.

Bernard, H. S., & Schwartz, A. J. (1977). Impact of a human sexuality program on sex related knowledge, attitudes, behavior and guilt of college undergraduates. *Journal of the American College Health Association*, *25*, 182–185.

DeHaan, C. B., & Wallander, J. L. (1988). Self-concept, sexual knowledge and attitudes, and parental support in the sexual adjustment of women with early- and late-onset physical disability. *Archives of Sexual Behavior*, *17*, 145–161.

Driscoll, C. E., Coble, R. J., & Caplan, R. M. (1982). The sexual practices, attitudes and knowledge of family physicians. *Family Practice Research Journal*, *1*, 200–210.

Ebert, R. K., & Lief, H. I. (1974). Why sex education for medical students? In R. Green (Ed.), *Human sexuality: A health practitioner's text* (pp. 1–6). Baltimore: Williams & Wilkins.

Elstein, M., Dennis, K. J., & Buckingham, M. S. (1977). Sexual knowledge and attitudes of Southamptom medical students. *Lancet*, *2*, 495–497.

Fyfe, B. (1979). Effects of a sexual enhancement workshop on young adults. *Journal of Clinical Psychology*, *35*, 873–875.

Garrard, J., Vaitkus, A., Held, J., & Chilgren, R. A. (1976). Follow-up effects of a medical school course in human sexuality. *Archives of Sexual Behavior*, *5*, 331–340.

Hoch, Z., Kubat, H., Fisher, M., & Brandes, J. M. (1978). Background and sexual experience of Israeli medical students. *Archives of Sexual Behavior*, *7*, 429–441.

Johnson, M. N., & Boren, Y. (1982). Sexual knowledge and spouse abuse: A cultural phenomenon. *Issues in Mental Health Nursing*, *4*, 217–231.

Leary, M. R., & Dobbins, S. E. (1983). Social anxiety, sexual behavior, and contraceptive use. *Journal of Personality and Social Psychology*, *45*, 1347–1354.

Lief, H. I. (undated). *Preliminary technical manual: Sex Knowledge and Attitude Test (SKAT, 2nd ed.)*. Unpublished paper.

Lief, H. I. (1974). Sexual knowledge, attitudes and behavior of medical students: Implications for medical practice. In W. Abse, E. M. Nash, & L. M. R. Louden (Eds.), *Marital and sexual counseling in medical practice* (2nd ed.) (pp. 474–494). Hagerstown, MD: Harper & Row.

Lief, H. I. (1988). The Sex Knowledge and Attitude Test (SKAT). In C. M. Davis, W. L. Yarber, & S. L. Davis (Eds.), *Sexuality-related measures: A compendium* (pp. 213–216). Syracuse: Editors.

Lief, H. I., & Payne, T. (1975). Sexuality: Knowledge and attitudes. *American Journal of Nursing, 75*, 2026–2029.

Marcotte, D. B., Kilpatrick, D. G., & Willis, A. (1977). The Sheppe and Hain study revisited: Professional students and their knowledge and attitudes about human sexuality. *Medical Education, 11*, 201–204.

Martin, C. V. (1983). Treatment of homophobia: Part I. *Corrective and Social Psychiatry and Journal of Behavior Technology, Methods and Therapy, 29*(3), 70–73.

McNab, W. L. (1976). Sexual attitude development in children and the parents' role. *Journal of School Health, 46*, 537–542.

Miller, W. R., & Lief, H. I. (1976). Masturbatory attitudes, knowledge, and experience: Data from the Sex Knowledge and Attitude Test (SKAT). *Archives of Sexual Behavior, 5*, 447–467.

Miller, W. R., & Lief, H. I. (1979). The Sex Knowledge and Attitude Test (SKAT). *Journal of Sex and Marital Therapy, 5*, 282–287.

Mims, F. H., Brown, L., & Lubow, R. (1976). Human sexuality course evaluation. *Nursing Research, 25*, 187–191.

Mims, F., Yeaworth, R., & Hornstein, S. (1974). Effectiveness of an interdisciplinary course in human sexuality. *Nursing Research, 23*, 248–253.

Moracco, J., & Zeidan, M. (1982). Assessment of sex knowledge and attitude of non-Western medical students. *Psychology, 19*(2/3), 13–21.

Padilla, E. R., & O'Grady, K. E. (1987). Sexuality among Mexican Americans: A case of sexual stereotyping. *Journal of Personality and Social Psychology, 52*, 5–10.

Payne, T. (1976). Sexuality of nurses: Correlations of knowledge, attitudes, and behavior. *Nursing Research, 25*, 286–292.

Raboch, J. (1984). The sexual development and life of female schizophrenic patients. *Archives of Sexual Behavior, 13*, 341–349.

Raboch, J. (1986). Sexual development and life of psychiatric female patients. *Archives of Sexual Behavior, 15*, 341–353.

Ray, R. E., & Kirkpatrick, D. R. (1983). Two time formats for teaching human sexuality. *Teaching of Psychology, 10*, 84–88.

Ray, S., & Miederhoff, P. A. (1984). The role of pharmacists in sexual health. *American Journal of Pharmaceutical Education, 48*, 268–271.

Schinke, S. P., Blythe, B. J., & Gilchrist, L. D. (1981). Cognitive-behavioral prevention of adolescent pregnancy. *Journal of Counseling Psychology, 28*, 451–454.

Schnarch, D. M. (1981). Impact of sex education on medical students' projections of patients' attitudes. *Journal of Sex and Marital Therapy, 7*, 141–155.

Schnarch, D. M. (1982). The role of medical students' stereotype of physicians in sex education. *Journal of Medical Education, 57*, 922–930.

Schnarch, D. M., & Jones, K. (1981). Efficacy of sex education courses in medical school. *Journal of Sex and Marital Therapy, 7*, 307–317.

Schover, L. R. (1981). Male and female therapists' responses to male and female client sexual material: An analogue study. *Archives of Sexual Behavior, 10*, 477–492.

Smith, P., Flaherty, C., & Webb, L. (1981). Training teachers in human sexuality: Effect on attitude and knowledge. *Psychological Reports, 48*, 527–530.

Smith, P. B., Flaherty, L. J., Webb, L. J., & Mumford, D. M. (1984). The long-term effects of human sexuality training programs for public school teachers. *Journal of School Health, 54*(4), 157–159.

Wheeler, J., & Kilmann, P. R. (1983). Comarital sexual behavior: Individual and relationship variables. *Archives of Sexual Behavior, 12*, 295–306.

BIBLIOGRAPHY:

Buros, O. K. (1978). *The eighth mental measurements yearbook*. Highland Park, NJ: Gryphon Press.

SEX MYTH INVENTORY

AUTHOR: Donald L. Mosher

DATE: 1979

VARIABLE: Knowledge regarding sexuality

TYPE OF INSTRUMENT: Alternate choice: true/false

DESCRIPTION: The Sex Myth Inventory contains 41 statements regarding human sexual behavior and physiology. Twelve of the statements are factually accurate; the others are myths. The respondent indicates whether each statement is true or false.

SAMPLE ITEMS: Boys who masturbate excessively harm themselves by losing protein and blood through the semen which is ejaculated.

Sexual intercourse should be avoided during pregnancy to ensure the health of the infant and mother.

PREVIOUS SUBJECTS: College students

APPROPRIATE FOR: College students and older

ADMINISTRATION: Self-administered; about 15–20 minutes

SCORING: Items are scored by assigning 1 point each time the respondent endorses a myth. Twelve items are keyed "false," and the respondent is assigned 1 point for selecting the answer "false." The remaining 29 items are keyed "true," and 1 point is assigned for selecting the answer "true." Total scores can range from 0 (correctly answered each item; did not endorse any myths) to 41 (endorsed all of the myths). Mosher (1979) reported the percentage of males and the percentage of females endorsing each of the 41 items.

DEVELOPMENT: The items on the Sex Myth Inventory were adapted from a list of 70 myths given in the textbook *Human Sexuality* (McCary, 1967). A subset of 41 items was selected on the grounds that the selected items were "appropriate to the concerns and educational level of the students" (Mosher, 1979, p. 226).

RELIABILITY: No information was provided.

VALIDITY: Mosher (1979) correlated scores on the Sex Myth Inventory with scores on the Mosher Guilt Inventory (Mosher, 1966) (see separate entry for Revised Mosher Guilt Inventory) and the Sexual Experience Inventory (Brady & Levitt, 1965) (see separate entry). Correlations were computed separately for males and females; the correlations were quite similar. Scores on the Sex Myth Inventory were significantly correlated with sex guilt (r = .36 for males and .32 for females) and nonsignificantly correlated with sex experience (r = −.15 for males and −.12 for females). When Mosher (1979) correlated sex guilt scores with responses to each of the 41 myths, he obtained eight significant correlations for males and four significant correlations for females.

Mendelsohn and Mosher (1979) correlated scores from the Sex Myth Inventory with scores on the Mosher Guilt Inventory, the Reiss Premarital Sexual Permissiveness Scale (Reiss, 1964) (see separate entry), and three measures of the accuracy of sex-related information communicated by the subject. Scores on the Sex Myth Inventory were significantly correlated with scores on the sex guilt measure (r = .29) and with all three measures of the accuracy of information that was communicated (r = −.28, −.39, −.28).

NOTES & COMMENTS: (1) Mosher (1979) found that college men endorsed significantly more myths than did college women. He also found that "this significant difference emerged in large part from responses to 12 specific myths that were endorsed by significantly more males than females" (p. 227).

(2) Andre, Fretwell, and Cheng (1986) used a variety of measures including a subset of 26 items from the Sex Myth Inventory in their study of various sources of sex education.

AVAILABLE FROM: Mosher, 1979

USED IN:

Andre, T., Fretwell, C., & Cheng, Y. (1986, April). *Sources of sex education as a function of sex, coital activity, and type of information.* Paper presented at the meeting of the American Educational Research Association, San Francisco.

Mendelsohn, M. J., & Mosher, D. L. (1979). Effects of sex guilt and premarital sexual permissiveness on role-played sex education and moral attitudes. *Journal of Sex Research, 15,* 174–183.

Mosher, D. L. (1979). Sex guilt and sex myths in college men and women. *Journal of Sex Research, 15,* 224–234.

BIBLIOGRAPHY:

Brady, J. P., & Levitt, E. E. (1965). The scalability of sexual experiences. *Psychological Record, 15,* 377–384.

McCary, J. L. (1967). *Human sexuality*. Princeton, NJ: Van Nostrand.

Mosher, D. L. (1966). The development and multitrait-multimethod matrix analysis of three measures of three aspects of guilt. *Journal of Consulting Psychology, 30*, 25–29.

Reiss, I. L. (1964). The scaling of premarital sexual permissiveness. *Journal of Marriage and the Family, 26*, 188–198.

4

Contraception and Abortion

This chapter contains descriptions of 17 scales organized into two sections: contraception and abortion. Eight scales pertain to various aspects of contraception, with some measures dealing with contraception in general and others considering specific forms of contraception. The scales, presented in alphabetical order by title, purport to measure attitudes, behavior, and knowledge. Seven of the eight scales were initially used during the 1980s. Only one scale is older; the Reasons for Not Using Birth Control was first described in the literature in 1970 (Bauman, 1970). Several types of measures are described here: four summated rating scales, two alternate choice measures, a semantic differential, and a role-play measure. Scale length is quite variable, with the shortest scale, not considering the role-play measure, containing only 8 items and the longest scale containing 66 items. Most of the scales have been used with adolescents, sometimes high school–age adolescents and sometimes college-age adolescents. Several of the measures are appropriate for specific groups, such as females or sexually active persons.

Reliability estimates were provided for seven of the eight scales in this section; most often, the reliability estimates were alpha coefficients. Test-retest reliability estimates were available for only one scale: the Contraceptive Knowledge Test (Reichelt & Werley, 1975). There was some information regarding the validity of six of the eight scales, but the data for two scales were equivocal. None of the measures described in this first section has been used extensively. The Contraceptive Knowledge Test was used more often than the other scales, but still there were only six articles that described research involving the use of the Contraceptive Knowledge Test.

The second section contains descriptions of nine scales dealing with abortion. The scales are presented in alphabetical order. All nine scales are appropriate for persons of high school age and older. One scale measures knowledge about abortion; the other eight measure attitudes regarding abortion. A common approach to measuring abortion attitudes is to provide the respondent with a list of conditions and ask him or her to indicate which conditions provide sufficient justification for an abortion. Sometimes the conditions are divided into two categories: hard reasons are those that have a medical or physical basis, and soft reasons are those that reflect that a child is not wanted. Many measures that used this approach were not included in this chapter because they failed to meet the criteria for inclusion. However, three measures using this approach are described: Favorability Toward Abortion Scale (Finlay, 1981), NORC Survey of Abortion Attitudes (Blake, 1971), and Smetana Permissible Circumstances for Abortion scale (Smetana, 1979).

There was evidence regarding the reliability of all scales described in this chapter, and there was evidence regarding the validity of eight of the measures. However, some of the data pertaining to validity were weak at best. Only one scale described in this section was used extensively. The NORC Survey of Abortion Attitudes and variations of the scale were used in research reported in at least 25 journal articles.

Researchers interested in studying attitudes regarding abortion should be very careful in selecting a scale. Item content should be carefully reviewed before a measure is selected because items that were appropriate at one time may be outdated. Similarly, normative data may quickly be outdated in an area that receives so much public attention.

Because the topics of contraception and abortion were not covered in my original handbook (Beere, 1979), none of the measures described here was described in that handbook. It will be interesting to see how many of these scales will still be used 10 years from now.

BIBLIOGRAPHY:

Bauman, K. E. (1970). Selected aspects of the contraceptive practices of unmarried university students. *American Journal of Obstetrics and Gynecology, 108*, 203–209.

Beere, C. A. (1979). *Women and women's issues: A handbook of tests and measures.* San Francisco: Jossey-Bass.

Blake, J. (1971). Abortion and public opinion: The 1960–1970 decade. *Science, 171*, 540–555.

Finlay, B. A. (1981). Sex differences in attitudes toward abortion among college students. *Journal of Marriage and the Family, 43*, 571–582.

Reichelt, P. A., & Werley, H. H. (1975). Contraception, abortion and venereal disease: Teenagers' knowledge and the effect of education. *Family Planning Perspectives, 7*(2), 83–88.

Smetana, J. G. (1979). Beliefs about the permissibility of abortion and their relationship to decision regarding abortion. *Journal of Population, 24*, 294–305.

ATTITUDES TOWARD CONDOMS SCALE (ATC)

AUTHOR: Idalyn S. Brown

DATE: 1984

VARIABLE: Attitudes toward the condom as a method of birth control

TYPE OF INSTRUMENT: Summated rating scale

DESCRIPTION: The Attitudes Toward Condoms Scale (ATC) consists of 40 statements, half expressing a favorable attitude toward the use of condoms and half expressing a negative attitude. Each statement is accompanied by five response options: "strongly disagree, disagree, undecided, agree, strongly agree."

SAMPLE ITEMS: I just don't like the idea of using condoms.

The neatness of condoms, for example, no wet spot on the bed, makes them attractive.

PREVIOUS SUBJECTS: College students

APPROPRIATE FOR: College students and older, or sexually active high school students

ADMINISTRATION: Self-administered; about 15 minutes

SCORING: Items are individually scored on a 5-point scale, with 5 points assigned to the response that reflects a positive attitude toward condoms. Item scores are summed to yield a total score that ranges from 40 (very negative attitudes toward condoms) to 200 (very positive attitudes toward condoms).

DEVELOPMENT: As the first step in scale development, undergraduate students were asked to write a paragraph regarding their perceptions of condoms as contraceptive devices. Sixteen students cooperated. The authors used this material, in combination with statements supplied by graduate students and faculty, to construct a pool of 77 items. The items were reviewed by two male and two female raters. Based on their review, they deleted some items, revised others, and reduced the item pool to 55 items—30 negatively worded and 25 positively worded. The item pool was administered to a sample of over 200 college students, and an item discrimination analysis was performed comparing the responses from the highest-scoring 25% of the students and the lowest-scoring 25% of the students. For each item, a *t* test was performed comparing the mean scores for the two groups. The *t* values were rank ordered separately for the positive and the negative items, and the 20 items with the highest *t* values were selected from each set. These 40 items, all of which had highly significant *t* values, comprise the scale.

RELIABILITY: Reliability was computed based on testing another sample of almost 200 students. Coefficient alpha was .93. Interitem correlations ranged from .10 to .76, with an average interitem correlation of .24.

VALIDITY: Brown (1984) compared ATC scores of students who read stories in which the condom was used during sexual activity with scores from students who read similar stories that did not involve the use of

condoms. The scores of those who read about condoms were significantly higher (more positive toward condoms).
NOTES & COMMENTS: (1) Based on a factor analysis of the responses from 187 college students, Brown labeled five factors. The major factor concerned "satisfaction with the safety and reliability of condoms" (Brown, 1984, p. 262). The other factors concerned "comfort, embarrassment, sexual arousal/excitement, and interruption of sexual activity" (p. 262).

(2) Tanner and Pollack (1988) used the ATC to test the hypothesis that erotic experiences with condoms lead to more positive attitudes toward condoms.
AVAILABLE FROM: Brown, 1984
USED IN:

Brown, I. S. (1984). Development of a scale to measure attitude toward the condom as a method of birth control. *Journal of Sex Research, 20,* 255–263.

Tanner, W. M., & Pollack, R. H. (1988). The effect of condom use and erotic instructions on attitudes toward condoms. *Journal of Sex Research, 25,* 537–541.

ATTITUDES TOWARD FAMILY PLANNING
AUTHOR: Joyce McDonough Mercier
DATE: 1980
VARIABLE: Attitudes toward family planning
TYPE OF INSTRUMENT: Summated rating scale
DESCRIPTION: The Attitudes Toward Family Planning scale consists of 66 items representing eight dimensions. Community Effect is represented by 7 items designed to measure "attitudes of those people living in the same geographical area which affect family planning education" (Mercier, 1980, p. 101). Educational Setting is represented by 5 items to measure "attitudes that are associated with the teaching and taking of a family planning course" (p. 101). Family Integration is represented by 10 items designed to measure the "amount and quality of communication and interaction between family members affecting solidarity, unity, and cohesiveness of the primary group" (p. 101). Family Size and Spacing is represented by 6 items that measure "the number and spacing of children in the nuclear family, and the importance of numbers in determining how parents and children live their lives in a family" (p. 101). Goals is represented by 6 items designed to assess "educational, career, family aspirations and the levels of each that the primary group desires" (p. 102). Premarital Sex is represented by 5 items regarding "attitudes that relate to adolescent sexual activity before marriage" (p. 102). Religious/Morals is represented by 17 items relating to "issues from religious and moral beliefs that relate to family planning education" (p. 102). Responsibility is represented by 10 items to measure "the making of

choices, accepting consequences of decisions, and taking of initiative and obligation'' (p. 102). For each item, respondents are to indicate whether they agree or disagree with the statement and the certainty of their feelings. Certainty is rated on a 5-point scale.

SAMPLE ITEMS: (Community Effect) This community would feel that a course on family planning is unnecessary.

(Educational Setting) Family planning should be part of a parenting course.

(Family Integration) Family planning can help couples to improve their relationship.

(Family Size and Spacing) It is important for a couple to plan its family so that no unwanted children are born.

(Goals) Planning when to have children has no effect upon educational goals.

(Premarital Sex) Premarital sex would not increase as a result of a family planning course.

(Religious/Morals) Birth control violates the purpose of the marital relationship.

(Responsibility) Parents who have planned for a child should be able to provide for this child.

PREVIOUS SUBJECTS: High school students, high school teachers, adults

APPROPRIATE FOR: High school students and older

ADMINISTRATION: Self-administered; about 30 minutes

SCORING: Items are individually scored by assigning one of the following numbers to each item: 0, 3, 5, 6, 7, 8, 9, 10, 11, 13, or 16. The ends of the scoring continuum are used for responses that are given high certainty rating. For example, ''agree'' with a certainty of 5 is 16 points, ''agree'' with a certainty of 4 is 13 points, and ''agree'' with a certainty of 3 is 11 points. After scoring of selected items is reversed, item scores are summed to yield a total score on each of 12 factors representing the eight dimensions. Mercier (1980) provided more specific details on scoring.

DEVELOPMENT: An open-ended questionnaire was constructed based on a review of the literature related to ''adolescent sexuality, adolescent pregnancy, adolescent parenthood, and sexuality education'' (Mercier, 1980, p. 101). The questionnaire was completed by high school students. Eight dimensions for the final questionnaire were identified from the students' responses to the open-ended questionnaire, from the literature search, from materials used in an international family planning program, and from inputs from family planning professionals. The eight dimensions and the items representing each dimension were reviewed by a panel of four family planning specialists. Based on their inputs, a preliminary version of the scale was developed containing 108 items. The preliminary version was completed by 88 high school students, and their responses were analyzed. As a result of this process, the scale was reduced to 84 items.

The 84-item version of the scale was administered to 735 high school students. Using coefficient alpha estimates, interitem correlations, and the results of a factor analysis of responses, Mercier (1980) reduced the scale to the current 66-item version. The factor analysis produced 12 factors with eigenvalues greater than .80, less than the typical requirement of 1.00. Five dimensions were each represented by one factor: Family Integration—I, Educational Setting—VII, Premarital Sex—IX, Family Size and Spacing—XII, and Goals—XI. Religious/Morals was represented by three factors: II, IV, and X. Community Effect was represented by two factors: III and VIII. Responsibility was also represented by two factors: V and VI.

RELIABILITY: Mercier (1980) reported coefficient alpha for each factor of each of the eight dimensions: Community Effect Factor III = .77, Community Effect Factor VIII = .80, Educational Setting = .75, Family Integration = .85, Family Size and Spacing = .73, Goals = .58, Premarital Sex = .56, Religious/Morals Factor II = .87, Religious/Morals Factor IV = .77, Religious/Morals Factor X = .63, Responsibility Factor V = .72, and Responsibility Factor VI = .76.

Mercier (1984) reported alpha coefficients ranging from .69 to .88 on the 8 dimensions/12 factors. For 11 of 12 factors, alpha was higher for the adults in this study than it was for the high school students in Mercier's (1980) earlier study.

VALIDITY: No information was provided. However, Mercier and Hughes (1981) related scores on the 12 factors to sex, age, religion, occupation of mother, and occupation of father, and Mercier (1984) related scores on the 12 factors to age, religion, and occupation. These results, which varied across the factors, can be interpreted as relevant to the scale's validity.

NOTES & COMMENTS: (1) Mercier (1980) reported the average interitem correlations, separately by sex and for both sexes combined, for each of the 12 factors. In addition, she reported, separately by sex, the intercorrelations among the 12 factors.

(2) The length of the 12 subscales is quite variable, as is the size of the alpha coefficients.

AVAILABLE FROM: Mercier, 1980

USED IN:

Mercier, J. M. (1980). Development of an instrument to measure attitudes toward family planning education. *Iowa State Journal of Research*, *55*, 99–118.

Mercier, J. M. (1984). Family planning education: How do adults feel about it. *Family Relations*, *33*, 523–530.

Mercier, J. M., & Hughes, R. P. (1981). Attitudes of selected secondary students toward family planning education. *Home Economics Research Journal, 10,* 127–136.

ATTITUDES TOWARD USING BIRTH CONTROL PILLS

AUTHORS: Edward S. Herold and Marilyn Shirley Goodwin

DATE: 1979

VARIABLE: Attitudes toward using birth control pills

TYPE OF INSTRUMENT: Semantic differential

DESCRIPTION: The concept "I think that using birth control pills is . . . " is followed by 14 bipolar adjective scales. Following the typical format for a semantic differential, each adjective scale is represented by a 7-point scale, with the bipolar adjectives placed at opposite ends of the scale.

SAMPLE ITEMS: reliable-unreliable
effective-uneffective

PREVIOUS SUBJECTS: Females, ages 13–20

APPROPRIATE FOR: Ages 13 and older

ADMINISTRATION: Self-administered; about 5 minutes

SCORING: Each bipolar adjective scale is assigned a score from 1 to 7, with 1 assigned to the favorable end of the continuum, 7 assigned to the unfavorable end of the continuum, and 2 through 6 assigned to the intermediate points. Scale scores can be summed to yield three factor scores (see factor analysis below) and a total score.

DEVELOPMENT: Initially the scale consisted of 17 pairs of bipolar adjectives set up as a semantic differential. "The choice of adjectives was based on their relevance to the concept and for their representativeness of the three factors of Evaluation, Potency, and Activity" (Herold & Goodwin, 1980, p. 117). A factor analysis of responses from 486 adolescent females led Herold and Goodwin to identify three orthogonal factors accounting for 61.7% of the variance. The three factors were labeled Effectiveness, Safety, and Anxiety. Only items with loadings greater than .50 were included on a factor; this led to the elimination of three bipolar adjective pairs and a final scale of 14 adjective pairs. A second factor analysis was performed with the three items deleted. The results of the second factor analysis were comparable to the first.

RELIABILITY: Herold, Goodwin, and Lero (1979) reported that coefficient alpha for the full scale was .91. Herold and Goodwin (1980) reported coefficient alpha for the three factor scores: Effectiveness = .88, Safety = .85, and Anxiety = .84.

VALIDITY: Herold and Goodwin (1980) compared the scores of 68 pill users with the scores from 17 persons who had discontinued pill use. As expected, continuing pill users had significantly more positive attitudes on all three subscales. Compared to those who discontinued pill use, the continuing users thought the pill was more effective and safer, and they were less anxious about using birth control pills. Furthermore, the two groups differed in total score on the Attitudes Toward Using Birth Control Pills scale. Herold and Goodwin also compared the results obtained from 48 pill users who were sexually inexperienced with those obtained from sexually active nonusers. Again the results were consistent with expectations: pill users who were sexually inexperienced thought the pill was more effective and safer, and they were less anxious about using it. Also, a comparison of total scores from the two groups showed that the sexually inexperienced pill users were more favorable toward the pill than were sexually active nonusers.

NOTES & COMMENTS: (1) Herold and Goodwin (1980) reported the intercorrelations between the factor scores and the correlations between factor and total scores. The intercorrelations between the factor scores were relatively high: .49, .58, and .66. The correlations between factor scores and total scores were quite high: .82, .90, and .82.

(2) Regression analysis showed that Effectiveness was the most important predictor when the pill users were compared with those who discontinued pill use. Safety was the single most important predictor when sexually inexperienced pill users were compared with sexually active nonusers.

(3) Herold et al. (1979) used Attitudes Toward Using Birth Control Pills to test the hypothesis that "young women with an internal locus of control and those with high self-esteem would have a more positive attitude toward using contraception" (p. 84).

AVAILABLE FROM: Herold, Goodwin, and Lero, 1979; Herold, 1988

USED IN:

Herold, E. S. (1988). Attitudes Toward Using Birth Control Pill scale. In C. M. Davis, W. L. Yarber, & S. L. Davis (Eds.), *Sexuality-related measures: A compendium* (pp. 61–62). Syracuse: Editors.

Herold, E. S., & Goodwin, M. S. (1980). Development of a scale to measure attitudes toward using birth control pills. *Journal of Social Psychology, 110,* 115–122.

Herold, E. S., Goodwin, M. S., & Lero, D. S. (1979). Self-esteem, locus of control, and adolescent contraception. *Journal of Psychology, 101,* 83–88.

CONTRACEPTIVE EMBARRASSMENT SCALE

AUTHOR: Edward S. Herold

DATE: 1981

VARIABLE: Embarrassment over visiting a physician or pharmacy to obtain contraceptive devices

TYPE OF INSTRUMENT: Summated rating scale

DESCRIPTION: The Contraceptive Embarrassment Scale is a brief scale consisting of a stem, "I am embarrassed or would be embarrassed about the following:" and eight statements pertaining to condoms, contraceptive foam, birth control pills, and a birth control prescription. One statement regarding each of these forms of birth control includes the phrase "close to where my parents live"; there is a second statement regarding each of these forms of birth control, but the location is changed to "distant from where my parents live." Each statement is accompanied by nine response options ranging from "strongly agree" to "strongly disagree."

SAMPLE ITEMS: Obtaining condoms from a pharmacy close to where my parents live.

Obtaining contraceptive foam from a pharmacy distant from where my parents live.

PREVIOUS SUBJECTS: Females, ages 13–22

APPROPRIATE FOR: Females, high school ages and older

ADMINISTRATION: Self-administered; a couple of minutes

SCORING: Each item is scored on a 9-point scale with a score of 1 assigned to "strongly disagree" (the response showing no embarrassment), and a score of 9 assigned to "strongly agree" (the response showing strong embarrassment). Total scores can range from 8 to 72, with higher scores showing greater embarrassment. In actuality, the scores from 265 females who had experienced sexual intercourse ranged from 8 to 67. The mean total score for this group was 31.7, and the standard deviation was 15.6.

DEVELOPMENT: No information was provided.

RELIABILITY: Coefficient alpha for 265 females was .88 for the total scale. For the close embarrassment items, coefficient alpha was .87, and for the distant embarrassment items, it was .79.

VALIDITY: As would be expected, Herold (1981a) found consistently greater embarrassment expressed on the items that dealt with obtaining birth control close to the parental home. Herold also found significant correlations between contraceptive use and each of the following: total score, a close-to-home score, and a distant-from-home score. As would be expected, the distant-from-home score showed the weakest correlation. These findings were consistent across two different measures of contraceptive use.

NOTES & COMMENTS: (1) Herold (1981a) looked at the relationship between contraceptive embarrassment and numerous other variables, including premarital intercourse attitudes, friends' reaction to intercourse, parents' reaction to intercourse, number of sex partners, sex guilt, attitudes toward contraceptive planning, difficulty in obtaining contraception, religiosity, career aspirations, partner reaction to contraception, dating commitment, frequency of intercourse, and whether the respondent attended a lecture on contraception.

(2) Herold (1981b) studied numerous variables that might predict contraceptive use. His measures included the Contraceptive Embarrassment Scale.

AVAILABLE FROM: Herold, 1981a, 1981b, 1988
USED IN:

Herold, E. S. (1981a). Contraceptive embarrassment and contraceptive behavior among young single women. *Journal of Youth and Adolescence, 10*, 233–242.

Herold, E. S. (1981b). Measurement issues involved in examining contraceptive use among young single women. *Population and Environment, 4*, 128–144.

Herold, E. S. (1988). Contraceptive Embarrassment Scale. In C. M. Davis, W. L. Yarber, & S. L. Davis (Eds.), *Sexuality-related measures: A compendium* (p. 63). Syracuse: Editors.

CONTRACEPTIVE KNOWLEDGE TEST

AUTHORS: Paul A. Reichelt and Harriet H. Werley
DATE: 1975
VARIABLE: Knowledge of oral contraception, interuterine devices (IUDs), diaphragms, condoms, spermicides, and miscellaneous other methods of birth control
TYPE OF INSTRUMENT: Alternate choice: true/false
DESCRIPTION: The Contraceptive Knowledge Test contains 25 statements covering six types of birth control: 6 items relate to the birth control pill; 4 items refer to IUDs; 4 items refer to diaphragms; 3 items pertain to condoms; 5 items deal with spermicidal foams, creams, and jellies; and 1 item refers to each of the following: rhythm, withdrawal, and douching. In addition to the contraceptive items, the scale contains 5 items dealing with reproduction, 3 items relating to abortion, and 6 items pertaining to venereal disease. The researcher can use either the 25-item Contraceptive Knowledge Test or all 39 items relating to sexual knowledge. Each item is accompanied by three response options: "true, false, don't know." The last option is provided to allow researchers to differentiate teenagers who are uninformed from those who are misinformed.
SAMPLE ITEMS: (oral contraception) The pill must be stopped every year for three months.

(IUDs) The IUD is inserted before each act of intercourse (making love).

(diaphragm) The diaphragm must be worn at all times.

(condom) A rubber should be tested before use.

(spermicides) They should be inserted just before each intercourse.

(miscellaneous methods) Rhythm is a highly effective method of birth control.

(reproduction) Menstruation (monthly period) is a clearing of the uterus to prepare again for possible pregnancy.

(abortion) An abortion can be done safely and easily by a doctor during the first 12 weeks of pregnancy.

(venereal disease) Many cases of VD are caught by contact with toilet seats, drinking fountains and swimming pools.

PREVIOUS SUBJECTS: Adolescents, ages 13–19; college students
APPROPRIATE FOR: Ages 13 and older
ADMINISTRATION: Self-administered; about 15–20 minutes
SCORING: The final score is the number of correct answers minus the number of incorrect answers. Answering "don't know" neither adds to nor subtracts from the final score. A score can be obtained for the 25 items of the Contraceptive Knowledge Test, and a score can be obtained for all 39 items included on the original Reichelt and Werley scale. The higher the score, the more the respondent is knowledgeable about contraception and the related topics.
DEVELOPMENT: No information was provided.
RELIABILITY: Using a slightly revised version of the Contraceptive Knowledge Test, Berger (cited in Berger, Jacques, Brender, Gold, & Andres, 1985) obtained a test-retest reliability of .97 when the test was administered to university students on two occasions with a 3-week interval between testings.
VALIDITY: As would be expected, Reichelt and Werley (1975, 1976) found differences in the scores of different groups, but they did not report whether the differences were statistically significant. Contraceptive Knowledge scores and Total Knowledge scores increased with increasing age for age groups from 13 to 17; thereafter they decreased. Higher socioeconomic groups scored higher than lower socioeconomic groups. Sexually experienced adolescents scored higher than sexually inexperienced adolescents. Those who had previously used birth control scored higher than those who had not previously used birth control.

Amonker (1980) tested a sample of teenagers who visited a Planned Parenthood Clinic and largely confirmed the findings of Reichelt and Werley. Amonker, however, found that mean scores continued to increase with increasing age, even after age 17.

Reichelt and Werley (1975, 1976) found that Contraceptive Knowledge scores and Total Knowledge scores increased considerably after the adolescents attended a rap session intended to increase their knowledge of contraception.
NOTES & COMMENTS: (1) Berger et al. (1985) used a slightly revised version of the 25-item Contraceptive Knowledge Test to test the following two hypotheses: "low-sex-guilt students would have acquired more birth control information as measured before they heard a lecture about contraception and, furthermore, would retain more information from the lecture than their high-sex-guilt counterparts" (p. 73).

(2) Pope, Westerfield, and Walker (1985) examined two sources of contraceptive knowledge: structured/organized sources included schools, colleges, churches, planned parenthood and health services; unstructured/unorganized sources included family, peers, sexual partners, and the mass media. Using the Contraceptive Knowledge Test,

the researchers looked at the relationship between source of contraceptive knowledge and accuracy of that knowledge.

(3) Marcy, Brown, and Danielson (1983) used the Contraceptive Knowledge Test and the other 14 items used by Reichelt and Werley (1975) to test the hypothesis that contraceptive use is not determined by contraceptive knowledge; that is, they hypothesized that "adolescents who become effective users of contraceptives do not differ from those who do not in the amount of their knowledge about sex and contraception" (Marcy et al., 1983, p. 179).

AVAILABLE FROM: Reichelt and Werley, 1975, 1976; Amonker, 1980

USED IN:

Amonker, R. G. (1980). What do teens know about the facts of life? *Journal of School Health, 50,* 527–530.

Berger, C., Jacques, J., Brender, W., Gold, D., & Andres, D. (1985). Contraceptive knowledge and use of birth control as a function of sex guilt. *International Journal of Women's Studies, 8,* 72–79.

Marcy, S. A., Brown, J. S., & Danielson, R. (1983). Contraceptive use by adolescent females in relation to knowledge, and to time and method of contraceptive counseling. *Research in Nursing and Health, 6,* 175–182.

Pope, A. J., Westerfield, C., & Walker, J. (1985). The effect of contraceptive knowledge source upon knowledge accuracy and contraceptive behavior. *Health Education, 16*(3), 41–44.

Reichelt, P. A., & Werley, H. H. (1975). Contraception, abortion and venereal disease: Teenagers' knowledge and the effect of education. *Family Planning Perspectives, 7,* 83–88.

Reichelt, P. A., & Werley, H. H. (1976). Sex knowledge of teenagers and the effect of an educational rap session. *Journal of Research and Development in Education, 10,* 13–22.

CONTRACEPTIVE SELF-EFFICACY INSTRUMENT (CSE)

AUTHOR: Ruth Andrea Levinson

DATE: 1986

VARIABLE: Likelihood of contraceptive use

TYPE OF INSTRUMENT: Summated rating scale

DESCRIPTION: The Contraceptive Self-Efficacy Instrument (CSE) consists of 15 numbered items, 1 of which contains four parts, giving a total of 18 items. The items "describe situations that involve obtaining contraceptives; using contraceptives with a partner; talking to a partner about contraceptive use; using contraceptives in spite of partner or parental disapproval; interrupting an episode of highly aroused, unplanned sex to talk about (or use) a contraceptive; and preventing episodes of unprotected intercourse" (Levinson, 1986, p. 350). All of the items focus on the respondent's behavior. For each item, respondents select one of five options ranging from "not at all true of me" to "completely true of me."

SAMPLE ITEMS: When I am with a boyfriend, I feel that I can always be responsible for what happens sexually with him.

There are times when I should talk to my boyfriend about using contraceptives, but I can't seem to do it in the situation.

PREVIOUS SUBJECTS: Adolescent females, ages 14–20

APPROPRIATE FOR: Sexually active females

ADMINISTRATION: Self-administered; about 5–10 minutes

SCORING: Little information was provided regarding scoring. Apparently scores can be obtained for each of the four factors and for the total scale. Items appear to be scored on a 5-point scale, with 5 points assigned to the response "completely true of me" and 1 point assigned to the response "not at all true of me."

DEVELOPMENT: It was assumed that contraceptive use would be more likely for a girl who is "(a) assertive in preventing unprotected sexual intercourse, (b) competent in obtaining and utilizing contraceptives, (c) communicative about sexual relationships and contraceptive issues, and (d) accepting of her own sexuality" (Levinson, 1986, p. 350). Therefore, items for the CSE were written to tap these four areas. The items were generated from three areas of published research: family planning, psychology, and social psychology. According to Levinson (1986), "the appearance and content of the original CSE instrument was changed several times, based on information derived from pretesting the instrument among different populations and from consulting experts in self-efficacy assessment" (p. 355).

Item-total correlations were computed, and one item was deleted because it was not significantly correlated with the total score.

RELIABILITY: The alpha coefficient for the 18-item scale was .73.

VALIDITY: Factor analysis of responses to the CSE led to the identification of four factors: "(a) conscious acceptance of sexual activity by planning for it . . . , (b) assumption of responsibility for the direction of sexual activity and for using contraception, (c) assertiveness in preventing sexual intercourse in an involved situation, and (d) strong feelings of sexual arousal" (Levinson, 1986, p. 356). These factors did not completely coincide with the four conceptual categories presumed to influence contraceptive behavior and thus used to develop the scale. (See DEVELOPMENT.)

As evidence of validity, Levinson (1986) reported significant correlations between various factor scores and measures of contraceptive behavior. For example, the first factor, conscious acceptance of sexual activity by planning for it, and the second factor, assumption of responsibility for the direction of sexual activity and contraception, were both significantly correlated with contraceptive method efficacy. However, the correlations were .15 and .22, both quite low. Similarly, Factors 2, 3, and 4 were significantly correlated with frequent episodes of unprotected intercourse. Again the correlations, although statistically significant, were low.

NOTES & COMMENTS: Levinson (1986) used the CSE to help understand adolescent girls' contraceptive behavior.

AVAILABLE FROM: Levinson, 1986, 1988

USED IN:

Levinson, R. A. (1986). Contraceptive self-efficacy: A perspective on teenage girls' contraceptive behavior. *Journal of Sex Research*, *22*, 347–369.

Levinson, R. A. (1988). The Contraceptive Self Efficacy Scale. In C. M. Davis, W. L. Yarber, & S. L. Davis (Eds.), *Sexuality-related measures: A compendium* (pp. 65–68). Syracuse: Editors.

HYNES CONTRACEPTIVE PROBLEM SITUATIONS

AUTHOR: Mary Jean Hynes

DATE: 1982

VARIABLE: Effectiveness, within social situations, of learning about, obtaining, and discussing the use of contraceptives

TYPE OF INSTRUMENT: Behavioral role play

DESCRIPTION: There are two forms of the Hynes Contraceptive Problem Situations scale—one for males and one for females. Each form consists of five situations. On the female form, two situations relate to learning about contraception, two relate to obtaining contraception, and one relates to discussing contraception with one's partner. On the male form, one situation relates to learning about contraception, two relate to obtaining contraception, and two relate to discussing contraception with one's partner. The male form contains situations likely to be encountered by unmarried men, and the female form contains situations likely to be encountered by unmarried women. An audiotape recorder is used to read the situation to the respondent, and responses are tape recorded for later scoring by a trained person.

SAMPLE ITEMS: (female form) You are going to visit your boyfriend for the weekend, and as you leave the bus station to walk to his apartment you realize that you will most likely have sexual intercourse with him and that in the rush of packing you forgot to bring your diaphragm. You know there is a Planned Parenthood clinic near his house because you've kidded him about it in the past. It is open as you walk by, and although you feel a bit embarrassed, you decide you'll stop there and see what they suggest as a safe method for you to use for the weekend. So, you walk into the reception room and a woman at the desk says, "May I help you?" What do you say?

(male form) You have been dating a woman for several weeks whom you've come to care for very much. Lately, it feels like you've come close to the point where you'd like to have sexual intercourse with her.

From her physical expressiveness to you, it seems like she feels the same way. You've decided to go camping together this weekend and feel you will probably sleep together then. You've never talked with her about birth control and are wondering if she has her own method or if you should be prepared with condoms. You've decided to bring this up with her. You're having a conversation about the weekend and she says, "I'm really looking forward to spending so much time alone with you this week-end." You decide now's the time to talk with her about birth control. What do you say?

PREVIOUS SUBJECTS: Unmarried college students involved in a dating situation

APPROPRIATE FOR: Unmarried college students

ADMINISTRATION: The scale is administered by a tape recorder, and responses are recorded on tape. Administration time is a function of the length of the individual's responses; however, 10–20 minutes is a reasonable time estimate for each administration.

SCORING: Items are individually scored on a 5-point scale using guidelines and examples provided in a scoring manual. (See Hynes, 1982/1983.)

DEVELOPMENT: Fifty college students were asked to describe problem situations relating to learning about birth control, obtaining birth control, and discussing birth control with a partner. Vague and redundant situations were eliminated, leaving a set of 13 female and 12 male situations. Another group of college students were asked to respond to the situations written for their sex. Some were asked to provide ideal responses and others to provide typical responses. About 20 responses were generated for each situation. Three women and three men, professionals working in the area of adolescent sexuality, served as judges to rate the effectiveness of the solutions and give a rationale for their ratings. They also provided samples of what they considered to be inferior, average, and effective responses to each situation. The evaluations provided by the judges were used to reduce the set of situations from 25 to 16: on each form, there were 4 situations relating to discussing contraception with a partner, 2 relating to learning about contraception, and 2 relating to obtaining contraception. "High interjudge agreement, range of effectiveness, and proportionate numbers of situations for each sex were the criteria used for retaining situations" (Hynes & Bruch, 1985, p. 428).

The scale was administered to 87 undergraduate and graduate college students, and the responses from about 30% of them were used to estimate interrater agreement and interrater reliability for each item. The results for some items were unacceptable, so three situations were eliminated from each form of the measure.

RELIABILITY: Percentage of interrater agreement ranged from 54% to 100% (mean = 79%) for the 10 situations; interrater reliability estimates ranged from .75 to .98 (mean = .87).
VALIDITY: No information was provided.
NOTES & COMMENTS: (1) Hynes (1982/1983) tested the hypothesis that sex role orientation and assertiveness level affect behaviors regarding contraceptive use. The Hynes Contraceptive Problem Situations scale was one of several measures used in the study.

(2) The Hynes and Bruch (1985) article is based on Hyne's (1982/1983) doctoral dissertation, which includes extensive detail about the development of the measure.
AVAILABLE FROM: The entire text of the situations is in Hynes, 1982/1983; a one-sentence description of each situation appears in Hynes and Bruch, 1985.
USED IN:

Hynes, M. J. (1983). An investigation of the relationship between sex role orientation, level of assertiveness, affective orientation to sexuality and a model of contraceptive behavior (Doctoral dissertation, State University of New York, 1982). *Dissertation Abstracts International, 43*, 3075B.

Hynes, M. J., & Bruch, M. A. (1985). Social skills and responses in simulated contraceptive problem situations. *Journal of Sex Research, 21*, 422–436.

REASONS FOR NOT USING BIRTH CONTROL

AUTHOR: Karl E. Bauman
DATE: 1970
VARIABLE: Reasons for not using birth control
TYPE OF INSTRUMENT: Alternate choice: yes/no
DESCRIPTION: Reasons for Not Using Birth Control is a list of 10 or 11 reasons that persons might give for not using birth control. For each reason, the respondent answers "yes" or "no" to indicate whether the statement represents a reason for the respondent's not using contraception on those occasions when contraception was not used.
SAMPLE ITEMS: Didn't expect intercourse to occur when it did
Didn't want to appear overly prepared
PREVIOUS SUBJECTS: College students
APPROPRIATE FOR: Sexually active adolescents and older
ADMINISTRATION: Self-administered; less than 5 minutes
SCORING: The measure is not scored. Rather, results have been tallied across respondents, and the percentage of people giving each answer has been reported.
DEVELOPMENT: No information was provided.
RELIABILITY: No information was provided.
VALIDITY: Maxwell, Sack, Frary, and Keller (1977) briefly described a factor analytic study of a 74-item questionnaire including the Reasons

for Not Using Birth Control. Without providing much information about the results, they concluded: "The factor loadings of the rotated matrix readily yielded plausible interpretations of underlying factor structure congruent with the content areas of the questionnaire. This outcome was interpreted as favorable evidence of reliability and validity of responses" (p. 267).

NOTES & COMMENTS: (1) The Reasons for Not Using Birth Control is not a scale in the sense that most other measures in this book are scales. It has been included here, however, because it has been used by several researchers and may be of interest to future researchers.

(2) The Reasons for Not Using Birth Control has been used to study the contraceptive practices of college students (Bauman, 1970; Maxwell et al., 1977; Needle, 1975).

AVAILABLE FROM: Bauman, 1970; Maxwell, Sack, Frary, and Keller, 1977; Needle, 1975

USED IN:

Bauman, K. E. (1970). Selected aspects of the contraceptive practices of unmarried university students. *American Journal of Obstetrics and Gynecology, 108*, 203–209.

Maxwell, J. W., Sack, A. R., Frary, R. B., & Keller, J. F. (1977). Factors influencing contraceptive behavior of single college students. *Journal of Sex and Marital Therapy, 3*, 265–273.

Needle, R. H. (1975). The relationship between first sexual intercourse and ways of handling contraception among college students. *Journal of the American College Health Association, 24*, 106–111.

ABORTION ATTITUDE SCALE

AUTHOR: Linda A. Sloan

DATE: 1983

VARIABLE: Attitudes toward abortion

TYPE OF INSTRUMENT: Summated rating scale

DESCRIPTION: The Abortion Attitude Scale contains 14 statements, each accompanied by six response options ranging from "strongly agree" to "strongly disagree." Half of the items are phrased so that agreement reflects a positive attitude toward abortion, and the other half are phrased so that agreement reflects a negative attitude.

SAMPLE ITEMS: Abortion is a good way of solving an unwanted pregnancy.

A mother should feel obligated to bear a child she has conceived.

PREVIOUS SUBJECTS: High school students, college students, adults

APPROPRIATE FOR: High school students and older

ADMINISTRATION: Self-administered; about 5–10 minutes

SCORING: Items are objectively scored on a 5-point system so that a score of 5 is assigned to the strongest pro-choice position and a score of 0 is assigned to the strongest pro-life position. Total scores range from

70 (strong pro-choice) to 0 (strong pro-life). Sloan (1983) suggested the following interpretations for scores: 0–15 indicates strong pro-life, 16–26 indicates moderate pro-life, 27–43 means unsure, 44–55 indicates moderate pro-abortion, and 56–70 indicates strong pro-abortion. She did not give a rationale for these groupings.

DEVELOPMENT: No information was provided.

RELIABILITY: Sloan (1983) reported a reliability of .92 but did not indicate the type of reliability being estimated. Iyriboz and Carter (1986) reported coefficient alpha equal to .95 (pretest) and .94 (posttest) based on using the scale with college undergraduates.

VALIDITY: The information on validity was rather vague: "The validation process involved interrater agreement, pilot testing, reliability estimates, factor analysis to determine unidimensionality and hypothesis testing. . . . Five hypotheses were supported on the construct validity assessment. Right to Life members' mean scores were 16.2, while abortion service associates' scores were 55.6. All other groups' mean scores fell in the middle range" (Sloan, 1983, p. 42).

AVAILABLE FROM: Sloan, 1983; Berne, 1988

USED IN:

Berne, L. A. S. (1988). Abortion Attitude Scale. In C. M. Davis, W. L. Yarber, & S. L. Davis (Eds.), *Sexuality-related measures: A compendium* (p. 1). Syracuse: Editors.

Iyriboz, Y., & Carter, J. A. (1986). Attitudes of a southern university human sexuality class toward sexual variance, abortion and homosexuality. *College Student Journal, 20*, 89–93.

Jones, H., & Henriksen, L. (1987). The impact of the "scream": To use or not to use. *Health Education, 18*, 9–11.

Sloan, L. A. (1983). Abortion Attitude Scale. *Health Education, 14*, 41–42.

ABORTION ATTITUDE SCALE

AUTHOR: Stanley Snegroff

DATE: 1976 (used 1973)

VARIABLE: Attitudes toward abortion as a method of birth control

TYPE OF INSTRUMENT: Summated rating scale

DESCRIPTION: The Abortion Attitude Scale consists of 30 statements pertaining to abortion, each accompanied by five response options ranging from "strongly agree" to "strongly disagree." Half of the items are expressed so that agreement reflects a positive attitude toward abortion; the other half are phrased in the reverse direction. The items pertain to the moral and social aspects of abortion, legal aspects of abortion, abortion as birth control, women's rights in regard to abortion, rights of the unborn, and health aspects of abortion.

SAMPLE ITEMS: Abortion penalizes the unborn for the mother's mistake.

If a woman feels that a child might ruin her life she should have an abortion.

PREVIOUS SUBJECTS: College students

APPROPRIATE FOR: High school students and older

ADMINISTRATION: Self-administered; about 15 minutes

SCORING: Items are scored so that 5 points are assigned to the response that reflects the most positive attitude toward abortion, and 1 point is assigned to the response that reflects the most negative attitude. Item scores are summed to yield a total score ranging from 30 (strongly opposed to abortion) to 150 (strongly supportive of abortion rights). For a sample of 527 college students, Snegroff (1976) reported a mean of 116.6 and a standard deviation of 27.3.

DEVELOPMENT: Based on a review of the literature, the authors constructed an initial item pool of 300 items. The pool was reduced by eliminating items that were factual, items that 12 professionals involved in abortion work or sex education programs judged as not directly relevant to abortion, and items that 60 college students judged as unclear. The remaining pool of 52 items was administered to 62 male and 59 female college students. Items were selected for the final scale if they differentiated between the pro-abortion respondents (students with the highest 25% of the scores) and the anti-abortion respondents (students with the lowest 25% of the scores). In selecting items, care was taken to ensure that half of the items would be phrased in a positive direction and the other half in a negative direction.

RELIABILITY: Split-half reliability was reported as .91.

VALIDITY: According to Snegroff (1976), "content validity was achieved" (p. 274) by specifying the six content areas before the item pool was developed.

NOTES & COMMENTS: (1) This scale was developed along with the Abortion Knowledge Inventory (see separate entry). The two measures may be used together or separately. Snegroff (1976) found a correlation of .36 between scores on the two scales.

(2) The development of this measure was consistent with good psychometric procedures, and despite the age of the Abortion Attitude Scale, the items are not outdated.

AVAILABLE FROM: Snegroff, 1988; available for purchase from Family Life Publications, 219 Henderson Street, P.O. Box 427, Saluda, NC 28733

USED IN:

Snegroff, S. (1976). The development of instruments to measure attitudes toward abortion and knowledge of abortion. *Journal of School Health, 46*, 273–277.

Snegroff, S. (1988). Abortion Attitude Scale and Abortion Knowledge Inventory. In C. M. Davis, W. L. Yarber, & S. L. Davis (Eds.), *Sexuality-related measures: A compendium* (pp. 5–9). Syracuse: Editors.

ABORTION KNOWLEDGE INVENTORY

AUTHOR: Stanley Snegroff

DATE: 1976 (used 1973)

VARIABLE: Knowledge about abortion

TYPE OF INSTRUMENT: Multiple choice

DESCRIPTION: The Abortion Knowledge Inventory consists of 30 items, each presented with four response options. Most of the items pertain to the legality of abortion, the process of abortion, the types of abortions, the effects of abortion, birth control and family planning, women's reproductive system, and abortion statistics.

SAMPLE ITEMS: After the twelfth week of pregnancy which method of abortion would most likely be used? (a) x-ray radiation; (b) dilation and curettage ("D & C"); (c) "salting out"; (d) suction

If a birth takes place during the fifth month of pregnancy, the chances of survival for the offspring are most likely (a) 0 percent; (b) 10 percent (1 in 10); (c) 20 percent (1 in 5); (d) 30 percent (1 in 3).

PREVIOUS SUBJECTS: College students

APPROPRIATE FOR: High school students and older

ADMINISTRATION: Self-administered; about 15–20 minutes

SCORING: One point is assigned for each item answered correctly; item scores are summed to yield a total score ranging from 0 to 30. For a sample of 527 college students, Snegroff (1976) reported a mean of 16.1 and a standard deviation of 3.8.

DEVELOPMENT: From a review of the literature and consultation with 12 professionals involved in abortion work or sex education, an item pool of 80 items was constructed to cover eight content areas. The pool was reduced to 56 items based on inputs from the 12 professionals and on college students' inputs regarding item clarity. The 56 items were administered to 127 college students. An item discrimination analysis was performed, and the most discriminating items were selected from the various content areas. In selecting items, consideration was also given to the percentage of respondents answering the item correctly and the percentage choosing each of the four response options.

RELIABILITY: Split-half reliability was .79.

VALIDITY: Snegroff (1976) stated that the method of scale development ensured that "content validity was achieved" (p. 275).

NOTES & COMMENTS: (1) The split-half reliability coefficient, $r = .79$, is low. It is reasonable to expect a higher coefficient on a scale with right and wrong answers.

(2) Some of the items on the Abortion Knowledge Inventory need to be modified to account for regional differences and updated statistics.

(3) The Abortion Knowledge Inventory was developed along with the Abortion Attitude Scale (see separate entry), and the correlation between

the two measures is .36 (Snegroff, 1976). The two measures may be used together or separately.

AVAILABLE FROM: Snegroff, 1988; available for purchase from Family Life Publications, 219 Henderson Street, P.O. Box 427, Saluda, NC 28733

USED IN:

Snegroff, S. (1976). The development of instruments to measure attitudes toward abortion and knowledge of abortion. *Journal of School Health, 46*, 273–277.

Snegroff, S. (1988). Abortion Attitude Scale and Abortion Knowledge Inventory. In C. M. Davis, W. L. Yarber, & S. L. Davis (Eds.), *Sexuality-related measures: A compendium* (pp. 5–9). Syracuse: Editors.

ATTITUDES TOWARD SHARED RESPONSIBILITY IN DECISIONS ABOUT ABORTION

AUTHORS: Ione J. Ryan and Patricia C. Dunn

DATE: 1983 (used 1981)

VARIABLE: Attitudes regarding whether males should share in the abortion decision

TYPE OF INSTRUMENT: Multiple choice

DESCRIPTION: In the Attitudes Toward Shared Responsibility in Decisions About Abortion, respondents are presented with seven situations in which an abortion is being considered. The relationship between the couple is somewhat different in each situation: "a couple is engaged, married, dating steadily, dating casually, involved in a single sexual encounter, considering a repeat abortion, and no longer in a relationship" (Ryan & Dunn, 1983, p. 232). Each situation is accompanied by five response options describing the extent to which the male should be involved in the abortion decision. The response options range from "Completely involved (male should be informed of pregnancy and abortion should take place only with his complete agreement)" to "No involvement (male should not be informed—female should assume complete responsibility for decision)."

SAMPLE ITEMS: John and Mary are both college seniors, engaged to be married in June after graduation. In mid-February, Mary learns she is pregnant (approximately 6 weeks). She decides to have an abortion. To what extent do you feel John should be involved?

After a casual date with Jake two months earlier, Susan learns that she is pregnant. She and Jake have not dated since that time although they see each other occasionally in passing on campus and are friendly. Susan decides she wants to have an abortion. To what extent should Jake be involved?

PREVIOUS SUBJECTS: Undergraduate college students

APPROPRIATE FOR: High school students and older

ADMINISTRATION: Self-administered; about 5–10 minutes

SCORING: Items are scored from 1 (greatest involvement) to 5 (least involvement) and then summed to yield a total score ranging from 7 to 35. Higher scores indicate less support for males being involved in the abortion decision.
DEVELOPMENT: The seven situations described in the scale are based on actual counseling cases of unplanned pregnancies.
RELIABILITY: Using a 2-week interval and data obtained from 16 college students, test-retest reliability was computed for a longer measure that included these seven items. The reliability was .76.
VALIDITY: No information was provided.
NOTES & COMMENTS: Given the low test-retest reliability and the lack of data regarding validity, this attitude scale needs further study and refinement before it is used extensively.
AVAILABLE FROM: Ryan and Dunn, 1988
USED IN:

Ryan, I. J., & Dunn, P. C. (1983). College students' attitudes toward shared responsibility in decisions about abortion: Implications for counseling. *Journal of American College Health, 31*, 231–235.

Ryan, I. J., & Dunn, P. C. (1988). Perceptions of shared responsibility: An attitude survey about abortion decision making. In C. M. Davis, W. L. Yarber, & S. L. Davis (Eds.), *Sexuality-related measures: A compendium* (pp. 3–4). Syracuse: Editors.

DUAL-FORM ABORTION SCALE
AUTHORS: John K. Bowers and Herbert B. Weaver
DATE: 1979
VARIABLE: Attitudes toward abortion
TYPE OF INSTRUMENT: Summated rating scale
DESCRIPTION: There are two 20-item forms of the Dual-Form Abortion Scale. Form A contains 12 pro-abortion items and 8 anti-abortion items; Form B contains 11 pro-abortion items and 9 anti-abortion items. The items cover a variety of topics related to abortion. Each item is accompanied by five response options ranging from "strongly agree" to "strongly disagree."
SAMPLE ITEMS: (Form A) To allow an unwanted child to be born is unfair to the child.

(Form B) It is unthinkable not to want a baby to be born after it has been conceived.
PREVIOUS SUBJECTS: College students, faculty, parents, other adults
APPROPRIATE FOR: High school students and older
ADMINISTRATION: Self-administered; each form takes less than 10 minutes
SCORING: Items are individually scored on a 5-point scale, with 5 points assigned to the most pro-abortion response. For some items, this is the

"strongly agree" end of the continuum; for other items, it is the "strongly disagree" end of the continuum. Item scores are summed to yield a total score ranging from 20 (strongly opposed to abortion) to 100 (strongly supportive of abortion).

DEVELOPMENT: A pool of 76 items was administered to a sample of 200 persons representing different ethnic, educational, socioeconomic, and religious backgrounds. Total scores were obtained for each respondent, and two subgroups were identified: those with the highest 10% of the scores and those with the lowest 10% of the scores. For each item, the mean difference between the two groups was calculated as an indication of the item's discrimination. Forty items with mean differences of 2 .05 or greater were selected for the two forms of the Dual-Form Abortion Scale. The items were divided for the two forms in such a way that the sums of the mean score differences were approximately equal on each form.

RELIABILITY: A sample of 175 college students and adults completed Form A and Form B, with half of the subjects completing Form A first and the other half of the subjects completing Form B first. The correlation between the two forms was .96. The Spearman-Brown formula was used to estimate the reliability of a 40-item form. The resulting coefficient was .98. Coefficient alpha was calculated for the entire set of 40 items. The coefficient was .98. For each set of 20 items, coefficient alpha was .97. Bowers and Weaver (1979) identified three religious groups: Catholics and Mormons, Protestants, and atheists/agnostics. When coefficient alpha was computed separately for each of the three somewhat homogeneous groups and then averaged across the three groups, the result was a coefficient of .92.

VALIDITY: As expected, Bowers and Weaver (1979) found that the group including Catholics and Mormons scored significantly lower (more anti-abortion) than the other two religious groups. These results were consistent for Form A, Form B, and for both forms combined. There were no significant differences between the Protestant group and the atheist/agnostic group.

AVAILABLE FROM: Order from NAPS c/o Microfiche Publications, P.O. Box 3513, Grand Central Station, New York, NY 10163–3513; NAPS document no. 04708; for microfiche, in the United States remit $4.00 with order.

USED IN:

Bowers, J. K., & Weaver, H. B. (1979). Development of a Dual-Form Abortion Scale. *Journal of Sex Research, 15*, 158–165.

FAVORABILITY TOWARD ABORTION SCALE

AUTHOR: Barbara Finlay

DATE: 1981 (used 1978)

TYPE OF INSTRUMENT: Checklist
VARIABLE: Conditions under which abortion should be allowed
DESCRIPTION: The Favorability Toward Abortion Scale describes eight circumstances for which a woman might want an abortion. Respondents are asked to circle those items that name a situation in which the woman is justified in desiring an abortion.
SAMPLE ITEMS: The pregnancy is the result of rape.
The "woman" is an unmarried 14-year-old.
PREVIOUS SUBJECTS: College students
APPROPRIATE FOR: High school students and older
ADMINISTRATION: Self-administered; less than 5 minutes
SCORING: The score is equal to the number of circled items. Total scores range from 0 to 8, with higher scores indicating more favorable attitudes. For a sample of 132 college males, Finlay (1981) obtained a mean of 4.94 (standard deviation of 2.4), and for a sample of 130 college females, she obtained a mean of 4.96 (standard deviation of 2.16).
DEVELOPMENT: No information was provided.
RELIABILITY: Based on responses from 277 college students, Guttman scalogram analysis yielded a coefficient of reproducibility of .92 and a coefficient of scalability of .74.
VALIDITY: Finlay (1981) found a high correlation (r = .77) between scores on the Favorability Toward Abortion Scale and scores on a single-item measure that asked the respondent's opinion of legalized abortion.
NOTES & COMMENTS: Half of the items overlap with items on the NORC Survey of Abortion Attitudes (see separate entry).
AVAILABLE FROM: Finlay, 1981, 1988
USED IN:

Finlay, B. A. (1981). Sex differences in attitudes toward abortion among college students. *Journal of Marriage and the Family*, *43*, 571–582.

Finlay, B. A. (1985). Correlates of abortion attitudes and implications for change. In P. Sachdev (Ed.), *Perspectives on abortion* (pp. 178–190). Metuchen, NJ: The Scarecrow Press.

Finlay, B. A. (1988). Scale of Favorability Toward Abortion. In C. M. Davis, W. L. Yarber, & S. L. Davis (Eds.), *Sexuality-related measures: A compendium* (p. 2). Syracuse: Editors.

GOUGH ABORTION ATTITUDE SCALE
AUTHOR: Harrison G. Gough
DATE: 1975
VARIABLE: Attitudes toward abortion
TYPE OF INSTRUMENT: Summated rating scale
DESCRIPTION: The Gough Abortion Attitude Scale consists of eight items pertaining to various aspects of abortion. Each item is accompanied by a 5-point scale ranging from "agree strongly" to "disagree strongly."

SAMPLE ITEMS: The decision to ask for an abortion must be in part a moral decision.

Abortion should be free of any and all legal restrictions.

PREVIOUS SUBJECTS: College students and adults

APPROPRIATE FOR: High school students and older

ADMINISTRATION: Self-administered; about 5 minutes

SCORING: Individual items are scored on a 5-point scale, with higher scores being assigned to the response that is "pro-choice" and lower scores assigned to the "right-to-life" response. Item scores are summed to yield a total score ranging from 8 (strong anti-abortion sentiment) to 40 (strong pro-choice sentiment). Gough (1975) reported means and standard deviations separately for males and females, for samples of college students and nonstudents. The means ranged from 27.78 to 29.44.

DEVELOPMENT: A pool of 25 items was administered to 46 college males and 76 college females. The F scale, which measures authoritarianism (Adorno, Frenkel-Brunswik, Levinson, & Sanford, 1950), was also administered, as were item pools being used to develop three other scales: Attitudes Toward Birth Control, Attitudes Toward Family Planning, and Attitudes Toward Population Management. Three criteria were used for eliminating items: a low correlation with the total score on the subset of items, a high correlation with the F scale, or a large sex difference in endorsement rates for the item. Eight items remained from the original pool of 25.

RELIABILITY: Alpha coefficients were computed for several groups. For a sample of 392 college and adult males, the coefficient was .70; for a sample of 374 college and adult females, the coefficient was .72; and for a sample of 287 adults, the coefficient was .70.

VALIDITY: There were no direct tests of the scale's validity. However, Gough (1975) did find that scale scores correlated in the predicted direction with attitudes toward birth control, family planning, population management, and modernity. He also found that, as expected, scores were negatively correlated with the number of children respondents expected to have.

Werner (1978) tested a large sample of adults and found a strong relationship between expressed attitudes and a measure of activism (in regard to abortion).

NOTES & COMMENTS: (1) Although the development of the Gough Abortion Attitude Scale was specifically designed to reduce the relationship between scale scores and scores on authoritarianism, Gough (1975) found a correlation of −.38 between the two measures.

(2) Gough, Gendre, and Lazzari (1976) used English, French, and Italian versions of the Gough Abortion Attitude Scale.

AVAILABLE FROM: Gough, 1975

USED IN:

Gough, H. G. (1975). An attitude profile for studies of population psychology. *Journal of Research in Personality, 9*, 122–135.

Gough, H. G., Gendre, F., & Lazzari, R. (1976). Attitudes related to the number of children wanted and expected by college students in three countries. *Journal of Cross-Cultural Psychology, 7*, 413–425.

Werner, P. D. (1978). Personality and attitude-activism correspondence. *Journal of Personality and Social Psychology, 36*, 1375–1390.

BIBLIOGRAPHY:

Adorno, T. W., Frenkel-Brunswik, E., Levinson, D. J., & Sanford, R. N. (1950). *The authoritarian personality*. New York: Harper.

NORC SURVEY OF ABORTION ATTITUDES

AUTHOR: James Allan Davis

DATE: 1965

VARIABLE: Conditions under which abortions should be allowed

TYPE OF INSTRUMENT: Guttman scale

DESCRIPTION: The NORC Survey of Abortion Attitudes consists of six conditions under which a woman might seek an abortion. For each condition, respondents are to answer "yes" if they believe that abortions should be legal under that condition or "no" if they believe that abortions should be illegal under the circumstances given. Of the six conditions, three are considered "hard" reasons, meaning that there is a medical or physical cause for the abortion, and three are considered "soft" reasons, meaning that a child is not wanted for one reason or another.

SAMPLE ITEMS: Please tell me whether or not *you* think it should be possible for a pregnant woman to obtain a *legal* abortion . . .

(hard reason) if there is a strong chance of serious defect in the baby.

(soft reason) if she is not married and does not want to marry the man.

PREVIOUS SUBJECTS: Ages 18 and older

APPROPRIATE FOR: High school students and older

ADMINISTRATION: The scale is simple enough to be self-administered or administered by telephone; it takes a few minutes to complete the scale.

SCORING: Some researchers obtained a total score by assigning 0 points to "no" responses and 1 point to "yes" responses and totaling across the six items. Other researchers obtained two summative scores: one for the three "soft" reasons and one for the three "hard" reasons. Some researchers did not total the items; instead they looked at responses to individual items.

DEVELOPMENT: No information was provided.

RELIABILITY: Several researchers have performed Guttman analyses on the items. Bock, Beeghley, and Mixon (1983) obtained a coefficient of reproducibility of .94 and a coefficient of scalability of .81. Granberg and Granberg (1985) looked at data from several years and reported coefficients of reproducibility ranging from .92 to .94. Jones and Westoff (1978) analyzed data from the National Fertility Study and reported a coefficient of reproducibility of .95 and a coefficient of scalability of .72 and .76. Cutler, Lentz, Miha, and Riter (1980) looked at seven sets of data gathered over 12 years. For the three "hard" reasons, they found coefficients of reproducibility ranging from .90 to .95 and coefficients of scalability ranging from .63 to .74. For the three "soft" reasons, the coefficients of reproducibility ranged from .92 to .94, and the coefficients of scalability ranged from .66 to .87. For the complete set of six items, the coefficients of reproducibility ranged from .92 to .94, and the coefficients of scalability ranged from .71 to .80.

VALIDITY: Granberg (1982) administered the scale to members of two politically active organizations: one "right-to-life" group and one abortion rights group. He obtained a point biserial correlation of .98, showing that the scale clearly differentiated between the two groups. Furthermore, he found that the two groups differed significantly on each of the six items.

Many researchers have found that scores related as expected to religious conservatism, religiosity, and education; that is, greater religious conservatism and greater religiosity were associated with less support for abortion, and higher education levels were associated with more support for abortion (Arney & Trescher, 1976; Barnartt & Harris, 1982; Bock et al., 1983; Granberg & Granberg, 1980, 1985; Hedderson, Hodgson, Bogan, & Crowley, 1974; Petersen & Mauss, 1976; Tedrow & Mahoney, 1979; Wagenaar & Knol, 1977).

NOTES & COMMENTS: (1) Many scales can be considered variations of the NORC Survey of Abortion Attitudes. The most important variation was used in the National Fertility Study (NFS) (e.g., Jones & Westoff, 1978, or Blake, 1971). The NFS measure contains conditions identical to those on the NORC scale. The only difference between the two measures is in the introductory statement. The NORC introduction is given above; the NFS introduction stated: "I'm going to read you a list of seven possible reasons why a woman might have a pregnancy interrupted. Would you tell me whether you think it would be all right for a woman to do this?" The seventh reason was, "If the woman wanted it for any reason." This last "reason" was also included in some of the studies using the NORC Survey of Abortion Attitudes. There are other variations on the NORC items. Singh and Leahy (1978) used the NORC data but looked at only three items; Clayton and Tolone (1973) used items similar to the NORC items; Perry and Trlin (1982) used similar items and tested attitudes in New Zealand; and Sell, Roghmann, and Doherty (1978) used the NORC items plus two other "soft" reasons. Gallup polls have also included some of the same items as used in the NORC scale (Blake, 1971).

(2) A factor analytic study by Arney and Trescher (1976) used data collected from the general public and revealed two factors. One factor included the "hard" reasons, and the other factor included the "soft" reasons. Granberg (1982) performed a factor analytic study using data he collected from members of a right-to-life group and members of a pro-choice group. He found a single factor including all 6 items. Furthermore, he included 6 additional items on the scale, and when he performed a factor analysis with all 12 items, he still found a single factor.

AVAILABLE FROM: Blake, 1971; Clayton and Tolone, 1973; Combs and Welch, 1982; Cutler, Lentz, Miha, and Riter, 1980; Ebaugh and Haney, 1980; Granberg, 1982; Hedderson, Hodgson, Bogan, and Crowley, 1974; Seals, Ekwo, Williamson, and Hanson, 1985; Sell, Roghmann, and Doherty, 1978; Tedrow and Mahoney, 1979; Wagenaar and Knol, 1977

USED IN:

Arney, W., & Trescher, W. (1976). Trends in attitudes toward abortion: 1972–1975. *Family Planning Perspectives, 8,* 117–124.

Barnartt, S. N., & Harris, R. J. (1982). Recent changes in predictors of abortion attitudes. *Sociology and Social Research, 66,* 320–334.

Blake, J. (1971). Abortion and public opinion: The 1960–1970 decade. *Science, 171,* 540–555.

Bock, E. W., Beeghley, L., & Mixon, A. J. (1983). Religion, socioeconomic status, and sexual morality: An application of reference group theory. *Sociological Quarterly, 24,* 545–559.

Clayton, R. R., & Tolone, W. L. (1973). Religiosity and attitudes toward induced abortion: An elaboration of the relationship. *Sociological Analysis, 34,* 26–39.

Combs, M. W., & Welch, S. (1982). Blacks, whites, and attitudes toward abortion. *Public Opinion Quarterly, 46,* 510–520.

Cutler, S. J., Lentz, S. A., Miha, M. J., & Riter, R. N. (1980). Aging and conservatism: Cohort changes in attitudes about legalized abortion. *Journal of Gerontology, 35,* 115–123.

Ebaugh, H. R., & Haney, A. C. (1980). Shifts in abortion attitudes: 1972–1978. *Journal of Marriage and Family, 42,* 491–499.

Gillespie, M. W., Ten Vergert, E. M., & Kingma, J. (1988). Secular trends in abortion attitudes: 1975–1980–1985. *Journal of Psychology, 122,* 323–341.

Granberg, D. (1982). Comparison of pro-choice and pro-life activists: Their values, attitudes, and beliefs. *Population and Environment: Behavioral and Social Issues, 5,* 75–94.

Granberg, D., & Granberg, B. W. (1980). Abortion attitudes 1965–1980: Trends and determinants. *Family Planning Perspectives, 12,* 250–261.

Granberg, D., & Granberg, B. W. (1985). A search for gender differences on fertility-related attitudes: Questioning the relevance of sociobiology theory for understanding social psychological aspects of human reproduction. *Psychology of Women Quarterly, 9,* 431–437.

Hall, E. J., & Ferree, M. M. (1986). Race differences in abortion attitudes. *Public Opinion Quarterly, 50,* 193–207.

Hedderson, J., Hodgson, L. G., Bogan, M., & Crowley, T. (1974). Determinants of abortion attitudes in the United States in 1972. *Cornell Journal of Social Relations, 9,* 261–276.

Henshaw, S. K., & Martire, G. (1982). Morality and legality. *Family Planning Perspectives, 14*(2), 53–62.

Jones, E. F., & Westoff, C. F. (1978). How attitudes toward abortion are changing. *Journal of Population, 1,* 5–21.

Perry, P., & Trlin, A. (1982). Attitudes toward abortion in a provincial area of New Zealand: Differentials and determinants. *Australian and New Zealand Journal of Sociology, 18,* 399–416.

Petersen, L. R., & Mauss, A. L. (1976). Religion and the "right to life": Correlates of opposition to abortion. *Sociological Analysis, 37,* 243–254.

Renzi, M. (1975). Ideal family size as an intervening variable between religion and attitudes toward abortion. *Journal for the Scientific Study of Religion, 14,* 23–27.

Seals, B. F., Ekwo, E. E., Williamson, R. A., & Hanson, J. W. (1985). Moral and religious influences on the amniocentesis decision. *Social Biology, 32,* 13–30.

Sell, R. R., Roghmann, K. J., & Doherty, R. A. (1978). Attitudes toward abortion and prenatal diagnosis of fetal abnormalities: Implications for educational programs. *Social Biology, 25,* 288–301.

Singh, B. K., & Leahy, P. J. (1978). Contextual and ideological dimensions of attitudes toward discretionary abortion. *Demography, 15,* 381–388.

Singh, B. K., & Williams, J. S. (1983). Attitudes and behavioral intentions about abortion. *Population and Environment: Behavioral and Social Issues, 6,* 84–95.

Tedrow, L. M., & Mahoney, E. R. (1979). Trends in attitudes toward abortion: 1972–1976. *Public Opinion Quarterly, 43,* 181–189.

Wagenaar, T. C., & Knol, I. W. (1977). Attitudes toward abortion: A comparative analysis of correlates for 1973 and 1975. *Journal of Sociology and Social Welfare, 4,* 927–944.

SMETANA PERMISSIBLE CIRCUMSTANCES FOR ABORTION

AUTHOR: Judith G. Smetana

DATE: 1979

VARIABLE: Circumstances under which an abortion is acceptable for oneself and for others

TYPE OF INSTRUMENT: Multiple choice

DESCRIPTION: The Smetana Permissible Circumstances for Abortion scale consists of 22 circumstances under which a woman might decide to have an abortion. The circumstances vary in terms of the responsibility for the pregnancy (e.g., rape), the woman's welfare (e.g., dangerous to the woman's health), and the child's welfare (e.g., the child would grow up in poverty). For each item, respondents are asked to choose one of four options indicating whether abortion was never justified, justified through the first trimester, the second trimester, or the third trimester. Respondents are then asked to respond a second time, using the same four response options, to indicate whether they would consider abortion for themselves.

SAMPLE ITEMS: The woman did not know about birth control.

Continuing the pregnancy would endanger the woman's mental health.

PREVIOUS SUBJECTS: Women, ages 13–31; pregnant women; women who had decided to have an abortion

APPROPRIATE FOR: High school and older; the scale would need to be modified for males

ADMINISTRATION: Self-administered; about 10 minutes

SCORING: Items are individually scored as follows: 0 points are given if abortion is never justified under the given circumstance; 1 point is given if abortion is justified through the first trimester; 2 points are given if abortion is justified through the second trimester; and 3 points are given if abortion is justified through the third trimester. A total score is obtained by summing item scores. Six factor scores can be obtained, based on Smetana's (1979) factor analysis. (See NOTES & COMMENTS.) Based on responses from 70 single women, Smetana reported means for these factor scores.

DEVELOPMENT: Smetana (1979) reported that items were "selected from a review of other research and pilot tested on a sample of university undergraduate women" (p. 297).

RELIABILITY: Faden et al. (1983) used a 10-item variation of Smetana's scale to assess the abortion attitudes of pregnant women. They calculated coefficient alpha to be .88 for the responses regarding women in general and .89 for the responses regarding "self."

VALIDITY: Based on the factor analysis described below, Smetana (1979) calculated factor scores in two ways. She used the ratings of the permissibility of abortion for women in general, and she used the ratings given for self. In comparing respondents who continued their pregnancy with respondents who had abortions and with never-pregnant respondents, the latter groups showed significantly more positive attitudes toward abortion on two of the three factors based on general permissibility for abortion. Comparisons of respondents who had abortions with respondents who continued their pregnancies revealed that the former group showed significantly more positive attitudes toward abortion on all four factors based on permissibility of abortion for oneself.

As expected, Faden et al. (1983) found that women were more accepting of abortion for women in general than they were of abortion for themselves. They also found that women who believed that the ideal family included a larger number of children were less likely to be accepting of abortion for women in general and for themselves.

NOTES & COMMENTS: (1) Three factors were identified from a factor analysis based on respondents' ratings of the general permissibility of abortion. The first factor, which accounted for 55% of the variance, contained 11 items describing a variety of "soft" reasons for obtaining an abortion (e.g., the woman is unmarried). Soft reasons are those that are under the woman's control, such as the child would strain the marriage or the relationship. The second factor, accounting for 10.5% of the variance, contained 6 items describing "hard" reasons (although some are less hard than others). Hard reasons are those that are beyond the woman's control, such as continuing the pregnancy would endanger the woman's mental health or the child would be born defective. The third factor accounted for 7.3% of the variance and contained 4 items concerning the quality of life for the unborn child (e.g., the child would grow up with only one parent).

A second factor analysis was performed using responses showing the acceptability of abortion for oneself. This analysis produced four factors, and Smetana (1979) explained how these factors related to the first set of factors.

(2) Faden et al. (1983) used a 10-item scale, with 7 of the items overlapping Smetana's scale. They also used Smetana's procedure of asking respondents to respond to the items in terms of the general permissibility of abortion and to respond a second time to indicate whether they would consider themselves justified in having an abortion under the particular circumstance. Faden et al. reported item-total correlations above .45 for all items.

AVAILABLE FROM: Smetana, 1979

USED IN:

Faden, R., Chwalow, A. J., Chase, G. A., Quaid, K., Leonard, C., & Holtzman, N. A. (1983). Pregnant women's attitudes toward the abortion of defective fetuses. *Population and Environment, 6,* 197–209.

Smetana, J. G. (1979). Beliefs about the permissibility of abortion and their relationship to decisions regarding abortion. *Journal of Population, 2,* 294–305.

5

Pregnancy and Childbirth

This chapter contains descriptions of 20 measures, organized into three categories: pregnancy (8 measures), labor and childbirth (7 measures), and the postpartum period (5 measures). In most cases, I placed the measures that deal with all three periods in the first category: pregnancy. However, to ensure that they do not overlook a potentially useful scale, researchers should consult all three categories before making a final selection.

Most of the measures in the first section are appropriate only for females. They cover a variety of topics: childbearing attitudes; new mother's perceptions of a variety of issues, including her body, her interpersonal relations, and her baby; attitudes toward pregnancy; maternal-fetal attachment during pregnancy; stressful events during pregnancy, childbirth, and the postpartum period; anxiety and depression during pregnancy; problems during pregnancy; and social support during pregnancy. One measure, the Maternal Adjustment and Maternal Attitudes scale (Kumar, Robson, & Smith, 1984), is available in two versions: a pregnancy version and a postpartum version.

With one exception, these scales have been used by few researchers. The exception is the Pregnancy Research Questionnaire (Schaefer & Manheimer, 1960), which has been used extensively and is also the oldest scale in this section. The newest scale is the Support Behaviors Inventory (Brown, 1986). Most of the scales in this section are summated rating scales, and they tend to be fairly long, ranging from 24 to 173 items. There was some evidence relating to the reliability of all of these scales; there was some evidence relating to the validity of most of these scales, but the data frequently provided weak or equivocal evidence regarding validity.

The second section in this chapter contains scales relating to labor and childbirth. Six of these seven scales are appropriate only for women. Three are summated rating scales; two are alternate choice measures, with one based on an interview; and two are behavioral observation measures. The two behavioral observation measures are intended for use with women in labor. There are two forms of one scale, the Schroeder Labor Locus of Control scale (Schroeder, 1985). One is to be completed while the woman is pregnant and one during the postpartum stage. There were data pertaining to the reliability of five scales and the validity of six scales in this section. Pain measures, such as the McGill Pain Questionnaire (Melzack, 1975), have also been used to measure the discomfort experienced during labor and childbirth. General pain measures are not described in this handbook because they were not developed especially for the study of women in labor.

The final section of this chapter contains descriptions of five measures pertaining to the postpartum period. The content of most of these scales pertains to postpartum adjustment, and all of these scales are to be completed by pregnant or postpartum women. None of these scales has been used extensively within the last 10 years. One scale, the Postnatal Research Inventory (Schaefer & Manheimer, 1960), may have been used by more researchers during the years prior to 1979. The other scales are not old enough to have been used before the late 1970s. Overall, one can place little confidence in the reliability of these scales. There were no reliability data for two of the measures, and the reliability coefficients were not very high for two other measures. Similarly, there was little convincing evidence regarding the validity of some of these measures.

Only one measure in this chapter was described in my original handbook (Beere, 1979): the Maternal Attitude to Pregnancy Instrument (Blau, Welkowitz, & Cohen, 1964).

BIBLIOGRAPHY:

Beere, C. A. (1979). *Women and women's issues: A handbook of tests and measures* (pp. 488–490). San Francisco: Jossey-Bass.

Blau, A., Welkowitz, J., & Cohen, J. (1964). Maternal Attitude to Pregnancy Instrument. *Archives of General Psychiatry, 10*, 324–331.

Brown, M. A. (1986). Social support during pregnancy: A unidimensional or multidimensional construct? *Nursing Research, 35*, 4–9.

Kumar, R., Robson, K. M., & Smith, A. M. (1984). Development of a self-administered questionnaire to measure maternal adjustment and maternal attitudes during pregnancy and after delivery. *Journal of Psychosomatic Research, 28*, 43–51.

Melzack, R. (1975). The McGill Pain Questionnaire: Major properties and scoring methods. *Pain, 1*, 277–299.

Schaefer, E. S., & Manheimer, H. (1960, April). *Dimensions of perinatal adjustment.*

Paper presented at the meeting of the Eastern Psychological Association, New York.

Schroeder, M. A. (1985). Development and testing of a scale to measure locus of control prior to and following childbirth. *Maternal Child Nursing Journal, 14*, 111–121.

CHILDBEARING ATTITUDES QUESTIONNAIRE (CAQ)

AUTHORS: Diane N. Ruble, Jeanne Brooks-Gunn, Alison Fleming, Garrett Fitzmaurice, Charles Stangor, and Francine Deutsch

DATE: 1981

VARIABLE: Childbearing attitudes

TYPE OF INSTRUMENT: Summated rating scale

DESCRIPTION: The Childbearing Attitudes Questionnaire (CAQ) consists of 60 items, with 2 to 6 items representing each of 16 factors: Maternal Worries, Maternal Self-Confidence, Relationship with Husband, Relationship with Mother, Body Image, Identification with Pregnancy, Feelings about Children, Negative Self-Image, Attitude toward Breastfeeding, Pain Tolerance, Interest in Sex, Denial, Negative Aspects of Caretaking, Feelings of Dependency, Social Boredom, and Information-Seeking. Some items are phrased to reflect a positive attitude toward childbearing, and others are phrased to reflect a negative attitude. The phrasing of the items is slightly altered depending on whether the CAQ is administered to women planning to become pregnant, women currently pregnant, or postpartum women. Each item is accompanied by a 7-point response scale, with the endpoints marked "disagree strongly" and "agree strongly."

SAMPLE ITEMS: (Maternal Worries) There is so much to know about babies, I wonder if I'll ever learn enough to feel comfortable.

(Maternal Self-Confidence) I feel completely ready for motherhood.

(Relationship with Husband) I expect to be bothered by my husband/mate's lack of involvement in the daily care of the baby.

(Relationship with Mother) My mother has been a great source of support.

(Body Image) I feel less attractive now that I'm pregnant.

(Identification with Pregnancy) I expect that being a mother will strengthen my sense of self.

(Feelings about Children) Just the sight of a small child makes me smile.

(Negative Self-Image) I feel inferior to most of the people I know.

(Attitude toward Breastfeeding) There is no difference between babies who are breastfed and those who are bottlefed.

(Pain Tolerance) I seem to be able to handle pain better than most people.

(Interest in Sex) I feel I am less interested in sex than I used to be.

(Denial) Most women make too much of the pain associated with delivery.

(Negative Aspects of Caretaking) I feel uncomfortable watching women breastfeeding their babies.

(Feelings of Dependency) I am concerned about becoming too dependent on others during my pregnancy.

(Social Boredom) My life lacks variety.

(Information-Seeking) I find I do not enjoy reading books on child care.

PREVIOUS SUBJECTS: Married women planning to get pregnant for the first time or currently pregnant for the first time and women who recently gave birth for the first time

APPROPRIATE FOR: Females, ages 16 and older

ADMINISTRATION: Self-administered; about 20–30 minutes

SCORING: Individual items are scored on a 7-point scale and summed to yield scores on each of the 16 factors. Scores can also be obtained for each of the four higher-order factors described below (see NOTES & COMMENTS).

DEVELOPMENT: A pool of 76 items was developed to measure attitudes toward pregnancy and birth, self-esteem, and interpersonal relationships. The items were pilot tested and then administered to 667 women, including women planning to become pregnant, women pregnant with their first child, and women who recently gave birth to their first child. Three items were initially deleted because of floor or ceiling effects, and responses to the remaining 73 items were factor analyzed. Twenty factors were identified; 15 were considered interpretable. The first factor consisted of a large number of items, and so it was divided into two smaller scales: one called Maternal Worries and reflecting negative feelings and one called Maternal Self-Confidence and reflecting positive feelings. Items were selected for the CAQ based on their factor loadings on the 16 factors.

RELIABILITY: Coefficient alpha for the 16 subscales ranged from .46 to .80. Ruble et al. (1988) reported coefficient alpha for three subgroups of the women respondents: prepregnant women, pregnant women, and postpartum women. On 15 of the 16 subscales, coefficient alpha was at least .50 for at least two of the three groups. Coefficient alpha on the Information-Seeking subscale was below .40 for two of the three groups.

Ruble et al. (1988) provided data regarding the test-retest reliability of the subscales. A group of about 40 women completed the CAQ when they were 1 month postpartum and again when they were 3 months postpartum. For 15 of the 16 subscales, the reliability coefficient was greater than .60; for 11 of the subscales, the reliability coefficient was at least .70.

VALIDITY: Ruble et al. (1988) found equality of covariance for all 16 subscales across the different childbearing groups. Furthermore, they identified four higher-order factors—self-confidence, awareness of negative aspects, social orientation, and identification with motherhood—that were comparable across the different childbearing groups.

Since women representing three phases of pregnancy (pre, during, post) completed the CAQ, it was possible to look at changes in scores across the different phases. Ten subscales showed significant changes across the three phases. There were significant increases across phase for four subscales: Maternal Self-Confidence, Identification with Pregnancy, Social Boredom, and Information-Seeking. There were significant decreases across phase for three subscales: Maternal Worries, Interest in Sex, and Negative Aspects of Caretaking. There were curvilinear relationships for three subscales: Relationship with Husband, Denial, and Body Image.

Longitudinal data were available for a sample of women tested during their pregnancy, at 1 month postpartum, and again at 3 months postpartum. Seven subscales showed significant changes over time, and three of those were large changes: "a decrease in endorsing Negative Aspects of Caretaking across time, an increase in Social Boredom, and an increase in Self-Confidence" (Ruble et al., 1988, p. 17). There were four subscales showing smaller yet significant changes: "Maternal worries decreased; positive Body Image increased; Denial decreased; and positive Attitudes about Breastfeeding decreased" (p. 18).

NOTES & COMMENTS: (1) A large sample of women in Toronto, Seattle, and the New York area provided the data for developing the CAQ and exploring some of its psychometric properties. Deutsch, Ruble, Fleming, Brooks-Gunn, and Stangor (1988) conducted research using a portion of these same data.

(2) The analyses for higher-order factors led to identifying four factors: Self-Confidence included Maternal Worries, Maternal Self-Confidence, Negative Self-Image, and Feelings of Dependency; Negative Aspects of Giving Birth included Attitude toward Breastfeeding, Pain Tolerance, Denial, and Negative Aspects of Caretaking; Social Orientation included Relationship with Husband, Body Image, Interest in Sex, and Social Boredom; and Identification with Motherhood included Relationship with Mother, Identification with Pregnancy, Feelings about Children, and Information-Seeking.

(3) The item content on this scale is unusually diverse, and the subscales cover a variety of topics. Caution should be exercised in using some of the subscales that are very short and have unacceptably low reliabilities.

AVAILABLE FROM: Diane Ruble, Department of Psychology, New York University, Washington Square, New York, NY 10003

USED IN:

Deutsch, F. M., Ruble, D. N., Fleming, A., Brooks-Gunn, J., & Stangor, C. S. (1988). Information-seeking and maternal self-definition during the transition to motherhood. *Journal of Personality and Social Psychology, 55*, 420–431.

Ruble, D. N., Brooks-Gunn, J., Fleming, A. S., Fitzmaurice, G., Stangor, C., & Deutsch, F. (1988). *Comparability of attitude constructs and self-definitional change across phases of childbearing*. Manuscript submitted for publication.

MATERNAL ADJUSTMENT AND MATERNAL ATTITUDES (MAMA)

AUTHORS: R. Kumar, K. M. Robson, and A. M. R. Smith
DATE: 1984
VARIABLE: "A [new] mother's perceptions of her body, of somatic symptoms, the marital relationship, attitudes to sex and attitudes to the pregnancy and the baby" (Kumar, Robson, & Smith, 1984, p. 43)
TYPE OF INSTRUMENT: Summated rating scale
DESCRIPTION: The Maternal Adjustment and Maternal Attitudes (MAMA) scale consists of 60 items, 12 representing each of five areas: Body Image, Somatic Symptoms, Marital Relationship, Attitudes to Sex, and Attitudes to Pregnancy and the Baby. There are two versions of the scale: a pregnancy version and a postpartum version. The content of the items is identical in the two versions, but the phrasing of 12 items is slightly different. Two different scales are provided for responding to items. Some items are accompanied by the options "very often, often, rarely, never," and other items are accompanied by the options "very much, a lot, a little, not at all." Responses are to be based on how the woman has been feeling during the prior 4 weeks.
SAMPLE ITEMS: (Body Image) Have you felt attractive?
(Somatic Symptoms) Have you been perspiring a lot?
(Marital Relationship) Has there been tension between you and your partner—irritability, unpleasant silence, etc.?
(Attitudes to Sex) Have you found your partner sexually desirable?
(Attitudes to Pregnancy and the Baby) Have you been worrying that you might not be a good mother?
PREVIOUS SUBJECTS: Pregnant women
APPROPRIATE FOR: Women in the prepartum and postpartum periods
ADMINISTRATION: Self-administered; about 10–12 minutes
SCORING: Items are individually scored on a 4-point scale, with the direction of the scoring varying according to the specific item. Item scores are totaled to yield scores on the five components. Kumar et al. (1984) indicated which items contributed to each component score.
DEVELOPMENT: A pool of 91 items was generated based on interviews with pregnant women and a search of the relevant literature. The 91 items covered six areas: body image, somatic symptoms, the marital

relationship, attitudes and feelings about sex, sexual activity, and attitudes to the pregnancy and the baby. The 91-item version of the scale was completed by 99 pregnant women who also commented on questions that they found objectionable, irrelevant, or ambiguous. Their responses were subjected to an item analysis, and "individual questions were removed if their association with the overall subscore was greater than .70, or if the percentage of subjects scoring 3 or 4 on a particular item was less than 10% or greater than 90%" (Kumar et al., 1984, p. 44). The items relating to sexual activity were deleted because the women had stopped having sexual intercourse and so could not respond to the items. Two other items were eliminated because of comments made by the women. This left a pool of 45 questions; 15 questions were added to the pool. The source of these 15 questions is not given, but the total of 60 questions now included 12 items representing each of five areas.

RELIABILITY: Test-retest reliability was computed using the responses from 38 women who were tested on two occasions separated by about 1 week. The interval of 1 week was selected because "this gap was, hopefully, long enough to minimise [*sic*] recall of previous responses and short enough to preclude too great a change in the subjects' attitudes and perceptions of their pregnancies" (Kumar et al., 1984, p. 45). The reliability coefficients were .89 for Body Image, .83 for Somatic Symptoms, .81 for Marital Relationship, .95 for Attitudes to Sex, and .84 for Attitudes to Pregnancy/Baby.

Split-half reliability coefficients were computed using the responses from 119 women. The resulting coefficients were .72 for Body Image, .58 for Somatic Symptoms, .74 for Marital Relationship, .82 for Attitudes to Sex, and .73 for Attitudes to Pregnancy/Baby.

VALIDITY: Kumar et al. (1984) compared information obtained from interviews and information obtained on the MAMA to obtain evidence of the validity of the subscales. Using interview data regarding frequency of nausea, they divided a sample of women into two groups. The Somatic Symptoms scores of these two groups were compared, and there was a significant difference between the group means ($p < .005$). Similarly, interview data regarding frequency of vomiting was used to divide the women into two groups, and again there was a significant difference between the mean scores on the Somatic Symptoms subscale ($p < .001$). The women were divided into two groups on the basis of interview data: those reporting considerable dissatisfaction with their marriages and those with little or no dissatisfaction. The Marital Relationship subscale scores for the two groups were significantly different from each other ($p < .001$). When the women were divided into two groups on the basis of their enjoyment of sex, there was a significant difference in scores on the Attitudes to Sex subscale ($p < .001$); similarly when they were divided into two groups based on reported frequency of intercourse, there were

significant differences on the Attitudes to Sex subscale ($p < .001$). Based on information obtained during the interview, the women were divided into two groups: those who expressed positive feelings about their babies and those who expressed mixed or negative feelings. A significant difference was found on the Attitude to Baby scores of these two groups ($p < .001$). Women were also divided into two groups depending on whether they perceived their babies as more difficult or not more difficult than the average baby. There was a significant difference between the scores of these two groups on the Attitude to Baby subscale ($p < .01$).
NOTES & COMMENTS: (1) No information was available regarding the validity of the Body Image subscale.

(2) Kumar et al. (1984) reported that three of the items were judged ambiguous, and they suggested new wording for them.
AVAILABLE FROM: Kumar, Robson, and Smith, 1984
USED IN:

Kumar, R., Robson, K. M., & Smith, A. M. (1984). Development of a self-administered questionnaire to measure maternal adjustment and maternal attitudes during pregnancy and after delivery. *Journal of Psychosomatic Research, 28,* 43–51.

MATERNAL ATTITUDE TO PREGNANCY INSTRUMENT (MAPI)
AUTHORS: Abram Blau, Joan Welkowitz, and Jacob Cohen
DATE: 1964
VARIABLE: Attitudes toward pregnancy
TYPE OF INSTRUMENT: Summated rating scale
DESCRIPTION: The Maternal Attitude to Pregnancy Instrument (MAPI) consists of 48 items representing four factors: Factor I, "a feeling of well-being during pregnancy and an acceptance of pregnancy, labor, and delivery without fear"; Factor II, "exaggerated feelings of well-being during pregnancy, pride of the pregnancy, positive maternal feelings to the child, and positive attitudes toward her doctor"; Factor III, "an unusual concern about the delivery and birth, a desire for active participation in the delivery, and a positive interest in breast nursing [*sic*]"; and Factor IV, "positive feelings toward the baby" (Blau, Welkowitz, & Cohen, 1964, p. 326). All items are phrased in the third person, so the MAPI can be completed by both males and females. It is not recommended for persons below age 16.
ARTICLES LISTED IN BEERE, 1979: 1
NOTES & COMMENTS: The scale is available in Spanish, as well as in English.
AVAILABLE FROM: Blau, Welkowitz, and Cohen, 1964
USED IN:

Blau, A., Welkowitz, J., & Cohen, J. (1964). Maternal Attitude to Pregnancy Instrument. *Archives of General Psychiatry, 10,* 324–331.
Blumberg, N. L. (1980). Effects of neonatal risk, maternal attitude, and cognitive

style on early postpartum adjustment. *Journal of Abnormal Psychology, 89,* 139–150.

Chalmers, B. (1983). Psychosocial factors and obstetric complications. *Psychological Medicine, 13,* 333–339.

Powers, P. S., Johnson, T., Knuppel, R., Cupoli, J. M., & Achenbach, K. E. (1986). Psychiatric disorders in high-risk pregnancy. *Comprehensive Psychiatry, 27,* 159–164.

Zax, M., Sameroff, A. J., & Babigian, H. M. (1977). Birth outcomes in the offspring of mentally disordered women. *American Journal of Orthopsychiatry, 47,* 218–230.

BIBLIOGRAPHY:

Beere, C. A. (1979). *Women and women's issues: A handbook of tests and measures* (pp. 488–490). San Francisco: Jossey-Bass.

MATERNAL FETAL ATTACHMENT (MFA)

AUTHOR: Mecca S. Cranley

DATE: 1981 (used 1979)

VARIABLE: Maternal-fetal attachment during pregnancy

TYPE OF INSTRUMENT: Summated rating scale

DESCRIPTION: The Maternal Fetal Attachment (MFA) scale is intended to measure "the extent to which women engage in behaviors that represent an affiliation and interaction with their unborn child" (Cranley, 1981, p. 282). The scale contains 24 items representing five subscales: differentiation of self from the fetus (4 items), interaction with the fetus (5 items), attributing characteristics and intentions to the fetus (6 items), giving of self (5 items), and role taking (4 items). Only one item is phrased negatively. All items are accompanied by five response options: "definitely yes, yes, uncertain, no, definitely no."

SAMPLE ITEMS: (differentiation of self from the fetus) I enjoy watching my tummy jiggle as the baby kicks inside.

(interaction with the fetus) I talk to my unborn baby.

(attributing characteristics and intentions to the fetus) I wonder if the baby feels cramped in there.

(giving of self) I feel all the trouble of being pregnant is worth it.

(role taking) I picture myself feeding the baby.

PREVIOUS SUBJECTS: Pregnant women and their husbands

APPROPRIATE FOR: Pregnant women; a modified version can be used with prospective fathers

ADMINISTRATION: Self-administered; about 5–10 minutes

SCORING: Items are individually scored on a 5-point scale, with 5 points assigned to the response expressing the greatest maternal-fetal attachment. Subscale scores are expressed as the average of the items on that subscale. The overall MFA score is the average of all item scores.

DEVELOPMENT: Six content areas were identified, and for each area, items were generated based on input from clinicians and Lamaze teachers. The items were reviewed by five nurses involved in maternal and child care and by a group of pregnant women. The purpose of these reviews was to ensure the content validity of the scale and the understandability of the individual items. The inputs from this review process led to a 37-item version of the scale, which was administered to 71 pregnant women. After using item analysis procedures, 13 of the 37 items were eliminated "for logical or empirical reasons or both" (Cranley, 1981, p. 282). One entire subscale, Nesting, was eliminated on the grounds that its internal consistency reliability was unacceptably low (alpha = .12). Four negatively worded items were deleted, leaving only one negative item on the final version of the scale. Cranley (1981) found that "women appeared reluctant to admit any annoyance from the fetus" (p. 282).

RELIABILITY: The responses from the 71 women who participated in scale development were used to compute coefficient alpha for each of the subscales and for the total score. The values obtained were: differentiation of self from the fetus = .62, interaction with the fetus = .68, attributing characteristics and intentions to the fetus = .67, giving of self = .52, role taking = .73, and total MFA = .85 (Cranley, 1981). The subscale reliabilities are rather low. Adding higher-quality items to the subscales would probably remedy this.

VALIDITY: Thirty pregnant women completed the MFA, and after their babies' births, they completed a measure of their perceptions of their infants. Contrary to expectation, there was no significant correlation between the two measures. Cranley (1981) offered several possible explanations for these unexpected findings.

As predicted, there was no relationship between MFA scores and age, number of pregnancies, or socioeconomic status. Self-esteem scores were also unrelated to MFA scores. There were significant correlations between MFA scores and the presence of a strong social support system ($r = .51$) and between MFA scores and stress ($r = -.41$). That is, those with more social support and less stress had stronger attachments to their fetuses (Cranley, 1981).

Using unpublished data, M. S. Cranley (personal communication, September 13, 1988) found that pregnant women had higher scores than their husbands on all subscales and on the total score. Furthermore, women who completed the test early in their pregnancy generally scored higher on subscales and total score than those completing the test later in their pregnancy. However, no statistical tests were reported, so it is not clear which of these differences were statistically significant.

NOTES & COMMENTS: (1) Intercorrelations among the subscales were all positive and ranged from .29 to .60. Subscale-total score correlations ranged from .61 to .83.

(2) Weaver and Cranley (1983) altered the original scale so that the

items were appropriate for a prospective father. Renaming the scale the Paternal-Fetal Attachment Scale, they obtained a coefficient alpha of .80 based on testing 100 expectant fathers. Weaver and Cranley used the scale to test two hypotheses: first, "the strength of the marital relationship as perceived by the expectant father during gestation is positively associated with the level of a father's attachment to the fetus," and second, "the incidence of physical symptoms related to pregnancy is positively associated with a father's attachment to the fetus" (Weaver & Cranley, 1983, p. 69).

AVAILABLE FROM: Mecca S. Cranley, University of Wisconsin—Madison, School of Nursing, 600 Highland Avenue, Madison, WI 53792

USED IN:

Cranley, M. S. (1981). Development of a tool for the measurement of maternal attachment during pregnancy. *Nursing Research, 30*(5), 281–284.

Weaver, R. H., & Cranley, M. S. (1983). An exploration of paternal-fetal attachment behavior. *Nursing Research, 32*(2), 68–72.

PERIPARTUM EVENTS SCALE (PES)

AUTHORS: Michael W. O'Hara, Michael W. Varner, and Susan R. Johnson

DATE: 1984

VARIABLE: An index of stressful events surrounding pregnancy, childbirth, and the postpartum period

TYPE OF INSTRUMENT: Checklist

DESCRIPTION: The Peripartum Events Scale (PES) was developed to provide a measure "to index stressful experiences in the peripartum period that would complement other measures of life events in studies of postpartum depression" (O'Hara, Varner, & Johnson, 1986, p. 86). The PES consists of 71 items representing 11 subscales, each containing 3 to 12 items. The subscales are: Demographic (3 items), Past Obstetric History (8 items), Medical Risk Factors (10 items), Obstetric Risk Factors (7 items), Indication for Admission to Labour and Delivery (8 items), Progress in Labour (4 items), Method of Delivery (5 items), Duration of Labour (3 items), Foetal Monitoring (6 items), Delivery Complications (5 items), and Infant Outcome (12 items). In addition, many of the subscales have a category labeled "other" in order to record other relevant stressful factors. The first three subscales refer to conditions present prior to the pregnancy: the Demographic subscale "reflect[s] a less than adequate social context for having a child" (O'Hara et al., 1986, p. 88); Past Obstetric History reflects problems from prior pregnancies that suggest an increased likelihood of problems with the current pregnancy; and Medical Risk Factors relate to preexisting medical conditions that increase the risk for peripartum complications. The remaining 8 subscales refer to conditions occurring immediately before, during, or after labor and childbirth. The PES can be completed from information contained in the medical chart.

SAMPLE ITEMS: (Demographic) Age < 18 or > 35

(Past Obstetric History) Previous Cesarean section, other uterine or cervical surgery, or uterine anomalies

(Medical Risk Factors) Hypertension

(Obstetric Risk Factors) Abnormal weight gain (< 4 kg or > 18 kg)

(Indication for Admission to Labour and Delivery) Ruptured membranes > 12 hours without labour

(Progress in Labour) Precipitous (< 3 hours)

(Method of Delivery) Midforceps

(Duration of Labour) First stage for primigravidas (> 20 hours)

(Foetal Monitoring) Electronic foetal heart rate monitoring (internal or external)

(Delivery Complications) Blood loss > 600 cc

(Infant Outcome) < 37 weeks or > 41 weeks

PREVIOUS SUBJECTS: Obstetricians have completed the scale for women who have just had babies

APPROPRIATE FOR: Persons trained to read medical charts can use the scale to rate women who have just had babies.

ADMINISTRATION: The scale is completed by a trained person using information contained in the medical chart.

SCORING: Most items are scored 1 point if they are checked as present. Exceptions include primary Cesarean section as the method of delivery and abnormal fetal blood sampling. These two items reflect particularly stressful events and thus are assigned 2 points. A total score is found for the PES by adding all of the points assigned. An exception to this is in the Demographic subscale where there are three items but the maximum score is 2. A score on the abbreviated PES is found by adding scores for the last eight subscales, that is, the subscales that refer only to the current labor and delivery experience.

DEVELOPMENT: The development of the PES was based on a rational rather than empirical approach. The items "were designed to represent the various contexts in which stress is manifested during the peripartum period" (O'Hara et al., 1986, p. 88). In order to facilitate completion of the scale, the organization of the PES was designed to coincide with the organization of medical charts.

RELIABILITY: Two obstetricians completed the scale for 98 women (O'Hara et al., 1986). The correlation between the total scores assigned by the two obstetricians was .92. Agreement on individual items was expressed by kappa, which was .91. The internal consistency of the full PES was .52. However, when only the last eight subscales were considered, that is, the abbreviated PES, coefficient alpha was .66.

VALIDITY: With the same data used to determine the scale's reliability,

O'Hara et al. (1986) reported information on the scale's validity. Of the eight subscales on the abbreviated PES, only Infant Outcome was not significantly correlated with a measure of "labour and delivery upset." However, many of the correlations, although significant, were rather low. The correlation between total scores on the abbreviated PES and labor and delivery upset rating was .39 ($p < .001$).

The Beck Depression Inventory (BDI) (Beck, 1967) was completed at 3, 6, and 9 weeks postpartum. As predicted, scores on both the full and the abbreviated PES were significantly correlated with the total BDI scores at all three times. Furthermore, when BDI scores were separated into somatic scores and cognitive scores, the somatic scores were significantly correlated with both full PES scores and abbreviated PES scores at all three times.

NOTES & COMMENTS: (1) O'Hara et al. (1986) suggested eliminating the first three subscales—Demographic, Past Obstetric History, and Medical Risk Factors—from the PES. Their exclusion increases the internal consistency of the scale. Unlike the other subscales, the three excluded subscales measure conditions occurring prior to the current pregnancy, and they add length to the scale while doing little to improve its validity.

(2) O'Hara (1986) used the PES as one of several measures of stress to examine the relationship of stress, social support, and postpartum depression. O'Hara, Neunaber, and Zekoski (1984) used the Obstetric Risk Factor subscale along with several other measures in a study of postpartum depression.

AVAILABLE FROM: O'Hara, Varner, and Johnson, 1986

USED IN:

O'Hara, M. W. (1986). Social support, life events, and depression during pregnancy and the puerperium. *Archives of General Psychiatry, 43*, 569–573.

O'Hara, M. W., Neunaber, D. J., & Zekoski, E. M. (1984). Prospective study of postpartum depression: Prevalence, course, and predictive factors. *Journal of Abnormal Psychology, 93*, 158–171.

O'Hara, M. W., Varner, M. W., & Johnson, S. R. (1986). Assessing stressful life events associated with childbearing: The Peripartum Events Scale. *Journal of Reproductive and Infant Psychology, 4*, 85–98.

BIBLIOGRAPHY:

Beck, A. T. (1967). *Depression.* Philadelphia: University of Pennsylvania Press.

PITT QUESTIONNAIRE

AUTHOR: Brice Pitt

DATE: 1968

VARIABLE: Anxiety and depression during pregnancy and the puerperium

TYPE OF INSTRUMENT: Multiple choice: yes/no/don't know

DESCRIPTION: The Pitt Questionnaire consists of 24 short questions, with 2 questions representing each of 12 areas: depression, anxiety, guilt, irritability, hypochondriasis, depersonalization, retardation, cognition, dependency, appetite, sleep, and libido. The order of the items is such that one question from each of the 12 areas is given, and then the second question from each area is given. The questions are accompanied by three response alternatives: "yes, no, don't know." Instructions direct respondents to answer in terms of how they feel "at the present time, that is today, or over the past few days."

SAMPLE ITEMS: Do you sleep well?

Do you worry a lot about the baby?

PREVIOUS SUBJECTS: Pregnant and postpartum women

APPROPRIATE FOR: Pregnant and postpartum women

ADMINISTRATION: Self-administered or administered by interview; about 10 minutes

SCORING: The response indicating morbidity is assigned 2 points, the healthy response is assigned 0 points, and the "don't know" response is assigned 1 point. Total scores can range from 0 (very healthy) to 48 (many problems). Pitt (1968) reported means and standard deviations for groups of women at the following times: 28 weeks pregnant, 34 weeks pregnant, 7–10 days postpartum, and 6–8 weeks postpartum.

DEVELOPMENT: The only information regarding scale development states that the questions were "based upon clinical experience of depressive illness and the special anxieties of childbearing women" (Pitt, 1968, p. 1333).

RELIABILITY: A sample of 49 pregnant women was administered the Pitt Questionnaire on two occasions separated by 6 weeks: at 28 weeks and 34 weeks into the pregnancy. The test-retest reliability was .76.

VALIDITY: Interviewers rated 40 pregnant and postpartum women on depression. The rated women also completed the Pitt Questionnaire, and correlations were computed between Pitt scores and interviewers' ratings. The correlation between the two measures was significant and substantial (r = .78).

NOTES & COMMENTS: Pitt (1968) used the Pitt Questionnaire in a study designed to determine the incidence of postpartum depression and the factors that differentiated those who became depressed after delivery from those who did not. Morsbach and Gordon (1984) studied the relationship between "maternity blues" and depression 6 to 8 weeks after childbirth. The Pitt Questionnaire was one measure used with their sample of 96 mothers. Affonso and Arizmendi (1986) looked at the relationship between disturbances in postpartum adaptation and depressive symptomatology. They studied women during the 3rd and 8th weeks postpartum.

AVAILABLE FROM: Pitt, 1968

USED IN:

Affonso, D. D., & Arizmendi, T. G. (1986). Disturbances in postpartum adaptation and depressive symptomatology. *Journal of Psychosomatic Obstetrics and Gynaecology, 5*, 15–32.

Morsbach, G., & Gordon, R. M. (1984). The relationship between "maternity blues" and symptom of puerperal (atypical) depression six to eight weeks after childbirth. *Psychologia, 27*, 171–175.

Pitt, B. (1968). "Atypical" depression following childbirth. *British Journal of Psychiatry, 114*, 1325–1335.

PREGNANCY RESEARCH QUESTIONNAIRE

AUTHORS: Earl S. Schaefer and Helen Manheimer

DATE: 1960

VARIABLE: Psychosomatic and psychological responses to pregnancy

TYPE OF INSTRUMENT: Primarily summated rating scale with some alternate choice and some multiple choice

DESCRIPTION: The Pregnancy Research Questionnaire is a lengthy instrument with two major sections. The first section consists of three parts: Health Problems During Pregnancy (46 items), Health Problems Before this Pregnancy (42 items), and Problems of Menstruation (17 items). The items on these three parts ask about a variety of symptoms, and the woman is to respond by indicating the frequency with which she is bothered by each symptom. Response options include "often, sometimes, rarely, never." There is considerable overlap in the items pertaining to health problems during pregnancy and health problems before pregnancy, and there is some overlap between the symptoms listed on these first two parts and the symptoms listed in the menstrual problem portion. The second section concerns psychological reactions to pregnancy and consists of seven subscales: Fears for Self (10 items), Desire for Pregnancy (8 items), Dependency (10 items), Fears for Baby (10 items), Irritability and Tension (10 items), Maternal Feeling (10 items), and Depression and Withdrawal (10 items). Each item is accompanied by fixed response alternatives. Generally there are four options, but many questions include more than four choices. Sometimes the options range from "strongly agree" to "strongly disagree" or from "often" to "never." Other times the responses are specific to the question.

SAMPLE ITEMS: (Health Problems During Pregnancy) Do you crave certain foods?

(Health Problems Before This Pregnancy) Were you troubled by headaches?

(Menstrual Problems) Were you ever troubled by diarrhea?

(Fears for Self) Most women go through labor without much difficulty . . . strongly agree . . . mildly agree . . . mildly disagree . . . strongly disagree

(Desire for Pregnancy) Before pregnancy, I had been looking forward to having a baby. (same options as above)

(Dependency) I would like to have my mother or some older woman help me take care of my baby. (same options as above)

(Fears for Baby) Some people may think it's silly to have superstitions during pregnancy, but I find that I have them . . . often . . . occasionally . . . rarely . . . never

(Irritability and Tension) I'm easily upset since pregnancy . . . frequently . . . occasionally . . . rarely . . . never

(Maternal Feeling) I would like to have . . . 1 child . . . 2 children . . . 3 children . . . 4 children . . . 5 children . . . 6 children . . . more than six children

(Depression and Withdrawal) I've lost interest in things during pregnancy . . . very much . . . somewhat . . . a little . . . not at all

PREVIOUS SUBJECTS: Pregnant women

APPROPRIATE FOR: Pregnant women

ADMINISTRATION: Self-administered; about 45–60 minutes

SCORING: Items are individually scored and summed to yield subscale scores on Health Problems During Pregnancy, Health Problems Before This Pregnancy, Menstrual Problems, Fears for Self, Desire for Pregnancy, Dependency, Fears for Baby, Irritability and Tension, Maternal Feeling, and Depression and Withdrawal. A key is available showing the items contributing to each subscale and the direction of scoring for each item.

DEVELOPMENT: A search of the relevant literature provided the information for writing items and identifying subscales. According to Schaefer and Manheimer (1960), "as much as possible, items were written that would appear to be reasonable to pregnant women and that would be subtle rather than obvious indicators of maladjustment" (p. 1).

RELIABILITY: Based on responses from 50 pregnant women, Schaefer and Manheimer (1960) computed internal consistency reliabilities for the subscales. Because these data were based on an administration of an earlier version of the scale, there were no data for Maternal Feeling, and the scales measuring symptoms before and during pregnancy were based on fewer items than are currently included. Internal consistency reliabilities were: Dependency = .94, Irritability and Tension = .91, Depression and Withdrawal = .86, Fears for Baby = .83, Desire for Pregnancy = .76, Fears for Self = .67, Health Problems Before This Pregnancy = .87, Health Problems During Pregnancy = .88, and Menstrual Problems = .88.

Freese and Thoman (1978) reported scale homogeneity and test-retest reliabilities for the seven subscales completed by a sample of 20 primiparae and a sample of 20 multiparae. The internal consistencies ranged from .39 to .89, with 9 of the 14 values being greater than .70. The test-retest reliabilities ranged from .79 to .98.

VALIDITY: When primigravida were compared with multigravida, the former group scored significantly higher on Dependency, Fears for Baby, and Fears for Self.

NOTES & COMMENTS: (1) Schaefer and Manheimer (1960) reported the intercorrelations among all the subscales.

(2) It is not unusual for researchers to use only a portion of the Pregnancy Research Questionnaire. It is also not unusual for researchers to use the Pregnancy Research Questionnaire during the pregnancy period and then to use the Postnatal Research Inventory (Schaefer & Manheimer, 1960) (see separate entry) during the postpartum period.

AVAILABLE FROM: ETS Tests in Microfiche, Educational Testing Service, Princeton, NJ 08540; order no. 012392

USED IN:

Barclay, R. L., & Barclay, M. L. (1976). Aspects of the normal psychology of pregnancy: The midtrimester. *American Journal of Obstetrics and Gynecology, 125*, 207–211.

Beck, N. C., Siegel, L. J., Davidson, N. P., Kormeier, S., Breitenstein, A., & Hall, D. G. (1980). The prediction of pregnancy outcome: Maternal preparation, anxiety and attitudinal sets. *Journal of Psychosomatic Research, 24*, 343–351.

Brody, H., Meikle, S., & Gerritse, R. (1971). Therapeutic abortion: A prospective study. I. *American Journal of Obstetrics and Gynecology, 109*, 347–353.

Egeland, B., Breitenbucher, M., & Rosenberg, D. (1980). Prospective study of the significance of life stress in the etiology of child abuse. *Journal of Consulting and Clinical Psychology, 48*, 195–205.

Egeland, B., & Farber, E. A. (1984). Infant-mother attachment: Factors related to its development and changes over time. *Child Development, 55*, 753–771.

Erickson, M. T. (1976). The influence of health factors on psychological variables predicting complications of pregnancy, labor and delivery. *Journal of Psychosomatic Research, 20*, 21–24.

Erickson, M. T. (1976). The relationship between psychological variables and specific complications of pregnancy, labor, and delivery. *Journal of Psychosomatic Research, 20*, 207–210.

Freese, M. P., & Thoman, E. B. (1978). The assessment of maternal characteristics for the study of mother-infant interactions. *Infant Behavior and Development, 1*, 95–105.

Klusman, L. E. (1975). Reduction of pain in childbirth by the alleviation of anxiety during pregnancy. *Journal of Consulting and Clinical Psychology, 43*, 162–165.

Lightfoot, E. C., Keeling, B., & Wilton, K. M. (1982). Characteristics distinguishing high-anxious and medium-/low-anxious women during pregnancy. *Journal of Psychosomatic Research, 26*, 345–350.

McCraw, R. K. (1984). Return of postnatal questionnaires. *Birth Psychology Bulletin, 5*, 23–32.

Meikle, S., Brody, H., Gerritse, R., & Maslany, G. (1973). Therapeutic abortion:

A perspective study. Part II. *American Journal of Obstetrics and Gynecology, 115*, 339–346.

Perez, R. (1983). Effects of stress, social support and coping style on adjustment to pregnancy among Hispanic women. *Hispanic Journal of Behavioral Sciences, 5*, 141–161.

Rapaport, J. L. (1965). American abortion applicants in Sweden. *Archives of General Psychiatry, 13*, 24–33.

Schaefer, E. S., & Manheimer, H. (1960, April). *Dimensions of perinatal adjustment*. Paper presented at the meeting of the Eastern Psychological Association, New York.

Vaughn, B. E., Bradley, C. F., Joffe, L. S., Seifer, R., & Barglow, P. (1987). Maternal characteristics measured prenatally are predictive of ratings of temperamental "difficulty" on the Carey Infant Temperament Questionnaire. *Developmental Psychology, 23*, 152–161.

Vaughn, B., Deinard, A., & Egeland, B. (1980). Measuring temperament in pediatric practice. *Journal of Pediatrics, 96*, 510–514.

Yang, R. K., Zweig, A. R., Douthitt, T. C., & Federman, E. J. (1976). Successive relationships between maternal attitudes during pregnancy, analgesic medication during labor and delivery, and newborn behavior. *Developmental Psychology, 12*, 6–14.

SUPPORT BEHAVIORS INVENTORY (SBI)

AUTHOR: Marie Annette Brown

DATE: 1986

VARIABLE: Social support during pregnancy

TYPE OF INSTRUMENT: Summated rating scale

DESCRIPTION: There are two forms of the Support Behaviors Inventory (SBI). The 45-item version contains approximately equal numbers of items relating to pregnancy and items not specific to pregnancy; the 11-item version does not directly relate to pregnancy. Items consist of brief descriptions of behaviors that one is likely to experience as helpful, supportive, or indicative of caring. On both forms, items are to be responded to twice. First, respondents indicate their degree of satisfaction with the amount the partner/spouse demonstrates the listed behavior; second, respondents indicate their degree of satisfaction with the amount that others (friends, relatives) demonstrate the listed behavior. Six response options are provided: "dissatisfied, somewhat dissatisfied, partly satisfied/partly dissatisfied, somewhat satisfied, satisfied, very satisfied."

SAMPLE ITEMS: (pregnancy-related) Reassures me that having a baby is a natural event and people "survive."

(not directly related to pregnancy) Goes out of his/her way to do special or thoughtful things for me.

PREVIOUS SUBJECTS: Expectant parents

APPROPRIATE FOR: Expectant or new parents for the 45-item version

ADMINISTRATION: Self-administered; the 45-item version requires about 15 minutes; the 11-item version can be completed in less than 5 minutes

SCORING: Individual items are scored on a 6-point scale, with higher scores associated with greater satisfaction. Separate scores can be obtained for partner support and support from others. Additionally, the two subscores can be added together to yield a single score indicating satisfaction with support.

DEVELOPMENT: In order to develop the SBI, 14 expectant couples were interviewed, and their responses were content analyzed to generate a list of supportive behaviors. House's (1981) typology provided a framework for the analysis. After a list of behaviors was generated, it was refined using two procedures. First, expectant parents rated the level of supportiveness in each item using a 5-point scale. Items with a mean rating of at least 4.5 were retained for the SBI. Second, three judges independently classified the items into House's categories: emotional, material, information, and appraisal support. Items for which there was unanimous agreement among the three judges were retained on the SBI.

RELIABILITY: Brown (1986) reported an alpha coefficient of .97 for items dealing with partner supportiveness. Item-total correlations on this subscale ranged from .44 to .62, and interitem correlations ranged from .10 to .74. For the items dealing with others' supportiveness, coefficient alpha was .98, and the item-total correlations ranged from .44 to .67. Interitem correlations ranged from .25 to .70. Brown also created subscales using House's (1981) four categories of emotional, material, information, and appraisal support. The alpha coefficients for the four subscales were .96, .89, .90, and .83, respectively.

Internal consistency reliability for the short-form SBI was .89.

VALIDITY: The intercorrelations among the four subscales—emotional, material, information, and appraisal—ranged from .86 to .93. These high intercorrelations raise doubts as to whether the scale is measuring four separate dimensions. Factor analysis suggested one interpretable factor that explained 48% of the variance for the spouse/partner responses and one interpretable factor that explained 61% of the variance for the responses regarding support from others.

NOTES & COMMENTS: The correlation between the supportiveness from partner score and the supportiveness from others score was .44.

AVAILABLE FROM: Marie Annette Brown, School of Nursing, Department of Community Health Care Systems, Mail Stop, SM-24, University of Washington, Seattle, WA 98195

USED IN:

Brown, M. A. (1986). Social support during pregnancy: A unidimensional or multidimensional construct? *Nursing Research, 35*, 4–9.

BIBLIOGRAPHY:

House, J. (1981). *Work, stress, and social support.* Menlo Park, CA: Addison-Wesley.

ATTITUDES TOWARD CHILDBIRTH

AUTHORS: Joanne Sullivan Marut and Ramona T. Mercer

DATE: 1979

VARIABLE: Attitudes about the labor and delivery experience

TYPE OF INSTRUMENT: Summated rating scale

DESCRIPTION: The Attitudes Toward Childbirth measure consists of 29 questions that ask the new mother about specific aspects of the labor and delivery experience. Of the 29 questions, 11 ask about labor only, 12 ask about delivery only, and 2 ask about both labor and delivery. Three questions focus on the initial contact with the infant after birth. Each question is followed by a line showing the numbers 1 through 5 and having the endpoints labeled "not at all" and "extremely" and the midpoint labeled "moderately." Respondents circle the number that "best describes the feeling state referred to in each question."

SAMPLE ITEMS: How successful were you in using the breathing or relaxation methods to help with contractions?

Did you worry about your baby's condition during delivery?

PREVIOUS SUBJECTS: Postpartum women

APPROPRIATE FOR: Postpartum women

ADMINISTRATION: Self-administered; about 10 minutes

SCORING: The score is equal to the sum of the circled ratings. Higher scores represent a more positive experience with labor and delivery.

DEVELOPMENT: The Attitudes Toward Childbirth measure is an adaptation of a 15-item measure Samko and Schoenfeld (1975) developed to measure women's attitudes toward their experience of giving birth. The adaptation was based on Marut's (1978) research regarding women who had Cesarean births and on literature relevant to the childbirth experience.

RELIABILITY: Marut and Mercer (1979) reported a coefficient alpha of .83. Cranley, Hedahl, and Pegg (1983) obtained a coefficient alpha of .76. They also computed three subscale scores and calculated reliabilities for the subscales: the labor subscale was .60, the delivery subscale was .69, and the baby subscale was .53. Wollaber (cited in Mercer, Hackley, & Bostrom, 1983) tested 20 women and obtained a coefficient alpha of .80. Mercer et al. (1983) tested 222 women and obtained a coefficient alpha of .87.

VALIDITY: Marut and Mercer (1979) used the Attitudes Toward Childbirth measure to test the hypotheses that women who have a vaginal delivery have a more positive childbirth experience than women who have an emergency Cesarean birth, and that women who have a Cesarean birth with a regional anesthesia have a more positive experience than women who have a Cesarean birth with a general anesthesia. Both hypotheses were supported.

NOTES & COMMENTS: (1) Cranley et al. (1983) created a 10-item subscale for women who had planned Cesarean deliveries. Since these women did not experience labor, they were asked questions about their experiences during the preoperative period. Cranley et al. used this subscale in place of the labor subscale for women with planned Cesareans.

(2) Cranley et al. (1983) used the Attitudes Toward Childbirth measure and their modified version of the measure to test five hypotheses relating to the causes and effects of a positive birth experience. Mercer et al. (1983) conducted a similar study using the Attitudes Toward Childbirth measure and looking at the correlates of a positive birth experience.

(3) V. G. Kottkamp (personal communication, March 25, 1989) developed a revised version of the Attitudes Toward Childbirth measure. A factor analysis using responses from 222 women who had completed the Attitudes Toward Childbirth measure led to the identification of two strong and one weak conceptually meaningful factors: Labor Experiences, Delivery Experiences, and Awareness and Realism of Events. On the basis of the analysis, several items were deleted from the Attitudes Toward Childbirth measure, two items were combined to form a new item, and several items were added to strengthen the third factor. A version of the measure was created to measure expectations; this version is appropriate for women who have not yet had a baby. Thus, there is both a prebirth and a postbirth questionnaire. These revised versions are available from Virginia G. Kottkamp, 25 Rowley Drive, Northport, NY 11768 (telephone: 516-754-5297).

AVAILABLE FROM: Marut, 1981

USED IN:

Cranley, M. S., Hedahl, K. J., & Pegg, S. H. (1983). Women's perceptions of vaginal and Cesarean deliveries. *Nursing Research, 32,* 10–15.

Marut, J. S. (1981). Effectuating change: The maternity staff nurse's role in the care of Cesarean mothers. In C. F. Kehoe (Ed.), *The Cesarean experience: Theoretical and clinical perspectives for nurses* (pp. 269–291). New York: Appleton-Century-Crofts.

Marut, J. S., & Mercer, R. T. (1979). Comparison of primiparas' perceptions of vaginal and Cesarean births. *Nursing Research, 28,* 260–266.

Mercer, R. T. (1985). Relationship of the birth experience to later mothering behaviors. *Journal of Nurse Mid-Wifery, 30,* 204–211.

Mercer, R. T., Hackley, K. C., & Bostrom, A. G. (1983). Relationship of psychosocial and perinatal variables to perception of childbirth. *Nursing Research, 32,* 202–207.

Mercer, R. T., & Stainton, M. C. (1984). Perceptions of the birth experience: A cross-cultural comparison. *Health Care for Women International, 5,* 29–47.

BIBLIOGRAPHY:

Marut, J. S. (1978). The special needs of the Cesarean mother. *American Journal of Maternal Child Nursing, 4*, 202–206.

Samko, M. R., & Schoenfeld, L. S. (1975). Hypnotic susceptibility and the Lamaze childbirth experience. *American Journal of Obstetrics and Gynecology, 121*, 631–636.

CHILDBIRTH PERCEPTIONS QUESTIONNAIRE (CPQ)

AUTHORS: Jill A. Padawer, Corey Fagan, Ronnie Janoff-Bulman, Bonnie R. Strickland, and Max Chorowski

DATE: 1988 (used 1984)

VARIABLE: Experience of pregnancy and childbirth

TYPE OF INSTRUMENT: Summated rating scale

DESCRIPTION: The Childbirth Perceptions Questionnaire (CPQ) consists of 27 items representing three subscales. The first subscale, Satisfaction with Sexuality, contains 5 items relating to the woman's physical appearance and sexuality during her pregnancy, during childbirth, and shortly after the birth. The second subscale, Satisfaction with Delivery, contains 13 items regarding the woman's conduct during labor and delivery. And the third subscale, Satisfaction with Spouse Interaction, contains 9 items dealing with interaction with the spouse during childbirth. Each item is accompanied by six response alternatives ranging from "agree completely" to "disagree completely."

SAMPLE ITEMS: (Satisfaction with Sexuality) I felt embarrassed about my physical appearance during pregnancy.

(Satisfaction with Delivery) I lost control of myself emotionally during labor.

(Satisfaction with Spouse Interaction) I felt my husband was aware of my needs during the childbirth experience.

PREVIOUS SUBJECTS: Women, 24 to 48 hours after delivery

APPROPRIATE FOR: Postpartum women

ADMINISTRATION: Self-administered; about 10–15 minutes

SCORING: Items are individually scored on a 6-point scale with higher scores assigned to responses reflecting less satisfaction. Scores are totaled for each of the three subscales: Satisfaction with Sexuality ranges from 5 to 30, Satisfaction with Delivery ranges from 13 to 78, and Satisfaction with Spouse Interaction ranges from 9 to 54.

DEVELOPMENT: Little information was provided regarding the development of the scale. Items were developed based on questions used in related studies and discussions with women attending Cesarean support groups.

RELIABILITY: Based on testing 44 women, coefficient alpha was .58 for Satisfaction with Sexuality, .82 for Satisfaction with Delivery, and .75 for Satisfaction with Spouse Interaction.

VALIDITY: Responses from women who had vaginal deliveries were

compared with responses from women who had Cesarean deliveries. There were no significant differences on Satisfaction with Sexuality or Satisfaction with Spouse Interaction, but there was a significant difference on Satisfaction with Delivery. As would be expected, women who had vaginal deliveries were more satisfied than women who had Cesarean deliveries.
AVAILABLE FROM: Padawer, Fagan, Janoff-Bulman, Strickland, and Chorowski, 1988
USED IN:
Padawer, J. A., Fagan, C., Janoff-Bulman, R., Strickland, B. R., & Chorowski, M. (1988). Women's psychological adjustment following emergency Cesarean versus vaginal delivery. *Psychology of Women Quarterly, 12,* 25–34.

FEAR OF CHILDBIRTH QUESTIONNAIRE
AUTHORS: B. Areskog, B. Kjessler, and N. Uddenberg
DATE: 1982
VARIABLE: Fear of childbirth
TYPE OF INSTRUMENT: Alternate choice: yes/no
DESCRIPTION: The Fear of Childbirth Questionnaire contains 19 items, most pertaining to fear of the childbirth process and fears regarding the health and safety of the child. Each item is accompanied by two response options: "yes" and "no." Eighteen of the items express a fear, so a "yes" response is an affirmation of fear; only one item is reversed.
SAMPLE ITEMS: I often have difficulty relaxing because I am thinking of the delivery.
I would prefer a Cesarean section to an ordinary delivery.
PREVIOUS SUBJECTS: Women in Sweden who were in their third trimester of pregnancy
APPROPRIATE FOR: Pregnant women
ADMINISTRATION: Although the scale can be self-administered and completed in a matter of 5 minutes, it is suggested that an interview approach be used because "the subject of fear of delivery can induce strong emotional tension during pregnancy" (Areskog, Uddenberg, & Kjessler, 1983, p. 103).
SCORING: The score is the number of "yes" responses from the 18 items phrased to express a fear; scoring is reversed on 1 item. Areskog et al. (1983) considered women scoring over 5 to be suffering from fear of childbirth.
DEVELOPMENT: No information was provided.
RELIABILITY: No information was provided.
VALIDITY: A sample of 139 women completed the Fear of Childbirth Questionnaire and also responded to a 15-minute unstructured interview in which the interviewer sought to determine whether the woman feared childbirth. The researchers found that "most women who had verbally

admitted any degree of fear of childbirth had also affirmed many items in the questionnaire" (Areskog, Kjessler, & Uddenberg, 1982, p. 103). Of the 19 items on the questionnaire, 15 discriminated between those who admitted fear and those who did not; that is, the items "attracted more affirmative answers from 'admittors' of fear than would be expected by chance alone" (Areskog et al., 1982, p. 101).

NOTES & COMMENTS: (1) Areskog et al. (1982) found that most women responded "no" to most or all items, and thus scores were quite low. The most common score was zero; the next most common score was 3.

(2) Areskog et al. (1983) administered the Fear of Childbirth Questionnaire to 793 women in their third trimester of pregnancy. They also administered extensive interviews to acquire the following information: demographic data, somatic history, gynecological history, information regarding present and past pregnancies, present life situation, attitudes and experiences regarding sexuality, childhood and parental relations, psychological well-being, attitudes toward pain and medical treatment, and expectations regarding delivery. Using the data obtained, the researchers were able to identify four groups of women: nulliparous women with a fear of childbirth, nulliparous women without a fear of childbirth, parous women with a fear of childbirth, and parous women without a fear of childbirth. Fear of childbirth was defined as a score greater than 5 on the Fear of Childbirth Questionnaire. The groups of women were then compared on a variety of issues included in the interviews.

AVAILABLE FROM: Areskog, Kjessler, and Uddenberg, 1982

USED IN:

Areskog, B., Kjessler, B., & Uddenberg, N. (1982). Identification of women with significant fear of childbirth during late pregnancy. *Gynecologic and Obstetric Investigation, 13,* 98–107.

Areskog, B., Uddenberg, N., & Kjessler, B. (1983). Background factors in pregnant women with and without fear of childbirth. *Journal of Psychosomatic Obstetrics and Gynaecology, 2,* 102–108.

GLOBAL BEHAVIORAL INDEX OF LABOR PAIN

AUTHORS: A. M. Bonnel and F. Boureau

DATE: 1985

VARIABLE: Labor pain

TYPE OF INSTRUMENT: Behavioral observation

DESCRIPTION: The "Present Behavioral Intensity" of pain is recorded continuously from the onset of labor, defined as 3 cm dilation, to full dilation, 10 cm. A 5-point system (0, 1, 2, 3, 4) is used to record an overall assessment of behavior reflecting respiratory changes, motor behavior, and agitation. A score of 0 indicates that no behavioral indicators of pain are apparent. For the remaining four categories, each behavioral

level reflects the changes observed at lower levels plus supplementary indicators of pain. For example, an intensity of 1 reflects respiratory changes; an intensity of 2 reflects respiratory changes and motor responses. The observer must record the behavioral level and its duration.
SAMPLE BEHAVIORAL CATEGORY: Intensity 1: The frequency or amplitude of respiratory rates is modified during contractions. All manifestations are considered as manifestations of pain, whether they be intentional (i.e., in relation to the psychological training), or purely reactive.
PREVIOUS SUBJECTS: Women in labor using natural childbirth methods in France
APPROPRIATE FOR: Women in labor
ADMINISTRATION: Observations must be made by a trained observer who records the behavioral level and its duration. The observer must be available for the entire period of labor.
SCORING: A "Global Behavioral Index of Labor Pain" is computed from records of the "Present Behavioral Intensity" and the duration of each level. Specifically, each behavioral level (0, 1, 2, 3, 4) is multiplied by its duration, and the values are summed to yield a single, overall score.
DEVELOPMENT: Very little information was provided. The authors stated that "in a preliminary study, 3 different manifestations were retained as reliable stereotyped criteria. These manifestations were respiratory modifications, motor responses such as grasping, and agitation" (Bonnel & Boureau, 1985, p. 83).
RELIABILITY: No direct assessment was made of reliability. Bonnel and Boureau (1985) defended the lack of data regarding interrater reliability by stating that "the behavioral levels have been defined in a sufficiently simple way so as to avoid ambiguity in the notation" (p. 85). The authors did, however, demonstrate that there were no significant differences in the mean scores on observations made by a midwife who observed 50 women and an obstetrician who observed a different sample of 50 women.
VALIDITY: Observations of 100 laboring women showed that there were no reversals in score assignments; that is, no woman went from a higher intensity of pain to a lower intensity of pain. Furthermore, as labor progressed, higher intensities of pain were observed more often, and lower intensities diminished. It is possible that both of these patterns were a function of observer bias since this is the expected pattern of observations.

Global Behavioral Index of Labor Pain scores were compared with patients' self-report scores obtained during labor. The correlation was .68, significant at the .001 level. When the length of labor was partialed out, the correlation was still significant, $r = .53$. Since self-reports were obtained at four times during labor (3, 5, 7, and 10 cm dilated), it was possible to examine the correlations for each of those four times. The results were correlations of .46, .50, .36, and .30, respectively, all significant at the .001 level.

Self-report indications of pain were consistently higher than Global Behavioral Index of Labor Pain scores.

Behavioral observations recorded during labor were not significantly correlated with patients' final assessment of their pain. However, when Bonnel and Boureau (1985) calculated a weighted Global Behavioral Index of Labor Pain, the correlation was significant. The weights used were 0, 4, 9, and 16 so that later observations were given the greater weight. This weighted score was significantly correlated with patients' final pain assessment offered immediately, with patients' overall pain assessment recorded at a later time, and with the observers' overall assessment and the patients' subjective feelings, both immediate and deferred.

A measure of anxiety was obtained from the patient at the time of her admission. Scores on this measure were significantly correlated with the behavioral measure of labor pain.

There was a relationship between behavioral observations made at the different points in labor and the use of psychological preparation for childbirth.

NOTES & COMMENTS: (1) Despite Bonnel and Boureau's (1985) contention that reliability can be presumed, evidence of interrater reliability is needed.

(2) Bonnel and Boureau (1985) suggested increasing the number of behavior categories if it can be done without causing problems with interrater reliability.

(3) More research is needed to determine whether the weighted or unweighted scores are the more valid indicators of labor pain.

AVAILABLE FROM: Bonnel and Boureau, 1985

USED IN:

Bonnel, A. M., & Boureau, F. (1985). Labor pain assessment: Validity of a behavioral index. *Pain, 22,* 81–90.

NATURALISTIC OBSERVATION OF THE CHILDBIRTH ENVIRONMENT

AUTHORS: Barbara J. Anderson and Kay Standley

DATE: 1977

VARIABLE: Physical state, social interactions, medical interventions, and verbal communications of a woman in labor

TYPE OF INSTRUMENT: Behavioral observation

DESCRIPTION: The Naturalistic Observation of the Childbirth Environment is a behavioral observation form designed for use by a trained observer who is unobtrusively present in the labor room. The observer does not interact with anyone in the labor room. The observation cycle is 30 seconds of observation followed by 30 seconds for recording those observations. A stopwatch is used to ensure that the proper observe-record periods are followed. One observation form, a single page, can be used to record 10 observations.

The observation system is organized into three areas: the woman's physical state, the stimulus contact she receives, and the verbal interactions involving the laboring woman. Six aspects of the woman's physical state are observed and recorded: (1) contraction (does she have a contraction during the observation period, is she at rest during the period, or does the observation period involve both a resting time and a contraction?), (2) breathing (would her breathing be best described as regular, irregular, deep, shallow, pant, or push?), (3) tension (is she relaxed, tense, or very tense?), (4) vocalization (if she makes any sound during the observation period, is it a laugh, cry, scream, or moan?), (5) body movement (is she moving around or remaining still?), and (6) body position (is she on her back, side, sitting, or squatting?).

Three aspects of the stimulus contact with the laboring woman are recorded: (1) who is in contact with the woman—the father, the nurse, the obstetrician, or another person; (2) what is the behavior directed at the laboring woman—conversation, touch (other than for medical procedures), provision of an item (such as ice chips), medical maintenance (such as blood pressure check), vaginal exam, provision of medication, adjusting medical equipment (such as fetal monitor), or demonstrating breathing techniques; and (3) what is the proximity between the laboring woman and each of the other persons in the room—facing the woman, near the woman, or distant from the woman.

The subject matter of verbal interactions involving the laboring woman is recorded. Nine categories (topics) are provided on the observational form: well-being of the laboring woman, the baby as a person, interpersonal relationship between laboring woman and other person, breathing, topics not related to the delivery, labor, pain, medication, and hospital procedures. The last four categories refer to medically related topics.

The period of observation is usually 1 hour; following this period, the observer rates five social relationships: the physical intimacy of the mother-father relationship, the quality of the mother-father relationship, the effectiveness of the mother-father system in comforting the mother, the quality of the nursing care, and the quality of the physician's care. All ratings are made on a 3-point scale, where 1 is a very negative evaluation, 2 is neither very positive nor very negative, and 3 is a positive evaluation.

PREVIOUS SUBJECTS: Women in labor
APPROPRIATE FOR: Women in labor

ADMINISTRATION: The observation schedule must be completed by trained observers. It is recommended that observations be made continuously for 1 hour.
SCORING: There is no scoring of this measure. Standley and Nicholson (1980) pointed out that the data can be used in a variety of ways. For example, they suggested deriving a behavioral index of pain by combining information from several categories: "irregular breathing; tense or very tense flexion; crying, screaming or moaning; and agitated, rapid body movement" (p. 18).
DEVELOPMENT: The only information on development is provided by Nicholson and Standley (1978) who stated that "from observations in the hospital labor setting, behaviors which were observed consistently were grouped into categories" (p. 3).
RELIABILITY: Standley and Nicholson (1980) reported that six members of their staff were able to obtain "better than 90% agreement within each coding category and rating scale" (p. 17).
VALIDITY: No information was provided.
NOTES & COMMENTS: (1) Standley and Nicholson (1980) reported using a videotape for training observers: "the training tape includes an introduction to naturalistic observation in general and the childbirth instrument in particular, with demonstrations of each of the behaviors which can be coded" (p. 17). In addition to using the tape for training, it is important that observers be given training in a hospital watching a woman during the laboring process. The length of training time depends on the observer's prior familiarity with labor and with hospital procedures.

(2) Nicholson and Standley (1978) suggested that the instrument be used for both research and training purposes: "as a training instrument, it can be useful to professionals in heightening their awareness of the process and procedures of labor and in orienting them to a view of the childbirth experience from the perspective of the woman in labor" (p. 4).
AVAILABLE FROM: Anderson and Standley, 1977
USED IN:

Anderson, B. J., & Standley, K. (1977). Manual for Naturalistic Observation of the Childbirth Environment. *Catalog of Selected Documents in Psychology, 7*, 6. (Ms. No. 1413)

Nicholson, J., & Standley, K. (1978, October). *A method for naturalistic observation of the childbirth environment: With application to theory building and research.* Paper presented at the meeting of the National Council on Family Relations, Philadelphia. (ERIC Document Reproduction Service No. 167 256)

Standley, K., & Nicholson, J. (1980). Observing the childbirth environment: A research model. *Birth and the Family Journal, 7*, 15–20.

SCHROEDER LABOR LOCUS OF CONTROL (SLLOC)
AUTHOR: Mary Ann Schroeder

DATE: 1985
VARIABLE: Expectation for locus of control during labor
TYPE OF INSTRUMENT: Summated rating scale
DESCRIPTION: There are two 20-item forms of the Schroeder Labor Locus of Control (SLLOC) scale. The items on the two forms differ only in terms of tense. One form is used before labor and delivery; the other is used after labor and delivery. Of the 20 items, 10 reflect an internal orientation, which is "a belief in one's own abilities and skills to determine the direction of one's behavior" (Schroeder, 1985, p. 114). Five items reflect an "external/powerful" orientation, which is the "belief that powerful others such as people, uterine contractions, or rules are in control" (p. 114). The remaining 5 items reflect an "external/chance" orientation, which is the "belief that one's destiny is controlled by fate, chance, or luck" (p. 114). Each item is accompanied by six response options ranging from "strongly agree" to "strongly disagree." There is no neutral point in the scale.
SAMPLE ITEMS: (sample items are phrased as in the prelabor form)
(internal) The more I can relax during labor, the faster my labor will progress.
(external/powerful) The doctors and nurses will be responsible for deciding what happens to me during my labor and delivery.
(external/chance) If I lose control during labor, I'll be lucky to regain it again.
PREVIOUS SUBJECTS: Women pregnant for the first time and women who have just had their first baby
APPROPRIATE FOR: Pregnant and postpartum women
ADMINISTRATION: Self-administered; about 10 minutes
SCORING: Items are individually scored on a 6-point scale, with higher points assigned to the response reflecting an internal orientation. Thus, "strongly agree" in response to an internal item is assigned 6 points, and "strongly disagree" in response to an external item is also assigned 6 points. Items are summed to yield an overall total score and three subscale scores: internal, external/powerful, and external/chance. Schroeder (1985) reported means and standard deviations for the three subscales of the SLLOC. Data are reported separately for the prelabor form and the postlabor form.
DEVELOPMENT: The SLLOC was developed to assess three areas of control: control of pain, defined as "the ability or inability to 'stay on top' of contractions by using breathing and relaxation techniques"; control of emotions, defined as "the ability to maintain composure in relation to feelings and behaviors during labor and delivery"; and control of relations with staff, defined as "the ability or inability to influence the decisions made for oneself during childbirth" (Schroeder, 1985, p. 114). Given these three areas of control and the three orientations—internal,

external/powerful, and external/chance—items were generated for the scale. Most of the items were generated by the researcher, but six items were adapted from a scale by Lederman (Lederman, Lederman, Work, & McCann, 1979). The items were submitted to four maternal-child nurse researchers who were asked to classify the items in terms of area of control (pain, emotion, and relations with staff) and control orientation. As a result of this process, items were modified and rejudged. Eventually there was 94% agreement on the area of control and at least 95% agreement on the control orientation for each item.

RELIABILITY: The prelabor form of the SLLOC was administered to 61 primigravidae on two occasions, separated by 1 week. The test-retest reliability coefficient was .81. The postlabor form of the SLLOC was completed by 50 postpartum women. Internal consistency reliability was .70 for the internal subscale and .71 for the external/chance subscale. The reliability for the external/powerful orientation was not given.

VALIDITY: Content validity for the SLLOC was built into it by the manner in which it was constructed. Feedback from the judges was used to ensure that the three areas of control and the three orientations were appropriately represented on the scale.

Schroeder (1985) obtained a nonsignificant correlation between scores on the SLLOC and the Marlowe-Crowne Social Desirability Scale (Crowne & Marlowe, 1964).

Women who attended childbirth education classes, compared to women who did not attend the classes, were significantly more internal on the prelabor form of the SLLOC. However, when prelabor and postlabor responses were compared, it was found that women who attended the childbirth classes experienced less control than they had expected, and women who did not attend the childbirth classes experienced more control than expected.

NOTES & COMMENTS: (1) Schroeder (1985) reported the intercorrelations among the subscales. All intercorrelations were moderate to high and were statistically significant; they ranged from .44 to .83. Schroeder claimed that these correlations provided evidence of the construct validity of the scale.

(2) Schroeder (1985) recommended that more research be conducted to establish further the psychometric properties of the scale.

AVAILABLE FROM: Order from NAPS c/o Microfiche Publications, P.O. Box 3513, Grand Central Station, New York, NY 10163–3513; NAPS document no. 04708; for microfiche, in the United States remit $4.00 with order.

USED IN:

Schroeder, M. A. (1985). Development and testing of a scale to measure locus of control prior to and following childbirth. *Maternal Child Nursing Journal, 14*, 111–121.

BIBLIOGRAPHY:
Crowne, D. P., & Marlowe, D. (1964). *The approval motive*. New York: Wiley.
Lederman, R., Lederman, E., Work, B., & McCann, D. (1979). Relationship of psychological factors in pregnancy to progress in labor. *Nursing Research*, *28*, 94–97.

UTAH TEST FOR THE CHILDBEARING YEAR: BELIEFS AND PERCEPTIONS ABOUT CHILDBEARING (UTAH TEST)

AUTHOR: Joyce Cameron Foster
DATE: 1981
VARIABLE: Beliefs and perceptions about childbearing
TYPE OF INSTRUMENT: Alternate choice: agree/disagree
DESCRIPTION: The Utah Test for the Childbearing Year: Beliefs and Perceptions About Childbearing (Utah Test) contains 100 items representing five domains: Fear of the Childbirth Process (21 items), Personal Values about Childbearing and Childrearing (15 items), Childbearing Health Locus of Control (20 items), Father's Role and Response in Childbearing (24 items), and Passive Compliance versus Active Participation in Childbirth Care Decision (20 items). The first domain, Fear of the Childbirth Process, relates to the idea that childbirth may be perceived as life threatening or permanently damaging to either mother or baby and that it is an unpleasant, frightening, and painful experience. The second domain, Personal Values about Childbearing and Childrearing, pertains to "desire to be a parent . . . personal meaning and value of childbearing and childrearing . . . enjoyment of babies and children . . . perceived effect of children on a marriage . . . and perceived risks and responsibilities of parenting" (Foster, 1981, p. 38). The third domain, Childbearing Health Locus of Control, contains items relating to three dimensions of locus of control: internality, powerful others (externality), and fate or chance (externality). The fourth domain, Father's Role and Response in Childbearing, pertains to the desirability and importance of father involvement, as well as the father's ability to become involved and the mother's ability to function without his involvement. The last domain, Passive Compliance in Childbirth Decisions, relates to the beliefs about the necessity and desirability of complying versus questioning decisions made by the "experts" during the childbirth procedure. Each item on the Utah Test is accompanied by two response options: "agree" and "disagree."
SAMPLE ITEMS: (Fear of Childbirth) The labor and delivery process is a life threatening event for the baby.

(Personal Values about Childbearing/rearing) Being a mother (father) is one of my most important personal goals.

(Childbearing Health Locus of Control) Even though it is difficult to arrange, I can have the kind of childbearing experience I want.

(Father's Role and Response in Childbearing) A woman needs the sustaining presence of her husband in order to function successfully during labor.

(Passive Compliance in Childbirth Decisions) For the safest outcome when you are in labor, you should do exactly what the hospital personnel tell you to do.

PREVIOUS SUBJECTS: New mothers, first-time expectant fathers, pregnant women

APPROPRIATE FOR: Ages 18 and older

ADMINISTRATION: Self-administered; about 30 minutes

SCORING: Scores are computed for each of the five domains by counting the number of items answered in the "scored direction." The scored directions are "toward fear of childbirth, external locus of control, minimal value of childbearing and childrearing, minimal father's role and response and social compliance with passive involvement" (Foster, 1981, p. 83). Foster reported means and standard deviations for subscale scores for a sample of 254 pregnant women. She also reported, for the same sample, the percentage who answered each item in the keyed direction. Fuchs (1981) reported normative data based on testing 253 first-time, expectant fathers.

DEVELOPMENT: Based on concepts identified during a thorough search of the literature, a pool of items was generated. A panel of eight experts reviewed the items, rated each item in terms of relevance to its particular domain, and suggested ideas for additional items. Based on their inputs, a 197-item version of the scale, with 35 to 42 items per subscale, was prepared. This scale was completed by 30 individuals. An item analysis was performed on their responses, and based on the results, the scale was reduced to 172 items, with 30 to 38 items on each subscale. This version of the scale was administered to 382 individuals. Analyses of these data led to the selection of 100 items for the final version of the scale.

RELIABILITY: The scale was completed by 254 pregnant women, and coefficient alpha was computed for each subscale. The results were: Fear of the Childbirth Process = .76, Childbearing Health Locus of Control = .71, Personal Values about Childbearing and Childrearing = .76, Father's Role and Response in Childbearing = .65, and Passive Compliance versus Active Participation in Childbirth Care Decisions = .63.

Based on testing 253 first-time expectant fathers, Fuchs (1981) reported coefficient alpha for each subscale: Fear of Childbirth = .68, Childbearing Health Locus of Control = .66, Personal Values about Childbearing/rearing = .78, Father's Role = .72, and Passive Compliance = .63.

VALIDITY: Content validity was built into the scale because of the procedures used for generating the item pool and selecting items for the domains.

Fuchs (1981) compared the scores from 253 first-time expectant fathers and 254 first-time expectant mothers. Fathers scored significantly higher than mothers on three of the five subscales: Fear of Childbirth (fathers showed greater fear), Childbearing Health Locus of Control (fathers were more external), and Father's Role and Responses in Childbearing and Childrearing (fathers believed they should play a lesser role).

NOTES & COMMENTS: (1) Foster (1981) reported the results of several different factor analyses of subscale scores. Foster also reported correlations between subscale scores on the Utah Test and numerous other variables including demographic data, health behavior data, and childbearing data.

(2) Alpha coefficients are too low; more work needs to be done to improve the internal consistency of the subscales.

(3) Fuchs (1981) used the Utah Test to determine expectant fathers' beliefs and perceptions regarding childbearing and child rearing. Poore and Foster (1985) used the Utah Test to compare women who used epidural anesthesia during childbirth with women who did not use it.

AVAILABLE FROM: Foster, 1981

USED IN:

Foster, J. C. (1981). Utah Test for the Childbearing Year: Beliefs and Perceptions About Childbearing (Doctoral dissertation, University of Utah, 1981). *Dissertation Abstracts International, 42,* 1811A.

Fuchs, D. A. (1981). *Beliefs and perceptions about childbirth of Utah first-time expectant fathers.* Unpublished master's thesis, University of Utah, Salt Lake City.

Poore, M., & Foster, J. C. (1985). Epidural and no epidural anesthesia: Differences between mothers and their experience of birth. *Birth, 12,* 205–212.

BRAVERMAN ROUX POSTPARTUM EMOTIONAL DISORDER QUESTIONNAIRE

AUTHORS: J. Braverman and J. F. Roux

DATE: 1978

VARIABLE: Prediction of postpartum emotional disorders

TYPE OF INSTRUMENT: Alternate choice: yes/no

DESCRIPTION: The Braverman Roux Postpartum Emotional Disorder Questionnaire consists of six questions that have been shown to be predictive of postpartum emotional disorders. Each question can be answered "yes" or "no."

SAMPLE ITEMS: Did you become very depressed or extremely nervous in the period following the birth of your last child?

Are you single or separated?

PREVIOUS SUBJECTS: Pregnant women

APPROPRIATE FOR: Pregnant women

ADMINISTRATION: Self-administered; less than 5 minutes
SCORING: The score is the number of "yes" responses.
DEVELOPMENT: A pool of 19 items was developed "by clinical intuition as well as derived from current knowledge concerning psychopathology in general, and in particular female psychology, and the theoretic dynamics apparently involved in postpartum reactions" (Braverman & Roux, 1978, p. 731). The 19 items were administered to 120 women attending a prenatal clinic. At the time of postpartum discharge, the ward nurses rated these same women for depression. Statistical analyses were then used to identify the questions that were the best predictors of postpartum depression.
RELIABILITY: No information was provided.
VALIDITY: The scores from the 120 women on whom the scale was developed, correctly identified 15 of the 16 women later classified as suffering from postpartum depression. There was a 15% rate of false positives. Based on some additional data gathering, Braverman and Roux (1978) were able to report that "had we decided to employ the additional data accumulated at the 6-week examinations, the predictive value of our questions . . . would have been slightly strengthened" (p. 735).
NOTES & COMMENTS: (1) Braverman and Roux (1978) felt that their patients were particularly honest and compliant with the requirements of their research. They questioned whether the same degree of cooperation would be attained in large-scale sampling.

(2) Saks et al. (1985) administered the entire set of 19 items from which Braverman and Roux (1978) selected the 6 most predictive items. They found that scores on the 19-item scale obtained during the 26th week of pregnancy and scores obtained during the 36th week of pregnancy were both significantly correlated with Beck Depression Inventory (Beck, 1967) scores obtained during the 26th week of pregnancy, the 36th week of pregnancy, and 6 weeks postpartum. There were no significant correlations with Beck Depression scores obtained 2 days postpartum. Saks et al. (1985) concluded that the 19-item scale is useful in predicting postpartum blues, but they did not look at whether specific items were more useful predictors than were other items.
AVAILABLE FROM: Braverman and Roux, 1978
USED IN:

Braverman, J., & Roux, J. F. (1978). Screening for the patient at risk for postpartum depression. *Obstetrics and Gynecology, 52*, 731–736.

Saks, B. R., Frank, J. B., Lowe, T. L., Berman, W., Naftolin, F., & Cohen, D. J. (1985). Depressed mood during pregnancy and the puerperium: Clinical recognition and implications for clinical practice. *American Journal of Psychiatry, 142*, 728–731.

BIBLIOGRAPHY:

Beck, A. T. (1967). *Depression*. Philadelphia: University of Pennsylvania Press.

MORSBACH MATERNITY BLUES SCALE

AUTHOR: Gisela Morsbach

DATE: 1983

VARIABLE: Experience of postpartum blues

TYPE OF INSTRUMENT: Summated rating scale

DESCRIPTION: The Morsbach Maternity Blues Scale contains 18 items; each is a short sentence giving a symptom—physical, cognitive, or emotional—a woman might experience during the postpartum period. Each item is accompanied by four response options: "yes, almost always; sometimes; never; don't know."

SAMPLE ITEMS: I slept more lightly than usual.

I lost my appetite.

PREVIOUS SUBJECTS: Women in Scotland and Japan during their first week after childbirth

APPROPRIATE FOR: Postpartum women

ADMINISTRATION: Self-administered; about 5 minutes

SCORING: Items are individually scored on a 2-point scale, with 2 points assigned to the "yes, almost always" response, 1 point assigned to "sometimes," and 0 points assigned to "never" or "don't know." Total scores can range from 0 (no symptoms) to 36 (considerable experience of symptoms). Morsbach and Gordon (1984) tested 96 postpartum women in Scotland. Their scores ranged from 0 to 35; their mean score was 13.21, with a standard deviation of 6.64.

DEVELOPMENT: The symptoms on the scale are those "most commonly mentioned in the literature" (Morsbach & Gordon, 1984, p. 172). No other information was provided regarding scale development.

RELIABILITY: No information was provided.

VALIDITY: Morsbach, Sawaragi, Riddell, and Carswell (1983) found that Japanese women scored significantly lower than Scottish women; that is, Japanese women reported less symptomatology. It is difficult to know whether this reflected a genuine lower incidence of symptomatology among Japanese women or whether Japanese women were more reluctant to admit to blues symptoms because they are less acceptable in their society.

Morsbach and Gordon (1984) administered the Morsbach Maternity Blues Scale to women who had given birth within the prior week. Six to 8 weeks later, the 18 women with the highest scores and the 18 women with the lowest scores completed a measure of depression. Morsbach and Gordon found that mothers who obtained high scores on the Morsbach Maternity Blues Scale were very likely to suffer from depression on the later measure. However, there was no predictive value to low scores on the Morsbach Scale.

Morsbach and Gordon (1984) also reported that there was no relationship between scores on the Morsbach Maternity Blues Scale and planned versus unplanned pregnancy, breast- versus bottle-feeding, or parity.

NOTES & COMMENTS: (1) The Morsbach Maternity Blues Scale was translated into Japanese and then backtranslated into English for use in Scotland (Morsbach et al., 1983). Nevertheless, the authors cautioned that "in a study such as this it is difficult to be entirely sure that the same statements are interpreted similarly by the subjects in two different cultures, even when care is taken to achieve accurate translation" (p. 34).

(2) Macy (1983) reanalyzed the data from Morsbach et al. (1983) and found that the seven items on which the Scottish women showed greater symptomatology than the Japanese women were all symptoms of depression. As a result Macy concluded that the authors "used the term 'blues' inappropriately, and . . . they were measuring a low level of depression, not emotional lability" (p. 62).

AVAILABLE FROM: Morsbach and Gordon, 1984

USED IN:

Macy, C. (1983). The occurrence of "maternity blues" in Scottish and Japanese women: A meta-analysis. *Journal of Reproductive and Infant Psychology, 1,* 61–62.

Morsbach, G., & Gordon, R. M. (1984). The relationship between "maternity blues" and symptom of puerperal (atypical) depression six to eight weeks after childbirth. *Psychologia, 27,* 171–175.

Morsbach, G., Sawaragi, I., Riddell, C., & Carswell, A. (1983). The occurrence of "maternity blues" in Scottish and Japanese mothers. *Journal of Reproductive and Infant Psychology, 1,* 29–35.

POSTNATAL RESEARCH INVENTORY

AUTHORS: Earl S. Schaefer and Helen Manheimer

DATE: 1960

VARIABLE: Reactions to the postpartum period

TYPE OF INSTRUMENT: Primarily summated rating scale; some multiple choice

DESCRIPTION: The Postnatal Research Inventory contains 91 items representing 20 subscales with 3 to 5 items on each subscale. The subscales are Happiness, Need for Assistance, Irritability, Positive Perception of Others, Fear or Concern for Baby, Negative Aspects of Childrearing, Acceptance, Intrapunitive, Ignoring, Need for Sharing Experiences, Protectiveness, Extrapunitive, Responsiveness to Infants Needs, Convalescence, Denial, Need for Consultation, Fears for Self, Confidence, Need for Reassurance, and Depression. Most items are followed by four response options. The options frequently range from "strongly agree" to "strongly disagree" or from "often" to "never."

SAMPLE ITEMS: (Because there are so many subscales on the Postnatal

Research Inventory, sample items will be given for only the first three subscales.)

(Happiness) The experience of having a baby has made me a happier person . . . strongly agree . . . mildly agree . . . mildly disagree . . . strongly disagree.

(Need for Assistance) The baby takes so much time I haven't been able to do my work without help. (same response options as above)

(Irritability) Taking care of the baby leaves me on edge and tense . . . often . . . sometimes . . . rarely . . . never.

PREVIOUS SUBJECTS: Postpartum women

APPROPRIATE FOR: Postpartum women

ADMINISTRATION: Self-administered; about 20–30 minutes

SCORING: Items are individually scored and summed to yield scores on all 20 subscales. A key is available to facilitate scoring.

DEVELOPMENT: No information was provided.

RELIABILITY: For 50 primiparae, internal consistency reliabilities for the 20 subscales ranged from .08 to .79. Only 11 subscales had reliabilities above .50, and only 5 had reliabilities above .70. For 50 multiparae, internal consistency reliabilities for the 20 subscales ranged from .23 to .74. Thirteen subscales had reliabilities above .50, and 4 subscales had reliabilities above .70.

Freese and Thoman (1978) reported scale homogeneity and test-retest reliabilities for the 20 subscales completed by a sample of 20 primiparae and 20 multiparae women. Separate values were reported for the two groups. Nine of the subscales had scale homogeneities greater than .50 for both groups. Test-retest reliabilities were considerably higher, and all 20 subscales had reliabilities greater than .50 for both groups. Four subscales had reliabilities greater than .75 for both groups.

VALIDITY: When primiparae were compared with multiparae (Schaefer & Manheimer, 1960), the primiparae scored significantly higher on Fear or Concern for Baby and Need for Reassurance.

NOTES & COMMENTS: (1) Schaefer and Manheimer (1960) reported intercorrelations among the 10 most reliable subscales.

(2) Researchers may use the Pregnancy Research Questionnaire (Schaefer & Manheimer, 1960) (see separate entry) during pregnancy and then use the Postnatal Research Inventory to study the same women during the postpartum period.

(3) Internal consistency reliabilities are unacceptably low for most subscales. Test-retest reliabilities are also too low.

AVAILABLE FROM: ETS Tests in Microfiche, Educational Testing Service, Princeton, NJ 08540; order no. 012392

USED IN:

Freese, M. P., & Thoman, E. B. (1978). The assessment of maternal characteristics for the study of mother-infant interactions. *Infant Behavior and Development, 1*, 95–105.

Ispa, J. (1984). A comparison of Soviet and American women's perceptions of the postpartum period. *Journal of Comparative Family Studies, 15,* 95–108.

Lounsbury, M. L., & Bates, J. E. (1982). The cries of infants of differing levels of perceived temperamental difficultness: Acoustic properties and effects on listeners. *Child Development, 53,* 677–686.

McCraw, R. K. (1984). Return of postnatal questionnaires. *Birth Psychology Bulletin, 5,* 23–32.

Schaefer, E. S., & Manheimer, H. (1960, April). *Dimensions of perinatal adjustment.* Paper presented at the meeting of the Eastern Psychological Association, New York.

Wright, B. M., & Zucker, R. A. (1980). Parental responses to competence and trauma in infants with reproductive casualty. *Journal of Abnormal Child Psychology, 8,* 385–395.

POSTPARTUM SELF-EVALUATION QUESTIONNAIRE (PSQ)

AUTHORS: Regina Placzek Lederman, Carol-Grace Toussie Weingarten, and Edward Lederman

DATE: 1981

VARIABLE: Eight factors related to maternal adaptation

TYPE OF INSTRUMENT: Summated rating scale

DESCRIPTION: The Postpartum Self-Evaluation Questionnaire (PSQ) consists of 81 items representing eight scales: (1) Quality of the Relationship with the Husband (13 items), (2) Mother's Perception of the Father's Participation in Child Care (11 items), (3) Mother's Gratification from Her Labor and Delivery Experience (10 items), (4) Mother's Satisfaction with Her Life Circumstances (10 items), (5) Mother's Confidence in Her Ability to Cope with the Tasks of Motherhood (13 items), (6) Mother's Satisfaction with Motherhood and Infant Care (13 items), (7) Support for the Maternal Role from Parents (6 items), and (8) Support for the Maternal Role from Friends and Other Family Members (5 items). For each item, the new mother indicates on a 4-point scale the extent to which the item expresses her feelings: "very much so, moderately so, somewhat so, not at all."

SAMPLE ITEMS: (Quality of Relationship with Husband) My husband cares about how I feel.

(Perception of Father's Participation in Child Care) My husband feels that caring for the baby is not his responsibility.

(Gratification with Labor and Delivery) I feel good about how I handled myself in labor and delivery.

(Satisfaction with Life Situation and Circumstances) I worry about how we will manage on our present income.

(Confidence in Motherhood Ability) I trust my own judgement in deciding how to care for the baby.

(Satisfaction with Motherhood and Infant Care) I would prefer to go to work or classes and have someone else care for the baby.

(Support from Parents) My parents are interested in the baby.

(Support from Friends and Other Relatives) I have friends or relatives who reassure me as a mother.

PREVIOUS SUBJECTS: Mothers at 3 days and 6 weeks postpartum, mothers and fathers (modified version of scale for fathers) who had babies 4 weeks and 6 weeks previously

APPROPRIATE FOR: Women who have recently given birth; the revised version is appropriate for men who have recently fathered a child

ADMINISTRATION: Self-administered; about 30–40 minutes

SCORING: Items are individually scored and summed to yield scores on each of the eight scales. Many items must be reversed before being added into the total. An overall score, based on totaling all item scores, can range from 82 to 328. Lederman, Weingarten, and Lederman (1981) reported means and standard deviations for women 3 days postpartum and 6 weeks postpartum. Lobo (1982) reported means and standard deviations for women 6 weeks postpartum; she also reported means and standard deviations for the fathers. Cronenwett (1985) reported means and standard deviations for mothers and fathers who had babies 4 to 6 weeks previously.

DEVELOPMENT: No information was provided.

RELIABILITY: Lederman et al. (1981) computed alpha coefficients for women tested 3 days postpartum and again 6 weeks postpartum. The sample size for the first testing was generally around 85; for the second testing, it was around 57. For the eight subscales, the coefficients ranged from .70 to .82 when the women were tested 3 days postpartum; at the later testing, the coefficients ranged from .73 to .90. Lobo (1982) reported alpha coefficients for approximately 70 women who were 6 weeks postpartum. The alpha coefficient for the total scale score was .90. For the eight subscales, the coefficients ranged from .64 to .89. Because the alpha coefficient for Support from Parents was low ($r = .64$), scores from this subscale were combined with those from the last subscale: Support from Friends and Other Relatives. The coefficient of the combined subscales was .79. Lobo also reported reliability data for the fathers whose wives had babies 6 weeks previously. For the overall score, coefficient alpha was .90. For the eight subscales, the coefficients ranged from .55 (Support from Parents) to .85. Again the two support subscales were combined; coefficient alpha for the combined subscale was .76.

VALIDITY: No information was provided.

NOTES & COMMENTS: (1) Lobo (1982) modified the phrasing of the items so that the scale could be completed by new fathers. She found low variability for two items and deleted those from the scoring.

(2) In general, the correlations among subscales tended to be low to moderate (Lederman et al., 1981). Because the correlation between Support from Parents and Support from Friends and Other Relatives tended

to be somewhat higher, it was suggested that scores on these two subscales be combined to produce a single Support score.

(3) There was a substantial correlation between scores on the Relationship with Husband and scores on Husband's Participation in Child Care. At 6 weeks postpartum, the correlation between the two subscales was .74.

(4) Lederman et al. (1981) compared PSQ scores from persons belonging to different groups. For example, they compared scores from primiparas with scores from multiparas; they compared scores from private patients and clinic patients; and they compared scores for those who attended childbirth classes with scores from those who did not. Lobo (1982) used the PSQ to determine how family resources and marital adjustment relate to mothers' and fathers' adjustment to parenthood. Cronenwett (1985) used the PSQ in a study examining the relationship of social network characteristics, perceived social support, and postpartum outcomes.

AVAILABLE FROM: Lobo, 1982

USED IN:

Cronenwett, L. R. (1985). Network structure, social support, and psychological outcomes of pregnancy. *Nursing Research*, *34*, 93–99.

Lederman, R. P., Weingarten, C. T., & Lederman, E. (1981). Postpartum Self-Evaluation Questionnaire: Measures of maternal adaptation. In R. Lederman, B. Raff, & P. Carroll (Eds.), *Perinatal parental behavior: Nursing research and implications for newborn health* (pp. 201–231). New York: Alan Liss.

Lobo, M. L. (1982). Mother's and father's perceptions of family resources and marital adjustment and their adaptation to parenthood (Doctoral dissertation, University of Washington, Seattle). *Dissertation Abstracts International*, *43*, 679B.

POSTPARTUM SOCIAL SUPPORT QUESTIONNAIRE (PSSQ)

AUTHOR: Joyce Hopkins

DATE: 1984

VARIABLE: Degree of social support received by mother during postpartum period

TYPE OF INSTRUMENT: Summated rating scale

DESCRIPTION: The Postpartum Social Support Questionnaire (PSSQ) as used by Hopkins (1984/1985) consists of 80 questions, 66 of which are answered three times. It appears, however, that only 64 items contribute to the scoring of the scale, and only two answers for each question are scored. There is no need to include the other items on the scale. The scored items are questions about the help and support received after childbirth. Named sources of support are the spouse (17 items), parents (11 items), in-laws (10 items), other relatives (11 items), friends (13 items), and other persons (2 items). Items pertain to both emotional support and instrumental support. Each question is answered twice—first in terms of how often the behavior actually occurs and next in terms of how often the respondent would like the behavior to occur. Both responses are recorded on 7-point scales, with the endpoints marked "almost never" and "very often" and the midpoint marked "sometimes."

SAMPLE ITEMS: (spouse instrumental support) How often does he [baby's father] help to feed the baby during the day?

(spouse emotional support) How often does he indicate to you by words or behavior that he knows that it is hard work to take care of a baby?

PREVIOUS SUBJECTS: Postpartum women

APPROPRIATE FOR: Postpartum women

ADMINISTRATION: Self-administered; about 30 minutes

SCORING: Individual items are scored on a 7-point scale. Hopkins (1984/1985) obtained eight subscale scores: spouse's actual emotional support, spouse's desired emotional support, spouse's actual instrumental support, spouse's desired instrumental support, others' actual emotional support, others' desired emotional support, others' actual instrumental support, and others' desired instrumental support.

DEVELOPMENT: According to Hopkins (1984/1985), "items were selected for their theoretical relevance in assessing emotional and instrumental support from family, friends, and a primary attachment figure following the birth of an infant" (p. 72).

RELIABILITY: Hopkins (1984/1985) reported that the PSSQ was pretested with 125 postpartum women, and internal consistency reliabilities ranged from .77 to .89. She reported the following test-retest reliabilities, with a 2-month interval between testings: .77 for spouse's emotional support, .76 for spouse's instrumental support, .75 for others' emotional support, and .70 for others' instrumental support.

O'Hara (1986) administered the PSSQ to 99 postpartum women and calculated difference scores by finding the difference between the ratings of actual behaviors and the ratings of desired behaviors. Internal consistency reliabilities for the difference scores ranged from .65 to .94.

VALIDITY: Hopkins (1984/1985) reported correlations between PSSQ scores and scores on the Interview Schedule for Social Interaction (ISSI) (Henderson, Byrne, & Duncan-Jones, 1981), a measure of the support received from primary group relationships. Significant correlations were reported between spouse's emotional support as measured by the PSSQ and availability of attachment as measured by the ISSI (r = .56), and between others' instrumental support as measured by the PSSQ and availability of social integration as measured by the ISSI (r = .66).

NOTES & COMMENTS: (1) Hopkins (1984/1985) compared depressed and nondepressed postpartum women on a variety of factors, including their scores on the PSSQ.

(2) In a study of husbands' and wives' depression during and after pregnancy, O'Hara (1985) used the spouse support items of the PSSQ to test the following hypothesis: "husbands' depressive symptomatology and marital satisfaction at 6 weeks postpartum would show a significant association with wives' satisfaction with spouse support at 9 weeks postpartum" (p. 50). In another study, O'Hara (1986) used the PSSQ to study the relationships among social support, stress, and depression in postpartum women.

AVAILABLE FROM: Hopkins, 1984/1985

USED IN:

Hopkins, J. (1985). Postpartum depression: The syndrome and its relationship to stress, infant characteristics, and social support (Doctoral dissertation, University of Pittsburgh, 1984). *Dissertation Abstracts International, 46,* 303B.

O'Hara, M. W. (1985). Depression and marital adjustment during pregnancy and after delivery. *American Journal of Family Therapy, 13*(4), 49–55.

O'Hara, M. W. (1986). Social support, life events, and depression during pregnancy and the puerperium. *Archives of General Psychiatry, 43,* 569–573.

BIBLIOGRAPHY:

Henderson, S., Byrne, D. G., & Duncan-Jones, P. (1981). *Neurosis and the social environment.* New York: Academic Press.

6

Somatic Issues

This chapter contains descriptions of 16 measures organized in three sections: menstruation (10 measures), menopause (4 measures), and breast examination (2 measures). Pregnancy and childbirth, which might be considered along with somatic issues, was the focus of Chapter 5.

Eight of the 10 measures in the first section deal with menstrual symptomatology. Moos' (1968) Menstrual Distress Questionnaire is the oldest measure in this section, the one used most often, and the only one described in my original handbook (Beere, 1979). Other researchers have used measures of menstrual symptomatology that are not described in this book but are similar to the measures described (e.g., Awaritefe, Awaritefe, Diejomaoh, & Ebie, 1980; Cox, 1983; Olatawura, Ayorinde, & Ogunlusi, 1977; Pepitone-Arreola-Rockwell, Sommer, Sassenrath, Rozee-Koker, & Stringer-Moore, 1981).

Nine of the 10 measures regarding menstruation are summated rating scales, and 9 of the 10 measures are appropriate only for females who menstruate. The Menstrual Attitude Questionnaire (MAQ) (Brooks-Gunn & Ruble, 1980) measures attitudes about menstruation and is the only scale in this section that can be used with males as well as females. There are two forms of the MAQ: a male form and a female form. Because there were no reliability data regarding some of the measures in this section and because the reliability data that exist were sometimes discouraging, researchers should carefully review these measures before selecting one for use. The same caution applies to validity because some of these measures lack adequate evidence of validity. Since measures of menstrual symptoms are often retrospective, relying on a person's memory of symptoms, validity can pose serious problems. For example, researchers have found that women who report premenstrual symptoms retrospectively tend to exaggerate their symptoms (e.g., Rapkin, Chang, & Reading, 1988). Perhaps they remember better their worst experiences. Researchers have also shown that retrospective ratings yield different information from that obtained from daily ratings (e.g., May, 1976). Researchers interested in studying premenstrual changes might find it useful to read Halbreich and Endicott's (1985) article that reviews the methodological issues to consider in the study of premenstrual change.

Four scales relating to menopause are described in this chapter. Three of the four deal with symptoms of menopause. The oldest menopausal symptom scale described here is the Neugarten-Kraines Menopausal Symptoms Scale (Neugarten & Kraines, 1965), which was described in my original handbook and is the basis for two other measures of menopausal symptoms, both described here. One scale in this section—the Menopause Attitude Scale (Bowles, 1986)—is a semantic differential scale intended to measure attitudes regarding menopause. As was the case with the scales in the first section, researchers need to evaluate carefully the reliability and validity of the scales in this section before adopting one for use. In contrast to retrospective ratings of menstrual symptomatology, Prakash and Murthy (1982) found that postmenopausal women underreported their menopausal symptoms on retrospective reports.

The last section of this chapter contains descriptions of two measures relating to breast self-examination. Both are summated rating scales intended for females over age 16. Neither of them has been used extensively nor is there strong evidence of their reliability and validity. However, researchers may find that these measures provide a good starting point for further scale development on this topic. Roberts, French, and Duffy (1984) described a measure assessing knowledge about breast cancer and breast self-examination. Although the measure did not satisfy the criteria for inclusion here, researchers might want to consider the scale.

In addition to the scales in this chapter, researchers study the effects of menstruation and menopause with general health questionnaires, such as the General Health Questionnaire (Goldberg, 1972; Goldberg & Hillier, 1979).

BIBLIOGRAPHY:

Awaritefe, A., Awaritefe, M., Diejomaoh, F. M., & Ebie, J. C. (1980). Personality and menstruation. *Psychosomatic Medicine, 42*, 237–251.

Beere, C. A. (1979). *Women and women's issues: A handbook of tests and measures.* San Francisco: Jossey-Bass.

Bowles, C. (1986). Measure of attitude toward menopause using the semantic differential model. *Nursing Research, 35*, 81–85.

Brooks-Gunn, J., & Ruble, D. N. (1980). The Menstrual Attitude Questionnaire. *Psychosomatic Medicine, 42*, 503–512.

Cox, D. J. (1983). Menstrual symptoms in college students: A controlled study. *Journal of Behavioral Medicine, 6,* 335–338.

Halbreich, U., & Endicott, J. (1985). Methodological issues in studies of premenstrual changes. *Psychoneuroendocrinology, 10,* 15–32.

Goldberg, D. P. (1972). *The detection of psychiatric illness by questionnaire.* London: Oxford University Press.

Goldberg, D. P., & Hillier, V. F. (1979). A scaled version of the General Health Questionnaire. *Psychological Medicine, 7,* 139–145.

May, P. R. (1976). Mood shifts and the menstrual cycle. *Journal of Psychosomatic Research, 20,* 125–130.

Moos, R. (1968). The development of a menstrual distress questionnaire. *Psychosomatic Medicine, 30,* 853–867.

Neugarten, B. L., & Kraines, R. J. (1965). Menopausal symptoms in women of various ages. *Psychosomatic Medicine, 27,* 266–273.

Olatawura, M. O., Ayorinde, A., & Ogunlusi, S. A. (1977). The premenstrual syndrome in Nigeria. *Nigerian Medical Journal, 7,* 57–65.

Pepitone-Arreola-Rockwell, F., Sommer, B., Sassenrath, E. N., Rozee-Koker, P., & Stringer-Moore, D. (1981). Job stress and health in working women. *Journal of Human Stress, 7,* 19–26.

Prakash, I. J., & Murthy, V. N. (1982). Menopausal symptoms in Indian women. *Personality Study and Group Behaviour, 2,* 54–58.

Rapkin, A. J., Chang, L. C., & Reading, A. E. (1988). Comparison of retrospective and prospective assessment of premenstrual symptoms. *Psychological Reports, 62,* 55–60.

Roberts, M. M., French, K., & Duffy, J. (1984). Breast cancer and breast self-examination: What do Scottish women know? *Social Science and Medicine, 18,* 791–797.

DAILY RATINGS FORM

AUTHORS: Jean Endicott, Sybil Schacht, and Uriel Halbreich

DATE: 1982

VARIABLE: Moods, behaviors, and physical changes that are sometimes associated with the premenstrual period

TYPE OF INSTRUMENT: Summated rating scale

DESCRIPTION: To some extent, the Daily Ratings Form is a method as much as a specific scale; that is, there is some variability in the specific items included in the scale. The version described here, dated September 1987, contains brief descriptions of 21 behaviors, moods, and physical conditions that sometimes relate to stages in the menstrual cycle. There are four items per page, and each item is accompanied by six ratings that are defined at the top of each page: "1 = not at all, 2 = minimal, 3 = mild, 4 = moderate, 5 = severe, and 6 = extreme." Ratings for each day of a 6-week period can be recorded on the same page. There is also a place to indicate whether the respondent is menstruating on the current day, and there is a place for comments to be recorded. Specific instructions appearing on the front of the booklet instruct the

respondent to complete the form each night just before going to sleep. Respondents are encouraged to rate items even if their ratings appear contradictory; for example, they might record that they feel happy and that they feel sad on a particular day. The instructions also encourage respondents to "comment . . . if anything has happened that may have affected your physical or psychological behavior that day."
SAMPLE ITEMS: Stay at home, avoid social activity
Increase enjoyment, creativity
PREVIOUS SUBJECTS: Adult women
APPROPRIATE FOR: Females who menstruate
ADMINISTRATION: Self-administered; requires about 5 minutes daily for 6 weeks
SCORING: Using results from factor analysis, Endicott, Nee, Cohen, and Halbreich (1986) suggested five summary scores: Dysphoric Mood, Physical Discomfort, Low Energy, Consumption, and More Alcohol/Sex/Active. The specific scales to be derived would depend on the specific items included on the scale. Two procedures were suggested for calculating scores: (1) if the focus is on premenstrual change, one can find the mean of the difference scores, which are obtained by comparing the 5 days premenses with the 5 days postmenses; (2) if the focus is on the pattern for one or more summary scores, then one can use the average ratings over a given period of time for the items contributing to the summary scores of interest.
DEVELOPMENT: Based on prior experience, the authors concluded that compliance in completing daily rating scales is related to the length of the rating scale. As a result, they limited the scale to 20 items, although the current version has 21 items. In selecting items, the authors chose those that "describe changes that are often more severe during the premenstrual than during the postmenstrual phase. . . . Two items were included to help determine severity of social impairment associated with reported changes. . . . Others were selected because of a particular interest of ours" (Endicott, Nee et al., 1986, p. 129).
RELIABILITY: No information was provided.
VALIDITY: Several researchers reported that the Daily Ratings Form improved on the validity of classifications made with the Premenstrual Assessment Form (PAF) (Endicott & Halbreich, 1982; McMillan & Pihl, 1987) (see separate entry). Additionally, research has shown that premenstrual change is not a unidimensional trait; that is, there is not a single form or type of premenstrual change (Endicott, Halbreich, & Nee, 1986; Endicott, Nee et al., 1986).
NOTES & COMMENTS: (1) The Daily Ratings Form is recommended to confirm findings obtained with the PAF. That is, whereas the PAF depends on retrospective ratings that are often known to be overstated,

the Daily Ratings Form provides for prospective ratings that can be used to substantiate or refute findings from the PAF.

(2) McMillan and Pihl (1987) were concerned that respondents' ratings on the Daily Ratings Form would be influenced by their seeing their ratings for prior days. They therefore changed the format of the rating form so that respondents would rate each day on a separate sheet of paper, which would then be put out of sight before the next day's ratings were made.

AVAILABLE FROM: Jean Endicott, Department of Research Assessment and Training, Box 123, New York State Psychiatric Institute, New York, NY 10032

USED IN:

Endicott, J., & Halbreich, U. (1982). Retrospective report of premenstrual depressive changes: Factors affecting confirmation by daily ratings. *Psychopharmacology Bulletin, 18,* 109–112.

Endicott, J., Halbreich, U., & Nee, J. (1986). Mood and behavior during the normal menstrual cycle. In L. Dennerstein & I. Fraser (Eds.), *Hormones and behaviour* (pp. 113–119). New York: Elsevier Science Publishers.

Endicott, J., Nee, J., Cohen, J., & Halbreich, U. (1986). Premenstrual changes: Patterns and correlates of daily ratings. *Journal of Affective Disorders, 10,* 127–135.

Halbreich, U., & Endicott, J. (1985). Relationship of dysphoric premenstrual changes to depressive disorders. *Acta Psychiatrica Scandinavica, 71,* 331–333.

McMillan, M., & Pihl, R. O. (1987). Premenstrual depression: A distinct entity. *Journal of Abnormal Psychology, 96,* 149–154.

MENSTRUAL ATTITUDE QUESTIONNAIRE (MAQ)

AUTHORS: Jeanne Brooks-Gunn and Diane Ruble

DATE: 1977

VARIABLE: Attitudes about menstruation

TYPE OF INSTRUMENT: Summated rating scale

DESCRIPTION: There are two forms of the Menstrual Attitude Questionnaire (MAQ), a female form and a male form, each consisting of 33 statements that load on five factors: menstruation as a debilitating event (12 items), menstruation as a bothersome event (6 items), menstruation as a positive event (5 items), anticipation and prediction of the onset of menstruation (5 items), and denial of any effect of menstruation (7 items). Two items each contribute to two factor scores, so there are 35 items contributing to the factor scores, but there are only 33 items on the questionnaire. Each item is accompanied by a 7-point scale, with the endpoints marked (1) "disagree strongly" and (7) "agree strongly." On the female form, some items are phrased in the first person, and others

are phrased in the third person. The 15 items phrased in the first person on the female form are phrased in the third person on the male form.
SAMPLE ITEMS: (menstruation as a debilitating event) A woman's performance in sports is not affected negatively by menstruation.

(menstruation as a bothersome event) Menstruation is something I just have to put up with.

(menstruation as a positive event) Menstruation is a reoccurring affirmation of womanhood.

(anticipation and prediction of the onset of menstruation) I can tell my period is approaching because of breast tenderness, backache, cramps, or other physical signs.

(denial of any effect of menstruation) Others should not be critical of a woman who is easily upset before or during her menstrual period.
PREVIOUS SUBJECTS: Girls in grades 5–12, college students, adult women
APPROPRIATE FOR: Age 13 and older
ADMINISTRATION: Self-administered; about 15 minutes
SCORING: Items are individually scored on a 7-point scale. The scoring on eight items must be reversed, and then five factor scores can be obtained by computing the mean of the item scores. Brooks-Gunn and Ruble (1980) reported means and standard deviations for each factor score for each of four groups who completed the MAQ: 191 college women, 154 college women, 82 college men, and 72 adolescent girls.
DEVELOPMENT: In the first stage of development, 191 undergraduate women completed a questionnaire including 46 statements designed to tap four dimensions of menstrual attitudes: "beliefs about physiological and psychological concomitants of menstruation; styles of dealing with menstruation; menstrual-related effects on performance; and general evaluations of menstruation" (Brooks, Ruble, & Clark, 1977, p. 290). The responses were factor analyzed, and five factors were identified: "menstruation as a psychologically and physically debilitating event, as a natural event, as a bothersome event, as an event whose onset can be predicted and anticipated, and as an event that does not and should not affect one's behavior" (Brooks-Gunn & Ruble, 1980, p. 505). Using the information acquired from the factor analysis, the authors prepared a shortened version of 33 items and administered it to 154 college women. First-person items were rephrased in the third person, and the scale was administered to 82 college men. The responses from this group were factor analyzed. The results were considered sufficiently similar to the results from the first sample that the same factor structure was retained.
RELIABILITY: Alpha coefficients were computed; they ranged from .95 to .97 (Brooks-Gunn & Ruble, 1980). Woods, Dery, and Most (1982)

administered the MAQ to women between the ages of 18 and 35. They obtained alpha coefficients ranging from .80 to .93.

VALIDITY: Brooks-Gunn and Ruble (1980) compared the factor scores of men and women. They found that college men saw menstruation as more debilitating and were less likely to deny the effects of menstruation. These findings were consistent with prior research that showed that men think menstrual distress is more severe than women do.

Brooks-Gunn and Ruble (1980) also administered the Menstrual Distress Questionnaire (MDQ) (Moos, 1977) (see separate entry), which is a measure of menstrual symptomatology. They found that "women who denied any effects of menstruation reported less severe symptomatology [on the MDQ]" (p. 508), a logical finding.

Ruble, Boggiano, and Brooks-Gunn (1982) administered the MAQ to college students. They predicted that those who believed that menstruation was debilitating would judge women who use menstrual-related excuses less harshly than those who believed that menstruation was not debilitating. Their prediction was supported.

As predicted, Brooks-Gunn (1985) found a relationship between menstrual flow/regularity and college women's scores on the MAQ. This finding was supported on four of the five factors; it was not supported by results on the "natural event" factor.

NOTES & COMMENTS: (1) There is an Adolescent Form of the MAQ consisting of 16 items loading on the following factors: I. menstruation as a debilitating event (3 items); II. menstruation as a bothersome event (6 items); III. menstruation as a natural event (1 item); IV. anticipation of the onset of menstruation (2 items); V. denial of any effect of menstruation (2 items); and VI. embarrassment about menstruation (2 items).

(2) Some researchers used slightly different versions of the MAQ or a variation of the Adolescent Menstrual Feeling Scale (Brooks et al., 1977; Clarke & Ruble, 1978; Brooks-Gunn & Ruble, 1982a, 1982b). Although the Adolescent Menstrual Feeling Scale is similar to the MAQ, the Adolescent Form of the MAQ is now the recommended measure.

AVAILABLE FROM: Brooks-Gunn and Ruble, 1980

USED IN:

Brooks, J., Ruble, D., & Clarke, A. (1977). College women's attitudes and expectations concerning menstrual-related changes. *Psychosomatic Medicine, 39*, 288–298.

Brooks-Gunn, J. (1985). The salience and timing of the menstrual flow. *Psychosomatic Medicine, 47*, 363–371.

Brooks-Gunn, J., & Ruble, D. N. (1980). The Menstrual Attitude Questionnaire. *Psychosomatic Medicine, 42*, 503–512.

Brooks-Gunn, J., & Ruble, D. N. (1982a). The development of menstrual-related beliefs and behaviors during early adolescence. *Child Development, 53*, 1567–1577.

Brooks-Gunn, J., & Ruble, D. N. (1982b). Psychological correlates of tampon use in adolescents. *Annals of Internal Medicine, 96,* 962–965.

Brooks-Gunn, J., & Ruble, D. N. (1986). Men's and women's attitudes and beliefs about the menstrual cycle. *Sex Roles, 14,* 287–299.

Clarke, A. E., & Ruble, D. N. (1978). Young adolescents' beliefs concerning menstruation. *Child Development, 49,* 231–234.

Gruber, V. A., & Wildman, B. G. (1987). The impact of dysmenorrhea on daily activities. *Behaviour Research and Therapy, 25,* 123–128.

Ruble, D. N., Boggiano, A. K., & Brooks-Gunn, J. (1982). Men's and women's evaluations of menstrual-related excuses. *Sex Roles, 8,* 625–638.

Siegel, S. J. (1985/1986). The effect of culture on how women experience menstruation: Jewish women and mikvah. *Women and Health, 10*(4), 63–74.

Woods, N. F. (1985). Relationship of socialization and stress to perimenstrual symptoms, disability, and menstrual attitudes. *Nursing Research, 34,* 145–149.

Woods, N. F., Dery, G. K., & Most, A. (1982). Recollections of menarche, current menstrual attitudes, and perimenstrual symptoms. *Psychosomatic Medicine, 44,* 285–293.

BIBLIOGRAPHY:

Moos, R. H. (1977). *Menstrual Distress Questionnaire Manual.* Palo Alto: Stanford University, Department of Psychiatry.

MENSTRUAL DISTRESS QUESTIONNAIRE (MDQ)

AUTHOR: Rudolf H. Moos

DATE: 1968

VARIABLE: Menstrual cycle symptomatology

TYPE OF INSTRUMENT: Summated rating scale

DESCRIPTION: The Menstrual Distress Questionnaire (MDQ) lists 46 symptoms that might be associated with a woman's menstrual cycle. Each symptom is rated on a 6-point scale ranging from "no experience of the symptom" to "an acute or partially disabling experience of the symptom." There are two forms of the MDQ. Form M is for recording ratings at three times: during the menstrual flow, during the week preceding the menstrual flow, and for the remainder of the cycle. Form T is for rating the experience of symptoms on the day the scale is being completed.

ARTICLES LISTED IN BEERE, 1979: 24

NOTES & COMMENTS: Researchers used modifications of the MDQ, which generally involved reducing the number of symptoms that were rated, changing the time in the cycle that ratings were made, or changing the number of points on the rating scale. For an example of a modification that is easier to use, see Clare and Wiggins (1979).

AVAILABLE FROM: Rudolf H. Moos, Stanford University School of Medicine, Stanford University, Stanford, CA 94305

USED IN:

Abplanalp, J. M., Donnelly, A. F., & Rose, R. M. (1979). Psychoendocrinology of the menstrual cycle: I. Enjoyment of daily activities and moods. *Psychosomatic Medicine, 41,* 587–604.

Abplanalp, J. M., Rose, R. M., Donnelly, A. F., & Livingston-Vaughan, L. (1979). Psychoendocrinology of the menstrual cycle: II. The relationship between enjoyment of activities, moods, and reproductive hormones. *Psychosomatic Medicine, 41,* 605–615.

Ammal, R. S. (1980). Personality correlates of college students with menstrual problems. *Indian Journal of Clinical Psychology, 7,* 13–16.

Biro, V., & Stukovsky, R. (1985). Changed self-ratings of young women during the phases of their cycle. *Studia Psychologica, 27,* 239–244.

Brattesani, K., & Silverthorne, C. P. (1978). Social psychological factors of menstrual distress. *Journal of Social Psychology, 106,* 139–140.

Brooks, J., Ruble, D., & Clark, A. (1977). College women's attitudes and expectations concerning menstrual-related changes. *Psychosomatic Medicine, 39,* 288–298.

Brooks-Gunn, J. (1985). The salience and timing of the menstrual flow. *Psychosomatic Medicine, 47,* 363–371.

Brooks-Gunn, J., & Ruble, D. N. (1982). The development of menstrual-related beliefs and behaviors during early adolescence. *Child Development, 53,* 1567–1577.

Brooks-Gunn, J., & Ruble, D. N. (1986). Men's and women's attitudes and beliefs about the menstrual cycle. *Sex Roles, 14,* 287–299.

Carrie, C. M. (1981). Reproductive symptoms: Interrelations and determinates. *Psychology of Women Quarterly, 6,* 174–186.

Chattopadhyay, P. K., & Das, M. (1980). Personality and menstrual distress: A preliminary study. *Indian Journal of Clinical Psychology, 7,* 117–123.

Chernovetz, M. E., Jones, W. H., & Hansson, R. O. (1979). Predictability, attentional focus, sex role orientation, and menstrual-related stress. *Psychosomatic Medicine, 41,* 383–391.

Clare, A. W., & Wiggins, R. D. (1979). The construction of a modified version of the Menstrual Distress Questionnaire for use in general practice populations. In L. Carenza & L. Zichella (Eds.), *Emotion and reproduction* (Vol. 20A, pp. 191–197). London: Academic Press.

Clarke, A. E., & Ruble, D. N. (1978). Young adolescents' beliefs concerning menstruation. *Child Development, 49,* 231–234.

Collins, A., Eneroth, P., & Landgren, B. M. (1985). Psychoneuroendocrine stress responses and mood as related to the menstrual cycle. *Psychosomatic Medicine, 47,* 512–527.

Doty, R. L., Snyder, P. J., Huggins, G. R., & Lowry, L. D. (1981). Endocrine, cardiovascular, and psychological correlates of olfactory sensitivity changes during the human menstrual cycle. *Journal of Comparative and Physiological Psychology, 95,* 45–60.

Dumas, M. C., Calliet, L. L., Tumblin, I. G., & King, A. R. (1984). Menstrual cycle influences on alcohol consumption among blacks. *Journal of Black Psychology, 11,* 9–18.

Feine, R., Belmaker, R. H., Rimon, R., & Ebstein, R. P. (1977). Platelet monoamine oxidase in women with premenstrual syndrome. *Neuropsychobiology, 3,* 105–110.

Fradkin, B., & Firestone, P. (1986). Premenstrual tension, expectancy, and mother-child relations. *Journal of Behavioral Medicine, 9,* 245–259.

Golub, S., & Harrington, D. M. (1981). Premenstrual and menstrual mood changes in adolescent women. *Journal of Personality Social Psychology, 41,* 961–965.

Good, P. R., & Smith, B. D. (1980). Menstrual distress and sex-role attributes. *Psychology of Women Quarterly, 4,* 482–491.

Hartley, L. R., Lyons, D., & Dunne, M. P. (1987). Memory and menstrual cycle. *Ergonomics, 30,* 111–120.

Haskett, R. F., Steiner, M., & Carroll, B. J. (1984). A psychoendrocrine study of premenstrual tension syndrome: A model for endogenous depression? *Journal of Affective Disorders, 6,* 191–199.

Haskett, R. F., Steiner, M., Osmun, J. N., & Carroll, B. J. (1980). Severe premenstrual tension: Delineation of the syndrome. *Biological Psychiatry, 15,* 121–139.

Israel, R. G., Sutton, M., & O'Brien, K. F. (1985). Effects of aerobic training on primary dysmenorrhea symptomatology in college females. *Journal of American College Health, 33,* 241–244.

Jensen, B. K. (1982). Menstrual cycle effects on task performance examined in the context of stress research. *Acta Psychologica, 50,* 159–178.

Jordan, J., & Meckler, J. R. (1982). The relationship between life change events, social supports, and dysmenorrhea. *Research in Nursing and Health, 5,* 73–79.

Lahmeyer, H. W., Miller, M., & DeLeon Jones, F. (1982). Anxiety and mood fluctuation during the normal menstrual cycle. *Psychosomatic Medicine, 44,* 183–194.

Leon, G. R., Phelan, P. W., Kelly, J. T., & Patten, S. R. (1986). The symptoms of bulimia and the menstrual cycle. *Psychosomatic Medicine, 48,* 415–422.

Marriott, A., & Faragher, E. B. (1986). An assessment of psychological state associated with the menstrual cycle and users of oral contraception. *Journal of Psychosomatic Research, 30,* 41–47.

Mathew, R. J., Claghorn, J. L., Largen, J. W., & Dobbins, K. (1979). Skin temperature control for premenstrual tension syndrome: A pilot study. *American Journal of Clinical Biofeedback, 2,* 7–10.

Matthews, K. A., & Carra, J. (1982). Suppression of menstrual distress symptoms: A study of Type A behavior. *Personality and Social Psychology Bulletin, 8,* 146–151.

Moos, R. H., & Leiderman, D. B. (1978). Toward a menstrual cycle symptom typology. *Journal of Psychosomatic Research, 22,* 31–40.

O'Rourke, M. W. (1983). Subjective appraisal of psychological well-being and self-reports of menstrual and nonmenstrual symptomatology in employed women. *Nursing Research, 32,* 288–292.

Osmun, J. N., Steiner, M., & Haskett, R. F. (1983). Psychosocial aspects of severe premenstrual tension. *International Journal of Women's Studies, 6,* 65–70.

Parlee, M. B. (1982). Changes in moods and activation levels during the menstrual cycle in experimentally naive subjects. *Psychology of Women Quarterly, 7,* 119–131.

Poirier, M. F., Loo, H., Dennis, T., Le Fur, G., & Scatton, B. (1986). Platelet monoamine oxidase activity and plasma 3,4-dihydroxyphenylethylene glycol levels during the menstrual cycle. *Neuropsychobiology, 14,* 165–169.

Prakash, I. J., & Rao, S. (1982). Prevalence of premenstrual symptoms in a college population. *Indian Journal of Clinical Psychology, 9,* 95–98.

Quillen, M. A., & Denney, D. R. (1982). Self-control of dysmenorrheic symptoms through pain management training. *Journal of Behavior Therapy and Experimental Psychiatry, 13,* 123–130.

Rao, S., Prakash, I. J., & Murthy, V. N. (1982). Prevalence of menstrual symptoms in college populations. *Indian Journal of Clinical Psychology, 9,* 89–94.

Rouse, P. (1978). Premenstrual tension: A study using the Moos Menstrual Questionnaire. *Journal of Psychosomatic Research, 22,* 215–222.

Ruble, D. N., & Brooks-Gunn, J. (1982). The experience of menarche. *Child Development, 53,* 1557–1566.

Sampson, G. A. (1979). Premenstrual syndrome: A double-blind controlled trial of progesterone and placebo. *British Journal of Psychiatry, 135,* 209–215.

Sampson, G. A., & Jenner, F. A. (1977). Studies of daily recordings from the Moos Menstrual Distress Questionnaire. *British Journal of Psychiatry, 130,* 265–271.

Sanders, D., Warner, P., Blackstrom, T., & Bancroft, J. (1983). Mood, sexuality, hormones and the menstrual cycle. I. Changes in mood and physical state: Description of subjects and method. *Psychosomatic Medicine, 45,* 487–501.

Scambler, A., & Scambler, G. (1985). Menstrual symptoms, attitudes and consulting behaviour. *Social Science and Medicine, 20,* 1065–1068.

Siegel, S. J. (1985/1986). The effect of culture on how women experience menstruation: Jewish women and mikvah. *Women and Health, 10,* 63–74.

Sirois, B. M., & de Koninck, J. (1982). Menstrual stress and dreams: Adaptation or interference. *Psychiatric Journal of the University of Ottawa, 7,* 77–86.

Slade, P. (1981). Menstrual cycle symptoms in infertile and control subjects: A re-evaluation of the evidence for psychological changes. *Journal of Psychosomatic Research, 25,* 175–181.

Slade, P. (1984). Premenstrual emotional changes in normal women: Fact or fiction? *Journal of Psychosomatic Research, 28,* 1–7.

Slade, P., & Jenner, F. A. (1980). Attitudes to female roles, aspects of menstruation and complaining of menstrual symptoms. *British Journal of Social and Clinical Psychology, 19,* 109–113.

Steiner, M., Haskett, R. F., & Carroll, B. J. (1980). Premenstrual syndrome: The development of research diagnostic criteria and new rating scales. *Acta Psychiatrica Scandinavica, 62,* 177–190.

Steiner, M., Haskett, R. F., Carroll, B. J., Hays, S. E., & Rubin, R. T. (1984). Plasma prolactin and severe premenstrual tension. *Psychoneuroendocrinology, 9,* 29–35.

Steiner, M., Haskett, R. F., Osmun, J. N., & Carroll, B. J. (1980). Treatment of premenstrual tension with lithium carbonate: A pilot study. *Acta Psychiatrica Scandinavica, 61,* 96–102.

Swandby, J. R. (1979, May). *Daily and retrospective mood and physical symptom self-reports and their relationship to the menstrual cycle.* Paper presented at the meeting of the Midwestern Psychological Association, Chicago. (ERIC Document Reproduction Service No. ED 176 190)

Tam, W. Y., Chan, M. Y., & Lee, P. H. (1985). The menstrual cycle and platelet 5-HT uptake. *Psychosomatic Medicine, 47,* 352–362.

Van den Akker, O., & Steptoe, A. (1985). The pattern and prevalence of symptoms during the menstrual cycle. *British Journal of Psychiatry, 147,* 164–169.

Vila, J., & Beech, H. R. (1980). Premenstrual symptomatology: An interaction hypothesis. *British Journal of Social and Clinical Psychology, 19,* 73–80.

Whitehead, W. E., Busch, C. M., Heller, B. R., & Costa, P. T. (1986). Social learning influences on menstrual symptoms and illness behavior. *Health Psychology, 5,* 13–23.

Woods, N. F. (1985). Relationship of socialization and stress to perimenstrual symptoms, disability, and menstrual attitudes. *Nursing Research, 34,* 145–149.

Woods, N. F., Dery, G. K., & Most, A. (1982a). Recollections of menarche, current menstrual attitudes, and perimenstrual symptoms. *Psychosomatic Medicine, 44,* 285–293.

Woods, N. F., Dery, G. K., & Most, A. (1982b). Stressful life events and perimenstrual symptoms. *Journal of Human Stress, 8*(2), 23–31.

Woods, N. F., Most, A., & Dery, G. K. (1982a). Estimating perimenstrual distress: A comparison of two methods. *Research in Nursing and Health, 5,* 81–91.

Woods, N. F., Most, A., & Dery, G. K. (1982b). Toward a construct of perimenstrual distress. *Research in Nursing and Health, 5,* 123–136.

Woods, N. F., Most, A., & Longenecker, G. D. (1985). Major life events, daily stressors, and perimenstrual symptoms. *Nursing Research, 34,* 263–267.

Zola, P., Meyerson, A. T., Reznikoff, M., Thornton, J. C., & Concool, B. M. (1979). Menstrual symptomatology and psychiatric admission. *Journal of Psychosomatic Research, 23,* 241–245.

BIBLIOGRAPHY:

Beere, C. A. (1979). *Women and women's issues: A handbook of tests and measures* (pp. 491–494). San Francisco: Jossey-Bass.

MENSTRUAL HISTORY QUESTIONNAIRE

AUTHORS: William E. Whitehead, Catherine M. Busch, Barbara R. Heller, and Paul T. Costa, Jr.

DATE: 1986 (used 1984)

VARIABLE: Encouragement of menstrual sick role, encouragement of cold sick role, and modeling of menstrual distress

TYPE OF INSTRUMENT: Summated rating scale

DESCRIPTION: The Menstrual History Questionnaire is a 16-item survey of three intermingled sets of items: Encouragement of Menstrual Sick Role contains 8 items, Encouragement of Cold Sick Role contains 4 items, and Modeling of Menstrual Sick Role contains 4 items. Each item is accompanied by four response options: "Never; Rarely, once or twice a year, if symptoms were severe; Sometimes, 3–6 times per year, if symptoms were worse than usual; Often, more than 6 times per year." There are two forms of the Menstrual History Questionnaire. On one form, the woman is asked to answer for herself and to relay information about her mother's modeling of menstrual distress; on the other form, the mother is asked to relay information about her daughter and to tell about her own modeling of menstrual distress.

SAMPLE ITEMS: (Encouragement of Menstrual Sick Role) Did your mother encourage you to stay home from school when you had your period before age 15?

(Encouragement of Cold Sick Role) Did your mother excuse you from school homework when you had a cold?

(Modeling of Menstrual Sick Role) How did your mother behave when she had her period? Did she stay home from work or cut back on household chores?

PREVIOUS SUBJECTS: Nursing students

APPROPRIATE FOR: Females who menstruate

ADMINISTRATION: Self-administered; about 10 minutes

SCORING: No information was provided regarding scoring except to indicate that separate scores are obtained for the three subscales.

DEVELOPMENT: The four questions dealing with parental encouragement of the "cold sick role" were taken from a previous survey (Whitehead, Winget, Fedoravicius, Wooley, & Blackwell, 1982). Modeling after these four questions, the authors developed a new set of eight items to assess parental responses to menstrual symptoms, and four items were written to measure maternal modeling of menstrual distress. Responses from 351 women, ages 18 to 39, were factor analyzed and, four factors were extracted. The first three factors corresponded to the three subscales of the Menstrual History Questionnaire. The fourth factor contained only two items and was not considered further.

RELIABILITY: Coefficient alpha was computed for the three subscales: Encouragement of Menstrual Sick Role = .81, Encouragement of Cold Sick Role = .79, and Modeling of Menstrual Sick Role = .82.

VALIDITY: Agreement between the results of mothers and daughters was computed by finding the correlations between their corresponding subscales. The results were: Encouragement of Menstrual Sick Role = .52, Encouragement of Cold Sick Role = .45, and Modeling of Menstrual Sick Role = .52.

As predicted, Whitehead, Busch, Heller, and Costa (1986) found that the number of menstrual and premenstrual symptoms reported on a symptom inventory and the severity of menstrual and premenstrual symptoms reported on the Menstrual Distress Questionnaire (Moos, 1977) (see separate entry) were significantly related to Encouragement of Menstrual Sick Role scores, Modeling of Menstrual Sick Role scores, and Encouragement of Cold Sick Role scores. The first two subscales were more strongly related to current menstrual symptoms than was the last subscale. Mothers' responses to the Menstrual History Questionnaire also related to the number and severity of symptoms reported by their daughters. Whitehead et al. (1986) found that the scores on the Encouragement of the Menstrual Sick Role were related to seeking medical treatment for menstrual disorders and absences from school or work due to menstrual/premenstrual symptoms.

In an unpublished study, Whitehead (personal communication, September, 1986) found the subscales of the Menstrual History Questionnaire had "low correlations with measures of personality and psychopathology indicative of neuroticism" (p. 3).

NOTES & COMMENTS: (1) Whitehead et al. (1986) examined the relationship between Menstrual History Questionnaire scores and a variety of other measures, including menstrual and premenstrual symptomatology, seeking of medical care, and absence from school and/or work.

(2) Whitehead (personal communication, September, 1986) stated that "although not empirically demonstrated, it can be assumed that the accuracy of mother's reports are inversely correlated with the age of their daughter and with the number of their female children" (p. 3).

AVAILABLE FROM: Health Instrument File, University of Pittsburgh, 211 Victoria Building, Pittsburgh, PA 15261

USED IN:

Whitehead, W. E., Busch, C. M., Heller, B. R., & Costa, P. T., Jr. (1986). Social learning influences on menstrual symptoms and illness behavior. *Health Psychology*, *5*, 13–23.

BIBLIOGRAPHY:

Moos, R. H. (1977). *Menstrual Distress Questionnaire Manual*. Palo Alto: Stanford University Department of Psychiatry.

Whitehead, W. E., Winget, C., Fedoravicius, A. S., Wooley, S., & Blackwell, B. (1982). Learned illness behavior in patients with irritable bowel syndrome and peptic ulcer. *Digestive Diseases and Sciences*, *27*, 202–208.

MENSTRUAL SYMPTOM QUESTIONNAIRE (MSQ)

AUTHORS: Margaret A. Chesney and Donald L. Tasto

DATE: 1975

VARIABLE: Two types of dysmenorrhea: spasmodic and congestive

TYPE OF INSTRUMENT: Summated rating scale

DESCRIPTION: The Menstrual Symptom Questionnaire (MSQ) consists of 25 items. The first 24 items describe symptoms that might be associated with menstruation: 12 of the symptoms are believed to indicate spasmodic dysmenorrhea, which is similar to labor pain, and the other 12 are believed to indicate congestive dysmenorrhea, which is a dull, aching pain. Respondents are told to indicate the degree to which they experience each of the symptoms. Five response options are provided: "never, rarely, sometimes, often, always." The last item, item 25, con-

tains two paragraphs describing menstrual discomfort. Respondents read the two paragraphs and select the one that more accurately describes their experience.
SAMPLE ITEMS: (congestive item) I feel irritable, easily agitated, and am impatient a few days before my period.
(spasmodic item) I have cramps that begin on the first day of my period.
PREVIOUS SUBJECTS: College women, adult women, women in India; samples preselected for experiencing menstrual discomfort and samples of women in general
APPROPRIATE FOR: Females who menstruate
ADMINISTRATION: Self-administered; about 10 minutes
SCORING: The 12 spasmodic items are assigned scores of 1 to 5, with 1 corresponding to "never" and 5 corresponding to "always." The 12 congestive items are scored in the reverse direction so that higher scores are assigned to the "never" end of the continuum. For item 25, 5 points are given if the respondent selects the paragraph describing spasmodic dysmenorrhea, and 1 point is given if the respondent selects the paragraph describing congestive dysmenorrhea. Thus high scores (maximum = 125) indicate spasmodic dysmenorrhea, and low scores (minimum = 25) indicate congestive dysmenorrhea.
DEVELOPMENT: The development of the MSQ was based on the work of Dalton (1969), who suggested that there are two types of primary dysmenorrhea: spasmodic and congestive. "The spasmodic type refers to spasms of pain similar to labor pains which begin the first day of menstruation. The congestive type refers to a variation or a symptom of the premenstrual syndrome with dull, aching pains accompanied by lethargy and depression prior to the onset of menstruation" (Chesney & Tasto, 1975a, p. 237). An item pool containing 51 items that tapped various aspects of spasmodic and congestive dysmenorrhea was administered twice to 56 college women who were selected because they described themselves as experiencing menstrual discomfort. Responses obtained from the second administration were used to perform a factor analysis that led the researchers to identify two factors: a spasmodic factor and a congestive factor. Items that did not correlate with the factors were eliminated, and other items were rewritten to increase their clarity. The resulting items constitute the current MSQ.
RELIABILITY: Using the scale development data obtained from the 56 college women, Chesney and Tasto (1975a) found a test-retest reliability coefficient of .87 based on a 2-week interval between testings. Cox (1977) obtained data from college women, some of whom experienced menstrual distress. With a 45-day interval between testings, he obtained test-retest reliabilities of .80 for the menstrually distressed females and .83 for the nondistressed females.

VALIDITY: Chesney and Tasto (1975a) found a large gap between scores indicating spasmodic dysmenorrhea and those indicating congestive dysmenorrhea; specifically there was a 14-point gap between the 29th and 30th ranked respondents. The authors concluded that "the ranked scores revealed a relatively continuous dimension within the higher scores (spasmodic) and within the lower scores (congestive), but with a large hiatus existing between these polar dimensions. This pattern of scores suggests that two types of dysmenorrhea can be identified by the MSQ" (Chesney & Tasto, 1975a, p. 242). In another study using 69 female volunteers, Chesney and Tasto (1975b) obtained similar results: "Ss clearly differentiated themselves into one of the two types with no one obtaining a score around the mid-point" (p. 247). In contrast, Cox (1977) found that 38% of menstrually distressed respondents and 43% of menstrually nondistressed respondents scored in the midrange on the MSQ; that is, they scored in the range where no one scored in Chesney and Tasto's (1975a, 1975b) studies. Data obtained by Nelson, Sigmon, Amodei, and Jarrett (1984) produced results similar to those obtained by Cox. To be as consistent as possible with the methods of Chesney and Tasto, Nelson et al. looked at data obtained from 80 college women who described themselves as "having only menstrual discomfort" and used Chesney and Tasto's method for scoring responses. They found that 57.5% of their sample scored in the midrange.

Webster, Martin, Uchalik, and Gannon (1979) obtained two scores for each respondent: a score on the spasmodic items and a score on the congestive items. If the two types of dysmenorrhea are, as Dalton (1969) hypothesized, "opposite types of dysmenorrhea" (p. 39), then the correlation between the two scores should be negative. Contrary to prediction, Webster et al. found a correlation of .56. They concluded that persons who reported symptoms reported lots of them. They also pointed out that persons who obtained midrange scores using Chesney and Tasto's scoring system may be high on both spasmodic and congestive dysmenorrhea, may be low on both types, or may be moderate but equivalent on both types of dysmenorrhea. Aberger, Denney, and Hutchings (1983) also found respondents who scored high on both congestive and spasmodic symptoms.

If congestive dysmenorrhea and spasmodic dysmenorrhea are two distinct, even opposite, syndromes, then one would expect that treatments designed to reduce symptoms would be differentially effective for the two groups. There are data both supporting and refuting this assumption. Chesney and Tasto (1975b) used the MSQ to divide subjects into two groups. They found that systematic desensitization was effective in reducing the symptoms for those identified as having spasmodic dysmenorrhea, but it was not effective for those with congestive dysmenorrhea. Similarly, Mathur, Sharma, and Likhari (1983) found that progressive muscle relaxation was more effective in reducing pain for spasmodics than for congestives. Other researchers performed similar studies, but their data led them to conclude that there were no differences in treatment effectiveness as a function of spasmodic/congestive classification (Cox, 1977; Cox & Meyer, 1978; Quillen & Denney, 1982).

Item 25, which contains one paragraph descriptive of the spasmodic syndrome and one paragraph descriptive of the congestive syndrome, can be used to classify respondents as spasmodic or congestive. Chesney and Tasto (1975a) found a moderate relationship between total MSQ scores and responses to item 25. For spasmodics, the correlation was .49 for one sample and .59 for a second sample. For congestives, the correlations were − .39 and − .54 for the two samples respectively.

Wildman and White (1986) looked at data from 302 female college students. They compared the classifications based on item 25 responses with the classifications based on a double median split procedure, that is, using two subscale scores, one on the spasmodic items and one on the congestive items, and classifying respondents as a function of how they scored in regard to the median on each subscale. The two procedures yielded different distributions. Similarly, Webster et al. (1979) used a chi square procedure to compare item 25 responses with responses to each of the other 24 items. They concluded that 3 items were misclassified, 10 differentiated in the predicted direction, and 11 were not significant. Both of these studies lead one to question the validity of the MSQ and the distinction between the congestive and the spasmodic syndromes.

Nelson et al. (1984) asked subjects to classify themselves as having only menstrual discomfort, as having only premenstrual discomfort, as having both, or as having neither. The authors then compared the self-classification results with the classifications that resulted from scoring the MSQ according to Chesney and Tasto's procedure. Consistent classification resulted for 27.5% of the women who had only menstrual discomfort, 53.8% of the women who had only premenstrual discomfort, and 62.4% of the women who had discomfort at both times. Nelson et al. also scored the MSQ on two subscales and compared the classifications produced with this method with the classifications resulting from the one item already mentioned. The researchers found that consistent classifications resulted for 7.5% of the women having only menstrual discomfort, 23.1% of the women having premenstrual discomfort, and 4.6% of the women having both. The researchers tried using a more liberal procedure for classifying respondents on the two subscales, and although the percentage of consistent classifications improved, they concluded that "the poor validity of the MSQ does not seem to rest with its reverse-scoring procedure. Even when the subscale scoring procedure is used, validity does not improve" (Nelson et al., 1984, p. 614).

Bloom, Shelton, and Michaels (1978), studying college women, looked at their MSQ scores in relation to their scores on the Minnesota Multiphasic Personality Inventory (MMPI) (Hathaway & McKinley, 1967), the Tennessee Self-Concept Scale (Fitts, 1964), and the Personality Research Form (Jackson, 1967). Although dysmenorrhea sufferers and nonsufferers differed from each other in many ways, the congestives and the spasmodics differed from each other only in terms of impulsivity.

NOTES & COMMENTS: (1) Some researchers have modified the MSQ. Stephenson, Denney, and Aberger (1983) modified the last item so that respondents would rate each paragraph on a 6-point scale rather than just select the one paragraph more descriptive of them. Stephenson et al. also altered the directions for the scale so that respondents would answer in terms of their most recent cycle (see also Gruber & Wildman, 1987; Wildman & White, 1986), and then they altered the response options, changing them to range from "0, no experience of this kind," to "5, very severe." Webster et al. (1979) modified item 25 to include the option that neither paragraph described the respondent.

(2) Some researchers scored the MSQ using a different method from that suggested by Chesney and Tasto. The most common alternate procedure results in separate scores on spasmodic dysmenorrhea and congestive dysmenorrhea (Aberger et al., 1983; Nelson et al., 1984; Webster, 1980; Webster et al., 1979; Wildman & White, 1986). Quillen and Denney (1982) scored the MSQ by finding the difference between the ratings on the spasmodic items and ratings on the congestive items.

(3) There have been many factor analyses performed using responses to the MSQ. Chesney and Tasto (1975a) reported finding two factors, both in their first analysis and again in their second analysis based on responses from different women. Their results, however, have not been confirmed by other researchers, and they have been justifiably criticized for the small size of the samples they used in performing the factor analysis. Wildman and White (1986) identified three factors that they labeled premenstrual symptoms, menstrual pain and use of aspirin, and psychophysiological discomfort. Other researchers found more factors, generally around six or seven (Stephenson et al., 1983; Webster et al., 1979; Webster, 1980).

(4) Overall, considerable criticism has been directed at the spasmodic/congestive dichotomy. These criticisms are warranted and should not be overlooked by researchers who are considering using the MSQ. As Nelson et al. (1984) pointed out: "The problem of validity of the congestive-spasmodic classification of dysmenorrheic women or symptoms may not lie so much with the MSQ as with the distinction itself. Not only is this distinction weak on psychometric grounds, but also this distinction has not shown great utility" (p. 614). To differentiate further the value of the MSQ from the value of the congestive/spasmodic di-

chotomy, Webster (1980) concluded: "The MSQ, as it stands, seems to be a good collection of symptoms and measures of their subjective frequency. Its application could be improved through the use of two subscales, one representing perceived frequency of premenstrual symptoms, the other the perceived frequency of intermenstrual symptoms" (p. 303).

AVAILABLE FROM: Chesney and Tasto, 1975a; Corcoran and Fischer, 1987

USED IN:

Aberger, E. W., Denney, D. R., & Hutchings, D. F. (1983). Pain sensitivity and coping strategies among dysmenorrheic women: Much ado about nothing. *Behaviour Research and Therapy, 21,* 119–127.

Amos, W. E., & Khanna, P. (1985). Life stress in spasmodic and congestive dysmenorrhea. *Psychological Reports, 57,* 245–253.

Bennink, C. D., Hulst, L. L., & Benthem, J. A. (1982). The effects of EMG biofeedback and relaxation training on primary dysmenorrhea. *Journal of Behavioral Medicine, 5,* 329–341.

Bloom, L. J., Shelton, J. L., & Michaels, A. C. (1978). Dysmenorrhea and personality. *Journal of Personality Assessment, 42,* 272–276.

Chesney, M. A., & Tasto, D. L. (1975a). The development of the Menstrual Symptom Questionnaire. *Behaviour Research and Therapy, 13,* 237–244.

Chesney, M. A., & Tasto, D. L. (1975b). The effectiveness of behavior modification with spasmodic and congestive dysmenorrhea. *Behavior Research and Therapy, 13,* 245–253.

Cox, D. J. (1977). Menstrual Symptom Questionnaire: Further psychometric evaluation. *Behaviour Research and Therapy, 15,* 506–508.

Cox, D. J., & Meyer, R. G. (1978). Behavioral treatment parameters with primary dysmenorrhea. *Journal of Behavioral Medicine, 1,* 297–310.

Gruber, V. A., & Wildman, B. G. (1987). The impact of dysmenorrhea on daily activities. *Behaviour Research and Therapy, 25,* 123–128.

Hart, A. D., Mathisen, K. S., & Prater, J. S. (1981). A comparison of skin temperature and EMG training for primary dysmenorrhea. *Biofeedback and Self Regulation, 6,* 367–373.

Mathur, C. N., Sharma, M., & Likhari, P. (1983). A study of progressive muscle relaxation on the treatment of dysmenorrhea. *Indian Journal of Clinical Psychology, 10,* 379–380.

Nelson, R. O., Sigmon, S., Amodei, N., & Jarrett, R. B. (1984). The Menstrual Symptom Questionnaire: The validity of the distinction between spasmodic and congestive dysmenorrhea. *Behaviour Research and Therapy, 22,* 611–614.

Plante, T. G., & Denney, D. R. (1984). Stress responsivity among dysmenorrheic women at different phases of their menstrual cycle: More ado about nothing. *Behaviour Research and Therapy, 22,* 249–258.

Quillen, M. A., & Denney, D. R. (1982). Self-control of dysmenorrheic symptoms through pain management training. *Journal of Behavior Therapy and Experimental Psychiatry, 13,* 123–130.

Rangaswamy, K., Premkumar, R., & Anatharaman, R. N. (1982). A study of menstrual distress. *Journal of Psychological Researches, 26,* 84–87.

Stephenson, L. A., Denney, D. R., & Aberger, E. W. (1983). Factor structure of the Menstrual Symptom Questionnaire: Relationship to oral contraceptives, neuroticism and life stress. *Behaviour Research and Therapy, 21,* 129–135.

Webster, S. K. (1980). Problems for diagnosis of spasmodic and congestive dysmenorrhea. In A. J. Dan, E. Graham, & C. Beecher (Eds.), *The menstrual cycle: Vol. 1. A synthesis of interdisciplinary research* (pp. 292–304). New York: Springer.

Webster, S. K., Martin, H. J., Uchalik, D., & Gannon, L. (1979). The Menstrual Symptom Questionnaire and spasmodic/congestive dysmenorrhea: Measurement of an invalid construct. *Journal of Behavioral Medicine, 2,* 1–19.

White, P. A., & Wildman, B. G. (1986). Factors related to medical help-seeking in women with menstrual discomfort. *Behaviour Research and Therapy, 24,* 471–474.

Wildman, B. G., & White, P. A. (1986). Assessment of dysmenorrhea using the Menstrual Symptom Questionnaire: Factor research and therapy. *Behaviour Research and Therapy,* 24, 547–551.

Woods, D. J., & Launius, A. L. (1979). Type of menstrual discomfort and psychological masculinity in college women. *Psychological Reports, 44,* 257–258.

BIBLIOGRAPHY:

Corcoran, K., & Fischer, J. (1987). *Measures for clinical practice: A sourcebook* (pp. 223–226). New York: Free Press.

Dalton, K. (1969). *The menstrual cycle.* New York: Pantheon Books.

Fitts, W. H. (1964). *Tennessee Self Concept Scale.* Los Angeles: Western Psychological Services.

Hathaway, S. R., & McKinley, J. C. (1967). *The Minnesota Multiphasic Personality Inventory.* Minneapolis: University of Minnesota Press.

Jackson, D. N. (1967). *Personality Research Form.* Goshen, NY: Research Psychologists Press.

MENSTRUAL SYMPTOMATOLOGY QUESTIONNAIRE

AUTHOR: Guy E. Abraham

DATE: 1980

VARIABLE: Presence, severity, and type of premenstrual tension (also called premenstrual syndrome, PMS)

TYPE OF INSTRUMENT: Summated rating scale

DESCRIPTION: Abraham (1980a) defines premenstrual tension (PMT) as "the sometimes disabling appearance or worsening of a group of symptoms experienced by many women before they menstruate" (p. 38). To measure premenstrual tension, the patient/client is asked to complete the Menstrual Symptomatology Questionnaire, a one-page rating scale listing 21 physical and psychological symptoms that may vary as a function of the phase of the menstrual cycle. The questionnaire divides the symptoms into four PMT categories. PMT-A, the most common type of PMT, is characterized by "anxiety, irritability, and nervous tension, occurring as early as the mid cycle, becoming progressively worse during the luteal phase, sometimes followed by mild to moderate depression, and improving with menses" (Abraham, 1980a, p. 11). PMT-H, the next most common type of PMT, is characterized by "weight gain, abdominal bloating and tenderness, breast congestion and imastalgia, and occasionally edema of the face and extremities" (p. 11). PMT-C is characterized by a craving for sweets, but ingestion of sweets is followed by a variety of negative symptoms. PMT-D is characterized by premenstrual depression that can be severe enough to lead to thoughts of suicide or even to suicide attempts. The Menstrual Symptomatology Questionnaire contains 4 symptoms relating to PMT-A, 6 symptoms relating to PMT-C, 5 symptoms relating to PMT-D, 4 symptoms relating to PMT-H, and 2 "other symptoms." Each of the 21 symptoms is to be rated for two different time periods: the week following menstruation and the week preceding menstruation. Symptoms are rated on a 4-point scale: none, mild, moderate, severe. In addition, the patient/client is asked to rate two symptoms—cramps and backache—for the "first two days" of the menstruation. Only the symptoms in the four PMT categories are used to diagnose PMT.

SAMPLE ITEMS: (PMT-A) nervous tension
(PMT-C) headache
(PMT-D) depression
(PMT-H) weight gain

PREVIOUS SUBJECTS: Females who menstruate

APPROPRIATE FOR: Females who menstruate

ADMINISTRATION: The questionnaire is self-administered. Abraham (1980a) did not specify any particular phase of the menstrual cycle when the questionnaire needs to be completed. Completing the questionnaire takes less than 10 minutes.

SCORING: Items are individually scored by assigning 1 point to "mild," 2 points to "moderate," and 3 points to "severe." The severity of PMT is rated as mild, moderate, or severe depending on the combination of scores for the four PMT portions of the questionnaire. For example, if scores on PMT-A and PMT-H total less than 5, PMT-D is less than 6, and PMT-C is less than 7, then PMT is classified as mild. Abraham (1980a) provided other criteria to rate PMT as moderate or severe. According to Abraham, for a patient to be labeled as having PMT, "the symptoms must be mild or absent during the follicular phase (the week following the patient's period) and moderate to severe for at least one subgroup during the luteal phase (the week preceding the period)" (p. 26).

DEVELOPMENT: The Menstrual Symptomatology Questionnaire is based on Abraham's (1980b) system of classifying PMT into four subgroups that "may exist alone or in combination with other

subgroups" (Abraham, 1980a, p. 11). Abraham (1980a) describes each of the four types of PMT and gives data on their incidence.
RELIABILITY: No information was provided.
VALIDITY: Content validity can be presumed because the symptoms listed on the Menstrual Symptomatology Questionnaire accurately represent Abraham's (1980b) theoretical formulation of the four types of PMT.
NOTES & COMMENTS: (1) Because the Menstrual Symptomatology Questionnaire is a retrospective questionnaire relying on a woman's memory of her symptoms, there is a strong possibility that ratings do not accurately reflect the experience. Many factors will influence what a woman remembers about symptomatology surrounding her menstrual cycle. Some of these factors are likely to relate to her expectations, self-perceptions, and knowledge of premenstrual tension.

(2) Peck (1982) used the Menstrual Symptomatology Questionnaire to identify patients suffering from PMS. She then tried to determine whether beta-endorphin levels were related to PMS. Giannini, Price, Loiselle, and Giannini (1985a) related scores on the Menstrual Symptomatology Questionnaire to caloric intake during the 10 days preceding and the 10 days following the menstrual cycle. In their 1985b study, they related Menstrual Symptomatology Questionnaire scores to pseudocholinesterase serum levels on the first day of menses and scores on the State Trait Anxiety Inventory (Spielberger, Gorusch, & Lushene, 1970).
AVAILABLE FROM: Abraham, 1980a; Peck, 1982
USED IN:

Abraham, G. E. (1980a). Premenstrual tension. *Current Problems in Obstetrics and Gynecology, 3,* 1–39.

Giannini, A. J., Price, W. A., Loiselle, R. H., & Giannini, M. C. (1985a). Hyperphagia in premenstrual tension syndrome. *Journal of Clinical Psychiatry, 46,* 436–438.

Giannini, A. J., Price, W. A., Loiselle, R. H., & Giannini, M. C. (1985b). Pseudocholinesterase and trait anxiety in premenstrual tension syndrome. *Journal of Clinical Psychiatry, 46,* 139–140.

Peck, S. D. (1982). Can increased beta-endorphins explain the etiology of premenstrual syndrome? *Journal of the American Osteopathic Association, 82,* 192–197.

BIBLIOGRAPHY:

Abraham, G. E. (1980b). The premenstrual tension syndrome. In L. K. McNall (Ed.), *Contemporary obstetric and gynecologic nursing* (Vol. 3). St. Louis: C. V. Mosby.

Spielberger, C. D., Gorusch, R. L., & Lushene, R. E. (1970). *Manual for the State-Trait Anxiety Inventory.* Palo Alto: Consulting Psychologists Press.

PREMENSTRUAL ASSESSMENT FORM (PAF)

AUTHORS: Uriel Halbreich, Jean Endicott, and Sybil Schacht

DATE: 1981
VARIABLE: Changes in mood, behavior, and physical condition during the premenstrual period
TYPE OF INSTRUMENT: Summated rating scale
DESCRIPTION: The purpose of the Premenstrual Assessment Form (PAF) is to allow for differentiation of different categories of premenstrual change. The scale contains 95 items describing a variety of changes in mood, behavior, and physical condition that may or may not be experienced during the premenstrual period. Some of the items express positive changes, and others express negative changes. Each item is rated on a 6-point scale to show the "severity of change from usual nonpremenstrual state." The rating options range from "1—not applicable or no change" to "6—extreme change." Each of the response options is defined for the respondent. For example, "extreme change" is defined as follows: "the degree of change in severity is so different from your usual state that it is very apparent to you OR even people who do not know you well might notice." The respondent is directed to respond in terms of "usual premenstrual changes" and answer in terms of the last three premenstrual periods. The original PAF is now used mainly for screening persons (U. Halbreich, personal communication, September, 1988). It is usually followed by a Daily Ratings Form (Endicott & Halbreich, 1982) (see separate entry) and the two PAF current forms, one to be filled out when the respondent has her "most severe premenstrual changes or on the first day of the menstrual bleeding" if no premenstrual changes were experienced. In completing this form, the respondent is to think about changes that she is currently experiencing or changes that have occurred during the prior few days. The other form is to be filled out "during the second week of the menstrual cycle (7–10 days after the beginning of menstrual bleeding)" and should be answered in terms of how the woman has been feeling during the past 24 hours. Items on this form are rated in terms of severity rather than severity of change. The items on all three forms are the same, and all three forms include explicit directions.
SAMPLE ITEMS: Have rapid changes in mood (e.g., laughing, crying, angry, happy, etc.) all within the same day
Have decreased energy or tend to fatigue easily
PREVIOUS SUBJECTS: Adult women
APPROPRIATE FOR: Females who menstruate
ADMINISTRATION: Self-administered; about 30 minutes
SCORING: The PAF is unusual in that it provides three scoring systems: (1) Bipolar Continua, 7 subscales; (2) Unipolar Continua, 18 subscales; and (3) Typological Categories, 12 typologies. The Bipolar Continua are (1) psychomotor activity (agitated-retarded), (2) appetite (increased-decreased), (3) sleep (increased-decreased), (4) sexual interest and ac-

tivity (increased-decreased), (5) energy (increased-decreased), (6) goal-oriented activity (increased-decreased), and (7) mood (depressed-increased well-being). The Unipolar Continua are: (1) low mood/loss of pleasure, (2) endogenous depressive features, (3) lability, (4) "atypical" depressive features, (5) hysteroid features, (6) hostility/anger, (7) social withdrawal, (8) anxiety, (9) increased well-being, (10) impulsivity, (11) "organic" mental features, (12) signs of water retention, (13) general physical discomfort, (14) autonomic physical changes, (15) nonspecific physical changes, (16) impaired functioning, (17) miscellaneous mood/ behavioral changes, and (18) miscellaneous physical changes. The Typological Categories are: (1) major depressive syndrome or minor depressive syndrome (with provisions for subtyping), (2) anxiety syndrome, (3) irritable/angry syndrome, (4) "organic" mental syndrome, (5) impulsivity, (6) signs of water retention, (7) general physical discomfort, (8) autonomic physical changes, (9) nonspecific physical changes, (10) impaired functioning, (11) increased well-being, and (12) no significant changes.

DEVELOPMENT: An initial pool of 200 items was developed based on a review of the literature, an examination of other questionnaires, consultation with staff members at the authors' institutions, and the authors' experience. The pool was reduced to 150 items by combining items that appeared to describe the same change. The 150-item pool was administered to 154 women, and their responses were used to reduce the size of the item pool. Item frequencies and item intercorrelations were used to determine which items could be combined. Alpha coefficients reflecting internal consistency and item-total correlations were also considered in selecting items. "The goal was to reduce redundancy while retaining sufficient coverage of dimensions to provide sensitive summary measures" (Halbreich, Endicott, Schacht, & Nee, 1982, p. 50).

RELIABILITY: Halbreich, Endicott, and Nee (1983) reported intraclass reliability coefficients ranging from .60 to .91. Halbreich, Endicott, and Schacht (1982) reported that "the relative stability of descriptions of the 'usual' changes associated with the premenstrual phase was indicated by the high intraclass correlation coefficients of reliability between changes reported to have occurred during the most recent premenstrual period and those typical of the last six premenstrual periods (80% greater than .90, 100% greater than .78)" (p. 164).

Halbreich, Endicott, Schacht, and Nee (1982) reported alpha coefficients for the 18 Unipolar subscales using data collected from 154 women. The coefficients ranged from .61 to .91. The number of items on the subscales ranged from 3 to 14.

Halbreich, Endicott, Schacht, and Nee (1982) compared the responses given by four groups of women that varied according to when in the cycle the measure was completed: during the premenstrual period, during menses, the week after menses, or the remainder of the cycle. Only one item was significantly different across the groups. They found no relationship between the responses on the items and phase of the menstrual cycle when the items were completed.

Endicott and Halbreich (1982) reported the results of a study in which women completed the PAF, then completed a cycle's worth of Daily Ratings Forms indicating moods and behavior, and finally completed a second PAF. They found that women reported symptoms as less severe when they completed the PAF after completing Daily Ratings Forms, but the pattern of symptoms was generally the same. Endicott and Halbreich suggested that women may report the "worst case" when giving retrospective data regarding premenstrual symptoms.

VALIDITY: Halbreich, Endicott, Schacht, and Nee (1982) had two psychiatric social workers rate the narrative description of the woman's premenstrual change. They found that the scores obtained from the PAF items varied in a manner consistent with the global ratings made by the social workers. They also found that age was not generally a factor in the pattern of responses on the PAF.

McMillan and Pihl (1987) used PAF scores to identify 28 women who suffered from premenstrual depression. Of the 28, they found that 6 experienced no depressed affect during the cycle studied with the Daily Ratings Form.

The issue of construct validity can be partially explored by determining whether the PAF is sensitive enough to yield different profiles for different "normal" women. Halbreich, Endicott, and Schacht (1982) found that the women's profiles differed in terms of both severity and pattern of responses. Endicott, Halbreich, Schacht, and Nee (1981) found that different types of premenstrual change, as measured by the PAF, related differentially to subtypes of mental disorders. The research that has been done leads to the conclusion that there are different types of premenstrual change, that premenstrual change can be divided into different categories, and that premenstrual change should not be treated as a unidimensional construct.

NOTES & COMMENTS: (1) The PAF is recommended as a screening tool to identify groups of women who are relatively homogeneous in regard to their type of premenstrual change. These groups can then be used to study the effectiveness of various treatment methods for reducing different types of premenstrual discomfort. However, it is important to remember that the PAF is a retrospective questionnaire whose results must be confirmed by daily ratings of mood and behavior. The Daily Ratings Form was developed in conjunction with the PAF.

(2) The PAF was administered to all women who sought treatment at the Duke University Medical Center Premenstrual Syndrome Clinic. Stout et al. (1986) looked at data from 50 of these women and selected

the items that were most strongly endorsed on seven of the Unipolar subscales. They then rewrote these items and used them as a scale in their research.

(3) Roy-Byrne et al. (1986) used an 18-item scale similar to the PAF; each item was accompanied by five response options: "not applicable, none, mild, moderate, severe." The items they used are included in their article.

AVAILABLE FROM: Jean Endicott, Department of Research Assessment and Training, Box 123, New York State Psychiatric Institute, New York, NY 10032

USED IN:

Endicott, J., & Halbreich, U. (1982). Retrospective report of premenstrual depressive changes: Factors affecting confirmation by daily ratings. *Psychopharmacology Bulletin, 18,* 109–112.

Endicott, J., Halbreich, U., Schacht, S., & Nee, J. (1981). Premenstrual changes and affective disorders. *Psychosomatic Medicine, 43,* 519–529.

Endicott, J., Nee, J., Cohen, J., & Halbreich, U. (1986). Premenstrual changes: Patterns and correlates of daily ratings. *Journal of Affective Disorders, 10,* 127–135.

Goldstein, S., Halbreich, U., Endicott, J., & Hill, E. (1986). Premenstrual hostility, impulsivity and impaired social functioning. *Journal of Psychosomatic Obstetrics and Gynaecology, 5,* 33–38.

Halbreich, U., & Endicott, J. (1982). Classification of premenstrual syndromes. In R. Friedman (Ed.), *Behavior and the menstrual cycle* (pp. 243–265). New York: Marcel Dekker.

Halbreich, U., & Endicott, J. (1985). Relationship of dysphoric premenstrual changes to depressive disorders. *Acta Psychiatrica Scandinavica, 71,* 331–338.

Halbreich, U., Endicott, J., & Nee, J. (1983). Premenstrual depressive changes: Value of differentiation. *Archives of General Psychiatry, 40,* 535–542.

Halbreich, U., Endicott, J., & Schacht, S. (1982). Premenstrual syndromes: A new instrument for their assessment. *Journal of Psychiatric Treatment and Evaluation, 4,* 161–164.

Halbreich, U., Endicott, J., Schacht, S., & Nee, J. (1982). The diversity of premenstrual changes as reflected in the Premenstrual Assessment Form. *Acta Psychiatrica Scandinavica, 65,* 46–65.

McMillan, M. J., & Pihl, R. O. (1987). Premenstrual depression: A distinct entity. *Journal of Abnormal Psychology, 96,* 149–154.

Roy-Byrne, P. P., Rubinow, D. R., Hoban, M. C., Parry, B. L., Rosenthal, N. E., Nurnberger, J. I., & Selma, B. (1986). Premenstrual changes: A comparison of five populations. *Psychiatry Research, 17,* 77–85.

Stout, A. L., Grady, T. A., Steege, J. F., Blazer, D. G., George, L. K., & Melville, M. L. (1986). Premenstrual symptoms in black and white community samples. *American Journal of Psychiatry, 143,* 1436–1439.

Youdale, J. V. M., & Freeman, R. J. (1987). Premenstrual Assessment Form typological categories: Classification of self-defined premenstrually symptomatic and asymptomatic women. *Journal of Consulting and Clinical Psychology, 55,* 418–422.

RATING SCALES FOR PREMENSTRUAL TENSION SYNDROME

AUTHORS: Meir Steiner, Roger F. Haskett, and Bernard J. Carroll

DATE: 1980

VARIABLE: Severity of the premenstrual tension syndrome

TYPE OF INSTRUMENT: Summated rating scale and alternate choice: yes/no

DESCRIPTION: There are actually two Rating Scales for Premenstrual Tension Syndrome. The first scale is a 10-item rating scale to be completed by a therapist/researcher based on information obtained from the subject. The 10 areas to be rated are irritability-hostility, tension, efficiency, dysphoria, motor coordination, mental-cognitive functioning, eating habits, sexual drive and activity, physical symptoms, and social impairment. Eight of the 10 items are rated on 5-point scales where 0 represents no problem and 4 represents a serious problem; 2 items, eating habits, and sexual drive and activities, are rated on 3-point scales ranging from 0 to 2 points. Verbal descriptions accompany each of the ratings.

The second Rating Scale for Premenstrual Tension Syndrome is a self-report scale that contains 36 questions, each answered "yes" or "no." The distribution of the 36 questions relates to the 10-item rating scale that is completed by a therapist/researcher. That is, there are 4 questions on the self-report scale representing each of the 8 items with 5-point rating scales, and there are 2 questions on the self-report scale representing each of the 2 items with 3-point rating scales. According to Steiner, Haskett, and Carroll (1980), the two rating scales are intended to be complementary.

SAMPLE ITEMS: (rating scale completed by researcher/therapist)

Irritability—Hostility (0–4)

(Irritable, hostile, negative attitude, angry, short-fused, yelling and screaming at others)

0. Not irritable
1. Doubtful, trivial. Not reported without direct questioning.
2. Mild. Occasional outbursts of anger and hostile behavior. Spontaneously reported.
3. Moderate. Irritable behavior evident. Frequent outbursts.
4. Severe. Affects most interactions between patient and significant others.

(self-report rating scale)

Do you find yourself avoiding some of your social commitments?

Have you gained 5 or more pounds during the past week?

PREVIOUS SUBJECTS: Women suffering from premenstrual tension

APPROPRIATE FOR: Females who menstruate

ADMINISTRATION: One rating scale must be completed by a trained

observer, generally a therapist or researcher, who has spent time interviewing the subject. The self-report rating scale is self-administered and can be completed in 10–15 minutes.
SCORING: For the 10-item rating scale, the score is the sum of the assigned ratings. For the self-report rating scale, the score is the sum of "yes" responses. For both scales, scores can range from 0 (no symptoms) to 36 (extreme symptomatology).
DEVELOPMENT: A sample of 42 women suffering from severe premenstrual symptoms completed a series of scales intended to measure their symptomatology. The scales included the Menstrual Distress Questionnaire (Moos, 1969) (see separate entry), the Multiple Affect Adjective Check List (Zuckerman & Lubin, 1965), the Visual Analogue Scale (Aitken, 1969; Maxwell, 1978), the State-Trait Anxiety Inventory (Spielberger, Gorsuch, & Lushene, 1970), the Hamilton Depression Scale (Hamilton, 1960), and the Carroll Depression Scale (Feinberg et al., 1979). Steiner et al. (1980) used the responses from these women to develop lists rank ordering the items from the MDQ and the Carroll Depression Scale. Using the rank-ordered lists, the researchers' own clinical observations, and information gleaned from the relevant literature, Steiner et al. developed a set of criteria for PMTS. The two rating scales relate directly to the criteria for diagnosing PMTS.
RELIABILITY: No information was provided.
VALIDITY: A sample of 24 women suffering from moderate to severe premenstrual tension was studied by Haskett and Abplanalp (1983) who tested them with the Rating Scales for Premenstrual Tension Syndrome and applied the diagnostic criteria mentioned earlier. After analyzing all of their data, Haskett and Abplanalp (1983) concluded that "although our results suggest that the use of the . . . [self-rating scale] score criteria alone may be sufficient to identify women for studies of severe PMTS, this finding needs replication and a clinical interview is still needed to exclude current physical and psychiatric illness" (p. 127).
NOTES & COMMENTS: Haskett and Abplanalp (1983) recommended using the self-report Rating Scales for Premenstrual Tension Syndrome to identify homogeneous samples for studying premenstrual tension.
AVAILABLE FROM: Steiner, Haskett, and Carroll, 1980
USED IN:

Haskett, R. F., & Abplanalp, J. M. (1983). Premenstrual tension syndrome: Diagnostic criteria and selection of research subjects. *Psychiatry Research, 9,* 125–138.

Steiner, M., Haskett, R. F., & Carroll, B. J. (1980). Premenstrual tension syndrome: The development of research diagnostic criteria and new rating scales. *Acta Psychiatrica Scandinavica, 62,* 177–190.

Steiner, M., Haskett, R. F., Carroll, B. J., Hays, S. E., & Rubin, R. T. (1984). Plasma prolactin and severe premenstrual tension. *Psychoneuroendocrinology, 9,* 29–35.

BIBLIOGRAPHY:
Aitken, R. C. B. (1969). Measurement of feelings using visual analogue scales. *Proceedings of the Royal Society of Medicine*, *62*, 989–993.
Feinberg, M., Carroll, B. J., Smouse, P., Rawson, R., Haskett, R. F., Steiner, M., Albala, A., & Zelnick, T. (1979). *Comparison of physician and self-ratings of depression*. Paper presented at the meeting of the Society of Biological Psychiatry, Chicago.
Hamilton, M. (1960). A rating scale for depression. *Journal of Neurology, Neurosurgery, and Psychiatry*, *23*, 56–62.
Maxwell, C. (1978). Sensitivity and accuracy of the Visual Analogue Scale: A psychophysical classroom experiment. *British Journal of Clinical Pharmacology*, *6*, 15–24.
Moos, R. H. (1969). *Menstrual Distress Questionnaire: Preliminary manual*. Palo Alto: Stanford University, Social Ecology Laboratory.
Spielberger, C. D., Gorsuch, R. L., & Lushene, R. E. (1970). *STAI Manual*. Palo Alto: Consulting Psychologists Press.
Zuckerman, M., & Lubin, B. (1965). *Manual for the Multiple Affect Adjective Check List*. San Diego: Educational and Industrial Testing Service.

SYMPTOM SEVERITY SCALE

AUTHORS: Margaret A. Chesney and Donald L. Tasto

DATE: 1975

VARIABLE: Experience of various symptoms in conjunction with menstruation

TYPE OF INSTRUMENT: Summated rating scale

DESCRIPTION: The Symptom Severity Scale consists of a list of 15 symptoms that a woman may or may not experience in conjunction with her menstrual period. For each of the 15 items, the respondent is to consider her last menstrual period and select one of five response options: "symptom not present, slightly, moderately, severely, very severely."

SAMPLE ITEMS: Cramps
 Dizziness

PREVIOUS SUBJECTS: College and adult women

APPROPRIATE FOR: Females who menstruate

ADMINISTRATION: Self-administered; about 5 minutes

SCORING: Each item is assigned a score from 1 to 5, with the higher scores being assigned to the greater severity. Total scores can range from a low of 15 (no symptoms present) to a high of 75 (all symptoms experienced "very severely"). Although Chesney and Tasto (1975) provided no guidelines for determining when someone should be labeled dysmenorrheic, Amos and Khanna (1985) used the criterion that subjects scoring one standard deviation (8.5) above the mean of 22 would be labeled dysmenorrheic. Goolkasian (1983) selected a nondysmenorrheic group that had a mean score of 19.8 (standard deviation = 2.9) and a dysmenorrheic group that had a mean score of 46.2 (standard deviation = 8.4).

DEVELOPMENT: Chesney and Tasto (1975) provided no information about the development of the scale except to say that it was adapted from Mullen (1971) "based on our previous research and requirements of this study" (p. 247).

RELIABILITY: Chesney and Tasto (1975) did not report reliability in their article, but Breckenridge, Gates, Hall, and Evans (1983) reported a test-retest reliability of .84 and cited "personal communication" from Chesney as their reference.

VALIDITY: Several research studies used the Symptom Severity Scale as a pretest/posttest measure to determine whether a particular treatment was effective in reducing menstrual symptomatology (Breckenridge et al., 1983; Chesney & Tasto, 1975; Cox, 1977; Hart, Mathisen, & Prater, 1981). As would be expected if the treatment were effective, scale scores changed after treatment.

NOTES & COMMENTS: Bennink, Hulst, and Benthem (1982) used selected items to form subscores of interest in their research.

AVAILABLE FROM: Chesney and Tasto, 1975

USED IN:

Amos, W. E., & Khanna, P. (1985). Life stress in spasmodic and congestive dysmenorrhea. *Psychological Reports, 57*, 216–218.

Bennink, C. D., Hulst, L. L., & Benthem, J. A. (1982). The effects of EMG biofeedback and relaxation training on primary dysmenorrhea. *Journal of Behavioral Medicine, 5*, 329–341.

Breckenridge, R. L., Gates, D. O., Hall, H. M., & Evans, D. S. (1983). Electromyographic biofeedback as a treatment for primary dysmenorrhea: A pilot study. *Southern Psychologist, 1*, 75–76.

Chesney, M. A., & Tasto, D. L. (1975). The effectiveness of behavior modification with spasmodic and congestive dysmenorrhea. *Behaviour Research and Therapy, 13*, 245–253.

Cox, D. J. (1977). Menstrual Symptom Questionnaire: Further psychometric evaluation. *Behaviour Research and Therapy, 15*, 506–508.

Goolkasian, P. (1983). An ROC analysis of pain reactions in dysmenorrheic and nondysmenorrheic women. *Perception and Psychophysics, 34*, 381–386.

Hart, A. D., Mathisen, K. S., & Prater, J. S. (1981). A comparison of skin temperature and EMG training for primary dysmenorrhea. *Biofeedback and Self Regulation, 6*, 367–373.

BIBLIOGRAPHY:

Mullen, F. G. (1971, September). *Treatment of dysmenorrhea by professional and student behavior therapists.* Paper presented at the meeting of the Association for the Advancement of Behavior Therapy, Washington, DC.

TAYLOR DAILY SYMPTOM RATING SCALE

AUTHOR: John W. Taylor

DATE: 1979

VARIABLE: The intensity of physical symptoms, behaviors, and moods, both positive and negative, that may or may not be associated with the menstrual cycle
TYPE OF INSTRUMENT: Summated rating scale
DESCRIPTION: The Taylor Daily Symptom Rating Scale contains a list of 17 symptoms, most expressed in a single word. Ten symptoms are taken from the affective domain and 7 from the somatic domain. Each symptom is to be rated at night before going to bed; responses for a 5-week period can be recorded on a single form. Ratings are made on a 6-point scale ranging from "0 = not at all" to "5 = very large amount."
SAMPLE ITEMS: Hopelessness
  Cheerfulness
  Breast swelling or tenderness
PREVIOUS SUBJECTS: Women, ages 17–46
APPROPRIATE FOR: Females who menstruate
ADMINISTRATION: Self-administered; less than 5 minutes daily
SCORING: Item scores can be summed to yield a total score, and separate scores can be obtained for the affective and the somatic items. Scores can be obtained for any portion of the menstrual cycle under study.
DEVELOPMENT: A list of symptoms was prepared based on reviewing the literature on premenstrual distress. Some items were unchanged, others were combined, some were eliminated, and attitudes relating to positive affect were added.
RELIABILITY: Using the data from 65 respondents, the authors estimated reliability for four different time periods: the premenstrual week, the period of menstruation, the remainder of the cycle, and the entire time period. Split-half reliability coefficients ranged from .92 (premenstrual week) to .94 (period of menstruation). Data from 25 respondents who completed the Taylor Daily Symptom Rating Scale for two consecutive cycles were used to estimate test-retest reliability. The estimates ranged from .80 (period of menstruation) to .92 (remainder of the cycle, and complete cycle).
VALIDITY: Four other measures of premenstrual discomfort were obtained and served as criteria for validating the Taylor Daily Symptom Rating Scale: amount of medication consumed during the premenstrual period (measured in terms of number of pills consumed); self-report of having previously consulted a physician regarding premenstrual distress; self-rating of the usual severity of premenstrual symptoms, made on a 5-point scale; and respondent's rating of the usual severity of her premenstrual symptoms in comparison to those of other women, another 5-point scale. All three premenstrual scores—total, affect, and somatic—correlated significantly with each of the four criterion measures. However, only two of the correlations exceeded .50: somatic score with self-rating on severity of symptoms and somatic score with history

of having sought medical help in dealing with premenstrual symptoms (Taylor, 1979a).

Symptom scores peaked at the onset of menstruation. This was particularly true for the somatic symptoms that were highest on day 1 or 2 of menstruation. The pattern for the affective symptoms was different and less clear-cut. Some affective symptoms showed virtually no cyclic pattern (Taylor, 1979a).

NOTES & COMMENTS: (1) Taylor (1979a) found that most negative symptoms had statistically significant intercorrelations, as did all positive symptoms. Furthermore, he found significant item correlations from phase to phase. This suggests that some women reported having lots of symptoms lots of the time; other women had few symptoms most of the time.

(2) Taylor (1979b) found a significant correlation ($r = .45$) between scores on the affective subscale and Neuroticism scores on the Eysenck Personality Inventory (EPI) (Eysenck, 1969). The correlation with the somatic subscore was nonsignificant, as were the correlations between the EPI Extraversion scores and both the affective and the somatic subscale scores.

AVAILABLE FROM: Taylor, 1979a

USED IN:

Taylor, J. W. (1979a). The timing of menstruation-related symptoms assessed by a daily symptom rating scale. *Acta Psychiatrica Scandinavica, 60,* 87–105.

Taylor, J. W. (1979b). Psychological factors in the aetiology of premenstrual symptoms. *Australian and New Zealand Journal of Psychiatry, 13,* 35–41.

BIBLIOGRAPHY:

Eysenck, H. J. (1969). *Eysenck Personality Inventory.* San Diego: Educational and Industrial Testing Service.

GREENE'S SYMPTOM RATING SCALE

AUTHOR: J. G. Greene

DATE: 1976

VARIABLE: Symptoms accompanying the climacterium (more colloquially referred to as menopausal symptoms)

TYPE OF INSTRUMENT: Summated rating scale

DESCRIPTION: Greene's Symptom Rating Scale contains 21 symptoms relating to moods, behavior, and physical conditions. Each item is accompanied by a 4-point rating scale ranging from "not at all" to "extremely—could not be worse."

SAMPLE ITEMS: Feeling tired or lacking in energy

Pressure or tightness in head or body

PREVIOUS SUBJECTS: Women, ages 25–65

APPROPRIATE FOR: Women

ADMINISTRATION: Self-administered; 5–10 minutes

SCORING: There are two subscale scores: 11 items contribute to the psychological factor score, and 7 items contribute to the somatic factor score. Within each subscale, items are scored 0 to 3, with a higher score being assigned to greater severity. Before totaling subscale scores, item scores are multiplied by a factor of 2 if the item's factor loading was above +.50.

DEVELOPMENT: A 30-item symptom rating scale was constructed, with most of the items coming from the Neugarten-Kraines Menopausal Symptoms Scale (Neugarten & Kraines, 1965) (see separate entry). Fifty women, ages 40–55, who were experiencing the climacterium and had been referred to a hormone replacement clinic completed the 30-item scale. A factor analysis of their responses led to three factors that accounted for a total of 38% of the variance. Factor I was interpreted as a psychological factor, and Factor II was a general somatic factor. The third factor, referred to as a vasomotor factor, was more difficult to interpret, and few items had high factor loadings on this factor. Items with factor loadings above .40 on one factor and less than .30 on the other two factors were retained. This procedure produced a 21-item scale with 11 psychological items, 7 general somatic items, and 3 vasomotor items (Greene, 1976). Later reports of using the scale continued to mention the 21 items, but items loading on the third factor were not scored (Greene & Cooke, 1980; Cooke & Greene, 1981).

RELIABILITY: Test-retest reliability was computed using data from 30 women who were tested on two occasions a week apart. The reliability for the psychological factor was .89, the reliability for the somatic factor was .85, and the reliability for the vasomotor factor was .83.

VALIDITY: Age trends on the psychological factor scores and the somatic factor scores suggested that symptoms increased in the late 30s, peaked in the early 40s, and then declined. Greene and Cooke (1980) claimed that "this elevation in symptoms therefore coincides remarkably closely with the period of the climacterium" (p. 488). Actually one could readily argue that these changes are somewhat early to be associated with the climacterium and may be caused by some other factors. In fact, Greene and Cooke's data supported the fact that symptom severity was related to life stress, although their later research showed that the relationship was quite complex (Cooke & Greene, 1981).

NOTES & COMMENTS: (1) The intercorrelation between the two subscale scores was .21, which Greene (1976) concluded was low enough to assume the factors were independent.

(2) The distributions derived from plotting scores on all three factors suggested that a woman's symptoms need to be described on all three factors; there are not three distinct categories of women.

(3) Prakash and Murthy (1982) used Greene's Symptom Rating Scale to examine menopausal symptoms of women in India.

AVAILABLE FROM: Greene (1976) lists the original set of 30 symptoms, their factor loadings, and the scoring weights for the 21 symptoms on Greene's Symptom Rating Scale.

USED IN:

Cooke, D. J., & Greene, J. G. (1981). Types of life events in relation to symptoms at the climacterium. *Journal of Psychosomatic Research, 25,* 5–11.

Greene, J. G. (1976). A factor analytic study of climacteric symptoms. *Journal of Psychosomatic Research, 20,* 425–430.

Greene, J. G. (1980). Stress at the climacterium: The assessment of symptomatology. In I. G. Sarason (Ed.), *Stress and anxiety* (Vol. 7, pp. 127–137). Washington, DC: Hemisphere Publishing.

Greene, J. G., & Cooke, D. J. (1980). Life stress and symptoms at the climacterium. *British Journal of Psychiatry, 136,* 486–491.

Prakash, I. J., & Murthy, V. N. (1982). Menopausal symptoms in Indian women. *Personality Study and Group Behaviour, 2,* 54–58.

BIBLIOGRAPHY:

Neugarten, B. L., & Kraines, R. J. (1965). Menopausal symptoms in women of varying ages. *Psychosomatic Medicine, 27,* 266–273.

MENOPAUSAL SYMPTOM CHECKLIST (MSC)

AUTHOR: Vinod Kumar Sharma

DATE: 1983 (used 1978)

VARIABLE: Symptomatology accompanying menopause

TYPE OF INSTRUMENT: Summated rating scale

DESCRIPTION: The Menopausal Symptom Checklist (MSC) consists of 33 symptoms: 11 somatic, 5 psychosomatic, and 17 psychological. For 30 symptoms, respondents are to indicate how frequently they experience the symptom. The response options are "always, often, occasionally, never." For the remaining 3 symptoms—hot flashes, night sweats, and sleeplessness—respondents provide more information. For example, for night sweats, respondents indicate whether they are currently experiencing the symptom, the intensity of the symptom, and the duration of the symptom.

SAMPLE ITEMS: (somatic symptoms) breast pains, cold hands and feet
(psychosomatic symptoms) black spots before the eyes, headaches
(psychological symptoms) crying spells, forgetfulness

PREVIOUS SUBJECTS: Women in India, ages 40–55

APPROPRIATE FOR: Women in India, ages 40–55

ADMINISTRATION: The MSC has been administered in an interview, but it could be self-administered; about 10–15 minutes

SCORING: The 30 items rated for frequency are scored as follows: 0 for "never," 1 for "sometimes," 2 for "often," and 3 for "always." Sharma (1983) provided a scoring key for the three symptoms for which there are several questions. Item scores are summed to yield a total score, ranging from 5 to 111, and three subscale scores: psychological symptoms, ranging from 1 to 53; somatic symptoms, ranging from 4 to 43; and psychosomatic symptoms, ranging from 0 to 15.

DEVELOPMENT: In developing the MSC, the author borrowed symptoms from the Neugarten-Kraines Menopausal Symptom Scale (Neugarten & Kraines, 1965) (see separate entry) and added some symptoms typical for Indian women. The initial version of the MSC was pretested on a sample of 87 women. Analysis of their responses led to the modification of some items and the elimination of others. According to Sharma (1983), the symptoms on the MSC were those "most frequently reported by clinicians and the interviewees as being typical and/or frequent complaints of the middle-aged Indian women" (p. 66).

RELIABILITY: A sample of 50 Indian women completed the MSC on two occasions with a 6-month interval between the two testings. The coefficients of stability were: overall score = .71, psychological symptom score = .70, psychosomatic symptom score = .37, and somatic symptom score = .59.

VALIDITY: No information was provided.

NOTES & COMMENTS: (1) When Sharma (1983) administered the MSC, the items were in Hindi.

(2) Sharma (1983) defended the extremely low reliability of the psychosomatic score by pointing out that the subscale contained few items. He showed that the coefficient of stability would be .79 if there were 33 items on that subscale. There are not 33 items on the subscale, however, and as the subscale now stands, scores show little stability over time. Sharma does not address the issue of whether the lack of stability could be attributable to real changes in psychosomatic symptoms over the 6-month period between testings.

AVAILABLE FROM: Sharma, 1983

USED IN:

Sharma, V. K. (1983). The construction and development of a menopausal symptom checklist. *Indian Journal of Clinical Psychology, 10,* 63–70.

BIBLIOGRAPHY:

Neugarten, B. L., & Kraines, R. J. (1965). Menopausal symptoms in women in various ages. *Psychosomatic Medicine, 27,* 266–273.

MENOPAUSE ATTITUDE SCALE (MAS)

AUTHOR: Cheryl Bowles

DATE: 1986

VARIABLE: Attitudes toward menopause

TYPE OF INSTRUMENT: Semantic differential

DESCRIPTION: The Menopause Attitude Scale (MAS) is a semantic differential consisting of 20 bipolar adjective scales. The bipolar scales are 7-point scales with the positions labeled "extremely [outermost position], quite, slightly." The center position is a neutral position. The items are preceded with a sentence stem that states, "During menopause a woman feels . . ."

SAMPLE ITEMS: Important . . . . . . unimportant

Passive . . . . . . active

PREVIOUS SUBJECTS: Women

APPROPRIATE FOR: College students and adults

ADMINISTRATION: Self-administered; about 10 minutes

SCORING: Items are individually scored and summed to yield a single score that can range from 20 to 140. For a sample of 419 adult females, the mean score was 82.31 with a standard deviation of 23.46.

DEVELOPMENT: A pool of 45 bipolar adjective scales was developed by selecting adjective pairs from Osgood, Suci, and Tannenbaum's (1957) original set of 50 adjectives, from literature regarding the menopause, and from two other semantic differentials used to study menopause (Kraines, 1963; Meltzer, 1974). Two individuals—experts on the subject of menopause—reviewed the adjectives to establish the content validity of the pool. Adjectives were selected to represent Osgood and Suci's (1955) three dimensions: evaluation, potency, and activity. Using the sentence stem, "During menopause a woman feels . . . ," 504 adult females responded to each adjective pair using a 7-point response scale. A factor analysis of their responses revealed one factor that accounted for 44% of the variance and six other factors that jointly accounted for 17% of the variance. Twenty bipolar adjective pairs with factor loadings greater than .70 were selected to represent the first factor. A second factor analysis was performed on responses to the 20 scales, and one factor was identified, accounting for 60% of the variance. These 20 scales comprise the MAS.

RELIABILITY: The data obtained from the 504 women used to develop the MAS were also used to compute coefficient alpha. For the 20 adjective scales, alpha was .96. When the MAS was administered to another sample of 419 women, coefficient alpha was again .96.

Test-retest reliability was computed using data from 39 subjects tested on two occasions with a 6-week interval between testings. The coefficient of stability was .87.

The interitem correlations, based on testing 419 women, ranged from .40 to .84 with a mean of .59.

VALIDITY: To assess the convergent validity of the MAS, a sample of 138 women completed the MAS and the Attitudes Toward Menopause Scale, a 35-item summated rating scale developed by Neugarten, Wood, Kraines, and Loomis (1963). The correlation between the two measures was .63.

To demonstrate the discriminant validity of the scale, Bowles (1986) administered the MAS and Kogan's (1961) Attitudes Toward Old People Scale to a sample of 135 women. The correlation between the two measures was .42, significantly lower than the correlation between the MAS and the Attitudes Toward Menopause Scale ($p < .02$). To demonstrate further the discriminant validity of the scale, the MAS and the Attitudes Toward Women Scale (Spence, Helmreich, & Stapp, 1973) (see Beere, 1990) were administered to a sample of 146 women. The correlation between the two scales was $-.04$.

NOTES & COMMENTS: Bowles (1986) performed a regression analysis on MAS scores using data from 419 women. Age and menopausal status were the two significant explanatory variables.

AVAILABLE FROM: Bowles, 1986

USED IN:

Bowles, C. (1986). Measure of attitude toward menopause using the semantic differential model. *Nursing Research, 35*, 81–85.

BIBLIOGRAPHY:

Beere, C. A. (1990). *Gender roles: A handbook of tests and measures.* Westport, CT: Greenwood.

Kogan, N. (1961). Attitudes Toward Old People: The development of a scale and an examination of correlates. *Journal of Abnormal and Social Psychology, 62*, 44–54.

Kraines, R. (1963). *The menopause and evaluations of the self: A study of middle-aged women.* Unpublished doctoral dissertation, University of Chicago.

Meltzer, L. (1974). The aging female: A study of attitudes toward aging and self-concept held by premenopausal, menopausal and postmenopausal women (Doctoral dissertation, Adelphi University, 1974). *Dissertation Abstracts International, 35*, 1055B.

Neugarten, B., Wood, V., Kraines, R., & Loomis, B. (1963). Women's attitudes toward the menopause. *Vita Humana, 6*, 140–151.

Osgood, C., & Suci, G. (1955). Factor analysis of meaning. *Journal of Experimental Psychology, 10*, 325–328.

Osgood, C., Suci, G., & Tannenbaum, P. (1957). *The measurement of meaning.* Illinois: University of Illinois Press.

Spence, J. T., Helmreich, R., & Stapp, J. (1973). A short version of the Attitudes Toward Women Scale (AWS). *Bulletin of the Psychonomic Society, 2*, 219–220.

NEUGARTEN-KRAINES MENOPAUSAL SYMPTOMS SCALE

AUTHORS: Bernice L. Neugarten and Ruth J. Kraines

DATE: 1965

VARIABLE: Presence of menopausal symptoms

TYPE OF INSTRUMENT: Checklist

DESCRIPTION: The Neugarten-Kraines Menopausal Symptoms Scale is a 28-item checklist consisting of symptoms that a woman might experience in connection with menopause. There are 12 somatic symptoms, 5 psychosomatic symptoms, and 11 psychological symptoms.

ARTICLES LISTED IN BEERE, 1979: 1
AVAILABLE FROM: Neugarten and Kraines, 1965
USED IN:

Davis, D. L. (1986). The meaning of menopause in a Newfoundland fishing village. *Culture, Medicine and Psychiatry, 10,* 73–94.

Engle, N. S. (1984). On the vicissitudes of health appraisal. *Advances in Nursing Science, 7,* 12–23.

Neugarten, B. L., & Kraines, R. J. (1965). Menopausal symptoms in women of various ages. *Psychosomatic Medicine, 27,* 266–273.

Prakash, I. J., & Murthy, V. N. (1982). Menopausal symptoms in Indian women. *Personality Study and Group Behaviour, 2,* 54–58.

BIBLIOGRAPHY:

Beere, C. A. (1979). *Women and women's issues: A handbook of tests and measures* (pp. 499–500). San Francisco: Jossey-Bass.

CHAMPION BREAST EXAMINATION SCALE
AUTHOR: Victoria Lee Champion
DATE: 1984 (used 1981)
VARIABLE: Beliefs relating to breast self-examination
TYPE OF INSTRUMENT: Summated rating scale
DESCRIPTION: The original version of the Champion Breast Examination Scale consists of 39 items representing five subscales: susceptibility to breast cancer (6 items), seriousness of breast cancer (12 items), benefits from breast self-examination (5 items), barriers to breast self-examination (8 items), and general health motivation (8 items). The items from the different areas are intermingled. Each is accompanied by five response options ranging from "strongly agree" to "strongly disagree." All items are phrased so that agreement indicates a "stronger feeling on each concept" (Champion, 1985, p. 375).

The second version of the Champion Breast Examination Scale consists of 33 items representing six subscales: susceptibility to breast cancer (5 items), seriousness of breast cancer (8 items), benefits of breast self-examination (5 items), barriers to breast self-examination (6 items), general health motivation (5 items), and perceived control (4 items). Items are accompanied by five response options: "strongly agree, agree, neutral, disagree, strongly disagree." Again items are phrased so that agreement indicates greater support for what is being measured.

SAMPLE ITEMS: (susceptibility) I worry a lot about getting breast cancer.

(seriousness) The thought of breast cancer scares me.

(benefits) Discovering lumps early would increase my chance of survival if I had breast cancer.

(barriers) It is embarrassing for me to do monthly breast exams.

(health motivation) I have yearly physical exams in addition to visits related to illness.

(control) If I get breast cancer I can do a lot myself to control what happens.

PREVIOUS SUBJECTS: Females, ages 16 and older

APPROPRIATE FOR: Females, ages 16 and older

ADMINISTRATION: Self-administered; about 10–15 minutes

SCORING: Items are individually scored, with "strongly agree" assigned 5 points and "strongly disagree" assigned 1 point. The items contributing to each subscale are summed to yield a subscale score; no overall score is obtained.

DEVELOPMENT: The development of the Champion Breast Examination Scale was based on the Health Belief Model (Becker, 1974), which posits that health-related behaviors are a function of perceived susceptibility to a potentially harmful condition, perceived seriousness of the condition, perceived benefits from the behavior, and perceived barriers to performing the behavior. Champion (1984) added the idea of general health motivation. Scale development was guided by conceptual definitions of these five terms. A group of 20 to 24 items was prepared for each area. Items for the first four areas were all directly relevant to breast self-examination and breast cancer; items for the last area related to general health. Eight judges—faculty and graduate students who were familiar with the Health Belief Model—reviewed the items and determined the area each item belonged to. The judges were also given the option to state that the item was not relevant to any of the areas. A set of 10 to 12 items was selected to represent each area; at least six of the eight judges agreed on the item classification of the selected items. Using responses from 301 women, the researchers reduced the number of items on each subscale by selecting items that produced the greatest internal consistency reliabilities.

In the second version of the Champion Breast Examination Scale, some items were revised to improve their clarity, and four items were added to measure perceived control. The bases for other changes between the two versions were not explained.

RELIABILITY: Internal consistency reliabilities for the five subscales on the first version of the Champion Breast Examination Scale were computed using the responses from 301 women. The coefficients were: susceptibility = .78, seriousness = .78, benefits = .61, barriers = .76, and motivation = .62 (Champion, 1984). On the second version of the scale, the responses from 585 women were used to calculate internal consistency reliabilities. The results ranged from .63 to .76 (Champion, 1987).

For the first version of the Champion Breast Examination Scale, test-retest reliabilities were computed using the responses from 57 women who were tested on two occasions separated by about 2 weeks. The results were: susceptibility = .86, seriousness = .76, benefits = .47, barriers = .83, and motivation = .81 (Champion, 1984). On the second version of the scale, test-retest reliabilities were based on a longer period between testings: 1 month as compared to 2 weeks. The reliabilities ranged from .47 to .62 (Champion, 1987).

VALIDITY: Champion (1984, 1985) also measured the behavior of breast self-examination by asking each woman how often she performed breast self-examination. Using multiple regression procedures, Champion found that barriers accounted for the largest portion of the variance in behavior; health motivation was second in importance. Benefits, susceptibility, and seriousness did not add to the prediction. Discriminant analysis led to similar conclusions.

NOTES & COMMENTS: (1) Champion (1984) reported the results of a factor analysis of responses given by 301 women. She identified seven factors: "with only one exception, all items on a factor were from the same construct" (p. 82).

(2) Champion (1987) examined the relationship between breast self-examination and the constructs of the Health Belief Model. In this study, she also considered the influence of knowledge of breast cancer.

AVAILABLE FROM: Victoria Champion, Indiana University, 610 Barnhill Drive, Indianapolis, IN 46202

USED IN:

Champion, V. L. (1984). Instrument development for Health Belief Model constructs. *Advances in Nursing Science*, 6(3), 73–85.

Champion, V. L. (1985). Use of the Health Belief Model in determining frequency of breast self-examination. *Research in Nursing and Health*, *8*, 373–379.

Champion, V. L. (1987). The relationship of breast self-examination to Health Belief Model variables. *Research in Nursing and Health*, *10*, 375–382.

BIBLIOGRAPHY:

Becker, M. H. (1974). *The Health Belief Model and personal health behavior*. Thorofare, New Jersey: Charles B. Slack.

PERCEIVED SUSCEPTIBILITY TO BREAST CANCER AND PERCEIVED BENEFITS FROM BSE

AUTHOR: Margot J. Stillman

DATE: 1977

VARIABLE: Perceptions of one's own susceptibility to breast cancer and perceptions of benefits to be derived from breast self-examination (BSE)

TYPE OF INSTRUMENT: Summated rating scale

DESCRIPTION: This measure of Perceived Susceptibility to Breast Cancer and Perceived Benefits from BSE consists of 10 items, with the first 9 accompanied by four response options ranging from "agree strongly" to "disagree strongly." The 10th item has three options: average, above average, and below average. The even-numbered items are intended to measure the respondent's belief in her own susceptibility to breast cancer, and the odd-numbered items pertain to beliefs about the impact of BSE in reducing the threat of breast cancer.

SAMPLE ITEMS: If more women examined their breast regularly, there would be fewer deaths from breast cancer.

My health is too good at present to even consider thinking that I might get breast cancer.

PREVIOUS SUBJECTS: Women

APPROPRIATE FOR: Females, ages 16 and over

ADMINISTRATION: Self-administered; less than 5 minutes

SCORING: For each of the first nine items, an item score of 1 to 4 is assigned to the item, with 1 point always assigned to the end of the continuum reflecting the lowest belief. Item 10 is scored on a 3-point scale. Item scores are totaled to yield a score that can range from 5 to 19 for perceived susceptibility and 5 to 20 for perceived benefits. For both subscales, scores of 15 and higher represent "high belief," and scores of 9 and lower indicate "low belief."

DEVELOPMENT: The scale, which was part of a larger questionnaire, was based on a review of the literature, and all items were original. After the questionnaire was developed, it was submitted to five graduate nursing students who were asked "to review the entire instrument for clarity, readability, and understandability and to evaluate the items on the attitude scale in terms of whether they measured the variables under investigation, perceived susceptibility, and perceived benefits" (Stillman, 1977, p. 124). The questionnaire was also reviewed by two women to determine whether respondents would have difficulty with the items. The questionnaire was pretested on a sample of 20 women, and it was found that "items . . . discriminated to some degree" (p. 124).

RELIABILITY: No information was provided.

VALIDITY: There is definitely a relationship between beliefs as expressed on the scales and behavior as measured by the frequency with which one practices BSE (Hallal, 1982; Stillman, 1977). Scores reflecting the perceived value of BSE increased in a community where there was a well-publicized BSE class (Calnan, Chamberlain, & Moss, 1983).

NOTES & COMMENTS: (1) Calnan et al. (1983) added three items to the scale.

(2) The questionnaire administered by Stillman (1977) also contained a 4-item multiple choice measure of factual knowledge regarding breast cancer. The measure appears in Stillman's article.

AVAILABLE FROM: Stillman, 1977

USED IN:

Calnan, M. W., Chamberlain, J., & Moss, S. (1983). Compliance with a class teaching breast self examination. *Journal of Epidemiology and Community Health, 37*, 264–270.

Calnan, M., & Rutter, D. R. (1986). Do health beliefs predict health behaviour? An analysis of breast self examination. *Social Science and Medicine, 22*, 673–678.

Hallal, J. C. (1982). The relationship of health beliefs, health locus of control, and self concept to the practice of breast self-examination in adult women. *Nursing Research, 31*, 137–142.

Schleuter, L. A. (1982). Knowledge and beliefs about breast cancer and breast self-examination among athletic and nonathletic women. *Nursing Research, 31*, 348–353.

Stillman, M. J. (1977). Women's health beliefs about breast cancer and breast self-examination. *Nursing Research, 26*, 121–127.

7

Homosexuality

The 10 scales described in this chapter have similar characteristics. Nine of the 10 measures assess attitudes regarding homosexuality, and all of these measures are appropriate for persons ages 16 and older. Seven of the measures in this chapter are summated rating scales, and 2 are alternate choice measures. The remaining scale has both a rating scale and a checklist. The scales range in length from 9 to 49 items. Most of the scales have been used in fewer than six research studies. There are more than 6 citations listed for only one scale: the MacDonald Attitudes Toward Homosexuality Scales (MacDonald, Huggins, Young, & Swanson, 1973), which is followed by 12 references. Not surprisingly, the scale is one of the oldest ones listed in this chapter.

There were data supporting the reliability of nine of these scales, at least in terms of internal consistency. Test-retest reliability was assessed for only two of the measures, and for one of those two, the data suggested that the measure was not sufficiently stable over time.

There was some evidence supporting the validity of all the measures described in this chapter. A common method for demonstrating the validity of a measure of attitudes toward homosexuality is to compare the scores from male and female respondents. This approach was used as evidence of the validity of five of the nine attitude measures described in this chapter. In every case, the data showed that males were less tolerant of homosexuality.

Interestingly, half of the scales in this chapter are old enough to have been included in my original handbook (Beere, 1979), but none was because the original handbook covered a narrower range of topics.

There is a difference of opinion as to whether attitudes toward lesbians and toward gay males should be measured as two separate constructs. Herek (1988) stated that "differences in attitudes can be assessed empirically only with instruments that yield separate scores for attitudes toward gay men and toward lesbians" (p. 454). Herek developed such a measure that includes different items for assessing attitudes toward each of the two groups. The scale yields separate scores for attitudes toward gay males and toward lesbians. Two other measures in this chapter also consider attitudes toward gay males separately from attitudes toward lesbians: the Homosexuality Attitude Scale (Millham, San Miguel, & Kellogg, 1976) and the MacDonald Attitudes Toward Homosexuality Scales (MacDonald et al., 1973).

Researchers interested in studying attitudes toward homosexuality should be able to find appropriate measures; however, with the exception of the Lesbian Degree of Involvement and Overtness scale (Ferguson & Finkler, 1978), I did not locate measures designed specifically for studying homosexual persons.

BIBLIOGRAPHY:

Beere, C. A. (1979). *Women and women's issues: A handbook of tests and measures.* San Francisco: Jossey-Bass.

Ferguson, K. D., & Finkler, D. C. (1978). An involvement and overtness measure for lesbians: Its development and relation to anxiety and social zeitgeist. *Archives of Sexual Behavior, 7,* 211–227.

Herek, G. M. (1988). Heterosexuals' attitudes toward lesbians and gay men: Correlates and gender differences. *Journal of Sex Research, 25,* 451–477.

MacDonald, A. P., Jr., Huggins, J., Young, S., & Swanson, R. A. (1973). Attitudes toward homosexuality: Preservation of sex morality or the double standard? *Journal of Consulting and Clinical Psychology, 40,* 161.

Millham, J., San Miguel, C. L., & Kellogg, R. (1976). A factor-analytic conceptualization of attitudes toward male and female homosexuals. *Journal of Homosexuality, 2,* 3–10.

ATTITUDES TOWARD LESBIANS AND GAY MEN (ATLG)

AUTHOR: Gregory M. Herek

DATE: 1988

VARIABLE: Attitudes toward homosexuals

TYPE OF INSTRUMENT: Summated rating scale

DESCRIPTION: The Attitudes Toward Lesbians and Gay Men (ATLG) scale consists of 20 items. The first 10 items refer to lesbians and are referred to as ATL items. The last 10 items refer to gay men and are referred to as ATG items. Seven of the ATL items reflect negative attitudes; 6 of the ATG items reflect negative attitudes. Responses are recorded on a 9-point scale ranging from "strongly disagree" to "strongly agree."

SAMPLE ITEMS: Lesbians just can't fit into our society.

Male homosexuality is merely a different kind of lifestyle that should *not* be condemned.

PREVIOUS SUBJECTS: College students, members of lesbian and gay organizations

APPROPRIATE FOR: Ages 16 and older

ADMINISTRATION: Self-administered; about 5 minutes

SCORING: Items are individually scored on a 9-point scale, with lower scores assigned to the responses reflecting positive attitudes. Item scores are summed to yield three scores. The ATL and ATG scores can each range from 10 (positive attitudes) to 90 (negative attitudes); the ATLG score can range from 20 to 180. Herek (1988) reported means and standard deviations for various groups who completed the ATLG.

DEVELOPMENT: The item pool for the ATLG scale consisted of 37 items that Herek (1984) had previously identified as loading on a single factor labeled "Condemnation-Tolerance." Two versions of the item pool were developed. For one version, the items were phrased in terms of gay males; for the other version, items were phrased in terms of lesbians. Each version was administered to a different sample of college students: 133 students responded to the version referring to lesbians; 147 students responded to the version referring to gay males. The ATLG is comprised of 20 items that had the highest item-total correlations on both versions of the questionnaire.

RELIABILITY: Herek (1988) reported alpha coefficients for the two subscales and the total scale: ATLG = .90, ATG = .89, and ATL = .77. Based on another sample of college students, Herek obtained the following values for coefficient alpha: ATLG = .95, ATG = .91, and ATL = .90.

Herek (1988) produced alternate forms of the ATG and the ATL by rewriting the items to refer to a person of the opposite sex. That is, the ATG items were rewritten to refer to lesbians, and the ATL items were rewritten to refer to gay males. Coefficient alpha for these new versions were as follows: ATG = .92, ATL = .92, and ATLG = .96. Alternate form reliabilities with a 3-week interval between testings were as follows: ATL = .84, ATG = .83, and ATLG = .90.

A sample of 368 college students completed the ATLG, with half of the students completing a version of the scale that presented the items in reverse order. The means on the two versions were not significantly different from each other.

VALIDITY: Consistent with other research, Herek (1988) found that males expressed more negative attitudes toward homosexuality than did females. Furthermore, males expressed more negative attitudes toward same-sex homosexuals than they did toward opposite-sex homosexuals. Herek replicated these findings with various different samples.

Comparing scores from the ATG and ATL with the scores from their alternate versions, Herek (1988) determined that the ATG items (which were also the alternate ATL items) elicited more negative responses than did the ATL items (also the alternate ATG items).

Herek (1988) correlated scores on the ATL and ATG with numerous other measures. As predicted, the correlations were significant and in the expected direction for "attitudes toward sex roles, traditional family ideology dogmatism, perceived agreement by friends, and positive contact with any lesbians or gay men" (p. 459). Furthermore, scores for females were significantly related to three measures of religiosity.

After correlating ATL and ATG scores with scores on the Marlowe-Crowne Social Desirability Scale (Crowne & Marlowe, 1960), Herek (1988) found that for females, neither ATL nor ATG scores were significantly correlated with social desirability, but for males, ATG scores were significantly correlated with social desirability ($r = -.27$).

NOTES & COMMENTS: (1) Herek (1988) developed a short version of the ATLG comprised of 5 ATG and 5 ATL items that had high item-total correlations and reflected positive and negative attitudes. Coefficient alpha for the short ATG was .87; it was .85 for the short ATL. Alpha for the short ATLG was .92. Herek provided evidence supporting the construct validity of the short ATLG; in particular, he reported correlations for a variety of other measures predicted to correlate with ATL and ATG scores.

(2) Because this scale is relatively new, it has not been used extensively. However, the data regarding reliability and validity are quite promising, the scale is short and easy to administer, and it is likely to be used in future research.

AVAILABLE FROM: Herek, 1988

USED IN:

Herek, G. M. (1988). Heterosexuals' attitudes toward lesbians and gay men: Correlates and gender differences. *Journal of Sex Research, 25*, 451–477.

BIBLIOGRAPHY:

Crowne, D. P., & Marlowe, D. (1960). A new scale of social desirability independent of psychopathology. *Journal of Consulting Psychology, 24*, 349–354.

Herek, G. M. (1984). Attitudes Toward Lesbians and Gay Men: A factor analytic study. *Journal of Homosexuality, 10*, 39–51.

HETEROSEXUAL ATTITUDES TOWARD HOMOSEXUALITY (HATH)

AUTHORS: Knud S. Larsen, Michael Reed, and Susan Hoffman

DATE: 1980

VARIABLE: Attitudes toward homosexuality

TYPE OF INSTRUMENT: Summated rating scale

DESCRIPTION: The Heterosexual Attitudes Toward Homosexuality (HATH) scale contains 20 statements pertaining to homosexuals and

homosexuality. Items cover a variety of issues, including the rights of homosexuals, labeling of homosexuality, and willingness to associate with homosexuals. Half of the statements reflect a positive attitude, and the other half reflect a negative attitude. Items are accompanied by five response options ranging from "strongly agree" to "strongly disagree."
SAMPLE ITEMS: I enjoy the company of homosexuals.

It would be beneficial to society to recognize homosexuality as normal.
PREVIOUS SUBJECTS: College students
APPROPRIATE FOR: Ages 16 and older
ADMINISTRATION: Self-administered; about 10 minutes
SCORING: Items are individually scored on a 5-point scale, with 5 points assigned to the end of the continuum reflecting a positive attitude. This means that half of the items must be reversed before scoring. Item scores are summed to yield a total score that can range from 20 (very negative attitudes toward homosexuality) to 100 (very positive attitudes toward homosexuality).
DEVELOPMENT: A pool of 70 items was developed to measure attitudes toward homosexuals and homosexuality. The pool, which included about half positive and half negative statements, was administered as a summated rating scale to 43 college men and 37 college women. An item analysis was performed on their results, and the 20 items with the highest item-total correlations were selected for the HATH scale. This produced items with item-total correlations between .57 and .76.
RELIABILITY: Internal consistency reliability was calculated using the data from the sample on which the HATH scale was developed. The reliability was .95 (Larsen, Reed, & Hoffman, 1980).

The HATH scale was administered to 32 college women and 38 college men. The split-half reliability, corrected by Spearman-Brown, was .92. The analysis was replicated using data from another sample of 72 college men, 106 college women, and 24 persons who had failed to report their sex. Corrected, split-half reliability for this sample was also .92 (Larsen et al., 1980).

Whitley (1987) administered the HATH scale to 222 college students. For this sample, the internal consistency reliability of the scale was .94.
VALIDITY: Using data from two different samples, Larsen et al. (1980) compared the responses from college men and college women. With both sets of data, they obtained significant differences, with women scoring higher, more positive toward homosexuals. Whitley (1987) also found significant sex differences on the HATH scale: college women were significantly more positive than college men in their attitudes toward homosexuality.

Consistent with expectations, Larsen et al. (1980) found that liberal arts' students compared to business majors scored higher (more positive) on the HATH scale, and students who attended church "often" were significantly more negative on the HATH scale than students who attended church "rarely" or "never." No significant differences were found in the attitudes expressed by freshman/sophomores and the attitudes expressed by juniors/seniors.

Larsen et al. (1980) compared scores on the HATH scale with several other variables. They found that HATH scores were positively correlated with beliefs about peers' attitudes; the correlation was even stronger for males than for females. Furthermore, religiosity and authoritarianism were both negatively correlated with HATH scores, showing that less religious and less authoritarian persons were more tolerant of homosexuality.

Larsen, Cate, and Reed (1983) found that for a sample of 314 college students, HATH scores were significantly correlated with antiblack attitudes ($r = .33$), religious orthodoxy ($r = -.32$), and intimacy permissiveness ($r = .19$). No significant correlations were found between HATH scores and sexual experience or extramarital sex attitudes.

Larsen et al. (1983) used the HATH scale in a pretest/posttest design to determine whether a course in human sexuality could change attitudes toward homosexuality. Whereas there was no significant difference between pretest scores for the treatment and control groups, there was a significant difference between posttest scores for the two groups: the treatment group scored significantly higher.

As expected, Greendlinger (1985) found that scores on the HATH scale were significantly related to scores on the F scale, a measure of authoritarianism (Cherry & Byrne, 1977).

Larsen (1988) reported a significant correlation ($r = .84$) between HATH scores and scores on a measure of attitudes toward acquired immune deficiency syndrome (AIDS).

NOTES & COMMENTS: (1) The response options and scoring procedures Larsen (1988) reported are different from those given here.

(2) Whitley (1987) used the HATH scale along with several other measures to study the relationships among sex role beliefs, sex role self-concept, sex role behaviors, and attitudes toward homosexuality. His research also considered respondents' age, self-esteem, and conservatism.

(3) Mathews, Booth, Turner, and Kessler (1986) used the HATH scale with members of the San Diego Medical Society.

AVAILABLE FROM: Larsen, Reed, and Hoffman, 1980; Larsen, 1988; Mathews, Booth, Turner, and Kessler, 1986

USED IN:

Greendlinger, V. (1985). Authoritarianism as a predictor of response to heterosexual and homosexual erotica. *High School Journal*, *68*(3), 183–186.

Larsen, K. S. (1988). Heterosexual Attitudes Toward Homosexuality (HATH) scale. In C. M. Davis, W. L. Yarber, & S. L. Davis (Eds.), *Sexuality-related measures: A compendium* (pp. 167–168). Syracuse: Editors.

Larsen, K. S., Cate, R., & Reed, M. (1983). Anti-black attitudes, religious orthodoxy, permissiveness, and sexual information: A study of the attitudes of heterosexuals toward homosexuality. *Journal of Sex Research, 19*, 105–118.

Larsen, K. S., Reed, M., & Hoffman, S. (1980). Attitudes of heterosexuals toward homosexuality: A Likert-type scale and construct validity. *Journal of Sex Research, 16*, 245–257.

Mathews, W. C., Booth, M. W., Turner, J. D., & Kessler, L. (1986). Physicians' attitudes toward homosexuality—survey of a California county medical society. *Western Journal of Medicine, 144*, 106–110.

Whitley, B. E., Jr. (1987). The relationship of sex-role orientation to heterosexuals' attitudes toward homosexuals. *Sex Roles, 17*, 103–113.

BIBLIOGRAPHY:

Cherry, F., & Byrne, D. (1977). Authoritarianism. In T. Blass (Ed.), *Personality variables in social behavior* (pp. 109–133). Hillsdale, NJ: Lawrence Erlbaum.

HOMOPHOBIA SCALE

AUTHOR: Kenneth T. Smith

DATE: 1971

VARIABLE: Negative or fearful responding to homosexuality

TYPE OF INSTRUMENT: Alternate choice: yes/no

DESCRIPTION: The Homophobia Scale consists of nine items pertaining to the rights of homosexuals, one's willingness to associate with homosexuals, and one's reactions to homosexuals. Six items reflect negative attitudes toward homosexuals; three items reflect positive attitudes. Each item is accompanied by two response options: "yes" and "no."

SAMPLE ITEMS: Homosexuals should be locked up to protect society.

It would be upsetting for me to find out I was alone with a homosexual.

PREVIOUS SUBJECTS: College students; homosexual men, male-to-female transsexuals, and heterosexual men

APPROPRIATE FOR: Ages 16 and older

ADMINISTRATION: Self-administered; about 5 minutes

SCORING: One point is assigned for each response reflecting a negative attitude toward homosexuality. Thus, higher scores are associated with greater homophobia.

DEVELOPMENT: No information was provided.

RELIABILITY: Thompson, Grisanti, and Pleck (1985) used the Homophobia Scale with a 7-point response scale ranging from "very strongly disagree" to "very strongly agree." Coefficient alpha was .89 for a sample of 233 college men.

Iyriboz and Carter (1986) administered the Homophobia Scale as both a pretest and a posttest to 45 college students. On both occasions, coefficient alpha was .78.

VALIDITY: Karr (1978) used an adaptation of the Homophobia Scale and tested 90 college men. He found that scores on the Homophobia

Scale were significantly correlated with scores on a measure of authoritarianism ($r = .43$).

Hellman, Green, Gray, and Williams (1981) found that heterosexuals were more homophobic than were transsexuals. They also found that religiosity was positively correlated with homophobia among heterosexuals and adult transsexuals.

NOTES & COMMENTS: (1) Smith (1971) used the Homophobia Scale to identify homophobics and nonhomophobics. From a sample of 99 college students, he considered those with the highest 21 scores to be the homophobic group and those with the lowest 21 scores to be the nonhomophobic group. Smith then compared the two groups in terms of their age, religious affiliation, and college major, as well as on their answers to 15 items measuring opinions on a variety of issues.

(2) Karr (1978) used the Homophobia Scale to examine whether homophobic men compared to nonhomophobic men would react differently to a person labeled as a homosexual. Hellman et al. (1981) used the Homophobia Scale in a study involving boyhood cross-gender behavior, religiosity, and homophobia among Catholic transsexuals, homosexuals, and heterosexuals. Thompson et al. (1985) looked at the relationship between college men's attitudes toward the male role, as measured by the Brannon Masculinity Scale (Brannon & Juni, 1984) (see Beere, 1990), and five other variables, including attitudes toward homosexuality. Iyriboz and Carter (1986) used the Homophobia Scale as one of several measures in a pretest/posttest study of the effects of a 3-hour university class on human sexuality. Although Homophobia scores declined between pretest and posttest, the difference was not significant.

(3) Lumby (1976) modified the Homophobia Scale for his study comparing the attitudes of heterosexual and homosexual men.

AVAILABLE FROM: Smith, 1971

USED IN:

Hellman, R. E., Green, R., Gray, J. L., & Williams, K. (1981). Childhood sexual identity, childhood religiosity, and 'homophobia' as influences in the development of transsexualism, homosexuality, and heterosexuality. *Archives of General Psychiatry, 38,* 910–915.

Iyriboz, Y., & Carter, J. A. (1986). Attitudes of a southern university human sexuality class toward sexual variance, abortion and homosexuality. *College Student Journal, 20,* 89–93.

Karr, R. G. (1978). Homosexual labeling and the male role. *Journal of Social Issues, 34,* 73–83.

Lumby, M. E. (1976). Homophobia: The quest for a valid scale. *Journal of Homosexuality, 2,* 39–47.

Smith, K. T. (1971). Homophobia: A tentative personality profile. *Psychological Reports, 29,* 1091–1094.

Thompson, E. H., Jr., Grisanti, C., & Pleck, J. H. (1985). Attitudes toward the male role and their correlates. *Sex Roles, 13,* 413–427.

BIBLIOGRAPHY:
Beere, C. A. (1990). *Gender roles: A handbook of tests and measures.* Westport, CT: Greenwood.
Brannon, R., & Juni, S. (1984). A scale for measuring attitudes about masculinity. *Psychological Documents, 14,* 6. (Ms. No. 2612)

HOMOSEXISM SCALE
AUTHOR: Gary L. Hansen
DATE: 1982
VARIABLE: Homosexism defined as prejudice against homosexuality
TYPE OF INSTRUMENT: Summated rating scale
DESCRIPTION: There are two forms of the Homosexism Scale: a long form consisting of 49 statements and a short form consisting of 15 statements. In the long form, 22 items are phrased to reflect negative attitudes toward homosexuals and homosexuality; in the short form, 10 items are phrased in a negative manner. The items cover a variety of topics such as the rights of homosexuals, beliefs about the characteristics of homosexuals, and willingness to associate with homosexuals. Items are accompanied by five response options ranging from "strongly agree" to "strongly disagree."
SAMPLE ITEMS: Sexual preference should not be a factor in employment opportunity.
Homosexuals should be isolated from heterosexuals.
PREVIOUS SUBJECTS: College students
APPROPRIATE FOR: Ages 16 and older
ADMINISTRATION: Self-administered; the long form requires about 20 minutes; the short form requires about 5–10 minutes
SCORING: Items are individually scored on a 5-point scale. For items reflecting negative attitudes toward homosexuals, the "strongly agree" end of the continuum is assigned 5 points; scoring is reversed for the items that reflect positive attitudes. Item scores are summed to yield a total score. Low scores reflect positive attitudes. For the long form of the Homosexism Scale, total scores range from 49 to 245; for the short form of the scale, total scores range from 15 to 75. In a study of 143 college students, Hansen (1982b) found that scores on the short form covered the entire range from 15 to 75, with a mean of 41.80 and a standard deviation of 14.52.
DEVELOPMENT: An initial pool of 182 items was developed to assess homosexist attitudes. This pool was reduced to 53 items, but the method of reduction was not explained. The 53-item version was administered to 143 college students, and an item analysis was performed on their responses. A pool of 49 items was identified with item-total correlations of .50 or larger. All 49 items were found to discriminate at the .001 level

between those with the highest 25% of the total scores and those with the lowest 25% of the total scores.

The short form of the Homosexism Scale was constructed by selecting the 15 items with item-total correlations of .75 or larger (Hansen, 1982b).

RELIABILITY: Based on testing 143 college students, coefficient alpha for the long form of the Homosexism Scale was .98; for the short form, it was .96 (Hansen, 1982b).

VALIDITY: The correlation between the long form and the short form of the Homosexism Scale was .98 (Hansen, 1982b).

To assess the validity of the Homosexism Scale, the short form of the scale was administered to 112 college students. As predicted, the mean score for males was significantly higher (more prejudiced against homosexuals) than the mean score for females. Furthermore, the mean score for persons who did not know any homosexuals was significantly higher (more prejudiced) than the mean score for persons who did know homosexuals. Although the mean score for persons from rural backgrounds was higher than the mean score for persons from urban backgrounds, the difference was not statistically significant.

In a study of 87 college men and 119 college women, Hansen (1982a) replicated the finding that men scored significantly higher (more negative) on the Homosexism Scale.

NOTES & COMMENTS: Hansen (1982a) compared the Homosexism scores of college men and women with their scores on several other variables. For college women, Hansen found Homosexism scores significantly correlated with androgyny ($r = .27$), sex role orientation ($r = -.55$), religiosity ($r = .28$), and age ($r = -.20$). Correlations between Homosexism scores and self-concept, size of home town, and parents' income were not significant. For college men, Homosexism scores significantly correlated with sex role orientation ($r = -.48$) but not with any of the other variables. Thus, both homosexist males and females were more traditional in their sex role orientation, and homosexist females tended to be more religious and younger than nonhomosexist females.

AVAILABLE FROM: The short form appears in Hansen, 1982b; for the long form, write to Gary L. Hansen, Department of Sociology, S-205 Agricultural Science Center–North, University of Kentucky, Lexington, KY 40546–0091; telephone (606) 257–7586

USED IN:

Hansen, G. L. (1982a). Androgyny, sex-role orientation, and homosexism. *Journal of Psychology, 112*, 39–45.

Hansen, G. L. (1982b). Measuring prejudice against homosexuality (homosexism) among college students: A new scale. *Journal of Social Psychology, 117*, 233–236.

HOMOSEXUALITY ATTITUDE SCALE (HAS)

AUTHORS: Mary E. Kite and Kay Deaux

DATE: 1986

VARIABLE: Attitudes toward homosexuality
TYPE OF INSTRUMENT: Summated rating scale
DESCRIPTION: The Homosexuality Attitude Scale (HAS) consists of 21 items pertaining to one's reactions to homosexuals, beliefs about homosexuals, and support for the rights of homosexuals. Eleven items reflect a positive attitude regarding homosexuality; 10 items reflect a negative attitude. The scale is accompanied by a 5-point scale, with the endpoints labeled "Strongly Agree" and "Strongly Disagree" and the midpoint labeled "Neutral."
SAMPLE ITEMS: I would not mind having homosexual friends.

Homosexuals should be kept separate from the rest of society (i.e., separate housing, restricted employment).
PREVIOUS SUBJECTS: College students
APPROPRIATE FOR: Ages 16 and older
ADMINISTRATION: Self-administered; less than 10 minutes
SCORING: Individual items are scored on a 5-point scale, with higher scores assigned to the response reflecting a positive attitude toward homosexuality. Item scores are summed to yield a total score that can range from 21 (very negative attitudes toward homosexuality) to 105 (very positive attitude toward homosexuality). Kite and Deaux (1986) provided means and standard deviations, separately by sex and combined for both sexes, for two different samples of college students.
DEVELOPMENT: A pool of 40 items was developed with ideas for the items coming from the following sources: prejudices and anxieties revealed in questions that psychology students asked of gay rights activists who gave guest presentations in their classes, prejudices communicated by the media, beliefs and anxieties gleaned from human sexuality and abnormal psychology textbooks, and items included on other homosexuality scales. Forty college students anonymously completed the 40-item pool and provided feedback regarding "item clarity, item ambiguity, how well they felt their attitude had been assessed, and any other comments they had on particular items" (Kite & Deaux, 1986, p. 139). Using the feedback from the students and item-total correlations, the authors reduced the item pool to 25 items.

The 25-item scale was administered to two samples of university students: 317 students from the University of Texas and 252 students from Purdue University. Using item analysis data, Kite and Deaux (1986) deleted 3 items. As a result of later analyses, they recommended omitting another item with a low factor loading and a low item-total correlation. These deletions produced the current 21-item version of the scale.
RELIABILITY: Kite and Deaux (1986) reported reliability data for several groups who completed the HAS. Based on a sample of 307 college students in Texas who completed a 21-item version of the scale with 1 item different from the current version, coefficient alpha was .94. Item-total correlations for this sample ranged from .42 to .79. Based on a sample

of 252 Purdue University students who completed a 22-item version of the scale, coefficient alpha was .93. Item-total correlations for this sample ranged from .44 to .75, excluding the 1 item not on the current version. Coefficient alpha was .93 using data from another sample of 1,342 Purdue University students. Item-total correlations for this sample ranged from .42 to .71, excluding the 1 item not on the current version. A sample of 97 Purdue University students completed a slightly different version of the scale; the phrase *gay male* was substituted for *homosexual*. Coefficient alpha was .93, and the item-total correlations ranged from .40 to .77. Similarly, a sample of 117 Purdue University students completed a version of the scale in which the word *lesbian* was substituted for *homosexual*. Coefficient alpha was .92, and the item-total correlations ranged from .40 to .77. Kite and Branscombe (1989) administered the HAS to 440 college students. Coefficient alpha was .92, and the item-total correlations ranged from .34 to .74.

A sample of 26 college men and 54 college women completed the HAS on two occasions, with a 1-month interval between testings. The test-retest reliability was .71 (Kite & Deaux, 1986).

VALIDITY: Kite and Deaux (1986) found that college men scored significantly lower (more negative) than college women on the HAS. They also found that the items on the HAS loaded on a single major factor that accounted for 42.4% of the variance. Although a second factor accounted for 5.7% of the variance, the second factor was highly correlated with the first ($r = .73$).

Kite and Deaux (1986) created two versions of the HAS. In one version, the term *gay male* was substituted for *homosexual*; in the other version, the word *lesbian* was substituted for *homosexual*. After comparing responses to the two versions of the scale, Kite and Deaux concluded that "the number of items showing a significant difference is small [6 items] relative to the total, and the direction of the results is inconsistent. Therefore, it seems reasonable to assume that the scale would have good predictive ability for either target group" (p. 143).

Kite and Deaux (1986) related scores on the HAS to scores on other scales, including the FEM Scale (Smith, Ferree, & Miller, 1975) (see Beere, 1990), which is a measure of attitudes toward feminism; the Personal Attributes Questionnaire (PAQ) (Spence, Helmreich, & Stapp, 1974) (see Beere, 1990), which is a gender role measure; the Bem Sex Role Inventory (BSRI) (Bem, 1974) (see Beere, 1990), which is another gender role measure; and the Self-Monitoring Scale (Snyder, 1974). The HAS was positively and significantly correlated with the FEM Scale ($r = .50$), showing that persons who expressed more traditional attitudes on the FEM scale were likely to express more negative attitudes toward homosexuals. The correlations between scores on the HAS and the PAQ, the BSRI, and the Self-Monitoring Scale were quite low and generally not significant.

Kite and Branscombe (1989) tested 440 college students with the HAS and several other measures: the Personal Attributes Questionnaire, the Marlowe-Crowne Social Desirability Scale (Crowne & Marlowe, 1964), Rosenberg's (1965) self-esteem scale, and two items assessing perceived masculinity and perceived femininity. The correlation between scores on the HAS and the Social Desirability Scale was −.03 (not significant). The other correlations involving the HAS were low, but because of the large sample size, they were statistically significant. Kite and Branscombe pointed out that "people with negative attitudes toward homosexuals see themselves as more masculine and less feminine than people with positive attitudes toward homosexuals" (p. [4]).

In a study looking at the behavioral consequences of attitudes regarding homosexuality, Kite and Deaux (1986) found that males with high scores on the HAS compared with males with low scores "react very differently when they believe they are interacting with a homosexual, as evidenced by their ratings of liking for that individual, the type of information they requested from him, the information they presented about themselves, and what they remembered about that person" (p. 137).

NOTES & COMMENTS: Many of the items on the HAS are phrased negatively; they use the word *not*. These items are sometimes confusing for respondents. It would be interesting to see whether the psychometric properties of the scale would change if the items were phrased affirmatively (of course, items can be phrased affirmatively and still express negative attitudes).

AVAILABLE FROM: Kite and Deaux, 1986

USED IN:

Kite, M. E., & Branscombe, N. R. (1989). *Psychometric properties of the Homosexuality Attitude Scale.* Paper submitted for presentation.

Kite, M. E., & Deaux, K. (1986). Attitudes toward homosexuality: Assessment and behavioral consequences. *Basic and Applied Social Psychology, 7,* 137–162.

BIBLIOGRAPHY:

Beere, C. A. (1990). *Gender role: A handbook of tests and measures.* Westport, CT: Greenwood.

Bem, S. L. (1974). The measurement of psychological androgyny. *Journal of Consulting and Clinical Psychology, 42,* 155–162.

Crowne, D., & Marlowe, D. (1964). *The approval motive.* New York: Wiley.

Rosenberg, M. (1965). *Society and the adolescent self-image.* Princeton: Princeton University Press.

Smith, E. R., Ferree, M. M., & Miller, F. E. (1975). A scale of attitudes toward feminism. *Representative Research in Social Psychology, 6,* 51–56.

Snyder, M. (1974). The self-monitoring of expressive behavior. *Journal of Personality and Social Psychology, 30,* 526–537.

Spence, J. T., Helmreich, R. L., & Stapp, J. (1974). The Personal Attributes

Questionnaire: A measure of sex role stereotypes and masculinity-femininity. *Catalog of Selected Documents in Psychology, 4,* 43–44. (Ms. No. 617)

HOMOSEXUALITY ATTITUDE SCALE (HAS)
AUTHORS: Jim Millham, Christopher L. San Miguel, and Richard Kellogg
DATE: 1976
VARIABLE: Attitudes toward male and female homosexuals
TYPE OF INSTRUMENT: Alternate choice: true/false
DESCRIPTION: There are two forms of the Homosexuality Attitude Scale (HAS): male homosexuals are the target of the questions on one form, and female homosexuals are the target of the questions on the other. Each form has 38 items, but not all of the items contribute to the scores, so not all need to be included when the scale is administered. Six factors are represented on each form of the HAS. Repressive-Dangerous is represented by 6 items reflecting the view that homosexuality is dangerous and homosexuals should be socially and legally restricted; Personal Anxiety is represented by 8 items that reflect responses of disgust, avoidance, and anxiety in response to homosexuals; Preference for Female over Male Homosexuals and Preference for Male over Female Homosexuals are each represented by 2 items; Cross-Sexed Mannerisms is represented by 2 items reflecting the belief that homosexuals display mannerisms associated with the opposite sex; and Moral Reprobation is represented by 5 items on the male-target form and 7 items on the female-target form. These items reflect the view that homosexuals are sinful and morally wrong. For each item, the respondents are to indicate whether they believe the statement is true or false.
SAMPLE ITEMS: (all items are from the female-target version of the HAS)

(Repressive-Dangerous) Female homosexuals are more likely to commit crimes (nonsexual) than are heterosexuals.

(Personal Anxiety) I think female homosexuals are disgusting.

(Preference for Female over Male Homosexuals) I would rather have a homosexual brother than a lesbian sister.

(Preference for Male over Female Homosexuals) Male homosexuals are more revolting than female homosexuals (lesbians).

(Cross-Sexed Mannerisms) Most female homosexuals have some identifiable masculine characteristics.

(Moral Reprobation) Homosexual behavior between women is just plain sick.

PREVIOUS SUBJECTS: College students
APPROPRIATE FOR: Ages 16 and older

ADMINISTRATION: Self-administered; for the two forms together, completion time is about 20–25 minutes if all 38 items are used on each form.

SCORING: Ten separate scores are obtained: four factors from the male-target version of the HAS, four factors from the female-target version of the HAS, and two factors reflecting attitudes toward both male and female homosexuals. The last two factors pertain to the preference of male over female homosexuals and preference for female over male homosexuals; item scores from the two versions of the HAS are combined so that two rather than four scores are obtained on these factors. One point is counted for each item answered in the keyed direction. Higher scores reflect more of what is being measured, that is, more personal anxiety, more cross-sexed mannerisms, and so forth. Because a different number of items contribute to the different factor scores, the factors cannot be compared unless scores are converted to item means. Millham, San Miguel, and Kellogg (1976) reported means and standard deviations, by sex, for the different scores on the Homosexuality Attitude Scale.

DEVELOPMENT: A pool of 38 items was developed and used to create two 38-item forms of the HAS: a female-target and a male-target version. The two forms were administered to 795 college students with instructions to respond "true" or "false" to each item. Their responses were factor analyzed, separately for the two versions of the HAS. The six factors are comprised of the items with loadings of .45 or greater on the factor. On the male form, 23 items load on the six factors, and 2 of those items contribute to more than one factor. On the female form, 24 items load on the six factors, and 3 of those items contribute to more than one factor.

RELIABILITY: No information was provided.

VALIDITY: When the responses from 795 heterosexuals were analyzed, it was found that overall, persons expressed more negative attitudes toward same-sex rather than opposite-sex homosexuals. Specifically, for both male and female respondents, more personal anxiety was expressed for same-sex homosexuals compared to opposite-sex homosexuals. Male respondents advocated more repression against male homosexuals than did female respondents.

Having a homosexual friend was associated with lower personal anxiety scores, less support for repression of homosexuals, and lower moral reprobation scores.

NOTES & COMMENTS: (1) Millham et al. (1976) reported the percentage of variance accounted for by each of the six factors.

(2) Weinberger and Millham (1979) studied attitudes regarding homosexuality in relation to sex role attitudes and sex role identity. A sample

of 267 college students completed the HAS in addition to MacDonald's (1974) Sex Role Survey (see Beere, 1990) and the Bem Sex Role Inventory (BSRI) (Bem, 1974) (see Beere, 1990).

(3) Black and Stevenson (1984) modified the HAS. Twenty items were selected from the HAS to represent the factors of Personal Anxiety, Moral Reprobation, and Repressive-Dangerous. Half of the items were phrased to reflect positive attitudes, and half reflected negative attitudes toward homosexuals. Response options were increased from two to three by adding an "uncertain or undecided" category. All items referred to homosexuals in general; there were not separate versions for male homosexual and female homosexual targets. A different scoring system was used. Separate acceptance and rejection scores were calculated for each of the three factors included on the HAS. Furthermore, a total acceptance score and a total rejection score were figured. Black and Stevenson used the modified HAS along with the BSRI and the Personal Attributes Questionnaire (Spence, Helmreich, & Stapp, 1974) (see Beere, 1990) in a study of college students' self-reported sex role in relation to their attitudes toward homosexuality.

AVAILABLE FROM: Millham, San Miguel, and Kellogg, 1976

USED IN:

Black, K. N., & Stevenson, M. R. (1984). The relationship of self-reported sex-role characteristics and attitudes toward homosexuality. *Journal of Homosexuality, 10*, 83–93.

Millham, J., San Miguel, C. L., & Kellogg, R. (1976). A factor-analytic conceptualization of attitudes toward male and female homosexuals. *Journal of Homosexuality, 2*, 3–10.

San Miguel, C. L., & Millham, J. (1976). The role of cognitive and situational variables in aggression toward homosexuals. *Journal of Homosexuality, 2*, 11–27.

Weinberger, L. E., & Millham, J. (1979). Attitudinal homophobia and support of traditional sex roles. *Journal of Homosexuality, 4*, 237–246.

BIBLIOGRAPHY:

Beere, C. A. (1990). *Gender roles: A handbook of tests and measures*. Westport, CT: Greenwood.

Bem, S. L. (1974). The measurement of psychological androgyny. *Journal of Consulting and Clinical Psychology, 42*, 155–162.

MacDonald, A. P., Jr. (1974). Identification and measurement of multidimensional attitudes toward equality between the sexes. *Journal of Homosexuality, 1*, 165–182.

Spence, J. T., Helmreich, R. L., & Stapp, J. (1974). The Personal Attributes Questionnaire: A measure of sex-role stereotypes and masculinity-femininity. *Catalog of Selected Documents in Psychology, 4*, 127. (Ms. No. 617)

HOMOSEXUALITY SCALE

AUTHORS: John Dunbar, Marvin Brown, and Donald M. Amoroso

DATE: 1973

VARIABLE: Attitudes toward homosexuality
TYPE OF INSTRUMENT: Summated rating scale
DESCRIPTION: The Homosexuality Scale consists of 14 items regarding homosexuals: 6 items reflect a positive attitude toward homosexuality, and 8 items reflect a negative attitude. Each item is accompanied by six response options ranging from "strongly agree" to "strongly disagree."
SAMPLE ITEMS: Homosexuality is a rotten perversion and ought to be suppressed.

Homosexuals constitute a minority group and as such they are being denied certain of their basic civil rights.
PREVIOUS SUBJECTS: College students
APPROPRIATE FOR: Ages 16 and older
ADMINISTRATION: Self-administered; about 5–10 minutes
SCORING: Items are scored on a 6-point scale, with 0 points assigned to the response reflecting no prejudice and 5 points assigned to the response showing the most prejudice. The Homosexuality Scale yields a single score that is the sum of the item scores. Dunbar, Brown, and Amoroso (1973) tested 126 college students and obtained scores that ranged from 13 to 70. They reported a mean score of 36.52 (standard deviation of 11.85) based on testing 129 students.
DEVELOPMENT: An item pool was generated by taking items from the California F Scale (Adorno, Frenkel-Brunswik, Levinson, & Sanford, 1950) and a *Psychology Today* magazine survey (Shaver & Athanasiou, 1969) and by writing some original items based on the "major tenets of Gay Liberation groups in North America" (Dunbar et al., 1973, p. 274). The authors did not explain the procedures used to reduce the item pool to 15 items, but they did indicate that, after the pool was reduced, "one item was dropped as a result of the item analysis, leaving 14" (p. 274).
RELIABILITY: The internal consistency reliability of the Homosexuality Scale was .86 based on the responses from 126 college students. Item-total correlations for the 14 items ranged from .39 to .70, with 12 of the correlations exceeding .54.
VALIDITY: Dunbar et al. (1973) administered the Homosexuality Scale along with a measure of liberal-conservative attitudes and a measure of personal sex guilt to 126 college students. The Homosexuality Scale correlated .39 with the liberal-conservative measure and .24 with the sex guilt measure. Both of these correlations were statistically significant, suggesting, as expected, some relationship between the variables.

When Dunbar et al. (1973) divided their subjects into two groups, pro-homosexual (scoring below 26 on the Homosexual Scale) and anti-homosexual (scoring above 44 on the Homosexual Scale), they found significant differences between the two groups on both liberal-conservative attitudes and sex guilt. The two groups also differed significantly on a sex stereotype measure in which they were asked to label adjectives and nouns as male, female, or sex irrelevant. The pro-homosexual group was more likely to label the terms as sex irrelevant. Furthermore, the anti-homosexual group was more likely to label as homosexual any male exhibiting feminine characteristics.

NOTES & COMMENTS: (1) The negatively worded items on this scale are more strongly negative than items found on other homosexuality scales.

(2) Stokes, Fuehrer, and Childs (1980) used the Homosexuality Scale to test the hypothesis that homophobia affects men's willingness to self-disclose about intimate topics to same-sex target persons.

AVAILABLE FROM: Order from NAPS c/o Microfiche Publications, P.O. Box 3513, Grand Central Station, New York, NY 10163–3513; NAPS document no. 02005; for microfiche, in the United States, remit $4 .00 with order.

USED IN:

Dunbar, J., Brown, M., & Amoroso, D. M. (1973). Some correlates of attitudes toward homosexuality. *Journal of Social Psychology, 89*, 271–279.

Stokes, J., Fuehrer, A., & Childs, L. (1980). Gender differences in self-disclosure to various target persons. *Journal of Counseling Psychology, 27*, 192–198.

BIBLIOGRAPHY:

Adorno, T. W., Frenkel-Brunswik, E., Levinson, D. J., & Sanford, R. N. (1950). *The authoritarian personality*. New York: Harper.

Shaver, P., & Athanasiou, R. (1969). A research questionnaire on sex. *Psychology Today, 3*(2), 64–69.

INDEX OF HOMOPHOBIA (IHP)

AUTHORS: Walter W. Hudson and Wendell A. Ricketts

DATE: 1977

VARIABLE: Responses of fear, disgust, anger, discomfort, and aversion in dealing with gay people

TYPE OF INSTRUMENT: Summated rating scale

DESCRIPTION: The Index of Homophobia (IHP) consists of 25 statements pertaining to homosexuals. All items deal with affective reactions to homosexuals; in fact, most items begin, "I would feel." About half the items are positive statements about homosexuals; the other half are negative statements. Only 4 items specify the sex of the homosexual; 3 items refer to male homosexuals and 1 item refers to female homosexuals. Item responses are recorded on a 5-point scale ranging from "strongly agree" to "strongly disagree."

SAMPLE ITEMS: I would enjoy attending social functions at which homosexuals were present.

I would feel uncomfortable if I learned that my neighbor was homosexual.

PREVIOUS SUBJECTS: College students and adults, pastoral counselors

APPROPRIATE FOR: Ages 16 and older

ADMINISTRATION: Self-administered; about 10 minutes. Hudson and Ricketts (1980) suggested titling respondents' copies of the scale "Index of Attitudes Toward Homosexuals (IAH)" in order to reduce the likelihood of responses being affected by a social desirability response bias.

SCORING: Items are scored on a 5-point scale, with 5 points assigned to the response reflecting the most negative attitudes. A formula is used to find total scores: total = $(\Sigma X - N)(100)/[(N)(4)]$. ΣX is the sum of the item scores; N refers to the number of items actually completed. The formula ensures that all scores will be between 0 and 100. Hudson and Ricketts (1988) provided the following guideline for interpreting scores: respondents with scores between 0 and 25 are considered "non-homophobics," those with scores between 25 and 50 are considered "moderate non-homophobics," those with scores between 50 and 75 are labeled "moderate homophobics," and those with scores between 75 and 100 are considered "strongly homophobic."

DEVELOPMENT: Items were developed to be consistent with the definition of homophobia as set forth by the authors of the scale. Described below are suggestions for substituting five new items for five items of the original scale.

RELIABILITY: Using responses from 300 persons, most of them college students, Hudson and Ricketts (1980) found coefficient alpha to be .90.

VALIDITY: Hudson and Ricketts (1980) hypothesized that persons scoring as homophobic on the IHP would have conservative sexual attitudes. Their hypothesis was supported. In a study relating responses to the IHP with responses to the Sexual Attitude Scale (Hudson & Murphy, 1978) (see separate entry), the correlation between the two measures was .53.

Hudson and Ricketts (1980) hypothesized that "a high level of homophobia is likely to be a signal that the person has experienced the kinds of social learning and training that would make them more susceptible to a variety of personal problems and difficulties with interpersonal relationships" (p. 364). The hypothesis was supported. When IHP scores were related to severity of problems in 20 areas, 12 correlations were nonsignificant, and 7 correlations were positive and statistically significant; only 1 correlation was negative and significant.

To examine the content validity of the IHP, Hudson and Ricketts (1980) examined each item in light of their definition of homophobia: "personal affective responses of disgust, anxiety, aversion, discomfort, fear, and anger with respect to either proximal or distal contact or involvement with homosexual individuals" (p. 366). Four of the 21 items on the IHP failed to conform to this definition of homophobia. Hudson and Ricketts suggested replacing these items on the IHP.

IHP scores were negatively and significantly correlated with age (older respondents were less homophobic) and education (respondents with more education were less homophobic).

As predicted, Greendlinger (1985) found that scores on the IHP were positively correlated with scores on the F Scale (Cherry & Byrne, 1977), a measure of authoritarianism.

NOTES & COMMENTS: (1) Hudson and Ricketts (1980) emphasized that their measure is unique in its adherence to a narrow definition of homophobia. They defined homophobia as "an affective response to homosexual men and women" (p. 359) and described homophobia as a subset of homonegativism, "a completely general set of negative responses" (p. 359) to homosexual men and women.

(2) Hudson and Ricketts (1980) suggested that the four items lacking content validity be replaced with four other items they provided. They also suggested replacing the one item that had a low item-total correlation with a new item they provided.

(3) Hudson and Ricketts (1980) computed item-total correlations. All but one correlation was at least .40, and the median item-total correlation was .54. When item-remainder correlations were computed, all but one correlation was at least .34 and the median was .48.

(4) Hochstein (1986) reported IHP scores and demographic correlates for a sample of pastoral counselors.

(5) Edgar (1983) used the IHP in a study looking at whether homophobia affects willingness to self-disclose to persons of the same sex. He found that homophobia was not significantly related to self-disclosure.

(6) Whitley (1987) used the IHP along with several other measures to study the relationship of sex role beliefs, sex role self-concept, sex role behaviors, and attitudes toward homosexuality. His research also considered respondents' age, self-esteem, and conservatism.

AVAILABLE FROM: Hudson and Ricketts, 1980, 1988

USED IN:

Edgar, T. M. (1983, May). *Homophobia and intimate self-disclosure: Why aren't men talking?* Paper presented at the meeting of the International Communication Association, Dallas. (ERIC Document Reproduction Service No. ED 230 998)

Greendlinger, V. (1985). Authoritarianism as a predictor of response to heterosexual and homosexual erotica. *High School Journal, 68*, 183–186.

Hochstein, L. M. (1986). Pastoral counselors: Their attitudes toward gay and lesbian clients. *Journal of Pastoral Care, 40*, 158–165.

Hudson, W. W., & Ricketts, W. A. (1980). A strategy for the measurement of homophobia. *Journal of Homosexuality, 5*, 357–372.

Hudson, W. W., & Ricketts, W. A. (1988). Index of Homophobia. In C. M. Davis, W. L. Yarber, & S. L. Davis (Eds.), *Sexuality-related measures: A compendium* (pp. 155–156). Syracuse: Editors.

Whitley, B. E., Jr. (1987). The relationship of sex-role orientation to heterosexuals' attitudes toward homosexuals. *Sex Roles, 17*, 103–113.
BIBLIOGRAPHY:
Cherry, F., & Byrne, D. (1977). Authoritarianism. In T. Blass (Ed.), *Personality variables in social behavior* (pp. 109–133). Hillsdale, NJ: Lawrence Erlbaum.
Hudson, W. W., & Murphy, G. J. (1978). *Liberal vs. conservative orientations toward human sexual expressions*. Honolulu: University of Hawaii School of Social Work.

MACDONALD ATTITUDES TOWARD HOMOSEXUALITY SCALES (ATHS)

AUTHORS: A. P. MacDonald and Jim Huggins
DATE: 1973
VARIABLE: Attitudes toward homosexuality
TYPE OF INSTRUMENT: Summated rating scale
DESCRIPTION: There are three forms of the MacDonald Attitudes Toward Homosexuality Scales (ATHS). One form is labeled G (for "general") and pertains to homosexuals, sex unspecified; a second form is labeled M (for "male") and pertains to male homosexuals; and a third form is labeled L (for "lesbian") and pertains to lesbians. The 28 statements are essentially identical across forms except that the words *male* or *male homosexual* and *female* or *female lesbian* are substituted in the items. Six items are phrased in a positive direction; the remaining items reflect a negative attitude toward homosexuals and homosexuality. Each item is accompanied by a 9-point scale ranging from "strongly disagree" to "strongly agree."
SAMPLE ITEMS: Homosexuals should not be allowed to hold responsible positions.

I believe that all homosexuals should be confined and not released until cured.

PREVIOUS SUBJECTS: College students, 11th- and 12th-grade high school students, adult men, nurses; both homosexuals and heterosexuals have completed the scales
APPROPRIATE FOR: Ages 16 and older
ADMINISTRATION: Self-administered; about 15 minutes
SCORING: Items are individually scored on a 9-point scale, with higher scores assigned to the response reflecting a negative attitude toward homosexuality. Total scores can range from 28 (very positive attitude) to 252 (very negative attitude). Goldberg (1982) specified score ranges for labeling respondents' attitudes as tolerant, moderate, and intolerant.
DEVELOPMENT: No information was provided regarding the development of the general form of the ATHS. However, the forms specific to male homosexuals and female homosexuals were developed by altering the wording of the original form.

RELIABILITY: MacDonald and Games (1974) reported the results from earlier research that yielded the following internal consistency coefficients for Form G: .93 for both males and females, .96 for males alone, and .89 for females alone. From their own sample of 94 college men and 103 college women, about half of whom completed Form M of the scale and half of whom completed Form L, MacDonald and Games obtained an internal consistency reliability for Form M of .94 for male and female respondents, .93 for female respondents alone, and .93 for male respondents alone. For Form L, they obtained a reliability of .93 for male and female respondents, .92 for female respondents alone, and .94 for male respondents alone.

VALIDITY: MacDonald, Huggins, Young, and Swanson (1973) tested university students and faculty members and found that persons with more negative attitudes toward homosexuals were more likely to support a double standard of sexual behavior. They also found significant correlations between ATHS scores and scores on measures of sexual permissiveness and sex roles.

MacDonald and Games (1974) related scores on the ATHS to numerous other variables. Many of their findings offered support for the construct validity of the measure. For example, they found that negative attitudes toward homosexuals were associated with opposition to equality between the sexes, with support for authoritarianism, with intolerance of ambiguity, and with cognitive rigidity.

Krulewitz and Nash (1980) correlated scores on the ATHS with scores on the FEM scale (Smith, Ferree, & Miller, 1975) (see Beere, 1990), a measure of attitudes toward feminism. For their sample of 188 persons, the correlation was .65.

Lieblich and Friedman (1985) found that the scores of males taking the ATHS were higher (more negative) than the scores of females.

NOTES & COMMENTS: (1) Herek (1984) factor analyzed ATHS responses from 40 females and 32 males. He identified three interpretable factors. The first factor, the largest, included items "expressing moral condemnation of homosexuality and advocating repression of homosexuals" (p. 43); the second factor denied similarities between heterosexuals and homosexuals; the third factor included items expressing revulsion to or threat regarding homosexuality. He reported interfactor correlations ranging from −.25 to .53.

(2) Goldberg (1982) used the ATHS as a pretest and posttest measure in a study designed to determine the effectiveness of a program intended to change attitudes toward homosexuality. The pretest measure was used to divide respondents into three groups: those with tolerant attitudes (scores below 126), those with moderate attitudes (scores between 126 and 153), and those with intolerant attitudes (scores above 153). Iyriboz and Carter (1986) also used the ATHS as one of several pretest/

posttest measures intended to determine whether a human sexuality course would lead to a change in attitudes toward homosexuality.

(3) Price (1982) used a slightly modified version of the ATHS to determine high school students' attitudes toward homosexuals and homosexuality. Price had a difficult time finding a high school that would agree to let him conduct the research. Yarber and Yee (1983) used the ATHS in a study examining the relationship between attitudes toward homosexuality and respondents' affective orientation and sex guilt. Lieblich and Friedman (1985) used the ATHS in a cross-cultural study comparing the attitudes of American and Israeli college students. Devlin and Cowan (1985) tested 130 heterosexual males with the ATHS and related their scores to scores on eight intimacy scales and four scales measuring recollection of father's parenting styles. Ernulf and Innala (1987) used a 10-item Swedish-language version of the ATHS. They included the items that had the highest loadings on Herek's (1984) condemnation-tolerance factor.

AVAILABLE FROM: The scales can be purchased from the Center for the Study of Human Sexuality, 1208 Somerset Avenue, Austin, TX 78753

USED IN:

Devlin, P. K., & Cowan, G. A. (1985). Homophobia, perceived fathering, and male intimate relationships. *Journal of Personality Assessment, 49*, 467–473.

Ernulf, K. E., & Innala, S. M. (1987). The relationship between affective and cognitive components of homophobic reaction. *Archives of Sexual Behavior, 16*, 501–509.

Goldberg, R. (1982). Attitude change among college students toward homosexuality. *Journal of American College Health, 30*, 260–268.

Herek, G. M. (1984). Attitudes toward lesbians and gay men: A factor-analytic study. *Journal of Homosexuality, 10*, 39–51.

Iyriboz, Y., & Carter, J. A. (1986). Attitudes of a southern university human sexuality class toward sexual variance, abortion and homosexuality. *College Student Journal, 20*, 89–93.

Krulewitz, J. E., & Nash, J. E. (1980). Effects of sex role attitudes and similarity on men's rejection of male homosexuals. *Journal of Personality and Social Psychology, 38*, 67–74.

Lieblich, A., & Friedman, G. (1985). Attitudes toward male and female homosexuality and sex-role stereotypes in Israeli and American students. *Sex Roles, 12*, 561–570.

MacDonald, A. P., Jr. (1988). The MacDonald Attitudes Toward Homosexuality Scales. In C. M. Davis, W. L. Yarber, & S. L. Davis (Eds.), *Sexuality-related measures: A compendium* (pp. 168–171). Syracuse: Editors.

MacDonald, A. P., Jr., & Games, R. G. (1974). Some characteristics of those who hold positive and negative attitudes toward homosexuals. *Journal of Homosexuality, 1*, 9–27.

MacDonald, A. P., Jr., Huggins, J., Young, S., & Swanson, R. A. (1973). Attitudes toward homosexuality: Preservation of sex morality or the double standard? *Journal of Consulting and Clinical Psychology, 40*, 161.

Price, J. H. (1982). High school students' attitudes toward homosexuality. *Journal of School Health, 52*, 469–474.

Yarber, W. L., & Yee, B. (1983). Heterosexuals' attitudes toward lesbianism and male homosexuality: Their affective orientation toward sexuality and sex guilt. *Journal of American College Health, 31*, 203–208.

BIBLIOGRAPHY:

Beere, C. A. (1990). *Gender roles: A handbook of tests and measures.* Westport, CT: Greenwood.

Smith, E. R., Ferree, M. M., & Miller, F. D. (1975). A short scale of attitudes toward feminism. *Representative Research in Social Psychology, 6*, 51–56.

LESBIAN DEGREE OF INVOLVEMENT AND OVERTNESS SCALES (DIOS)

AUTHORS: K. D. Ferguson and Deana C. Finkler

DATE: 1978

VARIABLE: Degree of lesbian overtness and involvement

TYPE OF INSTRUMENT: Rating scale and report of age of performance of various behaviors

DESCRIPTION: The Lesbian Degree of Involvement and Overtness Scales (DIOS) consists of 37 statements representing two dimensions. The Involvement Scale contains 11 unique items, the Overtness Scale contains 22 unique items, and 4 additional items are included on both scales. The items from the two different subscales are intermingled with each other. Each item is responded to twice. First, respondents rate each item on the degree of comfort they feel about it; responses are recorded on a 10-point scale that ranges from 10 ("most comfortable") to 1 ("least comfortable"). After the comfort ratings are recorded, respondents review the items a second time, circling the number of each item that represents a behavior they have performed and writing in the age of the first time they performed the behavior. Items (behaviors) that they have not performed are left blank.

SAMPLE ITEMS: (Involvement Scale) Admit to other relatives, if asked, that I am involved with a woman.

(Overtness Scale) Have lesbian literature sent to my home.

(both scales) Sleep in the same bed with a woman.

PREVIOUS SUBJECTS: College women and older, lesbians

APPROPRIATE FOR: College women and older

ADMINISTRATION: Self-administered; about 20 minutes

SCORING: Four scores can be obtained from the DIOS: the sum of the ratings assigned to the items on the Involvement Scale, the sum of the ratings assigned to the items on the Overtness Scale, the number of Involvement behaviors performed, and the number of Overtness behaviors performed. For the first two scores, higher scores reflect greater comfort. For the latter two scores, higher scores reflect greater involvement and overtness.

DEVELOPMENT: The first author and two members of lesbian organizations independently developed lists of behaviors reflecting "interpersonal homosexual involvement or overtness of homosexuality" (Ferguson & Finkler, 1978, p. 213). A pool of 39 items was developed by these procedures. The three persons then independently sorted the items into those reflecting an overt-covert dimension and those reflecting interpersonal homosexual involvement. This produced a 37-item scale with 11 items concerning overtness-covertness, 22 items concerning interpersonal homosexual involvement, and 4 items pertaining to both topics.

RELIABILITY: Using data from 69 lesbians, feminists, and female college students, Kuder-Richardson reliability was .78 for the Involvement Scale and .70 for the Overtness Scale. Corrected split-half reliability was .95 for the Involvement Scale and .92 for the Overtness Scale.

Using a different sample of 63 lesbians, Ferguson and Finkler (1978) computed corrected split-half reliability. For the Involvement Scale, the reliability was .86; for the Overtness Scale, it was .84.

VALIDITY: DIOS was administered to three groups of women who were expected to score differently on the two portions of the scale. The groups, in decreasing order of involvement with homosexuality, were women from a lesbian resource center, facilitators of women's rap groups and members of a feminist organization, and college women enrolled in introductory psychology classes. The mean scores on the degree of comfort reported on the Involvement items and on the Overtness items were in the predicted direction (lesbians scored higher than feminists, who scored higher than students), and the differences among all pairs of groups were statistically significant. On both the Overtness and the Involvement scales, lesbians reported a higher mean number of behaviors when compared to the feminists and the students; the feminists and the students did not differ from each other.

Ferguson and Finkler (1978) found that for a group of lesbians, behaviors that evoked greater discomfort had lower frequencies. This was true for items on both the Involvement and the Overtness scales.

NOTES & COMMENTS: Ferguson and Finkler (1978) used the DIOS as one measure in a research study designed to examine the relationships of overtness in homosexuality, involvement in homosexuality, anxiety, and occupational status. Their intent was to test some hypotheses regarding homosexuality and neuroticism.

AVAILABLE FROM: Ferguson and Finkler, 1978, 1988

USED IN:

Ferguson, K. D., & Finkler, D. C. (1978). An involvement and overtness measure for lesbians: Its development and relation to anxiety and social zeitgeist. *Archives of Sexual Behavior*, *7*, 211–227.

Ferguson, K. D., & Finkler, D. C. (1988). Lesbian Degree of Involvement and Overtness Scale. In C. M. Davis, W. L. Yarber, & S. L. Davis (Eds.), *Sexuality-related measures: A compendium* (pp. 161–162). Syracuse: Editors.

8

Rape and Sexual Coercion

The subjects of rape and sexual coercion have attracted considerable attention in the past decade, particularly on university campuses. It is not surprising, therefore, that these subjects have also been the focus of numerous research studies, and researchers have developed many measures for studying these topics.

This chapter contains descriptions of 25 measures relating to rape and sexual coercion. The measures are arranged alphabetically by title and cover a broad range of topics, such as rape knowledge, rape prevention, rape blame, effects of rape, attitudes regarding rape, and experience with sexually coercive fantasies or behaviors. There are scales dealing with acquaintance rape and with stranger rape. There are scales appropriate only for females, only for males, and for both sexes. Some scales are labeled as being appropriate for high school students and older, and others are labeled as being appropriate for college students and older. In actuality, the scales are probably all appropriate for the same age range: adolescents and older. Before using a particular scale with a particular population, researchers would be wise to pilot test the measure to ensure that the items and the concepts are understandable to the respondents.

Most of the scales in this chapter are summated rating scales, ranging in length from 6 to 120 items. All have been developed relatively recently. The oldest scale is Barnett and Feild's (1977) Attitudes Toward Rape Questionnaire. The newest is Malamuth's (1989a, 1989b) Attraction to Sexual Aggression Scale. Although most of these scales have been used by few researchers, two scales are accompanied by over 20 references: Acceptance of Interpersonal Violence (Burt, 1980) and the Rape Myth

Acceptance Scale (Burt, 1980). Another three scales have at least a dozen citations: the Attitudes Toward Rape Questionnaire (Barnett & Feild, 1977), the Modified Fear Survey (Veronen & Kilpatrick, 1980), and the Sexual Experiences Survey (Koss & Oros, 1980). None of the scales was described in my original handbook (Beere, 1979).

Lack of reliability and validity can be serious problems with the scales described in this chapter. There were no data regarding the reliability of six of the scales in this chapter, and the data for other scales often suggested that the scale is not adequately reliable. Although there was some information entered into the VALIDITY section of each description, the information frequently provided very weak evidence of the scale's validity. Malamuth's (1989a, 1989b) Attraction to Sexual Aggression Scale had the most complete evidence of validity. Before the other scales in this chapter are used in further research, more evidence is needed to show that the scales are valid for measuring the constructs they are presumed to measure.

A common approach to studying attitudes regarding rape, rapists, and rape victims has been to conduct an attribution study in which respondents read or hear a description of a rape incident and then make some judgments about the event. For example, Pallak and Davies (1982) conducted a study in which 40 college women read one of four versions of a rape incident. All versions began with the same first paragraph. The second paragraph indicated either that the victim did or did not take precautions to reduce the likelihood of being raped, and the third paragraph indicated that the assailant either did or did not plan the rape. These variations were subtly communicated by varying the details of the rape incident. After reading one version of the incident, respondents answered a series of questions pertaining to the ideal length of imprisonment for the assailant, the extent to which the victim and the assailant were each responsible for the rape, the extent to which the victim and the assailant were each at "fault," how careless the victim was, how much the victimization was the result of chance, feelings about the victim, and identification with the victim. This study was typical of many research studies focusing on rape, either acquaintance or stranger rape. In addition to using written vignettes, researchers have used "mock trials . . . , videotaped scenarios . . . , still photography . . . and newspaper reports . . . as bases for inferring attitudes toward rape and rape victims" (Ward, 1988, p. 128). The researchers conducting these studies typically presume that their dependent measure is both reliable and valid, and they rarely mention these issues in their articles. No measure associated with these studies met the criteria for inclusion in this book. Nevertheless, researchers might find the method useful.

The short-term and long-term effects of rape are frequently assessed by measures that have more general applications rather than by measures used exclusively in rape research. For example, psychological symptomatology following rape has been measured by many different scales, including the Beck Depression Inventory (Beck, Ward, Mendelson, Mock, & Erbaugh, 1961), the Hopkins Symptom Checklist (Derogatis, Lipman, Rickels, Uhlenhuth, & Covi, 1974), and the SCL-90 (Derogatis, 1977).

BIBLIOGRAPHY:

Barnett, N. J., & Feild, H. S. (1977). Sex differences in university students' attitudes toward rape. *Journal of College Student Personnel, 18,* 93–96.

Beck, A. T., Ward, C. H., Mendelson, M., Mock, J., & Erbaugh, J. (1961). An inventory for measuring depression. *Archives of General Psychiatry, 4,* 561–571.

Beere, C. A. (1979). *Women and women's issues: A handbook of tests and measures.* San Francisco: Jossey-Bass.

Burt, M. R. (1980). Cultural myths and supports for rape. *Journal of Personality and Social Psychology, 38,* 217–230.

Derogatis, L. R. (1977). *The SCL-90 manual I: Scoring, administration and procedures for the SCL-90-R.* Baltimore: Clinical Psychometrics.

Derogatis, L., Lipman, R., Rickels, K., Uhlenhuth, E. H., & Covi, L. (1974). The Hopkins Symptom Checklist (HSCL): A self-report symptom inventory. *Behavioral Science, 19,* 1–15.

Koss, M. P., & Oros, C. J. (1980, May). *Hidden rape: A survey of the incidence of sexual aggression and victimization on a university campus.* Paper presented at the meeting of the Midwestern Psychological Association, St. Louis. (ERIC Document Reproduction Service No. ED 188 095)

Malamuth, N. M. (1989a). The Attraction to Sexual Aggression Scale: Part one. *Journal of Sex Research, 26,* 26–49.

Malamuth, N. M. (1989b). The Attraction to Sexual Aggression Scale: Part two. *Journal of Sex Research, 26,* 324–354.

Pallak, S. R., & Davies, J. M. (1982). Finding fault versus attributing responsibility using facts differently. *Personality and Social Psychology Bulletin, 8,* 454–459.

Veronen, L. J., & Kilpatrick, D. G. (1980). Self-reported fears of rape victims: A preliminary investigation. *Behavior Modification, 4,* 383–396.

Ward, C. (1988). The Attitudes Toward Rape Victims Scale: Construction, validation, and cross-cultural applicability. *Psychology of Women Quarterly, 12,* 127–146.

ACCEPTANCE OF INTERPERSONAL VIOLENCE (AIV)

AUTHOR: Martha R. Burt

DATE: 1980 (used 1977)

VARIABLE: Endorsement of force and coercion, particularly against women, as a means of solving problems or gaining compliance

TYPE OF INSTRUMENT: Summated rating scale

DESCRIPTION: The Acceptance of Interpersonal Violence (AIV) scale consists of six items, five dealing specifically with violence against women. Three of these five items pertain to the use of violence in relation to sexual activities. Half of the items support the use of violence; the other half oppose it. Each item is accompanied by a 7-point response scale ranging from "strongly agree" to "strongly disagree."

SAMPLE ITEMS: Sometimes the only way a man can get a cold woman turned on is to use force.

A man is never justified in hitting his wife.

PREVIOUS SUBJECTS: College students; adults, ages 18 and older; convicted rapists; child molesters

APPROPRIATE FOR: Ages 18 and older

ADMINISTRATION: Self-administered (although it has been used in an interview format); a couple of minutes

SCORING: Items are individually scored on a 7-point scale, with the higher number of points assigned to the response that is supportive of violence, that is, "strongly agree" for three items and "strongly disagree" for the other three items. Items are totaled to yield one score that can range from 6 (opposed to violence) to 42 (very supportive of violence). Burt (1980) tested 598 adults and obtained a mean score of 18.2 and a standard deviation of 5.9.

DEVELOPMENT: This scale was developed concurrently with four other scales: Adversarial Sexual Beliefs (ASB) (see separate entry), Sexual Conservatism (see separate entry), the Sex Role Stereotyping Scale (see Beere, 1990), and the Rape Myth Acceptance Scale (see separate entry). Pretesting involving a large item pool was conducted, and based on the results, about twice the number of items to be included on each of the final scales was included on an interview form. The interview was administered to 598 adults in Minnesota, and item analyses were performed on their responses. Based on these analyses, the "best items" were selected for the scale.

RELIABILITY: Burt (1980, 1983) administered the scale to 598 adults in Minnesota. She obtained an alpha coefficient of .59. Burt also reported the item-total correlations for each of the items. The values she obtained ranged from .21 to .40. Malamuth (1986) tested 155 men and obtained an alpha coefficient of .61.

VALIDITY: Burt (1980) looked at the relationship between Rape Myth Acceptance scores and a variety of other variables. She found that, of the attitude measures, scores on the AIV were the strongest predictor of Rape Myth Acceptance scores.

Check and Malamuth (1983) gave college students the Sex Role Stereotyping Scale and the AIV. As predicted, the correlation between scores on the two measures was significant ($r = .39$).

A sample of 598 adults heard a description of a scene involving a man and a woman. The scene varied according to the degree of violence described (three levels) and the closeness of the relationship between the man and woman (strangers, acquaintances, and married persons). The respondents were asked to rate the violence, rate the man in the story, and indicate what the woman did to "deserve" the violence. In addition, respondents completed several attitude scales, including the AIV. For the general public, high scores on this scale were associated with perceiving less violence in the stories (Burt, 1983).

NOTES & COMMENTS: (1) Although I have presented Burt's measures as five separate scales, and they can be used independently of each other, Burt actually developed her five measures together. The five scales are: AIV, ASB, Rape Myth Acceptance Scale, Sex Role Stereotyping Scale, and Sexual Conservatism. A subset of 37 items from the Burt scales has been used in research looking at the characteristics of rape victims who never reported their assault (Koss, 1985) and sexual offenders who were never detected (Koss, Leonard, Beezley, & Oros, 1985). When these researchers factor analyzed responses to the 37 items, they identified five factors that were quite comparable to the scales developed by Burt. The factors were labeled "Acceptance of Sexual Aggression; Conservative Attitudes Toward Female Sexuality; Rejection of Rape Myths; Heterosexual Relationships as Game-playing; and Unacceptability of Aggression" (Koss, 1985, p. 198).

(2) Briere, Malamuth, and Check (1985) factor analyzed the responses from 452 male college students. They identified three factors: "Women Enjoy Sexual Violence," "Acceptance of Domestic Violence," and "Vengefulness."

(3) In Burt and Albin's (1981) study, subjects heard one of six rape depictions that varied in terms of the victim's reputation (good or bad), the relationship between assailant and victim (no relationship or dating) and the amount of force used (low or high force). The subjects completed a variety of measures including the AIV, and they answered two questions: "How much do you feel the situation was a rape or was not a rape?" and "How strongly do you feel that you would convict or would not convict the man?" (p. 219).

(4) Briere and Malamuth (1983) sought to identify the variables that could predict likelihood to rape or likelihood to use sexual force. They tested college men with a variety of measures, including the Rape Myth Acceptance Scale, the AIV, and the ASB. To examine the impact of these three scales, Briere and Malamuth, using results of earlier research, reformed the responses into nine attitude scales.

(5) In a study comparing men's laboratory aggression with their "real-world" aggression against women, Malamuth (1983) tested 42 men with a variety of measures including the AIV. In other studies, Malamuth (1988, 1989a, 1989b) used the AIV to study sexual aggression.

(6) Rapaport and Burkhart (1984) and Malamuth (1986) conducted studies to investigate the relationship between college men's coercive

sexual behaviors and their responses on a variety of measures including the AIV.

(7) Check and Malamuth (1985) conducted a study to determine whether scores on the AIV and other attitude scores can predict "(a) reactions to fictional rape, (b) reactions to a report of a real rape, and (c) males' actual predictions about their own likelihood of raping" (p. 417). They also looked at how scores on the AIV were affected by observing a sexually violent film as compared to watching a control film (Malamuth & Check, 1981).

(8) Overholser and Beck (1986) compared incarcerated rapists, incarcerated child molesters, and three control groups on a variety of measures, including the AIV. Pryor (1987) studied college men and compared their scores on a measure of their likelihood to commit sexual harassment with their scores on a variety of other measures including the AIV.

(9) Muehlenhard and Linton (1987) used the AIV as one of several measures in their study of the risk factors for date rape and other forms of male-to-female sexual aggression. Briere (1987) used the AIV in a study of the antecedents of wife abuse. Demare, Briere, and Lips (1988) used the AIV as one of several measures in order to study the relationships between violent pornography and sexual aggression.

(10) Mayerson and Taylor (1987) conducted a study with 98 college women. They used eight items from the Sex Role Stereotyping Scale and selected those females scoring in the highest third and in the lowest third on stereotyping. Mayerson and Taylor then compared these two groups in terms of how pornography affects them. More specifically, they looked at how pornographic depictions that varied in degree of consent and degree of sexual arousal affected the two groups of women's scores on a variety of measures, including five items from the AIV.

AVAILABLE FROM: Burt, 1980, 1983; Burt and Albin, 1981

USED IN:

Briere, J. (1987). Predicting self-reported likelihood of battering: Attitudes and childhood experiences. *Journal of Research in Personality, 21*, 61–69.

Briere, J., & Malamuth, N. M. (1983). Self-reported likelihood of sexually aggressive behavior: Attitudinal versus sexual explanations. *Journal of Research in Personality, 17*, 315–323.

Briere, J., Malamuth, N., & Check, J. V. P. (1985). Sexuality and rape-supportive beliefs. *International Journal of Women's Studies, 8*, 398–403.

Burt, M. R. (1980). Cultural myths and supports for rape. *Journal of Personality and Social Psychology, 38*, 217–230.

Burt, M. R. (1983). Justifying personal violence: A comparison of rapists and the general public. *Victimology: An International Journal, 8*, 131–150.

Burt, M. R., & Albin, R. S. (1981). Rape myths, rape definitions, and probability of conviction. *Journal of Applied Social Psychology, 11*, 212–230.

Check, J. V. P., & Malamuth, N. M. (1983). Sex role stereotyping and reactions to depictions of stranger versus acquaintance rape. *Journal of Personality and Social Psychology, 45*, 344–356.

Check, J. V. P., & Malamuth, N. M. (1985). An empirical assessment of some feminist hypotheses about rape. *International Journal of Women's Studies, 8*, 414–423.

Demare, D., Briere, J., & Lips, H. M. (1988). Violent pornography and self-reported likelihood of sexual aggression. *Journal of Research in Personality, 22*, 140–153.

Koss, M. P. (1985). The hidden rape victim: Personality, attitudinal, and situational characteristics. *Psychology of Women Quarterly, 9*, 193–212.

Koss, M. P., Leonard, K. E., Beezley, D. A., & Oros, C. J. (1985). Nonstranger sexual aggression: A discriminant analysis of the psychological characteristics of undetected offenders. *Sex Roles, 12*, 981–992.

Malamuth, N. M. (1983). Factors associated with rape as predictors of laboratory aggression against women. *Journal of Personality and Social Psychology, 47*, 432–442.

Malamuth, N. M. (1986). Predictors of naturalistic sexual aggression. *Journal of Personality and Social Psychology, 50*, 953–962.

Malamuth, N. M. (1988). Predicting laboratory aggression against female and male targets: Implications for sexual aggression. *Journal of Research in Personality, 22*, 474–495.

Malamuth, N. M. (1989a). The Attraction to Sexual Aggression Scale: Part one. *Journal of Sex Research, 26*, 26–49.

Malamuth, N. M. (1989b). The Attraction to Sexual Aggression Scale: Part two. *Journal of Sex Research, 26*, 324–354.

Malamuth, N. M., & Check, J. V. P. (1981). The effects of mass media exposure on acceptance of violence against women: A field experiment. *Journal of Research in Personality, 15*, 436–446.

Mayerson, S. E., & Taylor, D. A. (1987). The effects of rape myth pornography on women's attitudes and the mediating role of sex role stereotyping. *Sex Roles, 17*, 321–338.

Muehlenhard, C. L., & Linton, M. A. (1987). Date rape and sexual aggression in dating situations: Incidence and risk factors. *Journal of Counseling Psychology, 34*, 186–196.

Overholser, J. C., & Beck, S. (1986). Multimethod assessment of rapists, child molesters, and three control groups on behavioral and psychological measures. *Journal of Consulting and Clinical Psychology, 54*, 682–687.

Pryor, J. B. (1987). Sexual harassment proclivities in men. *Sex Roles, 17*, 269–290.

Rapaport, K., & Burkhart, B. R. (1984). Personality and attitudinal characteristics of sexually coercive college males. *Journal of Abnormal Psychology, 93*, 216–221.

BIBLIOGRAPHY:

Beere, C. A. (1990). *Gender roles: A handbook of tests and measures*. Westport, CT: Greenwood.

AGGRESSIVE SEXUAL BEHAVIOR INVENTORY

AUTHOR: Donald L. Mosher

DATE: 1986

VARIABLE: Frequency of aggressive sexual behavior

TYPE OF INSTRUMENT: Summated rating scale
DESCRIPTION: The Aggressive Sexual Behavior Inventory consists of 20 items loading on six factors: Sexual Force (6 items), Drugs and Alcohol (3 items), Verbal Manipulation (4 items), Angry Rejection (2 items), Anger Expression (3 items), and Threat (2 items). All items are phrased in the same direction; that is, agreement always reflects the use of sexually aggressive behavior. Each item is accompanied by a 7-point response scale ranging from "never" to "extremely frequent."
SAMPLE ITEMS: (Sexual Force) I have calmed a woman down with a good slap or two when she got hysterical over my advances.

(Drugs and Alcohol) I have turned a woman on to some expensive drugs so that she would feel obligated to do me a sexual favor.

(Verbal Manipulation) I have told a woman that her refusal to have sex with me was changing the way I felt about her.

(Angry Rejection) I have told a woman I was going out with that I could find someone else to give me sex if she wouldn't.

(Anger Expression) I have gripped a woman tightly and given her an angry look when she was not giving me the sexual response I wanted.

(Threat) I have promised a woman that I wouldn't harm her if she did everything that I told her to do.
PREVIOUS SUBJECTS: College men
APPROPRIATE FOR: College men and older; in some cases, the scale might be appropriate for older high school boys
ADMINISTRATION: Self-administered; about 10 minutes
SCORING: Items are scored on a 7-point scale, with higher scores assigned to the responses reflecting greater frequency. Item scores are averaged to yield scores on each of the six factors. Mosher and Anderson (1986) reported factor means and standard deviations based on testing a sample of 175 college men. They also reported the percentage of respondents admitting to each item.
DEVELOPMENT: A pool of 33 items was administered to 175 college men. Their responses were factor analyzed, and the results were used to identify factors and select items representing each factor. All selected items had factor loadings greater than .45; the average factor loading was .64.
RELIABILITY: Mosher and Anderson (1986) computed coefficient alpha for each factor score. They obtained the following values for alpha: Sexual Force = .83, Drugs and Alcohol = .81, Verbal Manipulation = .77, Angry Rejection = .79, Anger Expression = .73, and Threat = .76. Mosher (1988) reported a coefficient alpha of .94 for the full-length scale.
VALIDITY: Mosher and Anderson (1986) administered the Aggressive Sexual Behavior Inventory and the Hypermasculinity Inventory (Mosher & Sirkin, 1984) (see Beere, 1990) to 175 college men. The Hypermasculinity Inventory yields a total score and three subscale scores: calloused

sex attitudes, violence as manly, and danger as exciting. The four scores from the Hypermasculinity Inventory were correlated with the seven scores (six factor scores and a total score) from the Aggressive Sexual Behavior Inventory. Of the 28 correlations, 25 were statistically significant.

Mosher and Anderson (1986) also found that men who scored higher on the Aggressive Sexual Behavior Inventory were more likely to report experiencing sexual arousal while imagining committing a rape, and they were more likely to feel interested and excited. Somewhat surprisingly, the men with higher scores also experienced more "anger, distress, fear, shame, guilt, and disgust . . . as they imagined themselves committing the crime of rape" (p. 87).

Anderson (cited in Mosher, 1988) found a significant negative correlation between scores on the Aggressive Sexual Behavior Inventory, and sex-guilt and hostility-guilt as measured by the Mosher Forced-Choice Guilt Inventory (Mosher, 1966) (see separate entry for Revised Mosher Guilt Inventory).

Zaitchik (cited in Mosher, 1988) tested 55 male rock musicians and found significant positive correlations between scores on the Aggressive Sexual Behavior Inventory and macho scores, cocaine use, amphetamine use, and marijuana use. He found a significant negative correlation with a measure of life satisfaction.

NOTES & COMMENTS: (1) The sensitive and somewhat self-incriminating nature of the items on this scale may lead respondents to underreport using the behaviors on the scale.

(2) Given that some of the factors contain few items, the internal consistencies of the factor scores seem quite respectable.

(3) Mosher (1988) indicated that a 10-item short form of the scale can be used. The internal consistency of the short form was .87 when the scale was administered to 55 male rock musicians (Zaitchik cited in Mosher, 1988).

AVAILABLE FROM: Mosher and Anderson, 1986; Mosher, 1988

USED IN:

Mosher, D. L. (1988). Aggressive Sexual Behavior Inventory. In C. M. Davis, W. L. Yarber, & S. L. Davis (Eds.), *Sexuality-related measures: A compendium* (pp. 9–10). Syracuse: Editors.

Mosher, D. L., & Anderson, R. D. (1986). Macho personality, sexual aggression, and reactions to guided imagery of realistic rape. *Journal of Research in Personality, 20,* 77–94.

BIBLIOGRAPHY:

Beere, C. A. (1990). *Gender roles: A handbook of tests and measures.* Westport, CT: Greenwood.

Mosher, D. L. (1966). The development and multitrait-multimethod matrix analysis of three measures of guilt. *Journal of Consulting Psychology, 30,* 25–29.

Mosher, D. L., & Sirkin, M. (1984). Measuring a macho personality constellation. *Journal of Research in Personality, 18,* 150–163.

ATTITUDES TOWARD RAPE

AUTHOR: Hubert S. Feild

DATE: 1978

VARIABLE: Attitudes toward rape

TYPE OF INSTRUMENT: Summated rating scale

DESCRIPTION: The Attitudes Toward Rape scale contains 32 statements, half positively phrased and half negatively phrased. Three broad content domains are represented on the scale: the act of rape, the rape victim, and the rapist. The items, many of them reflecting rape myths, represent eight factors. Items are accompanied by a 6-point response scale ranging from "strongly agree" to "strongly disagree."

SAMPLE ITEMS: A woman can be raped against her will.

The reason most rapists commit rape is for the thrill of physical violence.

PREVIOUS SUBJECTS: General adult population, college students, incarcerated rapists, rape crisis counselors, police officers, physicians

APPROPRIATE FOR: High school students and older

ADMINISTRATION: Self-administered; about 10–15 minutes

SCORING: Items are individually scored on a 6-point scale. Eight factor scores are obtained using a procedure that produces "uncorrelated, standardized scores on the factors with M = 0 and SD = 1" (Feild, 1978, p. 161). Feild provided item means and standard deviations based on testing 1,448 subjects.

DEVELOPMENT: The author compiled a pool of 75 items including items relating to the "affective (feelings of liking-disliking), cognitive (beliefs, expectations), and conative (action orientation) components of rape attitudes" (Feild, 1978, p. 158). Using judgment, the author retained a pool of 37 statements that reflected comments or statements frequently found in the relevant literature and that were as "brief, unambiguous, and nonredundant as possible" (p. 158). The pool of 37 statements was administered to 400 college students—half female, half male—along with a 6-point response scale for expressing their attitudes. Based on item analysis procedures, a review of item content, and interviews with selected respondents, the author revised 4 items and deleted 5 items. The remaining 32 items comprise the scale.

After determining that the factor structures from the general adult respondents, the police officers, and the rape crisis counselors were quite similar, responses from 1,448 persons were factor analyzed in a single analysis. The factor analyses produced eight factors. The eight factors, accounting for 50% of the variance, were all considered interpretable and were labeled as follows: Factor 1, Woman's Responsibility in Rape Prevention; Factor 2, Sex as Motivation for Rape; Factor 3, Severe Punishment for Rape; Factor 4, Victim Precipitation of Rape; Factor 5, Normality of Rapists; Factor 6, Power as Motivation for Rape; Factor 7,

Favorable Perception of a Woman After Rape; and Factor 8, Resistance as Woman's Role During Rape. For five of these factors, high scores reflected either a pro- or anti-rape attitude. However, scores on three of the factors (Sex as Motivation for Rape, Normality of Rapists, and Power as Motivation for Rape) did not reflect either a positive or a negative attitude toward rape. Feild (1978) provided factor loadings for all items.

RELIABILITY: The lower bound of the reliability for each of the eight factors was .62 (Feild, 1978).

VALIDITY: Sex, race, and attitudes toward women were consistent predictors of factor scores for a sample of 1,056 adults (Feild, 1978). Specifically, sex was correlated with seven factors, attitudes toward women was correlated with six factors, and race was correlated with four factors.

Feild (1978) compared factor scores from four groups of respondents: adults, convicted rapists, police officers, and rape crisis counselors. As predicted, he found that rapists had more favorable views of rape than did rape crisis counselors. This was true on all five factors where it was possible to characterize the direction of scoring as positive or negative. Furthermore, as expected, rape crisis counselors perceived rape differently than did citizens, police officers, and rapists.

Larsen and Long (1987) tested college students and compared their scores on three measures: the Attitudes Toward Rape scale, the Rape Myth Acceptance Scale (Burt, 1980) (see separate entry), and the General Scale of Attitudes Toward Rape developed by Larsen and Long (see separate entry). The Attitudes Toward Rape scale was significantly and substantially correlated with both of the other scales. The correlation with the Rape Myth Acceptance Scale was .77; the correlation with the General Scale of Attitudes Toward Rape was .56.

NOTES AND COMMENTS: (1) Feild (1978) tested four groups of subjects: adults, convicted rapists, police officers, and rape crisis counselors. He also assessed their rape knowledge and their attitudes toward women, and he obtained the following personal information from them: age, sex, race, years of education, marital status, and personal knowledge of a rape victim. Feild was then able to examine which variables were the best predictors of rape attitudes in each of the four samples.

(2) Although I describe the Attitudes Toward Rape scale and the Attitudes Toward Rape Questionnaire (ATR) (Barnett & Feild, 1977) (see separate entry) as two separate scales, they are very closely related. The Attitudes Toward Rape scale contains 32 items, whereas the ATR contains only 25 items. The longer scale contains 22 items that are identical or nearly identical to items on the shorter scale. The longer scale also contains 2 items that are exactly opposite to 2 items on the shorter scale. Thus, there are only 7 items that are unique to the Attitudes Toward Rape scale.

(3) Larsen and Long (1988) used the Attitudes Toward Rape scale as one of several measures to establish the validity of their Traditional-Egalitarian Sex Role Scale (see Beere, 1990). Thomas (1982) used the Attitudes Toward Rape scale as one of several measures to assess the effectiveness of a program to train rape crisis counselors. Feild (1979) used the Attitudes Toward Rape scale to determine whether perceptions of a rape case would be affected by the "juror's" attitudes coming into the trial situation. Koss used a subset of 15 items from the Attitudes Toward Rape scale as one of several measures to examine the characteristics of rape victims who had never reported their rapes (Koss, 1985) and to examine the characteristics of undetected sexually aggressive men (Koss, Leonard, Beezley, & Oros, 1985). Garcia (1986) used the Attitudes Toward Rape scale in a study of the relationship between exposure to pornography and attitudes toward rape. Calhoun (1980) used the Attitudes Toward Rape scale to compare physicians and rape crisis counselors. Lester, Gronau, and Wondrack (1982) used the Attitudes Toward Rape scale as one of several measures to compare female police recruits with female college students.

(4) Costin, Kibler, and Crank (1982) used the Attitudes Toward Rape scale as the basis for developing a shorter scale of attitudes toward rape, which they named the R Scale (see separate entry). LeDoux and Hazelwood (1985) used a 39-item scale with many of their items adapted from the Attitudes Toward Rape scale. The scale had an alpha coefficient of .78. LeDoux and Hazelwood's article includes all 39 items and the results of a factor analysis.

AVAILABLE FROM: Feild, 1978

USED IN:

Calhoun, L. G. (1980, September). *Interpreting rape: Differences among professionals and non-professional resources*. Paper presented at the meeting of the American Psychological Association, Montreal. (ERIC Document Reproduction Service No. ED 198 472)

Costin, F., Kibler, K. J., & Crank, S. (1982, August). *Beliefs about rape and women's social roles*. Paper presented at the meeting of the American Psychological Association, Washington, DC. (ERIC Document Reproduction Service No. ED 222 533)

Feild, H. S. (1978). Attitudes Toward Rape: A comparative analysis of police, rapists, crisis counselors, and citizens. *Journal of Personality and Social Psychology, 36*, 156–179.

Feild, H. S. (1979). Rape trials and jurors' decisions: A psychological analysis of the effects of victim, defendant, and case characteristics. *Law and Human Behavior, 3*, 261–284.

Garcia, L. T. (1986). Exposure to pornography and attitudes about women and rape: A correlational study. *Journal of Sex Research, 22*, 378–385.

Koss, M. P. (1985). The hidden rape victim: Personality, attitudinal, and situational characteristics. *Psychology of Women Quarterly, 9*, 193–212.

Koss, M. P., Leonard, K. E., Beezley, D. A., & Oros, C. J. (1985). Nonstranger sexual aggression: A discriminant analysis of the psychological characteristics of undetected offenders. *Sex Roles, 12,* 981–992.

Larsen, K. S., & Long, E. (1987, April). *Attitudes toward rape.* Paper presented at the meeting of the Western Psychological Association, Long Beach, CA. (ERIC Document Reproduction Service No. ED 278 884)

Larsen, K. S., & Long, E. (1988). Attitudes toward sex-roles: Traditional or egalitarian? *Sex Roles, 19,* 1–12.

LeDoux, J. C., & Hazelwood, R. R. (1985). Police attitudes and beliefs toward rape. *Journal of Police Science and Administration, 13,* 211–220.

Lester, D., Gronau, F., & Wondrack, K. (1982). The personality and attitudes of female police officers: Needs, androgyny, and attitudes toward rape. *Journal of Police Science and Administration, 10,* 357–360.

Thomas, R. (1982). Training volunteers to provide crisis counseling to rape victims: An evaluation. *Crisis Intervention, 12,* 43–59.

BIBLIOGRAPHY:

Barnett, N. J., & Feild, H. S. (1977). Sex differences in university students' attitudes toward rape. *Journal of College Student Personnel, 18,* 93–96.

Beere, C. A. (1990). *Gender roles: A handbook of tests and measures.* Westport, CT: Greenwood.

Burt, M. R. (1980). Cultural myths and supports for rape. *Journal of Personality and Social Psychology, 38,* 217–230.

ATTITUDES TOWARD RAPE QUESTIONNAIRE (ATR)

AUTHORS: Nona J. Barnett and Hubert S. Feild

DATE: 1977

VARIABLE: Attitudes toward rape

TYPE OF INSTRUMENT: Summated rating scale

DESCRIPTION: The Attitudes Toward Rape Questionnaire (ATR) consists of 25 statements relating to rape, rapists, and rape victims. Most of the items relate to the following general topics: what causes rape, who is responsible for rape, how rape affects the victim, how the victim should respond during the rape, and how rapists should be treated. Each item is accompanied by a 6-point rating scale ranging from "strongly agree" to "strongly disagree." All of the items are phrased in the same direction; that is, a person who abhors rape would disagree with every item.

SAMPLE ITEMS: In most cases when a woman was raped, she was asking for it.

If a woman is going to be raped, she might as well relax and enjoy it.

PREVIOUS SUBJECTS: College students, adults

APPROPRIATE FOR: High school students and older

ADMINISTRATION: Self-administered; less than 10 minutes

SCORING: Items are individually scored on a 6-point scale, with 6 points assigned to the "strongly disagree" end of the continuum and 1 point assigned to the "strongly agree" end of the continuum. Item scores are summed to yield a total score. Low scores indicate an anti-victim, pro-rape sentiment. Barnett and Feild (1977) provided means and standard deviations, by sex, for each item on the scale.

DEVELOPMENT: Little information was provided regarding scale development. Barnett and Feild (1977) reported only that the 25 items were based on a comprehensive review of the relevant literature.

RELIABILITY: No information was provided.

VALIDITY: Barnett and Feild (1977) compared the item means for college men and college women. They found significant sex differences on 18 of the 25 items, with males scoring lower on 15 of those 18 items. A discriminant function analysis confirmed the sex differences.

NOTES & COMMENTS: (1) Thornton, Robbins, and Johnson (1981) factor analyzed responses from 173 college students and extracted four factors. Factor I, Victim Precipitation-Responsibility, contained 13 items and accounted for 56% of the variance; Factor II, Negative Evaluation, contained 3 items and accounted for 13% of the variance; Factor III, Sexual Motivation, contained 3 items and accounted for 12% of the variance; and Factor IV, Power Motivation, contained only 2 items. Four items did not load appreciably on any factor. Internal consistency was computed for each factor, and the results were .89, .54, .49, and .60 for Factors I, II, III, and IV, respectively. Yonker, Laubacher, and LaMarco (1986) conducted another factor analytic study using responses from 323 college students. They identified eight factors; all 25 items were included on the factors.

(2) Although I described the Attitudes Toward Rape scale (Feild, 1978) (see separate entry) and the ATR as two separate scales, they are very closely related. The Attitudes Toward Rape scale contains 32 items, whereas the ATR contains only 25 items. The longer scale contains 22 items that are identical or nearly identical to items on the shorter scale. The longer scale also contains 2 items that are exactly opposite to 2 items on the shorter scale. Thus, there are only 7 items that are unique to the Attitudes Toward Rape scale.

(3) Thornton et al. (1981) used scores on the Victim Precipitation-Responsibility factor to examine the relationship between differences in attributional tendencies and perceptions of victim's responsibility for her own victimization. In a similar study, Thornton, Ryckman, and Robbins (1982) obtained scores from the Victim Precipitation-Responsibility factor and examined their relationship to observers' sex, their attitudes toward women, and their degree of dogmatism.

(4) Yarmey and Jones (1983) showed college students a slide presentation of a sexual assault and implied rape and then assessed their memory for details of what they had seen. After measuring attitudes toward rape using the 21 items from the four factors identified by Thornton et

al. (1981), they tested the hypothesis that "witnesses who are more sympathetic to rape victims and hold stronger antirape attitudes may differ in memory performance from witnesses who have weaker antirape attitudes" (Yarmey & Jones, 1983, p. 90).

(5) Yonker et al. (1986) examined the relationships among scores on the eight factors they identified from the ATR, gender, and years in college.

AVAILABLE FROM: Barnett and Feild, 1977

USED IN:

Barnett, N. J., & Feild, H. S. (1977). Sex differences in university students' attitudes toward rape. *Journal of College Student Personnel, 18*, 93–96.

Thornton, B., Robbins, M. A., & Johnson, J. A. (1981). Social perception of the rape victim's culpability: The influence of respondents' personal-environmental causal attribution tendencies. *Human Relations, 34*, 225–237.

Thornton, B., Ryckman, R. M., & Robbins, M. A. (1982). The relationships of observer characteristics to beliefs in the causal responsibility of victims of sexual assault. *Human Relations, 35*, 321–330.

Yarmey, A. D., & Jones, H. P. (1983). Accuracy of memory of male and female eyewitnesses to a criminal assault and rape. *Bulletin of the Psychonomic Society, 21*, 89–92.

Yonker, R. J., Laubacher, C., & LaMarco, T. (1986). *Differences in college students' belief in common myths about rape by gender and year in college*. Unpublished manuscript. (ERIC Document Reproduction Service No. ED 280 332)

BIBLIOGRAPHY:

Feild, H. S. (1978). Attitudes toward rape: A comparative analysis of police, rapists, crisis counselors, and citizens. *Journal of Personality and Social Psychology, 36*, 156–179.

ATTITUDES TOWARD RAPE VICTIMS SCALE (ARVS)

AUTHOR: Colleen Ward

DATE: 1988

VARIABLE: Attitudes toward rape victims, particularly, "victim blame, credibility, deservingness, denigration, and trivialization" (Ward, 1988, p. 127).

TYPE OF INSTRUMENT: Summated rating scale

DESCRIPTION: The Attitudes Toward Rape Victims Scale (ARVS) contains 25 statements—8 reflecting positive attitudes about rape victims and 17 reflecting negative attitudes about rape victims. Two of the 25 items are taken verbatim from Feild's (1978) Attitudes Toward Rape Scale (see separate entry), and 5 items are revised from Feild's scale and from the Rape Myth Acceptance Scale (Burt, 1980) (see separate entry). Each item is accompanied by five response options: "disagree strongly, disagree mildly, neutral, agree mildly, agree strongly."

SAMPLE ITEMS: A raped woman is a less desirable woman.

A raped woman is usually an innocent victim.

PREVIOUS SUBJECTS: College students, doctors, lawyers, social workers, psychologists, and police in Singapore; college students in the United States; persons in New Zealand, West Germany, the United Kingdom, Malaysia, Israel, and Canada

APPROPRIATE FOR: High school students and older

ADMINISTRATION: Self-administered; about 10–15 minutes

SCORING: Items are individually scored on a 5-point scale ranging from 0 to 4. For 11 items, the "agree strongly" end of the continuum is assigned 4 points; for 9 items, scoring is reversed, and the "disagree strongly" end of the continuum is assigned 4 points. Item scores are summed to yield a total score that can range from 0 (favorable attitudes toward victims) to 100 (unfavorable attitudes toward victims). Ward (1988) provided normative information on total scores and on individual item responses.

DEVELOPMENT: There were three specific objectives for scale development: to develop a measure of attitudes toward rape victims rather than a measure of attitudes toward rape in general, rape tolerance, or rape prevention, to design items that were simple and concise and did not rely on idiomatic phrases, and to select items that had cross-cultural relevance. To achieve these objectives, a pool of 70 items—34 positively phrased statements and 36 negatively phrased statements—was developed. Approximately 15% of the statements were taken from existing rape measures (Feild, 1978; Burt, 1980). The items dealt with victim blame, victim responsibility for precipitating rape, victim denigration, victim believability, victim resistance, victim deservingness, and trivialization of victim's experiences. The item pool was administered to 411 college students in Singapore. The students were asked to express their own views on each item by using a 5-point scale ranging from "strongly agree" to "strongly disagree."

Item analyses were performed on the responses from the students. Those statements with item-total correlations below .30 were deleted, and the remaining items were subjected to a second item analysis. Three more items were deleted because of item-total correlations below .30. To refine the scale further, the author deleted 9 items because they only indirectly assessed attitudes toward victims, and 1 was deleted because it was culturally biased. This left a pool of 35 items from which 25 were selected to satisfy the following criteria: "the inclusion of the most varied, least repetitive items, the inclusion of favorable and unfavorable statements, and the omission of items with extreme responses" (Ward, 1988, p. 133).

RELIABILITY: Coefficient alpha based on testing 411 college students in Singapore was .83. Coefficient alpha for 572 college students in the United States was .86. A group of 48 college students in Singapore was tested on two occasions with a 6-week interval between testings. Test-retest reliability was .80. Ward (personal communication, November 1988) reported coefficient alpha for persons in different countries. For 330 persons in New Zealand, alpha was .88; for 196 persons in West Germany, alpha was .82; for 201 persons in the United Kingdom, alpha was .88; for 200 persons in Malaysia, alpha was .73; for 95 persons in Israel, alpha was .81; and for 181 persons in Canada, alpha was .88.

VALIDITY: A sample of 411 students completed the ARVS along with four other measures: Adversarial Sexual Beliefs, Sexual Conservatism, Acceptance of Interpersonal Violence, and Attitudes Toward Women. The first three measures are variations of Burt's (1980) scales (see separate entry for each title), and the last measure is a variation of Spence and Helmreich's (1972) Attitudes Toward Women Scale (see Beere, 1990). Correlations between the ARVS and the other four measures were all significant and in the predicted direction. The strongest relationship was with the Attitudes Toward Women Scale ($r = -.61$).

A sample of 510 adults including lawyers, social workers, psychologists, doctors, and police officers completed the ARVS. It was predicted that scores "would be differentiated by profession with social workers and psychologists producing the lowest scores . . . , police producing the highest scores . . . and doctors and lawyers falling between these two extremes" (Ward, 1988, p. 139). It was also predicted that women would score significantly lower than men. All of the predictions were supported by the data.

A sample of 411 college students in Singapore and another sample of 572 college students in the United States completed the ARVS. As predicted, males had significantly less favorable attitudes toward rape victims than did females. This was true for the total scale score for both groups of students. For the Singapore students, males had less favorable attitudes for 23 of the 25 items; for the American students, males had less favorable attitudes for 24 of the 25 items.

NOTES & COMMENTS: (1) For the scale development phase of this research and for one of the validity studies, the response rate was only 30%.

(2) Separate factor analyses were performed on the responses from college students in Singapore and college students in the United States. In both instances, the findings suggested that the ARVS is unidimensional, and both analyses produced similar loadings.

AVAILABLE FROM: Ward, 1988

USED IN:

Ward, C. (1988). The Attitudes Toward Rape Victims Scale: Construction, validation, and cross-cultural applicability. *Psychology of Women Quarterly*, *12*, 127–146.

BIBLIOGRAPHY:

Beere, C. A. (1990). *Gender roles: A handbook of tests and measures*. Westport, CT: Greenwood.

Burt, M. R. (1980). Cultural myths and supports for rape. *Journal of Personality and Social Psychology*, *38*, 217–230.

Feild, H. S. (1978). Attitudes Toward Rape: A comparative analysis of police, rapists, crisis counselors, and citizens. *Journal of Personality and Social Psychology, 36,* 156–179.

Spence, J. T., & Helmreich, R. L. (1972). The Attitudes Toward Women Scale: An objective instrument to measure attitudes toward the rights and roles of women in contemporary society. *Catalog of Selected Documents in Psychology, 2,* 66. (Ms. No. 153)

ATTRACTION TO SEXUAL AGGRESSION SCALE (ASA)

AUTHOR: Neil M. Malamuth

DATE: 1989

VARIABLE: Attraction to sexual aggression

TYPE OF INSTRUMENT: Questions followed by fixed response alternatives

DESCRIPTION: The Attraction to Sexual Aggression Scale (ASA) is a subset of items embedded in a longer questionnaire that assesses attraction to a variety of sexual acts. The longer questionnaire contains six different items/questions regarding whether the respondent has thought about engaging in various sexual activities, the attractiveness of the activities, the percentages of males and females who would find the activities arousing, the respondent's feelings of arousal in response to the activities, and the likelihood that one would perform the activities. Each item/question is followed by a list of 9 to 14 behaviors; the question is to be answered for each item in the list. There are 14 items that relate to rape, forcing a female (male) to do something sexual, and being forced to do something sexual. These 14 items comprise the ASA. A subset of 6 items comprises a short form of the ASA. The 6 items ask how likely the respondent is to rape and to force a female to do something sexual, what percentage of men are aroused by rape and forced sex, and what percentage of women are aroused by rape and forced sex.

SAMPLE ITEMS: If you could be assured that no one would know and that you could in no way be punished for engaging in the following acts, how likely, if at all, would you be to commit such acts? (followed by nine sexual behaviors; e.g., anal intercourse, bondage, pedophilia)

PREVIOUS SUBJECTS: College and adult men

APPROPRIATE FOR: College students and older

ADMINISTRATION: Self-administered; the complete scale can be completed in about 20–30 minutes

SCORING: To score the ASA, responses to the 14 questions are first standardized and then added together.

DEVELOPMENT: According to Malamuth (1989a), "the scale items were constructed a-priori to assess the construct of attraction to sexual aggression, although a couple of the items originally included were deleted from the final version" (p. 34).

RELIABILITY: Based on testing college men, coefficient alpha for the

ASA was .91. Item-total correlations for the 14 items ranged from .46 to .77, with a mean of .41. The short form of the ASA was administered twice, with about 1 week separating the two testings. The first administration yielded a coefficient alpha of .84; the second administration yielded a coefficient alpha of .91. The test-retest reliability between the two testings was .76 (Malamuth, 1989a).

Malamuth (1989b) used a 10-item version of the ASA in two studies. He obtained an alpha coefficient of .88 in both studies and item-total correlations ranging from .41 to .71 in the first study and .46 to .75 in the second study.

VALIDITY: The correlation between the short form ASA and the 14-item ASA was .75 (Malamuth, 1989a).

The longer scale containing the ASA allowed for the identification of the following five subscales: Attraction to Bondage, Attraction to Unconventional Sex, Attraction to Conventional Sex, Attraction to Deviant Sex, and Attraction to Homosexuality. There was a significant correlation between rape attitudes and only one of these subscales, Attraction to Bondage. The strongest relationship (r = .41), however, was between ASA scores and the measure of rape attitudes. Furthermore, when a regression analysis was performed, only ASA scores made a significant contribution to the regression equation (Malamuth, 1989a).

The short form of the ASA was also significantly correlated with rape attitudes (r = .46 at time 1, and r = .51 at time 2) (Malamuth, 1989a).

A measure of perceptions of a rape victim's experience was significantly correlated with scores on the 14-item ASA and with scores on the short form ASA at time 1 and time 2. Furthermore, correlations with different behavioral measures of sexual aggression were all significantly correlated with the 14-item ASA, and they were generally correlated with the short form of the ASA (Malamuth, 1989a).

Malamuth (1989b) related scores on a 10-item version of the ASA to numerous other variables, including eight other measures that are described in this book: the Sexual Functions Scale (Nelson, 1978); the Rape Myth Acceptance Scale (Burt, 1980); the Acceptance of Interpersonal Violence (Burt, 1980); the Adversarial Sexual Beliefs (Burt, 1980); the Heterosexual Behavior Assessment Inventory (Bentler, 1968); the strain gauge (Fisher, Gross, & Zuch, 1965); the Sexual Experiences Survey (Koss & Oros, 1980); and the Hostility Toward Women Scale (Check, Malamuth, Elias, & Barton, 1985). Malamuth (1989b) concluded that "on the whole, the findings provide additional support for the reliability, construct and discriminant validity of the Attraction to Sexual Aggression Scale. The data showed theoretically expected relationships between this scale and attitudinal, affective, motivational, emotional, personality, and behavioral measures" (p. 347).

Malamuth (1989b) found statistically significant but weak correlations between ASA scores and scores on the Marlowe-Crowne Social Desirability Scale (Crowne & Marlowe, 1960).

NOTES & COMMENTS: (1) A factor analysis of the ASA items produced one factor with an eigenvalue of 6.45; the factor accounted for 46.1% of the variance (Malamuth, 1989a). No other factors seemed to be worth retaining. Malamuth (1989b) conducted factor analyses using a 10-item version of the ASA with two different samples of respondents. In each factor analysis, the first factor had an eigenvalue greater than 5.00, accounted for over 50% of the variance, and yielded factor loadings above .45 on all items.

(2) Other measures of attraction to deviant behavior did not correlate with the various criterion measures. This refutes the argument that the ASA findings can be attributed to a "deviation hypothesis" or a "response set" explanation (Malamuth, 1989a).

(3) The number of response options is not consistent across questions. Malamuth (1989a) suggested that future research might use five or nine response options for every question.

AVAILABLE FROM: Malamuth, 1989a

USED IN:

Malamuth, N. M. (1989a). The Attraction to Sexual Aggression Scale: Part one. *Journal of Sex Research, 26,* 26–49.

Malamuth, N. M. (1989b). The Attraction to Sexual Aggression Scale: Part two. *Journal of Sex Research, 26,* 324–354.

BIBLIOGRAPHY:

Bentler, P. M. (1968). Heterosexual Behavior Assessment—I. Males. *Behaviour Research and Therapy, 6,* 21–25.

Burt, M. R. (1980). Cultural myths and supports for rape. *Journal of Personality and Social Psychology, 38,* 217–230.

Check, J. V. P., Malamuth, N. M., Elias, B., & Barton, S. A. (1985). On hostile ground. *Psychology Today, 19*(4), 56–61.

Crowne, D. P., & Marlowe, D. (1960). A new scale of social desirability independent of psychopathology. *Journal of Consulting Psychology, 24,* 349–354.

Fisher, C., Gross, J., & Zuch, J. (1965). Cycle of penile erection synchronous with dreaming (REM) sleep. *Archives of General Psychiatry, 12,* 29–45.

Koss, M. P., & Oros, C. J. (1980, May). *Hidden rape: A survey of the incidence of sexual aggression and victimization on a university campus.* Paper presented at the meeting of the Midwestern Psychological Association, St. Louis, MO. (ERIC Document Reproduction Service No. ED 188 095)

Nelson, P. A. (1978). Personality, sexual functions, and sexual behavior: An experiment in methodology (Doctoral dissertation, University of Florida, 1978). *Dissertation Abstracts International, 39,* 6134B.

ATTRIBUTION OF RAPE BLAME SCALE (ARBS)

AUTHORS: Margaret Anne Ward and Patricia A. Resick

DATE: 1980 (used 1976)

VARIABLE: Attribution of rape blame to victim, offender, society, or situation
TYPE OF INSTRUMENT: Summated rating scale
DESCRIPTION: The Attribution of Rape Blame Scale (ARBS) consists of 20 items, with 5 items attributing blame to each of four sources: the victim, the offender, society, and the situation. Each statement is accompanied by a 6-point response scale with the endpoints labeled "strongly disagree" and "strongly agree." An even number of response options is provided to prevent the choice of a neutral option.
SAMPLE ITEMS: (victim) Women entice men to rape them.
(offender) Most rapists are "mentally ill" or psychologically disturbed.
(society) There is a strong relationship between women being regarded as sex objects by our society and the crime of rape.
(situation) Rape is more likely to occur in slum or "bad" areas.
PREVIOUS SUBJECTS: College students, psychologists
APPROPRIATE FOR: High school students and older
ADMINISTRATION: Self-administered (although it has been administered by a telephone interview); about 10 minutes
SCORING: Items are individually scored, with 6 points assigned to the "strongly agree" end of the continuum and 1 point assigned to the "strongly disagree" end of the continuum. Scores can be obtained by summing items for four subscales: offender blame, victim blame, societal values blame, and situation blame.
DEVELOPMENT: Five graduate students and five community members were asked to generate statements accounting for blame in rape situations. Each person independently generated at least 40 statements, with at least 10 focusing on each of four sources of blame: victim, offender, society, and situation. The statements were then pooled, and the group that generated the items rank ordered them in terms of their relevance to each of the four sources of blame. The 8 statements judged most relevant to each factor were identified, and these 32 items were submitted to 15 undergraduate psychology students. The psychology students independently determined the blame source in each item. Five items for which there was consistent agreement on the blame source were selected for each of the four blame factors.
RELIABILITY: No information was provided.
VALIDITY: A factor analysis of responses from 409 college students (Ward, 1980) yielded four factors: Factor I, victim blame (6 items); Factor II, offender characteristics (4 items); Factor III, situational variables (4 items); and Factor IV, societal values (5 items). These results provided some confirmation for the construct validity of the ARBS. When the sample was divided into two subgroups—women who had not been assaulted and women who had been assaulted—the factor analytic results for the two groups were different. In general, the factor solution

for the women who had not been assaulted matched the factor solution for the entire sample. However, the four factors emerging from the factor analysis of responses from those who had been sexually assaulted were quite different. The factors were: Factor I, offender characteristics and situation blame; Factor II, victim blame; Factor III, societal values; and Factor IV, offender blame and not victim blame. In other words, the four sources of blame did not form four neat factors.

Resick and Jackson (1981) administered the ARBS to members of a state psychological association. They factor analyzed responses and extracted four factors: Factor I, victim blame (4 items); Factor II, societal values and sex and violence in the media (6 items); Factor III, offender blame (6 items); and Factor IV, sociological factors (4 items). After identifying the four factors, Resick and Jackson looked at whether there were age or gender differences on any of the factor scores. The only significant difference was on the societal values factor: women more than men tended to place the blame for rape on societal values.

NOTES & COMMENTS: (1) Ward (1980) looked at the relationship between factor scores on the ARBS and marital status, religion, and size of community.

(2) Resick and Jackson's (1981) factor analytic study was based on a sample that was very small ($n = 38$) relative to the number of items on the ARBS.

(3) The Jackson Incest Blame Scale (Jackson & Ferguson, 1983) (see separate entry) is an adaptation of the ARBS.

AVAILABLE FROM: Ward, 1980; Resick and Jackson, 1981

USED IN:

Resick, P. A., & Jackson, T. L., Jr. (1981). Attitudes toward rape among mental health professionals. *American Journal of Community Psychology, 9*, 481–490.

Ward, M. A. (1980). Attribution of blame in rape (Doctoral dissertation, University of South Dakota, Vermillion, 1980). *Dissertation Abstracts International, 41*, 1934B.

BIBLIOGRAPHY:

Jackson, T. L. & Ferguson, W. P. (1983). Attribution of blame in incest. *American Journal of Community Psychology, 11*, 313–322.

COERCIVE SEXUAL FANTASIES

AUTHORS: Virginia Greendlinger and Donn Byrne

DATE: 1987

VARIABLE: Experience of coercive sexual fantasies

TYPE OF INSTRUMENT: Summated rating scale

DESCRIPTION: The Coercive Sexual Fantasies scale consists of 10 items relating to the use of force, bondage, or pain in regard to sexual activity. The scale includes items in which the male is the recipient of the force, as well as items in which he is the perpetrator of the force. Each item is rated on a 7-point scale.

SAMPLE ITEMS: It would turn me on to be tied up and forced by a woman to have sex with her.

In my fantasies I am sometimes violent toward women.

PREVIOUS SUBJECTS: College men

APPROPRIATE FOR: Males, ages 16 and older

ADMINISTRATION: Self-administered; about 5 minutes

SCORING: Items are individually scored on a 7-point scale. Item scores are summed to yield a total score; higher scores reflect greater endorsement of sexually coercive fantasies.

DEVELOPMENT: College men responded to a 36-item questionnaire that asked them "to rate the frequencies of various sexual fantasies, preferences, and beliefs" (Greendlinger & Byrne, 1987, p. 4). Their responses were factor analyzed, and five factors had eigenvalues greater than 2.0. One factor—Coercive Sexual Fantasies—contained 10 items with factor loadings greater than .50, and these items comprise the scale.

RELIABILITY: Based on testing 114 college men, coefficient alpha was .91.

VALIDITY: Greendlinger and Byrne (1987) found a significant correlation (r = .51) between scores on the Coercive Sexual Fantasies scale and responses to a single-item question about the respondent's likelihood to commit rape if there was no chance of being caught.

Smeaton and Byrne (1987) tested 70 college men and obtained a correlation of .41 between scores on the Coercive Sexual Fantasies scale and the respondent's likelihood to commit rape; however, there was a nonsignificant correlation between Coercive Sexual Fantasies scores and the likelihood of acquaintance rape.

NOTES & COMMENTS: It was reported that "Greendlinger subdivided the 10-item scale into two 5-item scales involving bondage and mild pain (Items 1, 2, 3, 6, and 8) versus rape, force, and violence (Items 4, 5, 7, 9, and 10)" (Greendlinger & Byrne, 1987, p. 6). The two subscales produced more precise predictions of coercive sexual behavior.

AVAILABLE FROM: Greendlinger and Byrne, 1987

USED IN:

Greendlinger, V. (1986). Dispositional and situational variables as predictors of rape proclivity in college men (Doctoral dissertation, State University of New York, Albany, 1985). *Dissertation Abstracts International, 46,* 2852B.

Greendlinger, V., & Byrne, D. (1987). Coercive sexual fantasies of college men as predictors of self-reported likelihood to rape and overt sexual aggression. *Journal of Sex Research, 23,* 1–11.

Smeaton, G., & Byrne, D. (1987). The effects of R-rated violence and erotica, individual differences, and victim characteristics on acquaintance rape proclivity. *Journal of Research in Personality, 21,* 171–184.

COERCIVE SEXUALITY SCALE

AUTHOR: Karen Rapaport

DATE: 1982

VARIABLE: Frequency with which coercive sexuality is practiced
TYPE OF INSTRUMENT: Summated rating scale
DESCRIPTION: The Coercive Sexuality Scale consists of two parts. The first part lists 11 coercive sexual behaviors, and the second part lists 8 sexual methods, 7 of them coercive. All of the items begin with "I have" and most end with "against her wishes." The respondent is to indicate the frequency with which he has exhibited these behaviors and methods. The response options are "never, once or twice, several times, often."
SAMPLE ITEMS: (coercive sexual behaviors) I have placed my hand on a woman's thigh or crotch against her wishes.

(coercive sexual methods) I have used physical restraint with a woman.

PREVIOUS SUBJECTS: College men
APPROPRIATE FOR: High school males and older
ADMINISTRATION: Self-administered; about 5–10 minutes
SCORING: Items are individually scored on a 4-point scale, with higher scores assigned to greater frequencies.
DEVELOPMENT: No information was provided.
RELIABILITY: Internal consistency reliability, based on testing 201 college men, was .96.
VALIDITY: Although there is no direct evidence of validity, Rapaport and Burkhart's (1984) finding that "28% of this sample reported having used a directly coercive method at least once in the past, and 15% of the subjects reported having forced a woman to have intercourse at least once in the past" (p. 220) suggested that males were willing to admit to sexually coercive behaviors.
NOTES & COMMENTS: (1) Rapaport (1982) and Rapaport and Burkhart (1984) looked at the personality and attitudinal characteristics of sexually coercive college men.

(2) Smeaton and Byrne (1987) used the Coercive Sexuality Scale as one of several measures in a study looking at the effects of violence shown in R-rated films on proclivity for acquaintance rape.

AVAILABLE FROM: Rapaport, 1982
USED IN:

Rapaport, K. (1982). *Predicting sexually coercive behavior in college males*. Unpublished master's thesis, Auburn University, Auburn, AL.

Rapaport, K., & Burkhart, B. R. (1984). Personality and attitudinal characteristics of sexually coercive college males. *Journal of Abnormal Psychology, 93*, 216–221.

BIBLIOGRAPHY:

Smeaton, G., & Byrne, D. (1987). The effects of R-rated violence and erotica, individual differences, and victim characteristics on acquaintance rape proclivity. *Journal of Research in Personality, 21*, 171–184.

ENDORSEMENT OF FORCE SCALE

AUTHORS: Karen Rapaport and Barry R. Burkhart
DATE: 1982

VARIABLE: Endorsement of the use of force in sexual interactions
TYPE OF INSTRUMENT: Summated rating scale
DESCRIPTION: The Endorsement of Force Scale consists of descriptions of 20 situations in which a man and a woman are engaged in some activity when the man makes a physical overture that the woman rejects. The respondent indicates whether the man is justified in using force to continue his behavior. The situations vary in terms of "the degree of prior sexual contact, verbal behavior, clothing of participants, surroundings, type of relationship, and physical contact between participants" (Rapaport & Burkhart, 1984, p. 218). Items are accompanied by a 7-point scale ranging from "strongly agree" to "strongly disagree."
SAMPLE ITEMS: A man meets a woman in a bar and buys her several drinks. They go back to her apartment, turn the lights low and make out on the couch. He tells her that he would like to have sex, but she says no.

A steady couple goes to an X-rated movie. The woman says that she is excited, and invites the man to her house. She says that she wants to have sex, but then changes her mind and says no.
PREVIOUS SUBJECTS: College men
APPROPRIATE FOR: College students and older
ADMINISTRATION: Self-administered; about 10 minutes
SCORING: Items are scored on a 7-point scale, with higher scores associated with more support for the use of force in sexual interactions. Total scores can range from 20 (totally opposed to the use of force) to 140 (very supportive of the use of force).
DEVELOPMENT: No information was provided other than a statement that the scale was developed rationally.
RELIABILITY: Coefficient alpha for 201 college men was .89.
VALIDITY: Rapaport (1982) and Rapaport and Burkhart (1984) studied college men and reported a correlation of .23 ($p < .01$) between scores on the Endorsement of Force Scale and scores on a measure of the actual use of coercive behaviors in a sexual context.
NOTES & COMMENTS: Rapaport (1982) reported correlations between scores on the Endorsement of Force Scale and various other scales, including selected subscales of the California Psychological Inventory (Gough, 1975); several of Burt's (1980) scales, including Own Sex Role Satisfaction, Sex Role Stereotyping (see Beere, 1990), Adversarial Sexual Beliefs (see separate entry), Sexual Conservatism (see separate entry), and Acceptance of Interpersonal Violence (see separate entry); and the short form of the Attitudes Toward Women Scale (Spence, Helmreich, & Stapp, 1973) (see Beere, 1990).
AVAILABLE FROM: Rapaport, 1982
USED IN:

Rapaport, K. (1982). *Predicting sexually coercive behavior in college males*. Unpublished master's thesis, Auburn University, Auburn, AL.

Rapaport, K., & Burkhart, B. R. (1984). Personality and attitudinal characteristics of sexually coercive college males. *Journal of Abnormal Psychology, 93,* 216–221.

BIBLIOGRAPHY:

Beere, C. A. (1990). *Gender roles: A handbook of tests and measures.* Westport, CT: Greenwood.

Burt, M. R. (1980). Cultural myths and supports for rape. *Journal of Personality and Social Psychology, 38,* 217–230.

Gough, H. G. (1975). *California Psychological Inventory.* Palo Alto: Consulting Psychologists Press.

Spence, J., Helmreich, R. L., & Stapp, J. (1973). A short version of the Attitudes Toward Women Scale (AWS). *Bulletin of the Psychonomic Society, 2,* 219–220.

FEMINIST ATTITUDES TOWARD RAPE SCALE (FARS)

AUTHORS: Marsha B. Jacobson, Paula M. Popovich, and David W. Biers

DATE: 1980

VARIABLE: Attitudes toward rape on a traditional-to-feminist continuum

TYPE OF INSTRUMENT: Summated rating scale

DESCRIPTION: The Feminist Attitudes Toward Rape Scale (FARS) consists of 46 statements regarding rape. Items relate to such topics as definition of rape, prevention of rape, responsibility for rape, and consequences of rape. Half of the items are phrased to reflect a feminist attitude toward rape, and half are phrased to reflect a traditional attitude. Items are accompanied by four response options: "strongly agree, moderately agree, moderately disagree, strongly disagree."

SAMPLE ITEMS: The rape of a prostitute is just as serious as the rape of any other woman.

In a relationship, it's the woman's responsibility to set limits, and if things go too far, it's her fault.

PREVIOUS SUBJECTS: College students

APPROPRIATE FOR: High school students and older

ADMINISTRATION: Self-administered; about 15 minutes

SCORING: For each item, the most feminist response is assigned 3 points, and the most traditional response is assigned 0 points. Total scores can range from 0 to 138, but in actuality scores cover a narrower range. For a sample of 150 women, the range of scores was 71 to 132; for a sample of 150 men, the range of scores was 66 to 122. Jacobson, Popovich, and Biers (1980) provided normative information.

DEVELOPMENT: The initial version of the FARS consisted of 53 items that were included on the basis of face validity. These items were administered to 355 college students, and the analysis of their responses led to rewriting some items and omitting others. The second version of the FARS contained 46 items that were administered to another sample of college students. Statistical analysis of their responses led to further refinement of the scale; again some items were omitted, some were revised, and new items were added. The resulting 46-item scale constitutes the FARS.

RELIABILITY: Split-half reliability using the responses from 150 women and 150 men was .84 for women and .72 for men.

Jacobson et al. (1980) reported item-total correlations separately for males and females and for males and females considered together. Four items were not significantly correlated with total scores for women, but they were for men, and nine items that were not significantly correlated with total scores for men were significantly correlated for women. Only one item was not significantly correlated with total scores when data from men and women were considered together.

VALIDITY: On 33 of the 46 items and on total scores, women scored significantly higher (more feminist) than men.

A sample of 300 students who completed the FARS also completed the Attitudes Toward Women Scale (Spence & Helmreich, 1972) (see Beere, 1990). The correlations between the two scales were significant for both women (r = .69) and men (r = .54).

Assuming that students enrolled in a women's studies course were more profeminist than students in general, the FARS was administered to a sample from each group. For female respondents, there was the predicted significant difference between the two groups. Furthermore, when scores for men and women were considered together, the difference between the two groups was significant and in the predicted direction.

Jacobson et al. (1980) classified respondents on a feminism continuum, based on their agreement and/or disagreement with each of three definitions of rape. As expected, mean scores on the FARS were significantly higher for the most feminist group and lowest for the least feminist group.

NOTES & COMMENTS: Jacobson et al. (1980) factor analyzed male and female responses separately. They concluded that "the resultant factor structure is quite weak" (p. 18) and noted that the factor structures for men and women are quite different from each other.

AVAILABLE FROM: Jacobson, Popovich, and Biers, 1980

USED IN:

Jacobson, M. B., Popovich, P. M., & Biers, D. W. (1980). The Feminist Attitudes Toward Rape Scale. *Catalog of Selected Documents in Psychology, 10*(4), 88. (Ms. No. 2140)

BIBLIOGRAPHY:

Beere, C. A. (1990). *Gender roles: A handbook of tests and measures*. Westport, CT: Greenwood.

Spence, J. T., & Helmreich, R. L. (1972). The Attitudes Toward Women Scale:

An objective instrument to measure attitudes toward the rights and roles of women in contemporary society. *Catalog of Selected Documents in Psychology, 2,* 66. (Ms. No. 153)

FORCIBLE DATE RAPE SCALE

AUTHORS: R. Giarruso, P. Johnson, J. Goodchild, and G. Zellman
DATE: 1979
VARIABLE: Acceptability of forced sexual intercourse in a dating situation
TYPE OF INSTRUMENT: Summated rating scale
DESCRIPTION: The Forcible Date Rape Scale consists of nine items, each stating a condition preceding forced sexual intercourse. Respondents are to use a 5-point scale to indicate the acceptability or unacceptability of the male's behavior. The response options are "definitely acceptable, probably acceptable, not sure, probably unacceptable, definitely unacceptable."
SAMPLE ITEMS: If he had spent a lot of money on her.
If he was so sexually excited he couldn't stop.
PREVIOUS SUBJECTS: College students
APPROPRIATE FOR: High school students and older
ADMINISTRATION: Self-administered; a couple of minutes
SCORING: Items are scored on a 5-point scale, with 5 points assigned to the response "definitely unacceptable" and 1 point assigned to the response "definitely acceptable." Item scores are summed to yield a total score that can range from 9 (finds all conditions totally acceptable) to 45 (finds all conditions totally unacceptable).
DEVELOPMENT: No information was provided.
RELIABILITY: No information was provided.
VALIDITY: As predicted, Fischer (1986) found that lower scores on the Forcible Date Rape Scale were associated with more traditional attitudes toward women and greater sexual permissiveness. Also as predicted, Fischer (1987) found that Hispanic students were more accepting of date rape than were Caucasian students.
NOTES & COMMENTS: (1) Although there is not much information regarding this scale, it is included here because it measures a variable not measured by other scales.

(2) Fischer (1986) related scores on the Forcible Date Rape Scale to religiosity, tolerance of socially unapproved sexual behavior, sexual experience, sexual knowledge, attitudes toward women, a rape blame measure, and gender.
AVAILABLE FROM: Fischer, 1986
USED IN:

Fischer, G. J. (1986). College student attitudes toward forcible date rape: I. Cognitive predictors. *Archives of Sexual Behavior, 15,* 457–466.

Fischer, G. J. (1987). Hispanic and majority student attitudes toward forcible date rape as a function of differences in attitudes toward women. *Sex Roles, 17*, 93–101.

GENERAL SCALE OF ATTITUDES TOWARD RAPE (GATR)

AUTHORS: Knud S. Larsen and Ed Long
DATE: 1987
VARIABLE: Attitudes toward rape
TYPE OF INSTRUMENT: Summated rating scale
DESCRIPTION: The General Scale of Attitudes Toward Rape (GATR) contains 22 statements—10 positively keyed and 12 negatively keyed. The items cover a broad range of content, including the victim's responsibility for the rape, support for rape victims, marital rape, and rape and prostitution. About half of the items could be classified as rape myths. Items are accompanied by five response options ranging from "strongly agree" to "strongly disagree."
SAMPLE ITEMS: Some women at least secretly want to be raped.
Women who say no to sexual advances often mean yes.
PREVIOUS SUBJECTS: College students
APPROPRIATE FOR: Ages 16 and older
ADMINISTRATION: Self-administered; about 10 minutes
SCORING: Items are individually scored on a 5-point scale, with 5 points assigned to the response that indicates a negative attitude toward rape and 1 point assigned to the response indicating an accepting attitude regarding rape. Total scores range from 22 (very accepting of rape) to 110 (very opposed to rape).
DEVELOPMENT: A pool of 80 statements, half positively keyed and half negatively keyed, was administered to 72 college students. An item analysis was performed, and 22 statements were identified that had part-whole correlations above .54. These items comprise the final form of the GATR.
RELIABILITY: The split-half reliability, corrected by Spearman-Brown, was .68 for a sample of 71 college students. Based on responses from 356 college students, coefficient alpha was .92.
VALIDITY: As predicted, in two different samples, college females scored significantly higher than college males, indicating that males are more accepting of rape. Larsen and Long (1987) tested another group of 47 college men and 65 college women. These students completed the GATR along with Feild's (1978) Attitudes Toward Rape scale (see separate entry) and Burt's (1980) Rape Myth Acceptance Scale (see separate entry). As predicted, the correlation between the GATR and the Attitudes Toward Rape scale was significant ($r = .56$), as was the correlation between the GATR and the Rape Myth Acceptance Scale ($r = .63$).

To provide support for the construct validity of the scale, Larsen and

Long (1987) gave 356 college students the GATR, a locus of control scale, a measure of Machiavellianism, and an anomie scale. The correlations between GATR and the other measures were as follows: .31 for locus of control, .14 for Machiavellianism, and .13 for anomie. All of the correlations were significant in the predicted direction, but all were rather low.

NOTES & COMMENTS: (1) A factor analysis of the responses from 356 college students produced three factors: Factor 1 with 6 items was labeled "rape enjoyment," Factor 2 with 11 items was labeled "general attitude toward rape," and Factor 3 with 4 items was not interpreted because its eigenvalue was too low. The responses accounted, respectively, for 82.6%, 11.5%, and 5.9% of the variance.

(2) Item analysis procedures were used to select items for the GATR. In addition, Larsen and Long (1987) conducted an item analysis on the responses from another sample of students who completed the final version of the GATR. The results from this analysis were somewhat lower than the results obtained in the scale development phase of the research. Item-total correlations ranged from .33 to .72 (original results ranged from .54 to .91).

AVAILABLE FROM: Larsen and Long, 1987

USED IN:

Larsen, K. S., & Long, E. (1987, April). *Attitudes toward rape*. Paper presented at the meeting of the Western Psychological Association, Long Beach, CA. (ERIC Document Reproduction Service No. ED 278 884)

BIBLIOGRAPHY:

Burt, M. R. (1980). Cultural myths and supports for rape. *Journal of Personality and Social Psychology*, *38*(2), 217–230.

Feild, H. S. (1978). Attitudes Toward Rape: A comparative analysis of police, rapists, crisis counselors, and citizens. *Journal of Personality and Social Psychology*, *36*, 156–179.

MODIFIED FEAR SURVEY (MFS)

AUTHORS: Lois J. Veronen and Dean G. Kilpatrick

DATE: 1980

VARIABLE: Experience of rape-induced fear and anxiety

TYPE OF INSTRUMENT: Summated rating scale

DESCRIPTION: The Modified Fear Survey (MFS) is a list of 120 potentially fear-inducing objects, animals, and situations. For each item on the MFS, respondents indicate the extent to which they "are disturbed by each nowadays." There are five response options: "not at all, a little, a fair amount, much, very much."

SAMPLE ITEMS: Emergency rooms

Being awakened at night

Nude men

PREVIOUS SUBJECTS: Rape victims and nonrape victim controls

APPROPRIATE FOR: High school ages and older, particularly rape victims
ADMINISTRATION: Self-administered; about 30 minutes
SCORING: Each item is scored on a 5-point scale, with lower points assigned to the response indicating less fear. Thus "not at all" is assigned 1 point, and "very much" is assigned 5 points. Item scores are summed to yield an overall fear score. In addition, seven subscale scores can be computed: animal fears, classical fears, social-interpersonal fears, tissue damage fears, miscellaneous fears, failure/loss of self-esteem fears, and rape-related fears. An alternative scoring procedure involves obtaining scores on eight factors derived from the factor analytic study described below.
DEVELOPMENT: The MFS contains all 78 items from the Fear Survey Schedule III (Wolpe & Lang, 1964) and 42 additional items that were named most frequently by a group of five rape victims asked to recall fear-evoking situations and events relating to their rape experience.
RELIABILITY: Alpha coefficients for the subscales ranged from .81 to .94. The alpha coefficient for the total score was .98. Test-retest reliability over a 2.5-month interval ranged from .60 to .74 for the subscales. Test-retest reliability for the total score was .73.
VALIDITY: According to Seidner and Kilpatrick (1988), the MFS is generally able to differentiate between rape victims and nonvictims and is sensitive to treatment-induced changes. For example, Kilpatrick, Veronen, and Resick (1979b) reported that "rape victims were significantly more fearful than nonvictims, and victim fears declined somewhat over time but remained at high levels at the 6-month postrape period" (p. 133). The researchers also found that the content of victims' fears was rape related.

In some cases, however, significant differences were not found between victims and nonvictims. For example, the Rape subscale scores and total scores from a sample of 20 rape victims were compared to those from a comparison sample of 12 nonrape victims. There were no significant differences between the two groups on either of the scores (Veronen & Kilpatrick, 1980).

Ellis, Atkeson, and Calhoun (1981) found that victims of stranger rapes were significantly more fearful, as measured by the MFS, than were victims of nonstranger rapes.
NOTES & COMMENTS: (1) Resick, Veronen, Kilpatrick, Calhoun, and Atkeson (1986) factor analyzed MFS responses from 292 female rape victims and 163 nonvictims. They identified eight factors: Vulnerability, Classical Fear, Sexual Fears, Social Evaluation and Failure, Medical Fears, Agoraphobia, Unexpected or Loud Noises, and Weapons. Victims and nonvictims differed significantly on six of the eight factors.

(2) The MFS has been used to study the effects, including long-term effects, of rape (Calhoun, Atkeson, & Resick, 1982; Ellis et al., 1981; Girelli, Resick, Marhoefer-Dvorak, & Hutter, 1986; Kilpatrick, Resick, & Veronen, 1981; Kilpatrick, Veronen, & Resick, 1979a).

(3) Becker, Skinner, Abel, and Cichon (1984) used the MFS as one of several measures to evaluate the effectiveness of a treatment program for sexual assault victims.

AVAILABLE FROM: Lois Veronen, Human Development Center, Winthrop College, Rock Hill, SC 29733

USED IN:

Becker, J. V., Skinner, L. J., Abel, G. G., & Cichon, J. (1984). Time limited therapy with sexually dysfunctional sexually assaulted women. *Journal of Social Work and Human Sexuality, 3,* 97–115.

Calhoun, K. S., Atkeson, B. M., & Resick, P. A. (1982). A longitudinal examination of fear reactions in victims of rape. *Journal of Counseling Psychology, 29,* 655–661.

Ellis, E. M., Atkeson, B. M., & Calhoun, K. S. (1981). An assessment of long-term reaction to rape. *Journal of Abnormal Psychology, 90,* 263–266.

Girelli, S. A., Resick, P. A., Marhoefer-Dvorak, S., & Hutter, C. K. (1986). Subjective distress and violence during rape: Their effects on long-term fear. *Victims and Violence, 1,* 35–46.

Kilpatrick, D. G., Resick, P. A., & Veronen, L. J. (1981). Effects of a rape experience: A longitudinal study. *Journal of Social Issues, 37*(4), 105–122.

Kilpatrick, D. G., Veronen, L. J., & Resick, P. A. (1979a). The aftermath of rape: Recent empirical findings. *American Journal of Orthopsychiatry, 49,* 658–669.

Kilpatrick, D. G., Veronen, L. J., & Resick, P. A. (1979b). Assessment of aftermath of rape: Changing patterns of fear. *Journal of Behavioral Assessment, 1,* 133–148.

Resick, P. A., Veronen, L. J., Kilpatrick, D. G., Calhoun, K. S., & Atkeson, B. M. (1986). Assessment of fear reactions in sexual assault victims: A factor analytic study of the Veronen-Kilpatrick Modified Fear Survey. *Behavioral Assessment, 8,* 271–283.

Seidner, A. L., & Kilpatrick, D. G. (1988). Modified Fear Survey. In M. Hersen & A. S. Bellack (Eds.), *Dictionary of behavioral assessment techniques* (pp. 307–309). New York: Pergamon Press.

Veronen, L. J., & Kilpatrick, D. G. (1980). Self-reported fears of rape victims: A preliminary investigation. *Behavior Modification, 4,* 383–396.

Veronen, L. J., & Kilpatrick, D. G. (1983). Stress management for rape victims. In D. Meichenbaum & M. E. Jaremko (Eds.), *Stress reduction and prevention* (pp. 341–374). New York: Plenum.

Veronen, L. G., Kilpatrick, D. G., & Resick, P. A. (1979). Treating fear and anxiety in rape victims: Implications for the criminal justice system. In W. H. Parsonage (Ed.), *Perspectives on victimology* (pp. 148–159). Beverly Hills: Sage.

BIBLIOGRAPHY:

Wolpe, J., & Lang, P. J. (1964). A fear survey schedule for use in behavior therapy. *Behaviour Research and Therapy, 2,* 27–30.

INVENTORY OF SEXUAL PRESSURE DYNAMICS (ISPD)
AUTHOR: F. Scott Christopher
DATE: 1988
VARIABLE: Experience of sexual coercion
TYPE OF INSTRUMENT: Alternate choice, multiple choice, and open-ended
DESCRIPTION: The Inventory of Sexual Pressure Dynamics (ISPD) consists of a list of 21 sexual behaviors ranging from kissing to intercourse to mutual oral manipulation. For each of the behaviors, women are first asked if they have ever been pressured into the experience. If they have, they are asked to rank order the type of pressure they experienced: "(a) positive verbal statements (promises, statements of affection that later turned out to be untrue); (b) persistent physical attempts (continuous body contacts, roving hands); (c) verbal threats of force (threatened bodily injury or harm such as hitting or arm twisting); and (d) physical force (hit you, twisted your arm)" (Christopher, 1988, p. 258). They are next asked to describe their relationship to the man who most recently pressured them. The response options are "stranger, nonromantic friend, casually dating, seriously dating, engaged." Respondents are next asked to describe how the experience affected their relationships, and they are offered the following response options: "improved, got worse, stayed the same." Finally, an open-ended question asks women to describe how they felt about being pressured into the behavior. This series of questions is repeated for each of the 21 behaviors. When a woman says "no" to the initial question, thereby indicating that she has never been pressured into the behavior, she proceeds to the next behavior.
SAMPLE ITEMS: One minute continuous lip kissing
Mutual manipulation of genitals to mutual orgasm
Sexual intercourse face-to-back
PREVIOUS SUBJECTS: College women
APPROPRIATE FOR: Females, ages 16 and older
ADMINISTRATION: Self-administered; the time is a function of the number of behaviors that the respondent has been pressured into. If the woman has not been pressured into any, it would take about 5 minutes to complete; if the woman has been pressured into many of the listed behaviors, it could take a half-hour or longer, depending on the length of her responses to the open-ended question.
SCORING: Christopher (1988) did not report scores for individuals; rather he reported percentages associated with the various behaviors, the pressure types, and the relationship between the respondent and the person doing the pressuring. Responses to the open-ended question were content analyzed.
DEVELOPMENT: The list of 21 behaviors on the ISPD was taken from

Bentler's (1968) Heterosexual Behavior Assessment Inventory (see separate entry). This set of behaviors was selected for two reasons: the list contained sexual behaviors that often occur during premarital involvement, and it formed a Guttman scale progressing from the most common to the least common behaviors. The coefficient of reproducibility for Bentler's list was .99.

RELIABILITY: No information was provided regarding the reliability of the measure. However, for the content analysis of responses to the open-ended question, the percentage agreement between two coders was 92%.

VALIDITY: Women clearly reported sexual pressure. Over 95% of the respondents indicated that they had been pressured into at least one of the behaviors listed. The frequency with which women reported being pressured into sexual acts was greater with this measure than it was in other studies using other measures. Most likely the discrepancy existed because this study defined pressure more broadly. That is, other studies have looked only at sexually aggressive pressure, whereas this study included "positive statements" and "persistent physical attempts" as forms of pressure.

NOTES & COMMENTS: (1) In administering the ISPD, it is important to tell respondents whether they should answer only in terms of behaviors they actually performed or whether they should answer in terms of behaviors that a man tried to pressure them into but they resisted successfully.

(2) Christopher (1988) coded persistent physical attempts, positive verbal statements that later proved untrue, threats of force, and actual force as 1, 2, 3, and 4, respectively. He then applied Guttman analysis procedures and obtained a coefficient of reproducibility of .93. He found that this procedure produced a scale with a Kuder-Richardson reliability of .70.

AVAILABLE FROM: Christopher, 1988

USED IN:

Christopher, F. S. (1988). An initial investigation into a continuum of premarital sexual pressure. *Journal of Sex Research, 25,* 255–266.

BIBLIOGRAPHY:

Bentler, P. M. (1968). Heterosexual Behavior Assessment-II. Females. *Behavior Research and Therapy, 6,* 27–30.

R SCALE

AUTHORS: Frank Costin, Kathi J. Kibler, and Sharon Crank

DATE: 1982

VARIABLE: Support for stereotyped beliefs about rape

TYPE OF INSTRUMENT: Summated rating scale

DESCRIPTION: The R Scale contains 20 items pertaining to rape, rape victims, and rapists. Eleven of the items are phrased to reflect stereo-

typed or noncritical attitudes toward rape. Each item is accompanied by six response alternatives: "strongly agree, agree, not sure but probably agree, not sure but probably disagree, disagree, strongly disagree."
SAMPLE ITEMS: In order to protect the male, it should be difficult to prove that a rape has occurred.

No healthy adult female who resists vigorously can be raped by an unarmed man.

PREVIOUS SUBJECTS: College students, employed adults
APPROPRIATE FOR: High school ages and older
ADMINISTRATION: Self-administered; about 10 minutes
SCORING: Items are individually scored on a 6-point scale, with "strongly disagree" assigned 6 points for 9 of the items and "strongly agree" assigned 6 points for the other 11 items. Higher scores indicate greater agreement with negative stereotypes about rape. Costin, Kibler, and Crank (1982) provided means and standard deviations for college men, college women, employed women, and employed men.
DEVELOPMENT: The Attitudes Toward Rape scale (Feild, 1978) (see separate entry) provided the basis for scale development. Seven items were taken directly from Feild's scale, 9 items were revised from Feild's scale, and 4 items were written especially for the R Scale. A factor analysis of the 20 items yielded three factors: Factor 1, with 8 items, related to "women's responsibility and causal role in rape"; Factor 2, with 7 items, pertained to "role of consent in rape"; and Factor 3, with 5 items, dealt with "rapist's role and motivation" (Costin, 1985, p. 321).
RELIABILITY: Corrected split-half reliability estimates ranged from .67 for college men to .80 for employed women. Reliability coefficients were also computed for the factor scores. For Factor 1, they ranged from .57 to .67; for Factor 2, they ranged from .61 to .70; and for Factor 3, they ranged from .49 to .52.
VALIDITY: In addition to administering the R Scale to college students and employed adults, Costin et al. (1982) gave them a measure of attitudes toward women. As predicted, they found that "stereotyped beliefs about rape are positively related to restrictive beliefs about women's roles in society" (p. 3). These findings were true for total scores and factor scores for all four groups: college men, college women, employed men, and employed women.

Costin et al. (1982) and Costin (1985) also found, as expected, that the mean score for college women was lower than the mean score for college men, and the mean score for employed women was lower than the mean score for employed men.

NOTES & COMMENTS: (1) Items on the R Scale have been interspersed with items from a scale similar to Spence and Helmreich's (1972) Attitudes Toward Women Scale (Costin, 1985; Costin et al., 1982).

(2) Schwarz and Brand (1983) sought to determine whether thinking

about rape would affect women's self-esteem, their support for traditional sex roles, and their trust in other persons. Furthermore, they were interested in whether the impact of thinking about rape was mediated by one's attitudes about it. To measure rape attitudes, they used a subset of 10 items from the R Scale.

AVAILABLE FROM: Costin, Kibler, and Crank, 1982

USED IN:

Costin, F. (1985). Beliefs about rape and women's social roles. *Archives of Sexual Behavior, 14,* 319–325.

Costin, F., Kibler, K. J., & Crank, S. (1982, August). *Beliefs about rape and women's social roles.* Paper presented at the meeting of the American Psychological Association, Washington, DC. (ERIC Document Reproduction Service No. ED 222 533)

Schwarz, N., & Brand, J. F. (1983). Effects of salience of rape on sex role attitudes, trust, and self-esteem in non-raped women. *European Journal of Social Psychology, 13,* 71–76.

BIBLIOGRAPHY:

Feild, H. S. (1978). Attitudes Toward Rape: A comparative analysis of police, rapists, crisis counselors, and citizens. *Journal of Personality and Social Psychology, 36,* 156–179.

Spence, J. T., & Helmreich, R. L. (1972). The Attitudes Toward Women Scale: An objective instrument to measure attitudes toward the rights and roles of women in contemporary society. *Catalog of Selected Documents in Psychology, 2,* 66. (Ms. No. 153)

RAPE ATTITUDES SCALE

AUTHORS: Eleanor R. Hall, Judith A. Howard, and Sherrie L. Boezio

DATE: 1986

VARIABLE: Tolerance for rape

TYPE OF INSTRUMENT: Summated rating scale

DESCRIPTION: The Rape Attitudes Scale consists of 14 items pertaining to rape, rapists, and rape victims. Most of the items on the scale are phrased in such a way that agreement with the statement reflects the view that one is tolerant of rape and rapists and that women are often to blame for becoming rape victims. For adolescents, the wording of items is slightly altered so that the words *man* and *woman* are replaced with the words *guy* and *girl.*

SAMPLE ITEMS: Often, women falsely report a rape in order to get attention.

When a man is so turned on he can't stop, it is OK for him to force a woman to have sex even if she doesn't want to.

PREVIOUS SUBJECTS: Men convicted of rape, assault, and armed robbery; adult men from a city; females and males between the ages of 14 and 17; college students

APPROPRIATE FOR: High school students and older

ADMINISTRATION: Self-administered; about 5–10 minutes
SCORING: No information was provided. It was clear, however, that higher scores reflect greater tolerance for rape.
DEVELOPMENT: An item pool was compiled consisting largely of items taken from existing measures of attitudes toward rape. The pool was administered to three groups of men: men convicted and incarcerated for sexual assault, men convicted and incarcerated for other violent crimes (e.g., assault and armed robbery), and a control group of men from the community. The responses from the three groups of men were compared, and 15 items that differentiated between the control group and those convicted of sexual assault were selected for the scale. This 15-item version of the Rape Attitudes Scale was administered to high school and college students, and based on item-total correlations; 1 item was eliminated, leaving a 14-item scale.
RELIABILITY: Coefficient alpha for a sample of 973 adolescents was .66. For a sample of 293 college students, coefficient alpha was .78.

Hall, Howard, and Boezio (1986) reported item-total correlations for each of the 14 items on the Rape Attitudes Scale. For a sample of 973 adolescents, the correlations ranged from .16 to .49. For a sample of 293 college students, the correlations ranged from .21 to .64.
VALIDITY: Hall et al. (1986) found that college men showed greater tolerance for rape than did college women. These findings were consistent with results from other published studies, but they were not replicated in the analysis of the data from adolescents.

Hall et al. (1986) also gave college students the Heterosexual Relationships Scale (see separate entry) that they constructed to measure the degree of sexism in attitudes toward male-female relationships. As predicted, the correlation between the two measures was positive and significant. The authors concluded that "those who tolerated rape tended to perceive women as sex objects and to condone male dominance of women" (Hall et al., 1986, p. 112). The researchers also administered Gough's (1960) Socialization Scale and found a significant, negative correlation between Gough's scale and tolerance of rape; that is, those who were more tolerant of rape tended to be "reckless, rebellious, impulsive, and cynical rather than conforming, responsible, cooperative, and kind" (Hall et al., 1986, p. 114).
NOTES & COMMENTS: Howard (1984) used the Attitudes Toward Heterosexual Behavior Scale, a 45-item scale combining the Rape Attitudes Scale, items from the Heterosexual Relationships Scale, and some additional items. Howard was interested in whether gender role attitudes affected attributions of victim blame.
AVAILABLE FROM: Hall, Howard, and Boezio, 1986
USED IN:

Hall, E. R., Howard, J. A., & Boezio, S. L. (1986). Tolerance of rape: A sexist or antisocial attitude? *Psychology of Women Quarterly, 10,* 101–118.

Howard, J. A. (1984). Societal influences on attribution? Blaming some victims more than others. *Journal of Personality and Social Psychology, 47,* 494–505.
BIBLIOGRAPHY:
Gough, H. G. (1960). Theory and measurement of socialization. *Journal of Consulting Psychology, 24,* 23–30.

RAPE AWARENESS SCALE (RAS)

AUTHORS: Judy Schwartz, Heather Williams, and Fran Pepitone-Rockwell

DATE: 1983

VARIABLE: Knowledge about the causes, nature, and prevention of rape

TYPE OF INSTRUMENT: Summated rating scale

DESCRIPTION: The Rape Awareness Scale (RAS) consists of 19 items regarding the causes, nature, and prevention of rape. Each item is accompanied by five response options ranging from "strongly agree" to "strongly disagree."

SAMPLE ITEMS: Most rapists are motivated by sexual passion.

A rape victim's past sexual history should be relevant evidence in the courtroom during a rape trial.

PREVIOUS SUBJECTS: Adult women

APPROPRIATE FOR: Females, ages 16 and older

ADMINISTRATION: Self-administered; about 10 minutes

SCORING: Items are individually scored on a 5-point scale. Higher scores are associated with greater knowledge about the causes, nature, and prevention of rape. Total scores can range from 19 to 95.

DEVELOPMENT: Based on existing theory and data, a pool of 21 items was constructed and submitted to five judges who independently rated the face validity of the items. The judges were women who had expertise in the area of rape; most were experienced in working with rape victims. The judges were asked to rate each item on a 5-point scale ranging from irrelevant to very greatly associated with rape. Using the ratings provided by the judges, the authors eliminated 2 items because their average ratings were low. Two other items were rephrased as a result of constructive feedback from the judges.

RELIABILITY: Based on testing a sample of 200 women, coefficient alpha was .78. Schwartz, Williams, and Pepitone-Rockwell (1983) also reported the value of coefficient alpha for 19 different 18-item versions of the scale; that is, coefficient alpha is reported for each 18-item scale that would result from deleting each item, one at a time. The results ranged from .76 to .79.

Corrected item-total correlations were reported for each of the 19 items on the scale. The correlations ranged from .14 to .59, with an average of .36.

VALIDITY: Two independent samples of adult women were tested with the RAS—one group of 17 women and the other of 19 women. When the responses of those with the highest 25% of the scores were compared with the responses of those with the lowest 25% of the scores, all items were found to differentiate clearly between the two groups.

Contrary to prediction, there was not a significant difference ($p > .05$) between the scores obtained by women living in an area where a serial rapist had been operating and women living in a different area.

Women who identified strongly with the women's movement and younger women scored significantly higher on the RAS; that is, they showed greater rape awareness. Similarly politically liberal and politically uncommitted women, compared to politically conservative women, scored significantly higher on the RAS. There were no significant differences on the RAS as a function of respondents' education or income level.

NOTES & COMMENTS: Given that the RAS appears to be a reasonable instrument, it is surprising that the literature search for this book did not identify other published studies that used the scale.

AVAILABLE FROM: Schwartz, Williams, and Pepitone-Rockwell, 1983

USED IN:

Schwartz, J., Williams, H., & Pepitone-Rockwell, F. (1983). Construction of a Rape Awareness Scale. *Victimology, 6*, 110–119.

RAPE EMPATHY SCALE (RES)

AUTHORS: Sheila R. Deitz, Karen Tiemann Blackwell, Paul C. Daley, and Brenda J. Bentley

DATE: 1980

VARIABLE: Empathy toward the rape victim and the rapist in a heterosexual rape situation

TYPE OF INSTRUMENT: Summated rating scale

DESCRIPTION: The Rape Empathy Scale (RES) consists of 19 items, each a pair of statements. One statement in each pair expresses empathy for the rape victim, and the other expresses empathy for the rapist. Responses are expressed on a 7-point scale, with 1 indicating strong empathy for the rapist and 7 indicating strong empathy for the rape victim. A rating of 4 represents a neutral midpoint in which equal empathy is felt for the rapist and the victim.

SAMPLE ITEMS: (Pair 1, part a) I feel that the situation in which a man compels a woman to submit to sexual intercourse against her will is an unjustifiable act under any circumstances.

(Pair 1, part b) I feel that the situation in which a man compels a woman to submit to sexual intercourse against her will is a justifiable act under certain circumstances.

PREVIOUS SUBJECTS: College students, prospective jurors

APPROPRIATE FOR: High school ages and older
ADMINISTRATION: Self-administered; about 10 minutes
SCORING: Items are individually scored on a 7-point scale, with 7 assigned to the response indicating strong empathy for the rape victim and 1 assigned to the response indicating strong empathy for the rapist. Total scores can range from 19 (extreme empathy for the rapist) to 133 (extreme empathy for the rape victim).
DEVELOPMENT: The authors began with the following definition: "rape empathy . . . is the relative tendency for subjects to assume the psychological perspective of the rape victim or the rapist in viewing a rape incident" (Deitz, Blackwell, Daley, & Bentley, 1982, p. 374). The authors intended to develop a scale that reflected the adversarial process typical of a courtroom situation. That is, unlike the single-statement format of other rape attitude scales, they decided to present statements in pairs, on the grounds that paired, opposite statements more closely resemble the type of information presented to jurors by the defense and prosecution. Based on a thorough search of the relevant literature, they developed a scale of 20 pairs of statements, each pair accompanied by a 7-point response scale. A sample of 255 college men, 384 college women, 72 male prospective jurors, and 98 female prospective jurors completed the RES. Item-total correlations were computed using their responses. Other than 1 item, all were judged to have adequate item-total correlations, and so 19 items were retained for the final scale. The item-total correlations for jurors ranged from .33 to .75; for students, they ranged from .18 to .52.
RELIABILITY: Using the responses from the students and jurors, the authors computed coefficient alpha for the four sex-by-status groups. The results were .89 for female jurors, .85 for male jurors, .84 for female students, and .82 for male students.
VALIDITY: Deitz et al. (1982) tested many hypotheses to ascertain the validity of the RES. They found that females showed significantly more empathy for the rape victim than did males. Furthermore, women who had more contact with rape (rape victims and resisters) showed significantly more empathy for the rape victim than did women who had no direct experience with rape. There was a significant correlation between scores on the Attitudes Toward Women Scale (Spence, Helmreich, & Stapp, 1973) (see Beere, 1990) and scores on the RES, and there were significant correlations between the RES and support for a marital rape law, support for the women's movement, and support for the equal rights amendment. More positive attitudes toward women and women's issues were associated with more empathy for the rape victim. Male prospective jurors who expressed more empathy for the victim also reported less desire to rape a woman. Also, RES scores correlated sig-

nificantly with attributions of responsibility for rape and with social perceptions of rape victims and accused rapists. All of these relationships were predicted by Deitz et al. (1982).

To demonstrate the discriminant validity of the RES, Deitz et al. (1982) administered the Marlowe-Crowne Social Desirability Scale (Crowne & Marlowe, 1964) along with the RES. As predicted, the correlation was nonsignificant (r = .05).

Deitz and Byrnes (1981) reported that RES scores "have been significantly correlated with Ss' scores on . . . factors of the Attitudes Toward Rape Scale" (p. 21).

NOTES & COMMENTS: (1) The description given here indicates that the RES includes only 19 pairs of statements, but Deitz and Byrnes (1981) and Deitz, Littman, and Bentley (1984) reported using all 20 pairs of statements from the original version of the scale.

(2) Deitz and Byrnes (1981) and Deitz et al. (1984) tested whether rape empathy moderates judgments of a hypothetical rape case.

(3) Sedlak (1984a, 1984b) developed the 17-item Battering Empathy scale modeled after the RES. The scale assesses general attitudes about violence between intimates.

AVAILABLE FROM: Deitz, Blackwell, Daley, and Bentley, 1982

USED IN:

Deitz, S. R., Blackwell, K. T., Daley, P. C., & Bentley, B. J. (1982). Measurement of empathy toward rape victims and rapists. *Journal of Personality and Social Psychology, 43*, 372–384.

Deitz, S. R., & Byrnes, L. E. (1981). Attribution of responsibility for sexual assault: The influence of observer empathy and defendant occupation and attractiveness. *Journal of Psychology, 108*, 17–29.

Deitz, S. R., Littman, M., & Bentley, B. J. (1984). Attribution of responsibility for rape: The influence of observer empathy, victim resistance, and victim attractiveness. *Sex Roles, 10*, 261–280.

Sedlak, A. J. (1984a, August). *Understanding violence between intimate partners: The effects of personal experience and victim reactions on labelling it "battering" and allocating blame*. Paper presented at the meeting of the American Psychological Association, Toronto. (ERIC Document Reproduction Service No. ED 252 787)

Sedlak, A. J. (1984b, August). *Violence between intimate partners: Calling it "battering" and allocating blame*. Paper presented at the National Conference for Family Violence Researchers, Durham, NH. (ERIC Document Reproduction Service No. ED 253 789)

BIBLIOGRAPHY:

Beere, C. A. (1990). *Gender roles: A handbook of tests and measures*. Westport, CT: Greenwood.

Crowne, D. P., & Marlowe, D. (1964). *The approval motive*. New York: Wiley.

Spence, J. T., Helmreich, R. L., & Stapp, J. (1973). A short version of the Attitudes Toward Women Scale (AWS). *Bulletin of the Psychonomic Society, 2*, 219–220.

RAPE MYTH ACCEPTANCE SCALE (RMA)

AUTHOR: Martha R. Burt

DATE: 1980 (used 1977)

VARIABLE: Support for rape myths defined as "prejudicial, stereotyped, or false beliefs about rape, rape victims, and rapists" (Burt, 1980, p. 217).

TYPE OF INSTRUMENT: Summated rating scale

DESCRIPTION: The Rape Myth Acceptance Scale (RMA) consists of 19 items. The first 11 items are statements about women and rape; 10 of these statements are myths that reflect the belief that rape victims are somehow responsible for their own rape. One item indicates that any woman can be raped, thereby implying that a victim is not responsible for rape. Responses to these 11 items are recorded on 7-point scales ranging from "strongly agree" to "strongly disagree." The last 8 items ask questions. Two ask the respondent to estimate the percentage of reported rapes that are not really rape. Five response options are provided: "almost all, about 3/4, about half, about 1/4, almost none." Five items ask the likelihood of believing a claim of rape as a function of the type of person (e.g., best friend, Indian woman, young boy) reporting the rape. The response options are "always, frequently, sometimes, rarely, never."

SAMPLE ITEMS: A woman who goes to the home or apartment of a man on their first date implies that she is willing to have sex.

When women go around braless or wearing short skirts and tight tops, they are just asking for trouble.

PREVIOUS SUBJECTS: College students; adults, ages 18 and older; convicted rapists; child molesters

APPROPRIATE FOR: Ages 18 and older

ADMINISTRATION: Self-administered (although it has been administered in an interview format); about 10 minutes

SCORING: Items are individually scored on a 7-point scale and then summed to yield a total score. Higher scores reflect greater acceptance of rape myths.

DEVELOPMENT: This scale was developed concurrently with four other scales: Adversarial Sexual Beliefs (ASB) (see separate entry), Sexual Conservatism (see separate entry), Acceptance of Interpersonal Violence (AIV) (see separate entry), and Sex Role Stereotyping Scale (see Beere, 1990). Pretesting involving a large item pool was conducted, and based on the results, about twice the number of items to be included on each of the final scales was included on an interview form. The interview was administered to 598 adults in Minnesota, and item analyses were performed on their responses. Based on these analyses, the "best items" were selected for the scale.

RELIABILITY: Burt (1980, 1983) tested 598 adults and obtained an alpha coefficient of .875. She also computed item-total correlations and found they ranged from .27 to .62. Margolin, Miller, and Moran (1989) administered the RMA to 162 college women and 49 college men. Coefficient alpha was .874.

VALIDITY: Check and Malamuth (1983) gave college students the Sex Role Stereotyping Scale and the RMA. As expected, the correlation between the two measures was significant (r = .54).

In order to validate the RMA, Ashton (1982) administered it along with a dogmatism scale and a trustworthiness scale to 26 college students. As predicted, scores on the RMA correlated significantly with the dogmatism scale (r = .51) and the trustworthiness scale (r = −.46). Ashton also found a significant sex difference, with males scoring higher than females on the RMA.

A sample of 598 adults heard a description of a scene involving a man and a woman. The scene varied according to the degree of violence described (three levels) and the closeness of the relationship between the man and woman (strangers, acquaintances, and married persons). The respondents were asked to rate the violence and the man in the story and indicate what the woman did to "deserve" the violence. In addition, respondents completed several attitude scales, including the RMA. Rapists who had higher RMA scores perceived the man in the story as less violent and were more likely to exonerate him (Burt, 1983).

Larsen and Long (1987) administered the RMA along with their General Scale of Attitudes Toward Rape (GATR) (see separate entry) and Feild's (1978) Attitudes Toward Rape scale (see separate entry) to 112 college students. As expected, both of the correlations were significant and rather substantial. The correlation between the RMA and the GATR was .63; the correlation between the RMA and Feild's scale was .77.

Margolin et al. (1989) found a significant difference between the RMA scores of college women and college men.

NOTES & COMMENTS: (1) Although I have presented Burt's measures as five separate scales that can be used independently of each other, Burt actually developed the measures together. The five scales are AIV, ASB, RMA, Sex Role Stereotyping Scale, and Sexual Conservatism. Researchers have used 37 items from the Burt scales in research looking at the characteristics of rape victims who never reported their assault (Koss, 1985) and sexual offenders who were never detected (Koss, Leonard, Beezley, & Oros, 1985). When these researchers factor analyzed responses to the 37 items, they identified five factors that were quite comparable to the scales developed by Burt. The factors were labeled "Acceptance of Sexual Aggression; Conservative Attitudes Toward Female Sexuality; Rejection of Rape Myths; Heterosexual Relationships as Game-playing; and Unacceptability of Aggression" (Koss, 1985, p. 198).

(2) Briere, Malamuth, and Check (1985) factor analyzed the RMA responses from 452 male college students. They identified four independent factors and named them "Disbelief of Rape Claims," "Victim Responsible for Rape," "Rape Reports as Manipulation," and "Rape only happens to certain kinds of women."

(3) Burt (1980) looked at the relationship between RMA scores and a variety of attitude measures, personality characteristics, and personal experiences with rape or rape victims. The attitude measures included the Sex Role Stereotyping Scale, AIV, and the ASB.

(4) In Burt and Albin's (1981) study, subjects heard one of six rape depictions that varied in terms of the victim's reputation (good or bad), the relationship between assailant and victim (no relationship or dating), and the amount of force used (low or high force). The subjects completed a variety of measures including the RMA, and they answered two questions: "How much do you feel the situation was a rape or was not a rape?" and "How strongly do you feel that you would convict or would not convict the man?" (p. 219).

(5) In a study comparing men's laboratory aggression with their actual aggression against women, Malamuth (1983) tested 42 men with a variety of measures, including the RMA. Malamuth (1989a, 1989b) also used the RMA in his studies regarding sexual aggression in men.

(6) Briere and Malamuth (1983) sought to identify the variables that could predict likelihood to rape or to use sexual force. They tested college men with a variety of measures, including the RMA, the AIV, and the ASB. To examine the impact of these three scales, Briere and Malamuth, using results of earlier research, reformed the responses into nine attitude scales.

(7) Check and Malamuth (1985) conducted a study to determine whether acceptance of rape myths and other attitudes can predict "(a) reactions to fictional rape, (b) reactions to a report of a real rape, and (c) males' actual predictions about their own likelihood of raping" (p. 417). They also looked at how scores on the RMA were affected by observing a sexually violent film as compared to watching a control film (Malamuth & Check, 1981).

(8) Mayerson and Taylor (1987) conducted a study with 98 college women. They used the Sex Role Stereotyping Scale and selected those females scoring in the highest third and in the lowest third on stereotyping. Mayerson and Taylor then compared these two groups in terms of how pornography affects them. More specifically, they looked at how pornographic depictions that varied in degree of consent and degree of sexual arousal affected the two groups of women's scores on a variety of measures including 13 items of the RMA.

(9) Overholser and Beck (1986) compared incarcerated rapists, incarcerated child molesters, and three control groups on a variety of measures including the RMA. Pryor (1987) studied college men and

compared their scores on a measure of their likelihood to commit sexual harassment with their scores on a variety of other measures including the RMA. Larsen and Long (1988) used the RMA as one of several measures to establish the validity of their Traditional-Egalitarian Sex Role Scale (see Beere, 1990). Demare, Briere, and Lips (1988) used the RMA as one of several measures in a study of the relationship between violent pornography and sexual aggression. Muehlenhard and Linton (1987) used the RMA as one of several measures to study the risk factors for date rape and other forms of male-to-female sexual aggression. Byers (1988) used the RMA in a study looking at "the effects of acceptance of rape supportive beliefs [as measured by the RMA], sexual intimacy, and sexual arousal on behavior in sexual disagreement situations" (p. 235). Greendlinger and Byrne (1987) looked at the relationship between various measures, including the RMA and self-reported likelihood to exhibit male-to-female sexual aggression. Margolin et al. (1989) related RMA scores to reactions to a man kissing a woman after she had indicated she did not want to be kissed.

AVAILABLE FROM: Burt, 1980, 1983; Burt and Albin, 1981

USED IN:

Ashton, N. L. (1982). Validation of Rape Myth Acceptance Scale. *Psychological Reports, 50,* 252.

Briere, J., & Malamuth, N. M. (1983). Self-reported likelihood of sexually aggressive behavior: Attitudinal versus sexual explanations. *Journal of Research in Personality, 17,* 315–323.

Briere, J., Malamuth, N., & Check, J. V. P. (1985). Sexuality and rape-supportive beliefs. *International Journal of Women's Studies, 8,* 398–403.

Burt, M. R. (1980). Cultural myths and supports for rape. *Journal of Personality and Social Psychology, 38,* 217–230.

Burt, M. R. (1983). Justifying personal violence: A comparison of rapists and the general public. *Victimology: An International Journal, 8,* 131–150.

Burt, M. R., & Albin, R. S. (1981). Rape myths, rape definitions, and probability of conviction. *Journal of Applied Social Psychology, 11,* 212–230.

Byers, E. S. (1988). Effects of sexual arousal on men's and women's behavior in sexual disagreement situations. *Journal of Sex Research, 25,* 235–254.

Check, J. V. P., & Malamuth, N. M. (1983). Sex role stereotyping and reactions to depictions of stranger versus acquaintance rape. *Journal of Personality and Social Psychology, 45,* 344–356.

Check, J. V. P., & Malamuth, N. M. (1985). An empirical assessment of some feminist hypotheses about rape. *International Journal of Women's Studies, 8,* 414–423.

Demare, D., Briere, J., & Lips, H. M. (1988). Violent pornography and self-reported likelihood of sexual aggression. *Journal of Research in Personality, 22,* 140–153.

Greendlinger, V., & Byrne, D. (1987). Coercive sexual fantasies of college men as predictors of self-reported likelihood to rape and overt sexual aggression. *Journal of Sex Research, 23,* 1–11.

Koss, M. P. (1985). The hidden rape victim: Personality, attitudinal, and situational characteristics. *Psychology of Women Quarterly, 9,* 193–212.

Koss, M. P., Leonard, K. E., Beezley, D. A., & Oros, C. J. (1985). Nonstranger sexual aggression: A discriminant analysis of the psychological characteristics of undetected offenders. *Sex Roles, 12,* 981–992.

Larsen, K. S., & Long, E. (1987, April). *Attitudes toward rape.* Paper presented at the meeting of the Western Psychological Association, Long Beach, CA. (ERIC Document Reproduction Service No. ED 278 884)

Larsen, K. S., & Long, E. (1988). Attitudes toward sex-roles: Traditional or egalitarian? *Sex Roles, 19,* 1–12.

Malamuth, N. M. (1983). Factors associated with rape as predictors of laboratory aggression against women. *Journal of Personality and Social Psychology, 47,* 432–442.

Malamuth, N. M. (1989a). The Attraction to Sexual Aggression Scale: Part one. *Journal of Sex Research, 26,* 26–49.

Malamuth, N. M. (1989b). The Attraction to Sexual Aggression Scale: Part two. *Journal of Sex Research, 26,* 324–354.

Malamuth, N. M., & Check, J. V. P. (1981). The effects of mass media exposure on acceptance of violence against women: A field experiment. *Journal of Research in Personality, 15,* 436–446.

Margolin, L., Miller, M., & Moran, P. B. (1989). When a kiss is not just a kiss: Relating violations of consent in kissing to rape myth acceptance. *Sex Roles, 20,* 231–243.

Mayerson, S. E., & Taylor, D. A. (1987). The effects of rape myth pornography on women's attitudes and the mediating role of sex role stereotyping. *Sex Roles, 17,* 321–338.

Muehlenhard, C. L., & Linton, M. A. (1987). Date rape and sexual aggression in dating situations: Incidence and risk factors. *Journal of Counseling Psychology, 34,* 186–196.

Overholser, J. C., & Beck, S. (1986). Multimethod assessment of rapists, child molesters, and three control groups on behavioral and psychological measures. *Journal of Consulting and Clinical Psychology, 54,* 682–687.

Pryor, J. B. (1987). Sexual harassment proclivities in men. *Sex Roles, 17,* 269–290.

BIBLIOGRAPHY:

Beere, C. A. (1990). *Gender roles: A handbook of tests and measures.* Westport, CT: Greenwood.

Feild, H. S. (1978). Attitudes Toward Rape: A comparative analysis of police, rapists, crisis counselors, and citizens. *Journal of Personality and Social Psychology, 36,* 156–179.

RAPE PREVENTION BELIEFS

AUTHORS: Stephanie Riger and Margaret T. Gordon

DATE: 1979

VARIABLE: Belief in the effectiveness of various rape prevention strategies

TYPE OF INSTRUMENT: Summated rating scale

DESCRIPTION: The Rape Prevention Beliefs scale consists of 11 items, each describing a tactic that individual women or society as a whole could adopt to try to reduce the incidence of rape. Each item is accompanied by three response options: "help a great deal, help somewhat, help hardly at all." Four of the items describe strategies that restrict women's behavior, and these 4 items yield a subscale score called Restrictive Prevention Measures. Another 5 items describe changes that society must undertake and assertive actions that women could undertake. These 5 items yield a second subscale score called Assertive Prevention Measures. One item suggests improved security measures in the home, and the last item mentions women carrying weapons. These 2 items do not contribute to the subscale scores.

SAMPLE ITEMS: (Restrictive Prevention Measures) Women dressing more modestly, or in a less sexy way.

(Assertive Prevention Measures) Newspapers publicizing names and pictures of known rapists.

PREVIOUS SUBJECTS: Adults

APPROPRIATE FOR: High school students and older

ADMINISTRATION: Although the Rape Prevention Beliefs scale was administered as part of a telephone interview, it can easily be self-administered and completed in a few minutes.

SCORING: Items are individually scored on a 3-point scale, with "help a great deal" assigned a score of 3, "help somewhat" assigned a score of 2, and "help hardly at all" assigned a score of 1. Two subscale scores are obtained: Restrictive Prevention Measures and Assertive Prevention Measures. High scores reflect the belief that the specified rape prevention strategies would be effective. Riger and Gordon (1979) provided means, by sex and race, for each of the two subscales.

DEVELOPMENT: Based on a literature search, a list of 21 rape prevention strategies was compiled. The list was pretested in a telephone survey, and 11 items were retained. These items "a) attributed responsibility for preventing rape to society as a whole as well as to potential victims, and b) received variability in responses" (Riger & Gordon, 1979, p. 187). The 11 items were then administered in a telephone survey to approximately 1,600 adults. Responses from almost 1,200 persons were factor analyzed; data from minority groups other than blacks were eliminated because their group sizes were too small. Initially four factors were extracted, but a two-factor solution was used to identify the subscales. The first factor, containing 4 items, was labeled "Restrictive Prevention Measures"; the second factor, consisting of 5 items, was labeled "Assertive Prevention Measures," but this label does not accurately describe all of the items.

RELIABILITY: Coefficient alpha for Restrictive Prevention Measures was .52; for Assertive Prevention Measures, it was .59.

VALIDITY: In comparing the four race-by-sex groups, Riger and Gordon

(1979) found that, for both subscales, women rated the measures as more effective than men did, and blacks rated the measures as more effective than whites. The interaction between race and sex was nonsignificant.

NOTES & COMMENTS: (1) The correlation between the two subscales was .28, using the same data used to develop the subscales.

(2) Of the four race-by-sex groups, only black females rated the restrictive strategies as more effective than the assertive strategies. The other three groups rated the assertive strategies as more effective.

AVAILABLE FROM: Riger and Gordon, 1979

USED IN:

Riger, S., & Gordon, M. T. (1979). The structure of rape prevention beliefs. *Personality and Social Psychology Bulletin, 5,* 186–190.

RAPE RESPONSIBILITY QUESTIONNAIRE

AUTHORS: Sheila R. Deitz and Lynne E. Byrnes

DATE: 1981

VARIABLE: Reactions to a rape incident

TYPE OF INSTRUMENT: Rating scales

DESCRIPTION: The Rape Responsibility Questionnaire contains 12 items designed to assess persons' reactions to a hypothetical rape case. The items deal with the following topics: recommended length of imprisonment, degree of responsibility attributed to victim, degree of responsibility attributed to assailant, identification with the victim, identification with the defendant, personal feelings for victim, personal feelings for defendant, extent to which victim encouraged rape, extent to which victim's involvement was the result of chance, certainty of the defendant's guilt, psychological impact of rape, and seriousness of rape. Each item is accompanied by an 11-point response scale.

PREVIOUS SUBJECTS: College students, prospective jurors

APPROPRIATE FOR: High school students and older

ADMINISTRATION: The scale must be administered following the presentation of a description of a hypothetical or actual rape incident. The scale can be self-administered and completed in about 5 minutes, but the total testing time depends on the length and complexity of the case presentation.

SCORING: Items are individually scored. The authors did not use total scores.

DEVELOPMENT: The items were developed as a result of a review of previous research dealing with attribution of responsibility for rape.

RELIABILITY: No information was provided. Because there are no subscale or total scores, the only type of reliability that would be meaningful would be test-retest reliability, and then only if the questionnaire was used following an identical hypothetical or actual case description.

VALIDITY: Deitz, Blackwell, Daley, and Bentley (1982) used the Rape Responsibility Questionnaire in addition to several other scales. They found that each item on the questionnaire was significantly correlated with scores on the Rape Empathy Scale (Deitz et al., 1982) (see separate entry). For a sample of 186 prospective jurors, 2 of the 12 items were significantly correlated with scores on the Attitudes Toward Women Scale (AWS) (Spence, Helmreich, & Stapp, 1973) (see Beere, 1990); for a sample of 190 college students, 10 of the 12 items were significantly correlated with scores on the AWS.

Deitz and Byrnes (1981) reported data that provided some support for the validity of some items. They found predicted sex differences for 7 of the 12 items: "Males believed that the rape victim was more likely to have done something to encourage the rape, identified less with the victim, and had more negative feelings about the rape victim than did female Ss. Females attributed greater responsibility for the rape to the defendant, were more certain that the defendant was guilty, rated the seriousness of rape as greater, and rated the psychological impact of the rape for the victim as marginally greater than did the males" (p. 24).

Deitz, Littman, and Bentley (1984) also found significant sex differences for 7 of the 12 items. Six of the 7 items for which there were significant differences were the same items for which Deitz and Byrnes (1981) found significant differences.

NOTES & COMMENTS: Deitz and Byrnes (1981) used the Rape Responsibility Questionnaire as the dependent measure in a study assessing the impact of victim's occupational status and physical attractiveness and observer's empathy on perceptions of a rape incident. Deitz et al. (1984) used the Rape Responsibility Questionnaire as the dependent measure in a similar study. They assessed the influence of victim attractiveness, victim resistance, and observer empathy on perceptions of the rape incident.

AVAILABLE FROM: The items are described in Deitz and Byrnes, 1981; Deitz, Blackwell, Daly, and Bentley, 1982; Deitz, Littman, and Bentley, 1984

USED IN:

Deitz, S. R., Blackwell, K. T., Daley, P. C., & Bentley, B. J. (1982). Measurement of empathy toward rape victims and rapists. *Journal of Personality and Social Psychology, 43*, 372–384.

Deitz, S. R., & Byrnes, L. E. (1981). Attribution of responsibility for sexual assault: The influence of observer empathy and defendant occupation and attractiveness. *Journal of Psychology, 108*, 17–29.

Deitz, S. R., Littman, M., & Bentley, B. J. (1984). Attribution of responsibility for rape: The influence of observer empathy, victim resistance, and victim attractiveness. *Sex Roles, 10*, 261–280.

BIBLIOGRAPHY:

Beere, C. A. (1990). *Gender roles: A handbook of tests and measures.* Westport, CT: Greenwood.

Spence, J. T., Helmreich, R., & Stapp, J. (1973). A short version of the Attitudes Toward Women Scale (AWS). *Bulletin of the Psychonomic Society, 2,* 219–220.

RAPE TRAUMA SYMPTOM RATING SCALE (RTSRS)

AUTHOR: Peter DiVasto

DATE: 1985

VARIABLE: Presence of symptoms that commonly follow sexual assault

TYPE OF INSTRUMENT: Rating scale

DESCRIPTION: Most of the other scales described in this book are intended for use in research; the Rape Trauma Symptom Rating Scale (RTSRS) was developed for use "in measuring progress in therapy, planning treatment, or identifying particularly dysfunctional victims" (DiVasto, 1985, p. 33). The RTSRS has eight categories: sleep disorders, appetite, phobias, motor behavior, relations, self-blame, self-esteem, and somatic reactions. An interviewer asks an open-ended question about each item and then, based on the response, assigns a scale value of 1 to 5 to the answer. Descriptions of each rating are provided to assist the interviewer in scoring the response.

SAMPLE ITEMS: For "sleep disorders," the descriptions of the ratings are "(1) sleeping well; (2) mild; episodic nightmares; broken sleep; (3) moderate; difficulty falling asleep; nightmares; (4) severe; 1–3 hours sleep per night; early morn awaking; stressful nightmares; (5) no sleep; awake all night most nights; sleep deprived state" (DiVasto, 1985, p. 34).

PREVIOUS SUBJECTS: College women, sexual assault victims

APPROPRIATE FOR: The RTSRS could be administered to anyone, but it is intended for use with sexual assault victims.

ADMINISTRATION: Individually administered by a trained interviewer; administration time varies depending on the victim's need to talk or resistance to talking. The role of the interviewer is to read the items and to make a determination regarding the scale value assigned to each item. The role of the interviewer is extremely important: she or he is doing both the administration and the scoring.

SCORING: Scoring is somewhat subjective. Each item is assigned a scale value of 1 to 5, and the eight item scores are summed to yield a total score. Higher scores are indicative of more symptomatology. DiVasto (1985) provided item means and standard deviations separately for a sample of sexual assault victims and a sample of college women.

DEVELOPMENT: The author provided little information regarding the development of the scale. He said that "the Rape Trauma Symptom Rating Scale (RTSRS) was developed by the author after a review of the relevant literature and several years experience in supervising the SART [Sexual Assault Response Team at the University of New Mexico Medical School] project" (DiVasto, 1985, p. 34).

RELIABILITY: No information was provided.
VALIDITY: The RTSRS was administered to 62 college women (the control group) and 56 female rape victims. The rape victims were interviewed from 3 to 8 days after their assault. The victims were significantly different from the controls, with the victims showing significantly more symptomatology on every one of the eight categories.
NOTES & COMMENTS: (1) Because of the subjective nature of the scoring, it is very important that interrater reliability be established for the RTSRS.

(2) Burgess and Holmstrom (1974) provided a good explanation of the rape trauma syndrome.

(3) DiVasto (1985) recommended the RTSRS "to chart progress over time, to measure specific symptoms within target groups, or as a means of comparing differing victim populations" (p. 35).
AVAILABLE FROM: DiVasto, 1985
USED IN:

DiVasto, P. V. (1985). Measuring the aftermath of rape. *Journal of Psychosocial Nursing, 23*(2), 33–35.

BIBLIOGRAPHY:

Burgess, A. W., & Holmstrom, L. L. (1974). Rape trauma syndrome. *American Journal of Psychiatry, 131*, 981–986.

SEXUAL EXPERIENCES SURVEY

AUTHORS: Mary P. Koss and Cheryl J. Oros
DATE: 1980 (used 1978)
VARIABLE: Experiences with sexual aggression/sexual victimization
TYPE OF INSTRUMENT: Alternate choice: yes/no
DESCRIPTION: There are two parallel versions of the Sexual Experiences Survey—one for males and the other for females. Each form consists of 10 items describing sexual experiences. These experiences cover a continuum in terms of the amount of sexual contact and the amount of aggression associated with the sexual experience. Items earlier in the scale involve less sexual contact and less aggression. For each item, the respondent indicates whether he or she has ever experienced the behavior. The response options are "yes" or "no."
SAMPLE ITEMS: (items given here are from the female form; wording is altered, but the substance is preserved, on the male form)

(item 2) Have you had sex play (fondling, kissing, or petting, but not intercourse) when you didn't want to because a man used his position of authority (boss, teacher, camp counselor, supervisor) to make you?

(item 10) Have you had sex acts (anal or oral intercourse or penetration by objects other than the penis) when you didn't want to because a man threatened or used some degree of physical force (twisting your arm, holding you down, etc.) to make you?

PREVIOUS SUBJECTS: College students
APPROPRIATE FOR: High school students and older
ADMINISTRATION: Self-administered; about 5 minutes
SCORING: The most common method for using responses to the Sexual Experiences Survey is to categorize people on the basis of their responses. One coding system (Koss, 1985; Orlando & Koss, 1983) used the following categories of victimization for classifying women: none, low, moderate, high acknowledged (answered "yes" when asked if ever raped), high unacknowledged (answered "no" when asked if ever raped). Koss, Leonard, Beezley, and Oros (1985) classified male respondents into four categories: sexually assaultive, sexually abusive, sexually coercive, and sexually nonaggressive.
DEVELOPMENT: Initially each of the two parallel versions of the Sexual Experiences Survey contained 12 items. The items were written to represent a dimensional view of rape, that is, the idea that "rape represents an extreme behavior but one that is on a continuum with normal male behavior within the culture" (Koss & Oros, 1982, p. 455). The scale was later modified: "original items were reworded slightly to increase clarity, improve consistency with the legal definition of rape, and reflect more degrees of sexual aggression and victimization" (Koss & Gidycz, 1985, p. 422). The modified version of the scale is the 10-item version currently used.
RELIABILITY: Using responses from 305 college women and 143 college men, the authors found that internal consistency reliability was .74 for women and .89 for men. A sample of 71 college women and 67 college men completed the Sexual Experiences Survey on two occasions, separated by a 1-week interval. The mean item agreement was 93% (Koss & Gidycz, 1985).
VALIDITY: In discussing the validity of the Sexual Experiences Survey, Koss and Oros (1982) stated: "It is difficult to establish the validity of an instrument whose goal is to identify respondents who have been missed by traditional sources and are thus 'unlabeled' " (p. 457).

Theoretically one would expect that the amount of aggression that females report experiencing would be equal to the amount of aggression that males report perpetrating. However, Koss and Oros (1980a) found that females reported being victimized more than males reported being aggressive. Koss and Oros (1980a) offered several possible explanations: "many more males who engaged in sexual aggression failed to report it, or each aggressive male victimized more than one woman, or males and females differed in their perception of a given experience" (p. 9).

The Sexual Experiences Survey was administered to a sample of several hundred college students who were also interviewed regarding their reported experiences and who completed the survey a second time. The second administration of the survey was done in a one-to-one setting with the survey being administered by a same-sex, post-master's-level psychologist. Students were classified into one of four groups based on their first set of responses. For women, the correlation between the level of victimization reported on the Sexual Experiences Survey and the level of victimization based on interview responses was .73. For men, the correlation between the level of sexual aggression expressed on the survey and the level of sexual aggression based on interview responses was .61. Furthermore, for 23.5% of the women and 37% of the men, the classification based on the Sexual Experiences Survey was changed as a result of changing responses on the second administration of the survey. For women, 16% moved to a lower category of victimization, and 7.5% moved to a higher category of victimization. For men, 34% moved to a lower category of aggression, and 3% moved to a higher category of aggression. An important finding here was that there was "a tendency among male participants to deny behaviors during interviews that had been revealed on self-reports" (Koss & Gidycz, 1985, p. 423). This is particularly significant, because this inconsistency in responding was not found when the test was self-administered in a group setting both times, as was the case when determining test-retest reliability. The significant factor was the presence of the interviewer. "A substantial number of men were unwilling to admit to a trained male interviewer that they had engaged in any degree of sexual aggression whatsoever" (p. 423).

NOTES & COMMENTS: (1) About half of the published studies used the original 12-item version of the Sexual Experiences Survey. The other studies used the newer, 10-item version of the survey.

(2) Koss and Oros (1980a) factor analyzed responses from 3,862 college students. Three factors accounted for 51% of the variance: Factor 1 was "High Sexual Aggression/Victimization" (3 items), Factor 2 was "Moderate Sexual Aggression/Victimization" (3 items), and Factor 3 was "Low Sexual Aggression/Victimization" (5 items). In factor analytic results reported by Koss and Oros (1982), the authors reported finding one factor that accounted for 67.3% of the variance. The two different sets of results appear to be based on factor analyzing the same data.

(3) Many researchers have used the Sexual Experiences Survey to determine the incidence of sexual victimization of women and/or the perpetration of sexually aggressive behavior on the part of men (Koss, 1985; Koss, Gidycz, & Wisniewski, 1985, 1987; Koss, Leonard et al., 1985; Koss & Oros, 1980a; Levine-MacCombie & Koss, 1986).

(4) Koss and Oros (1980b) used the Sexual Experiences Survey to identify unacknowledged rape victims, that is, women who had experienced forced sexual intercourse but did not conceptualize their experience as rape. The researchers then compared unacknowledged rape victims with acknowledged rape victims on a variety of rape-related

attitude measures and on the situational characteristics associated with the sexual assault. Koss (1985) reported the results of a similar study in which she used the Sexual Experiences Survey to identify women who were not sexually victimized, women who were low sexually victimized, women who were moderately sexually victimized, and women who were highly sexually victimized. The women in these four groups were then compared on a variety of personality, attitudinal, and situational variables.

(5) Koss, Leonard et al. (1985) used the Sexual Experiences Survey to classify college men into one of four categories: sexually assaultive, sexually abusive, sexually coercive, and sexually nonaggressive. The researchers then compared the four groups of men on a variety of personality and attitudinal variables. Levine-MacCombie and Koss (1986) used the Sexual Experiences Survey to identify women who were victims of sexual aggression and acknowledged it, women who were victims of sexual assault but did not conceptualize the experience as rape, and women who had successfully avoided sexual victimization. The three groups were compared in terms of five variables: level of perceived violence, victim response strategies, number of responses, effect of resistance, and victim emotions. Orlando and Koss (1983) conducted a study examining the relationship between college women's sexually aggressive experiences and their level of sexual satisfaction. The Sexual Experiences Survey was used to identify the level of sexually aggressive victimization. Several researchers (Malamuth, 1986, 1989; Greendlinger & Byrne, 1987; Smeaton & Byrne, 1987) used the Sexual Experiences Survey in studies designed to identify factors related to male sexual aggression.

AVAILABLE FROM: The 10-item version is in Koss, Gidycz, and Wisniewski, 1987; the 12-item version is in Koss and Oros, 1982.

USED IN:

Greendlinger, V., & Byrne, D. (1987). Coercive sexual fantasies of college men as predictors of self-reported likelihood to rape and overt sexual aggression. *Journal of Sex Research, 23,* 1–11.

Koss, M. P. (1985). The hidden rape victim: Personality, attitudinal, and situational characteristics. *Psychology of Women Quarterly, 9,* 193–212.

Koss, M. P., & Gidycz, C. A. (1985). Sexual Experiences Survey: Reliability and validity. *Journal of Consulting and Clinical Psychology, 53,* 422–423.

Koss, M. P., Gidycz, C. A., & Wisniewski, N. (1985, August). *Hidden rape: Incidence and prevalence of sexual aggression and victimization in a national sample of students in higher education.* Paper presented at the meeting of the American Psychological Association, Los Angeles. (ERIC Document Reproduction Service No. ED 267 321)

Koss, M. P., Gidycz, C. A., & Wisniewski, N. (1987). The scope of rape: Incidence and prevalence of sexual aggression and victimization in a national sample of higher education students. *Journal of Consulting and Clinical Psychology, 55,* 162–170.

Koss, M. P., Leonard, K. E., Beezley, D. A., & Oros, C. J. (1985). Nonstranger sexual aggression: A discriminant analysis of the psychological characteristics of undetected offenders. *Sex Roles, 12,* 981–992.

Koss, M. P., & Oros, C. J. (1980a, May). *Hidden rape: A survey of the incidence of sexual aggression and victimization on a university campus.* Paper presented at the meeting of the Midwestern Psychological Association, St. Louis, MO. (ERIC Document Reproduction Service No. ED 188 095)

Koss, M. P., & Oros, C. J. (1980b, September). *The "unacknowledged" rape victim.* Paper presented at the meeting of the American Psychological Association, Montreal. (ERIC Document Reproduction Service No. ED 199 590)

Koss, M. P., & Oros, C. J. (1982). Sexual Experiences Survey: A research instrument investigating sexual aggression and victimization. *Journal of Consulting and Clinical Psychology, 50,* 455–457.

Levine-MacCombie, J., & Koss, M. P. (1986). Acquaintance rape: Effective avoidance strategies. *Psychology of Women Quarterly, 10,* 311–320.

Malamuth, N. M. (1986). Predictors of naturalistic sexual aggression. *Journal of Personality and Social Psychology, 50,* 953–962.

Malamuth, N. M. (1988). Predicting laboratory aggression against female and male targets: Implications for sexual aggression. *Journal of Research in Personality, 22,* 474–495.

Malamuth, N. M. (1989). The Attraction to Sexual Aggression Scale: Part two. *Journal of Sex Research, 26,* 324–354.

Orlando, J. A., & Koss, M. P. (1983). The effect of sexual victimization on sexual satisfaction: A study of the negative-association hypothesis. *Journal of Abnormal Psychology, 92,* 104–106.

Smeaton, G., & Byrne, D. (1987). The effects of R-rated violence and erotica, individual differences, and victim characteristics on acquaintance rape proclivity. *Journal of Research in Personality, 21,* 171–184.

THORNTON ATTRIBUTION OF RESPONSIBILITY FOR RAPE

AUTHOR: Bill Thornton

DATE: 1984

VARIABLE: Attribution of rape responsibility to the victim: behavioral and/or characterological responsibility on the part of the victim

TYPE OF INSTRUMENT: Summated rating scale

DESCRIPTION: In order to determine whether a person perceives a rape victim as responsible for her own rape, the Thornton Attribution of Responsibility for Rape scale is administered after a subject hears or reads a description of a rape incident. This 10-item scale contains 5 items that form a composite index of behavioral blame; that is, something about the victim's behavior led her to become a rape victim. The other 5 items form a composite index of characterological blame, meaning that something about the woman's character or personality led her to become a rape victim. The 10 items are interspersed with each other, and each is accompanied by a 7-point scale, with the endpoints labeled "strongly agree," and "strongly disagree."

SAMPLE ITEMS: (behavioral blame) The woman should not have been talking so openly with a stranger, letting him get so familiar with her.

(characterological blame) This woman is just too open and trusting of other people, especially where new acquaintances are concerned.

PREVIOUS SUBJECTS: College students, female volunteer rape crisis counselors

APPROPRIATE FOR: High school students and older

ADMINISTRATION: In order to complete this scale, the subject must first read or hear a description of a rape incident. The scale can then be self-administered and completed in a couple of minutes.

SCORING: Each item is scored on a 7-point scale, with the "strongly disagree" end of the continuum assigned 1 point and the "strongly agree" end assigned 7 points. Item scores are summed to yield two scores: characterological blame and behavioral blame; each can range from 5 to 35. A total score is obtained by summing scores on the two subscales.

DEVELOPMENT: No information was provided.

RELIABILITY: Thornton (1984) added two items to the scale: "Can the victim be considered responsible to some extent for being sexually assaulted because of something she did?" and "Can the victim be considered responsible to some extent for being sexually assaulted because of the kind of person she is?" The score on the former item was added to the behavioral blame score, and the score on the latter item was added to the characterological blame score. A sample of 48 college women completed the scale after reading an account, approximately 450 words long, of a sexual assault. Coefficient alpha for the 6-item characterological index was .68; for the 6-item behavioral index, it was .50. For the 12 items combined, coefficient alpha was .66. In a second experiment, reported in the same article, a sample of 56 college women participated in a similar study. Coefficient alpha was .72 and .75 for the behavioral and characterological indexes, respectively. For the 12 items combined, coefficient alpha was .80.

A sample of 54 college women read a transcript describing a sexual assault and then completed the Thornton Attribution of Responsibility for Rape scale. For the behavioral index, coefficient alpha was .81; for the characterological index, it was .85; and for the two indexes combined, it was .91 (Thornton, Hogate, Moirs, Pinette, & Presby, 1986). In a second study, reported in the same article, 50 college women completed the scale after reading a report of a sexual assault. Coefficient alpha was .82 and .76 for the behavioral and characterological indexes, respectively. It was .87 for the two indexes combined.

In another study, Thornton et al. (1988) used the scale with 55 female volunteer rape crisis counselors who had read a description of a sexual assault. Coefficient alpha was .71 and .63 for the behavioral and char-

acterological indexes, respectively. For the two indexes combined, coefficient alpha was .79.
VALIDITY: Thornton (1984) reported the results of two experiments in which, as predicted, observers attributed more behavioral blame to a personally similar victim and more characterological blame to a personally dissimilar victim. Furthermore, Thornton reported that less blame overall was attributed to a personally similar victim.
NOTES & COMMENTS: (1) In several studies, a correlation was computed to express the relationship between the behavioral and characterological indexes. Thornton (1984) reported a nonsignificant correlation of .19 in one study and a significant correlation of .46 ($p < .001$) in a second study. Thornton et al. (1986) reported a strong and significant correlation of .85 ($p < .001$) in one experiment and a moderate and significant correlation of .53 ($p < .001$) in a second experiment. Thornton et al. (1988) reported a significant correlation of .64 ($p < .001$).

(2) Thornton (1984) and Thornton et al. (1986) used both the behavioral and characterological indexes from the Thornton Attribution of Responsibility for Rape scale to study the effects of observer arousal on the attribution of rape responsibility to the victim.

(3) Thornton et al. (1988) studied the "potential impact of self-blame on observers' perceptions of sexual assault victims" (p. 418). Both rape crisis counselors and college students participated in the study so that responses from the two groups could be compared.
AVAILABLE FROM: Thornton, Hogate, Moirs, Pinette, and Presby, 1986
USED IN:

Thornton, B. (1984). Defensive attribution of responsibility: Evidence for an arousal-based motivational bias. *Journal of Personality and Social Psychology, 46*, 721–734.

Thornton, B., Hogate, L., Moirs, K., Pinette, M., & Presby, W. (1986). Physiological evidence of an arousal-based motivational bias in the defensive attribution of responsibility. *Journal of Experimental Social Psychology, 22*, 148–162.

Thornton, B., Ryckman, R. M., Kirchner, G., Jacobs, J., Kaczor, L., & Kuehnel, R. H. (1988). Reaction to self-attributed victim responsibility: A comparative analysis of rape crisis counselors and lay observers. *Journal of Applied Social Psychology, 18*, 409–422.

9

Family Violence

The nine scales described in this chapter are similar to each other in several ways: all first appeared in the literature after 1980; all are summated rating scales, and none has been used extensively. To organize the chapter, I divided the nine scales into two sections. The first section of five scales is intended for women, either currently or previously married or cohabiting. These scales deal with the experience of spouse abuse, the attitudes of abuse victims, or the risk of being an abuse victim. They are similar to each other in length, ranging from 22 to 35 items. There is no evidence of the reliability of two of the five scales, and the data are equivocal for one of the other three. Overall the data pertaining to validity are not particularly convincing.

The second section contains four scales: two assess attitudes and beliefs regarding wife abuse and two pertain to incest. Lack of reliability is a problem for three scales, and lack of validity is a problem for three scales. None of the four scales is psychometrically strong.

Despite the weaknesses associated with the scales described in this chapter, they provide a starting point for researchers interested in the study of family violence.

ABUSE RISK INVENTORY FOR WOMEN
AUTHOR: Bonnie L. Yegidis
DATE: 1989 (used 1985)
VARIABLE: Risk of being a victim of physical abuse by a husband or other intimate male partner
TYPE OF INSTRUMENT: Summated rating scale

DESCRIPTION: The Abuse Risk Inventory for Women is a 25-item scale with 15 items following the stem saying "My husband/partner" and 10 items following the stem saying "My husband/partner and I." Items pertain to a variety of topics, including alcohol and drug use, sources of frustration, intimacy, conflict, and communication. Each item is accompanied by four response options: "rarely or never, sometimes, often, always." Eleven items are phrased so that a woman at risk for wife abuse would respond "rarely or never," and 14 items are phrased so that she would respond "always." The inventory is labeled "Interpersonal Relationship Survey," so respondents are not sensitized to the issue of abuse when deciding their answers.

SAMPLE ITEMS: My husband/partner and I discuss minor problems before they blow up.

My husband/partner starts arguments with me about matters in the home.

PREVIOUS SUBJECTS: Married women and women involved in a live-in relationship, abused and not abused; college women

APPROPRIATE FOR: Married or cohabiting women; could be modified to refer to a previous relationship

ADMINISTRATION: Self-administered; about 10–15 minutes

SCORING: Items are individually scored on a 4-point scale, with 4 points assigned to the response associated with wife abuse. Total scores can range from 25 (very unlikely to be a victim of wife abuse) to 100 (very likely to be a victim of wife abuse). Scores above 50 suggest that the woman is at risk for abuse. Based on testing 59 college women, only one of whom had experienced abuse, Yegidis (1989) reported a mean of 44, a standard deviation of 7.9, and a range from 31 to 62. For this group, Yegidis also reported means and standard deviations for each item.

DEVELOPMENT: A pool of 40 items was generated based on a review of the relevant literature and interviews with battered women. The items were submitted to four content experts, who made suggestions for improving the wording of the items. The revised items were then administered to 11 residents of a shelter for abused women. This led to the retention of 34 items that were tested on a sample of 50 women. A total score based on the 34 items successfully discriminated between abused and nonabused women. Both the internal consistency reliability and the split-half reliability of the 34-item inventory were .90. Based on item means, standard deviations, and item-total correlations, the author eliminated 3 items, leaving 31 items for the next version of the inventory. The 31-item inventory correctly discriminated between abused and nonabused women. Using a cutoff score of 68, 88.1% of 193 respondents were correctly classified as abused or nonabused. A factor analysis led to the labeling of two factors, Communication and Conflict Resolution Skills, which contained 12 items, and Intimacy, which contained 10 items. Coefficient alpha for the inventory, based on testing 193 women, was .90.

The final version of the Abuse Risk Inventory for Women was created by deleting 6 items with item-total correlations below .38. The 25 remaining items comprise the current version of the Abuse Risk Inventory for Women.

RELIABILITY: The internal consistency reliability of the 25-item current version of the Inventory was .88.

When the Abuse Risk Inventory for Women was administered to a sample of 59 college women, the internal consistency of the inventory was .73.

VALIDITY: The Abuse Risk Inventory for Women was administered to 78 women seeking marital or relationship counseling from one of three family service agencies. The questionnaire they completed also included a question asking, "Within the last year, have you been hit, kicked, punched, or physically assaulted in other ways by your husband or partner?" Responses to this question were used to divide the women into two groups, abused and nonabused. Using a cutoff score of 50 on the Abuse Risk Inventory for Women (equivalent to a cutoff score of 68 on the 31-item version of the scale), the inventory discriminated between abused and nonabused women quite well.

Bagwell (cited in Yegidis, 1989) found that 94% of 35 women residing at a spouse abuse shelter obtained scores above 50 on the Abuse Risk Inventory for Women.

In another study reported by Yegidis (1989), 43.8% of a sample of abused women did not score above the cutoff score of 50 on the Abuse Risk Inventory for Women. In the same study, however, it was shown that Abuse Risk Inventory scores were moderately and significantly correlated with scores on a measure of child abuse potential.

NOTES & COMMENTS: (1) Yegidis (1989) cautioned that the Abuse Risk Inventory for Women should never be used as the sole basis for concluding that a woman is a victim or is at risk to be a victim of wife abuse. Rather, inventory results should be used in conjunction with other data obtained through interviews.

(2) Yegidis (1989) cautioned that the Abuse Risk Inventory for Women may not be appropriate for women with family incomes over $20,000. The development and later work with the inventory involved primarily samples of low- and moderate-income women.

(3) The earlier versions of the Abuse Risk Inventory for Women were called the Wife Abuse Inventory.

AVAILABLE FROM: Consulting Psychologists Press, 577 College Avenue, Palo Alto, CA 94306

USED IN:

Lewis, B. Y. (1985). The Wife Abuse Inventory: A screening device for the identification of abused women. *Social Work, 30*, 32–35.

Lewis, B. Y. (1987). Psychosocial factors related to wife abuse. *Journal of Family Violence, 2,* 1–10.

Yegidis, B. L. (1989). *Abuse Risk Inventory for Women: Manual.* Palo Alto: Consulting Psychologists Press.

ABUSED WIVES ATTITUDES REGARDING HUSBANDS

AUTHORS: Eileen M. Kelly and Larry C. Loesch

DATE: 1983

VARIABLE: Abused wives' perceptions of their husbands

TYPE OF INSTRUMENT: Summated rating scale

DESCRIPTION: The Abused Wives Attitudes Regarding Husbands scale contains 29 statements, 24 of them directly related to the respondent's husband. The item content deals with such areas as the husband's treatment of his wife; the husband's attitudes toward violence and abuse; the husband's behavior and attitudes in other areas such as jealousy, drinking, expressing emotions; and various other aspects of the marital relationship. Each item is accompanied by five response options: "strongly agree, agree, undecided, disagree, strongly disagree."

SAMPLE ITEMS: My husband very often says bad (i.e., nasty or hurtful) things to me or about me.

My husband believes it is "okay" for a man to beat his wife.

PREVIOUS SUBJECTS: Wife abuse victims

APPROPRIATE FOR: Wife abuse victims; wording can be modified for cohabiting abuse victims

ADMINISTRATION: Self-administered; about 10–15 minutes

SCORING: Items are individually scored. It appears that total scores are not computed. Kelly and Loesch (1983) provided means and standard deviations for each item based on the responses from 42 abused wives.

DEVELOPMENT: No information was provided.

RELIABILITY: No information was provided.

VALIDITY: The item intercorrelation matrix shows that only 20.4% of the correlations were statistically significant. This finding led the authors to conclude: "It seems that the women effectively discriminated among the items even though they were in what might be called 'emotionally (negatively) charged' situations. This, of course, adds credence to the validity of the responses" (Kelly & Loesch, 1983, p. 139). The authors labeled the situations as "emotionally charged" because the scale was administered as part of a counseling session immediately after an abuse incident.

NOTES & COMMENTS: (1) Item responses from 42 abused wives were compared with their answers to four questions: how long they were married, how long they knew their husband, how many years of school the wife completed, and how many years of school the husband completed. Only 7 of 116 correlations were statistically significant: Two items were significantly correlated with the length of the marriage, three items were significantly correlated with the number of years they had known each other, two items were significantly correlated with the wife's educational level, and no items were significantly correlated with the husband's educational level.

(2) Although little is known regarding the psychometric properties of these items, the scale is included here because there are relatively few measures available in the area of spouse abuse, and the area is attracting considerable attention, suggesting an increase in research activity in the future.

AVAILABLE FROM: Kelly and Loesch, 1983

USED IN:

Kelly, E. M., & Loesch, L. C. (1983). Abused wives: Perceptions during crisis counseling. *American Mental Health Counselors Association Journal, 5,* 132–140.

INDEX OF SPOUSE ABUSE (ISA)

AUTHOR: Walter W. Hudson

DATE: 1981

VARIABLE: Degree of spouse abuse experienced by a woman

TYPE OF INSTRUMENT: Summated rating scale

DESCRIPTION: The Index of Spouse Abuse (ISA) is a 30-item scale with 11 items relating to physical abuse and 19 items relating to nonphysical abuse. Each item is a statement beginning with the phrase "My partner" and ending with a behavior considered abusive. For each item, a respondent is to indicate how frequently the statement is true: "never, rarely, occasionally, frequently, very frequently."

SAMPLE ITEMS: (nonphysical abuse) My partner belittles me.

(physical abuse) My partner punches me with his fists.

PREVIOUS SUBJECTS: Married college women, married women

APPROPRIATE FOR: Married or cohabiting women; could be modified to refer to a previous relationship

ADMINISTRATION: Self-administered; about 10–15 minutes

SCORING: The ISA yields two scores: a physical abuse score (ISA-P) and a nonphysical abuse score (ISA-NP). Each score can range from 0 to 100, with higher scores reflecting more abuse. Scoring is more complicated than usual because each item is multiplied by a weight reflecting the seriousness of the type of abuse. When items are omitted, scoring becomes even more complex. According to Hudson and McIntosh (1981), a score above 10 on the physical abuse subscale is probably indicative of serious physical abuse, and a score above 25 on the nonphysical abuse subscale is probably indicative of serious nonphysical abuse. Item weights and specific scoring instructions are provided in Hudson and McIntosh and in Corcoran and Fischer (1987).

DEVELOPMENT: A sample of 398 college women completed the 30-item ISA as well as the 25-item Index of Marital Satisfaction (IMS) (Hudson & Glisson, 1976). A factor analysis was performed using responses to the 55 items. It was predicted that three factors would emerge: one for the IMS and two for the ISA. The results supported this prediction. Based on item content, Hudson and McIntosh (1981) assigned 6 items to the ISA-P subscale and 15 items to the ISA-NP subscale. For the remaining 9 items, the factor analytic results were used to determine which items would contribute to the ISA-P score and which to the ISA-NP score.

A sample of 188 respondents were asked to rate each of the ISA items in terms of the seriousness of the abuse described in the item. Their ratings were used to determine item weights for the 30 items.

RELIABILITY: Based on responses from a sample of 398 college women, coefficient alpha was .90 for ISA-P scores and .91 for ISA-NP scores. Based on a different sample of 107 women, coefficient alpha was .94 for ISA-P scores and .97 for ISA-NP scores.

Hudson and McIntosh (1981) reported a standard error of measurement of 3.68 for ISA-P and a standard error of measurement of 3.30 for ISA-NP.

VALIDITY: The factor analysis described above provided some evidence for the factorial validity of the scale.

Hudson and McIntosh (1981) claimed that the scale had excellent content validity because the items had face validity. Their logic on this point is questionable.

Hudson and McIntosh (1981) compared the responses from 64 women known to be victims of spouse abuse with responses from 43 women who were not victims of spouse abuse. There was a significant difference ($p < .0001$) in the mean scores for both ISA-P and ISA-NP. Furthermore, the point-biserial correlation between group membership and ISA scores was .73 for ISA-P scores and .80 for ISA-NP scores. Clearly the ISA discriminates between abused and nonabused women.

As predicted, Hudson and McIntosh (1981) found low correlations between ISA subscale scores and problems with work associates, quality of work, problems with friends, problems with mother, problems with father, and problems with children. Also as predicted, they found slightly higher correlations between ISA subscale scores and depression, self-esteem, marital problems, sexual relations, personal sex life, fearfulness, anxiety, nightmares, sense of identity, and unhappiness.

NOTES & COMMENTS: (1) Unlike most other measures included in this book, the ISA is intended for use in clinical settings. It is suggested for use in monitoring and evaluating progress in treatment.

(2) The sample size of 398 respondents was too small for a factor analytic study of 55 items.

(3) Hudson and McIntosh (1981) cautioned that cutoff scores were based on research with severely abused women in protective shelters. It is possible that the cutoff scores need to be adjusted to identify women who are less severely abused.

(4) The correlation between ISA-P and ISA-NP scores for a group of abused women was .86, suggesting considerable overlap in the two scores. However, the fact that the abused group included severely abused women may have led to spurious results. For a sample of married college women, the correlation between the two subscales was .66.

(5) Hudson and McIntosh (1981) offered suggestions for a 25-item version of the ISA.

AVAILABLE FROM: Hudson and McIntosh, 1981; Corcoran and Fischer, 1987

USED IN:

Hudson, W. W., & McIntosh, S. R. (1981). The assessment of spouse abuse: Two quantifiable dimensions. *Journal of Marriage and the Family, 43,* 873–885.

BIBLIOGRAPHY:

Corcoran, K., & Fischer, J. (1987). *Measures for clinical practice: A sourcebook* (pp. 447–450). New York: Free Press.

Hudson, W. W., & Glisson, D. H. (1976). Assessment of marital discord in social work practice. *Social Service Review, 50,* 293–311.

MARITAL PSYCHOLOGICAL ABUSE SCALE FOR WOMEN

AUTHORS: Kathy Greenberg Stein, Irene Gillman Bruschi, and Beth Raymond

DATE: 1982

VARIABLE: Experience with psychological spouse abuse

TYPE OF INSTRUMENT: Summated rating scale

DESCRIPTION: The Marital Psychological Abuse Scale for Women consists of 22 items. The first 19 items are statements about a husband's behavior; the behaviors are ones that could be considered psychologically abusive. The respondent is to indicate the frequency with which the behavior is displayed. Five response options are given: "never happened, happened just once or twice in our marriage, happens several times a year, happens several times a month, happens several times a week." The last 3 items are statements about thoughts and feelings that a woman might have about her husband and marriage. The woman is to indicate the frequency with which she thinks or feels the way described.

SAMPLE ITEMS: My husband tells me to "drop dead."

My husband destroys my personal belongings.

I let my husband have his own way because I'm afraid of what will happen if I don't.

PREVIOUS SUBJECTS: Married, separated, and divorced women
APPROPRIATE FOR: Women currently or previously married or cohabiting (wording would need slight revision for a cohabiting relationship)
ADMINISTRATION: Self-administered; about 10 minutes
SCORING: Each item is assigned a score of 0 or 1, with 1 assigned to responses indicative of psychological abuse. To identify the frequency indicative of psychological abuse, a group of psychologists determined, a priori, for each item the behavioral frequency that constitutes abuse. Their judgments determined the cutoff for scoring each item as 0 or 1. For total scores, a cutoff score of 6 or more leads to a label of psychological abuse.
DEVELOPMENT: A pool of 79 items was generated based on a search of relevant literature, the clinical experiences of persons who had worked with victims of psychological spouse abuse, and inputs from graduate psychology students. A sample of 30 psychologists independently rated each of the 79 items in terms of the level at which they believe the behavior in the item is psychologically abusive. The psychologists also offered suggestions for improving the items. Feedback from the psychologists led to revisions in the items. The items were rated by another sample of psychologists, and their ratings were used to reduce the pool to 40 items, including items representing differing "abuse-frequencies." For example, 9 items were considered abusive if they occurred just once or twice in the relationship, and 11 items were considered abusive if they occurred several times a year. The pool of 40 items was administered to 200 women. Using item-total and interitem correlations, the authors reduced the pool to the 22 items that constitute the Marital Psychological Abuse Scale for Women.
RELIABILITY: Split-half reliability was .83. Of the 22 items, 19 showed item-total correlations of at least .50.
VALIDITY: As predicted, scores on the Marital Psychological Abuse Scale for Women were significantly related to scores on the short form of the Locke-Wallace Marital Adjustment Test (Locke & Wallace, 1959) ($r = -.82$ in one sample and $r = -.75$ in another sample), and they were significantly related to a self-rating of abuse ($r = .72$ in one sample and $r = .77$ in another sample).

A sample of divorced/separated women scored differently from a sample of married women on the Marital Psychological Abuse Scale for Women.
NOTES & COMMENTS: Although no articles have yet been published using the Marital Psychological Abuse Scale for Women, it is included here because it seems to be a promising measure dealing exclusively with psychological abuse.

AVAILABLE FROM: Irene Gillman Bruschi, Psychology Department, Hofstra University, Hempstead, NY 11550; or Stein, 1982

USED IN:

Stein, K. G. (1982). Development and validity of a woman's marital psychological abuse scale (Doctoral dissertation, Hofstra University, 1982). *Dissertation Abstracts International, 43,* 2005B.

BIBLIOGRAPHY:

Locke, H., & Wallace, K. (1959). Short marital adjustment and prediction tests: Their reliability and validity. *Journal of Marriage and Family Living, 21,* 251–255.

PSYCHOLOGICAL ABUSE AND KINDNESS AMONG MARRIED WOMEN/PSYCHOLOGICAL ABUSE AND KINDNESS AMONG DATING WOMEN

AUTHORS: Beth Raymond and Irene Gillman Bruschi

DATE: 1988

VARIABLE: Psychological abuse and kindness in intimate heterosexual relationships

TYPE OF INSTRUMENT: Summated rating scale

DESCRIPTION: The Psychological Abuse and Kindness scales each contain 35 items. The items on the two scales are essentially parallel, differing only in whether the focus is on "husband" or "boyfriend." Fourteen items describe positive behaviors that a man may exhibit toward his wife/girlfriend, and 16 items describe negative behaviors that a man may exhibit toward his wife/girlfriend. Five items pertain to the wife's/girlfriend's feelings about her husband/boyfriend or their relationship. Two items express positive feelings, and 3 items express negative feelings. For each item, the woman responds on a 5-point scale to indicate the frequency of the behavior or the frequency of the stated feelings. Response options range from "never" to "several times a week."

SAMPLE ITEMS: When I see my husband (boyfriend), he says very little and seems more interested in whatever he happens to be doing at the time than me.

My husband (boyfriend) approves of my friends and supports me in being with them.

I think my life would be better if I were in a relationship with someone else.

PREVIOUS SUBJECTS: The married version has been administered to women ranging from 35 to 60 years old; the dating version has been administered to college women.

APPROPRIATE FOR: As written, the married version is appropriate for married women, but it could be slightly revised for use with previously married women or women cohabiting with men. The dating version is appropriate for a woman who has a boyfriend.

ADMINISTRATION: Self-administered; about 15 minutes

SCORING: Four separate scores can be obtained: behavioral abuse, behavioral kindness, positive feelings, and negative feelings.

DEVELOPMENT: The Psychological Abuse and Kindness scales were based on unpublished research by Raymond, Gillman, and Donner and on later work by Stein, Gillman, and Raymond (see Stein, 1982). As a result, the scales are closely related to the Marital Psychological Abuse Scale for Women (Stein, 1982) (see separate entry). The latter scale was lengthened and revised by rephrasing some items in a positive direction.

RELIABILITY: No information was provided.

VALIDITY: No information was provided.

NOTES & COMMENTS: Although there is little information available about the Psychological Abuse and Kindness scales, they are included here because of their potential and their uniqueness.

AVAILABLE FROM: Beth Raymond or Irene Gillman Bruschi, Department of Psychology, Hofstra University, Hempstead, NY 11550

USED IN:

Gillman Bruschi, I., & Raymond, B. (in press). What women think and what men think: Perceptions of abuse and kindness in dating relationships. *Psychological Reports*.

Raymond, B., & Gillman Bruschi, I. (1989). Psychological abuse among college women in dating relationships. *Perceptual and Motor Skills, 69*, 1283–1297.

BIBLIOGRAPHY:

Stein, K. G. (1982). Development and validation of a woman's marital psychological abuse scale (Doctoral dissertation, Hofstra University, 1982). *Dissertation Abstracts International, 43*, 2005B.

ATTITUDES TOWARD WIFE ABUSE (AWA)

AUTHOR: John Briere

DATE: 1987

VARIABLE: Attitudes toward wife abuse

TYPE OF INSTRUMENT: Summated rating scale

DESCRIPTION: The Attitudes Toward Wife Abuse (AWA) scale consists of eight items pertaining to violence against wives. Half of the items accept wife abuse, and half of them oppose it. Each item is accompanied by seven response options ranging from "strongly disagree" to "strongly agree."

SAMPLE ITEMS: A wife should move out of the house if her husband hits her.

A husband should have the right to discipline his wife when it is necessary.

PREVIOUS SUBJECTS: College men

APPROPRIATE FOR: High school students and older

ADMINISTRATION: Self-administered; less than 5 minutes
SCORING: Items are individually scored on a 7-point scale, with higher scores assigned to the response that reflects an attitude accepting of violence toward wives. Briere (1987) found that for a sample of 191 college men, the mean score on the AWA was 23.8; the standard deviation was 7.2, and the range was 8 to 47.
DEVELOPMENT: In describing the scale's development, Briere (1987) reported that "the items of the AWA were based on the author's clinical experience with over 100 wife batterers, which led him to hypothesize that certain attitudes and beliefs are common to this group" (p. 63). Two of the eight items on the AWA are taken from the Acceptance of Interpersonal Violence scale (Burt, 1980) (see separate entry).
RELIABILITY: The internal consistency of the AWA, based on the responses from 191 college men, was .63.
VALIDITY: For a sample of 191 college students, scores on the AWA were significantly though moderately correlated with responses to four of five self-report items regarding likelihood to batter.

Discriminant analysis showed that the AWA was quite effective in predicting likelihood to batter.
NOTES & COMMENTS: (1) Briere's (1987) research also included five items asking whether a man would be likely to hit his wife under each of the following conditions: "she refused to cook and keep the house clean"; "she had sex with another man"; "she refused to have sex" with her husband; "she made fun of [her husband] at a party"; and "she told friends that [her husband] was sexually pathetic" (p. 64).

(2) Briere (1987) justified the low alpha coefficient on the grounds that this brief scale samples attitudes toward wife abuse in a variety of situations. He suggested that future researchers might lengthen the scale or try dividing it into homogeneous subscales.
AVAILABLE FROM: Briere, 1987
USED IN:

Briere, J. (1987). Predicting self-reported likelihood of battering: Attitudes and childhood experiences. *Journal of Research in Personality, 21,* 61–69.

BIBLIOGRAPHY:

Burt, M. R. (1980). Cultural myths and supports for rape. *Journal of Personality and Social Psychology, 38,* 217–230.

INVENTORY OF BELIEFS ABOUT WIFE BEATING (IBWB)

AUTHORS: Daniel G. Saunders, Ann B. Lynch, Marcia Grayson, and Daniel Linz
DATE: 1987
VARIABLE: Beliefs and attitudes about wife beating
TYPE OF INSTRUMENT: Summated rating scale
DESCRIPTION: The Inventory of Beliefs About Wife Beating (IBWB)

consists of 30 items representing five factors: Wife Beating is Justified (WJ, 12 items), Wives Gain from Beatings (WG, 7 items), Help Should be Given (HG, 5 items), Offender Should be Punished (OP, 5 items), and Offender is Responsible (OR, 2 items plus 2 additional items from the OP scale). All but 1 item is accompanied by seven response alternatives ranging from "strongly agree" to "strongly disagree." The remaining item ("How long should a man who has beaten his wife spend in prison or jail?") is accompanied by eight response options: "0, 1 month, 6 months, 1 year, 3 years, 5 years, 10 years, don't know."
SAMPLE ITEMS: (Wife Beating is Justified) A husband has no right to beat his wife even if she breaks agreements she has made with him.

(Wives Gain from Beatings) Battered wives are responsible for their abuse because they intended it to happen.

(Help Should be Given) If I heard a woman being attacked by her husband, it would be best that I do nothing.

(Offender Should be Punished) If a wife is beaten by her husband, she should divorce him immediately.

(Offender Is Responsible) Cases of wife beating are the fault of the husband.
PREVIOUS SUBJECTS: College students, adults, men who batter, advocates for battered women
APPROPRIATE FOR: Ages 16 and older
ADMINISTRATION: Self-administered; about 10–15 minutes
SCORING: Items are individually scored on a 7-point scale. Saunders, Lynch, Grayson, and Linz (1987) provided a key to indicate the direction of scoring for each item. Item scores are summed to yield scores on each of the five subscales. A person who is totally opposed to wife beating and believes that the husband is responsible and should be held accountable would score low on subscales WJ and WG and high on subscales HG, OP, and OR.
DEVELOPMENT: A pool of 119 items was developed based on "rape-attitude scales, research and popular literature on wife abuse, consultation with the staff of a shelter for battered women, and clinical work with battered women and their partners" (Saunders et al., 1987, p. 42). The item pool was reduced by eliminating ambiguous or factual items. A sample of 106 college students responded to the items, and based on their responses, item intercorrelations were computed. The item pool was further reduced by eliminating any item that did not correlate with at least 2 other items. The remaining 41 items were administered to 675 college students who also completed the Rape Myth Acceptance Scale (RMA) (Burt, 1980) (see separate entry). The responses to the item pool were factor analyzed, and 12 factors were extracted. By examining the factors from both a statistical basis (intercorrelations between factors)

and a conceptual basis (similarity of content), the authors identified factors and items for the final scale.

RELIABILITY: Saunders et al. (1987) reported alpha coefficients based on the responses from the 675 college students used to develop the scale: WJ was .86, WG was .77, HG was .67, OP was .61, and OR was .62. Rose (1984/1985) tested nurses and physicians with a portion of the IBWB and reported alpha coefficients for two subscales: WJ was .73, and HG was .72.

VALIDITY: Saunders et al. (1987) administered the RMA along with the IBWB to 675 college students. Correlations between subscales of the IBWB and RMA scores were all statistically significant and in the predicted direction: WJ was .56, WG was .62, HG was −.42, OR was −.25, and OP was −.20.

To test further the construct validity of the IBWB, Saunders et al. (1987) tested various groups: nurses and physicians, batterers, advocates for battered women, and a group of Hispanics and Anglo-Americans. Although not all of the groups completed all of the measures, most groups completed the IBWB and most of the following measures: the Attitudes Toward Women Scale (AWS) (Spence, Helmreich, & Stapp, 1973) (see Beere, 1990), the Sex-Role Stereotyping Scale (Burt, 1980) (see Beere, 1990), the Hostility Toward Women Scale (Check & Malamuth, 1983) (see separate entry), two items assessing men's propensity toward violence against women, the Psychoticism Scale of the Symptom Checklist-90 (Derogatis, 1977), the Extroversion and Neuroticism subscales of the Eysenck Personality Questionnaire (Eysenck & Eysenck, 1969), and a portion of the Marlowe-Crowne Social Desirability Scale (Crowne & Marlowe, 1964). In general, the results were consistent with predictions. Scores on the AWS, the Sex-Role Stereotyping Scale, and the Hostility Toward Women Scale were significantly correlated with scores on the IBWB for most samples. Scores on the personality measures tended to be independent of scores on the IBWB; that is, only 2 of 15 correlations were statistically significant.

Further evidence of the construct validity of the IBWB was provided by the finding that female and male students differed significantly on four of the five subscales; there was no difference on the OR subscale. On the four subscales where there were significant differences, all were in the predicted direction.

As predicted, the scores of abusers were significantly different from the scores of advocates for battered women on all five subscales. Furthermore, as predicted, the scores of college students fell between the scores of the abusers and the scores of the advocates on all five subscales.

NOTES & COMMENTS: (1) The alpha coefficients for the subscales indicate that they are quite heterogeneous.

(2) Saunders et al. (1987) suggested using a longer subscale including items from three subscales: WJ, WG, and HG (item scores reversed). This larger factor, named Sympathy for Battered Wives, accounted for 79.8% of the variance in the data obtained from the 675 college students. Coefficient alpha for the longer subscale was .89.

(3) Saunders et al. (1987) reported evidence that IBWB scores are somewhat affected by the tendency to respond in socially desirable ways. Although the impact of this tendency seems to be rather small, they suggested that its effects be removed statistically, such as by using analysis of covariance.

(4) Rose (1984/1985) and Rose and Saunders (1986) reported using the IBWB with nurses and physicians to determine their attitudes about spouse abuse.

AVAILABLE FROM: Saunders, Lynch, Grayson, and Linz, 1987

USED IN:

Rose, K. (1985). Physicians' and nurses' attitudes toward woman abuse (Doctoral dissertation, University of Wisconsin-Madison, 1984). *Dissertation Abstracts International, 46,* 348B.

Rose, K., & Saunders, D. G. (1986). Nurses' and physicians' attitudes about woman abuse: The effects of gender and professional role. *Health Care for Women International, 7,* 427–438.

Saunders, D. G., Lynch, A. B., Grayson, M., & Linz, D. (1987). The Inventory of Beliefs About Wife Beating: The construction and initial validation of a measure of beliefs and attitudes. *Violence and Victims, 2,* 39–57.

BIBLIOGRAPHY:

Beere, C. A. (1990). *Gender roles: A handbook of tests and measures.* Westport, CT: Greenwood.

Burt, M. R. (1980). Cultural myths and supports for rape. *Journal of Personality and Social Psychology, 38,* 217–230.

Check, J. V. P., & Malamuth, N. M. (1983). Sex role stereotyping and reactions to depictions of stranger versus acquaintance rape. *Journal of Personality and Social Psychology, 45,* 344–356.

Crowne, D. P., & Marlowe, D. (1964). *The approval motive.* New York: John Wiley.

Derogatis, L. R. (1977). *SCL-90: Administration, scoring and procedures manual—I, for the revised version.* Unpublished manuscript, Johns Hopkins University, Baltimore.

Eysenck, H. J., & Eysenck, S. B. (1969). *Manual of the Eysenck Personality Questionnaire.* London: Hodder & Stoughton.

Spence, J. T., Helmreich, R., & Stapp, J. (1973). A short version of the Attitudes Toward Women Scale (AWS). *Bulletin of the Psychonomic Society, 2,* 219–220.

JACKSON INCEST BLAME SCALE (JIBS)

AUTHORS: Thomas L. Jackson and William P. Ferguson

DATE: 1983

VARIABLE: Attribution of blame in incest

TYPE OF INSTRUMENT: Summated rating scale
DESCRIPTION: The Jackson Incest Blame Scale (JIBS) consists of 20 statements, 19 of them offering an explanation for the cause of incest. The following causes of incest are equally represented on the JIBS: Situational Factors, Victim Behavior, Societal Values, and Offender Characteristics. Each item is accompanied by six response options ranging from strong disagreement to strong agreement.
SAMPLE ITEMS: (Situational Factor) Incest is more likely to occur in broken homes.

(Victim Behavior) It is the victim who entices the offender to commit incest.

(Societal Values) There is a strong connection between the current morality and the crime of incest.

(Offender Characteristics) Incest can be mainly attributed to peculiarities in the offender's personality.
PREVIOUS SUBJECTS: College students, attorneys and judges, mental health workers
APPROPRIATE FOR: Ages 16 and older
ADMINISTRATION: Self-administered; about 10 minutes
SCORING: Items are individually scored, with 1 point assigned to the "strongly disagree" response and 6 points assigned to the "strongly agree" response. Item scores are totaled to yield four factor scores and a total score.
DEVELOPMENT: The JIBS is essentially an adaptation of the 20-item Attribution of Rape Blame Scale (ARBS) (Resick & Jackson, 1981; Ward, 1980) (see separate entry). Most of the items on the JIBS are the ARBS items with the word *rape* changed to *incest.* "However, on primarily situational items, certain changes in the item content were required to reflect the hypothesized situational differences between rape and incest" (Jackson & Ferguson, 1983, p. 318). After the JIBS was constructed, it was completed by 412 college students, and their responses were factor analyzed. Four factors were extracted: Situational Variables, Victim Blame, Societal Values, and Offender Characteristics.
RELIABILITY: Coefficient alpha, based on the 412 respondents tested by Jackson and Ferguson (1983), was .71 for the total score. Reliability values for the factor scores were not reported.
VALIDITY: Jackson and Ferguson (1983) found significant sex differences on only Factor II: Victim Blame, with males blaming the victim more than females did. They also compared scores from physically abused versus nonphysically abused and sexually abused versus nonsexually abused persons. The only significant difference was that sexually abused persons attributed more blame to societal values than did persons not sexually abused.
NOTES & COMMENTS: (1) Jackson and Sandberg (1985) factor analyzed

the responses from 216 attorneys who completed the JIBS. They extracted four factors that were similar to those reported in the Jackson and Ferguson (1983) study; however, "the difference in the factor solution was apparent in that two offender blame items loaded inversely on the victim blame factor" (Jackson & Sandberg, 1985, p. 45). Jackson and Sandberg found significant sex differences on three of the four factors: males were more likely to blame the victim, females attributed more blame to the offender, and males ascribed more blame to situational variables.

(2) Factor scores from college students (Jackson & Ferguson, 1983) and from attorneys and judges (Jackson & Sandberg, 1985) showed that both groups rank ordered blame in the following sequence: Offender Characteristics, Situational Factors, Societal Values, and Victim Behavior.

(3) Jackson and Sandberg (1985) examined the relationship between attorneys' and judges' attribution of incest blame and their assignment of a sentence to a convicted rapist. Kalichman, Craig, and Crowe (1986) studied the attribution of incest blame among a group of mental health professionals including psychologists, social workers, psychiatrists, nurses, and adult and adolescent counselors.

AVAILABLE FROM: Jackson and Ferguson, 1983; Jackson and Sandberg, 1985

USED IN:

Jackson, T. L., & Ferguson, W. P. (1983). Attribution of blame in incest. *American Journal of Community Psychology, 11*, 313–322.

Jackson, T. L., & Sandberg, G. (1985). Attribution of incest blame among rural attorneys and judges. *Women and Therapy*, *4*(3), 39–56.

Kalichman, S. C., Craig, M. E., & Crowe, C. M. (1986, August). *Incestuous abuse: Licensed and non-licensed clinicians' attitudes and reporting*. Paper presented at the meeting of the American Psychological Association, Washington, DC. (ERIC Document Reproduction Service No. ED 281 136)

BIBLIOGRAPHY:

Resick, P. A., & Jackson, T. L., Jr. (1981). Attitudes toward rape among mental health professionals. *American Journal of Community Psychology*, *9*, 481–490.

Ward, M. A. (1980). Attribution of blame in rape (Doctoral dissertation, University of South Dakota, Vermillion, 1980). *Dissertation Abstracts International*, *41*, 1934B.

SIBLING INCEST AVERSION SCALE

AUTHORS: William B. Arndt, Jr. and Barbara Ladd

DATE: 1981

VARIABLE: Aversion to sibling incest "as a means of assessing the magnitude of the Oedipus conflict" (Arndt & Ladd, 1981, p. 52).

TYPE OF INSTRUMENT: Summated rating scale

DESCRIPTION: The Sibling Incest Aversion Scale contains 30 items, most of them relating to the consequences of sibling incest or expressing a judgment about such incest. Each item is accompanied by five response options ranging from "strongly agree" to "strongly disagree."

SAMPLE ITEMS: Sister-brother incest is tolerable under some conditions.

If I ever became involved in a brother-sister incest relationship, I would feel so ashamed as to take my own life.

PREVIOUS SUBJECTS: College students

APPROPRIATE FOR: Ages 16 and older

ADMINISTRATION: Self-administered; about 10–15 minutes

SCORING: Items are individually scored on a 5-point scale. Item scores are summed to yield a total score that can range from 30 to 150, with higher scores showing greater incest aversion. Arndt and Ladd (1981) reported a mean of 113.64 (standard deviation = 36.58) for 53 college males and a mean of 123.54 (standard deviation = 21.65) for 50 college females.

DEVELOPMENT: As the first step in scale development, a group of 37 college students provided information on their attitudes toward brother-sister incest. Using this information, the authors constructed a pool of 100 statements and administered it to 90 other college students with instructions to respond to each item on a 5-point scale ranging from "strongly agree" to "strongly disagree." An item discrimination analysis was performed, and the responses from the third of the students with the highest scores were compared with the responses from the third of the students with the lowest scores. The 30 items retained for the final scale discriminated between high and low scorers at the .001 level.

RELIABILITY: Using the responses from the sample used for scale development, the authors computed two estimates of reliability: split-half and Hoyt index of internal consistency. Both estimates were .98.

VALIDITY: No information was provided.

NOTES & COMMENTS: (1) Unlike the other scales in this book, the theoretical underpinnings prompting the development of the Sibling Incest Aversion Scale rely on psychoanalytic theory.

(2) Arndt and Ladd (1981) related scores on the Sibling Incest Aversion Scale to the following variables: birth position, guilt disposition, neuroticism, extroversion, and sensitization/repression.

(3) Arndt, Foehl, and Good (1985) related responses to their Sexual Fantasy Questionnaire (see separate entry) to a variety of variables, including scores on the Sibling Incest Aversion Scale.

AVAILABLE FROM: Arndt and Ladd, 1981

USED IN:

Arndt, W. B., Jr., Foehl, J. C., & Good, F. E. (1985). Specific sexual fantasy themes: A multidimensional study. *Journal of Personality and Social Psychology, 48*, 472–480.

Arndt, W. B., Jr., & Ladd, B. (1981). Sibling incest aversion as an index of Oedipal conflict. *Journal of Personality Assessment, 45*, 52–58.

10

Body Image and Appearance

This chapter contains descriptions of 17 measures organized into four sections: clothing and makeup (3 scales), attitudes and perceptions regarding one's own body (7 scales), self-perception of body size (5 scales), and stereotypes regarding physical attractiveness (2 scales). Because my original handbook (Beere, 1979) did not contain scales measuring body image and/or appearance, none of the scales described in this chapter was contained in the original handbook.

Of the first three measures, two deal with clothing, and one pertains to makeup. All three are summated rating scales that can be used with high school students, college students, and adults. The makeup scale is appropriate only for females. Although there were data relevant to the reliability of all three scales, only two of the three were sufficiently reliable. Furthermore, there was little or no evidence that any of these scales was valid. Nevertheless, I include them because they are relevant to a significant gender issue—appearance—and they measure variables not covered by other scales in the book.

The second section of this chapter describes seven scales to measure attitudes regarding one's body, satisfaction with one's body, and concern with body-related issues. Four of the seven measures include a list of body parts, and respondents either rate their satisfaction regarding the body parts or complete bipolar adjective scales for each body part. Five measures in this section are summated rating scales. One is appropriate only for males, one is appropriate only for females, and the other five are for both sexes. All are intended for use with adolescents or adults. The oldest scale in this section is the Body Cathexis scale (Secord & Jourard, 1953), and the newest scale is the Food, Fitness, and Looks

Questionnaire (Hall, Leibrich, & Walkey, 1983). The scales in this section tend to be longer than usual; five of the seven have at least 25 items. Only one scale in this section has been used extensively; the Body Cathexis scale is accompanied by a list of over 30 citations. There were data relevant to the reliability and validity of all measures in this section, but sometimes the data were equivocal or even suggested the scale lacked validity.

The third section of this chapter describes five estimation procedures. The different procedures require different equipment, but all have the same objective: to provide respondents with an opportunity to report their perceptions of the size of their own body. The procedures can be used to assess self-perceptions of actual body size and perceptions of ideal body size. All of the procedures can be used to score perceived body size as a function of actual body size or as a function of ideal body size. There were no data to indicate the minimum age for handling the requirements of the estimation tasks, but one can presume that 12-year-olds can handle the tasks. It is possible that younger persons could also complete the tasks required by some of these procedures, but I did not find any research that used the procedures with children. There were no data pertaining to the reliability of two of these procedures, but the reliability for the remaining three procedures suggested that they yield stable results. There were data to support the validity of all five measures. Researchers interested in more information regarding the assessment of body image should review *Body Image Disturbance: Assessment and Treatment* by Thompson (in press) and two articles: one by Garner and Garfinkel (1981/1982) and the other by Ruff and Barrios (1986).

The last section of this chapter contains two scales that are related to each other; the first author on both scales is A. Chris Downs (Downs & Currie, 1983; Downs, Reagan, Garrett, & Kolodzy, 1982). Both scales assess agreement with the stereotypes regarding physically attractive and unattractive persons. One scale is for use with high school ages and older; the other is for use with ages 6 to 11. The internal consistency reliability is satisfactory for both scales, and there was evidence relating to the validity of both scales. Neither scale has been used much.

BIBLIOGRAPHY:

Beere, C. A. (1979). *Women and women's issues: A handbook of tests and measures.* San Francisco: Jossey-Bass.

Downs, A. C., & Currie, M. V. (1983). Indexing elementary school-age children's views of attractive and unattractive people: The Attitudes Toward Physical Attractiveness Scale—Intermediate version. *Psychological Documents, 13,* 23. (Ms. No. 2579)

Downs, A. C., Reagan, M. A., Garrett, C., & Kolodzy, P. (1982). The Attitudes Toward Physical Attractiveness Scale (ATPAS): An index of stereotypes based on physical appearance. *Catalog of Selected Documents in Psychology, 12,* 44. (Ms. No. 2502)

Garner, D. M., & Garfinkel, P. E. (1981/1982). Body image in anorexia nervosa: Measurement, theory and clinical implications. *International Journal of Psychiatry in Medicine, 11*, 263–284.

Hall, A., Leibrich, J., & Walkey, F. H. (1983). The development of a Food, Fitness, and Looks Questionnaire and its use in a study of "weight pathology" in 204 nonpatient families. In P. L. Darby, P. E. Garfinkel, D. M. Garner, & D. V. Coscina (Eds.), *Anorexia nervosa: Recent developments in research* (pp. 41–55). New York: Alan R. Liss.

Ruff, G. A., & Barrios, B. A. (1986). Realistic assessment of body image. *Behavioral Assessment, 8*, 237–251.

Secord, P. F., & Jourard, S. M. (1953). The appraisal of body cathexis: Body cathexis and the self. *Journal of Consulting Psychology, 17*, 343–347.

Thompson, J. K. (1990). *Body image disturbance: Assessment and treatment.* New York: Pergamon.

CLOTHING INTEREST INVENTORY
AUTHOR: Holly Lois Schrank
DATE: 1970
VARIABLE: Interest in clothing
TYPE OF INSTRUMENT: Summated rating scale
DESCRIPTION: The Clothing Interest Inventory contains 20 statements relating to fashion and clothing. Each statement is accompanied by 5 response options: "DT—Definitely True; PT—Partially True, more true than false; U—Undecided, Uncertain; PF—Partially False, more false than true; DF—Definitely False." Half of the items are phrased to reflect a positive interest in clothing; the other half reflect a lack of interest in clothing.
SAMPLE ITEMS: I enjoy clothing like some people do such things as books, records, and movies.

I have no interest in keeping up with the latest fashion trends.
PREVIOUS SUBJECTS: College women
APPROPRIATE FOR: High school students and older; a few items need editing to be appropriate for males or for persons not in college
ADMINISTRATION: Self-administered; less than 10 minutes
SCORING: Items are scored on a 5-point scale. For positively keyed items, the end of the continuum stating "definitely true" is assigned 5 points; scoring is reversed for the negatively keyed items. A score of 3 is assigned for any item left blank. Item scores are summed to yield a total score ranging from 20 (no interest in clothing) to 100 (strong interest in clothing).
DEVELOPMENT: The Clothing Interest Inventory represents a modification of the Sharpe Clothing-Interest-and-Importance Scale (Sharpe, 1963). The items from Sharpe's scale were reviewed by eight graduate students and faculty members who made suggestions for revising and eliminating items. Based on their inputs, a pool of 16 items was pre-

tested. The pool was reduced to 12 items using a "scale discrimination technique" (Schrank, 1970/1971, p. 53). Eight statements were added to the pool to create the current 20-item version of the Clothing Interest Inventory.
RELIABILITY: Schrank (1970/1971) reported a corrected split-half reliability of .94.
VALIDITY: No information was provided other than the suggestion that the review by expert judges ensured that the items possessed face validity.
NOTES & COMMENTS: (1) Schrank (1970/1971) and Schrank and Gilmore (1973) used the Clothing Interest Inventory in their study of fashion leadership. Davis (1985) looked at the relationship between clothing interest and perceived body type.

(2) Since Schrank (1970/1971) provided no justification for the response options, it would be a good idea to change them to "strongly agree, agree, neutral, disagree, strongly disagree." These options are consistent with those commonly used in research and thus are more likely to be familiar to respondents.
AVAILABLE FROM: Schrank, 1970/1971; Schrank and Gilmore, 1973
USED IN:

Davis, L. L. (1985). Perceived somatotype, body-cathexis, and attitudes toward clothing among college females. *Perceptual and Motor Skills, 61*, 1199–1205.

Schrank, H. L. (1971). Fashion innovativeness and fashion opinion leadership as related to social insecurity, attitudes toward conformity, clothing interest and socioeconomic level (Doctoral dissertation, Ohio State University, 1970). *Dissertation Abstracts International, 31*, 5459B.

Schrank, H. L., & Gilmore, D. L. (1973). Correlates of fashion leadership: Implications for fashion process theory. *Sociological Quarterly, 14*, 534–543.

BIBLIOGRAPHY:

Sharpe, E. S. (1963). *Development of a clothing interest-and-importance scale*. Unpublished master's thesis, Ohio State University, Columbus.

CREEKMORE IMPORTANCE OF CLOTHING QUESTIONNAIRE

AUTHOR: Anna Creekmore
DATE: 1967
VARIABLE: Attitudes toward the importance of clothing
TYPE OF INSTRUMENT: Summated rating scale
DESCRIPTION: The Creekmore Importance of Clothing Questionnaire contains 89 items divided into eight areas. Each area is represented by 11 items, and there is an introductory item at the beginning of the scale that does not contribute to the scoring. *Aesthetic* items pertain to the use of clothing to enhance one's own appearance; *Approval* items pertain to the use of clothing to achieve acceptance from one's peer group; the *Attention* items relate to the use of clothing to seek attention—either

positive or negative (i.e., the attention may be in the form of social approval or disapproval); the *Comfort* items focus on dressing for personal comfort; the *Dependence* items pertain to the relationship between one's mood and one's clothing; the *Interest* items reflect the extent of one's interest in clothing as reflected in the time and energy one devotes to their appearance; the *Management* items pertain to the extent to which one plans ahead in terms of clothing and appearance; and the *Modesty* items relate to a preference for inconspicuous or conservative dress. The respondent rates each of the 89 items on a 5-point scale: "5. Almost Always—very few exceptions; 4. Usually—majority of the time; 3. Sometimes; 2. Seldom—not very often; 1. Almost Never—very few exceptions."

SAMPLE ITEMS: (Aesthetic) The way I look in my clothes is important to me.

(Approval) I check with my friends about what they are wearing to a gathering before I decide what to wear.

(Attention) When new fashions appear on the market, I am one of the first to own them.

(Comfort) The way my clothes feel to my body is important to me.

(Dependence) Certain clothes make me feel more sure of myself.

(Interest) My friends and I try each others clothes to see how we look in them.

(Management) I plan for and prepare clothes to wear several days in advance.

(Modesty) Unlined sheer dresses or blouses reveal too much of the body.

PREVIOUS SUBJECTS: High school and college students

APPROPRIATE FOR: High school students and older

ADMINISTRATION: Self-administered; about 30 minutes

SCORING: Creekmore (1971) suggested nine scores: one score representing each of the eight categories plus another score based on the last statement in each category. "The last statement in each of the scales measures the subject's searching for understanding of self and others relative to the behavior" (Creekmore, 1971, p. 97). Item scores are equal to the rating assigned by the subject, except that scores on a few items must be reversed. Subscale scores are obtained by summing item scores. The eight category scores can each range from 11 to 55, with higher scores indicating more of what is being measured (e.g., more modesty, more dependence, more value on aesthetics).

Results from factor analytic studies using the Creekmore Importance of Clothing Questionnaire can also serve as the basis for determining subscales.

DEVELOPMENT: The development of the questionnaire began with Creekmore's (1963) theoretical notions regarding "the relationship between clothing behaviors and general values and striving for satisfaction of needs" (Creekmore, 1971, p. 97). An initial measure containing 170 items was pretested three times with samples of 28 college students, 21 high school students, and 68 college students. Each pretest led to additional deletions and revisions. The initial measure included seven categories; after most of the pretesting was completed, the eighth category, Dependence, was added.

RELIABILITY: Fetterman (cited in Creekmore, 1971) reported internal consistency reliability, separately by sex, based on testing 236 high school boys and 269 high school girls. For boys, the reliability estimates were: Aesthetic = .77, Approval = .71, Attention = .71, Comfort = .57, Dependence = .75, Interest = .77, Management = .67, and Modesty = .71. For girls, the reliability estimates were Aesthetic = .58, Approval = .71, Attention = .77, Comfort = .61, Dependence = .78, Interest = .81, Management = .65, and Modesty = .65.

VALIDITY: Gurel and Deemer (1975) administered the Creekmore Importance of Clothing Questionnaire to 500 college students enrolled in a clothing and textiles course. They identified eight factors and found that 80 of the 89 items could easily be assigned to one of the factors; these 80 items had factor loadings of at least .30 and loaded substantially higher on one factor than on any of the others. Gurel and Deemer used their judgment in determining the appropriate factor for the remaining 9 items. Factor 1, Concern with Personal Appearance, contained 16 items; Factor 2, Experimenting with Appearance, contained 12 items; Factor 3, Conformity, contained 13 items; Factor 4, Modesty, contained 10 items; Factor 5, Heightened Awareness of Clothes, contained 9 items; Factor 6, Clothing as Enhancement of Security, contained 9 items; Factor 7, Clothing as Enhancement of Individuality, contained 11 items; and Factor 8, Sensitivity to Comfort, contained 9 items (Gurel & Gurel, 1979).

Gurel and Deemer (1975) computed phi coefficients between the factor scores (resulting from their factor analysis) and the subscale scores normally obtained from the Creekmore Importance of Clothing Questionnaire. Their findings provided some evidence for the construct validity of the questionnaire. For six of the eight factor scores, Gurel and Deemer found that the factors were significantly correlated with one subscale score; the remaining two factor scores each correlated significantly with two subscale scores. From the perspective of the subscale scores, seven of the eight subscale scores correlated significantly with one, and only one, factor score. The remaining subscale score was significantly correlated with two factor scores.

NOTES & COMMENTS: (1) The Creekmore Importance of Clothing Questionnaire is older than most other scales described in this book, and some of the items may be outdated. Despite its age, the scale has been used in the last 10 years, and of the various clothing measures that have been developed, the Creekmore Importance of Clothing Questionnaire has probably been used most often.

(2) Gurel and Gurel (1979) reported the intercorrelations between the eight factors they identified. The factors were definitely not independent. Of the 28 correlation coefficients, all but 3 were significantly different from 0; many, however, were quite low. Half of the 28 correlations were below .30. After examining the pattern of correlations, Gurel and Gurel concluded that "clothing interest is, in fact, multidimensional and is made up of at least five related but distinguishable dimensions . . . Concern with Personal Appearance, Experimenting with Appearance, Use of Clothing as Enhancement of Security, Use of Clothing as Enhancement of Individuality, and Heightened Awareness of Clothes" (p. 281). These factors can provide the framework for scoring the Creekmore Importance of Clothing Questionnaire.

(3) Davis (1985) used the Creekmore Importance of Clothing Questionnaire as one of three clothing measures in a study examining the relationships among perceived somatotype, body cathexis, and attitudes regarding clothing.

(4) Creekmore (1971) reported that five master's theses were written in conjunction with the development of the Creekmore Importance of Clothing Questionnaire (Engel, 1967; Humphrey, 1967; Hundley, 1967; Klaasen, 1967; Young, 1967).

AVAILABLE FROM: Creekmore, 1971; Gurel, 1974; Gurel and Gurel, 1979

USED IN:

Creekmore, A. M. (1971). *Methods of measuring clothing variables* (pp. 96–101). East Lansing: Michigan Agricultural Experiment Station Project No. 783, Michigan State University.

Davis, L. L. (1985). Perceived somatotype, body-cathexis, and attitudes toward clothing among college females. *Perceptual and Motor Skills, 61,* 1199–1205.

Engel, K. (1967). *The relationship of self-concept and clothing.* Unpublished master's thesis, Michigan State University, East Lansing.

Gurel, L. M. (1974). Dimensions of clothing interest based on factor analysis of Creekmore's 1968 clothing measure (Doctoral dissertation, University of North Carolina, 1974). *Dissertation Abstracts International, 35,* 1778B.

Gurel, L. M., & Deemer, E. M. (1975). Construct validity of Creekmore's clothing questionnaire. *Home Economics Research Journal, 4,* 42–47.

Gurel, L. M., & Gurel, L. (1979). Clothing interest: Conceptualization and measurement. *Home Economics Research Journal, 7,* 274–282.

Humphrey, C. A. (1967). *The relationship of stability of self concept to the clothing of adolescents.* Unpublished master's thesis, Michigan State University, East Lansing.

Hundley, W. S. (1967). *The relationship of clothing to social class, high school position and status inconsistency of adolescent boys and girls.* Unpublished master's thesis, Michigan State University, East Lansing.

Klaasen, M. G. (1967). *Self esteem and its relationship to clothing*. Unpublished master's thesis, Michigan State University, East Lansing.

Young, M. J. (1967). *The relationship of social acceptance to personal appearance of adolescents*. Unpublished master's thesis, Michigan State University, East Lansing.

BIBLIOGRAPHY:

Creekmore, A. M. (1963). Clothing and its relation to the satisfaction of basic needs and to general values (Doctoral dissertation, Pennsylvania State University, 1963). *Dissertation Abstracts, 24*, 1599.

MILLER COX ATTITUDES ABOUT MAKEUP

AUTHORS: Lynn Carol Miller and Cathryn Leigh Cox
DATE: 1982
VARIABLE: Attitudes and feelings about wearing makeup
TYPE OF INSTRUMENT: Summated rating scale
DESCRIPTION: The Miller Cox Attitudes About Makeup scale contains seven items regarding a woman's attitudes and feelings about her own use of makeup. Items pertain to the effect makeup has on the woman's behavior toward others and the effect it has on others' behavior toward the woman. Each item is accompanied by a 5-point scale ranging from "1—not at all characteristic" to "5—extremely characteristic."
SAMPLE ITEMS: I feel that makeup enhances my appearance.
People react more positively toward me when I wear make-up.
PREVIOUS SUBJECTS: College women
APPROPRIATE FOR: Females, ages 16 and older; if items were modified, the scale could be used with males
ADMINISTRATION: Self-administered; less than 5 minutes
SCORING: Items are individually scored on a 5-point scale and summed to yield a total score. Total scores range from 7 (very negative attitude toward the use of makeup) to 35 (very positive attitude toward the use of makeup).
DEVELOPMENT: No information was provided.
RELIABILITY: Based on responses from 42 college women, coefficient alpha was .89.
VALIDITY: Miller and Cox (1982) administered the Miller Cox Attitudes About Makeup scale, the Public Self-Consciousness Scale (Fenigstein, Scheier, & Buss, 1975), and several other measures to 42 college women. As expected, scores on the Miller Cox Attitudes About Makeup scale were significantly correlated with scores on the Public Self-Consciousness Scale ($r = .40$).
NOTES & COMMENTS: Although this scale has been used in only one published study, I have included it because it measures a variable not measured by other scales described in this book.
AVAILABLE FROM: Miller and Cox, 1982

USED IN:

Miller, L. C., & Cox, C. L. (1982). For appearances' sake: Public self-consciousness and makeup use. *Personality and Social Psychology Bulletin, 8*, 748–751.

BIBLIOGRAPHY:

Fenigstein, A., Scheier, M., & Buss, A. (1975). Public and private self-consciousness: Assessment and theory. *Journal of Consulting and Clinical Psychology, 43*, 522–527.

BODY CATHEXIS (BC)

AUTHORS: Paul F. Secord and Sidney M. Jourard

DATE: 1953

VARIABLE: Body cathexis, defined as "the degree of feeling of satisfaction or dissatisfaction with the various parts or processes of the body" (Secord & Jourard, 1953, p. 343)

TYPE OF INSTRUMENT: Summated rating scale

DESCRIPTION: The Body Cathexis (BC) scale contains a list of 46 body parts and functions. Items pertain to almost every part of the body except those parts related to sexual and excretory functions. Respondents rate each item in terms of themselves. A 5-point rating scale is provided: "1. Have strong feelings and wish change could somehow be made; 2. Don't like, but can put up with; 3. Have no particular feelings one way or the other; 4. Am satisfied; 5. Consider myself fortunate."

SAMPLE ITEMS: hair
 digestion
 back view of head

PREVIOUS SUBJECTS: College students, adolescent girls with and without bulimia, adults, patients with bulimia, chronic schizophrenics, postmastectomy patients, women addicted to alcohol or opiates, women with amenorrhea, pregnant and postpartum women, infertile and previously infertile couples, preorgasmic women, high school students

APPROPRIATE FOR: Ages 12 and up

ADMINISTRATION: Self-administered; about 15–20 minutes

SCORING: Each item is assigned a score equal to the rating assigned to it. An overall BC average is obtained by summing the item scores and dividing the total by 46. Overall, scores can vary from 1 to 5, with lower scores reflecting more positive feelings. Young, Reeve, and Elliott (cited in Young & Reeve, 1980) recommended scoring each item separately rather than obtaining a composite score on the BC.

DEVELOPMENT: Extensive pilot testing of earlier versions of the BC led to the elimination of items that were "difficult to understand, difficult for the subject to assign a meaningful rating, or which resulted in little variability from subject to subject" (Secord & Jourard, 1953, p. 344). If the deletion of an item would result in the omission or underrepresentation of an important body part, the item was retained despite its failure to satisfy the criteria.

RELIABILITY: Secord and Jourard (1953) administered the BC to 70 college men and 56 college women. Before computing split-half reliability, they removed the responses from persons who did not show considerable variability in their responses. More specifically, persons' data were excluded if they responded with "4" at least 32 times, if they responded with "5" at least 28 times, or if they responded with "5" at least 24 times and had fewer than 2 responses of "1" and "2" combined. Applying these criteria reduced the pool of subjects to 45 men and 43 women. Split-half reliability was .78 for the men and .83 for the women.

Johnson (1956) administered the BC, with slightly revised instructions, to 52 college men who were retested after a 6- to 8-week interval. Test-retest reliability was .72.

VALIDITY: In addition to the BC, Secord and Jourard (1953) administered a Self-Cathexis scale (SC) and a Homonym Test of Body-Cathexis (H test) to 70 college men and 56 college women. Another group of 47 college students completed the BC, the SC, and Maslow's Test of Psychological Security-Insecurity (Maslow, Hirsh, Stein, & Honigmann, 1945). The correlation between the H test and BC was significant for females ($r = -.41$) but nonsignificant for males ($r = -.18$). The correlation between BC and Maslow's test was significant ($r = -.37$), and the correlation between BC and SC was significant for both females ($r = .66$) and males ($r = .58$).

Secord and Jourard (1953) found a significant sex difference on the BC: "females cathect their bodies, irrespective of direction, more highly than do males" (p. 346). Secord and Jourard demonstrated this by showing that there was a significant difference in the number of "3" responses ("Have no particular feelings one way or the other") selected by females and by males.

Johnson (1956) administered the BC to 52 college men and 95 female student nurses who also completed the SC and the Cornell Medical Index Health Questionnaire. The males had a significantly more positive attitude toward their bodies than did the females. The correlation between the BC and the SC was .66 for males and .79 for females. The correlation between BC scores and scores on the Cornell Medical Index Health Questionnaire was $-.33$ for males and $-.40$ for females; both correlations were statistically significant.

Mintz and Betz (1986), using a shortened verson of the BC with different response options, found a significant difference between the responses from males and from females: males were more positive toward their body.

NOTES & COMMENTS: Researchers have related scores on the BC to many other variables. Many of these researchers used modified versions of the BC. Among the variables studied in relation to BC scores were menarcheal status (Koff, Rierdan, & Silverstone, 1978); amenorrhea (Schreiber, Florin, & Rost, 1983); importance of cosmetics (Theberge & Kernaleguen, 1979); attitudes toward clothing (Davis, 1985); sexual behavior (MacCorquodale & DeLamater, 1979; Young, 1980); sexual preference (LaTorre & Wendenburg, 1983); contraceptive use (McKinney, Sprecher, & DeLamater, 1984; Young, 1981); reactions to infertility (Adler & Boxley, 1985); effectiveness of treatments for bulimia (Connors, Johnson, & Stuckey, 1984; Huon & Brown, 1985; Ordman & Kirschenbaum, 1985; White & Boskind-White, 1981); effects of a program to improve body image (Bergner, Remer, & Whetsell, 1985); effectiveness of a program for improving the appearance of inpatients with chronic schizophrenia (Callis & Dickey, 1982); effectiveness of treatment for lack of orgasm (Bogat, Hamernik, & Brooks, 1987); experience of mastectomy (Gerard, 1982); use of alcohol or opiates (Weathers & Billingskley, 1982); experience of breast-feeding (Hughes, 1984); percentage of body fat (Young & Reeve, 1980); bulimia (Post & Crowther, 1985); compulsive eating (Golden, Buzcek, & Robbins, 1986); weight change (Rosen, Gross, & Vara, 1987); impact of dance team participation (Blackman, Hunter, Hilyer, & Harrison, 1988); personality variables (Mable, Balance, & Galgan, 1986); self-esteem (McCaulay, Mintz, & Glenn, 1988; Rackley, Warren, & Bird, 1988); depression (McCaulay et al., 1988); and morphological variables (Ward & McKeown, 1987).

(2) Researchers have modified the BC scale. For example, Koff et al. (1978) selected 17 items from the BC and asked each respondent to use the 17 items to rate a figure drawing she had just completed. Responses were recorded on a 5-point scale ranging from "very satisfied" to "not satisfied." In addition to using the BC, Theberge and Kernaleguen (1979) used a Facial Cathexis scale with 14 face-related items excerpted from the BC. MacCorquodale and DeLamater (1979) and McKinney et al. (1984) initially used 25 items from the BC; later the number was reduced to 16 items. Factor analysis suggested that the 16 items loaded on two factors. Schreiber et al. (1983) used a 40-item German-language version of the BC scale. Other researchers used slightly longer or slightly shorter verions of the BC scale (e.g., Callis & Dickey, 1982; Davis, 1985; Golden et al., 1986; Hughes, 1984; McCaulay et al., 1988; Mintz & Betz, 1986). Researchers have frequently varied the response options, using a 5-point scale ranging from "very satisfied" to "very dissatisfied."

(3) Jourard and Secord (1955) developed a 12-item version of the BC scale. Some of the researchers listed here used the 12-item version.

AVAILABLE FROM: Secord and Jourard, 1953

USED IN:

Adler, J. D., & Boxley, R. L. (1985). The psychological reactions to infertility: Sex roles and coping styles. *Sex Roles, 12,* 271–279.

Bergner, M., Remer, P., & Whetsell, C. (1985). Transforming women's body image: A feminist counseling approach. *Women and Therapy, 4*, 25–38.

Blackman, L., Hunter, G., Hilyer, J., & Harrison, P. (1988). The effects of dance team participation on female adolescent physical fitness and self-concept. *Adolescence, 23*, 437–448.

Bogat, G. A., Hamernik, K., & Brooks, L. A. (1987). The influence of self-efficacy expectations on the treatment of preorgasmic women. *Journal of Sex and Marital Therapy, 13*, 128–136.

Callis, C., & Dickey, L. E. (1982). An appearance program with female psychiatric patients: Effect on self-concept, body cathexis, and appearance. *Catalog of Selected Documents in Psychology, 12*, 48. (Ms. No. 2512)

Connors, M. E., Johnson, C. L., & Stuckey, M. K. (1984). Treatment of bulimia with brief psychoeducational group therapy. *American Journal of Psychiatry, 141*, 1512–1516.

Davis, L. L. (1985). Perceived somatotype, body-cathexis, and attitudes toward clothing among college females. *Perceptual and Motor Skills, 61*, 1199–1205.

Gerard, D. (1982). Sexual functioning after mastectomy: Life vs. lab. *Journal of Sex and Marital Therapy, 8*, 305–315.

Golden, B. R., Buzcek, T., & Robbins, S. B. (1986). Parameters of bulimia: Examining the Compulsive Eating Scale. *Measurement and Evaluation in Counseling and Development, 19*, 84–92.

Hughes, R. B. (1984). Satisfaction with one's body and success in breastfeeding. *Issues in Comprehensive Pediatric Nursing, 7*, 141–153.

Huon, G. F., & Brown, L. B. (1985). Evaluating a group treatment for bulimia. *Journal of Psychiatric Research, 19*, 479–483.

Johnson, L. C. (1956). Body cathexis as a factor in somatic complaints. *Journal of Consulting Psychology, 20*, 145–149.

Jourard, S. M., & Secord, P. J. (1955). Body-cathexis and the ideal female figure. *Journal of Abnormal and Social Psychology, 50*, 243–246.

Koff, E., Rierdan, J., & Silverstone, E. (1978). Changes in representation of body image as a function of menarcheal status. *Developmental Psychology, 14*, 635–642.

LaTorre, R. A., & Wendenburg, K. (1983). Psychological characteristics of bisexual, heterosexual and homosexual women. *Journal of Homosexuality, 9*, 87–97.

Mable, H. M., Balance, W. D. G., & Galgan, R. J. (1986). Body-image distortion and dissatisfaction in university students. *Perceptual and Motor Skills, 63*, 907–911.

MacCorquodale, P., & DeLamater, J. (1979). Self-image and premarital sexuality. *Journal of Marriage and the Family, 41*, 327–339.

McCaulay, M., Mintz, L., & Glenn, A. A. (1988). Body image, self-esteem, and depression-proneness: Closing the gender gap. *Sex Roles, 18*, 381–391.

McKinney, K., Sprecher, S., & DeLamater, J. (1984). Self images and contraceptive behavior. *Basic and Applied Social Psychology, 5*, 37–57.

Mintz, L. B., & Betz, N. E. (1986). Sex differences in the nature, realism, and correlates of body image. *Sex Roles, 15*, 185–195.

Ordman, A. M., & Kirschenbaum, D. S. (1985). Cognitive-behavioral therapy for bulimia: An initial outcome study. *Journal of Consulting and Clinical Psychology, 53,* 305–313.

Post, G., & Crowther, J. H. (1985). Variables that discriminate bulimic from nonbulimic adolescent females. *Journal of Youth and Adolescence, 14,* 85–95.

Rackley, J. V., Warren, S. A., & Bird, G. W. (1988). Determinants of body image in women at midlife. *Psychological Reports, 62,* 9–10.

Rosen, J. C., Gross, J., & Vara, L. (1987). Psychological adjustment of adolescents attempting to lose or gain weight. *Journal of Consulting and Clinical Psychology, 55,* 742–747.

Schreiber, C., Florin, I., & Rost, W. (1983). Psychological correlates of functional secondary amenorrhoea. *Psychotherapy and Psychosomatics, 39,* 106–111.

Secord, P. F., & Jourard, S. M. (1953). The appraisal of body cathexis: Body cathexis and the self. *Journal of Consulting Psychology, 17,* 343–347.

Theberge, L., & Kernaleguen, A. (1979). Importance of cosmetics related to aspects of the self. *Perceptual and Motor Skills, 48,* 827–830.

Ward, T. E., & McKeown, B. C. (1987). Association of body cathexis and morphological variables on college-aged females in an exercise setting. *Perceptual and Motor Skills, 64,* 179–190.

Weathers, C., & Billingskley, D. (1982). Body image and sex-role stereotype as features of addiction in women. *International Journal of the Addictions, 17,* 343–347.

White, W. C., Jr., & Boskind-White, M. (1981). An experiential-behavioral approach to the treatment of bulimarexia. *Psychotherapy: Theory, Research and Practice, 18,* 501–507.

Young, M. (1980). Body image and females' sexual behavior. *Perceptual and Motor Skills, 50,* 425–426.

Young, M. (1981). Body image and contraceptive use by college females. *Perceptual and Motor Skills, 53,* 456–458.

Young, M., & Reeve, T. G. (1980). Discriminant analysis of personality and body-image factors of females differing in percent body fat. *Perceptual and Motor Skills, 50,* 547–552.

BIBLIOGRAPHY:

Maslow, A. H., Hirsh, E., Stein, M., & Honigmann, I. (1945). A clinically derived test for measuring psychological security-insecurity. *Journal of Genetic Psychology, 33,* 21–41.

BODY CONSCIOUSNESS QUESTIONNAIRE

AUTHORS: Lynn C. Miller, Richard Murphy, and Arnold H. Buss

DATE: 1981

VARIABLE: Body awareness and competence

TYPE OF INSTRUMENT: Summated rating scale

DESCRIPTION: The Body Consciousness Questionnaire consists of 15 items representing three factors: Private Body Consciousness (5 items), Public Body Consciousness (6 items), and Body Competence (4 items). Respondents rate each item on a 5-point scale ranging from "0 (extremely uncharacteristic)" to "4 (extremely characteristic)."

SAMPLE ITEMS: (Private Body Consciousness) I am sensitive to internal bodily tensions.

(Public Body Consciousness) When with others, I want my hands to be clean and look nice.

(Body Competence) For my size, I'm pretty strong.

PREVIOUS SUBJECTS: College students in Australia and the United States

APPROPRIATE FOR: High school students and older

ADMINISTRATION: Self-administered; about 5–10 minutes

SCORING: Individual items are scored on a 4-point scale and summed to yield a score on each of the three subscales (factors). Using responses from 275 college men and 353 college women, Miller, Murphy, and Buss (1981) provided means and standard deviations, separately by sex.

DEVELOPMENT: A pool of items dealing with both the private and the public aspects of the body was reduced to 15 items based on pilot testing. The 15 items were rated by 561 college men and 720 college women. Factor analysis of their responses yielded three factors, similar to results obtained during pilot testing. Later administrations involving 460 college students and 680 college students produced comparable factor structures. Miller et al. (1981) reported the factor analytic results from 1,281 persons analyzed together. The lowest factor loading was .39, and no item loaded on a factor other than its own.

RELIABILITY: Miller et al. (1981) administered the Body Consciousness Questionnaire to 130 college students on two occasions, separated by a 2-month interval. They obtained the following test-retest reliabilities: Private Body Consciousness = .69, Public Body Consciousness = .73, and Body Competence = .83.

VALIDITY: Based on testing 275 college men and 353 college women, Miller et al. (1981) noted a significant difference between men and women on the Public Body Consciousness subscale. There were no significant sex differences on the other two subscales.

NOTES & COMMENTS: (1) Miller et al. (1981) correlated scores on the Body Consciousness Questionnaire with the following other measures: Private Self-Consciousness, Public Self-Consciousness, and Social Anxiety, which are the three subscales from the Self-Consciousness Inventory (Fenigstein, Scheier, & Buss, 1975); 14 items from the Hypochondriasis scale of the Minnesota Multiphasic Personality Inventory (Hathaway & McKinley, 1967); and the Emotionality scale of the EASI Temperament Survey (Buss & Plomin, 1975).

(2) Miller et al. (1981) tested college students with the Body Consciousness Questionnaire and the Self-Consciousness Inventory. The researchers then looked at how scores on these measures related to the impact that caffeine had on the students.

(3) Snell, Belk, and Hawkins (1986a) compared scores on the Body

Consciousness Questionnaire with scores on their Masculine and Feminine Self-Disclosure Scales (see separate entry). Snell, Belk, and Hawkins (1986b) compared scores on the Body Consciousness Questionnaire with scores on their Stereotypes About Male Sexuality Scale (see Beere, 1990).

(4) Tiggemann and Rothblum (1988) compared students from the University of Vermont with students from Flinders University of South Australia. The researchers used several measures, including the Body Consciousness Questionnaire.

AVAILABLE FROM: Miller, Murphy, and Buss, 1981

USED IN:

Miller, L. C., Murphy, R., & Buss, A. H. (1981). Consciousness of body: Private and public. *Journal of Personality and Social Psychology, 41,* 397–406.

Snell, W. E., Jr., Belk, S. S., & Hawkins, R. C., II. (1986a). The Masculine and Feminine Self-Disclosure Scale: The politics of masculine and feminine self-presentation. *Sex Roles, 15,* 249–267.

Snell, W. E., Jr., Belk, S. S., & Hawkins, R. C., II. (1986b). The Stereotypes About Male Sexuality Scale (SAMSS): Components, correlates, antecedents, consequences and counselor bias. *Social and Behavioral Science Documents, 16,* 9. (Ms. No. 2746)

Tiggemann, M., & Rothblum, E. D. (1988). Gender differences in social consequences of perceived overweight in the United States and Australia. *Sex Roles, 18,* 75–86.

BIBLIOGRAPHY:

Beere, C. A. (1990). *Gender roles: A handbook of tests and measures.* Westport, CT: Greenwood.

Buss, A. H., & Plomin, R. (1975). *A temperament theory of personality development.* New York: Wiley.

Fenigstein, A., Scheier, M., & Buss, A. H. (1975). Public and private self-consciousness: Assessment and theory. *Journal of Consulting and Clinical Psychology, 43,* 522–527.

Hathaway, S. R., & McKinley, J. C. (1967). *Minnesota Multiphasic Personality Inventory.* New York: Psychological Corporation.

BODY PARTS SATISFACTION SCALE (BPSS)

AUTHORS: Ellen Berscheid, Elaine Walster, and George Bohrnstedt

DATE: 1973

VARIABLE: Satisfaction and dissatisfaction with one's own body parts

TYPE OF INSTRUMENT: Summated rating scale

DESCRIPTION: The Body Parts Satisfaction Scale (BPSS) contains 24 body parts, each accompanied by six response options: "Extremely satisfied, Quite satisfied, Somewhat satisfied, Somewhat dissatisfied, Quite dissatisfied, Extremely dissatisfied." There is a 25th item referring to "Overall body appearance" and accompanied by the same six response options.

SAMPLE ITEMS: Height

Nose

PREVIOUS SUBJECTS: Readers of the *Psychology Today* magazine, college students, anorexics and bulimics, and their families

APPROPRIATE FOR: Ages 12 and older

ADMINISTRATION: Self-administered; about 5–10 minutes

SCORING: Items are individually scored on a 6-point scale, with 6 points assigned to the "Extremely satisfied" end of the continuum. A total score can be obtained by summing the scores across all items, and a mean score can be obtained by finding the average item score. Higher scores reflect more positive attitudes toward one's own body.

DEVELOPMENT: The BPSS was originally part of a *Psychology Today* survey (1972, July) on body image. The survey contained 109 items, including numerous items requesting demographic information. No information regarding scale development was provided.

RELIABILITY: Based on testing 163 college women and 61 college men, Noles, Cash, and Winstead (1985) obtained a coefficient alpha of .89. Kimlicka, Cross, and Tarnai (1983) tested 204 unmarried college women and obtained a corrected split-half reliability coefficient of .92.

VALIDITY: Noles et al. (1985) obtained four body image scores from each of 224 college students: an Appearance Satisfaction score equal to the rating assigned to the BPSS item concerned with overall appearance, a BPSS score based on summing the ratings for the remaining 24 items of the BPSS, a self-perceived physical attractiveness score based on 3 items from the Body-Self Relations Questionnaire (BSRQ) (Winstead & Cash, 1984), and a score based on a 19-item Physical Appearance subscale from the BSRQ. The intercorrelations among the four measures were all statistically significant and ranged from .53 to .87. Noles et al. also looked at the relationship between these scores and a measure of depression. As predicted, depressed persons compared to nondepressed persons were significantly less satisfied with their bodies, as measured by the BPSS.

Kimlicka et al. (1983) used the Bem Sex Role Inventory (Bem, 1974) (see Beere, 1990) to classify college students into four groups: androgynous, masculine, feminine, and undifferentiated. Multiple regression analysis showed that BPSS scores were significantly related to masculinity but not to femininity.

Butters and Cash (1987) used the BPSS as one of several measures to evaluate the effectiveness of a treatment program to reduce negative body image. As expected, the treatment produced significant improvement in body image as measured by the single BPSS item relating to overall appearance and significant improvement in body image as measured by a cumulative score based on the entire BPSS scale.

NOTES & COMMENTS: (1) The original *Psychology Today* survey, which included the BPSS, elicited responses from 62,000 readers. Berscheid,

Walster, and Bohrnstedt (1973) analyzed the responses from a subset of 2,000 readers.

(2) Bohrnstedt (cited in Noles et al., 1985) found that the BPSS consists of five factors for each sex. According to Butters and Cash (1987), the BPSS can yield six factor scores and an overall appearance rating score.

(3) The Body Dissatisfaction Scale (BDS), an 18-item adaptation from the BPSS, has been used in several studies of eating disorders (Garfinkel et al., 1983; Garner & Garfinkel, 1981; Garner, Olmsted, Bohr, & Garfinkel, 1982; Toner, Garfinkel, & Garner, 1986).

AVAILABLE FROM: The full *Psychology Today* survey is in the July 1972 issue of the magazine (pp. 58–64).

USED IN:

Berscheid, E., Walster, E., & Bohrnstedt, G. (1973, November). Body image. The happy American body: A survey report. *Psychology Today*, 119–131.

Body image. (1972, July). *Psychology Today*, pp. 58–64.

Butters, J. W., & Cash, T. F. (1987). Cognitive-behavioral treatment of women's body-image dissatisfaction. *Journal of Consulting and Clinical Psychology, 55*, 889–897.

Garfinkel, P. E., Garner, D. M., Rose, J., Darby, P. L., Brandes, J. S., O'Hanlon, J., & Walsh, N. (1983). A comparison of characteristics in the families of patients with anorexia nervosa and normal controls. *Psychological Medicine, 13*, 821–828.

Garner, D. M., & Garfinkel, P. E. (1981). Body image in anorexia nervosa: Measurement, theory and clinical implications. *International Journal of Psychiatry in Medicine, 11*, 263–284.

Garner, D. M., Olmsted, M. P., Bohr, Y., & Garfinkel, P. E. (1982). The Eating Attitudes Test: Psychometric features and clinical correlates. *Psychological Medicine, 12*, 871–878.

Kimlicka, T., Cross, H., & Tarnai, J. (1983). A comparison of androgynous, feminine, masculine, and undifferentiated women on self-esteem, body satisfaction, and sexual satisfaction. *Psychology of Women Quarterly, 7*, 291–294.

Noles, S. W., Cash, T. F., & Winstead, B. A. (1985). Body image, physical attractiveness, and depression. *Journal of Consulting and Clinical Psychology, 53*, 88–94.

Toner, B. B., Garfinkel, P. E., & Garner, D. M. (1986). Long-term follow-up of anorexia nervosa. *Psychosomatic Medicine, 48*, 520–529.

BIBLIOGRAPHY:

Beere, C. A. (1990). *Gender roles: A handbook of tests and measures*. Westport, CT: Greenwood.

Bem, S. L. (1974). The measurement of psychological androgyny. *Journal of Consulting and Clinical Psychology, 42*, 155–162.

Winstead, B. A., & Cash, T. F. (1984, March). *Reliability and validity of the Body-Self Relations Questionnaire: A new measure of body image*. Paper presented at the meeting of the Southeastern Psychological Association, New Orleans.

FOOD, FITNESS, AND LOOKS QUESTIONNAIRE (FFL)
AUTHORS: Anne Hall, Julie Leibrich, and Frank H. Walkey
DATE: 1983
VARIABLE: "Concern about weight, appearance, fitness and diet, and food control" (Hall, Leibrich, Walkey, & Welch, 1986, p. 72)
TYPE OF INSTRUMENT: Summated rating scale
DESCRIPTION: The Food, Fitness, and Looks Questionnaire (FFL) consists of 52 items representing five subscales: Weight (11 items), Appearance (18 items), Fitness (10 items), Values (14 items), and Eating (5 items). The sum of the items on the subscales is 58 because 6 items each contribute to two subscales. Each item is accompanied by five response alternatives: "definitely agree, agree, neutral, disagree, definitely disagree." Some items are phrased so that a person with concerns in the area would answer "definitely agree"; other items are phrased in the reverse direction.
SAMPLE ITEMS: (Weight) I don't worry about how "fattening" different foods are.

(Appearance) Women who don't look after their skin will be sorry.

(Fitness) Fitness is the key to attractiveness.

(Values) Family mealtimes should not be prolonged into social sessions.

(Eating) It's a good idea to have an eating "binge" from time to time.

PREVIOUS SUBJECTS: Mothers of adolescents, mothers of patients being treated for anorexia nervosa, and female members of Weight Watchers, all in New Zealand.
APPROPRIATE FOR: Women; one item would be inappropriate for women without families
ADMINISTRATION: Self-administered; about 30 minutes
SCORING: Items are individually scored on a 5-point scale, with the response showing greater concern assigned the higher score: "Definitely agree" is assigned 5 points for 36 of the items; "definitely disagree" is assigned 5 points for 16 items. Item scores are summed to yield five subscale scores: Weight, Appearance, Fitness, Values, and Eating.
DEVELOPMENT: The authors developed a pool of items pertaining to "attention to appearance, fitness consciousness, weight consciousness, and careful diet and food control" (Hall, Leibrich, & Walkey, 1983, p. 42). Using their own ideas and inputs from colleagues, the authors eliminated some items, modified others, and added new items. The resulting pool of 74 items was administered in New Zealand to two different samples of mothers of female adolescents. The first sample contained 142 mothers, and the second contained 204 mothers. The responses from the two groups were factor analyzed separately. The results were similar. According to Hall et al. (1983), the only difference between the two sets of factors was the order in which the first two factors emerged. To be

included on a factor, an item had to have a loading of .30 in one of the analyses and a loading of .25 on the same factor in the other analysis. These criteria resulted in the five subscales of the FFL as they currently exist. The names of four subscales—Weight, Appearance, Fitness, and Eating—clearly connote their content. The content of the Values subscale is less obvious, and in fact, the authors acknowledged that "this proved to be a more difficult factor to label" (Hall et al., 1983, p. 45). According to the authors, the items on this subscale relate to a value system involving restraint.

RELIABILITY: Coefficient alpha was reported for each subscale, for each sample. The values were: Weight = .88 for both sample 1 and sample 2, Appearance = .90 for sample 1 and .93 for sample 2, Fitness = .82 for sample 1 and .86 for sample 2, Values = .76 for both sample 1 and sample 2, and Eating = .60 for sample 1 and .66 for sample 2.

VALIDITY: From the sample of 204 mothers, Hall et al. (1983) collected additional information that allowed them to compute the following variables: current weight as a percentage of average weight, minimum weight as a percentage of average weight, maximum weight as a percentage of ideal weight, and weight variation as a percentage of ideal weight. The authors also collected data regarding age and current health status, and the mothers completed the Restraint Scale (Herman & Polivy, 1975) (see separate entry). These seven variables were correlated with the five subscale scores from the FFL. None of the variables was significantly correlated with the Appearance subscale, and only one of the variables—current health status—was significantly correlated with the Fitness subscale. Two variables were significantly correlated with the Values subscale—Restraint Scale scores and Age—and two variables were significantly correlated with the Eating subscale—maximum weight as a percentage of ideal weight and weight variation as a percentage of ideal weight. The greatest number of significant correlations was with the Weight subscale, which was significantly related to four of the variables: Restraint Scale scores, current weight as a percentage of average weight, maximum weight as a percentage of ideal weight, and weight variation as a percentage of ideal weight. Although Hall et al. (1983) interpreted these findings as providing evidence for the scale's validity, the findings seem ambiguous.

Hall et al. (1986) compared FFL scores from four groups of women: 58 mothers of anorexia nervosa patients, 204 mothers of female adolescents, 142 mothers of adolescents, and 446 members of Weight Watchers. While their data showed that mothers of anorexics did not show greater concern with the areas measured by the FFL (in most cases, the mothers of "normals" showed greater concern than the mothers of anorexics), the study did provide some evidence for the validity of the scale. The members of Weight Watchers scored significantly higher than the moth-

ers of anorexic patients on all five subscales. Furthermore, the mothers of the two control groups scored significantly lower than the Weight Watchers group on the Weight subscale and the Eating subscale.
NOTES & COMMENTS: (1) Both of the factor analytic studies were based on unacceptably small sample sizes. The consistency in findings between the two analyses is encouraging, yet the combined sample size was only 346, nowhere near the requisite 10 persons per item.

(2) The internal consistency reliability for the Eating subscale was unacceptably low. Although the brevity of the subscale helps explain the low reliability, it does not excuse it.
AVAILABLE FROM: Hall, Leibrich, and Walkey, 1983; Hall, Leibrich, Walkey, and Welch, 1986
USED IN:

Hall, A., Leibrich, J., & Walkey, F. H. (1983). The development of a Food, Fitness, and Looks Questionnaire and its use in a study of "weight pathology" in 204 nonpatient families. In P. L. Darby, P. E. Garfinkel, D. M. Garner, & D. V. Coscina (Eds.), *Anorexia nervosa: Recent developments in research* (pp. 41–55). New York: Alan R. Liss.

Hall, A., Leibrich, J., Walkey, F. H., & Welch, G. (1986). Investigation of "weight pathology" of 58 mothers of anorexia nervosa patients and 204 mothers of schoolgirls. *Psychological Medicine, 16*, 71–76.

BIBLIOGRAPHY:

Herman, C. P., & Polivy, J. (1975). Anxiety, restraint, and eating behaviour. *Journal of Abnormal Psychology, 84*, 666–672.

KURTZ BODY ATTITUDE SCALE

AUTHOR: Richard M. Kurtz
DATE: 1969
VARIABLE: Attitudes toward one's own body
TYPE OF INSTRUMENT: Semantic differential
DESCRIPTION: The Kurtz Body Attitude Scale consists of 30 body concepts, each to be rated on nine 7-point semantic differential scales. There are three bipolar adjective scales for each of the three dimensions on the semantic differential: Evaluative dimension—good-bad, awkward-graceful, beautiful-ugly; Potency dimension—weak-strong, hard-soft, thin-thick; and Activity dimension—active-passive, cold-hot, fast-slow.
SAMPLE ITEMS: Color of my hair

Size of my hands

PREVIOUS SUBJECTS: College students
APPROPRIATE FOR: High school ages and older
ADMINISTRATION: Self-administered; about 45 minutes
SCORING: Each response is assigned a score between 1 and 7, with higher scores assigned to the end of the continuum more strongly associated with the dimension being measured. A score can be obtained

for each of the three dimensions—Evaluative, Potency, Activity—by summing 90 item scores (i.e., responses to three bipolar adjective scales for each of 30 body parts), and an overall score can be obtained by summing all 270 item scores.
DEVELOPMENT: According to Kurtz and Hirt (1970), "the nine adjectival scales were chosen for the purity of their factor loadings and their relative freedom from denotative association with the concepts being noted" (p. 150).
RELIABILITY: Kurtz (1969) and Kurtz and Hirt (1970) reported results from a generalizability study that yielded generalizability coefficients ranging from .86 to .95 for all three dimensions.
VALIDITY: In a study of 89 college men and 80 college women, Kurtz (1969) provided evidence of the construct validity of the scale by the fact that he confirmed the following hypotheses: (1) women have a more clearly differentiated idea of what they like and what they dislike about their bodies, (2) women score higher than men do on the Evaluative dimension, and (3) men score higher than women do on the Potency and Activity dimensions.

Kurtz and Hirt (1970) compared 20 chronically ill women with 20 college women. As predicted, they found that the healthy group scored higher on the Evaluative dimension. However, contrary to prediction, the healthy group did not score significantly higher on the Potency dimension. In terms of the Activity dimension, the healthy group judged their bodies to be less passive than did the chronically ill group.

Kurtz (1966) confirmed several hypotheses relating body size and body build to responses to the Kurtz Body Attitude Scale. On the other hand, Kurtz failed to confirm many other hypotheses relating these variables to each other. Overall, Kurtz concluded that body attitude is "a function of the sex, size, and shape of their bodies" (p. 1929A).
NOTES & COMMENTS: (1) The Kurtz Body Attitude Scale was developed as part of Kurtz's (1966) doctoral dissertation, which contains more information about the scale.

(2) The generalizability of the findings regarding the Evaluative dimension is questionable. Of the three bipolar adjective pairs on the Evaluative dimension, two are sex typed; that is, men are not expected to be "graceful," nor are they likely to perceive themselves as graceful. Similarly, "beautiful" is a positive trait for women, but men are unlikely to perceive themselves as beautiful.

(3) Katzman and Wolchik (1984) used the Evaluative dimension subscale of the Kurtz Body Attitude Scale as one of several measures to compare bulimics and binge eaters to each other and to a control group of normal eaters.
AVAILABLE FROM: Kurtz, 1969; Kurtz and Hirt, 1970

USED IN:

Katzman, M. A., & Wolchik, S. A. (1984). Bulimia and binge eating in college women: A comparison of personality and behavioral characteristics. *Journal of Consulting and Clinical Psychology, 52*, 423–428.

Kurtz, R. M. (1966). The relationship of body attitude to sex, body size, and body build in a college population (Doctoral dissertation, University of Cincinnati, 1966). *Dissertation Abstracts International, 27*, 1928A-1929A.

Kurtz, R. M. (1969). Sex differences and variations in body attitudes. *Journal of Consulting and Clinical Psychology, 33*, 625–629.

Kurtz, R., & Hirt, M. (1970). Body attitude and physical health. *Journal of Clinical Psychology, 26*, 149–151.

PERCEIVED SOMATOTYPE SCALE

AUTHOR: Larry A. Tucker

DATE: 1982

VARIABLE: Perceived and ideal somatotype

TYPE OF INSTRUMENT: Picture preference

DESCRIPTION: The Perceived Somatotype Scale consists of a set of seven line drawings of a male figure, 78 mm high. The drawings "represent seven different body builds or somatotypes ranging from very thin and fragile (ectomorph) to very muscular (mesomorph) to very fat and rounded (endomorph)" (Tucker, 1982, p. 984). When taking the Perceived Somatotype Scale, a person first indicates the drawing that most resembles his own body build and then indicates the drawing that most resembles the body build he desires to have. A modification of the scale for females is described under NOTES & COMMENTS.

PREVIOUS SUBJECTS: College men

APPROPRIATE FOR: High school boys and older; the modification described below can be used with high school girls and older

ADMINISTRATION: Individually or self-administered; less than 5 minutes

SCORING: The Perceived Somatotype Scale is not scored per se. Rather data analysis is based on the choices the respondents made. Tucker (1982) suggested creating a dichotomous variable to show whether there is a difference between perceived and desired somatotype.

DEVELOPMENT: The drawings in the Perceived Somatotype Scale were based on Sheldon's (1940) work relating body type to temperament and the photographs and sketches Sheldon (1954) provided as reflective of the basic male somatotypes.

RELIABILITY: Based on data from 63 college men who completed the Perceived Somatotype Scale on two occasions, separated by a 2-week interval, the test-retest reliability of the scale was .96 for perceived somatotype and .94 for ideal somatotype.

VALIDITY: Tucker (1982) administered the Body Cathexis scale (BC)

(Secord & Jourard, 1953) (see separate entry) and the Perceived Somatotype Scale to 86 college men. BC measures the extent to which one is satisfied or dissatisfied with one's body parts. Perceived somatotype and the discrepancy between perceived and ideal somatotype were each significantly related to BC scores. Together they accounted for over 30% of the variance in BC scores. Tucker found that males who perceived themselves as mesomorphic had higher BC scores (more satisfaction with body) than any other group, and males who perceived themselves as mesoectomorphic had higher BC scores than did those who perceived themselves as mesoendomorphs, ectomorphs, or endomorphs. Males who perceived themselves to be at the extremes of thinness or fatness felt more negatively about their body parts on the BC scale. Males whose perceived somatotype differed from their ideal somatotype were more likely to have lower BC scores, reflecting greater dissatisfaction with their body parts.

NOTES & COMMENTS: Davis (1985) modified the Perceived Somatotype Scale to make it appropriate for use with females. Davis's modification used seven drawings of females in place of the seven drawings of males; in all other respects, the measure was the same as Tucker's measure. Davis tested 91 college women with the modified Perceived Somatotype Scale, the BC, the Creekmore Importance of Clothing Questionnaire (Creekmore, 1971) (see separate entry), the Clothing Interest Inventory (Schrank & Gilmore, 1973) (see separate entry), and a Fashion Opinion Leadership and Innovativeness Scale (Hirschman & Adcock, 1978). Consistent with Tucker's findings, Davis found significant relationships between BC scores and results on the Perceived Somatotype Scale. Females who perceived themselves as ectomorphs had significantly higher BC scores compared to those who perceived themselves as average or somewhat mesomorphic, and those who perceived themselves as endomorphs had significantly lower BC scores than those who perceived themselves as average or somewhat mesomorphic. Thus, contrary to the males, females who saw themselves as more muscular and fatter were less satisfied with their bodies. As was the case with males, females who perceived a discrepancy between their real and their ideal selves had lower BC scores, expressing less satisfaction with their bodies. Davis also found that perceived somatotype was unrelated to the fashion and clothing measures used in her study.

AVAILABLE FROM: The drawings are shown in Tucker, 1982; the drawings for the modified version are shown in Davis, 1985.

USED IN:

Davis, L. L. (1985). Perceived somatotype, body-cathexis, and attitudes toward clothing among college females. *Perceptual and Motor Skills, 61,* 1199–1205.

Tucker, L. A. (1982). Relationship between perceived somatotype and body cathexis of college males. *Psychological Reports, 50,* 983–989.

BIBLIOGRAPHY:
Creekmore, A. M. (1971). *Methods of measuring clothing variables* (pp. 96–101). East Lansing: Michigan Agricultural Experiment Station Project No. 783, Michigan State University.
Hirschman, E. C., & Adcock, W. O. (1978). An examination of innovative communicators, opinion leaders and innovators for men's fashion apparel. *Advances in Consumer Research, 5,* 303–314.
Schrank, H. L., & Gilmore, D. L. (1973). Correlates of fashion leadership: Implications for fashion process theory. *Sociological Quarterly, 14,* 534–543.
Secord, P. F., & Jourard, S. M. (1953). The appraisal of body-cathexis: Body-cathexis and the self. *Journal of Consulting Psychology, 17,* 343–347.
Sheldon, W. H. (1940). *The varieties of human physique*. New York: Harper.
Sheldon, W. H. (1954). *Atlas of men*. New York: Harper.

SELF PERCEPTION SCALES
AUTHORS: Gerald M. Rosen and Alan O. Ross, extended by Richard M. Lerner, Stuart A. Karabenick, and Joyce L. Stuart; also based on the Adjective Check List by Harrison Gough (1952)
DATE: 1968 (extended 1973)
VARIABLE: Self-perception in terms of physical attractiveness, personality traits, and physical effectiveness
TYPE OF INSTRUMENT: Summated rating scale
DESCRIPTION: There are three parts to the Self Perception Scales (Lerner, Orlos, & Knapp, 1976). Part I contains a list of 24 body parts (e.g., facial complexion, ears, and chest), and respondents rate themselves in terms of how attractive they are in regard to each body part. Five response options are provided: "very attractive, moderately attractive, midpoint of this scale, moderately unattractive, very unattractive." Part II contains 16 pairs of bipolar adjectives (e.g., mature-immature, masculine-feminine, and independent-dependent), and respondents rate where they fall on each pair. The following five response options are provided: "word on *left* end of continuum is *most like me*; word on *left* end of the continuum is *somewhat like me*; I fall on the midpoint of this scale; word on *right* end of the continuum is *somewhat like me*; word on *right* end of the continuum is *most like me*." Part III pertains to the effectiveness of various body parts. Respondents are presented with the same list of 24 body parts used in Part I. They rate the effectiveness of each body part using the following five response options: "very effective, moderately effective, midpoint of this scale, moderately ineffective, very ineffective."
PREVIOUS SUBJECTS: College students
APPROPRIATE FOR: High school students and older
ADMINISTRATION: Self-administered; about 20–30 minutes
SCORING: Scores are either reported for individual items or summed to yield a score on each of the three scales. A score of 1 point is assigned

for responses "very attractive" and "very effective," so that lower scores represent more positive self-perceptions. Similarly, the more positive end of the continuum for the bipolar adjective scales is assigned 1 point.
DEVELOPMENT: Lerner, Karabenick, and Stuart (1973) used four scales adapted from Rosen and Ross (1968) whose scale "contained 24 body parts judged to be of relevance to an S's satisfaction with his physical appearance" (p. 100), and 17 adjectives selected from the Adjective Check List (Gough, 1952). The first three scales from Lerner et al. used the list of 24 body parts. For Part I, respondents were to "judge how important *you feel* each of these characteristics is in determining how attractive you are to members of the opposite sex." Five response options were provided, ranging from "very important" to "very unimportant." For Part II, respondents were to "judge how important *you feel* each of these characteristics is in determining how attractive members of the opposite sex are to you." The same five response options were provided. For Part III, respondents were to rate how satisfied they were with each of the body parts on their own body, and Part IV was the same as Part II on the current version of the Self Perception Scales; that is, respondents reported their self-perceptions in terms of 16 bipolar adjective scales. Lerner and Karabenick (1974) used two of these parts: Respondents rated the importance of each characteristic to them and completed the 16 bipolar adjective scales. In addition, respondents rated how attractive they felt in terms of each of the 24 body parts. Lerner et al. (1976) varied the Self Perception Scales again, modifying them to match their current description. There was no information to explain the basis for the various modifications.
RELIABILITY: Lerner et al. (1976) tested 124 college men and 218 college women. The internal consistency reliability was .90 for both the males' attractiveness and effectiveness ratings. For females, the internal consistency reliabilities were .88 and .90 for attractiveness and effectiveness ratings, respectively.
VALIDITY: As predicted, Lerner and Karabenick (1974) found that the mean scores for body parts attractiveness were significantly correlated with self-concept scores for females ($r = .40, p < .01$) but not for males.

Lerner et al. (1976) reported a significant correlation between the mean attractiveness ratings from men and from women. Across all 24 items, the correlation was .66. Similarly the correlation between the effectiveness ratings from men and women was .87. They also found that, for both sexes, there was a significant correlation between attractiveness and effectiveness ratings, but the correlation was significantly higher for males.

Lerner et al. (1976) found that for females, attractiveness ratings were more closely associated with self-concept than were effectiveness ratings. "Five attractiveness items were significant predictors of females' self-concepts . . . , [but] only two effectiveness items are significantly related to self-concepts in females" (p. 321). The results were reversed for males: Effectiveness ratings were more closely associated with self-concept than were attractiveness ratings. "Eleven effectiveness items significantly predicted males' self-concepts . . . , [but] only two attractiveness items were significant predictor variables" (p. 323).

NOTES & COMMENTS: (1) Lerner and Brackney (1978) used an extension of the Self Perception Scales in order to study whether self-ratings of attractiveness and effectiveness of inner and outer body parts relate to self-concept and whether this relationship was different in college men compared to college women.

(2) Grant and Fodor (1986) used the Self Perception Scales to study the relationship between self-concept in terms of physical attractiveness, physical effectiveness, and personality traits and to see how these aspects of self-concept relate to eating disorders and to sex.

AVAILABLE FROM: Lerner, Karabenick, and Stuart, 1973, list the 24 body parts; the Adjective Check List can be purchased from Consulting Psychologists Press, 577 College Avenue, Palo Alto, CA 94306; for a list of the bipolar adjectives, write to Dr. Richard M. Lerner, Department of Child/Adolescent Development, Pennsylvania State University, University Park, PA 16802.

USED IN:

Grant, C. L., & Fodor, I. G. (1986). Adolescent attitudes toward body image and anorexic behavior. *Adolescence, 21*, 269–281.

Lerner, R. M., & Brackney, B. E. (1978). The importance of inner and outer body parts attitudes in the self-concept of late adolescents. *Sex Roles, 4*, 225–238.

Lerner, R. M., & Karabenick, S. A. (1974). Physical attractiveness, body attitudes, and self-concept in late adolescents. *Journal of Youth and Adolescence, 3*, 307–316.

Lerner, R. M., Karabenick, S. A., & Stuart, J. L. (1973). Relations among physical attractiveness, body attitudes, and self-concept in male and female college students. *Journal of Psychology, 85*, 119–129.

Lerner, R. M., Orlos, J. B., & Knapp, J. R. (1976). Physical attractiveness, physical effectiveness, and self-concept in late adolescents. *Adolescence, 11*, 313–326.

Rosen, G. M., & Ross, A. O. (1968). Relationship of body image to self-concept. *Journal of Consulting and Clinical Psychology, 32*, 100.

BIBLIOGRAPHY:

Gough, H. (1952). *The Adjective Check List*. Palo Alto, CA: Consulting Psychologists Press.

BODY IMAGE DETECTION DEVICE (BIDD)

AUTHORS: Gary A. Ruff and Billy A. Barrios

DATE: 1986

VARIABLE: Self perception of body size
TYPE OF INSTRUMENT: Estimation procedure
DESCRIPTION: The Body Image Detection Device (BIDD) requires an overhead projector, black posterboard, and pieces of wood. Two pieces of posterboard are situated on the overhead transparency plate in such a way as to allow a band of light, 1 cm wide, to be projected onto a white wall, 8 feet away. When using the BIDD, subjects are asked to operate the BIDD to estimate the width of five body parts: "the face across the zygomas (cheekbones), the chest across the axillae, the waist at its narrowest, the hips at their broadest, and the thighs with legs together, where the fingertips fall when the arms are at one's side" (Ruff & Barrios, 1986, p. 241). Participants are asked to make their estimates twice: one estimate involves a diverging line, and the other estimate involves two converging lines. For the estimate using a diverging line, the participant moves a piece of cardboard, with a triangular portion removed, across the transparency plate to increase or decrease the length of the projected line. To produce a converging estimate, the participant moves a triangular-shaped piece of cardboard across the transparency plate so that the projected image consists of two white lines, each 1 cm wide, separated by blackness. By moving the triangular piece of cardboard, the participant increases or decreases the distance between the two white lines.
PREVIOUS SUBJECTS: Bulimic and normal college women
APPROPRIATE FOR: Ages 12 and older
ADMINISTRATION: Individually administered with the research participant operating the BIDD; about 10–15 minutes
SCORING: The width of each body part is considered to be the average of the converging estimate and the diverging estimate for that body part.
DEVELOPMENT: No information was provided.
RELIABILITY: Using a linear composite of the estimates of the five body parts, Ruff and Barrios (1986) computed coefficient alpha for testing done at two different times. They obtained a coefficient alpha of .91 for the earlier testing involving 40 persons and a coefficient alpha of .93 for the later testing involving 34 persons. Sixteen "normal" females and 18 female bulimics completed the BIDD on two occasions, separated by a 3-week interval. For the normals, test-retest reliability for each of the five body parts ranged from .72 (thighs) to .85 (hips); for the bulimics, test-retest reliabilities ranged from .82 (chest and waist) to .87 (face and hips); and for the two groups combined, the reliabilities ranged from .84 (waist) to .92 (hips) (Ruff & Barrios, 1986).

Ruff and Barrios (1986) compared responses using the converging lines to responses using the diverging line. Correlations ranged from .61 to .84, with a mean of .73.

The estimates given on the wall were independently measured by two raters. Ruff and Barrios (1986) reported interrater reliabilities of at least .98.

VALIDITY: Ruff and Barrios (1986) compared normals and bulimics in terms of their BIDD scores relative to the actual size of their body parts. They found that bulimics tended to overestimate their body size more than did normals for every body part.

Cash and Green (1986) found that underweight college women were more likely than normal-weight college women to overestimate their own body size. In addition, underweight college women were more likely than normal-weight college women to overestimate the body size of a mannequin. Overweight college women, on the other hand, did not differ from normal-weight college women in terms of their estimate of their own body weight or the mannequin's body weight.

NOTES & COMMENTS: (1) Researchers (Butters & Cash, 1987; Cash & Green, 1986; Ruff & Barrios, 1986) asked respondents to provide a subjective rating indicating, for each of the five body parts, whether they were grossly below the norm (0), at the norm (50), above the norm (100), or somewhere in between.

(2) The BIDD results can be used to compute a Body Perception Index. According to Cash and Green (1986), the Body Perception Index is equal to the perceived size (as measured by the BIDD) divided by the actual size and multiplied by 100. This formula, which yields a separate value for each body part, requires that the actual size of each body part be assessed. Similarly, the subjective ratings can be used to compute a Subjective Rating Index. The Subjective Rating Index is equal to the subjective rating divided by 50 and multiplied by 100.

(3) Butters and Cash (1987) used the BIDD as one of several measures in a study evaluating the effectiveness of a treatment program designed to improve body image.

(4) An advantage to the BIDD is the easy availability of the required apparatus.

AVAILABLE FROM: The procedure is described fully in Ruff and Barrios, 1986.

USED IN:

Butters, J. W., & Cash, T. F. (1987). Cognitive-behavioral treatment of women's body-image dissatisfaction. *Journal of Consulting and Clinical Psychology, 55*, 889–897.

Cash, T. F., & Green, G. K. (1986). Body weight and body image among college women: Perception, cognition, and affect. *Journal of Personality Assessment, 50*, 290–301.

Ruff, G. A., & Barrios, B. A. (1986). Realistic assessment of body image. *Behavioral Assessment, 8*, 237–251.

BODY IMAGE PERCEPTION SCALE

AUTHORS: P. D. Slade and G. F. M. Russell

DATE: 1973

VARIABLE: Self-perception of body size
TYPE OF INSTRUMENT: Estimation procedure
DESCRIPTION: Administration of the Body Image Perception Scale requires a physical measurement of four body parts and measures of the subject's perceptions of the same four body parts. The four body parts are the face (across the zygomas), the chest (high in the axillae), the narrowest point of the waist, and the widest point of the hips. The physical measures are obtained with an anthropometer. After the physical measures are obtained, the subject's perceptions of the sizes are obtained with an estimation apparatus that Slade and Russell (1973a) described in the following manner: "The apparatus consist[s] of a movable horizontal bar, 155 cm long, 10.2 cm wide, mounted on a stand approximately 183 cm in height. Two lights attached to runners [are] mounted on tracks set into the horizontal bar" (p. 190). Originally a pulley device was used by the experimenter to move the two lights equal distances outward or inward from a center point. More recently, the lights are moved electrically. The back of the horizontal bar holds a measuring instrument from which the experimenter can record the distance between the lights.

To administer the procedure, the bar is first set at the subject's eye level. As the experimenter moves the lights outward or inward, the subject is to stop the experimenter when the distance between the lights matches the subject's perception of the distance across his or her face. After two practice trials, the subject is given four test trials. In two trials, the lights are placed close together, and the experimenter moves them outward until the subject feels they match the width of his or her face. In the other two trials, the lights are placed far apart, and the experimenter moves them inward until they match the subject's perceptions. The procedure is repeated for the three remaining body parts.
PREVIOUS SUBJECTS: Anorexia nervosa patients, bulimics, college students, secretaries, mothers, nurses, obese females
APPROPRIATE FOR: Ages 12 and older
ADMINISTRATION: Individually administered; about 20 minutes
SCORING: In order to obtain a perceived score for each of the four body parts, the results (read off the back of the bar) are averaged for the four trials on that body part. A body image perception index is computed for each body part by dividing the perceived size by the real size and multiplying the results by 100. Thus, a score of 100 reflects accurate perception, scores above 100 reflect overestimations of the size of the body parts, and scores below 100 reflect underestimations of the size of the body parts.
DEVELOPMENT: The Body Image Perception Scale is a modification of Reitman and Cleveland's (1964) visual estimation task.
RELIABILITY: The fact that each index is based on four trials with a

single body part should increase the reliability compared to a similar procedure based on only a single trial for each body part.

Slade and Russell (1973a) reported the intercorrelations among the four body indexes. For a group of 14 anorexics, the correlations were all statistically significant and rather substantial; they ranged from .72 to .93. For a group of 20 normals, all but one of the correlations were statistically significant. The significant correlations were somewhat lower than those from the anorexic group; the significant correlations for the normal group ranged from .53 to .79.

Halmi, Goldberg, and Cunningham (1977) and Pierloot and Houben (1978) also found significant correlations among the four body perception indexes.

Halmi et al. (1977) used a composite score found by taking a mean of the scores on five body parts. They reported a reliability of .84 for the composite score.

VALIDITY: Slade and Russell (1973a) compared the Body Image Perception indexes from a group of anorexics with the indexes from a control group of persons with no history of eating disorders. There were statistically significant differences on each of the four body parts. Whereas the normal females slightly underestimated the size of three body parts, the anorexics overestimated by a considerable amount the size of all four body parts.

Slade and Russell (1973a) tested whether anorexics displayed a general perceptual disorder rather than simply displaying an error in their own body size perception. They asked each anorexic to judge the size of a 10-inch wooden block and a 5-inch wooden block. The distortion measure for the 5-inch block was not significantly correlated with any of the four perceptual indexes; the distortion measure for the 10-inch block was significantly correlated with only one (the chest) of the four body parts. The distortion measures for the two blocks were strongly and significantly correlated with each other (r = .84). These findings, in combination with the strong intercorrelations between the perception indexes for the four body parts, suggested that "the observed disorder of 'body perception' cannot be accounted for by a general factor of perceptual disturbance" (Slade & Russell, 1973a, p. 192).

Garner, Garfinkel, Stancer, and Moldofsky (1976) used the Body Image Perception Scale with four groups of subjects: anorexia patients, females who had been obese prior to age 14 and were currently 25% to 75% overweight, thin normal females, and a normal control group. Included in the last group were females who had no history of psychiatric treatment or weight problems. Contrary to expectation, there were no significant differences on the four body perception indexes derived from the Body Image Perception Scale.

The findings of Slade and Russell (1973a) were replicated by Pierlott and Houben (1978), but they were not replicated in the study by Button, Fransella, and Slade (1977). The last researchers did not find significant differences in the perception indexes of anorexics and normals. The anorexics in the Button et al. study did not overestimate their weight as much as those in the Slade and Russell study, and the estimates from the normal group were higher in the Button et al. study than they were in the Slade and Russell study.

Birtchnell, Lacey, and Harte (1985) did not find significant differences when bulimics were compared with a control group.

Garner et al. (1976) correlated scores on the Body Image Perception Scale with scores obtained with the Distorting Photograph Technique (Glucksman & Hirsch, 1969) (see separate entry). For a sample of 18 anorexics, the correlation between the two measures was .50 ($p < .05$); for a sample of 16 obese persons, the correlation was .44 ($p < .05$).

Ben-Tovim, Whitehead, and Crisp (1979) found that accuracy of estimation is related to the size of the body part being estimated.

Fichter, Meister, and Koch (1986) compared three approaches to measuring body image: the Image Marking Procedure (Askevold, 1975) (see separate entry), the Body Image Perception Scale, and a procedure similar to the Freeman Body Image Distortion measure (Freeman, Thomas, Solyom, & Hunter, 1984) (see separate entry). Using discriminant analysis, the researchers concluded that the Image Marking Procedure correctly classified all cases, and the Body Image Perception Scale was the next most effective measure, with 87.5% correct classifications.

NOTES & COMMENTS: (1) Slade and Russell (1973a, 1973b) compared anorexics' tendency to overestimate their own body width with their ability to judge the body width of other females. The researchers also looked at the body perception indexes of anorexics after they gained weight. Slade (1977) used the Body Image Perception Scale to compare the body images of anorexics, pregnant women, and a "normal" group of women. Goldberg, Halmi, Casper, Eckert, and Davis (1977) studied numerous variables that might be effective predictors of weight change during treatment of anorexia nervosa. The Body Image Perception Scale was one of the measures they used. Eckert, Goldberg, Halmi, Casper, and Davis (1982) studied hospitalized anorexia patients with a variety of measures, including the Body Image Perception Scale.

(2) Researchers have varied the procedures of the Body Image Perception Scale. Some researchers (Button et al., 1977; Slade, 1977) have included a fifth body part: stomach depth. Halmi et al. (1977) included seven body parts: the original four plus body depth, foot length, and arm length. Researchers (Button et al., 1977; Garner et al., 1976; Pierlott & Houben, 1978) have used two trials on each body part rather than the

four originally recommended. Button et al. (1977) stated: "Based on an analysis of variance we have found no evidence that 4 trials produce significantly different average indices from 2 trials" (p. 236).

AVAILABLE FROM: The procedure is described by Slade and Russell, 1973a.

USED IN:

Ben-Tovim, D. I., Whitehead, J., & Crisp, A. H. (1979). A controlled study of the perception of body width in anorexia nervosa. *Journal of Psychosomatic Research, 23*, 267–272.

Birtchnell, S. A., Lacey, J. H., & Harte, A. (1985). Body image distortion in bulimia nervosa. *British Journal of Psychiatry, 147*, 408–412.

Button, E. J., Fransella, F., & Slade, P. D. (1977). A reappraisal of body perception disturbance in anorexia nervosa. *Psychological Medicine, 7*, 235–243.

Eckert, E. D., Goldberg, S. C., Halmi, K. A., Casper, R. C., & Davis, J. M. (1982). Depression in anorexia nervosa. *Psychological Medicine, 12*, 115–122.

Fichter, M. M., Meister, I., & Koch, H. J. (1986). The measurement of body image disturbances in anorexia nervosa: Experimental comparison of different methods. *British Journal of Psychiatry, 148*, 453–461.

Garner, D. M., Garfinkel, P. E., Stancer, H. C., & Moldofsky, H. (1976). Body image disturbances in anorexia nervosa and obesity. *Psychosomatic Medicine, 38*, 327–335.

Goldberg, S. C., Halmi, K. A., Casper, R., Eckert, E., & Davis, J. M. (1977). Pretreatment predictors of weight change in anorexia nervosa. In R. A. Vigersky (Ed.), *Anorexia nervosa* (pp. 31–41). New York: Raven Press.

Halmi, K. A., Goldberg, S. C., & Cunningham, S. (1977). Perceptual distortion of body image in adolescence. *Psychological Medicine, 7*, 253–257.

Pierloot, R. A., & Houben, M. E. (1978). Estimation of body dimensions in anorexia nervosa. *Psychological Medicine, 8*, 317–324.

Slade, P. D. (1977). Awareness of body dimensions during pregnancy: An analogue study. *Psychological Medicine, 7*, 245–252.

Slade, P. D., & Russell, G. F. M. (1973a). Awareness of body dimensions in anorexia nervosa: Cross-sectional and longitudinal studies. *Psychological Medicine, 3*, 188–199.

Slade, P. D., & Russell, G. F. M. (1973b). Experimental investigations of bodily perception in anorexia nervosa and obesity. *Psychosomatics, 22*, 359–363.

BIBLIOGRAPHY:

Askevold, F. (1975). Measuring body image. *Psychotherapy and Psychosomatics, 26*, 71–77.

Freeman, R. J., Thomas, C. D., Solyom, L., & Hunter, M. A. (1984). A modified video camera for measuring body image distortion: Technical description and reliability. *Psychological Medicine, 14*, 411–416.

Glucksman, M. L., & Hirsch, J. (1969). The response of obese patients to weight reduction. III. The perception of body size. *Psychosomatic Medicine, 31*, 1–7.

Reitman, E. E., & Cleveland, S. E. (1964). Changes in body image following sensory deprivation in schizophrenic and control groups. *Journal of Abnormal and Social Psychology, 68*, 168–176.

DISTORTING PHOTOGRAPH TECHNIQUE

AUTHORS: Myron L. Glucksman and Jules Hirsch
DATE: 1969
VARIABLE: Self-perception of body size
TYPE OF INSTRUMENT: Estimation procedure
DESCRIPTION: The apparatus for the Distorting Photograph Technique consists of "a Hilux 102 variable anamorphic lens with a magnification of 1.0 to 2.0 times and with a regular, fixed-distance, corrector lens" (Glucksman & Hirsch, 1969, p. 2). The lens is attached to a slide projector and is motorized so that the subject can easily alter the projected image. A slide of the subject is projected onto a screen. When the lens is moved in one direction, the image on the screen is made to look more obese; moving the lens in the other direction makes the image look thinner. A dial is connected to the lens. Hidden from the subject, the dial allows the experimenter to measure the amount of distortion without the subject being influenced by the reading on it.

Before beginning the procedure, the experimenter must obtain a slide of the subject showing a full frontal view, preferably in a two-piece bathing suit. To administer the Distorting Photograph Technique, the experimenter projects the slide of the subject on the screen, and the subject is directed to adjust the lens until the projected image matches the subject's appearance. The task is presented four times. In two trials, the slide is initially presented in the most obese direction; in the other two trials, the slide is initially presented in the thinnest direction. To provide a basis for comparison (i.e., to measure whether the subject has a general tendency to distort the size of objects or other persons), subjects are also asked to match a slide of a vase to an undistorted slide they had seen previously. This procedure is repeated for a slide of an average man and an average woman.
PREVIOUS SUBJECTS: Obese adults, anorexics, bulimics, college women, parents of adolescent girls rating their daughters
APPROPRIATE FOR: Ages 12 and older
ADMINISTRATION: Individually administered by a trained examiner; about 10 minutes
SCORING: The dial retained by the examiner is divided into 10 measuring units, and the amount of distortion on a trial is read directly from the dial. A size estimation score is computed by summing the self-perception scores (from the dial) for the four trials.
DEVELOPMENT: No information was provided.
RELIABILITY: No information was provided.
VALIDITY: Glucksman and Hirsch (1969) found that obese persons overestimated their body size; after they lost weight, obese subjects continued to overestimate their body size, even to the point that they perceived themselves as having lost little, if any, weight. Stated differently, the

obese subjects were even more in error in their self-perceptions after they lost weight than they were before they lost weight.

Garner, Garfinkel, Stancer, and Moldofsky (1976) found that anorexics and obese subjects did not score differently from each other on the Distorting Photograph Technique, but they did differ from three normal control groups. Interestingly, about half of the anorexic and obese subjects overestimated their size and half underestimated their size. In general, control subjects appeared to underestimate their size. Garner et al. compared data obtained with the Distorting Photograph Technique to measures of neuroticism, extraversion, lack of self-control, and locus of control scores. For anorexics, they found that results on the Distorting Photograph Technique were significantly related to neuroticism and lack of self-control; for the obese subjects, results on the Distorting Photograph Technique were significantly related to locus of control.

Garner et al. (1976) correlated scores on the Distorting Photograph Technique with scores from Slade and Russell's (1973) Body Image Perception Scale (see separate entry). The correlation for anorexics was .50; the correlation for obese persons was .44.

Garner, Olmsted, Bohr, and Garfinkel (1982) related scores on the Distorting Photograph Technique to scores on the Eating Attitudes Test (EAT) (Garner & Garfinkel, 1979) (see separate entry). Using data from both anorexics and a normal control group, the researchers found that body size estimates and estimates of ideal body size were both significantly correlated with total scores on the EAT (r = .41 and −.41) and with total scores on the shortened version of the EAT (EAT-26) (r = .42 and −.38). Furthermore, they found that body size estimates and estimates of ideal body size were both significantly correlated with two of the three factors of the EAT. The two significantly related factors were Dieting (r = .50 and −.47) and Bulimia and Food Preoccupation (r = .36 and −.47); the factor that was not significantly correlated with results from the Distorting Photograph Technique was Oral Control.

NOTES & COMMENTS: (1) Garfinkel, Moldofsky, and Garner (1979) used the Distorting Photograph Technique as one of several measures to study anorexics who had also been studied one year earlier; the researchers looked at the stability of body perception distortion. Strober (1981) used the Distorting Photograph Technique to study the relationship between body image distortion and personality variables as measured by the Minnesota Multiphasic Personality Inventory (Hathaway & McKinley, 1967). Using a variety of measures including the Distorting Photograph Technique, Garfinkel et al. (1983) compared anorexic and nonanorexic adolescent girls. They also had parents of the girls rate their daughters in terms of actual size and ideal size on the Distorting Photograph Technique. Garner, Garfinkel, and O'Shaughnessy (1985) compared women with bulimia and anorexia, normal-weight bulimic women, and anorexic women of the restricting type. They used a variety of measures including the Distorting Photograph Technique.

(2) The Distorting Photograph Technique can be used to measure ideal body size as well as perception of current body size (Garfinkel et al., 1979, 1983; Garner et al., 1976, 1982, 1985).

(3) After describing a study using both the Distorting Photograph Technique and the Body Image Perception Scale, Garner et al. (1976) concluded: "The distorting photograph technique involves a more direct confrontation with the visual appearance of one's body, whereas the size estimation apparatus does not involve making judgements from one's actual appearance. This suggests that the distorting photograph technique may be a more sensitive measure of one's perceptions and feelings about one's overall appearance" (p. 333).

AVAILABLE FROM: The procedure is described by Glucksman and Hirsch (1969), who included a picture of the apparatus with their article.

USED IN:

Garfinkel, P. E., Garner, D. M., Rose, J., Darby, P. L., Brandes, J. S., O'Hanlon, J., & Walsh, N. (1983). A comparison of characteristics in the families of patients with anorexia nervosa and normal controls. *Psychological Medicine, 13*, 821–828.

Garfinkel, P. E., Moldofsky, H., & Garner, D. M. (1979). The stability of perceptual disturbances in anorexia nervosa. *Psychological Medicine, 9*, 703–708.

Garner, D. M., Garfinkel, P. E., & O'Shaughnessy, M. (1985). The validity of the distinction between bulimia with and without anorexia nervosa. *American Journal of Psychiatry, 142*, 581–587.

Garner, D. M., Garfinkel, P. E., Stancer, H. C., & Moldofsky, H. (1976). Body image disturbances in anorexia nervosa and obesity. *Psychosomatic Medicine, 38*, 327–335.

Garner, D. M., Olmsted, M. P., Bohr, Y., & Garfinkel, P. E. (1982). The Eating Attitudes Test: Psychometric features and clinical correlates. *Psychological Medicine, 12*, 871–878.

Glucksman, M. L., & Hirsch, J. (1969). The response of obese patients to weight reduction. III. The perception of body size. *Psychosomatic Medicine, 31*, 1–7.

Strober, M. (1981). The relation of personality characteristics to body image disturbances in juvenile anorexia nervosa: A multivariate analysis. *Psychosomatic Medicine, 43*, 323–330.

BIBLIOGRAPHY:

Garner, D. M., & Garfinkel, P. E. (1979). The Eating Attitudes Test: An index of the symptoms of anorexia nervosa. *Psychological Medicine, 9*, 273–279.

Hathaway, S. R., & McKinley, J. C. (1967). *Minnesota Multiphasic Personality Inventory*. New York: Psychological Corporation.

Slade, P. D., & Russell, G. F. M. (1973). Awareness of body dimension in anorexia nervosa: Cross-sectional and longitudinal studies. *Psychological Medicine, 3*, 188–193.

FREEMAN BODY IMAGE DISTORTION

AUTHORS: Richard J. Freeman, Cheryl D. Thomas, Leslie Solyom, and Michael A. Hunter

DATE: 1984

VARIABLE: Body image distortion

TYPE OF INSTRUMENT: Estimation procedure

DESCRIPTION: The Freeman Body Image Distortion measure involves the use of a video camera, two video monitors, and a distortion meter. The video camera is modified in such a way that variable voltage can be applied to the horizontal deflection circuit of the camera. "The visual effect [on] the image produced by the camera varies as a function of the voltage, becoming apparently broader or narrower as the speed of the scan is increased or decreased" (Freeman, Thomas, Solyom, & Hunter, 1984, p. 413). Human images can appear up to 20% thinner and 40% fatter than they really are without distorting the quality of the image. A control apparatus, plugged directly into the camera and outfitted with a dial, is used to alter the voltage and thus the image. A voltmeter is used to read the degree of distortion. To measure body image distortion, the subject wears a solid-colored bathing suit or a leotard and stands equidistant from two monitors. One monitor is directly ahead of the subject and projects a full frontal image; one monitor is to the side of the subject and projects an image of the subject's profile. The control apparatus is operated by the experimenter who, on the first trial, moves the dial from a thin image to a fatter image, and on the second trial, moves the dial from a fat image to a thinner image. The subject informs the experimenter when the subject believes the image matches the subject's appearance. The procedure is repeated for the frontal view and for the profile view.

PREVIOUS SUBJECTS: Anorexics, bulimics, psychiatric patients, normal women

APPROPRIATE FOR: Ages 12 and older

ADMINISTRATION: Individually administered; about 10–15 minutes

SCORING: The results from the two trials—thin to fat and then fat to thin—are averaged to yield one value. This value, the perceived size, is divided by the actual size, and the result is multiplied by 100. The final score is referred to as the Body Image Distortion score. A researcher can compute a separate frontal Body Image Distortion score and a profile Body Image Distortion score, or the two values can be averaged.

DEVELOPMENT: The Freeman Body Image Distortion measure represents a modification of a video procedure previously developed by Allebeck, Hallberg, and Espmark (1976). Freeman et al. (1984) modified the Allebeck et al. procedure because it "proved to be unnecessarily cumbersome, and it seemed to produce undesirable distortions of the image, as well as being limited to a maximum of 15% distortion" (p. 412).

RELIABILITY: For a sample of 70 women, including normal women, anorexics, bulimics, and psychiatric patients, the correlation between the frontal scores and the profile scores was .62. If the profile and frontal scores are considered together, the correlation coefficient reported here provides an estimate of the internal consistency of the scale.

Twenty normal women and 20 women with anorexia nervosa or bulimia completed the measure on two occasions, with an interval of 7 to 22 days between testings. The test-retest reliability for the frontal scores was .90; the test-retest reliability for the profile scores was .86.

VALIDITY: Freeman et al. (1984) reported a correlation of .56 between Body Image Distortion scores and scores on the Eating Attitudes Test (Garner & Garfinkel, 1979) (see separate entry).

Freeman, Thomas, Solyom, and Miles (cited in Freeman et al., 1984) reported that patients with anorexia or bulimia differed from normals and psychiatric patients in terms of both frontal scores and profile scores.

Freeman et al. (1984) calculated a "body image dissatisfaction" score by subtracting ideal body image from perceived body image. They found "substantial correlations between this dissatisfaction index and measures of depression, particularly in patients with bulimia nervosa" (p. 415).

Garner (cited in Freeman et al., 1984) found a "substantial" correlation between body image as measured by the Distorting Photograph Technique (Garner, Garfinkel, Stancer, & Moldofsky, 1976) (see separate entry) and body image as measured by the Freeman Body Image Distortion measure.

NOTES & COMMENTS: Independently of Freeman et al. (1984), Fichter, Meister, and Koch (1986) developed a procedure to measure body image that was based on the work of Allebeck et al. (1976). The procedure by Fichter et al. involved the use of a video camera whose image could be increased or decreased in width. Based on discriminant analysis using data from anorexics and healthy females, they concluded that the discriminative ability of this video procedure was unsatisfactory.

AVAILABLE FROM: The procedure is described in Freeman, Thomas, Solyom, and Hunter, 1984.

USED IN:

Fichter, M. M., Meister, I., & Koch, H. J. (1986). The measurement of body image disturbances in anorexia nervosa: Experimental comparison of different methods. *British Journal of Psychiatry, 148*, 453–461.

Freeman, R. J., Thomas, C. D., Solyom, L., & Hunter, M. A. (1984). A modified video camera for measuring body image distortion: Technical description and reliability. *Psychological Medicine, 14*, 411–416.

BIBLIOGRAPHY:

Allebeck, P., Hallberg, D., & Espmark, S. (1976). Body image—An apparatus for measuring disturbances in estimation of size and shape. *Journal of Psychosomatic Research, 20*, 583–589.

Garner, D., & Garfinkel, P. (1979). The Eating Attitudes Test: An index of the symptoms of anorexia nervosa. *Psychological Medicine, 9,* 273–279.
Garner, D. M., Garfinkel, P. E., Stancer, H. C., & Moldofsky, H. (1976). Body image disturbances in anorexia nervosa and obesity. *Psychosomatic Medicine, 38,* 327–335.

IMAGE MARKING PROCEDURE
AUTHOR: Finn Askevold
DATE: 1975
VARIABLE: Self-perception of body size
TYPE OF INSTRUMENT: Estimation procedure
DESCRIPTION: The Image Marking Procedure requires the following equipment: a piece of paper 1.5 m by 1 m, taped to a wall, two black marking pencils, one red marking pencil, an angle, and a yardstick. The subject, with a black marking pencil in each hand, stands in front of the paper and faces the paper while the experimenter stands directly behind the subject. The subject is told to imagine that she is standing in front of the mirror looking at the reflection of her own body. When the experimenter touches a part of her body, she is to place an "X" on the paper where the image of that part would be reflected. In order to prevent the subject from starting out with the marking pencil near the body part to be marked, and hence "measuring" the location of the body part, the subject is instructed to keep both pencils close to the paper in front of her until all marking is completed. To administer the procedure, the experimenter touches seven points on the subject's body: the top of the head, the highest point of each shoulder (acromioclavicular joints), the point on each side of the waist that corresponds to the narrowest point on the waist, and the widest point on each hip (trochanters of the femoral bones). When marking the points on the paper, the subject uses her right hand to mark points on the right side of the body and her left hand to mark points on the left side of her body. After the subject marks the seven points, she turns her back to the paper, and the experimenter, with the help of the angle, uses the red marking pencil to place an X where each of the seven points would actually be reflected. The yardstick is then used to measure the width of the shoulders, waist, and hips as perceived by the subject and the width of the three body parts as recorded by the experimenter.
PREVIOUS SUBJECTS: Female anorexics and obese patients; psychoneurotic females; adolescent female anorexics, depressives, and those with conduct disorders
APPROPRIATE FOR: Ages 12 and older
ADMINISTRATION: Individually administered; about 10 minutes
SCORING: Several researchers followed Pierloot and Houben's (1978) procedure for calculating scores: estimated size (width) was divided by

actual size, and the result was multiplied by 100. With this procedure, a score of 100 reflects perfect agreement between estimated and actual size; a score above 100 indicates that the estimated size is greater than the actual size; and a score below 100 indicates that the estimated size is less than the actual size. This approach to scoring yields three scores—shoulders, waist, hips—that can be averaged to yield a composite score.
DEVELOPMENT: No information was provided.
RELIABILITY: Pierloot and Houben (1978) reported the intercorrelations for the three scores they computed: a body perception index for shoulders, waist, and hips. They estimated the correlations separately for two groups: 31 female hospitalized anorexics and 20 female hospitalized neurotics. For the anorexics, the three intercorrelations were .30, .55, and .61; for the neurotics, the three intercorrelations were .75, .52, and .75. Pierloot and Houben concluded that the intercorrelations were sufficiently high to justify combining the three scores into a single score.

Strober, Goldenberg, Green, and Saxon (1979) also intercorrelated the three body perception scores. For a sample of 18 anorexics, they obtained the following correlations: .51, .64, and .66. For a sample of 24 nonanorexics, the correlations were .68, .49, and .72.
VALIDITY: Pierloot and Houben (1978) compared the four mean scores from 31 anorexics and 20 neurotics. There was a significant difference for the body perception index for shoulders and the body perception index for waist, but the differences for hips and the composite score were nonsignificant. For the two significant comparisons, the anorexics obtained higher scores, reflecting the fact that they were more likely to overestimate their body widths or likely to overestimate them by a greater amount.

Pierloot and Houben (1978) compared several approaches to measuring body image. They concluded that the Image Marking Procedure produced results with anorexics that were quite comparable to those produced by an estimation task adapted from Slade and Russell's (1973) Body Image Perception Scale (see separate entry). The results for the neurotic group, however, were different on the two measures, at least in terms of the hips: using the Image Marking Procedure led to significantly higher overestimations of the width of the hips.

Wingate and Christie (1978) tested 15 hospitalized female anorexics and 15 nonhospitalized normal females. They found that the anorexic group overestimated the size of all three widths—shoulders, waist, and hips—with the waist being overestimated by the largest amount. The control group, on the other hand, underestimated the width of the shoulders and hips but slightly overestimated the width of the waist. The researchers also found that ego strength, for the anorexic group, was significantly correlated with perception of shoulders, waist, and hips, but the correlations for the normal group were nonsignificant. As expected, both the anorexics and the normals estimated their height accurately.

Strober et al. (1979) tested 18 anorexics and 24 nonanorexics with the Image Marking Procedure, the Fisher Body Distortion Questionnaire (Fisher, 1970), which measures body image aberrations, and the Sophistication of Body Concept Scale (Witkin, Dyk, Paterson, Goodenough, & Karp, 1962), which reflects the degree of differentiation in the body concept. They obtained the following correlations for the anorexics: Image Marking Procedure with Fisher Body Distortion Questionnaire = .27 and Image Marking Procedure with Sophistication of Body Concept Scale = .17. For the normals, the two correlations were .18 and .11.

Strober et al. (1979) compared hospitalized anorexics and hospitalized nonanorexics (personality disorders, neurotics, and depressives) in terms of the three body perception indexes from the Image Marking Procedure. The differences between the two groups were nonsignificant, both during the acute phase of anorexia (3 days after admission to a hospital) and during the recuperative phase (during the first week of their sixth month of hospitalization). Both groups tended to overestimate the width of the three body parts. Strober et al. also found no significant differences between the testings done at the two different times—acute time versus recuperative time.

Fichter, Meister, and Koch (1986) compared three approaches to measuring body image: a technique using a video monitor similar to the Freeman Body Image Distortion Measure (Freeman, Thomas, Solyom, & Hunter, 1984) (see separate entry), Slade and Russell's (1973) Body Image Perception Scale, and the Image Marking Procedure. After analyzing data from 12 acute anorexics, 9 chronic anorexics, and a control group of healthy female volunteers, Fichter et al. concluded that: "the best discrimination between an anorectic and control group was found for the Image Marking Procedure" (p. 457).

NOTES & COMMENTS: (1) Strober (1981) compared binge-eating anorexics and nonbinge-eating anorexics on a variety of measures including the Image Marking Procedure, the Anorexic Behavior Scale (Slade, 1973) (see separate entry), the Psychiatric Rating Scale for Anorexia Nervosa (Goldberg, Halmi, Casper, Eckert, & Davis, 1977) (see separate entry), and the Moos' (1974) Family Environment Scale. Strober (1982) compared 30 hospitalized adolescent females with anorexia nervosa, 30 hospitalized adolescent females with depression, and 30 hospitalized adolescent females with conduct disorders. He used three measures: the Image Marking Procedure, the Psychiatric Rating Scale for Anorexia Nervosa, and the Nowicki-Strickland Locus of Control Scale (Nowicki & Strickland, 1973).

(2) The simplicity of the Image Marking Procedure in combination with the evidence for the scale's validity makes it a desirable measure

of body image. Although no researcher has demonstrated the test-retest reliability of the scale, the findings from Strober et al. (1979) that there were no significant differences in scores between the acute and recuperative phases of anorexia—6 months apart—suggests that the measure tends to yield stable results.

AVAILABLE FROM: The procedure is described in Askevold, 1975.

USED IN:

Askevold, F. (1975). Measuring body image. *Psychotherapy and Psychosomatics, 26*, 71–77.

Fichter, M. M., Meister, I., & Koch, H. J. (1986). The measurement of body image disturbances in anorexia nervosa: Experimental comparison of different methods. *British Journal of Psychiatry, 148*, 453–461.

Pierloot, R. A., & Houben, M. E. (1978). Estimation of body dimensions in anorexia nervosa. *Psychological Medicine, 8*, 317–324.

Strober, M. (1981). The significance of bulimia in juvenile anorexia nervosa: An exploration of possible etiologic factors. *International Journal of Eating Disorders, 1*, 28–43.

Strober, M. (1982). Locus of control, psychopathology, and weight gain in juvenile anorexia nervosa. *Journal of Abnormal Child Psychology, 10*, 97–106.

Strober, M., Goldenberg, I., Green, J., & Saxon, J. (1979). Body image disturbance in anorexia nervosa during the acute and recuperative phase. *Psychological Medicine, 9*, 695–701.

Wingate, B. A., & Christie, M. J. (1978). Ego strength and body image in anorexia nervosa. *Journal of Psychosomatic Research, 22*, 201–204.

BIBLIOGRAPHY:

Fisher, S. (1970). *Body experience in fantasy behavior*. New York: Appleton-Century-Crofts.

Freeman, R. J., Thomas, C. D., Solyom, L., & Hunter, M. A. (1984). A modified video camera for measuring body image distortion: Technical description and reliability. *Psychological Medicine, 14*, 411–416.

Goldberg, S. C., Halmi, K. A., Casper, R. C., Eckert, E., & Davis, J. M. (1977). Pretreatment predictors of weight change in anorexia nervosa. In R. A. Vigersky (Ed.), *Anorexia nervosa* (pp. 31–41). New York: Raven Press.

Moos, R. (1974). *Family Environment Scale*. Palo Alto: Consulting Psychologists Press.

Nowicki, S., & Strickland, B. R. (1973). A locus of control scale for children. *Journal of Consulting and Clinical Psychology, 40*, 148–154.

Slade, P. D. (1973). A short anorexic behaviour scale. *British Journal of Psychiatry, 122*, 83–85.

Slade, P. D., & Russell, G. F. M. (1973). Awareness of body dimensions in anorexia nervosa. *Psychological Medicine, 3*, 188–199.

Witkin, H. A., Dyk, R. B., Paterson, H. F., Goodenough, D. R., & Karp, S. A. (1962). *Psychological differentiation*. New York: Wiley.

ATTITUDES TOWARD PHYSICAL ATTRACTIVENESS SCALE (ATPAS)

AUTHORS: A. Chris Downs, Mary A. Reagan, Celia Garrett, and Perry Kolodzy

DATE: 1982
VARIABLE: Adherence to stereotypes regarding physically attractive and physically unattractive persons
TYPE OF INSTRUMENT: Summated rating scale
DESCRIPTION: The Attitudes Toward Physical Attractiveness Scale (ATPAS) contains 34 items. There are 17 statements pertaining to attractive people, and 15 of them are positive stereotypes. Similarly, there are 17 statements pertaining to unattractive people, and 15 of them are negative stereotypes. Agreement or disagreement with each statement is recorded using a 7-point scale ranging from "disagree strongly" to "agree strongly."
SAMPLE ITEMS: Attractive people are young looking.
Unattractive people are rude and offensive.
PREVIOUS SUBJECTS: Adolescents and adults
APPROPRIATE FOR: High school ages and older
ADMINISTRATION: Self-administered; less than 15 minutes
SCORING: Items are individually scored on a 7-point scale, with 1 point assigned to the most nonstereotyped response and 7 points assigned to the most stereotyped response. Thus, strongly agreeing with a positive statement about attractive persons earns 7 points, and strongly agreeing with a negative statement about unattractive persons earns 7 points. Four items are reversed before scoring. Item scores are summed to yield a total score that can range from 34 (strong disagreement with stereotypes about attractive and unattractive persons) to 238 (strong agreement with stereotypes about attractive and unattractive persons). Downs, Reagan, Garrett, and Kolodzy (1982) provided means, medians, and ranges, separately by sex, for two groups of respondents: college students and adolescents.
DEVELOPMENT: An item pool was constructed including 88 stereotypes of physically attractive or physically unattractive persons. The item pool was administered to 37 male and 72 female graduate students on two occasions separated by about 1 week. Item-total correlations and test-retest correlations were computed for each item. Thirty-four items that had significant item-total correlations and significant test-retest correlations were retained for the ATPAS.
RELIABILITY: Coefficient alpha was computed for each of the following groups: 333 adolescent males, 438 adolescent females, 98 college men, and 270 college women. For each group, the value of coefficient alpha was greater than .90. For the 431 males, considered together, coefficient alpha was .91; for the 708 females, considered together, coefficient alpha was .92.

Test-retest reliability estimates were computed for several groups that completed the ATPAS. The following test-retest reliabilities were obtained: .83 for 119 adolescent males, .91 for 203 adolescent females, .82

for 37 college men, and .87 for 112 college women. When the scores for adolescents and college students were combined, the test-retest reliabilities were .83 and .89 for males and females, respectively.

VALIDITY: As evidence of the validity of the ATPAS, Downs et al. (1982) tested the following hypotheses: adolescents would score higher than college students, males would score higher than females, and whites would score higher than blacks or Chicanos. All three hypotheses were supported. There were, however, also unexpected interactions: Chicano college students scored higher than adolescent Chicanos, and the predicted ethnic difference was supported among adolescents but not among college students.

NOTES & COMMENTS: (1) The self-report of stereotypes is fraught with opportunities for providing socially desirable responses or responses that are influenced by other extraneous variables. Research has shown that it is often difficult to obtain honest responses with this type of measure. At the very least, it would be interesting to compare ATPAS scores with scores on a social desirability measure.

(2) Downs and Currie (1983) developed a measure of attitudes toward physical attractiveness that is intended for use with children; it is titled the Attitudes Toward Physical Attractiveness Scale—Intermediate Version (ATPAS-I) (see separate entry).

(3) Downs et al. (1982) compared self-ratings of attractiveness with scores on the ATPAS. Downs and Abshier (1982) looked at the relationships among self-perceptions regarding attractiveness, sex-typed characteristics as measured by the Personal Attributes Questionnaire (Spence & Helmreich, 1978) (see Beere, 1990), and scores on the ATPAS.

(4) A factor analysis showed that the 30 stereotyped items all loaded above .30 on a single factor. This one factor accounted for 64.5% of the variance. As a result, Downs et al. (1982) suggested that "additional research using the ATPAS could, then, score only the stereotyped items [not the reversed items] for purposes of analyses while retaining the reversed items only for better scale construction" (p. 13).

AVAILABLE FROM: Downs, Reagan, Garrett, and Kolodzy, 1982

USED IN:

Downs, A. C., & Abshier, G. R. (1982). Conceptions of physical appearance among young adolescents: The interrelationships among self-judged appearance, attractiveness stereotyping, and sex-typed characteristics. *Journal of Early Adolescence, 2,* 255–265.

Downs, A. C., Reagan, M. A., Garrett, C., & Kolodzy, P. (1982). The Attitudes Toward Physical Attractiveness Scale (ATPAS): An index of stereotypes based on physical appearance. *Catalog of Selected Documents in Psychology, 12,* 44. (Ms. No. 2502)

BIBLIOGRAPHY:

Downs, A. C., & Currie, M. V. (1983). Indexing elementary school-age children's views of attractive and unattractive people: The Attitudes Toward Physical

Attractiveness Scale—Intermediate version. *Psychological Documents, 13,* 23. (Ms. No. 2579)

Spence, J. T., & Helmreich, R. L. (1978). *Masculinity and femininity: Their psychological dimensions, correlates, and antecedents.* Austin: University of Texas.

ATTITUDES TOWARD PHYSICAL ATTRACTIVENESS SCALE—INTERMEDIATE VERSION (ATPAS-I)

AUTHORS: A. Chris Downs and Marie V. Currie

DATE: 1983

VARIABLE: Adherence to stereotypes regarding physically attractive and physically unattractive persons

TYPE OF INSTRUMENT: Summated rating scale

DESCRIPTION: The Attitudes Toward Physical Attractiveness Scale—Intermediate Version (ATPAS-I) contains 16 items, 2 of them filler items. Of the 14 scorable items, 7 are positive stereotypes about "good-looking people," and 7 are negative stereotypes about "ugly-looking people." One of the 2 filler items expresses a negative view of good-looking people, and 1 expresses a positive view of ugly-looking people. Each item is accompanied by five response options: "very true, true, don't know, not true, not at all true."

SAMPLE ITEMS: Ugly-looking people are rude and mean.

Good-looking people are smart.

PREVIOUS SUBJECTS: Ages 6–11

APPROPRIATE FOR: Ages 6–11

ADMINISTRATION: The scale is administered to children in groups of 15 or fewer children. Items are read aloud, and children record their responses by marking the appropriate box on the test page. About 20–30 minutes is required for administering the ATPAS-I.

SCORING: Items are scored on a 5-point scale, with 5 points reflecting disagreement with the stereotype and 1 point reflecting agreement with the stereotype. Item scores are summed to yield an overall score that can range from 14 (complete agreement with all the stereotypes) to 70 (complete disagreement with all the stereotypes). Downs and Currie (1983) reported means and standard deviations, separately by sex, for 338 boys and 360 girls. They also reported means by age for 6-, 7-, 8-, 9-, 10-, and 11-year-olds.

DEVELOPMENT: An item pool was constructed including 53 stereotypes of physically attractive or physically unattractive persons. After duplicate items were deleted, 36 items remained. These items were pretested with 35 boys and 35 girls in grades 1–6. Based on their responses, excessively difficult items were revised. The items were then administered to 200 boys and 200 girls on two occasions separated by 2 weeks. Item-total correlations and test-retest correlations were computed for each item. Items with low item-total correlations or test-retest correla-

tions below .65 were eliminated, leaving a scale of 16 items. The 2 nonstereotyped items that were retained were excluded from scoring.
RELIABILITY: Coefficient alpha using the data from 338 boys was .90. Coefficient alpha using the data from 360 girls was .84. Coefficient alpha for both sexes considered jointly was .89. Using responses from 200 boys tested on two occasions separated by about 2 weeks, the authors calculated test-retest reliability as .85; using responses from 200 girls also tested on two occasions separated by about 2 weeks, they calculated test-retest reliability as .84. (These were not the same 200 boys and 200 girls used for scale development.)
VALIDITY: To provide evidence of the validity of the ATPAS-I, Downs and Currie (1983) tested the following hypotheses: younger children would show greater stereotyping than older children; boys would show greater stereotyping than girls; and more attractive children—objectively judged or self-judged—would show greater stereotyping than less attractive children. All hypotheses were supported.
NOTES & COMMENTS: (1) Downs, Reagan, Garrett, and Kolodzy (1982) developed the Attitudes Toward Physical Attractiveness Scale (ATPAS) (see separate entry) for use with adolescents and adults.

(2) Downs and Currie (1983) factor analyzed responses to the ATPAS-I. All 14 scorable items had loadings of at least .45 on a single factor. This one factor accounted for 82.5% of the variance.

(3) Because self-report measures of stereotyping are susceptible to faking, further evidence of the scale's validity would be useful. In particular, how do scores on the ATPAS-I relate to a more subtle measure of stereotyping of attractive and unattractive persons or to behavior? Are scores affected by a social desirability response bias?
AVAILABLE FROM: Downs and Currie, 1983
USED IN:

Downs, A. C., & Currie, M. V. (1983). Indexing elementary school-age children's views of attractive and unattractive people: The Attitudes Toward Physical Attractiveness Scale—Intermediate version. *Psychological Documents, 13,* 23. (Ms. No. 2579)

BIBLIOGRAPHY:

Downs, A. C., Reagan, M. A., Garrett, C., & Kolodzy, P. (1982). The Attitudes Toward Physical Attractiveness Scale (ATPAS): An index of stereotypes based on physical appearance. *Catalog of Selected Documents in Psychology, 12,* 44. (Ms. No. 2502)

11

Eating Disorders

During the past 10 to 15 years, eating disorders have attracted the attention of many researchers who have developed numerous measures to assist them in better understanding anorexia nervosa and bulimia. Because these phenomena are generally associated with females, it is reasonable to label eating disorders as a gender issue and to include measures pertaining to eating disorders in this handbook. Rather than trying to decide what constitutes an eating disorder measure and what constitutes a measure of eating behavior in general, I decided to include measures of eating behavior that satisfied the general criteria for inclusion in the handbook (i.e., evidence of reliability and/or validity, use reported in several research articles, or scale development as the focus of a journal article). As a result of applying these criteria, this chapter includes measures relating to dieting behavior, restrained eating, and other eating behaviors, as well as measures relating to bulimia and anorexia nervosa. The chapter contains descriptions of 20 measures, arranged alphabetically.

The earliest publication date associated with the scales in this chapter was 1973, the date for the Anorexic Behaviour Scale (Slade, 1973). The newest publication date was 1987, the date for the Bulimic Investigatory Test, Edinburgh (Henderson & Freeman, 1987). Just over half of the scales in this chapter are summated rating scales; they range from 4 to 142 items. Two of the remaining scales—Anorexic Behaviour Scale (Slade, 1973) and Psychiatric Rating Scale for Anorexia Nervosa (Goldberg, Halmi, Casper, Eckert, & Davis, 1977)—are rating scales that require a member of a nursing staff or another trained person to rate the research participants. Most of the measures in this chapter are appropriate for use with persons who are in seventh grade or older, although some are more appropriate with persons who are at least in high school. Two of the measures are recommended for use in inpatient settings; one scale is appropriate only with female respondents.

The evidence regarding the reliability of these scales is somewhat mixed. There are no data pertaining to the reliability of two measures, and for the two rating scales that use outside raters, the only reliability pertained to interrater reliability. There are data regarding the internal consistency of most other measures. Although many of the scales are sufficiently reliable, the data for five measures lead one to question the internal consistency of the scales. There are data pertaining to the test-retest reliability of half of the scales in this chapter. In seven cases, the measures show adequate stability over time, and in three cases, there are problems in this area.

Generally there are data relevant to the validity of these measures. Sometimes the data suggest that the scale or some of its subscales are not measuring what the author intended for it to measure. Factor analysis was used in the development or further study of 12 of these measures. In some cases, the factor analytic results provided support for the scale's validity. Validity may be a particular problem for self-report measures used with anorexia nervosa patients. Anorexia nervosa is considered to be a disease of denial in that patients deny they have a problem. In order to maintain their facade, anorexia patients may be more interested in communicating a particular image of themselves than in providing honest answers to the questions asked.

Compared to other topics covered in this handbook, there seems to be greater consensus on what measures to use to study eating behaviors. Three scales in this chapter are accompanied by more than 35 references to studies where the scale was used. These commonly used scales are the Eating Attitudes Test (Garner & Garfinkel, 1979), which was used far more than any other scale in this chapter, the Eating Disorder Inventory (Garner & Olmsted, 1984), and the Restraint Scale (Herman & Polivy, 1975). Two other measures that have been used by more than a handful of researchers are the Anorexic Behaviour Scale (Slade, 1973) and the Binge Scale (Hawkins & Clement, 1980). Space did not permit me to provide details regarding all studies involving these popularly used measures. Instead I described the studies most relevant to the scale's reliability and validity in the sections headed RELIABILITY and VALIDITY, and I gave a general idea of the focus of the other studies by mentioning them in the NOTES & COMMENTS sections. Many of the studies that were only briefly mentioned provide data relevant to the scale's validity, particularly the construct or concurrent validity of the scale.

Researchers considering these scales should carefully examine all of the studies that involved the use of the measures. Furthermore, researchers would be wise to extend the literature review beyond what I have included; I believe that the USED IN lists in this chapter are less complete than they are for other chapters in this handbook. Chapter 1 provides a list of the search terms that I used to identify articles. Articles that were not indexed on the terms I used were not identified by me, yet these articles might include valuable information for the researcher who wants to adopt one of these measures.

Persons interested in knowing more about measurement issues in regard to eating behaviors are advised to consult Williamson's book *Assessment of Eating Disorders* (in press). He reviews various approaches to measurement in this area.

BIBLIOGRAPHY:

Garner, D. M., & Garfinkel, P. E. (1979). The Eating Attitudes Test: An index of the symptoms of anorexia nervosa. *Psychological Medicine, 9,* 273–279.

Garner, D. M., & Olmsted, M. P. (1984). *Manual for Eating Disorder Inventory (EDI).* Odessa, FL: Psychological Assessment Resources.

Goldberg, S. C., Halmi, K. A., Casper, R., Eckert, E., & Davis, J. M. (1977). Pretreatment predictors of weight change in anorexia nervosa. In R. A. Vigersky (Ed.), *Anorexia nervosa* (pp. 31–41). New York: Raven Press.

Hawkins, R. C., II, & Clement, P. F. (1980). Development and construct validation of a self-report measure of binge eating tendencies. *Addictive Behaviors, 5,* 219–226.

Henderson, M., & Freeman, C. P. L. (1987). A self-rating scale for bulimia: The "BITE." *British Journal of Psychiatry, 150,* 18–24.

Herman, C. P., & Polivy, J. (1975). Anxiety, restraint, and eating behavior. *Journal of Abnormal Psychology, 84,* 666–672.

Slade, P. D. (1973). A short Anorexic Behaviour Scale. *British Journal of Psychiatry, 122,* 83–85.

Williamson, D. A. (1990). *Assessment of eating disorders.* New York: Pergamon Press.

ANOREXIC BEHAVIOUR SCALE

AUTHOR: P. D. Slade

DATE: 1973

VARIABLE: Behavior indicative of and related to anorexia nervosa

TYPE OF INSTRUMENT: Rating scale

DESCRIPTION: The Anorexic Behaviour Scale is a 22-item rating scale containing 8 items relating to "resistance to eating," 8 items dealing with methods of "disposing of food," and 6 items pertaining to "overactivity." The scale was designed for use in an inpatient setting, and the items are to be completed by the nursing staff based on their observations of the patient. Each item is accompanied by three response options: "yes," "no," or "?" depending on the presence or absence of the behavior.

SAMPLE ITEMS: (resistance to eating) Delays as much as possible before coming to the dining table.

(disposing of food) Vomits after meals.

(over-activity) Stands as much as possible rather than sits.

PREVIOUS SUBJECTS: Hospitalized anorexia nervosa patients and hospitalized psychiatrically disturbed adolescents, normal adolescent girls

APPROPRIATE FOR: Hospitalized patients, primarily those with eating disorders

ADMINISTRATION: The rating scale is to be completed independently by two members of the nursing staff. Instructions direct the raters to use the "yes" option only if they observed the behavior in the hospital or if the behavior was reported to the nursing staff. It takes about 10 minutes to complete the Anorexic Behaviour Scale, but the staff must have had ample opportunity to observe the patient before the ratings are made. In Slade's (1973) original work, the nursing staff had observed the patients for over 1 month before they made the ratings.

SCORING: Each item is individually scored, with 2 points assigned to the "yes" response, 1 point assigned to the "?" response, and 0 points assigned to the "no" response. Item scores are summed to yield a total score. When two nurses complete the rating scale, scores are averaged across the two raters. A score greater than 12 is considered indicative of anorexia nervosa.

DEVELOPMENT: The only information regarding scale development stated: "On the basis of a series of discussions with senior nurses who had had considerable experience in the management of anorexia nervosa patients, a 22-item scale was developed, dealing with the patients' behaviour while in hospital" (Slade, 1973, p. 83).

RELIABILITY: Interrater reliability was based on two members of the nursing staff independently rating 12 anorexia nervosa patients and 12 psychiatric patients in the same age range. The reliability was .90 (Slade, 1973).

VALIDITY: There was a large and statistically significant difference ($p < .001$) in the mean scores of anorexia nervosa patients compared to psychiatric patients. No psychiatric patient received a total rating greater than 12 from either rater. Using 12 as the cutoff score, 9 of the 12 anorexia patients were correctly classified by rater 1, and 10 of the 12 were correctly classified by rater 2 (Slade, 1973).

Nine anorexia patients in Slade's (1973) research also completed a measure of body-size misperception, which yielded scores on face, chest, waist, and hips. Using the ratings assigned by rater 1, Anorexic Behaviour Scale scores related to misperception of chest, waist, and hips. Using the ratings assigned by rater 2, the Anorexic Behaviour Scale scores related to misperception of face, chest, and waist.

Steinhausen (1985) used the Anorexic Behaviour Scale as one of several measures to compare anorexic patients at the time of hospital admission and the time of hospital discharge. Scores on the Anorexic Behaviour Scale were significantly different between the two time periods.

Steinhausen (1986) tested 23 anorexia nervosa patients with a variety of measures including the Anorexic Behaviour Scale and the Goldberg Anorectic Attitude Scale (GAAS) (Goldberg et al., 1980) (see separate entry). The GAAS was scored on seven subscales: Staff Exploits, Fear of Fat, Parents at Fault, Denial of Illness, Hunger, Hypothermia, and Poor Self Care. Two of the seven subscales—Fear of Fat and Denial of Illness—were significantly correlated with scores on the Anorexic Behaviour Scale.

NOTES & COMMENTS: (1) Goldberg, Halmi, Casper, Eckert, and Davis (1977) used the Anorexic Behaviour Scale as one of several measures intended to predict success in an inpatient program for treating anorexia nervosa. They scored the scale in the following categories: unusual food habits, vomiting, purgative abuse, and hyperactivity. Halmi, Goldberg, Casper, Eckert, and Davis (1979) and Fichter, Doerr, Pirke, and Lund (1982) also used the Anorexic Behaviour Scale as one of several measures to assess the effectiveness of an in-patient treatment program. Steinhausen and Glanville (1983) used the Anorexic Behaviour Scale as one of several measures in a follow-up study of anorexia nervosa patients.

(2) Ben-Tovim, Whitehead, and Crisp (1979) compared self-estimates of body width for two groups: patients with anorexia nervosa and a control group of adolescents. They verified that the two groups were different by comparing their scores on the Anorexic Behaviour Scale.

(3) Researchers (Casper, Eckert, Halmi, Goldberg, & Davis, 1980; Eckert, Goldberg, Halmi, Casper, & Davis, 1982; Strober, 1981) have used the Anorexic Behaviour Scale as one of several measures to study hospitalized patients suffering from anorexia nervosa.

AVAILABLE FROM: Pauline Slade, Department of Psychiatry, University of Manchester, Rawnsley Building, Manchester Royal Infirmary, Oxford Road, Manchester, England M13 9WL

USED IN:

Ben-Tovim, D. I., Whitehead, J., & Crisp, A. H. (1979). A controlled study of the perception of body width in anorexia nervosa. *Journal of Psychosomatic Research, 23,* 267–272.

Casper, R. C., Eckert, E. D., Halmi, K. A., Goldberg, S. C., & Davis, J. M. (1980). Bulimia: Its incidence and clinical importance in patients with anorexia nervosa. *Archives of General Psychiatry, 37,* 1030–1035.

Eckert, E. D., Goldberg, S. C., Halmi, K. A., Casper, R. C., & Davis, J. M. (1982). Depression in anorexia nervosa. *Psychological Medicine, 12,* 115–122.

Fichter, M. M., Doerr, P., Pirke, K. M., & Lund, R. (1982). Behavior, attitude, nutrition and endocrinology in anorexia nervosa: A longitudinal study in 24 patients. *Acta Psychiatrica Scandinavica, 66*, 429–444.

Goldberg, S. C., Halmi, K. A., Casper, R., Eckert, E., & Davis, J. M. (1977). Pretreatment predictors of weight change in anorexia nervosa. In R. A. Vigersky (Ed.), *Anorexia nervosa* (pp. 31–41). New York: Raven Press.

Halmi, K. A., Goldberg, S. C., Casper, R. C., Eckert, E. D., & Davis, J. M. (1979). Pretreatment predictors of outcome in anorexia nervosa. *British Journal of Psychiatry, 134*, 71–78.

Slade, P. D. (1973). A short Anorexic Behaviour Scale. *British Journal of Psychiatry, 122*, 83–85.

Steinhausen, H. C. (1985). Evaluation of inpatient treatment of adolescent anorexic patients. *Journal of Psychiatric Research, 19*, 371–375.

Steinhausen, H. C. (1986). Attitudinal dimensions in adolescent anorexic patients: An analysis of the Goldberg Anorectic Attitude Scale. *Journal of Psychiatric Research, 20*, 83–87.

Steinhausen, H. C., & Glanville, K. (1983). Retrospective and prospective follow-up studies in anorexia nervosa. *International Journal of Eating Disorders, 2*, 221–235.

Strober, M. (1981). The significance of bulimia in juvenile anorexia nervosa: An exploration of possible etiologic factors. *International Journal of Eating Disorders, 1*, 28–43.

BIBLIOGRAPHY:

Goldberg, S. C., Halmi, K. A., Eckert, E. D., Casper, R. C., Davis, J. M., & Roper, M. (1980). Attitudinal dimensions in anorexia nervosa. *Journal of psychiatric research, 15*, 239–252.

BINGE-EATING QUESTIONNAIRE

AUTHORS: Katherine A. Halmi, James R. Falk, and Estelle Schwartz

DATE: 1981

VARIABLE: Prevalence of bulimia

TYPE OF INSTRUMENT: Questionnaire with open-ended, multiple choice, and alternate choice items

DESCRIPTION: The Binge-Eating Questionnaire contains 23 items, some with several parts. The item content pertains to "sex, college major and year of study, age and physical stature, including one year weight change and history of highest and lowest weight, use of diet aids and medication, and the behavioural symptoms of bulimia according to the diagnostic criteria of the DSM-III" (Halmi, Falk, & Schwartz, 1981, p. 698). Eleven items are open-ended, requiring a brief answer; often it is a number. There are 3 multiple choice items and 9 alternate choice items.

SAMPLE ITEMS: Do you get uncontrollable urges to eat and eat until you feel physically ill? No Yes

In order to control your weight, do you use diet pills: never, less than once every four weeks, 1 to 3 times every four weeks, once every week, 2 to 6 times every week, once every day, more than once every day.

PREVIOUS SUBJECTS: College students, high school students, female bank employees
APPROPRIATE FOR: Grades 7 and older
ADMINISTRATION: Self-administered; about 10–15 minutes
SCORING: The Binge-Eating Questionnaire is used to determine the prevalence of bulimia in a particular group. Therefore, users are more likely to determine item frequencies across persons rather than obtain total scores for individuals.
DEVELOPMENT: Although no information was provided, it is clear that the questions were written to reflect the criteria for bulimia as specified in the DSM-III (American Psychiatric Association, 1980).
RELIABILITY: No information was provided, but since no scores were computed, one would not expect a report of reliability.
VALIDITY: Halmi et al. (1981) found a strong interrelationship among the following symptoms: "(a) considering oneself a binge-eater; (b) having an uncontrollable urge to eat; (c) feelings of guilt and self-deprecating thoughts; (d) actual bingeing on food; and (e) experiencing a fear of not being able to stop eating" (p. 703). These symptoms are an integral part of the definition of bulimia.

Lachenmeyer and Muni-Brander (1988) used adolescents' responses to the Binge-Eating Questionnaire to classify the adolescents into five groups: bingers, vomiters, clinical bulimics, bulimics-1, and bulimics-2. Clinical bulimics met all DSM-III criteria for bulimia, bulimics-1 met all criteria except one "menu" item, and bulimics-2 met all criteria except two "menu" items.
NOTES & COMMENTS: (1) Halmi et al. (1981) factor analyzed responses from 539 college students. They identified six factors: Weight, Bingeing, Vomiting, Sex differences (including items likely to show a sex difference, such as height and opinion of one's own weight), Weight change, and Diuretics.

(2) This questionnaire was not developed to be a scale in that it does not yield scores for individuals; however, since the Binge-Eating Questionnaire has been used by other researchers and may prove useful to future researchers, it is included here.

(3) Ruderman (1985) used five items from the Binge-Eating Questionnaire to assess "bulimic tendencies." Each item was scored on a 7-point scale, and the item scores were summed to yield a single score.
AVAILABLE FROM: Halmi, Falk, and Schwartz, 1981
USED IN:

Halmi, K. A., Falk, J. R., & Schwartz, E. (1981). Binge-eating and vomiting: A survey of a college population. *Psychological Medicine, 11*, 697–706.

Hart, K. J., & Ollendick, T. H. (1985). Prevalence of bulimia in working and university women. *American Journal of Psychiatry, 142*, 851–854.

Lachenmeyer, J. R., & Muni-Brander, P. (1988). Eating disorders in a nonclinical adolescent population: Implications for treatment. *Adolescence*, *23*, 303–312.

Ruderman, A. J. (1985). Restraint, obesity and bulimia. *Behaviour Research and Therapy*, *23*, 151–156.

BIBLIOGRAPHY:

American Psychiatric Association. (1980). *Diagnostic and statistical manual of mental disorders* (3rd ed.). Washington, DC: APA.

BINGE EATING SCALE

AUTHORS: Jim Gormally, Sionag Black, Sandy Daston, and David Rardin

DATE: 1982

VARIABLE: Severity of binge eating

TYPE OF INSTRUMENT: Multiple choice

DESCRIPTION: The Binge Eating Scale consists of 16 groups of statements. Each group contains three or four statements relating to behaviors that may be associated with bingeing (9 groups emphasize behaviors) and/or feelings and cognitions that may be associated with bingeing (7 groups emphasize feelings or cognitions). The three or four statements in each group comprise a continuum of increasing intensity or severity. For each group of statements, respondents mark the one statement that most accurately describes them.

SAMPLE ITEM: Group #1: (1) I don't feel self-conscious about my weight or body size when I'm with others. (2) I feel concerned about how I look to others, but it normally does not make me feel disappointed with myself. (3) I do get self-conscious about my appearance and weight which makes me feel disappointed in myself. (4) I feel very self-conscious about my weight and frequently, I feel intense shame and disgust for myself. I try to avoid social contacts because of my self-consciousness.

PREVIOUS SUBJECTS: Obese adults, bulimics and anorexics

APPROPRIATE FOR: Grades 7 and older

ADMINISTRATION: Self-administered; about 10 minutes

SCORING: Item scores for 14 groups of statements range from 0 to 3; item scores for the other 2 groups range from 0 to 2. Gormally, Black, Daston, and Rardin (1982) provided a scoring key showing the number of points assigned to each response in each of the 16 groups of statements. Totaling the item scores produces an overall score that can range from 0 (no bingeing) to 46 (severe bingeing). Marcus, Wing, and Lamparski (1985) considered total scores below 17 to indicate little or no problem with bingeing, scores between 17 and 27 to reflect a moderate bingeing problem, and scores above 27 to reflect a serious bingeing problem.

DEVELOPMENT: Using their own experiences treating bulimics and the characteristics specified for bulimia in the DSM-III (American Psychiatric

Association, 1980), the authors specified the characteristics of binge eating. For each of the 16 characteristics they listed, the authors developed three or four statements reflecting a severity continuum. The authors independently assigned scoring weights to each statement and then discussed their differences to determine a final set of weights.

RELIABILITY: To obtain information regarding the internal consistency of the scale, Gormally et al. (1982) looked at the total scores as a function of the weighted statement that was endorsed. An example is helpful in understanding their procedure: "for item one, total scale scores of persons endorsing statement one or two (both weighted 0) were compared with those endorsing statement three (weighted 1) and statement four (weighted 3)" (Gormally et al., 1982, p. 50). Using the Kruskal-Wallis analysis of variance test for comparing ranked data, they showed that, for the first sample, the results for 15 items were significant at the .01 level: those with the highest ranks were those who endorsed the highest weighted statement in the group.

VALIDITY: Gormally et al. (1982) administered the Binge Eating Scale to two samples of obese persons who were also interviewed and independently rated in regards to severity of bingeing. The raters classified persons into three groups: None, Moderate, and Severe. A one-way analysis of variance was used to compare the mean scores for the three groups in the first sample. There was a significant difference among the groups; post hoc tests showed that the respondents classified as "None" and as "Moderate" did not differ from each other, but both groups differed from the respondents classified as "Severe." A similar analysis for the second sample also yielded a statistically significant difference, and post hoc tests showed that all groups differed from each other.

Gormally et al. (1982) hypothesized that Binge Eating scores would relate to scores on a Cognitive Factors Scale that they developed to measure "the tendency to set unrealistic standards for a diet (e.g., eliminating 'favorite foods') and low efficacy expectations for sustaining a diet" (p. 47). As predicted, correlations between the two scales were significant ($r = .56$ in one sample and $r = .53$ in a second sample).

Marcus et al. (1985) classified 430 subjects into three groups (little or no problem, moderate problem, and serious problem) as a function of their total scores on the Binge Eating Scale. Separate one-way analyses of variance showed significant differences on age, weight, and percentage overweight. Moderate and serious bingers weighed more than those with no bingeing problem, serious bingers were more overweight than nonbingers, and serious and moderate bingers were significantly younger than nonbingers.

A sample of 66 obese women completed the Binge Eating Scale and the Eating Inventory (EI) (Stunkard, 1981) (see separate entry for Three-Factor Eating Questionnaire). There was a significant correlation (r =

.54) between scores on the two measures (Marcus et al., 1985). There was also a significant correlation between Binge Eating scores and scores on two of the three subscales of the EI: tendency toward disinhibition = .61 and perceived hunger = .54. Marcus et al. (1985) performed separate one-way analyses of variance and post hoc tests to look at the subscale and total score means on the EI in regard to the women's classification based on the Binge Eating Scale.

Ross and Todt (1984) compared the Binge Eating scores of anorexics (AN), bulimics (BUL), and those suffering from both anorexia and bulimia (BULAN). As expected, the AN group scored significantly lower than the BUL group and the BULAN groups. Furthermore, Ross and Todt found significant correlations between Binge Eating scores and scores on the Cognitive Factors Scale (Gormally et al., 1982) for the BUL group but not for the AN group or the BULAN group.

NOTES & COMMENTS: (1) Some groups of statements on the Binge Eating Scale do not appear to form a continuum nor do all the statements in a group necessarily reflect the same concept. That is, one statement in the group may contain a single idea, and another statement in the same group may include that idea as well as another one.

(2) The articles listed here used the Binge Eating Scale only with obese persons or persons with eating disorders. There is, however, nothing in the items that restrict their use to special populations.

(3) Gormally et al. (1982) labeled the scale "Eating Habits Checklist" when they administered it. Wilson, Rossiter, Kleifield, and Lindholm (1986) labeled it the same way and used the scale as one of numerous dependent measures in a study comparing two methods of treating bulimia.

(4) Kolotkin, Revis, Kirkley, and Janick (1987) used the Binge Eating Scale to measure bingeing severity among obese women seeking treatment in a weight management program. The researchers compared the women's Binge Eating scores with their scores on the Minnesota Multiphasic Personality Inventory (Hathaway & McKinley, 1967).

AVAILABLE FROM: Gormally, Black, Daston, and Rardin, 1982

USED IN:

Gormally, J., Black, S., Daston, S., & Rardin, D. (1982). The assessment of binge eating severity among obese persons. *Addictive Behaviors*, *7*, 47–55.

Kolotkin, R. L., Revis, E. S., Kirkley, B. G., & Janick, L. (1987). Binge eating in obesity: Associated MMPI characteristics. *Journal of Consulting and Clinical Psychology*, *55*, 872–876.

Marcus, M. D., Wing, R. R., & Lamparski, D. M. (1985). Binge eating and dietary restraint in obese patients. *Addictive Behaviors*, *10*, 163–168.

Ross, S. M., & Todt, E. H. (1984, April). *Further clinical validation of the Binge-Eating Scale*. Paper presented at the meeting of the Rocky Mountain Psychological Association, Las Vegas. (ERIC Document Reproduction Service No. ED 247 509)

Wilson, G. T., Rossiter, E., Kleifield, E. I., & Lindholm, L. (1986). Cognitive-behavioral treatment of bulimia nervosa: A controlled evaluation. *Behaviour Research and Therapy, 24*, 277–288.
BIBLIOGRAPHY:
American Psychiatric Association. (1980). *Diagnostic and statistical manual of mental disorders* (3rd ed.). Washington, DC: APA.
Hathaway, S. R., & McKinley, J. C. (1967). *Minnesota Multiphasic Personality Inventory*. New York: Psychological Corporation.
Stunkard, A. J. (1981). "Restrained eating": What it is and a new scale to measure it. In L. A. Cioffi, W. B. T. James, & T. B. Van Itallie (Eds.), *The body weight regulatory system: Normal and disturbed mechanisms* (pp. 243–251). New York: Raven Press.

BINGE SCALE (BS)
AUTHORS: Raymond C. Hawkins, II and Pamelia F. Clement
DATE: 1980 (used before 1978)
VARIABLE: Binge eating tendencies
TYPE OF INSTRUMENT: Multiple choice
DESCRIPTION: The Binge Scale (BS) consists of 9 items embedded in a 19-item questionnaire. The 9 items pertain to frequency and duration of bingeing behavior, behavior and feelings during and after a binge, and overall concern about bingeing. Each item is accompanied by three or four response options. The items are appropriate only for persons who have binged at least once. The remaining items on the questionnaire pertain to such things as reaction to one's nude image in a mirror, frequency of dieting, precipitating event for bingeing, age at starting bingeing, and place of bingeing.
SAMPLE ITEMS: How often do you binge eat? (a) seldom, (b) once or twice a month, (c) once a week, (d) almost every day

Which best describes your feelings during a binge? (a) I feel that I could control the eating if I chose. (b) I feel that I have at least some control. (c) I feel completely out of control.
PREVIOUS SUBJECTS: College students, bulimia nervosa patients, women with a history of anorexia nervosa, obese women, women in general
APPROPRIATE FOR: Grades 7 and older
ADMINISTRATION: Self-administered; the 19-item questionnaire takes about 5–10 minutes to complete
SCORING: Hawkins and Clement (1980) provided a scoring key for the 9 items comprising the BS. Individual items are scored on a 0–1 scale, a 0–2 scale, or a 0–3 scale. Item scores are summed to yield a total score for the 9 items. The total score can range from 0 to 23. Hawkins (personal communication, March 5, 1985) reported that total scores less than 10 are essentially normal, scores above 12 are suggestive of bulimia, and scores greater than 15 are strongly suggestive of bulimia.

Hawkins and Clement (1984) provided response frequencies and percentages for each item on the BS, separately for each of three groups: 663 normal-weight females, 39 normal-weight males, and 86 overweight females.

DEVELOPMENT: No information was provided.

RELIABILITY: Coefficient alpha for the BS was .68, and test-retest reliability with a 1-month interval between testings was .88 (Hawkins & Clement, 1980).

VALIDITY: Hawkins and Clement (1980) reported the following significant differences in BS scores. Females scored higher than males, overweight persons scored higher than normal-weight persons, and those with onset of weight concern before age 12 scored higher than those with onset of weight concern after age 12.

As evidence of the discriminant validity of the BS, Hawkins and Clement (1980) tested 65 college men and 182 college women with the BS and the Marlowe-Crowne Social Desirability Scale (Crowne & Marlowe, 1960). The correlations were nonsignificant for both males (r = .07) and females (r = .03). Hawkins and Clement also compared the BS scores from these respondents with their scores on several other measures: the Restraint Scale (Herman & Polivy, 1975) (see separate entry), which measures degree of dieting concern, the Negative Self-Image Scale (Nash & Ormiston, 1978), and a measure of deviation from desired weight. For females, BS scores were significantly correlated with all three measures; for males, BS scores were significantly correlated with Restraint Scale scores and Negative Self-Image scores but not with scores on the measure of deviation from desired weight.

Hawkins and Clement (1980) tested another sample of 73 college women and 45 college men using the four measures named above plus three others: Rotter's (1966) Locus of Control Scale, the College Self-Expression Scale (Galassi, Delo, Galassi, & Bastien, 1974) which is a measure of assertiveness, and a life change measure (Price & Price, 1974). For college women, the BS was significantly correlated with three of the six measures: Restraint Scale (r = .61), Negative Self-Image Scale (r = .55), and the life change measure (r = .27). For college men, the BS was significantly correlated with two of the four measures: Restraint Scale (r = .39) and Negative Self-Image Scale (r = .44).

Williams, Spencer, and Edelmann (1987) tested college students with a lengthy questionnaire including the items from the BS, as well as numerous other items and measures relating to weight. When scores on the BS were correlated with other scores extracted from the questionnaire, 11 of the 15 correlations were statistically significant.

Smith and Thelen (1984) developed a measure of bulimia called the Bulimia Test (BULIT) (see separate entry). To validate the BULIT, the researchers correlated BULIT scores and BS scores from 89 normal controls and 20 bulimics. The correlation was .93, extremely high. Smith and Thelen also reported a point-biserial correlation of .79 between total scores on the BS and group membership (normal or bulimic). When a cutoff score of 9 was used to separate bingers and nonbinge eaters, 1 person in the bulimic group was misclassified, and 10 persons in the normal group were misclassified.

NOTES & COMMENTS: (1) A factor analysis produced one factor—"guilt and concern"—that accounted for 71% of the variance and a second factor—"duration and satiety feelings associated with binges"—that accounted for another 16% of the variance (Hawkins & Clement, 1980). According to Hawkins (personal communication, March 5, 1985), one item—Do you ever vomit after a binge—did not load highly on either factor.

(2) Hawkins and Clement (1984) administered the BS along with six other measures: the Eating Attitudes Test (Garner & Garfinkel, 1979) (see separate entry), the Negative Self-Image Scale (Nash & Ormiston, 1978), the Beck Depression Inventory (Beck, 1970), the neuroticism subscale from the Maudsley Personality Inventory (Jensen, 1958), the Dating and Assertion Questionnaire (Levenson & Gottman, 1978) (see separate entry), and an experimental measure of dating relationships developed by Clement. Their results provided information regarding the personality correlates of bingeing. Hawkins, Turell, and Jackson (1983) administered a variety of personality measures to normal-weight and overweight college students. The scales they used included the BS, the Personal Attributes Questionnaire (Spence & Helmreich, 1978) (see Beere, 1990), the Restraint Scale, the Texas Social Behavior Inventory, which is a measure of social self-esteem (Helmreich, Stapp, & Ervin, 1974), the Negative Self-Image Scale, Langston's (1975) modification of the Mosher Forced-Choice Sex-Guilt Scale (Mosher, 1968) (see separate entry for Revised Mosher Guilt Inventory), and the Work and Family Orientation Scale (Spence & Helmreich, 1978) (see Beere, 1990). They reported the interrelationships between the scores on the various measures.

(3) In addition to the work of Hawkins and his colleagues, other researchers have used the BS along with a variety of other measures to study the personality and behavior of persons with eating disorders and control subjects (Edwards & Nagelberg, 1986; Krueger & Bornstein, 1987; Yates & Sambrailo, 1984).

(4) Researchers have used the BS as one of several measures in a study designed to compare bulimics with and without a history of anorexia nervosa (Katzman & Wolchik, 1983) and to compare college women with bulimia and college women who binged (Katzman & Wolchik, 1984).

(5) Crowther, Lingswiler, and Stephens (1984) used the BS to identify binge eaters and nonbinge eaters. They used a cutoff score of 10 for

identifying the two groups. Williamson, Kelley, Davis, Ruggiero, and Blouin (1985) used the BS as part of a comprehensive pretreatment assessment of 45 women. Ruff and Barrios (1986) used the BS as one of several measures to validate self-report information used for identifying a sample of bulimics and a sample of normal controls. Ordman and Kirschenbaum (1985) used the BS as one of numerous dependent measures in a study of the effectiveness of cognitive-behavioral therapy in the treatment of bulimia.

(6) Hawkins (personal communication, March 5, 1985) recommended improving the BS by "specifying the actual frequency of self-induced vomiting and by adding item(s) tapping other forms of purging (e.g., diuretics, laxatives) and perhaps other self-destructive behaviors (e.g., self-mutilation, abuse of alcohol or drugs)."

AVAILABLE FROM: Hawkins and Clement, 1980; for the 19-item questionnaire, order from NAPS c/o Microfiche Publications, P.O. Box 3513, Grand Central Station, New York, NY 10163–3513; NAPS document no. 04753; for microfiche, in the United States, remit $4.00 with order.

USED IN:

Crowther, J. H., Lingswiler, V. M. & Stephens, M. A. P. (1984). The topography of binge eating. *Addictive Behaviors, 9,* 299–303.

Edwards, F. E., & Nagelberg, D. B. (1986). Personality characteristics of restrained/binge eaters versus unrestrained/nonbinge eaters. *Addictive Behaviors, 11,* 207–211.

Hawkins, R. C., II, & Clement, P. F. (1980). Development and construct validation of a self-report measure of binge eating tendencies. *Addictive Behaviors, 5,* 219–226.

Hawkins, R. C., II, & Clement, P. F. (1984). Binge eating: Measurement problems and a conceptual model. In R. C. Hawkins, II., W. J. Fremouw, & P. F. Clement (Eds.), *The binge-purge syndrome: Diagnosis, treatment, and research* (pp. 229–251). New York: Springer.

Hawkins, R. C., II, Turell, S., & Jackson, L. J. (1983). Desirable and undesirable masculine and feminine traits in relation to students' dieting tendencies and body image dissatisfaction. *Sex Roles, 9,* 705–718.

Katzman, M. A., & Wolchik, S. A. (1983, April). *Bulimics with and without prior anorexia nervosa: A comparison of personality characteristics.* Paper presented at the meeting of the Rocky Mountain Psychological Association, Snowbird, UT. (ERIC Document Reproduction Service No. ED 236 463)

Katzman, M. A., & Wolchik, S. A. (1984). Bulimia and binge eating in college women: A comparison of personality and behavioral characteristics. *Journal of Consulting and Clinical Psychology, 52,* 423–428.

Krueger, H. K., & Bornstein, P. H. (1987). Depression, sex-roles, and family variables: Comparison of bulimics, binge-eaters, and normals. *Psychological Reports, 60,* 1106.

Ordman, A. M., & Kirschenbaum, D. S. (1985). Cognitive-behavioral therapy for bulimia: An initial outcome study. *Journal of Consulting and Clinical Psychology, 53,* 305–313.

Ruff, G. A., & Barrios, B. A. (1986). Realistic assessment of body image. *Behavioral Assessment, 8,* 237–251.

Smith, M. C., & Thelen, M. H. (1984). Development and validation of a test for bulimia. *Journal of Consulting and Clinical Psychology, 52,* 863–872.

Williams, A., Spencer, C. P., & Edelmann, R. J. (1987). Restraint theory, locus of control and the situational analysis of binge eating. *Personality and Individual Differences, 8,* 67–74.

Williamson, D. A., Kelley, M. L., Davis, C. J., Ruggiero, L., & Blouin, D. C. (1985). Psychopathology of eating disorders: A controlled comparison of bulimic, obese, and normal subjects. *Journal of Consulting and Clinical Psychology, 53,* 161–166.

Yates, A. J., & Sambrailo, F. (1984). Bulimia nervosa: A descriptive and therapeutic study. *Behavior Research and Therapy, 22,* 503–517.

BIBLIOGRAPHY:

Beck, A. T. (1970). *Depression: Causes and treatment.* Philadelphia: University of Pennsylvania Press.

Beere, C. A. (1990). *Gender roles: A handbook of tests and measures.* Westport, CT: Greenwood.

Crowne, D. P., & Marlowe, D. (1960). A new scale of social desirability independent of psychopathology. *Journal of Consulting Psychology, 24,* 349–354.

Galassi, J. P., Delo, J. S., Galassi, M. D., & Bastien, S. (1974). The College Self-Expression Scale: A measure of assertiveness. *Behavior Therapy, 5,* 165–171.

Garner, D. M., & Garfinkel, P. E. (1979). The Eating Attitudes Test: An index of the symptoms of anorexia nervosa. *Psychological Medicine, 9,* 273–279.

Helmreich, R., Stapp, J., & Ervin, C. (1974). The Texas Social Behavior Inventory (TSBI): An objective measure of self-esteem or social competence. *Catalog of Selected Documents in Psychology, 4,* 79. (Ms. No. 681)

Herman, C. P., & Polivy, J. (1975). Anxiety, restraint, and eating behavior. *Journal of Abnormal Psychology, 84,* 666–672.

Jensen, A. R. (1958). The Maudsley Personality Inventory. *Acta Psychologica, 14,* 314–325.

Langston, R. D. (1975). Stereotyped sex behavior and guilt. *Journal of Personality Assessment, 39,* 77–81.

Levenson, R. W., & Gottman, J. M. (1978). Toward the assessment of social competence. *Journal of Consulting and Clinical Psychology, 46,* 453–462.

Mosher, D. L. (1968). Measurement of guilt in females by self-report measures. *Journal of Consulting and Clinical Psychology, 32,* 690–695.

Nash, T. D., & Ormiston, L. H. (1978). *Taking charge of your weight and well being.* Palo Alto: Bull Publishing.

Price, G. H., & Price, K. P. (1974). *Instructor's manual and resource book for G. C. Davison & J. M. Neale's Abnormal Psychology: An experimental clinical approach.* New York: Wiley.

Rotter, J. B. (1966). Generalized expectations for internal versus external control of reinforcement. *Psychological Monographs, 80* (1, Whole No. 609).

Spence, J. T., & Helmreich, R. L. (1978). *Masculinity and femininity: Their psychological dimensions, correlates, and antecedents.* Austin: University of Texas Press.

BULIMIA COGNITIVE DISTORTIONS SCALE (BCDS)
AUTHORS: Richard G. Schulman, Bill N. Kinder, Pauline S. Powers, Mark Prange, and Alice Gleghorn
DATE: 1986
VARIABLE: Cognitive distortions and irrational beliefs associated with bulimia
TYPE OF INSTRUMENT: Summated rating scale
DESCRIPTION: The Bulimia Cognitive Distortions Scale (BCDS) contains 25 items representing two factors. The first factor consists of 16 items measuring "cognitive distortions associated with automatic eating behaviors" (Schulman, Kinder, Powers, Prange, & Gleghorn, 1986, p. 630); the second factor consists of 9 items measuring "cognitive distortions associated with physical appearance" (p. 630). Each item is accompanied by five response options: "strongly disagree, disagree, neutral, agree, strongly agree." All items are phrased in the same direction; bulimics are likely to agree with the statements.
SAMPLE ITEMS: (automatic eating behaviors) No matter what I do I'll never be able to stay on a normal diet.
(physical appearance) If my hair isn't perfect I'll look terrible.
PREVIOUS SUBJECTS: Female bulimics, ages 17–45; females, ages 18–40
APPROPRIATE FOR: Females, high school ages and older
ADMINISTRATION: Self-administered; about 10–15 minutes
SCORING: Items are individually scored on a 5-point scale, with 5 points assigned to the "strongly agree" end of the continuum. Item scores are summed to yield two factor scores and a total score. A cutoff score of 61 on the overall scale is considered effective in separating bulimics and nonbulimics. Schulman et al. (1986) reported means and standard deviations on the two factor scores and the total score for bulimics and nonbulimics.
DEVELOPMENT: A pool of 90 items was developed based on the cognitive distortions expressed by 15 bulimic women who were individually interviewed. Item content related to "eating, purging, dieting, weight, appearance, emotional triggers for bingeing, and control" (Schulman et al., 1986, p. 633). The suggestions from a psychiatrist, a psychologist, and a psychiatric social worker, all experienced in working with bulimics, were used to modify the items, which were then pilot tested on 12 bulimic women. The bulimic women independently sorted the items into three categories based on the frequency with which they would agree with the item. Eight of the 12 women indicated that they "always" or "sometimes" agreed with 47 items in the pool. These items were retained.

Five criteria were used to reduce further the size of the item pool. Items that strongly discriminated between bulimic and control groups were retained, as were items with high item-total correlations. Items were also retained if they were sensitive to the severity of bulimia, if they loaded in a desirable way in the factor analysis, or if they were needed to represent adequately the various domains of interest. The following domains were desired on the scale: "(a) beliefs that the only way to deal with stress or negative emotions is by binge eating; (b) beliefs that purging is necessary after eating; (c) beliefs that bulimics are out of control in both eating and other areas of their lives, loss of control is represented by weight gain, emotional reasoning about loss of control (assumption that negative emotions are the way things are); and (d) negative interpretations about how others view them, perfectionist attitudes in relation to their own appearance, self-esteem determined by weight" (Schulman et al., 1986, p. 634).

RELIABILITY: Based on responses from 55 bulimics and 55 nonbulimics, coefficient alpha for the full scale was .97. As further evidence of the internal consistency of the BCDS, the authors reported that 16 of the 25 items had item-total correlations of at least .75.

VALIDITY: To provide evidence of the scale's validity, 55 bulimic and 55 nonbulimic women completed the BCDS and three other measures: the Irrational Beliefs Test (Ellis, 1962), which has been shown in previous research to have two subscales—demand for approval (DA) and high self-expectations (HSE)—that differentiated between bulimics and nonbulimics (Katzman & Wolchik, 1984); the Beck Depression Inventory (Beck, 1967); and the Bizarre Sensory Experiences scale (BSE) (Harris & Lingoes, 1955), a subscale of the Minnesota Multiphasic Personality Inventory. As expected, the BCDS correlated significantly with scores on DA, HSE, and the Beck Depression Inventory for both the bulimics and the bulimics and nonbulimics considered together. Also as predicted, for bulimics, the BSE was not significantly correlated with BCDS scores, but contrary to expectation, the correlation between BCDS and BSE was significant when bulimics and nonbulimics were considered together.

A discriminant analysis was performed to determine the effectiveness of the various measures in predicting the presence or absence of bulimia. "The BCDS was the only variable significant in the prediction of group membership" (Schulman et al., 1986, p. 635). The BCDS correctly predicted group membership for all 55 nonbulimics and for 48 of the 55 bulimics (87.3%). Thus, the overall rate of correct classification was 93.6%. To test further the discriminative ability of the BCDS, the bulimics were divided into four groups representing the frequency with which they binged: "daily, at least once a week, at least once a month, and less than once a month" (p. 636). A discriminant analysis showed that the BCDS was again the only variable able to predict group membership. The overall rate of correct classification was 66.4%.

NOTES & COMMENTS: (1) A factor analysis of responses from 110 bulimics and nonbulimics yielded two factors. The first factor—cognitive distortions associated with automatic eating behaviors—included 16 items and accounted for 91% of the variance. The second factor—cognitive distortions associated with physical appearance—included 9 items and accounted for 9% of the variance. However, given the small sample size, these results cannot be presumed stable.

(2) Schulman et al. (1986) reported that a small group of anorexics completed the BCDS. There was a large difference in the mean scores of the six anorexics who reported no bingeing compared to the four anorexics who reported bingeing. These findings need to be replicated with larger samples.

AVAILABLE FROM: Bill Kinder, University of South Florida, College of Social and Behavioral Sciences, Department of Psychology, Tampa, FL 33620–8200

USED IN:

Schulman, R. G., Kinder, B. N., Powers, P. S., Prange, M., & Gleghorn, A. (1986). The development of a scale to measure cognitive distortions in bulimia. *Journal of Personality Assessment, 50*, 630–639.

BIBLIOGRAPHY:

Beck, A. T. (1967). *Depression: Clinical, experimental and theoretical aspects*. New York: Harper & Row.

Ellis, A. (1962). *Reason and emotion in psychotherapy*. New York: Lyle Stuart.

Harris, R., & Lingoes, J. (1955). *Subscales for the Minnesota Multiphasic Personality Inventory*. San Francisco: Langley Porter Clinic.

Katzman, M. A., & Wolchik, S. A. (1984). Bulimia and binge eating in college women: A comparison of personality and behavioral characteristics. *Journal of Consulting and Clinical Psychology, 52*, 423–428.

BULIMIA TEST (BULIT)

AUTHORS: Marcia C. Smith and Mark H. Thelen

DATE: 1984

VARIABLE: Bulimia

TYPE OF INSTRUMENT: Multiple choice

DESCRIPTION: The Bulimia Test (BULIT) consists of 32 items pertaining to eating behaviors, bingeing, use of laxatives or suppositories, vomiting, and dieting behaviors. Each item is accompanied by five response alternatives that vary depending on the specific question. The keyed response is sometimes the first response and sometimes the last response listed.

SAMPLE ITEMS: Do you ever eat uncontrollably to the point of stuffing yourself (i.e., going on eating binges)? (a) Once a month or less (or never); (b) 2–3 times a month; (c) Once or twice a week; (d) 3–6 times a week; (e) Once a day or more.

I don't like myself after I eat too much. (a) Always; (b) Frequently; (c) Sometimes; (d) Seldom or never; (e) I don't eat too much.
PREVIOUS SUBJECTS: Bulimics, college women
APPROPRIATE FOR: Grades 7 and older
ADMINISTRATION: Self-administered; about 15–20 minutes
SCORING: Smith and Thelen (1984) provided a key to indicate for each item which end of the response continuum is assigned 5 points. For about two-thirds of the items, this is the first response listed. Item scores are summed to yield a single score, and higher scores are more strongly indicative of bulimia. A cutoff score of 102 is used to differentiate between bulimics and nonbulimics.
DEVELOPMENT: A pool of 75 items was developed to reflect the characteristics listed in the DSM-III criteria for bulimia (American Psychiatric Association, 1980). The item pool, with each item accompanied by five response alternatives, was administered to 18 bulimics and 119 normal controls. Significant differences ($p < .0001$) between the two groups were found for 45 of the 75 items. To shorten the scale, 5 of the 45 items were eliminated because they correlated very highly with items that had stronger discriminating power. An additional 10 items were eliminated because they pertained to symptoms that were well represented on the scale by items with better discriminating power. This left a scale with 30 items representing all but two of the DSM-III criteria for bulimia. The omitted criteria were "(a) behaviors related to extreme attempts to lose weight (i.e., strict dieting, vomiting, laxative and diuretic abuse), and (b) criteria to rule out a diagnosis of anorexia nervosa" (Smith & Thelen, 1984, p. 865). These criteria were omitted because none of the items representing these criteria was found to discriminate sufficiently well between the two groups.

The scale was revised by adding 2 items, both pertaining to vomiting and strict dieting behaviors. In addition, 4 items that did not discriminate adequately were retained because they provided information "about laxative and diuretic abuse, and dysmenorrhea" (Smith & Thelen, 1984, p. 866). This led to a 36-item scale, later reduced to 32 items by ignoring responses to the 4 items added last.
RELIABILITY: Test-retest reliability was based on a sample of 69 respondents who were "retested several weeks later" (Smith & Thelen, 1984, p. 865). The reliability was .87.
VALIDITY: Bulimics and normal controls obtained significantly different means on the original 30-item version of the BULIT. The point-biserial correlation between group membership and these BULIT scores for the two groups was .80 (Smith & Thelen, 1984).

Bulimics and normal controls obtained significantly different means on the 32-item version of the BULIT administered to 20 bulimics and 94 normal controls. There were significant differences in group means for each of the 32 items; 30 of the differences were significant at the .0001 level. The point-biserial correlation between group membership and BULIT scores for these two groups was .82 (Smith & Thelen, 1984).

Using a cutoff score of 102 to classify respondents as bulimic or non-bulimic, the BULIT correctly classified 19 of 20 bulimics and 92 of 94 normal controls.

A subgroup of those who completed the BULIT were independently interviewed and rated as "bulimic" or "non-bulimic." Thirteen of 69 subjects were classified differently by the BULIT and the raters; more specifically, 8 bulimics and 5 nonbulimics, as judged by the raters, were classified differently by the BULIT. However, Smith and Thelen cautioned against judging these findings too harshly because the sampling procedure led to an overrepresentation of subjects whose scores were close to the cutoff: "these subjects were presumably more difficult to classify than subjects with extreme scores" (Smith & Thelen, 1984, p. 867).

Smith and Thelen (1984) administered the Binge Scale (BS) (Hawkins & Clement, 1980) (see separate entry) and the Eating Attitudes Test (EAT) (Garner & Garfinkel, 1979) (see separate entry) to about 90 bulimics and about 20 normal controls. The correlation between the BULIT and the BS was .93; the correlation between the BULIT and the EAT was .68.

NOTES & COMMENTS: (1) Smith and Thelen (1984) factor analyzed responses from 135 persons. They identified seven factors that offered support for the factorial validity of the scale, that is, "items targeted for each criterion area [on the DSM-III] indeed cluster together" (p. 867). Acknowledging that the sample size was small relative to the number of items, the authors replicated the factor analysis using another set of data. The results of the second analysis closely paralleled those from the first: "all but three items maintained the same highest row loading" (p. 867).

(2) Ruderman (1986) used the BULIT in a study looking at the relationship between bulimia and several other variables, including irrational beliefs as measured by the Rational Beliefs Inventory (Shorkey & Whiteman, 1977), depressive distortions and depressive nondistortions as measured by the Cognitive Bias Questionnaire (Krantz & Hammen, 1979), and relative weight.

AVAILABLE FROM: Smith and Thelen, 1984; Corcoran and Fischer, 1987

USED IN:

Ruderman, A. J. (1986). Bulimia and irrational beliefs. *Behaviour Research and Therapy, 24,* 193–197.

Smith, M. C., & Thelen, M. H. (1984). Development and validation of a test for bulimia. *Journal of Consulting and Clinical Psychology, 52,* 863–872.

BIBLIOGRAPHY:
American Psychiatric Association. (1980). *Diagnostic and statistical manual of mental disorders* (3rd ed.). Washington, DC: APA.
Corcoran, K., & Fischer, J. (1987). *Measures for clinical practice: A sourcebook* (pp. 111–117). New York: Free Press.
Garner, D. M., & Garfinkel, P. E. (1979). The Eating Attitudes Test: An index of the symptoms of anorexia nervosa. *Psychological Medicine, 9*, 273–279.
Hawkins, R. C., & Clement, P. F. (1980). Development and construct validation of a self-report measure of binge eating tendencies. *Addictive Behaviors, 5*, 219–226.
Krantz, S., & Hammen, C. (1979). Assessment of cognitive bias in depression. *Journal of Abnormal Psychology, 88*, 611–619.
Shorkey, C. T., & Whiteman, V. L. (1977). Development of the Rational Behavior Inventory: Initial validation and reliability. *Educational and Psychological Measurement, 37*, 527–534.

BULIMIC INVESTIGATORY TEST, EDINBURGH (BITE)
AUTHORS: M. Henderson and C. P. L. Freeman
DATE: 1987 (used 1985)
VARIABLE: Behaviors and feelings related to bulimia
TYPE OF INSTRUMENT: Alternate choice: yes/no
DESCRIPTION: The Bulimic Investigatory Test, Edinburgh (BITE), consists of 33 numbered items, with 1 item containing four questions. Thus, there are 36 questions on the BITE. The scale contains two subscales. The Symptom subscale contains 30 questions relating to "symptoms, behaviour and dieting" (Henderson & Freeman, 1987, p. 20), and the Severity subscale contains 6 questions "measuring the severity of behaviour as defined by its frequency" (p. 20). Although the questions on the Severity subscale are intermingled with the questions on the Symptom subscale, they differ in format. Each question on the Severity subscale is followed by 5 to 7 response options, and each question on the Symptom subscale is followed by the options "yes" and "no." Twenty-five of the 30 questions on the Symptom subscale are likely to be answered in the affirmative by persons with bulimia.

When the BITE is used as a screening instrument, the instructions direct respondents to answer "based on their feelings and behaviour over the past 3 months (Henderson & Freeman, 1987, p. 23). When the BITE is used to assess progress in treatment, respondents should consider their feelings and behavior only during the immediately prior month.

SAMPLE ITEMS: (Symptom subscale) Does your pattern of eating severely disrupt your life?

(Symptom subscale) Do you have a regular daily eating pattern?

(Severity subscale) If you do binge, how often is this? hardly ever, once a month, once a week, 2–3 times a week, daily, 2–3 times a day

PREVIOUS SUBJECTS: Female binge eaters, hospital staff members, medical school students, female bulimics
APPROPRIATE FOR: Grades 7 and older
ADMINISTRATION: Self-administered; about 10–15 minutes
SCORING: The Symptom and Severity subscales are scored separately. On the Symptom subscale, the keyed response is "yes" for 25 items and "no" for the remaining 5 items. The keyed response is assigned 1 point, so total scores range from 0 to 30. Higher scores are indicative of bulimia. Henderson and Freeman (1987) recommended three scoring categories. A score of 20 or more "indicates a highly disordered eating pattern and the presence of binge eating. There is a high probability that a subject who achieves such a score will fulfill DSM-III criteria for a diagnosis of bulimia" (p. 23). Scores in the 10–19 range suggest "an unusual eating pattern, but not to the extent that a subject in this range would meet all the criteria for a diagnosis of bulimia" (p. 23). Henderson and Freeman recommended that persons with scores in the 15–19 range be interviewed to determine what is causing the high score. Scores between 0 and 10 are considered normal.

For the six items comprising the Severity subscale, each response option is numbered, with higher numbers assigned to the responses reflecting greater frequency. The numbers accompanying the selected options are summed to yield a Severity subscale score. Scores on this subscale can range from 0 to 39. According to Henderson and Freeman (1987), "a score of 5 or more on this scale is considered clinically significant. A score of 10 or more indicates a high degree of severity" (p. 23).

A total score can be obtained by adding the Severity score and the Symptom score. A total score of 25 or greater suggests pathology. Total scores between 10 and 25 "are likely to reflect a subclinical group of subjects who have a disordered eating pattern" (Henderson & Freeman, 1987, p. 22).
DEVELOPMENT: A list of symptoms was compiled including those described by Palmer (1979), Russell (1979), and Bruch (1975) and those listed in the DSM-III (American Psychiatric Association, 1980). A list of questions was developed from these symptoms, and the questions were administered to a small group of bulimics and normal controls. The feedback from these subjects was used to revise some questions and delete others. A list of 40 questions remained: 7 questions about dieting behavior, 27 questions about symptoms and behavior of bulimia, and 6 questions dealing with the frequency of some specific behaviors related to bulimia. These 40 questions were completed by 15 female binge eaters and 40 normal controls. A cutoff score of 20 was used to divide respondents into two groups: high scorers and low scorers. Fourteen of the 15 binge eaters were correctly classified as high scorers, and 38 of the 40

normal controls were correctly classified as low scorers. The individual items were analyzed to determine whether they significantly differentiated between bulimics and normals. Using the results of the statistical analyses and their own judgment, the authors decided to combine the 27 symptom questions and 3 questions regarding dieting behavior. Together these 30 questions comprise the Symptom subscale. All 6 of the severity questions were retained and comprise the Severity subscale.

RELIABILITY: Henderson and Freeman (1987) calculated both internal consistency reliability and test-retest reliability for the BITE. Based on responses from 32 female binge eaters and 32 normal females, coefficient alpha was .96 for the Symptom subscale and .62 for the Severity subscale. A different sample of 30 normal females completed the BITE on two occasions separated by 1 week. The test-retest reliability for this group was .86. Another sample of 10 bulimic women completed the BITE on two occasions, separated by 15 weeks during which they did not experience treatment. Test-retest reliability for the bulimic women was .68.

VALIDITY: Using data from 32 female binge eaters and 32 normal females, Henderson and Freeman (1987) found that all binge eaters and all normal females were correctly classified on the Symptom subscale (using a cutoff score of 20). All normal subjects were also correctly classified on the Severity subscale; 62.5% of the normal controls had Severity scores of 0. Thirty of the 32 binge eaters were correctly classified by the Severity subscale (using a cutoff score of 5), and the 2 not correctly classified had scores of 4. Total scores correctly classified all participants (using a cutoff score of 25). Henderson and Freeman also reported significant mean differences between the two groups. They differed significantly on the Symptom score, the Severity score, and the total score.

Turnbull, Freeman, Barry, and Annandale (1987) tested five bulimic males with the BITE, the Eating Attitudes Test (EAT) (Garner & Garfinkel, 1979) (see separate entry) and the Eating Disorders Inventory (EDI) (Garner, Olmsted, & Polivy, 1983) (see separate entry). Only the BITE would have correctly identified the five men as bulimic.

NOTES & COMMENTS: (1) King and Williams (1987) raised some pointed and valid criticisms of Henderson and Freeman's (1987) work. They criticized the BITE on the following grounds: the authors claimed that it is effective as both a screening measure and as a diagnostic instrument; the authors did not adequately specify the criteria for labeling someone as a binge eater; the research methods were likely to overestimate the scale's validity; and the authors failed to provide sufficient information regarding various aspects of their research. Researchers considering using the BITE should review King and Williams (1987) before proceeding.

(2) Freeman, Sinclair, Turnbull, and Annandale (1985) used the BITE

as one of several eating scales in a study comparing several methods for treating bulimia.

AVAILABLE FROM: Henderson and Freeman, 1987

USED IN:

Freeman, C., Sinclair, F., Turnbull, J., & Annandale, A. (1985). Psychotherapy for bulimia: A controlled study. *Journal of Psychiatric Research, 19,* 473–478.

Henderson, M., & Freeman, C. P. L. (1987). A self-rating scale for bulimia: The "BITE." *British Journal of Psychiatry, 150,* 18–24.

King, M., & Williams, P. (1987). BITE: Self-rating scale for bulimia. *British Journal of Psychiatry, 150,* 714–715.

Turnbull, J. D., Freeman, C. P. L., Barry, F., & Annandale, A. (1987). Physical and psychological characteristics of five male bulimics. *British Journal of Psychiatry, 150,* 25–29.

BIBLIOGRAPHY:

American Psychiatric Association. (1980). *Diagnostic and statistical manual of mental disorders* (3rd ed.). Washington, DC: APA.

Bruch, H. (1975). *Eating disorders.* New York: Basic Books.

Garner, D. M., & Garfinkel, P. E. (1979). The Eating Attitudes Test: An index of the symptoms of anorexia nervosa. *Psychological Medicine, 9,* 273–279.

Garner, D. M., Olmsted, M. P., & Polivy, J. (1983). Development and validation of a multi-dimensional eating disorder inventory for anorexia nervosa and bulimia. *International Journal of Eating Disorders, 2,* 15–34.

Palmer, R. L. (1979). The dietary chaos syndrome: A useful new term? *British Journal of Medical Psychology, 52,* 187–190.

Russell, G. (1979). Bulimia nervosa: An ominous variant of anorexia nervosa. *Psychological Medicine, 9,* 429–448.

COMPULSIVE EATING SCALE (CES)

AUTHOR: Patricia A. Ondercin

DATE: 1979 (revised 1981)

VARIABLE: Behaviors and attitudes related to food and eating; assessment of bulimic symptomatology

TYPE OF INSTRUMENT: Summated rating scale

DESCRIPTION: The Compulsive Eating Scale (CES) contains 16 items. Item content pertains to attitudes toward food and eating; feelings leading to eating behavior; dieting, bingeing, and compulsive eating; and self-perception in regard to weight. Six items follow the stem, "I've noticed that I eat when I'm . . . " Fourteen items are accompanied by five response options: "never or rarely, occasionally, sometimes, frequently, almost always." The remaining 2 items are multiple choice items, 1 with five response options and 1 with three response options.

SAMPLE ITEMS: I get pleasure just thinking about food or eating.

I've noticed that I eat when I'm sad or depressed.

PREVIOUS SUBJECTS: College students

APPROPRIATE FOR: Grades 7 and older

ADMINISTRATION: Self-administered; about 5–10 minutes

SCORING: Individual items are scored on a 5-point scale, with the higher number of points assigned to the responses associated with eating disorders. Total scores can range from 16 (no evidence of bulimic symptomatology) to 80 (strong evidence of bulimic symptomatology).
DEVELOPMENT: Ondercin (1979) administered a 77-item questionnaire to 279 college women. Designed "to assess various aspects of eating behavior such as eating binges and their characteristics, general eating patterns, and weight and diet information" (p. 154), this questionnaire was followed by 20 items concerning "behaviors, attitudes, and feelings related to food and eating" (p. 154). The respondents were divided into three groups based on their answer to the question, "Would you label yourself a compulsive eater? . . . definitely, sometimes, or no" (p. 154). The three groups differed significantly on 12 of the 20 items and on several of the items from the 77-item portion of the questionnaire. Dunn and Ondercin (1981) administered a 32-item version of the CES to 252 college women and scored the 16 items that discriminated between compulsive and noncompulsive eaters. These 16 discriminating items comprise the current version of the CES.
RELIABILITY: Dunn and Ondercin (1981) reported a test-retest reliability of .96 based on a 4-week interval between successive administrations of the test. Golden, Buzcek, and Robbins (1986) tested 137 college women and obtained a coefficient alpha of .82.
VALIDITY: Dunn and Ondercin (1981) used the CES to identify a group who were low on compulsive eating (scores below 30) and a group who were high on compulsive eating (scores above 58). Most women (87%) in the high compulsive eating group were not overweight. Dunn and Ondercin compared the two groups on several measures, including Rotter's Internal-External Locus of Control Scale (I-E) (Rotter, 1966), the Marlowe-Crowne Social Desirability Scale (Crowne & Marlowe, 1960), the Sixteen Personality Factor Questionnaire (16PF) (Cattell, Eber, & Tatsuoka, 1970), and the Bem Sex Role Inventory (BSRI) (Bem, 1974) (see Beere, 1990), which is a measure of gender role identity. There were significant differences on Rotter's I-E Scale, the Marlowe-Crowne Social Desirability Scale, and 6 of the 16 factors from the 16PF: Emotional Stability, Suspiciousness, Shrewdness, Guilt-proneness, Control, and Inner Tension. The BSRI was used to measure masculine and feminine self-concepts and masculine and feminine ideal self. There were no significant differences between groups on the two self-concept measures nor was there a significant difference on the feminine ideal self. There was a significant difference on the male ideal self, with those scoring higher on the CES also scoring higher on the masculine ideal self score.

Nagelberg, Hale, and Ware (1984) tested college women, including 14 bingers, 10 purgers, and 7 normal controls. They found that bingers and purgers scored significantly higher than normals on the CES.

Golden et al. (1986) tested 137 college women and found that scores on the CES were not significantly related to self-esteem or depression, but they were significantly related to body image, DSM-III criteria for bulimia (American Psychiatric Association, 1980), and weight.

NOTES & COMMENTS: (1) Golden et al. (1986) factor analyzed responses from 137 college women. They identified three factors and used a factor loading of at least .40 to identify the items that would be included on each factor. Factor 1 contained six items and was labeled "Negative Affect" because the items reflected a negative affect in relation to food and eating. Factor 2 contained five items and was labeled "Dietary Restraint" because the items pertained to diet and body size. Factor 3 contained five items and was labeled "Positive Affect" because the items reflected the belief that eating produces pleasure and reduces tension. One item loaded above .40 on all three factors, and two items did not load above .40 on any factor. Golden et al. reported the intercorrelations between the subscales. They ranged from .38 to .87, and all but one were significant. Golden et al. also reported coefficient alpha for each subscale: Factor 1 = .84, Factor 2 = .75, and Factor 3 = .65.

(2) Williams, Spencer, and Edelmann (1987) used a subset of 12 items from the CES. Their subset included the items pertaining to reasons for eating, and they called their "scale" the "Situations for Eating Scale."

AVAILABLE FROM: Dunn and Ondercin, 1981

USED IN:

Dunn, P. K., & Ondercin, P. (1981). Personality variables related to compulsive eating in college women. *Journal of Clinical Psychology, 37*, 43–49.

Golden, B. R., Buzcek, T., & Robbins, S. B. (1986). Parameters of bulimia: Examining the Compulsive Eating Scale. *Measurement and Evaluation in Counseling and Development, 19*, 84–92.

Nagelberg, D. B., Hale, S. L., & Ware, S. L. (1984). The assessment of bulimic symptoms and personality correlates in female college students. *Journal of Clinical Psychology, 40*, 440–445.

Ondercin, P. A. (1979). Compulsive eating in college women. *Journal of College Student Personnel, 20*, 153–157

Williams, A., Spencer, C. P., & Edelmann, R. J. (1987). Restraint theory, locus of control and the situational analysis of binge eating. *Personality and Individual Differences, 8*, 67–74.

BIBLIOGRAPHY:

American Psychiatric Association. (1980). *Diagnostic and statistical manual of mental disorders* (3rd ed.). Washington, DC: APA.

Beere, C. A. (1990). *Gender roles: A handbook of tests and measures*. Westport, CT: Greenwood.

Bem, S. L. (1974). The measurement of psychological androgyny. *Journal of Consulting and Clinical Psychology, 42*, 155–162.

Cattell, R. B., Eber, H. W., & Tatsuoka, M. M. (1970). *Handbook for the Sixteen Personality Factor Questionnaire (16PF)*. Champaign, IL: Institute for Personality and Ability Testing.

Crowne, D. P., & Marlowe, D. (1960). A new scale of social desirability independent of psychopathology. *Journal of Consulting Psychology, 24,* 349–354.
Rotter, J. B. (1966). Generalized expectancies for internal versus external control of reinforcement. *Psychological Monographs, 80*(1).

EATING ATTITUDES TEST (EAT)
AUTHORS: David M. Garner and Paul E. Garfinkel
DATE: 1979
VARIABLE: Symptoms of anorexia nervosa
TYPE OF INSTRUMENT: Summated rating scale
DESCRIPTION: The Eating Attitudes Test (EAT) consists of 40 items regarding behaviors or feelings associated with eating, food, or weight. For each item, responses are indicated by placing an "X" under one of six columns headed "always, very often, often, sometimes, rarely, never." For 5 items, the "never" end of the continuum is associated with anorexia nervosa; for 34 items, the "always" end of the continuum is associated with anorexia nervosa; 1 item is not scored. One item, "Have regular menstrual periods," is not appropriate for male respondents. A 26-item version of the EAT is described below (see NOTES & COMMENTS).
SAMPLE ITEMS: Like eating with other people.
Aware of the calorie content of foods that I eat.
PREVIOUS SUBJECTS: Persons diagnosed with anorexia nervosa or bulimia, college students, high school students, obese females, professional dance students, modeling students, persons previously hospitalized because of anorexia nervosa, parents of anorexics, nonanorexic sisters of anorexic patients, depressed persons, attenders at a family planning clinic, normal-weight and overweight undergraduates, young adult females, cheerleaders, female diabetics, nursing students, twins and triplets, chronic schizophrenics, psychiatric outpatients, Hispanic females, Arab students in London, persons in England, Canada, Scotland, and Germany
APPROPRIATE FOR: High school students and older
ADMINISTRATION: Self-administered; about 15 minutes
SCORING: Each item is assigned between 0 and 3 points. For the 34 items where "always" is the response most indicative of anorexia nervosa, the responses "always," "very often" and "often" are assigned 3, 2, and 1 points, respectively. For these items, the remaining three responses are assigned 0 points. Scoring is reversed for the 5 items where "never" is the response most indicative of anorexia nervosa. Total scores range from 0 (no indication of anorexia nervosa) to 117 (strong indication of anorexia nervosa). A decision rule in which scores of 30 and higher were considered indicative of anorexia nervosa led to 13% false positives.
Steinhausen and Glanville (1983b) provided means and standard de-

viations for different groups of persons who completed the EAT. Rosen et al. (1988) provided normative data based on testing 1,373 adolescent boys and girls.

DEVELOPMENT: A pool of 35 items was developed based on a survey of the relevant literature. The items covered "a range of reported 'anorexic' behaviours and attitudes" (Garner & Garfinkel, 1979, p. 274). Each item was accompanied by five response alternatives ranging from "very often" to "never," and each was scored 0, 1, or 2, with higher scores reflecting anorexia nervosa. The item pool was administered to 32 anorexics and 34 normal controls. There was a significant difference in group means for 23 of the 35 items. These items were retained for the final version. In addition, "the remaining items were eliminated or re-worded and new items were added to the second version of the EAT" (Garner & Garfinkel, 1979, p. 274). No information was provided to indicate whether item analyses were performed for these new and revised items. A sixth response option, "always," was added, and scoring was revised so that each item could receive a maximum score of 3 points (rather than the 2 points used with the original item pool).

The development of the 26-item version of the EAT is described in the NOTES & COMMENTS section below.

RELIABILITY: Coefficient alpha based on testing 33 anorexics was .79; coefficient alpha based on testing 92 anorexics and normal controls was .94 (Garner & Garfinkel, 1979). Coefficient alpha for 160 anorexics was .92; coefficient alpha for 140 nonanorexics was .83 (Garner, Olmsted, Bohr, & Garfinkel, 1982).

P. I. Carter and Moss (1984) administered the EAT to a subset of 56 females between the ages of 18 and 39. The women completed the scale on two occasions separated by a 2- to 3-week interval. The test-retest reliability was .84.

VALIDITY: Garner and Garfinkel (1979) administered the EAT to a sample of 33 anorexics and 59 normal controls. The correlation between group membership and the original set of 23 items was .85. The correlation between group membership and the full 40-item version of the EAT was .87 ($p < .001$). The correlation between individual items and group membership was significant ($p < .001$) for 37 of the 40 items.

Garner and Garfinkel (1979) reported a significant difference when the mean total score for anorexics ($M = 58.9$, $s = 13.3$) was compared with the mean total score for the normal controls ($M = 15.6$, $s = 9.3$). Other researchers also reported significant differences when they compared the mean of EAT scores for a group with eating disorders to the mean of EAT scores for a group of normal controls (Button & Whitehouse, 1981; P. J. Cooper & Fairburn, 1983; Garfinkel et al., 1983; Harding & Lachenmeyer, 1986; Maloney & Shepard-Spiro, 1983; Post & Crowther, 1985).

Garner and Garfinkel (1979) found that 7% of their sample of normal controls obtained scores that overlapped with the lowest scoring anorexics. Interviews with these high-scoring nonanorexics indicated that these respondents "experience[d] significant concerns about their weight" (p. 277).

To provide evidence of the discriminant validity of the EAT, Garner and Garfinkel (1979) correlated scores on the EAT with scores on the Restraint Scale (Herman & Polivy, 1975) (see separate entry), a measure intended to assess degree of dieting behavior. For a sample of 43 nonanorexics, the correlation between the two measures was .28 (not significant). As further evidence of discriminant validity, Garner and Garfinkel tested a group of nonanorexics and obtained the following correlations, all nonsignificant: a correlation of .17 between EAT and weight fluctuations, a correlation of .30 between EAT and a measure of extraversion, a correlation of .10 between EAT and a measure of neuroticism, and a correlation of .10 between EAT and scores on the Eysenck Personality Inventory (Eysenck & Eysenck, 1964).

Garner and Garfinkel (1979) reported that recovered anorexics obtained scores in the normal range, "suggesting that the EAT is sensitive to clinical remission" (p. 276).

Garner and Garfinkel (1980) found that 69 of 183 dance students (37.7%) obtained EAT scores above 30. Clinical interviews showed that 11 of the 69 students were anorexic. One dance student with an EAT score below 30 was also found to be anorexic. The researchers found that of 56 modeling students, 16 had EAT scores above 30 (28.5%), and 3 of the 16 were identified as anorexic based on clinical interviews. One anorexic modeling student scored below 30 on the EAT.

Button and Whitehouse (1981) found that scores for female anorexics were significantly higher ($p < .001$) than scores for female students in a college of technology. Using a cutoff score of 32, the researchers found that 28 of 446 students (6.3%) scored in the anorexic range, and 5 of 13 female anorexics obtained EAT scores in the normal range. (Two patients obtained scores as low as 12.) From their analysis, Button and Whitehouse concluded: "A high score, while by no means diagnostic of anorexia nervosa, is of value in detecting subclinical cases. . . . The EAT is more accurately viewed as a measure of concern about weight and food intake, rather than exclusively a measure of the symptoms of anorexia nervosa" (p. 514).

Mann et al. (1983) related scores on the shortened version of the EAT to data obtained in an interview. They concluded that the EAT-26 "has value as a screening instrument, that is to identify subjects at risk who are to be further assessed" (p. 579).

P. I. Carter and Moss (1984) tested 162 females between the ages of 18 and 39. With a cutoff score of 30, 21.6% of the women scored in the anorexic range, but interview data suggested that only 2 women satisfied the DSM-III (American Psychiatric Association, 1980) criteria for anorexia. Thus, these researchers found that the EAT gave a very high false positive rate.

Turnbull, Freeman, Barry, and Annandale (1987) tested five men who satisfied the DSM-III criteria for bulimia. The researchers found that the EAT scores of these men would not have identified them as having an eating disorder.

The validity of the EAT was also considered by Nasser (1986), who studied female Arab students enrolled in a London university, and by Gross, Rosen, Leitenberg, and Willmuth (1986), who studied 82 women with bulimia.

NOTES & COMMENTS: (1) Garner and Olmsted (1984) compared the EAT and their Eating Disorder Inventory (EDI) (see separate entry). They noted that the approach to scale development was different for the two scales, with the development of the EAT based on an empirical approach and the development of the EDI beginning with a theoretical approach to determining subscales. They concluded that "the EAT is a sound measure of a range of symptoms common in anorexia nervosa, and the EDI focuses more on the specific cognitive and behavioral dimensions that may meaningfully differentiate subgroups of patients or which may distinguish those with serious psychopathology from 'normal' dieters" (p. 9).

(2) Garner and Garfinkel (1979) factor analyzed responses and identified seven factors: Food Preoccupation, Body Image for Thinness, Vomiting and Laxative Abuse, Dieting, Slow Eating, Clandestine Eating, and Perceived Social Pressure to Gain Weight. The authors acknowledged that their sample size was small but stated that "the results add tentative support for content validity of several symptom dimensions measured by the EAT" (Garner & Garfinkel, 1979, p. 276).

(3) Garner et al. (1982) developed a shorter form of the EAT by using results from a factor analytic study of the responses from 160 anorexics. The researchers identified three factors: Dieting, defined as "an avoidance of fattening foods and a preoccupation with being thinner" (p. 873); Bulimia and Food Preoccupation, "reflecting thoughts about food as well as those indicating bulimia" (p. 873); and Oral Control, "relating to self-control of eating and the perceived pressure from others to gain weight" (p. 873). Garner et al. acknowledged that the results of the factor analysis must be considered tentative since the sample size was small relative to the number of items. The three factors indicated above included 26 of the 40 items. These 26 items comprise a scale referred to as EAT-26. Coefficient alpha for EAT-26 was .90 for a sample of 160 anorexics and 83 for a sample of 140 nonanorexics. The correlation between EAT-26

and the full EAT was .98 for the anorexics and .97 for the nonanorexics. A cutoff score of 20 or 21 is recommended for the EAT-26.

(4) Wells, Coope, Gabb, and Pears (1985) factor analyzed responses from 749 girls between the ages of 12 and 18. Their analysis yielded four factors similar to those obtained by Garner et al. (1982): Dieting, Food Preoccupation, Vomiting/Laxatives, and Social Pressure to Eat. Twenty-seven items loaded on these four factors.

(5) Researchers have related EAT scores to scores on other measures including the Hopkins Symptom Checklist, a measure of somatization, depression, obsessive-compulsive tendencies, interpersonal sensitivity, and anxiety (Garner & Garfinkel, 1980; Garner et al., 1982); various measures of body satisfaction (Garner et al., 1982); a measure of locus of control (Garner et al., 1982; Harding & Lachenmeyer, 1986; Hood, Moore, & Garner, 1982); the Crown Crisp Experiential Index, a measure of neurotic symptoms (Clarke & Palmer, 1983; Meadows, Palmer, Newball, & Kenrick, 1986); the General Health Questionnaire, a measure of psychiatric disorder (J. A. Carter & Duncan, 1984; P. J. Cooper & Fairburn, 1983; P. J. Cooper, Waterman, & Fairburn, 1984; Mann et al., 1983); a sex role measure (Hawkins, Turell, & Jackson, 1983; Pettinati, Franks, Wade, & Kogan, 1987); the EDI (Z. Cooper, Cooper, & Fairburn, 1985; Grant & Fodor, 1986; Gross et al., 1986); the Desire for Thinness Scale (Lundholm & Littrell, 1986); a measure of self-esteem (Grant & Fodor, 1986); a measure of physical effectiveness (Grant & Fodor, 1986); a measure of physical attractiveness (Grant & Fodor, 1986); the Structural Family Interaction Scale (Harding & Lachenmeyer, 1986); and the Goldberg Anorectic Attitude Scale (see separate entry) (Steinhausen, 1986). EAT scores have also been related to college major (Joseph, Wood, & Goldberg, 1982); frequency of binge eating (P. J. Cooper & Fairburn, 1983); weight history (P. J. Cooper & Fairburn, 1983; Garner, Olmsted, & Garfinkel, 1985); induced vomiting (J. A. Carter & Duncan, 1984); socioeconomic status (Eisler & Szmukler, 1985; Pumariega, 1986; Rosen, Silberg, & Gross, 1988; Steinhausen, 1984); age (Rosen et al., 1988; Steinhausen, 1984); weight (Channon & DeSilva, 1985; Steinhausen, 1984); food consumption (Rosen, Leitenberg, Gross, & Willmuth, 1985); sleep patterns (Hicks & Rozette, 1986); acculturation (Pumariega, 1986); and sex (Rosen et al., 1988; Silberstein, Striegel-Moore, Timko, & Rodin, 1988). Many of these studies directly or indirectly relate to the validity of the EAT.

(6) The EAT has been used to measure the effectiveness of treatment programs for eating disorders (Bauer, 1984; Freeman, Sinclair, Turnbull, & Annandale, 1985; Giles, Young, & Young, 1985; Hsu, 1984; Jenkins, 1987; Kirkley, Schneider, Agras, & Bachman, 1985; Leitenberg, Gross, Peterson, & Rosen, 1984; Leitenberg, Rosen, Gross, Nudelman, & Vara,

1988; Oakley, 1986; Ordman & Kirschenbaum, 1985; Schneider & Agras, 1985; Steinhausen, 1985; Stewart, Walsh, Wright, Roose, & Glassman, 1984).

(7) The EAT has been used to identify the prevalence of eating disorders among various populations (Brooks-Gunn & Warren, 1985; Button & Whitehouse, 1981; J. A. Carter & Duncan, 1984; P. I. Carter & Moss, 1984; Clarke & Palmer, 1983; P. J. Cooper & Fairburn, 1983; P. J. Cooper et al., 1984; Eisler & Szmukler, 1985; Garner & Garfinkel, 1980; Joseph et al., 1982; Lachenmeyer & Muni-Brander, 1988; Lyketsos, Paterakis, Beis, & Lyketsos, 1985; Mann et al., 1983; Meadows et al., 1986; Moss, Jennings, McFarland, & Carter, 1984; Rodin, Johnson, Garfinkel, Daneman, & Kenshole, 1986/1987; Segal & Figley, 1985; Steiner-Adair, 1986; Steinhausen, 1984; Szmukler, Eisler, Gillies, & Hayward, 1985).

(8) Thompson and Schwartz (1982) used the EAT to screen college women for a research study concerning the impact of anorexia on the life adjustment of college women. Fairburn and Cooper (1984) used the EAT as one of several measures to understand better persons suffering from bulimia. Toner, Garfinkel, and Garner (1986) used the 26-item EAT to compare restricting anorexics, bulimic anorexics, and a control group. The researchers compared the three groups in terms of their three factor scores: Dieting, Bulimia and Food Preoccupation, and Oral Control. Wolf and Crowther (1983) used the EAT scores as one of several variables to predict binge eating and weight deviation.

(9) Williams, Hand, and Tarnopolsky (1982) discussed the problem of using the EAT as a screening device for identifying persons at risk for anorexia nervosa.

(10) Vacc and Rhyne (1987) reported the development of an "adapted language form" of the EAT (A-EAT). The A-EAT is appropriate for persons with a third-grade reading level and has a correlation of .75 with the regular EAT.

(11) As part of the process of validating their new scale, the Bulimic Investigatory Test (BITE) (see separate entry), Henderson and Freeman (1987) compared BITE scores with EAT scores.

(12) The EAT was developed in Canada. It has been used in Canada, the United States, England, Scotland, Germany, and New Zealand. The EAT has been translated into German and Arabic.

AVAILABLE FROM: Garner and Garfinkel, 1979, includes the full-length EAT; Garner et al., 1982, includes the EAT-26; also see Corcoran and Fisher, 1987

USED IN:

Bauer, B. G. (1984). Bulimia: A review of a group treatment program. *Journal of College Student Personnel, 25,* 221–227.

Brooks-Gunn, J., & Warren, M. P. (1985). The effects of delayed menarche in different contexts: Dance and nondance students. *Journal of Youth and Adolescence, 14,* 285–300.

Buree, B., Papageorgis, D., & Solyom, L. (1984). Body image perception and preference in anorexia nervosa. *Canadian Journal of Psychiatry, 29,* 557–563.

Button, E. J., & Whitehouse, A. (1981). Subclinical anorexia nervosa. *Psychological Medicine, 11,* 509–516.

Carter, J. A., & Duncan, P. A. (1984). Binge-eating and vomiting: A survey of a high school population. *Psychology in the Schools, 21,* 198–203.

Carter, P. I., & Moss, R. A. (1984). Screening for anorexia and bulimia nervosa in a college population: Problems and limitations. *Addictive Behaviors, 9,* 417–419.

Channon, S., & DeSilva, W. P. (1985). Psychological correlates of weight gain in patients with anorexia nervosa. *Journal of Psychiatric Research, 19,* 267–271.

Clarke, M. G., & Palmer, R. L. (1983). Eating attitudes and neurotic symptoms in university students. *British Journal of Psychiatry, 142,* 299–304.

Clinton, D. N., & McKinlay, W. W. (1986). Attitudes to food, eating and weight in acutely ill and recovered anorectics. *British Journal of Clinical Psychology, 25,* 61–67.

Cooper, P. J., & Fairburn, C. G. (1983). Binge-eating and self-induced vomiting in the community: A preliminary study. *British Journal of Psychiatry, 142,* 139–144.

Cooper, P. J., Waterman, G. C., & Fairburn, C. G. (1984). Women with eating problems: A community survey. *British Journal of Clinical Psychology, 23,* 45–52.

Cooper, Z., Cooper, P. J., & Fairburn, C. G. (1985). The specificity of the Eating Disorder Inventory. *British Journal of Clinical Psychology, 24,* 129–130.

Eisler, I., & Szmukler, G. I. (1985). Social class as a confounding variable in the Eating Attitudes Test. *Journal of Psychiatric Research, 19,* 171–176.

Fairburn, C. G., & Cooper, P. J. (1984). The clinical features of bulimia nervosa. *British Journal of Psychiatry, 144,* 238–246.

Freeman, C., Sinclair, F., Turnbull, J., & Annandale, A. (1985). Psychotherapy for bulimia: A controlled study. *Journal of Psychiatric Research, 19,* 473–478.

Garfinkel, P. E., Garner, D. M., Rose, J., Darby, P. L., Brandes, J. S., O'Hanlon, J., & Walsh, N. (1983). A comparison of characteristics in the families of patients with anorexia nervosa and normal controls. *Psychological Medicine, 13,* 821–828.

Garner, D. M., & Garfinkel, P. E. (1979). The Eating Attitudes Test: An index of the symptoms of anorexia nervosa. *Psychological Medicine, 9,* 273–279.

Garner, D. M., & Garfinkel, P. E. (1980). Socio-cultural factors in the development of anorexia nervosa. *Psychological Medicine, 10,* 647–656.

Garner, D. M., & Olmsted, M. P. (1984). *Manual for Eating Disorder Inventory (EDI).* Odessa, FL: Psychological Assessment Resources.

Garner, D. M., Olmsted, M. P., Bohr, Y., & Garfinkel, P. E. (1982). The Eating Attitudes Test: Psychometric features and clinical correlates. *Psychological Medicine, 12,* 871–878.

Garner, D. M., Olmsted, M. P., & Garfinkel, P. E. (1985). Similarities among bulimic groups selected by different weights and weight histories. *Journal of Psychiatric Research, 19,* 129–134.

Giles, T. R., Young, R. R., & Young, D. E. (1985). Behavioral treatment of severe bulimia. *Behavior Therapy, 16,* 393–405.

Grant, C. L., & Fodor, I. G. (1986). Adolescent attitudes toward body image and anorexic behavior. *Adolescence, 21,* 269–281.

Gross, J., Rosen, J. C., Leitenberg, H., & Willmuth, M. E. (1986). Validity of the Eating Attitudes Test and the Eating Disorders Inventory in bulimia nervosa. *Journal of Consulting and Clinical Psychology, 54,* 875–876.

Harding, T. P., & Lachenmeyer, J. R. (1986). Family interaction patterns and locus of control as predictors of the presence and severity of anorexia nervosa. *Journal of Clinical Psychology, 42,* 440–448.

Hawkins, R. C. II, Turell, S., & Jackson, L. J. (1983). Desirable and undesirable masculine and feminine traits in relation to students' dieting tendencies and body image dissatisfaction. *Sex Roles, 9,* 705–718.

Henderson, M., & Freeman, C. P. L. (1987). A self-rating scale for bulimia: The BITE. *British Journal of Psychiatry, 150,* 18–24.

Herzog, D. B., & Norman, D. K. (1985). Subtyping eating disorders. *Comprehensive Psychiatry, 26,* 375–380.

Hicks, R. A., & Rozette, E. (1986). Habitual sleep duration and eating disorders in college students. *Perceptual and Motor Skills, 62,* 209–210.

Holland, A. J., Hall, A., Murray, R., Russell, G. F. M., & Crisp, A. H. (1984). Anorexia nervosa: A study of 34 twin pairs and one set of triplets. *British Journal of Psychiatry, 145,* 414–419.

Hood, J., Moore, T. E., & Garner, D. M. (1982). Locus of control as a measure of ineffectiveness in anorexia nervosa. *Journal of Consulting and Clinical Psychology, 50,* 3–13.

Hsu, L. K. G. (1984). Treatment of bulimia with lithium. *American Journal of Psychiatry, 141,* 1260–1262.

Jenkins, M. E. (1987). An outcome study of anorexia nervosa in an adolescent unit. *Journal of Adolescence, 10,* 71–81.

Johnson-Sabine, E. C., Wood, K. H., & Wakeling, A. (1984). Mood changes in bulimia nervosa. *British Journal of Psychiatry, 145,* 512–516.

Joseph, A., Wood, I. K., & Goldberg, S. C. (1982). Determining populations at risk for developing anorexia nervosa based on selection of college major. *Psychiatry Research, 7,* 53–58.

Kirkley, B. G., Schneider, J. A., Agras, W. S., & Bachman, J. A. (1985). Comparison of two group treatments for bulimia. *Journal of Consulting and Clinical Psychology, 53,* 43–48.

Lachenmeyer, J. R., & Muni-Brander, P. (1988). Eating disorders in a nonclinical adolescent population: Implications for treatment. *Adolescence, 23,* 303–312.

Leitenberg, H., Gross, J., Peterson, J., & Rosen, J. C. (1984). Analysis of an anxiety model and the process of change during exposure plus response prevention treatment of bulimia nervosa. *Behavior Therapy, 15,* 3–20.

Leitenberg, H., Rosen, J. C., Gross, J., Nudelman, S., & Vara, L. S. (1988). Exposure plus response-prevention treatment of bulimia nervosa. *Journal of Consulting and Clinical Psychology, 56,* 535–541.

Lindy, D. C., Walsh, B. T., Roose, S. P., Gladis, M., & Glassman, A. H. (1985).

The dexamethasone suppression test in bulimia. *American Journal of Psychiatry, 142,* 1375–1376.

Lundholm, J. K., & Littrell, J. M. (1986). Desire for thinness among high school cheerleaders: Relationship to disordered eating and weight control behaviors. *Adolescence, 21,* 573–579.

Lyketsos, G. C., Paterakis, P., Beis, A., & Lyketsos, C. G. (1985). Eating disorders in schizophrenia. *British Journal of Psychiatry, 146,* 255–261.

Maloney, M. J., & Shepard-Spiro, P. (1983). Eating attitudes and behaviors of anorexia nervosa patients and their sisters. *General Hospital Psychiatry, 5,* 285–288.

Mann, A. H., Wakeling, A., Wood, K., Monck, E., Dobbs, R., & Szmukler, G. (1983). Screening for abnormal eating attitudes and psychiatric morbidity in an unselected population of 15-year-old schoolgirls. *Psychological Medicine, 13,* 573–580.

Meadows, G. N., Palmer, R. L., Newball, E. U. M., & Kenrick, J. M. T. (1986). Eating attitudes and disorder in young women: A general practice based survey. *Psychological Medicine, 16,* 351–357.

Moss, R. A., Jennings, G., McFarland, J. H., & Carter, P. (1984). Binge eating, vomiting, and weight fear in a female high school population. *Journal of Family Practice, 18,* 313–320.

Nasser, M. (1986). The validity of the Eating Attitude Test in a non-Western population. *Acta Psychiatrica Scandinavica, 73,* 109–110.

Oakley, S. J. (1986, November). *A short-term cognitive-behavioral approach to the treatment of bulimia.* Paper presented at the Meeting on Anorexia and Bulimia, New York. (ERIC Document Reproduction Service No. ED 283 059)

Ordman, A. M., & Kirschenbaum, D. S. (1985). Cognitive-behavioral therapy for bulimia: An initial outcome study. *Journal of Consulting and Clinical Psychology, 53,* 305–313.

Pettinati, H. M., Franks, V., Wade, J. H., & Kogan, L. G. (1987). Distinguishing the role of eating disturbance from depression in the sex role self-perceptions of anorexic and bulimic inpatients. *Journal of Abnormal Psychology, 96,* 280–282.

Post, G., & Crowther, J. H. (1985). Variables that discriminate bulimic from nonbulimic adolescent females. *Journal of Youth and Adolescence, 14,* 85–98.

Pumariega, A. J. (1986). Acculturation and eating attitudes in adolescent girls: A comparative and correlational study. *Journal of the American Academy of Child Psychiatry, 25,* 276–279.

Rodin, G. M., Johnson, L. E., Garfinkel, P. E., Daneman, D., & Kenshole, A. B. (1986/1987). Eating disorders in female adolescents with insulin dependent diabetes mellitus. *International Journal of Psychiatry in Medicine, 16,* 49–57.

Rosen, J. C., Leitenberg, H., Gross, J., & Willmuth, M. (1985). Standardized test meals in the assessment of bulimia nervosa. *Advances in Behaviour Research and Therapy, 7,* 181–197.

Rosen, J. C., Silberg, N. T., & Gross, J. (1988). Eating Attitudes Test and Eating

Disorder Inventory: Norms for adolescent girls and boys. *Journal of Consulting and Clinical Psychology, 56,* 305–308.

Schneider, J. A., & Agras, W. S. (1985). A cognitive behavioural group treatment of bulimia. *British Journal of Psychiatry, 146,* 66–69.

Segal, S. A., & Figley, C. R. (1985). Bulimia: Estimate of incidence and relationship to shyness. *Journal of College Student Personnel, 26,* 240–244.

Silberstein, L. R., Striegel-Moore, R. H., Timko, C., & Rodin, J. (1988). Behavioral and psychological implications of body dissatisfaction: Do men and women differ? *Sex Roles, 19,* 219–232.

Steiner-Adair, C. (1986). The body politic: Normal female adolescent development and the development of eating disorders. *Journal of the American Academy of Psychoanalysis, 14,* 95–114.

Steinhausen, H. C. (1984). Transcultural comparison of eating attitude in young females and anorectic patients. *European Archives of Psychiatry and Neurological Science, 234,* 198–201.

Steinhausen, H. C. (1985). Evaluation of inpatient treatment of adolescent anorexic patients. *Journal of Psychiatric Research, 19,* 371–375.

Steinhausen, H. C. (1986). Attitudinal dimensions in adolescent anorexic patients: An analysis of the Goldberg Anorectic Attitude Scale. *Journal of Psychiatric Research, 20,* 83–87.

Steinhausen, H. C., & Glanville, K. (1983a). A long-term follow-up of adolescent anorexia nervosa. *Acta Psychiatrica Scandinavica, 68,* 1–10.

Steinhausen, H. C., & Glanville, K. (1983b). Retrospective and prospective follow-up studies in anorexia nervosa. *International Journal of Eating Disorders, 2,* 221–235.

Stewart, J. W., Walsh, B. T., Wright, L., Roose, S. P., & Glassman, A. H. (1984). An open trial of MAO inhibitors in bulimia. *Journal of Clinical Psychiatry, 45,* 217–219.

Szmukler, G. I., Eisler, I., Gillies, C., & Hayward, M. E. (1985). The implications of anorexia nervosa in a ballet school. *Journal of Psychiatric Research, 19,* 177–181.

Thompson, M. G., & Schwartz, D. M. (1982). Life adjustment of women with anorexia nervosa and anorexic-like behavior. *International Journal of Eating Disorders, 1,* 47–60.

Toner, B. B., Garfinkel, P. E., & Garner, D. M. (1986). Long-term follow-up of anorexia nervosa. *Psychosomatic Medicine, 48,* 520–529.

Turnbull, J. D., Freeman, C. P. L., Barry, F., & Annandale, A. (1987). Physical and psychological characteristics of five male bulimics. *British Journal of Psychiatry, 150,* 25–29.

Vacc, N. A., & Rhyne, M. (1987). The Eating Attitudes Test: Development of an adapted language form for children. *Perceptual and Motor Skills, 65,* 335–336.

Wells, J. E., Coope, P. A., Gabb, D. C., & Pears, R. K. (1985). The factor structure of the Eating Attitudes Test with adolescent schoolgirls. *Psychological Medicine, 15,* 141–146.

Williams, P., Hand, D., & Tarnopolsky, A. (1982). The problem of screening for uncommon disorders: A comment on the Eating Attitudes Test. *Psychological Medicine, 12,* 431–434.

Wolf, E. M., & Crowther, J. H. (1983). Personality and eating habit variables as predictors of severity of binge eating and weight. *Addictive Behaviors, 8,* 335–344.

Yates, A. J., & Sambrailo, F. (1984). Bulimia nervosa: A descriptive and therapeutic study. *Behaviour Research and Therapy, 22,* 503–517.

BIBLIOGRAPHY:

American Psychiatric Association. (1980). *Diagnostic and statistical manual of mental disorders* (3rd ed.). Washington, DC: Author.

Corcoran, K., & Fischer, J. (1987). *Measures for clinical practice: A sourcebook* (pp. 146–149). New York: Free Press.

Eysenck, H. J., & Eysenck, S. B. G. (1964). *Manual of the EPI.* London: University of London Press.

Herman, C. P., & Polivy, J. (1975). Anxiety, restraint, and eating behavior. *Journal of Abnormal Psychology, 84,* 666–672.

EATING DISORDER INVENTORY (EDI)

AUTHORS: David M. Garner and Marion P. Olmsted

DATE: 1983

VARIABLE: Psychological and behavioral traits common in anorexia nervosa and bulimia

TYPE OF INSTRUMENT: Summated rating scale

DESCRIPTION: The Eating Disorder Inventory (EDI) is a 64-item scale that contains eight subscales. Drive for Thinness is defined as "excessive concern with dieting, preoccupation with weight and entrenchment in an extreme pursuit of thinness" (Garner, Olmsted, & Polivy, 1983a, p. 17); this subscale contains 7 items, one of them negatively keyed. The Bulimia subscale contains 7 items and measures "the tendency toward episodes of uncontrollable overeating (bingeing) and may be followed by the impulse to engage in self-induced vomiting" (p. 17). Body Dissatisfaction concerns "the belief that specific parts of the body associated with shape change or increased 'fatness' at puberty are too large" (p. 18); this subscale contains 9 items, including 5 negatively keyed items. Ineffectiveness relates to "feelings of general inadequacy, insecurity, worthlessness and the feeling of not being in control of one's life" (p. 18); this subscale contains 10 items, 3 negatively keyed. Perfectionism contains 6 items and assesses "excessive personal expectations for superior achievement" (p. 18). Interpersonal Distrust concerns "a sense of alienation and a general reluctance to form close relationships" (p. 18). Interpersonal Distrust contains 7 items, 5 of them negatively keyed. Interoceptive Awareness deals with "one's lack of confidence in recognizing and accurately identifying emotions and sensations of hunger or satiety" (p. 18); this subscale contains 10 items, with 1 negatively keyed. Maturity Fears assesses "one's wish to retreat to the security of the preadolescent years because of the overwhelming demands of adulthood" (p. 19); this subscale contains 8 items, with 3 negatively keyed.

To summarize, the items on the first two subscales—Drive for Thinness and Bulimia—relate directly to eating and food; the items on the Body Dissatisfaction subscale relate to self-perceptions regarding parts of one's body; the items on the last five subscales generally relate to personality. Each item on each subscale is rated on a 6-point scale: "always, usually, often, sometimes, rarely, never."

SAMPLE ITEMS: (These items are reproduced by special permission of PAR, Inc., Lutz, Florida 33549, from the Eating Disorder Inventory, by Garner, Olmsted, Polivy, Copyright 1984 by Psychological Assessment Resources, Inc. Further reproduction is prohibited without prior permission from PAR, Inc.)

(Drive for Thinness) I eat sweets and carbohydrates without feeling nervous.

(Bulimia) I eat when I am upset.

(Body Dissatisfaction) I think that my stomach is too big.

(Ineffectiveness) I feel ineffective as a person.

(Perfectionism) Only outstanding performance is good enough in my family.

(Interpersonal Distrust) I am open about my feelings.

(Interoceptive Awareness) I get frightened when my feelings are too strong.

(Maturity Fears) I wish that I could return to the security of childhood.

PREVIOUS SUBJECTS: High school students, college students, anorexics, bulimics, working women, cheerleaders, female psychiatric patients, ballet students, female athletes, diabetics

APPROPRIATE FOR: Grades 7 and older

ADMINISTRATION: Self-administered; about 20 minutes

SCORING: Hand scoring keys are available for scoring the EDI (see AVAILABLE FROM). The extreme response in the keyed direction is assigned 3 points, with the two adjacent responses receiving 2 and 1 points, respectively. The three responses not in the keyed direction are all assigned 0 points. Item scores are summed to yield a score on each of the eight subscales. Garner and Olmsted (1984) provided materials to assist in score interpretation. These include profile forms that facilitate comparisons with anorexics and with female college students, the standard error of measurement for each subscale, and percentile scores. Norms are available for anorexia nervosa patients, college women, high school girls, and college men. Garner and Olmsted recommended that subscale scores not be computed for any subscale where the respondent has omitted more than one item.

Garner, Olmsted, and Polivy (1983b) provided percentile norms based on testing 127 anorexics and 770 "normal" females. Rosen, Silberg, and Gross (1988) also provided normative data; their data were based on testing 1,373 high school students.

DEVELOPMENT: Experienced clinicians generated a pool of 146 items representing 11 constructs, but only 8 of the constructs were retained for the final version of the scale. The item pool was administered to a sample of anorexics and a comparison group of college women. Items were retained if they met two criteria: successfully differentiated between the two groups of subjects and were more highly correlated with their intended subscale than with any other subscale. In general, the minimum acceptable item-subscale correlation was .40 for the anorexic group; however, 3 items with item-subscale correlations below the cutoff were retained "because they were considered conceptually important" (Garner et al., 1983a, p. 20). After this analysis, additional items were written for the Interoceptive Awareness and Maturity Fears subscales, and these items, in combination with the items that survived the first pretest, were administered to new samples of anorexics and college women. The pool of items was reduced using the same two statistical criteria previously used. Data from a third group of anorexics and a third group of college women were analyzed with the expectation that the item pool would be further refined. However, these data confirmed the prior analyses, and no further changes were required.

RELIABILITY: Garner and Olmsted (1984) reported item-subscale correlations separately for anorexic and "normal" respondents; they also reported coefficient alpha for each subscale, separately for anorexic and "normal" respondents. They obtained the following values for coefficient alpha: Drive for Thinness, anorexics = .86, college women = .87; Bulimia, anorexics = .88, college women = .83; Body Dissatisfaction, anorexics = .90, college women = .92; Ineffectiveness, anorexics = .93, college women = .88; Perfectionism, anorexics = .85, college women = .76; Interpersonal Distrust, anorexics = .85, college women = .80; Interoceptive Awareness, anorexics = .83, college women = .81; and Maturity Fears, anorexics = .89, college women = .72. Item-subscale correlations ranged from .23 to .79 with an average of .63.

Grant and Fodor (1986) reported a reliability of .86 for scores based on the full EDI.

VALIDITY: To demonstrate that scores do not reflect a response set (i.e., a tendency to select one end of the continuum regardless of the item content), Garner et al. (1983a) correlated scores on the negatively phrased items with scores on the positively phrased items. The correlation was .74 for anorexics and .67 for college women, suggesting little, if any, impact of a response set.

Experienced clinicians who were familiar with a group of 49 anorexics rated each of the anorexics on one 10-point analogue scale representing each of the eight subscales. Each analogue scale included a description of the subscale content, and the raters were instructed to "rate the relevancy of each of these traits or characteristics for this patient compared to other anorexics that you have treated" (Garner & Olmsted, 1984, p. 6). Correlating the ratings with scores obtained by the anorexics yielded the following correlations: Drive for Thinness = .53, Bulimia = .57, Body Dissatisfaction = .44, Ineffectiveness = .68, Perfectionism = .47, Interpersonal Distrust = .56, Interoceptive Awareness = .51, and Maturity Fears = .43.

In order to provide evidence for the validity of the EDI, subscale scores from several groups of respondents were compared. Restricter anorexics are those "who exclusively restrict their dietary intake" (Garner et al., 1983a, p .16). As predicted, anorexia patients with bulimia scored significantly higher than restricter anorexics on Bulimia and Body Dissatisfaction (Garner et al., 1983a). Garner and Olmsted (1984) showed that anorexics scored significantly higher than restricter anorexics on these two subscales plus Drive for Thinness, Ineffectiveness, and Interoceptive Awareness. Further analysis led them to conclude that higher scores on Drive for Thinness, Ineffectiveness, and Interoceptive Awareness are related to bulimia, and higher scores on Body Dissatisfaction are related to higher body weight.

Garner et al. (1983a) also found that bulimics scored high on Drive for Thinness, Bulimia, and Body Dissatisfaction, and on these subscales, the bulimics were not significantly different from anorexia patients with bulimia.

Anorexic patients scored significantly higher than recovered anorexics on every subscale on the EDI, and recovered anorexics did not differ from a group of college women on any subscale of the EDI (Garner & Olmsted, 1984; Garner et al., 1983a).

Using scores on the Bulimia subscale, Garner et al. (1983a) were able to classify correctly 85% of anorexics into two subtypes: bulimics and restricters. Depending on the particular subscale score used as the basis for classification, the EDI was able to classify correctly between 87.6% and 93.1% of anorexics and normal college women.

Scores on the Eating Attitudes Test (EAT) (Garner & Garfinkel, 1979) (see separate entry) were correlated with scores on the EDI. For anorexic patients and for college women, EAT scores correlated most highly with Drive for Thinness scores (r = .51 for anorexics and .88 for college women) (Garner et al., 1983a, p. 27).

Garner and Olmsted (1984) reported the results of research in which anorexics completed a variety of measures: EDI, EAT, Restraint Scale (Herman & Polivy, 1975) (see separate entry); a measure of body dissatisfaction modified from the Body Parts Satisfaction Scale (Berscheid, Walster, & Bohrnstedt, 1973) (see separate entry); a measure of dissatisfaction with specific body parts that change as a result of maturation; locus of control (Reid & Ware, 1973); feelings of inadequacy (Janis & Field, 1959); the Beck Depression Inventory (Beck, 1978); physical anhedonia (Chapman, Chapman, & Raulin, 1976); and five scales selected from the Hopkins Symptom Checklist (Derogatis, Lipman, Rickels, Uhlenhuth, & Covi, 1974). After reporting and reviewing the pattern of correlation coefficients among the measures, Garner and Olmsted (1984) concluded: "All of the expected correlations were obtained, although many other correlations are also significant. . . . More importantly, the obtained pattern of correlations is quite consistent with current formulations about anorexia nervosa" (p. 8).

Garner, Olmsted, Polivy, and Garfinkel (1984) demonstrated that each of the subscales of the EDI is a significant contributor to a discriminative function to identify anorexics, weight-preoccupied persons, and not-weight-preoccupied persons.

Rosen, Leitenberg, Gross, and Willmuth (1985) showed that scores on two subscales of the EDI—Drive for Thinness and Bulimia—were significantly related to amount of food consumed during three different test meals.

Johnson and Flach (1985) found that bulimics scored significantly higher than a group of normal controls on each of the subscales of the EDI. Similarly, Gross, Rosen, Leitenberg, and Willmuth (1986) showed that bulimics scored significantly higher than a group of normal controls on each of the subscales of the EDI. These researchers correlated EDI scores with EAT scores and found that EAT scores were significantly related to the three eating-related subscales of the EDI, to Perfectionism, and to Interoceptive Awareness. Gross et al. also looked at the relationship between EDI subscale scores and several behavioral measures. Bulimia subscale scores were significantly related to vomiting frequency, and Body Dissatisfaction subscale scores were significantly related to body size estimation. Scores were not related to behavior during test meals.

Cooper, Cooper, and Fairburn (1985) compared EDI scores from female psychiatric outpatients with the Garner et al. (1983a) data from anorexics and college women. They found that the outpatients scored significantly higher than the college women on four subscales: Ineffectiveness, Interpersonal Distrust, Interoceptive Awareness, and Maturity Fears. The psychiatric outpatients had significantly lower scores than the anorexics on seven of the eight subscales; the difference was not significant for Maturity Fears. After reviewing the relationships between EDI scores, scores on the EAT, and scores on the General Health Questionnaire (GHQ) (Goldberg & Hillier, 1979), Cooper et al. (1985) concluded: "Although the patients with anorexia nervosa had high scores on these EDI subscales, they showed few differences from the psychiatric out-patients who had high scores on the GHQ. This suggests that these subscales may reflect the general level of psychological disturbance rather than features specific to patients with eating disorders" (p. 130).

Grant and Fodor (1986) obtained a correlation of .58 between EDI and EAT scores.

Turnbull, Freeman, Barry, and Annandale (1987) tested five bulimic men using the EDI. The researchers concluded that "the scores that subjects obtained on the EDI . . . would not have identified these men as having eating problems" (p. 27).

After testing over 1,300 high school students, Rosen et al. (1988) concluded that boys' scores did not differ by age, race, or socioeconomic level for any of the subscales of the EDI. Girls' scores on three subscales—Drive for Thinness, Bulimia, and Body Dissatisfaction—did not differ by age, race, or socioeconomic level.

Henderson and Freeman (1987) tested 57 persons and found significant correlations between scores on six subscales of the EDI and scores on their Bulimic Investigatory Test (BITE) (see separate entry). Only the Perfectionism subscale and the Interpersonal Distrust subscale failed to correlate significantly with the BITE.

NOTES & COMMENTS: (1) Garner and Olmsted (1984) compared the EAT and EDI. They noted that the approach to scale development was different for the two scales, with the development of the EAT based on an empirical approach and the development of the EDI starting with a theoretical approach. They concluded that "the EAT is a sound measure of a range of symptoms common in anorexia nervosa, and the EDI focuses more on the specific cognitive and behavioral dimensions that may meaningfully differentiate subgroups of patients or which may distinguish those with serious psychopathology from 'normal' dieters" (p. 9).

(2) Garner and Olmsted (1984) intercorrelated the subscales of the EDI. They presented the data separately for a sample of 155 anorexics and a sample of 271 college women. Garner et al. (1984) reported results from a cluster analysis using data from a group of weight-preoccupied women.

(3) The EDI has been used to evaluate the effectiveness of treatment programs designed to correct eating disorders (Connors, Johnson, & Stuckey, 1984; Freeman, Sinclair, Turnbull, & Annandale, 1985; Kirkley, Schneider, Agras, & Bachman, 1985; Steinhausen, 1985). Snodgrass, Szekely, and Raffeld (1987) used the EDI as part of the treatment process; that is, in the course of treatment for bulimia, EDI profiles were discussed with patients.

(4) The EDI has been used to help understand or identify persons with eating disorders (Borgen & Corbin, 1987; Bourke, Taylor, & Crisp, 1985; Eisele, Hertsgaard, & Light, 1986; Garner, Garfinkel, & O'Shaughnessy, 1985; Garner, Olmsted, & Garfinkel, 1985; Hart & Ollendick, 1985; Johnson, Lewis, Love, Lewis, & Stuckey, 1984; Lundholm & Littrell, 1986; Mickalide & Andersen, 1985; Olmsted & Garner, 1986; Rodin,

Daneman, Johnson, Kenshole, & Garfinkel, 1985; Rodin, Johnson, Garfinkel, Daneman, & Kenshole, 1986/1987; Swift, Kalin, Wamboldt, Kaslow, & Ritholz, 1985; Toner, Garfinkel, & Garner, 1986; VanThorre & Vogel, 1985). Information regarding the validity of the EDI can be inferred from many of these studies, and some of these studies provided normative data.

(5) Scores on the EDI have been related to other variables including neuroticism (Hollin, Houston, & Kent, 1985); body image (Grant & Fodor, 1986); cognitive restraint, tendency toward disinhibition, and perceived hunger (Lundholm & Anderson, 1986); and gender (Papini & Lloyd, 1987; Rosen et al., 1988).

(6) Some researchers use only selected subscales from the EDI (Bourke et al., 1985; Eisele et al., 1986; Johnson et al., 1984; Lundholm & Littrell, 1986; Rosen et al., 1985; Rosen, Gross, & Vara, 1987).

(7) Hart and Ollendick (1985) altered the scoring of the EDI. This produced several published letters and responses. To follow the communication, see, in order, Garner and Olmsted, 1986b; Ollendick and Hart, 1986; and Garner and Olmsted, 1986a.

(8) A description and review of the EDI is given in *Test Critiques* (Vol. 6) (Keyser & Sweetland, 1987). Also the EDI is entry 100 in the *Tenth Mental Measurements Yearbook*.

AVAILABLE FROM: Psychological Assessment Resources, Inc., P.O. Box 998, Odessa, FL 33556 (1–800–331–8378)

USED IN:

Borgen, J. S., & Corbin, C. B. (1987). Eating disorders among female athletes. *Physician and Sportsmedicine, 15,* 89–95.

Bourke, M. P., Taylor, G., & Crisp, A. H. (1985). Symbolic functioning in anorexia nervosa. *Journal of Psychiatric Research, 19,* 273–278.

Connors, M. E., Johnson, C. L., & Stuckey, M. K. (1984). Treatment of bulimia with brief psychoeducational group therapy. *American Journal of Psychiatry, 141,* 1512–1516.

Cooper, Z., Cooper, P. J., & Fairburn, C. G. (1985). The specificity of the Eating Disorder Inventory. *British Journal of Clinical Psychology, 24,* 129–130.

Eberly, C. C., & Eberly, B. W. (1985). A review of the Eating Disorder Inventory. *Journal of Counseling and Development, 64,* 285.

Eisele, J., Hertsgaard, D., & Light, H. K. (1986). Factors related to eating disorders in young adolescent girls. *Adolescence, 21,* 283–290.

Freeman, C., Sinclair, F., Turnbull, J., & Annandale, A. (1985). Psychotherapy for bulimia: A controlled study. *Journal of Psychiatric Research, 19,* 473–478.

Garner, D. M., Garfinkel, P. E., & O'Shaughnessy, M. (1985). The validity of the distinction between bulimia with and without anorexia nervosa. *American Journal of Psychiatry, 142,* 581–587.

Garner, D. M., & Olmsted, M. P. (1984). *Manual for Eating Disorder Inventory (EDI).* Odessa, FL: Psychological Assessment Resources.

Garner, D. M., & Olmsted, M. P. (1986a). More on the Eating Disorder Inventory. *American Journal of Psychiatry, 143,* 805–806.

Garner, D. M., & Olmsted, M. P. (1986b). Scoring the Eating Disorder Inventory. *American Journal of Psychiatry, 143*, 680.

Garner, D. M., Olmsted, M. P., & Garfinkel, P. E. (1985). Similarities among bulimic groups selected by different weights and weight histories. *Journal of Psychiatric Research, 19*, 129–134.

Garner, D. M., Olmsted, M. P., & Polivy, J. (1983a). Development and validation of a multidimensional eating disorder inventory for anorexia nervosa and bulimia. *International Journal of Eating Disorders, 2*(2), 15–34.

Garner, D. M., Olmsted, M. P., & Polivy, J. (1983b). The Eating Disorder Inventory: A measure of cognitive-behavioral dimensions of anorexia nervosa and bulimia. In P. L. Darby, P. E. Garfinkel, D. M. Garner, & D. V. Coscina (Eds.), *Anorexia nervosa: Recent developments in research* (pp. 173–184). New York: Alan R. Liss.

Garner, D. M., Olmsted, M. P., Polivy, J., & Garfinkel, P. E. (1984). Comparison between weight-preoccupied women and anorexia nervosa. *Psychosomatic Medicine, 46*, 255–266.

Grant, C. L., & Fodor, I. G. (1986). Adolescent attitudes toward body image and anorexic behavior. *Adolescence, 21*, 269–281.

Gross, J., Rosen, J. C., Leitenberg, H., & Willmuth, M. E. (1986). Validity of the Eating Attitudes Test and the Eating Disorders Inventory in bulimia nervosa. *Journal of Consulting and Clinical Psychology, 54*, 875–876.

Hart, K. J., & Ollendick, T. H. (1985). Prevalence of bulimia in working and university women. *American Journal of Psychiatry, 142*, 851–854.

Henderson, M., & Freeman, C. P. L. (1987). A self-rating scale for bulimia: The "BITE." *British Journal of Psychiatry, 150*, 18–24.

Hollin, C. R., Houston, J. C., & Kent, M. F. (1985). Neuroticism, life stress and concern about eating, body weight and appearance in a non-clinical population. *Personality and Individual Differences, 6*, 485–492.

Johnson, C., & Flach, A. (1985). Family characteristics of 105 patients with bulimia. *American Journal of Psychiatry, 142*, 1321–1324.

Johnson, C., Lewis, C., Love, S., Lewis, L., & Stuckey, M. (1984). Incidence and correlates of bulimic behavior in a female high school population. *Journal of Youth and Adolescence, 13*, 15–26.

Kirkley, B. G., Schneider, J. A., Agras, W. S., & Bachman, J. A. (1985). Comparison of two group treatments for bulimia. *Journal of Consulting and Clinical Psychology, 53*, 43–48.

Lundholm, J. K., & Anderson, D. F. (1986). Eating disordered behaviors: A comparison of male and female university students. *Addictive Behaviors, 11*, 193–196.

Lundholm, J. K., & Littrell, J. M. (1986). Desire for thinness among high school cheerleaders: Relationship to disordered eating and weight control behaviors. *Adolescence, 21*, 573–579.

Mickalide, A. D., & Andersen, A. E. (1985). Subgroups of anorexia nervosa and bulimia: Validity and utility. *Journal of Psychiatric Research, 19*, 121–128.

Ollendick, T. H., & Hart, K. J. (1986). Drs. Ollendick and Hart reply. *American Journal of Psychiatry, 143*, 680–681.

Olmsted, M. P., & Garner, D. M. (1986). The significance of self-induced vomiting as a weight control method among nonclinical samples. *International Journal of Eating Disorders, 5,* 683–700.

Papini, D. R., & Lloyd, P. J. (1987, April). *Gender related attitudes towards eating and health among college students.* Paper presented at the annual meeting of the Southwestern Psychological Association, New Orleans. (ERIC Document Reproduction Service No. ED 279 956)

Rodin, G. M., Daneman, D., Johnson, L. E., Kenshole, A., & Garfinkel, P. (1985). Anorexia nervosa and bulimia in female adolescents with insulin dependent diabetes mellitus: A systematic study. *Journal of Psychiatric Research, 19,* 381–384.

Rodin, G. M., Johnson, L. E., Garfinkel, P. E., Daneman, D., & Kenshole, A. B. (1986/1987). Eating disorders in female adolescents with insulin dependent diabetes mellitus. *International Journal of Psychiatry in Medicine, 16,* 49–57.

Rosen, J. C., Gross, J., & Vara, L. (1987). Psychological adjustment of adolescents attempting to lose or gain weight. *Journal of Consulting and Clinical Psychology, 55,* 742–747.

Rosen, J. C., Leitenberg, H., Gross, J., & Willmuth, M. (1985). Standardized test meals in the assessment of bulimia nervosa. *Advances in Behaviour Research and Therapy, 7,* 181–197.

Rosen, J. C., Silberg, N. T., & Gross, J. (1988). Eating Attitudes Test and Eating Disorders Inventory: Norms for adolescent girls and boys. *Journal of Consulting and Clinical Psychology, 56,* 305–308.

Snodgrass, G., Szekely, B., & Raffeld, P. C. (1987, April). *Group treatment of eating disorders in a university counseling center.* Paper presented at the meeting of the Southwestern Psychological Association, New Orleans. (ERIC Document Reproduction Service No. ED 279 952)

Steinhausen, H. C. (1985). Evaluation of inpatient treatment of adolescent anorexic patients. *Journal of Psychiatric Research, 19,* 371–375.

Swift, W. J., Kalin, N. H., Wamboldt, F. S., Kaslow, N., & Ritholz, M. (1985). Depression in bulimia at 2- to 5-year followup. *Psychiatry Research, 16,* 111–122.

Toner, B. B., Garfinkel, P. E., & Garner, D. M. (1986). Long-term follow-up of anorexia nervosa. *Psychosomatic Medicine, 48,* 520–529.

Turnbull, J. D., Freeman, C. P. L., Barry, F., & Annandale, A. (1987). Physical and psychological characteristics of five male bulimics. *British Journal of Psychiatry, 150,* 25–29.

VanThorre, M. D., & Vogel, F. X. (1985). The presence of bulimia in high school females. *Adolescence, 20,* 45–51.

BIBLIOGRAPHY:

Beck, A. T. (1978). *Depression Inventory.* Philadelphia: Center for Cognitive Therapy.

Berscheid, E., Walster, E., & Bohrnstedt, G. (1973, November). Body image. The happy American body: A survey report. *Psychology Today,* 119–131.

Chapman, L. J., Chapman, J. P., & Raulin, M. L. (1976). Scales for physical and social anhedonia. *Journal of Abnormal Psychology, 85,* 374–382.

Conoley, J. C., & Kramer, J. J. (1989). *The Tenth Mental Measurements Yearbook.*

Lincoln, NE: Buros Institute of Mental Measurements, University of Nebraska.

Derogatis, L., Lipman, R., Rickels, K., Uhlenhuth, E. H., & Covi, L. (1974). The Hopkins Symptom Checklist (HSCL): A self-report symptom inventory. *Behavioral Science, 19,* 1–15.

Garner, D. M., & Garfinkel, P. E. (1979). The Eating Attitudes Test: An index of the symptoms of anorexia nervosa. *Psychological Medicine, 9,* 1–17.

Goldberg, D. P., & Hillier, V. F. (1979). A scaled version of the General Health Questionnaire. *Psychological Medicine, 9,* 139–145.

Herman, C. P., & Polivy, J. (1975). Anxiety, restraint, and eating behavior. *Journal of Abnormal Psychology, 84,* 666–672.

Janis, I. L., & Field, P. B. (1959). Sex differences and personality factors related to persuasibility. In C. J. Hovland & I. L. Janis (Eds.), *Personality and persuasibility* (pp. 55–68). New Haven: Yale University.

Keyser, D. J., & Sweetland, R. C. (Eds.). (1987). *Test Critiques* (Vol. 6, pp. 177–182). Kansas City: Test Corporation of America.

Reid, D. W., & Ware, E. E. (1973). Multidimensionality of internal-external control: Implications for past and future research. *Canadian Journal of Behavioral Science, 5,* 264–271.

EATING PRACTICES INVENTORY

AUTHORS: Janet E. Helms, Jane A. Domke, and Janet A. Simons

DATE: 1981 (used before 1980)

VARIABLE: Eating practices, including eating-related behaviors and eating-related cognitions

TYPE OF INSTRUMENT: Summated rating scale

DESCRIPTION: The Eating Practices Inventory consists of 102 items pertaining to eating-related habits, which are "situations or circumstances in which eating may occur" (Helms, Domke, & Simons, 1981, p. 4) and eating-related cognitions, which are "cognitions that increase or decrease eating" (p. 4). The 102 items are divided into four subscales: Common Habits (17 items), Common Cognitions (17 items), Uncommon Habits (40 items), and Uncommon Cognitions (28 items). The Habits items are accompanied by five response options ranging from "rarely" to "usually," and the Cognitions items are accompanied by five response options ranging from "rarely effective" to "very effective." In describing the Common Habits items, Helms et al. (1981) stated: "Most can be characterized as leisure or relaxed eating practices. . . . Affective, external, and family oriented eating appear to be primary components of the common eating habits scale" (p. 8). In describing the items on the Common Cognitions subscale, the authors stated that "the items . . . reflect an emphasis on internal self-control and on self-control as influenced by the person's interpretation of external influences" (p. 8). The items on the Uncommon Habits subscale seem to lack a common theme. For the Uncommon Cognitions subscale, "most of the items seem to suggest a person who is struggling with self-control, perhaps not too successfully" (p. 8).

SAMPLE ITEMS: (Common Habits) I eat most of the calories I consume in the evening.

(Common Cognitions) Look at that overweight person gulping the food down.

(Uncommon Habits) I snack throughout the day.

(Uncommon Cognitions) I'll eat better tomorrow.

PREVIOUS SUBJECTS: College women

APPROPRIATE FOR: Most of the items are appropriate for grades 7 and older

ADMINISTRATION: Self-administered; about 45 minutes

SCORING: Items are individually scored on a 5-point scale, with 5 points assigned to the response "usually" for the eating habits items and 5 points assigned to the response "very effective" for the cognitions items. Item scores are summed to yield scores on the four subscales. Helms et al. (1981) reported means and standard deviations for scores on the four subscales. In addition, they reported item means and standard deviations for each item of the Eating Practices Inventory.

DEVELOPMENT: Three considerations guided the development of the Eating Practices Inventory: the Inventory should include cognitive, affective, and interpersonal factors, it should provide an opportunity for expressing the degree to which each eating habit is true for an individual, and it should include both common and uncommon behaviors. With these considerations in mind, the authors constructed a pool of 300 items based on their own experiences in gaining and losing weight and data obtained from interviews with obese women. The items represented four categories: "(a) cognitions that increase or decrease eating; (b) situations or circumstances in which eating occurs; (c) frequency of eating high caloric foods; [and] (d) amount of high caloric foods consumed" (Helms et al., 1981, p. 4). (The last two categories were later eliminated because the relevant items lacked adequate internal consistency reliability.)

The 300 items were administered to 59 college women. An item was retained as a Common Habits item if more than half the respondents answered with "often" or "usually"; an item was retained as a Common Cognitions item if more than half the respondents answered with "usually effective" or "very effective"; an item was retained as an Uncommon Habits item if more than half of the respondents answered "not often" or "sometimes"; and an item was retained as an Uncommon Cognitions item if more than half of the respondents answered "not often effective" or "sometimes effective." The items that met these criteria were grouped into the four subscales and administered to 207 college women. Using their responses and the responses from the original sample of 59 college

women, the authors computed the item-subscale correlations. Items having correlations of at least .20 were retained for the final scale.
RELIABILITY: The scores from 266 college women were used to compute coefficient alpha for each of the four subscales. The following results were obtained: Common Habits = .89, Common Cognitions = .87, Uncommon Habits = .88, and Uncommon Cognitions = .89.

A subset of 33 items was randomly selected from the full scale: 9 Common Habits, 6 Common Cognitions, 14 Uncommon Habits, and 4 Uncommon Cognitions. This subset of items was administered to a sample of 24 women on two occasions, about 2 weeks apart. These women monitored their weight during the intervening 2 weeks. Correlations between the two testings ranged from a low of .50 to a high of .69. The same 33 items were completed on two occasions, 2 weeks apart, by 10 women who were not directed to monitor their weight. Correlations between the two testings for this group ranged from .51 to .87. No data were available for the test-retest reliability of the full scale.
VALIDITY: The Eating Practices Inventory was administered to 59 overweight college women, and their scores were compared to the scores of those on whom the scale was developed. The overweight women scored significantly higher ($p < .001$) on the Common Habits subscale and the Uncommon Habits subscale. The two groups did not differ on the Common Cognitions and the Uncommon Cognitions subscales.

The overweight women also completed the Marlowe-Crowne Social Desirability Scale (Crowne & Marlowe, 1964). The overweight women had a significantly lower score on the Social Desirability Scale compared to the mean reported by Crowne and Marlowe, and two of the subscales from the Eating Practices Inventory—Uncommon Habits and Uncommon Cognitions—had low but significant correlations with scores on the Social Desirability Scale ($r = -.27$ and $-.33$ for the two subscales, respectively). The other two subscales from the Eating Practices Inventory were independent of Social Desirability scores. From this, the authors concluded that "a desire to 'look good' probably did not unduly influence subjects' responses to the scales and the hypothesis that the 'common' scales measure normal behavior is further substantiated" (Helms et al., 1981, p. 16).
NOTES & COMMENTS: (1) Helms et al. (1981) reported the intercorrelations among the four subscales. The values ranged from .26 (Uncommon Habits with Uncommon Cognitions) to .78 (Common Habits with Uncommon Habits and Common Cognitions with Uncommon Cognitions).

(2) Helms et al. (1981) made several recommendations for improving the Eating Practices Inventory. They suggested that further work be done with several items that have higher correlations with another subscale than they do with the subscale they are scored on. They also

suggested that factor analyses be performed to verify that the subscales are unidimensional.

(3) The internal consistency reliability estimates included data from the college women who were used for scale development. Since one of the criteria for item selection was high item-subscale correlations, the values of alpha may have been inflated by including the scale development sample in the computation of alpha.

(4) Helms et al. (1981) did not report the instructions accompanying the Eating Practices Inventory. Different results could be expected depending on whether the instructions are clear in asking respondents to answer in terms of their own behaviors and the effectiveness of the cognitions for themselves, or whether respondents assume they should answer for people in general.

AVAILABLE FROM: Helms, Domke, and Simons, 1981

USED IN:

Helms, J. E., Domke, J. A., & Simons, J. A. (1981). Development of an inventory to measure the eating practices of college women. *Catalog of Selected Documents in Psychology, 11,* 28. (Ms. No. 2240)

BIBLIOGRAPHY:

Crowne, D. P., & Marlowe, D. (1964). *The approval motive: Studies in evaluative dependence.* New York: Wiley.

EATING-RELATED CHARACTERISTICS QUESTIONNAIRE (ECQ)

AUTHOR: Albert Mehrabian

DATE: 1986

VARIABLE: Behavior related to food consumption

TYPE OF INSTRUMENT: Summated rating scale

DESCRIPTION: The Eating-Related Characteristics Questionnaire (ECQ) is a lengthy questionnaire containing 142 items. The items, presented in mixed order, represent 12 factors: Dieting, 26 items with 15 negatively keyed; Preoccupation with, and Fear of, Gaining Weight, 18 items with 5 negatively keyed; Obesity, 7 items with 1 negatively keyed; Eating Momentum Beyond Control, 19 items with 10 negatively keyed; Food a Panacea and Constant Temptation, 14 items, all positively keyed; Secret Bingeing, 9 items with 3 negatively keyed; Voracious Eating, 6 items with 3 negatively keyed; Insufficient Eating Obvious to Others, 8 items, all positively keyed; Food Phobia, 9 items with 2 negatively keyed; Inability to Eat, 14 items with 5 negatively keyed; Vomiting After Meals, 4 items with 1 negatively keyed; and Lack of Appetite, 8 items with 2 negatively keyed. Respondents are asked to rate each item on a 9-point scale ranging from "+4 = very strong agreement" to "−4 = very strong disagreement."

SAMPLE ITEMS: (Dieting) I can eat as much as I want without gaining weight.

(Preoccupation with, and Fear of, Gaining Weight) I would panic if I gained three pounds.

(Obesity) I cannot seem to do anything to lose weight and keep it off.

(Eating Momentum Beyond Control) When I start eating, it is hard for me to stop.

(Food a Panacea and Constant Temptation) When I am upset, food comforts me.

(Secret Bingeing) I eat moderately when others are present and binge eat when I am alone.

(Voracious Eating) One piece of pie is enough for me.

(Insufficient Eating Obvious to Others) Though I know food is necessary, I still do not eat enough.

(Food Phobia) I tend to get somewhat anxious or upset before eating.

(Inability to Eat) There have always been a large number of foods that I could not eat.

(Vomiting After Meals) I make myself vomit after meals.

(Lack of Appetite) I would have to force myself to eat a very large meal.

PREVIOUS SUBJECTS: College students

APPROPRIATE FOR: Grades 7 and older

ADMINISTRATION: Self-administered; about 45–60 minutes

SCORING: Item scores range from +4 to −4. After reversing the scoring of the negatively keyed items, item scores are summed to yield scores on the 12 factors listed above. In addition, the factor scores are used to compute scores on three primary-level factors. Predisposition to Obesity is based on the two factors Dieting, and Preoccupation with, and Fear of, Gaining Weight. Uncontrollable Urges to Eat is based on three factors: Eating Momentum Beyond Control, Food a Panacea and Constant Temptation, and Secret Bingeing. Predisposition to Anorexia is based on four factors: Insufficient Eating Obvious to Others, Food Phobia, Inability to Eat, and Vomiting After Meals. When the original factor scores are used to compute the primary-level factor scores, the original factor scores are first converted to *z* scores using the means and standard deviations available from Mehrabian (1987) and Mehrabian and Riccioni (1986).

DEVELOPMENT: An Eating Habits Questionnaire containing 108 items was administered to 179 college men and 219 college women (Mehrabian, Nahum, & Duke, 1985/86). Their responses were factor analyzed, and six factors were identified: Predisposition to Obesity, Binge Eating, Physical Activity, Food Phobia, Inability to Eat, and Abhorrence of Full Stomach. The ECQ represents an extension of this 108-item scale. The item pool was expanded to include 179 items that represented two areas: "One subset assessed eating characteristics relating to obesity. Item groups in this subset tapped tendencies to diet, to overeat, to be hungry frequently and be tempted by food easily, to lose control while eating, to binge eat, and to be overweight'' (Mehrabian, 1987, p. 63). The second group of items related to characteristics of anorexia: ''groups of items in this subset tapped anxiety associated with eating, insufficient eating, inability to eat, lack of appetite, and vomiting after meals'' (p. 64). The 179 items were administered to 109 college men and 151 college women, and their responses were factor analyzed. Twelve factors were identified, and the items that best represented each factor were selected for the ECQ. After the elimination of three factors—Voracious Eating, Lack of Appetite, and Obesity—the scores from the remaining factors were subjected to a factor analysis, and three primary factors were identified: Predisposition to Obesity, Uncontrollable Urges to Eat, and Predisposition to Anorexia.

RELIABILITY: Mehrabian (1987) reported the Kuder Richardson (KR) 20 reliabilities for each of the original factor scores. Based on testing 260 college students, he obtained the following results: Dieting = .97; Preoccupation with, and Fear of, Gaining Weight = .92; Obesity = .78; Eating Momentum Beyond Control = .94; Food a Panacea and Constant Temptation = .86; Secret Bingeing = .88; Voracious Eating = .67; Insufficient Eating Obvious to Others = .73; Food Phobia = .79; Inability to Eat = .77; Vomiting After Meals = .78; and Lack of Appetite = .69.

VALIDITY: As evidence of the validity of the ECQ, Mehrabian and Riccioni (1986) and Mehrabian (1987) reported that all but one of the 15 scores from the ECQ correlated significantly with sex. Women scored higher than men on the various scales. A person's ponderal index, equal to height divided by the cube root of weight, reflects the long versus round quality of body shape. Through correlational analysis, Mehrabian and Riccioni showed that persons with a greater Predisposition to Obesity and persons with higher scores on Uncontrollable Urges to Eat were more likely to show the round appearance. Although the third primary factor, Predisposition to Anorexia, was not significantly correlated with the ponderal index, one of the factors included in Predisposition to Anorexia (i.e., Insufficient Eating Obvious to Others) was significantly related to the ponderal index (r = .30).

As further evidence of the validity of the ECQ, Mehrabian and Riccioni (1986) showed that Predisposition to Anorexia was significantly correlated with Uncontrollable Urges to Eat (r = .23). In fact, all three primary factor scores were significantly correlated with each other, although the correlations were of a rather low magnitude.

NOTES & COMMENTS: (1) Mehrabian (1987) reported intercorrelations among the 12 factor scores and the three primary factor scores.

(2) Mehrabian (1987) developed measures of trait pleasure, trait arousability, and trait dominance and correlated scores on these three scales with the factor scores and primary factor scores from the ECQ.

(3) Mehrabian (1987) developed a Supplementary Eating-Related Char-

acteristics Questionnaire. A pool of 196 items was administered to 385 college students, and their responses were factor analyzed. Twenty-four factors were extracted: Continues eating when full, 10 items, alpha = .88; Eats rapidly without attending to food, 6 items, alpha = .69; Eats when it is unsuitable or undesirable, 8 items, alpha = .66; Eats alone and sloppily, 6 items, alpha = .58; Loses appetite when upset or tense, 5 items, alpha = .65; Dieting, 10 items, alpha = .94; Eats starches with meals, 2 items, alpha = .66; Full feeling inhibits work and sex, 7 items, alpha = .69; Fasts occasionally, 2 items, alpha = .69; Eats before sleep or napping, 5 items, alpha = .70; Tries new, unfamiliar foods, 5 items, alpha = .77; Prefers variety of courses, 2 items, alpha = .71; Prefers spicy and hot foods, 5 items, alpha = .81; Appreciates aesthetics of meals, 5 items, alpha = .61; Savors foods that take time to eat, 7 items, alpha = .53; Eats less when overstimulated or hot, 6 items, alpha = .46; Eats less when feeling submissive, 2 items, alpha = .56; Prefers arousing settings for meals, 6 items, alpha = .65; Plans and eats three males a day, 7 items, alpha = .80; Reads during meals, 3 items, alpha = .65; Sips beverages outside mealtimes, 3 items, alpha = .70; Likes and eats desserts, 8 items, alpha = .80; Snacks frequently, especially when bored, 11 items, alpha = .82; and Prefers proteins to starches, 4 items, alpha = .63. Obviously, the homogeneity of many of the subscales on the Supplementary Eating-Related Characteristics is unacceptably low.

AVAILABLE FROM: Mehrabian, 1987

USED IN:

Mehrabian, A. (1987). *Eating characteristics and temperament: General measures and interrelationships*. New York: Springer Verlag.

Mehrabian, A., Nahum, I. V., & Duke, V. (1985/1986). Individual difference correlates and measures of predisposition to obesity and to anorexia. *Imagination, Cognition and Personality, 5*, 339–355.

Mehrabian, A., & Riccioni, M. (1986). Measures of eating-related characteristics the general population: Relationships with temperament. *Journal of Personality Assessment, 50*, 610–629.

EATING SELF-EFFICACY SCALE (ESES)

AUTHORS: Shirley M. Glynn and Audrey J. Ruderman

DATE: 1986

VARIABLE: Eating self-efficacy, defined as "the belief that one is capable of making the change [necessary to control one's weight]" (Glynn & Ruderman, 1986, p. 403)

TYPE OF INSTRUMENT: Summated rating scale

DESCRIPTION: The Eating Self-Efficacy Scale (ESES) consists of 25 items representing two subscales: 15 items pertain to eating in response to negative affect (NA), and 10 items pertain to eating in socially acceptable circumstances (SAC). Each item is a situation in which dieters may have difficulty controlling their food consumption. The items are preceded by the single stem, "How difficult is it to control your. . . ." Each item begins with the word *overeating* and then states a condition or situation. Responses are recorded on a 7-point scale, with the endpoints labeled "No difficulty controlling eating" and "Most difficulty controlling eating." The midpoint of the scale is labeled "Moderate difficulty controlling eating."

SAMPLE ITEMS: (negative affect) Overeating when you feel upset
(socially acceptable circumstances) Overeating around holiday time

PREVIOUS SUBJECTS: College students, participants in a weight-loss program, bulimic women

APPROPRIATE FOR: Grades 7 and older

ADMINISTRATION: Self-administered; about 10 minutes

SCORING: Items are individually scored on a 7-point scale, with 7 points assigned to the end of the continuum labeled "Most difficulty controlling eating." Item scores are summed to yield scores on each of the two factors and a total score. Higher scores represent less self-efficacy. Glynn and Ruderman (1986) provided means and standard deviations on the factor scores and total scores for various groups who completed the ESES.

DEVELOPMENT: A list of 79 eating situations was constructed by adapting 37 situations from a measure Condiotte and Lichtenstein (1981) used to study smoking behavior, adding 37 situations written by Glynn and Ruderman and 5 situations gleaned from lists of eating situations written by college students. The list of 79 situations was administered to 328 college students with instructions to rate the degree of difficulty they experienced in controlling their eating in each situation. Responses were factor analyzed, and 15 factors were identified. Items with factor loadings greater than .4 and factors with a minimum of 3 items were retained. This left 59 items representing five factors: socially acceptable circumstances, negative affect, being alone, passing time, and social awkwardness.

The 59-item scale was administered to another sample of 362 college students, and their responses were factor analyzed. Twelve factors were extracted, but again only five factors satisfied the two criteria of factor loadings greater than .4 and at least 3 items on a factor. The first two factors were comparable to the first two factors in the prior analysis, although the order in which the factors emerged was reversed. The remaining factors did not match the results in the first analysis, and the factors were not interpretable. The final scale consists of the 25 items that loaded on the first two factors.

RELIABILITY: Reliability estimates were calculated using responses from another sample of 484 college students. Coefficient alpha was .94 for the NA subscale, .85 for the SAC subscale, and .92 for the full ESES.

Item-total correlations were also computed. For the full ESES, the coefficients ranged from .29 to 73; for the NA subscale, item-subscale correlations ranged from .53 to .80; and for the SAC subscale, item-subscale correlations ranged from .42 to .64. Test-retest reliability based on 85 college students who completed the measure on two occasions with a 7-week interval between testings was .70 (Glynn & Ruderman, 1986). Using data from another sample of 618 college students, Glynn and Ruderman obtained alpha coefficients greater than .88 for the full ESES and for each of the two factor scores.

VALIDITY: To verify the factorial validity of the scale, the responses from the 484 college students were factor analyzed. Three factors were extracted. The first factor paralleled the NA factor, included the 15 items on the NA subscale, and accounted for 33% of the variance. The second factor included 7 items from the SAC subscale and accounted for 15% of the variance. The third factor included 3 items from the SAC subscale and accounted for 7% of the variance. The factor analysis was repeated using data from obese persons and again using data from dieters. According to Glynn and Ruderman (1986), "the results were essentially the same" (p. 409).

In order to ascertain the construct validity of the ESES, the following hypotheses were tested: "ESES scores would be significantly and positively related to percentage overweight, Restraint Scale scores [(Ruderman, 1982) (see separate entry)], previous dieting experience, and current dieting behavior, but negatively related to self-esteem as measured by the TSCS [Tennessee Self-Concept Scale (Fitts, 1965)]" (Glynn & Ruderman, 1986, p. 410). There was a low but significant correlation (r = .15) between ESES scores and percentage overweight. The ESES scores were significantly correlated (r = .47) with Restraint Scale scores and with two factor scores from the Restraint Scale: Concern with Dieting factor (r = .45) and Weight Fluctuation factor (r = .38). The ESES scores were significantly correlated with previous dieting (r = .23) and with current dieting (r = .24). The ESES scores were negatively and significantly correlated with TSCS scores (r = − .51).

Using data from 303 college men and 315 college women, Glynn and Ruderman (1986) found significant sex differences. As would be expected, women obtained significantly higher scores than men. Using data from this group of students, Glynn and Ruderman replicated many of the findings reported earlier. The factor analytic results were comparable to those obtained with prior samples, and ESES scores were significantly correlated with percentage overweight, total Restraint Scale scores, and both subscales of the Restraint Scale. For both male and female students, dieters obtained significantly higher scores on the ESES than did nondieters.

A sample of 79 college women was intentionally made to feel dysphoric or nondysphoric. It was predicted that NA scores would predict food consumption for those in the dysphoric group but not for those in the nondysphoric group. The results showed that "NA subscale predicted food consumption, regardless of the individuals' mood state" (Glynn & Ruderman, 1986, p. 415).

In another study, Glynn and Ruderman (1986) involved 32 persons enrolled in weight-loss programs. They believed that ESES scores would predict weight loss in the program and increases in ESES scores would be correlated with weight loss. As expected, ESES scores increased over the course of the weight-loss program. Also as expected, greater weight loss was associated with increases in ESES scores. However, at any single point in the treatment program, ESES scores were not significantly related to previous or subsequent weight loss. This last finding may have been an artifact of the research procedures, and further research is needed to clarify its implications.

NOTES & COMMENTS: (1) Glynn and Ruderman (1986) reported a correlation of .39 between the two subscales, NA and SAC.

(2) Because Glynn and Ruderman's (1986) work focused primarily on college students, they suggested that research be carried out to determine the psychometric properties of the scale in other populations, particularly middle-age women, the majority of the participants in weight-loss programs.

(3) Wilson, Rossiter, Kleifield, and Lindholm (1986) used the original list of 79 situations from which the ESES was developed. The measure was used as one of several dependent measures to compare the effectiveness of two methods of treating bulimia.

AVAILABLE FROM: Glynn and Ruderman, 1986

USED IN:

Glynn, S. M., & Ruderman, A. J. (1986). The development and validation of an Eating Self-Efficacy Scale. *Cognitive Therapy and Research, 10,* 403–420.

Wilson, G. T., Rossiter, E., Kleifield, E. I., & Lindholm, L. (1986). Cognitive-behavioral treatment of bulimia nervosa: A controlled evaluation. *Behaviour Research and Therapy, 24,* 277–288.

BIBLIOGRAPHY:

Condiotte, M., & Lichtenstein, E. (1981). Self-efficacy and relapse in smoking cessation programs. *Journal of Consulting and Clinical Psychology, 49,* 648–658.

Fitts, W. H. (1965). *Tennessee Self-Concept Scale.* Nashville: Counselor Recordings and Tests.

Ruderman, A. (1982). The Restraint Scale: A psychometric investigation. *Behaviour Research and Therapy, 21,* 253–258.

GOLDBERG ANORECTIC ATTITUDE SCALE (GAAS)

AUTHOR: Solomon C. Goldberg

DATE: 1977

VARIABLE: Attitudes indicative of anorexia nervosa
TYPE OF INSTRUMENT: Summated rating scale
DESCRIPTION: The Goldberg Anorectic Attitude Scale (GAAS) contains 63 items covering a wide variety of topics directly or indirectly relating to anorexia nervosa. Each item is accompanied by four response options: "Not at all, A little, Quite a bit, Extremely." Goldberg, Halmi, Casper, Eckert, and Davis (1977) stated that the GAAS includes items representing eight categories: "(a) denial of illness, (b) loss of appetite, (c) interpersonal control, (d) thin body ideal, (e) hypothermia, (f) hyperactivity, (g) psychosexual immaturity, and (h) independence seeking" (p. 32).
SAMPLE ITEMS: (Sample items from the four largest factors are given here.)

(Denial) There was nothing really wrong with me that a few days rest couldn't cure.

(Psychosexual immaturity) If I could choose an age to be, it would be 10 or 11.

(Loss of appetite) I feel hungry by the time mealtime comes around.

(Interpersonal control) I have complete confidence in the way the medical staff is treating me.

PREVIOUS SUBJECTS: Hospitalized anorexics and persons previously hospitalized for anorexia nervosa
APPROPRIATE FOR: Hospitalized anorexics
ADMINISTRATION: Self-administered; about 20–30 minutes
SCORING: No information was provided. It can be presumed that items are scored on a 4-point scale. The specific scores to be computed depend on which set of factors one is using, but since the measure is not unidimensional, no overall score should be computed.
DEVELOPMENT: No information was provided.
RELIABILITY: Goldberg et al. (1980) identified 19 factors on the GAAS and considered 15 of them to be interpretable. They reported the internal consistency reliability of each of the factors using a modification of the Kuder-Richardson reliability procedure. Using a cutoff of .80 as an acceptable reliability level, they found that 5 factors had acceptable reliabilities. Three factors were close, with reliabilities between .70 and .79. The reliability coefficients for 6 factors were unacceptably low, with the lowest reliability coefficient being .23, and 1 factor contained only a single item, so the computation of internal consistency reliability was not possible.
VALIDITY: No information was provided regarding the full scale, but data presented by Goldberg et al. (1980) cause one to question the scale's validity. Goldberg et al. hypothesized that nine factors would emerge from a factor analysis of the GAAS. Their factor analytic study yielded numerous factors, but only five of the nine hypothesized factors were

identified, and three of those five factors contained only one or two items. Goldberg et al. acknowledged that "some items that were constructed to reflect an hypothesized factor, emerged as an independent factor" (p. 248).

Steinhausen (1986) tested 23 hospitalized anorexics with the Eating Attitudes Test (EAT) (Garner & Garfinkel, 1979) (see separate entry), the Anorexic Behaviour Scale (Slade, 1973) (see separate entry), a German checklist of bodily complaints, a German mood scale, and 7 of the 19 factor scales from Goldberg et al. (1980) (see NOTES & COMMENTS). The 7 factor scores were: Staff (called Staff Exploits), Fear of Fat, Parents (called Parents at Fault), Denial (called Denial of Illness), Hunger, Hypothermia, and Self Care (called Poor Self Care). Steinhausen intercorrelated the 7 factor scores, producing a matrix of 21 correlations. Five of the correlations were significantly different from zero; the highest correlation was .58 (Fear of Fat correlated with Poor Self Care). Steinhausen correlated scores on the 7 factors with each of the other four measures. Of the 28 correlations, 9 were statistically significant. Fear of Fat correlated significantly with EAT scores and scores on the Anorexic Behaviour Scale; Denial of Illness correlated significantly with scores on the Anorexic Behaviour Scale and the mood scales; Hypothermia correlated significantly with EAT scores, the bodily complaints measure, and the mood scale; and Poor Self Care correlated significantly with EAT scores and the bodily complaints measure.

Steinhausen (1986) relied on clinical judgments from the patients' therapists to identify anorexics who admitted their disease and anorexics who denied their disease. They found no significant differences between the two groups on any of the seven subscales, not even on the Denial of Illness subscale. They also found no relationship between the seven scores from the GAAS and age at onset of the disease, weight loss, hyperactivity, bulimia, vomiting, laxative abuse, intelligence, or socioeconomic status. When the scores obtained at the time of admission were compared with those at the time of discharge, there were significant differences on three of the seven subscales: Fear of Fat, Hunger, and Hypothermia.

NOTES & COMMENTS: (1) Goldberg et al. (1977) grouped the items on the GAAS into eight categories based on a factor analytic study using data from 44 hospitalized anorexics. In the appendix of their article, Halmi, Goldberg, Casper, Eckert, and Davis (1979) listed the items of the GAAS under nine categories: Denial (10 items), Psychosexual immaturity (8 items), Loss of appetite (12 items), Interpersonal control (19 items), Thin body ideal (4 items), Hypothermia (2 items), Compulsivity (3 items), Hyperactivity (3 items), and Purgatives (2 items). Seven of these categories overlap the list given by Goldberg et al. (1977); independence seeking, listed by Goldberg et al., was not listed by Halmi et al.; and two categories—Compulsivity and Purgatives—were added by Halmi et al. Interestingly, the text of the Halmi et al. article mentioned only eight categories of items even though the appendix listed nine categories. Casper, Eckert, Halmi, Goldberg, and Davis (1980) and Eckert, Goldberg, Halmi, Casper, and Davis (1982) also mentioned eight categories of items in the text of their articles. Goldberg et al. (1980) reported using factor analysis with data from 105 hospitalized anorexics. They identified 19 factors, with 15 considered interpretable: Staff (11 items), Fear of Fat (7 items), Parents (8 items), Denial (5 items), Hunger (4 items), Hypothermia (2 items), Bloated (4 items), Self Care (3 items), Effort for Achievement (2 items), Food Sickens Me (2 items), My Problems—Mental or Physical? (2 items), Helpful Authority (2 items), Physical Problems (2 items), Hobby Cooking (1 item), and Heterosexual Disinterest (2 items).

(2) The GAAS has been used in studies designed to identify the predictors of weight change in patients with anorexia nervosa (Goldberg et al., 1977, 1980; Halmi et al., 1979) and to look at the characteristics of bulimics (Casper et al., 1980). Eckert et al. (1982) studied hospitalized anorexics and looked at the relationships between depression and various pretreatment measures including the GAAS. Steinhausen (1985) and Steinhausen and Glanville (1983a, 1983b) used portions of the GAAS to evaluate persons treated for anorexia nervosa.

(3) Researchers have used a subset of the items on the GAAS. Steinhausen and Glanville (1983a, 1983b) used the items from 7 of the 15 factors identified by Goldberg et al. (1980). Steinhausen and Glanville used the items from the following factors: Fear of Fat, Parents, Denial, Hunger, Hypothermia, Self Care, and Effort for Achievement. Steinhausen (1986) also used data from 7 of the 15 factors.

(4) The usefulness of the GAAS is not clear from the information available. The factor analytic studies that have been completed were based on unacceptably small sample sizes. The reliabilities of several of the factor scores are unacceptably low. Since the GAAS has been used in quite a few published studies, further work is probably warranted to identify and improve its psychometric properties.

AVAILABLE FROM: Halmi, Goldberg, Casper, Eckert, and Davis, 1979; Goldberg, Halmi, Eckert, Casper, Davis, and Roper, 1980

USED IN:

Casper, R. C., Eckert, E. D., Halmi, K. A., Goldberg, S. C., & Davis, J. M. (1980). Bulimia: Its incidence and clinical importance in patients with anorexia nervosa. *Archives of General Psychiatry, 37*, 1030–1035.

Eckert, E. D., Goldberg, S. C., Halmi, K. A., Casper, R. C., & Davis, J. M. (1982). Depression in anorexia nervosa. *Psychological Medicine, 12*, 115–122.

Goldberg, S. C., Halmi, K. A., Casper, R., Eckert, E., & Davis, J. M. (1977).

Pretreatment predictors of weight change in anorexia nervosa. In R. A. Vigersky (Ed.), *Anorexia nervosa* (pp. 31–41). New York: Raven Press.

Goldberg, S. C., Halmi, K. A., Eckert, E. D., Casper, R. C., Davis, J. M., & Roper, M. (1980). Attitudinal dimensions in anorexia nervosa. *Journal of Psychiatric Research, 15,* 239–251.

Halmi, K. A., Goldberg, S. C., Casper, R. C., Eckert, E. D., & Davis, J. M. (1979). Pretreatment predictors of outcome in anorexia nervosa. *British Journal of Psychiatry, 134,* 71–78.

Steinhausen, H. C. (1985). Evaluation of inpatient treatment of adolescent anorexic patients. *Journal of Psychiatric Research, 19,* 371–375.

Steinhausen, H. C. (1986). Attitudinal dimensions in adolescent anorexic patients: An analysis of the Goldberg Anorectic Attitude Scale. *Journal of Psychiatric Research, 20,* 83–87.

Steinhausen, H. C., & Glanville, S. (1983a). A long-term follow-up of adolescent anorexia nervosa. *Acta Psychiatrica Scandinavica, 68,* 1–10.

Steinhausen, H. C., & Glanville, S. (1983b). Retrospective and prospective follow-up studies in anorexia nervosa. *International Journal of Eating Disorders, 2,* 221–235.

BIBLIOGRAPHY:

Garner, D. M., & Garfinkel, P. E. (1979). The Eating Attitudes Test: An index of the symptoms of anorexia nervosa. *Psychological Medicine, 9,* 273–279.

Slade, P. D. (1973). A short Anorexic Behaviour Scale. *British Journal of Psychiatry, 122,* 83–85.

GOLDFARB FEAR OF FAT SCALE (GFFS)

AUTHORS: Lori A. Goldfarb, Elisabeth M. Dykens, and Meg Gerrard

DATE: 1985 (used 1984)

VARIABLE: Abnormal fear of fat; scale is intended to identify persons at risk for developing eating disorders

TYPE OF INSTRUMENT: Summated rating scale

DESCRIPTION: The Goldfarb Fear of Fat Scale (GFFS) contains 10 items, each directly related to a fear of becoming fat or to steps taken to prevent becoming fat. Each item is accompanied by four response alternatives: "very untrue, somewhat untrue, somewhat true, very true." All items are phrased in the same direction: a person with a fear of becoming fat would respond "very true" to the items.

SAMPLE ITEMS: My biggest fear is of becoming fat.

Staying hungry is the only way I can guard against losing control and becoming fat.

PREVIOUS SUBJECTS: High school girls; college women including bulimics, repeat dieters, and nondieters; male and female distance runners

APPROPRIATE FOR: Grades 7 and older

ADMINISTRATION: Self-administered; about 5 minutes

SCORING: Items are individually scored on a 4-point scale, with 4 points assigned to the "very true" end of the continuum. Item scores are totaled to yield an overall score that can range from 10 (no fear of becoming fat) to 40 (extreme fear of becoming fat).

DEVELOPMENT: The only information regarding scale development indicated that the items were "generated from the first author's clinical contact with anorexia nervosa and bulimia patients" (Goldfarb, Dykens, & Gerrard, 1985, p. 329).

RELIABILITY: Based on testing 98 high school girls, coefficient alpha was .85. A sample of 23 college women completed the GFFS on two occasions, 1 week apart. The test-retest reliability was .88.

VALIDITY: Seven anorexics and 73 college women completed the GFFS. There was a large and statistically significant difference between the means of the two groups ($p < .01$), with anorexics showing greater fear of becoming fat.

Goldfarb et al. (1985) tested 23 bulimics, 20 repeat dieters (without bulimia), and 20 nondieters (without bulimia). As predicted, bulimics scored significantly higher than repeat dieters, and repeat dieters scored significantly higher than nondieters. The three groups also completed the following measures: the Tennessee Self-Concept Scale (Fitts, 1965), the Beck Depression Inventory (Beck, 1976), the State-Trait Anxiety Inventory (Spielberger, Gorsuch, & Lushene, 1970), and the Family Environment Scale (Moos, 1974). A step-wise discriminant function analysis showed that "fear of fat emerged as the most powerful discriminating variable." (Goldfarb et al., 1985, p. 331). The GFFS accounted for 36% of the variance. For the bulimic group but not for the other two groups, GFFS scores were positively and significantly correlated with anxiety, neuroticism, depression, maladjustment, and the two subscales of the Family Environment Scales. Also for the bulimics but not for the other two groups, GFFS scores were negatively and significantly correlated with six indicators of self-esteem.

NOTES & COMMENTS: Goldfarb and Plante (1984) used the GFFS to determine whether distance runners experience an abnormally high fear of becoming fat.

AVAILABLE FROM: Goldfarb, Dykens, and Gerrard, 1985; Corcoran and Fischer, 1987

USED IN:

Goldfarb, L. A., Dykens, E. M., & Gerrard, M. (1985). The Goldfarb Fear of Fat Scale. *Journal of Personality Assessment, 49*, 329–332.

Goldfarb, L. A., & Plante, T. G. (1984). Fear of fat in runners: An examination of the connection between anorexia nervosa and distance running. *Psychological Reports, 55*, 296.

BIBLIOGRAPHY:

Beck, A. (1976). *Depression: Causes and treatment*. Philadelphia: University of Pennsylvania Press.

Corcoran, K., & Fischer, J. (1987). *Measures for clinical practice: A sourcebook* (pp. 172–173). New York: Free Press

Fitts, W. (1965). *Tennessee Self-Concept Scale*. Nashville: Counselor Recordings and Tests.
Moos, R. (1974). *Family Environment Scale*. Palo Alto: Consulting Psychologists Press.
Spielberger, C., Gorsuch, R., & Lushene, R. (1970). *State-Trait Anxiety Inventory*. Palo Alto: Consulting Psychologists Press.

PSYCHIATRIC RATING SCALE FOR ANOREXIA NERVOSA

AUTHORS: Solomon C. Goldberg, Katherine A. Halmi, Regina Casper, Elke Eckert, and John M. Davis
DATE: 1977
VARIABLE: Ratings of characteristics associated with anorexia nervosa
TYPE OF INSTRUMENT: Rating scale
DESCRIPTION: The Psychiatric Rating Scale for Anorexia Nervosa contains 14 traits or characteristics associated with anorexia nervosa. Psychiatrists, psychologists, psychiatric nurses, or other trained persons use a 7-point rating scale to rate a person on each trait. The points on the rating scale are labeled as follows: "absent = 1; nearly absent = 2; mild = 3; moderate = 4; substantial = 5; severe = 6; most extreme = 7."
SAMPLE ITEMS: Denial
Fear of Fat
PREVIOUS SUBJECTS: Hospitalized patients with anorexia nervosa, depression, or conduct disorders
APPROPRIATE FOR: Grades 7 and older
ADMINISTRATION: The Psychiatric Rating Scale for Anorexia Nervosa must be completed by a trained person who has had ample opportunity to observe the subject. Although the scale has been used in inpatient facilities, its use is not limited to that environment.
SCORING: Items are given a score equal to the rating assigned by the observer. Total scores are not obtained; rather researchers have looked at the ratings on the individual items.
DEVELOPMENT: No information was provided.
RELIABILITY: Strober (1981) reported that 44 adolescent female anorexic inpatients were independently rated by two senior ward nurses. The interrater reliabilities ranged from .76 to .90. Strober (1982) studied 90 hospitalized females, including 30 with anorexia nervosa. A senior nurse clinician and the researcher independently rated 18 of the anorexic patients. Interrater reliabilities ranged from .79 to .92.
VALIDITY: Strober's (1981) research involved 44 adolescent female anorectic inpatients, half of them bulimics and half restricters (meaning they rely exclusively on restricting their intake of food). Multivariate analysis of variance followed by univariate *F* tests showed that bulimics

were rated higher than restricters on four items: Fear of Fat, Fear of Compulsive Eating, Depressed Mood, and Use of Purgative and Diuretics. Restricters were rated higher than bulimics on Psychosexual Immaturity. There were no significant differences on the remaining nine items.

Steinhausen (1985) and Steinhausen and Glanville (1983) used the Psychiatric Rating Scale for Anorexia Nervosa as one of several measures to compare anorexic patients at the time of hospital admission and the time of hospital discharge. Scores on the Psychiatric Rating Scale were significantly different between the two time periods.

NOTES & COMMENTS: Strober (1982) tested 30 hospitalized, female anorexics with the Psychiatric Rating Scale for Anorexia Nervosa and with the Nowicki-Strickland Locus of Control Scale (Nowicki & Strickland, 1973). Strober reported the correlations between each item on the Psychiatric Rating Scale and scores on the Nowicki-Strickland Locus of Control Scale. Five of the correlation coefficients were statistically significant: Denial of illness, Fear of fat, Fear of compulsive eating, Desire for control, and Use of purgatives and diuretics.

AVAILABLE FROM: Goldberg, Halmi, Casper, Eckert, and Davis, 1977; Strober, 1981, 1982

USED IN:

Goldberg, S. C., Halmi, K. A., Casper, R., Eckert, E., & Davis, J. M. (1977). Pretreatment predictors of weight change in anorexia nervosa. In R. A. Vigersky (Ed.), *Anorexia nervosa* (pp. 31–41). New York: Raven Press.

Steinhausen, H. C. (1985). Evaluation of inpatient treatment of adolescent anorexic patients. *Journal of Psychiatric Research, 19*, 371–375.

Steinhausen, H. C., & Glanville, K. (1983). Retrospective and prospective follow-up studies in anorexia nervosa. *International Journal of Eating Disorders, 2*, 221–235.

Strober, M. (1981). The significance of bulimia in juvenile anorexia nervosa: An exploration of possible etiologic factors. *International Journal of Eating Disorders, 1*, 28–43.

Strober, M. (1982). Locus of control, psychopathology, and weight gain in juvenile anorexia nervosa. *Journal of Abnormal Child Psychology, 10*, 97–106.

BIBLIOGRAPHY:

Nowicki, S., & Strickland, B. R. (1973). A locus of control scale for children. *Journal of Consulting and Clinical Psychology, 40*, 148–154.

RESTRAINT SCALE

AUTHORS: C. Peter Herman and Janet Polivy

DATE: 1975 (revised 1978)

VARIABLE: "Extent to which individuals exhibit behavioral and attitudinal concern about dieting and keeping their weight down" (Herman & Polivy, 1975, p. 668)

TYPE OF INSTRUMENT: Short answers and multiple choice items

DESCRIPTION: The original Restraint Scale consists of 11 items: 7 items are presented in a multiple choice format; the remaining 4 items ask questions about weight, and answers are expressed in terms of number of pounds. Six items pertain to Diet and Weight History; 5 items reflect concern with Food and Eating.

The revised Restraint Scale consists of 10 items: 5 of the 6 items from the Diet and Weight History subscale of the original Restraint Scale and all 5 items from the Concern with Food and Eating subscale. The order of the items on the revised Restraint Scale differs from that on the original Restraint Scale, and the wording of one item is altered. All items on the revised Restraint Scale are presented in a multiple choice format; for the items that were previously presented in an open-ended format, the response options are given as ranges of pounds (e.g., 0–1; 1.1–2; 2.1–3; 3.1–5; 5.1+)

SAMPLE ITEMS: How many pounds over your desired weight were you at your maximum weight?

Would a weight fluctuation of 5 pounds affect the way you live your life?—not at all, slightly, moderately, very much.

PREVIOUS SUBJECTS: College students in the United States and Canada; underweight, overweight, and normal-weight college females; anorexics; bulimics; parents of patients being treated for anorexia nervosa; participants in Weight Watchers programs; alcoholic women

APPROPRIATE FOR: High school students and older

ADMINISTRATION: Self-administered; less than 5 minutes

SCORING: Herman and Polivy (1975) provided a scoring key with simple directions for scoring each item on the original Restraint Scale. Multiple choice items are scored on a 0–2 or 0–3 basis. Open-ended items are scored as a function of the number of pounds mentioned in the answer: 1 point is given for every 3 pounds or every 5 pounds, depending on the question. Herman and Polivy used total scores and a median split procedure to identify restrained and unrestrained eaters. Their median score was 17. Herman and Polivy also suggested the use of two subscale scores: Diet and Weight History, and Concern with Food and Eating.

Herman, Polivy, Pliner, Threlkeld, and Munic (1978) provided a simple scoring key for scoring each item on the revised Restraint Scale. Half of the items are scored on a scale of 0–3, and the other half are scored on a scale of 0–4. A score of 14 was used as the median to separate restrained from unrestrained eaters (Herman et al., 1978).

DEVELOPMENT: Little information was provided regarding the development of the Restraint Scale. Herman and Polivy (1975) reported that "the restraint scale was adapted from a previous study . . . in which restraint scores successfully predicted differential responses to a preload manipulation" (p. 668). A study by Herman and Mack (1975) used a questionnaire composed of 38 items; 10 were determined, a priori, to be relevant to their study of restrained and unrestrained eating. Of the 10 items, 5 pertained to attitudes toward food and eating, and the other 5 concerned dieting and weight fluctuation. No information was given regarding the source of the items. Herman and Mack used 5 of the 10 items as a restraint scale. The original Restraint Scale was an adaptation of this measure used by Herman and Mack.

Herman et al. (1978) indicated that the revised Restraint Scale was developed on the basis of a psychometric study of the original Restraint Scale. Information regarding the psychometric study was reported in an unpublished paper.

RELIABILITY: Based on testing 42 college women, Herman and Polivy (1975) reported a coefficient alpha of .75 for total scores on the original Restraint Scale. The alpha coefficients for the two subscales were .68 for Diet and Weight History and .62 for Concern with Food and Eating. The correlation between the two subscales was .48.

Herman et al. (1978) stated that the revised Restraint Scale had "substantial reliability" (p. 543), but they did not provide the supporting data.

Hibscher and Herman (1977) tested 86 college men with the Restraint Scale. The college men completed the scale on two occasions, separated by several weeks. The test-retest reliability was .92.

Ruderman (1983) tested 58 obese college women and 89 normal-weight college women. Internal consistency reliability was .51 for the former group and .86 for the latter group. Item-total correlations ranged from .39 to .69 for the normal-weight women and from −.21 to .53 for the obese women. These data suggest that the Restraint Scale is not sufficiently reliable for obese subjects.

VALIDITY: In defending the validity of the scale, Herman and Polivy (1975) stated: "The validity of the scale is currently based on its predictive power. However, the significant correlation between restraint and a physiological measure of deprivation, as reported by Hibscher (1974) lends some evidence of construct validity to the scale" (p. 669).

An unpublished study by Polivy, Herman, Younger, and Erskine (cited in Herman et al., 1978) provided evidence of the predictive validity of the revised Restraint Scale.

Garner and Garfinkel (1979) administered their Eating Attitudes Test (see separate entry) and the Restraint Scale to 59 normal college women. The correlation between the two measures was nonsignificant ($r = .28$).

Hawkins and Clement (1980) reported the results from two samples of college students who completed the Restraint Scale along with several other measures. The first sample completed only the 5 items listed in the Herman and Mack (1975) article, and they completed the Binge Scale (BS) (Hawkins & Clement, 1980) (see separate entry), the Negative Self-Image Scale (Nash & Ormiston, 1978), and the Marlowe-Crowne Social

Desirability Scale (Crowne & Marlowe, 1960). The second sample completed the 10 items in the Herman and Polivy (1975) article, along with the BS, the Negative Self-Image Scale, the College Self-Expression Scale (Galassi, Delo, Galassi, & Bastien, 1974), which is a measure of assertiveness, the Locus of Control Scale (Rotter, 1966), and the Life Change measure (Price & Price, 1974). For both samples and for both males and females analyzed separately, significant correlations were found between Restraint Scale scores and BS scores and between Restraint Scale scores and Negative Self-Image Scale scores. For both males and females in the first sample, scores on the Restraint Scale and the Marlowe-Crowne Social Desirability Scale were independent. For the second sample, scores on the Restraint Scale were significantly correlated with scores on the Life Change measure for both males and females, but they were significantly correlated with the Locus of Control Scale and the College Self-Expression Scale for males only. For both samples and both sexes, Restraint Scale scores were significantly related to deviation from desirable weight.

Garfinkel et al. (1983) found a significant difference in the Restraint Scale scores of 23 anorexics who were compared with 12 normal controls. Significant differences were not found between the mothers or the fathers of the two groups.

Ruderman (1983) pointed out that "numerically-equivalent Restraint scores may represent a lower degree of restraint in obese individuals than they do in normal-weight subjects" (p. 254) because 4 of the 10 items on the scale assess weight changes, with more points assigned to greater weight fluctuations. Obese persons are likely to show greater weight fluctuations; thus their high scores reflect weight fluctuation rather than restraint. Ruderman also suggested that the scale taps different constructs in normal-weight and obese subjects. To test these ideas, Ruderman tested 58 obese college women and 89 normal-weight college women. Separate factor analyses were performed for the responses from the two groups. For the normal-weight women, two factors were identified: Concern with Dieting and Weight Fluctuation. For the obese women, four factors were identified: Weight Fluctuation, Bingeing, Tendency to Diet, and Overconcern with Dieting. Thus, only the Weight Fluctuation factor is consistent across the two groups. Ruderman argued that if the Restraint Scale measures the same construct for obese and normal-weight subjects, then scores for both groups should correlate similarly with measures of the need to respond in socially desirable ways. Ruderman administered the Restraint Scale, the Marlowe-Crowne Social Desirability Scale, and the Lie Scale of the Eysenck Personality Inventory (Eysenck & Eysenck, 1963) to 69 obese college students and 176 normal-weight college students. The relationships between scores on the Restraint Scale and the Marlowe-Crowne Social Desirability Scale were similar for the two groups, but the relationships between the Lie Scale scores and the Restraint Scale scores were quite different for the two groups. Ruderman also found that Restraint Scale scores were higher and more homogeneous in obese subjects than in normal-weight subjects. Ruderman interpreted all of her findings as evidence that the Restraint Scale measures a different construct in obese subjects than it does in normal-weight subjects.

Drewnowski, Riskey, and Desor (1982) scored the measure on two factors they identified through factor analysis. Like Ruderman (1983), they named the factors Weight Fluctuation and Dietary Concern. Drewnowski et al. found that Weight Fluctuation scores correlated significantly with percentage overweight, but Dietary Concern scores did not. Lowe (1984), on the other hand, found that Dietary Concern scores were more strongly related to being overweight than were Weight Fluctuation scores. Lowe also found that restrained normals, as identified by the total restraint score, were more likely than unrestrained normals to have a history of being overweight.

Glynn and Ruderman (1986) developed the Eating Self-Efficacy Scale (ESES) (see separate entry). As they predicted, scores on the ESES were significantly correlated with both Restraint Scale factors identified by Ruderman (1983). The correlation between ESES and Concern with Dieting was .45 ($p < .001$); the correlation between ESES and Weight Fluctuation was .38 ($p < .001$). Furthermore, the correlation between total Restraint Scale scores and ESES was .47 ($p < .001$).

Several researchers have reported significant differences between the Restraint Scale scores of persons with and without an eating disorder (Buree, Papageorgis, & Solyom, 1984; Katzman & Wolchik, 1984; Nagelberg, Hale, & Ware, 1984). Tiggemann and Rothblum (1988) found significant differences in Restraint Scale scores as a function of sex; females scored significantly higher than males. Furthermore, Tiggemann and Rothblum found that college students from the University of Vermont scored significantly higher than college students in Australia.

NOTES & COMMENTS: (1) Stunkard and Messick (1985) criticized the Restraint Scale on several grounds: the scale failed to predict that obese persons would overeat following a preload, the scale measured weight fluctuation in addition to dietary restraint, and scores for obese persons were confounded by social desirability. As a result of their negative assessment of the Restraint Scale, Stunkard and Messick developed another eating scale. Items from the Restraint Scale were part of the item pool they used to develop the Three-Factor Eating Questionnaire (see separate entry) that measures cognitive restraint regarding eating, disinhibition, and hunger.

(2) Wardle (1986) reported several criticisms directed toward the ESES: the subscale structure is questionable, the total score is not a pure mea-

sure of restraint, and persons who are not concerned with their weight are likely to be unable to answer the weight fluctuation items.

(3) The Restraint Scale has often been used to identify restrained and unrestrained eaters, so that the two groups could be compared on other variables, such as response to anxiety (Herman & Polivy, 1975); perception of calories and eating behavior (Polivy, 1976); affective responsiveness as a function of arousal (Polivy, Herman, & Warsh, 1978); distractibility (Herman et al., 1978); binge eating (Spencer & Fremouw, 1979); internality (Hood, Moore, & Garner, 1982); eating behaviors (Hibscher & Herman, 1977; Ruderman, 1985a; Ruderman & Christensen, 1983; Ruderman & Wilson, 1979); body image (Counts & Adams, 1985); depression (Edwards & Nagelberg, 1986); cognitive restructuring performance (Etaugh & Hall, 1989); and personality characteristics (Edwards & Nagelberg, 1986).

(4) Restraint Scale scores have been related to a variety of other measures, including the Personal Attributes Questionnaire (see Beere, 1990) (Hawkins, Turell, & Jackson, 1983); the Texas Social Behavior Inventory (Hawkins et al., 1983); the Negative Self-Image Scale (Hawkins et al., 1983); the Mosher Forced-Choice Guilt Scale (see separate entry for Revised Mosher Guilt Inventory) (Hawkins et al., 1983); the Binge Scale (Hawkins et al., 1983) (see separate entry); the Dutch Eating Behavior Questionnaire (Wardle, 1986); the Food, Fitness, and Looks Questionnaire (see separate entry) (Hall, Leibrich, & Walkey, 1983); and the Work and Family Orientation Questionnaire (see Beere, 1990) (Hawkins et al., 1983). Restraint Scale scores have also been related to other variables including bulimia (Ruderman, 1985b); obesity (Ruderman, 1985b); checking behavior (Frost, Sher, & Geen, 1986); eating disorder within the family (Hall, Leibrich, Walkey, & Welch, 1986); and alcohol and food consumption (Rand, Lawlor, & Kuldau, 1986).

(5) Researchers have used the Restraint Scale as one of several measures to compare bulimics with and without a history of anorexia nervosa (Katzman & Wolchik, 1983) and to compare college women with bulimia and college women who binged (Katzman & Wolchik, 1984).

(6) Responses to the Restraint Scale have been factor analyzed in several studies (Blanchard & Frost, 1983; Drewnowski et al., 1982; Ruderman, 1983; Williams, Spencer, & Edelmann, 1987).

(7) The Restraint Scale has been used in the United States, Canada, Australia, England, and New Zealand.

AVAILABLE FROM: The original Restraint Scale is given in Herman and Polivy, 1975; the revised Restraint Scale is given in Polivy, Herman, and Warsh, 1978, and Corcoran and Fischer, 1987

USED IN:

Blanchard, F. A., & Frost, R. O. (1983). Two factors of restraint: Concern for dieting and weight fluctuation. *Behaviour Research and Therapy, 21*, 259–267.

Buree, B., Papageorgis, D., & Solyom, L. (1984). Body image perception and preference in anorexia nervosa. *Canadian Journal of Psychiatry, 29*, 557–563.

Counts, C. R., & Adams, H. E. (1985). Body image in bulimic, dieting, and normal females. *Journal of Psychopathology and Behavioral Assessment, 7*, 289–300.

Drewnowski, A., Riskey, D., & Desor, J. A. (1982). Feeling fat yet unconcerned: Self-reported overweight and the Restraint Scale. *Appetite, 3*, 273–279.

Edwards, F. E., & Nagelberg, D. B. (1986). Personality characteristics of restrained/binge eaters versus unrestrained/nonbinge eaters. *Addictive Behaviors, 11*, 207–211.

Etaugh, C., & Hall, P. (1989). Restrained eating: Mediator of gender differences on cognitive restructuring tasks. *Sex Roles, 20*, 465–471.

Freeman, C., Sinclair, F., Turnbull, J., & Annandale, A. (1985). Psychotherapy for bulimia: A controlled study. *Journal of Psychiatric Research, 19*, 473–478.

Frost, R. O., Sher, K. J., & Geen, T. (1986). Psychopathology and personality characteristics of nonclinical compulsive checkers. *Behaviour Research Therapy, 24*, 133–143.

Garfinkel, P. E., Garner, D. M., Rose, J., Darby, P. L., Brandes, J. S., O'Hanlon, J., & Walsh, N. (1983). A comparison of characteristics in the families of patients with anorexia nervosa and normal controls. *Psychological Medicine, 13*, 821–828.

Garner, D. M., & Garfinkel, P. E. (1979). The Eating Attitudes Test: An index of the symptoms of anorexia nervosa. *Psychological Medicine, 9*, 273–279.

Giles, T. R., Young, R. R., & Young, D. E. (1985). Behavioral treatment of severe bulimia. *Behavior Therapy, 16*, 393–405.

Glynn, S. M., & Ruderman, A. J. (1986). The development and validation of an eating self-efficacy scale. *Cognitive Therapy and Research, 10*, 403–420.

Hall, A., Leibrich, J., & Walkey, F. H. (1983). Development of a Food, Fitness, and Looks Questionnaire and its use in a study of "weight pathology" in 204 nonpatient families. In P. L. Darby, P. E. Garfinkel, D. M. Garner, & D. V. Coscina (Eds.), *Anorexia nervosa: Recent developments in research* (pp. 41–55). New York: Alan R. Liss.

Hall, A., Leibrich, J., Walkey, F. H., & Welch, G. (1986). Investigation of "weight pathology" of 58 mothers of anorexia nervosa patients and 204 mothers of schoolgirls. *Psychological Medicine, 16*, 71–76.

Hawkins, R. C., & Clement, P. F. (1980). Development and construct validation of a self-report measure of binge eating tendencies. *Addictive Behaviors, 5*, 219–226.

Hawkins, R. C., Turell, S., & Jackson, L. J. (1983). Desirable and undesirable masculine and feminine traits in relation to students' dieting tendencies and body image dissatisfaction. *Sex Roles, 9*, 705–718.

Herman, C. P., & Mack, D. (1975). Restrained and unrestrained eating. *Journal of Personality, 43*, 647–660.

Herman, C. P., & Polivy, J. (1975). Anxiety, restraint, and eating behavior. *Journal of Abnormal Psychology, 84*, 666–672.

Herman, C. P., Polivy, J., Pliner, P., Threlkeld, J., & Munic, D. (1978). Distractibility in dieters and nondieters: An alternative view of "externality". *Journal of Personality and Social Psychology, 36*, 536–548.

Hibscher, J. A., & Herman, C. P. (1977). Obesity, dieting, and the expression of "obese" characteristics. *Journal of Comparative and Physiological Psychology, 91,* 374–380.

Hood, J., Moore, T. E., & Garner, D. M. (1982). Locus of control as a measure of ineffectiveness in anorexia nervosa. *Journal of Consulting and Clinical Psychology, 50,* 3–13.

Katzman, M. A., & Wolchik, S. A. (1983, April). *Bulimics with and without prior anorexia nervosa: A comparison of personality characteristics.* Paper presented at the meeting of the Rocky Mountain Psychological Association, Snowbird, UT. (ERIC Document Reproduction Service No. ED 236 463)

Katzman, M. A., & Wolchik, S. A. (1984). Bulimia and binge eating in college women: A comparison of personality and behavioral characteristics. *Journal of Consulting and Clinical Psychology, 52,* 423–428.

Lowe, M. R. (1984). Dietary concern, weight fluctuation and weight status: Further explorations of the Restraint Scale. *Behaviour Research and Therapy, 22,* 243–248.

Nagelberg, D. B., Hale, S. L., & Ware, S. L. (1984). The assessment of bulimic symptoms and personality correlates in female college students. *Journal of Clinical Psychology, 40,* 440–445.

Polivy, J. (1976). Perception of calories and regulation of intake in restrained and unrestrained subjects. *Addictive Behaviors, 1,* 237–243.

Polivy, J., & Herman, C. P. (1985). Dieting and bingeing. *American Psychologist, 40,* 193–201.

Polivy, J., Herman, C. P., & Warsh, S. (1978). Internal and external components of emotionality in restrained and unrestrained eaters. *Journal of Abnormal Psychology, 87,* 497–504.

Rand, C. S. W., Lawlor, B. A., & Kuldau, J. M. (1986). Patterns of food and alcohol consumption in a group of bulimic women. *Bulletin of the Society of Psychologists in Addictive Behaviors, 5,* 95–104.

Rosen, J. C., Silberg, N. T., & Gross, J. (1988). Eating Attitudes Test and Eating Disorder Inventory: Norms for adolescent girls and boys. *Journal of Consulting and Clinical Psychology, 56,* 305–308.

Ruderman, A. J. (1983). The Restraint Scale: A psychometric investigation. *Behaviour Research and Therapy, 21,* 253–258.

Ruderman, A. J. (1985a). Dysphoric mood and overeating: A test of restraint theory's disinhibition hypothesis. *Journal of Abnormal Psychology, 94,* 78–85.

Ruderman, A. J. (1985b). Restraint, obesity and bulimia. *Behaviour Research and Therapy, 23,* 151–156.

Ruderman, A. J., & Christensen, H. (1983). Restraint theory and its applicability to overweight individuals. *Journal of Abnormal Psychology, 92,* 210–215.

Ruderman, A. J., & Wilson, G. T. (1979). Weight, restraint, cognitions and counterregulation. *Behaviour Research and Therapy, 17,* 581–590.

Ruff, G. A., & Barrios, B. A. (1986). Realistic assessment of body image. *Behavioral Assessment, 8,* 237–251.

Spencer, J. A., & Fremouw, W. J. (1979). Binge eating as a function of restraint and weight classification. *Journal of Abnormal Psychology, 88,* 262–267.

Stunkard, A. J. (1981). "Restrained eating": What it is and a new scale to measure it. In L. A. Cioffi, W. P. T. James, & T. B. Van Itallie (Eds.), *The body weight regulatory system: Normal and disturbed mechanisms* (pp. 243–251). New York: Raven Press.

Stunkard, A. J., & Messick, S. (1985). The Three-Factor Eating Questionnaire to measure dietary restraint, disinhibition and hunger. *Journal of Psychosomatic Research, 29*, 71–83.

Tiggemann, M., & Rothblum, E. D. (1988). Gender differences in social consequences of perceived overweight in the United States and Australia. *Sex Roles, 18*, 75–86.

Wardle, J. (1986). The assessment of restrained eating. *Behaviour Research and Therapy, 24*, 213–215.

Williams, A., Spencer, C. P., & Edelmann, R. J. (1987). Restraint theory, locus of control and the situational analysis of binge eating. *Personality and Individual Differences, 8*, 67–74.

BIBLIOGRAPHY:

Beere, C. A. (1990). *Gender roles: A handbook of tests and measures*. Westport, CT: Greenwood.

Corcoran, K., & Fischer, J. (1987). *Measures for clinical practice: A sourcebook* (pp. 284–285). New York: Free Press.

Crowne, D. P., & Marlowe, D. (1960). A new scale of social desirability independent of psychopathology. *Journal of Consulting Psychology, 24*, 349–354.

Eysenck, H. J., & Eysenck, S. B. G. (1963). *Eysenck Personality Inventory*. San Diego: Educational & Industrial Testing Service.

Galassi, J. P., Delo, J. S., Galassi, M. D., & Bastien, S. (1974). The College Self-Expression Scale: A measure of assertiveness. *Behavior Therapy, 5*, 165–171.

Nash, T. D., & Ormiston, L. H. (1978). *Taking charge of your weight and well being*. Palo Alto: Bull Publishing.

Price, G. H., & Price, K. P. (1974). *Instructor's manual and resource book for G. C. Davison & J. M. Neale's abnormal psychology: An experimental clinical approach*. New York: Wiley.

Rotter, J. B. (1966). Generalized expectations for internal versus external control of reinforcement. *Psychological Monographs, 80* (1, Whole No. 609).

SURVEY OF EATING BEHAVIOR

AUTHORS: Morton G. Harmatz and Bruce B. Kerr

DATE: 1981

VARIABLE: Reasons for eating and attitudes toward eating

TYPE OF INSTRUMENT: Summated rating scale

DESCRIPTION: The Survey of Eating Behavior consists of 18 items, each describing a possible reason for eating or an attitude regarding food or eating. Each item is accompanied by five response options: "always, frequently, occasionally, seldom, never."

SAMPLE ITEMS: I eat in order to keep myself from slowing down.

Preparing food is part of the enjoyment of eating it.

PREVIOUS SUBJECTS: College students in the United States and England

APPROPRIATE FOR: High school students and older
ADMINISTRATION: Self-administered; about 5–10 minutes
SCORING: Items are individually scored on a 5-point scale, with higher points assigned to the responses reflecting greater frequency. A total score is obtained as well as scores on each of the factors (See NOTES & COMMENTS). Williams, Spencer, and Edelmann (1987) reported means and standard deviations for binge eaters and nonbinge eaters. They reported the data for total scores, as well as for each of the six factor scores identified in their factor analysis.
DEVELOPMENT: No information was provided.
RELIABILITY: No information was provided.
VALIDITY: Harmatz and Kerr (1981) found that normal-weight and overweight college students differed on three of the five factor scores (see NOTES & COMMENTS) on the Survey of Eating Behavior. Overweight students scored significantly higher on the Tension-Reduction and Craving-Habit factors.

Williams et al. (1987) compared responses from binge-eating and nonbinge-eating college students in England. They found that binge eaters scored significantly higher on the total scale score and on three factor scores: Negative Emotions, Stimulation, and Eating—a habit. (The factors Williams et al. used were slightly different from the factors used by Harmatz and Kerr. [See NOTES & COMMENTS]).

Williams et al. (1987) correlated scores on the Survey of Eating Behavior with scores on the Binge Scale (BS) (Hawkins & Clement, 1980) (see separate entry). There were significant correlations between BS scores and four of the six factor scores, as well as the total score on the Survey of Eating Behavior.
NOTES & COMMENTS: (1) Harmatz and Kerr (1981) factor analyzed responses from 49 college men and 130 college women. They identified five factors. Factor 1, Tension-Reduction, contained three items dealing with eating as a response to negative affect and accounted for just over 14% of the variance. Factor 2, Stimulation, contained three items dealing with eating to maintain energy and accounted for 11% of the variance. Factor 3, Craving-Habit, contained four items dealing with craving food or eating out of habit and accounted for another 11% of the variance. Factor 4, Handling, contained three items regarding food preparation, handling, and arrangement and accounted for 8% of the variance. Factor 5, Pleasurable Relaxation, contained two items reflecting that eating is pleasurable and relaxing and accounted for 6.5% of the variance.

(2) Williams et al. (1987) factor analyzed responses from 110 college students in England. They identified six factors that were remarkably similar to those identified by Harmatz and Kerr (1981). The major difference between the results from the two factor analyses was that Williams et al. identified two factors in place of the Craving-Habit factor

Harmatz and Kerr identified. The similarity in the results of the two analyses is particularly noteworthy because both analyses were done with relatively small samples.

(3) Williams et al. (1987) reported the intercorrelations between their six factors. Six of the 15 intercorrelations were statistically significant.

(4) Williams et al. (1987) referred to the Survey of Eating Behavior as the "Reasons for Eating Scale."

AVAILABLE FROM: Harmatz and Kerr, 1981; Williams, Spencer, and Edelmann, 1987

USED IN:

Harmatz, M. G., & Kerr, B. B. (1981). Overeating behavior: A multicausal approach. *Obesity and Metabolism, 1*, 134–139.

Williams, A., Spencer, C. P., & Edelmann, R. J. (1987). Restraint theory, locus of control and the situational analysis of binge eating. *Personality and Individual Differences, 8*, 67–74.

BIBLIOGRAPHY:

Hawkins, R. C., & Clement, P. F. (1980). Development and construct validation of a self-report measure of binge eating tendencies. *Addictive Behaviors, 5*, 219–226.

THREE-FACTOR EATING QUESTIONNAIRE

AUTHORS: Albert J. Stunkard and Samuel Messick

DATE: 1981

VARIABLE: Three factors relating to eating: restraint, disinhibition, and hunger

TYPE OF INSTRUMENT: Multiple choice and alternate choice: true/false

DESCRIPTION: The Three-Factor Eating Questionnaire contains 51 items representing three factors: cognitive restraint of eating, disinhibition, and hunger. The 51 items are presented in two sections. Part I contains 36 statements accompanied by the response options "true" and "false." Item content pertains to a variety of topics, including motivations for eating, dieting behaviors, eating habits, and hunger. Part II contains 15 multiple choice items, each accompanied by four or five response options that form a continuum, for example, "not at all, slightly, moderately, extremely." Item content is similar to item content on Part I. "Cognitive restraint of eating" is represented by 12 items on Part I and 9 items on Part II; "disinhibition" is represented by 13 items on Part I and 3 items on Part II; and "hunger" is represented by 11 items on Part I and 3 items on Part II.

SAMPLE ITEMS: (Part I) When I smell a sizzling steak or see a juicy piece of meat, I find it very difficult to keep from eating, even if I have just finished a meal.

(Part II) How often are you dieting in a conscious effort to control your weight? (1) rarely, (2) sometimes, (3) usually, (4) always

PREVIOUS SUBJECTS: Members of a weight reduction group, adults,

persons seeking treatment for obesity, college students, high school cheerleaders, bulimics
APPROPRIATE FOR: High school students and older
ADMINISTRATION: Self-administered; about 20 minutes
SCORING: The keyed response is given for the true/false items, and the keyed direction is indicated for the multiple choice items. For the 36 true/false items, the keyed response is assigned 1 point. For the multiple choice items, selecting one of the two responses in the keyed direction earns 1 point; selecting one of the two responses in the nonkeyed direction earns 0 points. Item scores are summed to yield scores on each of the three factors.
DEVELOPMENT: A pool of 67 items was compiled: the 10 items from the Restraint Scale (Herman & Polivy, 1975) (see separate entry), 40 items from Pudel, Metzdorff, and Oetting's (1975) Latent Obesity Questionnaire, which was repeatedly translated and backtranslated, and 17 items written specifically for the item pool. The 67 items were completed by 200 persons (dieters, normal-weight persons who were heavy eaters, and neighbors of the dieters). Their responses were factor analyzed, and three factors were identified: "Factor 1 [with 20 items] involved behavioral restraint, particularly conscious control of eating behavior. Factor II [with 19 items] reflected lability in both behavior and weight, and Factor III [with 20 items] [concerns] hunger and its behavior ramifications" (Stunkard & Messick, 1985, p. 74). Coefficient alpha was computed for each of the factors: Factor I = .90, Factor II = .87, and Factor III = .82. The intercorrelations between the factors were computed: Factor I with Factor II = .60, Factor I with Factor III = .37, and Factor II with Factor III = .63. The reliabilities remained consistent when the three groups—dieters, free eaters, and neighbors—were looked at separately, but the scale intercorrelations were different for the different subsamples. Factor analysis for the separate subgroups yielded fairly consistent results for the neighbors and the dieters groups, but four salient factors emerged from a factor analysis of responses from the free eaters group.

As a result of the provisional factor analysis, "new items were written to conform to the tentative rationale and, at the same time, to heighten the distinctiveness of each factor vis-a-vis the other two" (Stunkard & Messick, 1985, p. 75), and some original items were revised to emphasize the distinction among the factors. The three factors were now interpreted as follows: Factor I was "cognitive control of eating behavior," Factor II was "disinhibition of control," and Factor III was "susceptibility to hunger" (p. 76). The new questionnaire contained 93 items that were administered to a sample of 53 dieters and 45 free eaters. Using multiple item analyses and partial correlations looking at each item in relation to its factor, the authors retained 58 items:

23 items for Factor I, 20 items for Factor II, and 15 items for Factor III. This version of the scale was described in Stunkard (1981). Alpha coefficients were computed: Factor I = .92, Factor II = .91, and Factor III = .85. Factor intercorrelations were as follows: Factor I with Factor II = .43, Factor I with Factor III = −.03, and Factor II with Factor III = .42.

Responses were factor analyzed from 98 dieters and free eaters who completed the 58-item version of the scale. Fifty-five of the 58 items loaded highest on their designated factors. The factor analysis was repeated using responses to the 55 items, and three factors were identified: "Factor I reflected conscious mechanisms for restraining food intake. Factor II involved a variety of disinhibitors. . . . Factor III reflected feelings of hunger and its behavioral consequences" (Stunkard & Messick, 1985, p. 77). As a final step in scale construction, 4 items pertaining to weight fluctuation were deleted, largely because they distorted the results obtained from obese persons. According to Stunkard and Messick (1985), "the deletion of these items did not substantially affect either the stability of the scale or the pattern of scale intercorrelations among the scales for dieters, free eaters or the combined second sample" (p. 78).

RELIABILITY: Alpha coefficients for the 55-item version of the Three-Factor Eating Questionnaire were computed separately for dieters, free eaters, and the two groups combined. Coefficient alpha for Factor I was .79, .92, and .93 for the three groups, respectively; coefficient alpha for Factor II was .84, .84, and .91 for the three groups, respectively; and coefficient alpha for Factor III was .83, .87, and .85 for the three groups (Stunkard & Messick, 1985).

Ganley (cited in Stunkard & Messick, 1985) obtained respectable test-retest reliabilities when the scale was used with 17 college students tested on two occasions separated by 1 month: Factor I = .93, Factor II = .80, and Factor III = .83.

VALIDITY: Stunkard and Messick (1985) reported that scores from Factors I and II discriminated significantly between dieters and free eaters ($p < .001$), but the difference on Factor III was nonsignificant.

Stunkard and Messick (1985) also reported intercorrelations between the factor scores. For the combined sample, the correlation between Factor 1 and Factor II was .43 ($p < .01$), the correlation between Factor I and Factor III was −.04 (not significant), and the correlation between Factors II and III was .40 ($p < .01$). When Stunkard and Messick looked at the factor intercorrelations separately for the dieters and the free eaters, they found significant differences in the pattern of intercorrelations for the two groups.

Marcus and Wing (cited in Stunkard & Messick, 1985) found that severity of bingeing was significantly related to scores on Factors II and III but not with Factor I scores.

Shrager, Wadden, Miller, Stunkard, and Stellar (cited in Stunkard & Messick, 1985) found that Factor II scores were significantly related to overeating during a laboratory study involving food intake under ambiguous circumstances.

Marcus, Wing, and Lamparski (1985) administered the Binge Eating Scale (Gormally, Black, Daston, & Rardin, 1982) (see separate entry) and the Three-Factor Eating Questionnaire to overweight persons. Binge-Eating scores, which reflect binge-eating severity, were significantly related to total scores on the Three-Factor Eating Questionnaire and to scores on Factors II and III but not to Factor I, the cognitive restraint factor.

NOTES & COMMENTS: (1) Stunkard and Messick (1985) found that Factor II, disinhibition, predicted weight change during depression, but Factor I, dietary restraint, was not related to weight changes for depressed persons.

(2) Lundholm and Anderson (1986) used the 1981 version of the Three-Factor Eating Questionnaire along with another measure of disordered eating in order to compare the eating behaviors of male and female college students. In a study focusing on adolescent cheerleaders' desire for thinness in relation to disordered eating behaviors and attitudes, Lundholm and Littrell (1986) used the Three-Factor Eating Questionnaire as one of several measures of eating attitudes and behavior. Cooper and Bowskill (1986) used a portion of the Three-Factor Eating Questionnaire in a study relating mood to eating behavior.

(3) Fairburn and Cooper (1984) modified the Three-Factor Eating Questionnaire for use in the United Kingdom. They used the scale as one of several measures to better understand persons suffering from bulimia.

AVAILABLE FROM: Stunkard and Messick, 1985

USED IN:

Cooper, P. J., & Bowskill, R. (1986). Dysphoric mood and overeating. *British Journal of Clinical Psychology, 25*, 155–156.

Fairburn, C. G., & Cooper, P. J. (1984). The clinical features of bulimia nervosa. *British Journal of Psychiatry, 144*, 238–246.

Lundholm, J. K., & Anderson, D. F. (1986). Eating disordered behaviors: A comparison of male and female university students. *Addictive Behaviors, 11*, 193–196.

Lundholm, J. K., & Littrell, J. M. (1986). Desire for thinness among high school cheerleaders: Relationship to disordered eating and weight control behaviors. *Adolescence, 21*, 573–579.

Marcus, M. D., Wing, R. R., & Lamparski, D. M. (1985). Binge eating and dietary restraint in obese patients. *Addictive Behaviors, 10*, 163–168.

Stunkard, A. J. (1981). "Restrained eating": What it is and a new scale to measure it. In L. A. Cioffi, W. P. T. James, & T. B. Van Itallie (Eds.), *The body weight regulatory system: Normal and disturbed mechanisms* (pp. 243–251). New York: Raven Press.

Stunkard, A. J., & Messick, S. (1985). The Three-Factor Eating Questionnaire to measure dietary restraint, disinhibition and hunger. *Journal of Psychosomatic Research*, *29*, 71–83.

BIBLIOGRAPHY:

Gormally, J., Black, S., Daston, S., & Rardin, D. (1982). The assessment of binge eating severity among obese persons. *Addictive Behaviors*, *7*, 47–55.

Herman, C. P., & Polivy, J. (1975). Anxiety, restraint, and eating behavior. *Journal of Abnormal Psychology*, *84*, 666–672.

Pudel, V. E., Metzdorff, M., & Oetting, M. X. (1975). Zur Persoehnlichkeit Adipoeser in psychologischen Tests unter Beruecksichtigung latent Fettsuechtiger. *Zeitschrift Fuer Psychosomatische Medizin und Psychoanalyse*, *21*, 345–350.

WEIGHT LOCUS OF CONTROL (WLOC)

AUTHOR: Eleanor B. Saltzer

DATE: 1982 (used 1978)

VARIABLE: Locus of control with respect to one's own weight

TYPE OF INSTRUMENT: Summated rating scale

DESCRIPTION: The Weight Locus of Control (WLOC) scale consists of four items: two reflecting an internal orientation and two reflecting an external orientation. Each item is accompanied by a 6-point scale ranging from "strongly disagree" to "strongly agree."

SAMPLE ITEMS: (internal orientation) Whether I gain, lose, or maintain my weight is entirely up to me.

(external orientation) Being the right weight is largely a matter of good fortune.

PREVIOUS SUBJECTS: College students, women beginning a weight reduction program

APPROPRIATE FOR: Grades 7 and older

ADMINISTRATION: Self-administered; less than 5 minutes

SCORING: Items are individually scored on a 6-point scale. Total scores range from 4 (extremely internal orientation) to 24 (extremely external orientation). Saltzer (1982) provided normative data—medians, means, and standard deviations—for two groups of college students and a group of females beginning a weight control program.

DEVELOPMENT: No information was provided.

RELIABILITY: A group of 110 college students completed the WLOC on two occasions, 24 days apart. Coefficient alpha for the first testing was .58; for the second testing, it was .56. Test-retest reliability was .67.

VALIDITY: To establish the convergent validity of the scale, Saltzer (1982) correlated scores on the WLOC with scores on five other indicators of locus of control. Four of the five correlations were moderate and statistically significant. One was nonsignificant. To provide evidence of discriminant validity, Saltzer compared WLOC scores with scores on a shortened version of the Marlowe-Crowne Social Desirability Scale (Strahan & Gerbasi, 1972). The correlation between the two measures was nonsignificant.

Saltzer (1982) studied college students' behavioral intentions in regard to weight loss. She found that those who were internal on the WLOC and who valued health and/or physical appearance were influenced by personal attitudes toward weight loss, and those who were external on the WLOC and who valued health and/or physical appearance were influenced by perceived social normative beliefs. These findings were not replicated when locus of control was assessed by other locus of control measures.

Saltzer (1982) studied 115 women beginning a weight loss program. She administered a variety of measures, including the WLOC. As expected, there was a significant (though rather low) correlation ($r = -.20$) between program completion and internality, as measured by the WLOC. Furthermore, "completers" were significantly more internal on the WLOC than were "noncompleters." In this study, Saltzer also found that WLOC interacted with value placed on health and physical appearance to moderate the relationship between behavioral intentions in regard to weight loss and actual weight loss.

Williams, Spencer, and Edelmann (1987) tested college students with a variety of eating-related measures, including the WLOC. They found no significant difference on the WLOC scores of binge eaters and nonbinge eaters. Similarly, they found a nonsignificant correlation ($r = -.03$) between WLOC scores and scores on the Binge Scale (Hawkins & Clement, 1980) (see separate entry).

NOTES & COMMENTS: Although the evidence in Saltzer's (1982) research convinced me that a weight loss locus of control measure is more useful in weight loss research than is a general locus of control measure or a general health-related locus of control measure, there is a major problem with the WLOC. The reliability of the scale—both internal consistency and test-retest—was unacceptably low. The low internal consistency reliability was not surprising given the brevity of the scale. Nevertheless, the scale should be improved before further use.

AVAILABLE FROM: Saltzer, 1982

USED IN:

Saltzer, E. B. (1982). The Weight Locus of Control (WLOC) scale: A specific measure for obesity research. *Journal of Personality Assessment, 46*, 620–628.

Williams, A., Spencer, C. P., & Edelmann, R. J. (1987). Restraint theory, locus of control and the situational analysis of binge eating. *Personality and Individual Differences, 8*, 67–74.

BIBLIOGRAPHY:

Hawkins, R. C., & Clement, P. F. (1980). Development and construct validation of a self-report measure of binge eating tendencies. *Addictive Behavior, 5,* 219–226.

Strahan, R., & Gerbasi, K. C. (1972). Short, homogeneous versions of the Marlowe-Crowne Social Desirability Scale. *Journal of Clinical Psychology, 28,* 191–193.

12

Other Scales

This is the shortest chapter in the handbook. The five scales described here have potential value for researchers studying gender-related issues, yet they do not fit into any of the other chapters. First is the Hostility Toward Women Scale (Check, Malamuth, Elias, & Barton, 1985), recommended for use in studies of rape. Since the scale assesses the extent to which men are hostile toward women, it did not fit with the scales in Chapter 8, "Rape and Sexual Coercion."

The second scale is the Masculine and Feminine Self-Disclosure Scale (MFSDS) (Snell, Belk, & Hawkins, 1986). As its name implies, it measures self-disclosure, a topic that has not been included in this handbook, although two measures of self-disclosure are briefly described in the introduction to Chapter 2. The MFSDS is included, however, because it is directly related to gender issues; the MFSDS measures people's willingness to disclose information about the masculine and feminine aspects of themselves.

The third measure in this chapter is the Nonsexist Personal Attribute Inventory for Children (NPAIC) (Parish & Rankin, 1982), a measure of self-concept in children. Although self-concept is a topic that is not included in this handbook, this scale is here because it is specifically nonsexist, suggesting that it might be relevant for gender-related research.

The fourth scale is the Same Sex Touching Scale (SSTS) (Larsen & LeRoux, 1984), a measure of attitudes toward same-sex touching. Although this scale might appear to fit in Chapter 7, "Homosexuality," the SSTS is not a measure of sexual expression between same-sex persons. Rather it measures attitudes toward touching a person of the same sex; the touch may be, for example, an expression of warmth, comfort, or affection.

The final scale in this chapter, the Wallin Women's Neighborliness Scale (Wallin, 1953), was described in my original handbook (Beere, 1979). It measures a woman's knowledge of and friendliness with her neighbors. Indirectly related to the topic of neighborliness is the topic of loneliness, which has also been studied extensively in women. Measures of loneliness are not described in this book, but researchers might want to obtain information about the most frequently used measures of loneliness: the UCLA Loneliness Scale (Russell, Peplau, & Ferguson, 1978) and the Revised UCLA Loneliness Scale (Russell, Peplau, & Cutrona, 1980), 20-item summated rating scales that have been used in over 30 studies.

BIBLIOGRAPHY:

Beere, C. A. (1979). *Women and women's issues: A handbook of tests and measures* (pp. 523–524). San Francisco: Jossey-Bass.

Check, J. V. P., Malamuth, N. M., Elias, B., & Barton, S. A. (1985). On hostile ground. *Psychology Today, 19*(4), 56–61.

Larsen, K. S., & LeRoux, J. (1984). A study of same sex touching attitudes: Scale development and personality predictors. *Journal of Sex Research, 20*, 264–278.

Parish, T. S., & Rankin, C. I. (1982). The Nonsexist Personal Attribute Inventory for Children: A report on its validity and reliability as a self-concept scale. *Educational and Psychological Measures, 42*, 339–343.

Russell, D., Peplau, L. A., & Cutrona, C. E. (1980). The Revised UCLA Loneliness Scale: Concurrent and discriminant validity evidence. *Journal of Personality and Social Psychology, 39*, 472–480.

Russell, D., Peplau, L. A., & Ferguson, M. L. (1978). Developing a measure of loneliness. *Journal of Personality Assessment, 42*, 290–294.

Snell, W. E., Jr., Belk, S. S., & Hawkins, R. C., II. (1986). The Masculine and Feminine Self-Disclosure Scale: The politics of masculine and feminine self-presentation. *Sex Roles, 15*, 249–267.

Wallin, P. (1953). A Guttman scale for measuring women's neighborliness. *American Journal of Sociology, 59*, 243–246.

HOSTILITY TOWARD WOMEN SCALE

AUTHORS: James V. P. Check and Neil M. Malamuth

DATE: 1983

VARIABLE: Hostility toward women with the following definition: "Hostility *toward women* is typically implicit, consisting of the mulling over of past attacks *from women*, rejections *from women*, and deprivations *from women*, and may be inferred when aggression *against a woman* is motivated by a desire to hurt rather than by a desire to attain some extrinsic reinforcer" (Check, 1984/1985, p. 35., based on Buss, 1961, p. 12).

TYPE OF INSTRUMENT: Alternate choice: true/false

DESCRIPTION: The Hostility Toward Women Scale contains 30 statements about women. The statements reflect "resentment," "suspicion of women," "guilt," and "miscellaneous forms of indirect hostility" (Check, 1984/1985, p. 40). For each statement, respondents are to indicate whether they think the statement is "true" or "false."
SAMPLE ITEMS: I feel that many times women flirt with men just to tease them or hurt them.

I feel upset even by slight criticism by a woman.
PREVIOUS SUBJECTS: College and adult men
APPROPRIATE FOR: College and adult men
ADMINISTRATION: Self-administered; about 10–15 minutes
SCORING: Half of the items are keyed true, and half are keyed false. One point is assigned for each response in the keyed direction, so total scores can range from zero to 30. Higher scores are associated with greater hostility toward women. For a sample of 305 college men, the average score was 8.79 (Check, Malamuth, Elias, & Barton, 1985).
DEVELOPMENT: A pool of 118 nonredundant items was constructed by adapting items from hostility measures by Buss and Durkee (1957), Comrey (1964), Siegel (1956), and Evans and Stangeland (1971) and by adding some new items written by Check. The item pool was administered to 136 college men, and the 30 items with the highest item-total correlations were selected for the first version of the Hostility Toward Women Scale. All items on the first version of the scale were keyed in the same direction; the items were all considered "protrait" items.

Another study was undertaken to create and select equivalent items that would be keyed in the opposite direction, that is, "contrait" items. Based on pilot testing, the contrait items were selected by considering three criteria: "(a) the contrait item's correlation with the original item . . . , (b) the degree to which the proportion of individuals responding 'false' to the contrait item approximated the proportion of individuals responding 'true' to the original protrait item . . . , and (c) the degree to which the contrait item's standard deviation approximated the original item's standard deviation" (Check, 1984/1985, p. 67). The current version of the Hostility Toward Women Scale has equal numbers of contrait and protrait items.
RELIABILITY: Two studies using the original version of the Hostility Toward Women Scale yielded Kuder-Richardson 20 (KR 20) coefficients of .89 (Check, 1984/1985). To determine the reliability of the second (current) version of the Hostility Toward Women Scale, a sample of 61 college men completed the scale on two occasions with a 1-week interval between testings. The test-retest reliability was .83. The KR 20 reliability for a sample of 80 college men was .81. When a subset of 61 men completed the scale a second time, the KR 20 coefficient was .87 for the second testing.

VALIDITY: A factor analysis of responses to the original version of the Hostility Toward Women Scale led to the identification of one factor that accounted for 25% of the total variance. All items had factor loadings of at least .30 on the one factor. A factor analysis of responses to the current version of the Hostility Toward Women Scale also led to the identification of one factor, but there was a suggestion of a second and perhaps a third factor. The first factor accounted for 19% of the variance, and the factor loadings were above .30 for 20 of the 30 items. Factor analysis for the second testing with the scale also produced a single factor, this time accounting for 23% of the variance. The factor loadings for 25 items were above .30; for 21 items, the factor loadings were greater than .40.

In order to obtain data relevant to the validity of the Hostility Toward Women Scale, Check (1984/1985) tested 275 college men with the Hostility Toward Women Scale, the Rape Myth Acceptance Scale (Burt, 1980) (see separate entry), the Acceptance of Interpersonal Violence (Burt, 1980) (see separate entry), the Adversarial Sexual Beliefs scale (Burt, 1980) (see separate entry), the General Acceptance of Violence scale (Malamuth, Check, & Briere, 1983), two subscales from the Sexual Functions Scale (Nelson, 1978/1979) (see separate entry), the Trait Anger Scale (Spielberger, Jacobs, Russell, & Crane, 1982), a measure of past acts of sexual aggression taken from the Sexual Experiences Survey (Koss & Oros, 1982) (see separate entry), a self-report measure of the likelihood to commit rape, and Reynolds's (1982) short form of the Marlowe-Crowne Social Desirability Scale (Crowne & Marlowe, 1960). Check correlated Hostility Toward Women scores with each of the other measures. He found significant correlations with Social Desirability ($r = -.36$), Rape Myth Acceptance ($r = .32$), Acceptance of Interpersonal Violence ($r = .20$), Adversarial Sexual Beliefs ($r = .45$), power motivation for sex ($r = .29$), past acts of sexual aggression ($r = .16$), likelihood to rape ($r = .23$), and the Trait Anger Scale ($r = .49$). Scores from the Hostility Toward Women Scale were not significantly correlated with General Acceptance of Violence or with a love and affection motivation for sex.

Check (1984/1985) found that scores on the Hostility Toward Women Scale generally predicted aggressive behavior toward both males and females in laboratory conditions and also predicted subjects' reported desire to hurt someone; scores on the Hostility Toward Women Scale did not predict desire to help a person.

Malamuth (1986) attempted to identify predictors of males' sexual aggression against women. He tested men with a variety of measures expected to predict sexual aggression: Acceptance of Interpersonal Violence scale, the Psychoticism scale of the Eysenck Personality Questionnaire (Eysenck, 1978), the Heterosexual Behavior Assessment Inventory (Bentler, 1968) (see separate entry), the Sexual Experiences Survey, a subscale from Nelson's Sexual Functions Scale, a self-reported index of sexual arousal in response to a rape depiction, and a physiological measure of sexual arousal in response to a rape depiction. Malamuth intercorrelated the predictors and used them in regression analysis. He found that scores on the Hostility Toward Women Scale were a significant predictor of aggression and they were significantly correlated with all of the other predictors used in the study except the Psychoticism measure.

Malamuth (1989) conducted a study looking at the relationship between scores on the Attraction to Sexual Aggression Scale and numerous other variables, including the Hostility Toward Women Scale. The results, as predicted, showed that the scores on the two measures were significantly correlated with each other.

NOTES & COMMENTS: Check (1984/1985) concluded: "Whatever the reason for the Hostility Toward Women scale's ability to predict aggressive behavior against both male and female targets, the scale has at least shown substantial validity in predicting all of the hostility toward women criterion variables used in this research. It seems reasonable to conclude, therefore, that further research on rape would benefit from the use of the Hostility Toward Women scale, especially in testing certain theoretical questions regarding the underlying motivations for rape" (p. 129).

AVAILABLE FROM: Check, Malamuth, Elias, and Barton, 1985

USED IN:

Check, J. V. P. (1985). The Hostility Toward Women Scale (Doctoral dissertation, University of Manitoba, Canada, 1984). *Dissertation Abstracts International, 45*, 3993B.

Check, J. V. P., Malamuth, N. M., Elias, B., & Barton, S. A. (1985). On hostile ground. *Psychology Today, 19*(4), 56–61.

Malamuth, N. M. (1986). Predictors of naturalistic sexual aggression. *Journal of Personality and Social Psychology, 50*, 953–962.

Malamuth, N. M. (1989). The Attraction to Sexual Aggression Scale: Part two. *Journal of Sex Research, 26*, 324–354.

BIBLIOGRAPHY:

Bentler, P. M. (1968). Heterosexual Behavior Assessment—1: Males. *Behaviour Research and Therapy, 6*, 21–25.

Burt, M. R. (1980). Cultural myths and supports for rape. *Journal of Personality and Social Psychology, 38*, 217–230.

Buss, A. H. (1961). *The psychology of aggression*. New York: Wiley.

Buss, A. H., & Durkee, A. (1957). An inventory for assessing different kinds of hostility. *Journal of Consulting Psychology, 21*, 343–349.

Comrey, A L. (1964). Personality factors, compulsion, dependence, hostility, and neuroticism. *Education and Psychological Measurement, 24*, 74–84.

Crowne, D. P., & Marlowe, D. (1960). A new scale of social desirability independent of psychopathology. *Journal of Consulting Psychology, 24*, 349–354.

Evans, D. R., & Stangeland, M. (1971). Development of the Reaction Inventory to measure anger. *Psychological Reports, 29*, 412–414.

Eysenck, H. J. (1978). *Sex and personality*. London: Open Books.

Koss, M. P., & Oros, C. (1982). Sexual Experiences Survey: A research instrument investigating sexual aggression and victimization. *Journal of Consulting and Clinical Psychology, 50*, 455–457.

Malamuth, N. M., Check, J. V. P., & Briere, J. (1983, August). *Is violence sexually arousing?* Paper presented at the meeting of the American Psychological Association, Anaheim, CA.

Nelson, P. A. (1979). Personality, sexual functions, and sexual behavior: An experiment in methodology (Doctoral dissertation, University of Florida, 1978). *Dissertation Abstracts International, 39*, 6134B.

Reynolds, W. M. (1982). Development of reliable and valid short forms of the Marlowe-Crowne Social Desirability scale. *Journal of Clinical Psychology, 38*, 119–125.

Siegel, S. M. (1956). The relationship of hostility to authoritarianism. *Journal of Abnormal and Social Psychology, 52*, 368–372.

Spielberger, C. D., Jacobs, G. A., Russell, S., & Crane, R. S. (1982). Assessment of anger: The State-Trait Anger Scale. In J. N. Butcher & C. D. Spielberger (Eds.), *Advances in personality assessment* (vol. 2, pp. 161–189). Hillsdale, NJ: Lawrence Erlbaum.

MASCULINE AND FEMININE SELF-DISCLOSURE SCALE (MFSDS)

AUTHORS: William E. Snell, Jr., Sharyn S. Belk, and Raymond C. Hawkins II

DATE: 1986

VARIABLE: Willingness to disclose information about the "masculine" and "feminine" aspects of the self

TYPE OF INSTRUMENT: Summated rating scale

DESCRIPTION: The Masculine and Feminine Self-Disclosure Scale (MFSDS) consists of 40 items: 7 items on each of four subscales plus 12 filler items that are not scored. The four subscales are Masculine Traits, Masculine Behaviors, Feminine Traits, and Feminine Behaviors. Each item is a phrase describing an aspect of the self that one may or may not be willing to discuss. In the original study reported by Snell, Belk, and Hawkins (1986), respondents were asked to respond to each item four times, once for each of four disclosure recipients: a male friend, a female friend, a male interviewer, and one's spouse-partner. Responses were recorded on a 5-point scale ranging from "not at all willing to discuss this topic" to "totally willing to discuss this topic."

SAMPLE ITEMS: (Masculine Traits) How self-sufficient you believe you are.

(Masculine Behavior) The extent to which you speak up when you want something.

(Feminine Traits) How warm a person you believe you are.

(Feminine Behavior) How often you tell people you really like their friendship.

PREVIOUS SUBJECTS: College students
APPROPRIATE FOR: High school students and older
ADMINISTRATION: Self-administered; about 10 minutes for each disclosure recipient listed
SCORING: Items are scored on a 5-point scale ranging from 0 (not at all willing to discuss this topic) to 4 (totally willing to discuss this topic). Separate totals are obtained for each of the four subscales for each disclosure recipient. Higher scores reflect greater willingness to disclose.
DEVELOPMENT: The authors of the MFSDS did not provide information regarding the development and selection of items. They did, however, provide definitions of masculinity and femininity that guided scale development: " 'masculinity' refers to those instrumental personality characteristics associated with being an independent, self-assertive, and self-reliant individual; 'femininity' refers to those expressive-communal personality characteristics associated with being a person who is kind, warm, and interpersonally concerned about others" (Snell et al., 1986, p. 252).
RELIABILITY: Snell et al. (1986) reported alpha coefficients based on administering the MFSDS to 55 college men and 168 college women. Given there were four subscales and four disclosure recipients, there were a total of 16 alpha coefficients, ranging from .80 to .94. Corrected item-subscale correlations were computed for each item for each disclosure recipient. All correlations were above .30, and almost half of the correlations were above .70.
VALIDITY: The MFSDS and the Jourard Self-Disclosure Scale (Jourard, 1971) were administered to 55 college men and 168 college women. Correlations between the two measures led Snell et al. (1986) to conclude that there is "a pattern of moderate relationships between the two self-disclosure measures" (p. 256). Thus, correlations between the two scales provided evidence of convergent validity, but they also suggested that the MFSDS measures something different from what the widely used Jourard Self-Disclosure Scale measures.
NOTES & COMMENTS: (1) Snell et al. (1986) reported subscale intercorrelations ranging from .55 to .91. They concluded that "the disclosure of masculine-instrumental and feminine-expressive traits and behaviors are highly related to each other" (p. 254).

(2) Snell et al. (1986) related MFSDS scores to scores on a variety of other self-report measures, including the Jenkins Activity Survey (Jenkins, 1978), designed to assess Type A behavior; the Self-Consciousness Inventory (Fenigstein, Scheier, & Buss, 1975); the Body Consciousness Questionnaire (Miller, Murphy, & Buss, 1981) (see separate entry); and the Extended Personal Attributes Questionnaire (Spence & Helmreich, 1978) (see Beere, 1990). Snell et al. (1986) used the MFSDS in a study to determine whether there are differences in willingness to disclose mas-

culine and feminine traits and behaviors as a function of the discloser's sex and the identity of the disclosure recipient. Belk, Martin, and Snell (1982) and Belk and Snell (1988) used the MFSDS in a study of the avoidance strategies that people use to contend with unwelcome persuasion attempts from their partners. The researchers were interested in whether there was a relationship between the choice of an avoidance strategy and a variety of other traits, including willingness to self-disclose. Snell, Belk, Flowers, and Warren (1988) used the MFSDS to study college students' willingness to disclose to male and female therapists and to male and female friends.

Snell (1989) related MFSDS scores to social anxiety as measured by the Social Anxiety subscale of the Self-Consciousness Inventory.

(3) Snell, Miller, and Belk (1988) developed a related scale, the Emotional Self-Disclosure Scale (ESDS). The ESDS consists of five items relating to each of eight specific emotions: depression, happiness, jealousy, anxiety, anger, calmness, apathy, and fear. Like the MFSDS, the ESDS asks respondents to indicate how willing they would be to discuss each topic with several different disclosure recipients.

AVAILABLE FROM: Snell, Belk, and Hawkins, 1986

USED IN:

Belk, S. S., Martin, H. P., & Snell, W. E., Jr. (1982, April). *Avoidance strategies in intimate relationships*. Paper presented at the meeting of the Southwestern Psychological Association, Dallas. (ERIC Document Reproduction Service No. ED 229 698)

Belk, S. S., & Snell, W. E., Jr. (1988). Avoidance of strategy use in intimate relationships. *Journal of Social and Clinical Psychology, 7*, 80–96.

Snell, W. E., Jr. (1989). Willingness to self-disclose to female and male friends as a function of social anxiety and gender. *Personality and Social Psychology Bulletin, 15*, 113–125.

Snell, W. E., Jr., Belk, S. S., Flowers, A., & Warren. J. (1988). Women's and men's willingness to self-disclose to therapists and friends: The moderating influence of instrumental, expressive, masculine, and feminine topics. *Sex Roles, 18*, 769–776.

Snell, W. E., Jr., Belk, S. S., & Hawkins, R. C., II. (1986). The Masculine and Feminine Self-Disclosure Scale: The politics of masculine and feminine self-presentation. *Sex Roles, 15*, 249–267.

BIBLIOGRAPHY:

Beere, C. A. (1990). *Gender roles: A handbook of tests and measures*. Westport, CT: Greenwood.

Fenigstein, A., Scheier, M. F., & Buss, A. H. (1975). Public and private self-consciousness: Assessment and theory. *Journal of Consulting and Clinical Psychology, 43*, 522–527.

Jenkins, C. D. (1978). A comparative review of the interview and questionnaire methods in the assessment of the coronary-prone-behavior pattern. In T. M. Dembroski, S. M. Weiss, J. L. Shields, S. Hayes, & M. Feinleib (Eds.) *Coronary-prone behavior* (pp. 71–88). New York: Springer.

Jourard, S. (1971). *Self-disclosure: An experimental analysis of the transparent self.* New York: Wiley-Interscience.

Miller, L. C., Murphy, R., & Buss, A. H. (1981). Consciousness of body: Private and public. *Journal of Personality and Social Psychology, 41,* 397–406.

Snell, W. E., Jr., Miller, R. S., & Belk, S. S. (1988). Development of the Emotional Self-Disclosure Scale. *Sex Roles, 18,* 59–73.

Spence, J. T., & Helmreich, R. L. (1978). *Masculinity and femininity: Their psychological dimensions, correlations, and antecedent.* Austin: University of Texas Press.

NONSEXIST PERSONAL ATTRIBUTE INVENTORY FOR CHILDREN (NPAIC)

AUTHORS: Thomas S. Parish and Charles I. Rankin
DATE: 1982
VARIABLE: Self-concept in children
TYPE OF INSTRUMENT: Checklist
DESCRIPTION: The Nonsexist Personal Attribute Inventory for Children (NPAIC) consists of 32 adjectives, 16 positive and 16 negative, arranged in alphabetical order. The respondents are to mark the 10 adjectives that best describe themselves.
SAMPLE ITEMS: (positive items) calm, fair-minded
(negative items) angry, wrongful
PREVIOUS SUBJECTS: Children in grades 5 through 8
APPROPRIATE FOR: Children in grades 5 through 8, although additional work might show that the scale could be used with older children
ADMINISTRATION: Self-administered; about 10 minutes
SCORING: The score is the number of positive items selected. The range is 0 to 10.
DEVELOPMENT: The Personal Attribute Inventory for Children (Parish & Taylor, 1978a, 1978b), which consists of 24 positive and 24 negative terms, arranged alphabetically, was administered to 686 children in grades 5 through 8. The children were asked to choose the 15 words that best described themselves. Chi-square analyses were performed to determine which traits were more likely to be endorsed by one sex over the other sex. From the traits that were not preferred by one sex over the other, 16 positive terms and 16 negative terms were selected for the NPAIC.
RELIABILITY: The NPAIC was administered to 272 children in grades 5 through 8 on two occasions, 1 month apart. The test-retest reliability was .62. Additionally test-retest reliabilities were computed for each sex by grade combination. These coefficients ranged from .35 (5th-grade girls) to .74 (7th-grade boys).
VALIDITY: A sample of 297 children in grades 5 through 8 completed the NPAIC and the Piers-Harris Children's Self-Concept Scale (Piers &

Harris, 1969). The overall correlation between the two scales was .49. Correlation coefficients for each sex by grade combination were also computed; they ranged from .29 (8th-grade boys) to .72 (6th-grade boys).
NOTES & COMMENTS: The NPAIC was developed to offer an alternative to existing self-concept scales for children, which confound self-concept with masculinity and femininity.
AVAILABLE FROM: Parish and Rankin, 1982
USED IN:

Parish, T. S., & Rankin, C. I. (1982). The Nonsexist Personal Attribute Inventory for Children: A report on its validity and reliability as a self-concept scale. *Educational and Psychological Measurement*, *42*, 339–343.

BIBLIOGRAPHY:

Parish, T., & Taylor, J. (1978a). A further report on the validity and reliability of the Personal Attribute Inventory for Children as a self-concept scale. *Educational and Psychological Measurement*, *38*, 1225–1228.

Parish, T., & Taylor, J. (1978b). The Personal Attribute Inventory for Children: A report on its validity and reliability as a self-concept scale. *Educational and Psychological Measurement*, *38*, 565–569.

Piers, E., & Harris, D. (1969). *The Piers-Harris Children's Self-Concept Scale*. Nashville: Counselor Recordings and Tests.

SAME SEX TOUCHING SCALE (SSTS)
AUTHORS: Knud S. Larsen and Jeff LeRoux
DATE: 1984
VARIABLE: Attitudes toward same-sex touching
TYPE OF INSTRUMENT: Summated rating scale
DESCRIPTION: The Same Sex Touching Scale (SSTS) consists of 20 statements that pertain to touching behavior between same-sex persons; 17 of the items pertain to feelings of comfort about one's own touching behavior with same-sex persons, and 3 pertain to feelings of comfort regarding other same-sex persons touching each other. Seventeen items are phrased to reflect positive attitudes toward touching behavior; 3 items reflect negative attitudes. Larsen and LeRoux (1984) reported that the SSTS is administered with the "usual Likert-type instructions and response categories" (p. 270), but they did not indicate how many response categories are used.
SAMPLE ITEMS: I would rather avoid touching persons of the same sex.

I appreciate a hug from a person of my sex when I need comforting.
PREVIOUS SUBJECTS: College students and adults
APPROPRIATE FOR: High school students and older
ADMINISTRATION: Self-administered; less than 10 minutes
SCORING: Information about scoring was not provided, but it can be presumed that items are individually scored and summed to yield one

overall score. Higher scores indicate more positive attitudes toward same sex touching.

DEVELOPMENT: A pool of 80 items was generated and administered to 29 men and 33 women. The 20 items with item-total correlations of .72 or higher comprise the SSTS.

RELIABILITY: Coefficient alpha was computed based on testing three different samples. The results were .98, .99, and .95—all very high.

VALIDITY: To provide evidence of the validity of the SSTS, Larsen and LeRoux (1984) compared SSTS scores with scores on numerous other measures. Testing a sample of 18 men and 41 women, they found that for males and females separately and for the total sample, SSTS scores were negatively and significantly correlated with a measure of authoritarianism and a measure of rigidity of attitudes, and SSTS scores were positively and significantly correlated with a measure of femininity. The correlations between SSTS scores and two other variables, masculinity and androgyny, were not significant. Testing another sample of 25 college men and 39 college women, they obtained similar results, except that for women the negative correlation between SSTS scores and the rigidity measure was not statistically significant.

In another phase of the research, Larsen and LeRoux (1984) compared SSTS scores obtained by 61 college men and 39 college women with their scores on Machiavellianism, religious orthodoxy, and locus of control. For men, there was a significant negative correlation between the SSTS scores and Machiavellianism and between SSTS scores and religious orthodoxy; for women, none of the three correlations was significant; for the sexes combined, there was a significant negative correlation between SSTS scores and Machiavellianism and a significant positive correlation between SSTS scores and locus of control.

In another phase of the research, SSTS scores for 61 men and 39 women were compared with scores on measures of radicalism-conservatism, self-esteem, same-sex touch avoidance, and opposite-sex touch avoidance. For males, there was only one significant correlation: the correlation between SSTS and same-sex touch avoidance was positive. For women, all of the correlations were significant. The first three were negative correlations, and the correlation between SSTS scores and opposite sex touch avoidance was positive. For men and women combined, there were significant negative correlations between SSTS scores and radicalism-conservatism and between SSTS scores and same-sex touch avoidance. All of the significant correlations reported in these various phases of the research were in the predicted direction.

Larsen and LeRoux (1984) compared responses from graduate students enrolled in counseling programs and graduate students enrolled in science programs. As predicted, the counseling students were more positive in their views regarding same-sex touching. Furthermore, female counseling students were significantly more positive than male counseling students. In a study with another sample of college students, peer rankings on ease of same-sex touching discriminated scores on the SSTS.

NOTES & COMMENTS: (1) Larsen and LeRoux (1984) calculated the reliability of shorter versions of the SSTS. In particular, they considered a scale consisting of only the first 5 items of the SSTS and a scale consisting of the last 10 items of the SSTS. Since the internal consistency reliabilities of the shorter scales were lower than that for the full scale, Larsen and LeRoux recommended using the full scale.

(2) Larsen and Long (1988) used the SSTS as one of several measures to establish the validity of their Traditional-Egalitarian Sex Role Scale (see Beere, 1990).

AVAILABLE FROM: Larsen and LeRoux, 1984

USED IN:

Larsen, K. S., & LeRoux, J. (1984). A study of same sex touching attitudes: Scale development and personality predictors. *Journal of Sex Research, 20,* 264–278.

Larsen, K. S., & Long, E. (1988). Attitudes toward sex-roles: Traditional or egalitarian? *Sex Roles, 19,* 1–12.

BIBLIOGRAPHY:

Beere, C. A. (1990). *Gender roles: A handbook of tests and measures.* Westport, CT: Greenwood.

WALLIN WOMEN'S NEIGHBORLINESS SCALE

AUTHOR: Paul Wallin

DATE: 1953 (used 1948)

VARIABLE: Women's knowledge of and friendliness with neighbors

TYPE OF INSTRUMENT: Guttman Scale

DESCRIPTION: The Wallin Women's Neighborliness Scale is a 12-item Guttman scale designed to determine one's friendliness with the neighbors. Originally administered as an interview, the questions can be asked as open-ended items or accompanied by fixed response options. If fixed response options are used, the scale can be adapted for use as a self-administered measure.

ARTICLES LISTED IN BEERE, 1979: 5

AVAILABLE FROM: Wallin, 1953

USED IN:

Orzek, A. M. (1977). Women's neighborliness and disengagement potential. *Essence, 1,* 157–162.

Wallin, P. (1953). A Guttman scale for measuring women's neighborliness. *American Journal of Sociology, 59,* 243–246.

BIBLIOGRAPHY:

Beere, C. A. (1979). *Women and women's issues: A handbook of tests and measures* (pp. 523–524). San Francisco: Jossey-Bass.

Index of Scale Titles

Index of Scale Authors

Index of Variables Measured by Scales

Index of Scale Users

About the Author

CAROLE A. BEERE is Associate Dean for Graduate Study and Research at Central Michigan University. She is the author of *Women and Women's Issues* and *Gender Roles: A Handbook of Tests and Measures* (Greenwood Press, 1990) and she has contributed articles to *Sex Roles* and *Psychology in the Schools*.